"Tired of traveling cross-country on boring, endless Interstates? Take the next exit and get yourself onto a two-lane highway. You will have an unforgettable experience. A stylish retro experience. An American experience. And the book to guide you down these soulful and charismatic routes is *Road Trip USA*."

—Roadside

"A fantastic guide, easily the best book of its type. The lively text celebrates the pleasures of the open road without ever getting too preachy about it, and vintage WPA photography provides a gorgeous finishing touch."

—Money

"Graphically handsome, the book adroitly weaves together sightseeing advice with history and restaurant and lodging recommendations. For budding myth collectors, I can't think of a better textbook."

—Los Angeles Times

"A diamond mine for the Harley-Davidson rider, this might just be the perfect book about hitting the summoning highway . . . It's impossible not to find something enticing in *Road Trip USA* to add to your next cycling expedition."

—Harley-Davidson Enthusiast

"Although over a dozen writers contributed to *Road Trip USA,* it speaks with a singular, consistent voice that celebrates the pleasures of the open road and small-town America without delving into kitsch or condescension . . . Extensive cross-referencing makes it easy to switch from one section of the book to another, and smartly placed margin notes provide useful nuggets of information on things like the best radio stations and where to watch out for speed traps."

—Condé Nast *Epicurious*

"Jamie Jensen and the 12 intrepid contributors to *Road Trip USA* have been everywhere and seen everything in the course of compiling this exhaustive, delightful, destination-anywhere guide to American road-tripping. As attuned to middle-lowbrow discoveries as it is to the usual roadside kitsch and the possibility of an even finer slice of pie along the next mile, *Road Trip USA* offers any possible traveler his brand of a good time."

—Washington D.C. *Citybooks*

ROAD TRIP USA

CALIFORNIA
AND THE
SOUTHWEST

ROAD TRIP USA

CALIFORNIA AND THE SOUTHWEST

FIRST EDITION

JAMIE JENSEN

CONTRIBUTING WRITERS:

Deke Castleman

Andy Collins

Doug Pappas

Barry Parr

Ivan Parr

Kevin Roe

Julian Smith

AVALON
TRAVEL
publishing

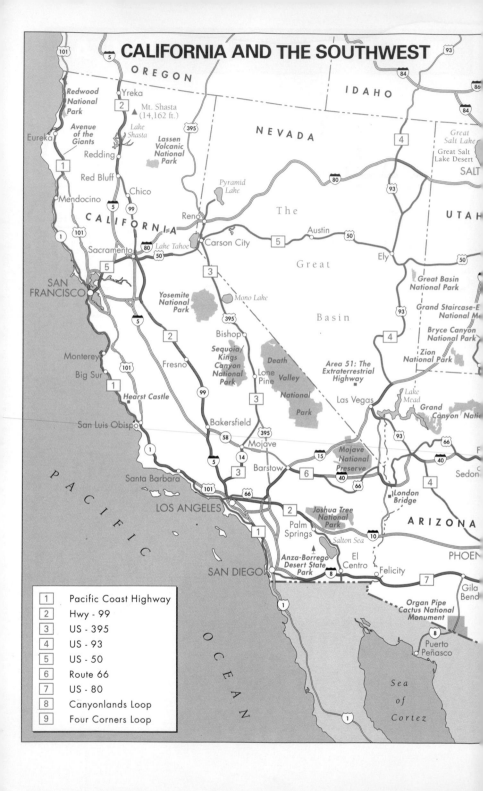

CALIFORNIA AND THE SOUTHWEST

OREGON

IDAHO

NEVADA

Redwood National Park

Yreka

Mt. Shasta (14,162 ft.)

Lake Shasta

Lassen Volcanic National Park

Avenue of the Giants

Eureka

Redding

Red Bluff

Chico

Mendocino

C A L I F O R N I A

Pyramid Lake

Reno

Sacramento

Lake Tahoe

Carson City

Austin

The

Great

Basin

Great Salt Lake

Great Salt Lake Desert

SALT

UTAH

SAN FRANCISCO

Yosemite National Park

Mono Lake

Great Basin National Park

Grand Staircase-E National M

Monterey

Big Sur

Hearst Castle

San Luis Obispo

Bishop

Fresno

Sequoia/ Kings Canyon National Park

Lone Pine

Death Valley National Park

Area 51: The Extraterrestrial Highway

Las Vegas

Lake Mead

Bryce Canyon National Park

Zion National Park

Grand Canyon Natio

Bakersfield

Mojave

Barstow

Mojave National Preserve

Sedon

Santa Barbara

LOS ANGELES

Joshua Tree National Park

Palm Springs

Salton Sea

London Bridge

ARIZONA

PHOEN

P A C I F I C

Anza-Borrego Desert State Park

SAN DIEGO

El Centro

Felicity

Gila Bend

Organ Pipe Cactus National Monument

Puerto Peñasco

O C E A N

Sea of Cortez

1	Pacific Coast Highway
2	Hwy - 99
3	US - 395
4	US - 93
5	US - 50
6	Route 66
7	US - 80
8	Canyonlands Loop
9	Four Corners Loop

**ROAD TRIP USA: CALIFORNIA
AND THE SOUTHWEST**
FIRST EDITION

Published by
Avalon Travel Publishing, Inc.
5855 Beaudry St.
Emeryville, CA 94608, USA

Printed by
Colocraft, Ltd.

© Text and photographs copyright Jamie Jensen,
2000. All rights reserved.

© Illustrations and maps copyright
Avalon Travel Publishing, Inc., 2000.
All rights reserved.

Please send all comments,
corrections, additions,
amendments, and critiques to:

**ROAD TRIP USA:
CALIFORNIA AND THE
SOUTHWEST**
AVALON TRAVEL PUBLISHING
5855 BEAUDRY STREET
EMERYVILLE, CA 94608, USA
e-mail: info@travelmatters.com
www.travelmatters.com

Printing History
1st edition—August 2000

5 4 3 2 1 0

Some photos and illustrations are used by permission
and are the property of the original copyright owners.

ISBN: 1-56691-190-7
ISSN: Library of Congress Cataloging-in-Publication data has been applied for.

Main Contributors:
Deke Castleman
Andy Collins
Doug Pappas
Barry Parr
Kevin Roe
Julian Smith

Other Contributors:
Sheri Cutter
Eric Finley
John Johnson
Jill Livingston
Patti Rowe

Editors: Emily Lunceford, Gregor Johnson Krause, Jeannie Trizzino
Production & Design: Dave Hurst
Cartography: Chris Folks
Index: Emily Lunceford

Front cover photo: Santa Rosa, New Mexico, © Ellen Barone/Dave G. Houser

Distributed in the United States and Canada by Publishers Group West

Printed in China

When you come to a fork in the road, take it.

—Yogi Berra

ON THE ROAD

The journeys in this book are as wild and varied as the landscapes they traverse. All celebrate the notion that freedom and discovery await us on the open road. Poets and artists from Walt Whitman to Muddy Waters have long sung the praises of rolling down the highway, and no matter how times have changed, there's still nothing more essentially American than hitting the road and seeing the country.

Despite the relentless roadside sprawl that keeps gobbling up the American landscape, if you turn off the fast-food-lined Interstates and turn onto the parallel universe of two-lane America, you can still experience the exhilarating freedom of the open road. The contrast between the Interstates and these older two-lane highways is big: driving along the Interstates is like watching a baseball game in a climate-controlled dome, while cruising these scenic two-lanes is like basking in the sun at Fenway Park or Wrigley Field.

For those of you who are happiest looking at the world through your windshield, you're in luck: California and the Southwest holds many of the most amazing drives on the planet. From the clifftop cruise Hwy-1 follows through Big Sur, to the breathtaking Million Dollar Highway along the crest of the Rockies, there are thousands of miles of great roads ahead of you, guaranteed to heighten your experience of the splendid scenery these roads pass through. Admiring a vista from a viewpoint is one thing, but the dynamic experience of driving over a mountain pass with a river crashing alongside you, or winding along the Pacific Coast at sunset, is the stuff of which road trip dreams are made.

Unlike the freeways, where the law and common sense dictate that you maintain your speed at all times, the sorts of scenic roads described in this book allow and often seem designed to encourage you to stop along the way—to read some fading historical plaque, to eat fresh dates straight from a palm tree at some desert oasis, or to sleep in a motel with rooms shaped like Indian teepees. Traveling along these older, more winding roads not only gets you wherever you want to go, but it also increases your chances of happening upon some state and local park preserving a perfect beach or a piece of history, or to stop at one of those kitschy souvenir shacks, flaunting giant dinosaurs and still selling the same postcards they've sold for decades.

In this book, the traditional "tourist attractions"—national parks like Yosemite, Zion, and the Grand Canyon, the Native American Pueblos of New Mexico, and the bright lights of big cities from San Francisco to Santa Fe—are all fully covered, but what I've really tried to do is to point you toward the less-hyped, less-visited places you might not otherwise find. If you want to get to know California and the Southwest, and want to have something truly your own to remember it by, take time to explore these roads less traveled, the parks less picnicked in, the sights less often seen. California and the Southwest is absolutely packed with world-famous places to spend your vacation time, but don't overlook the many magical places you can enjoy along the way. I've traveled thousands of miles searching for these classic stretches of highway, and this is the guide I wish I'd had with me all along. So without further ado, turn the key, turn on the radio—and hit the road.

Jamie Jensen

CONTENTS

Winding along the 1,000-mile coast of California, from the lush forests of Oregon to the Mexican deserts, the Pacific Coast Highway is one of the world's greatest long-distance drives. There's something for everyone along the way—majestic redwood forests and the pastoral vineyards of the legendary Wine Country, energetic big cities and sleepily quaint small towns, golden sand beaches and rocky coves—all connected by the most scenic stretches of highway anywhere.

INCLUDING: Kinetic Sculpture Race 38 • Avenue of the Giants 40-41 • Mendocino 45-46 • San Francisco 55-57 • Mystery Spot 61 • Big Sur 71 • El Camino Real and the California Missions 74-75 • Hearst Castle 77 • James Dean Memorial 77 • World's First Motel 79 • Mulholland Drive 86 • Disneyland 92-93 • Nixon Library 93 • Legoland 98

Running through the heart of California, this route captures the multiple personalities of the Golden State. From the small towns and fertile farmlands of the Central Valley, detour up into the foothills to visit historic remnants of mining camps founded 150 years ago, or even farther up into the mountains to explore the amazingly diverse parks and wildlands of the Cascade and Sierra Nevada Mountains. In the south, choose from deluxe desert resorts like Palm Springs or the deserted desert wilderness of Joshua Tree and Anza Borrego.

INCLUDING: Mount Shasta 109 • Lake Shasta 112-113 • Weaverville 115 • Mount Lassen Volcanic National Park 116-118 • Feather River Scenic Byway 119-120 • Grass Valley and Nevada City 122-125 • Sutter Creek and

HIGH SIERRA AND DEATH VALLEY: US-395 . . . . . . 156~193

Hemmed in by some of the most impressive mountain ranges in North America, and running north to south along the diagonal border that separates Nevada and California, US-395 is one of the last great roads left in the country. Linking Reno and Los Angeles, but otherwise hardly passing through anything approaching urban in its 600-mile journey, US-395 takes you to some of the most extreme, and extremely beautiful, places you'll ever see: the wild heart of the High Sierra, the otherworldly landscapes surrounding Pyramid and Mono Lakes, and the aptly named desert of Death Valley.

INCLUDING: Reno: National Automobile Museum 158 • Pyramid Lake 159-160 • Virginia City 160-161 • Bodie Ghost Town 169-170 • Mono Lake 172-173 • Yosemite National Park: Tioga Pass 173-174 • Devil's Postpile National Monument 176 • Oldest Living Things on Earth 180-181 • Manzanar National Monument 183 • Mount Whitney 185 • Death Valley National Park 185-188 • Edwards Air Force Base 191

GREAT BASIN AND SONORA DESERT: US-93 . . . . . . 196~227

Running from the volcanic plains of Idaho to the surprisingly green deserts of southern Arizona, this highway takes in the two extremes of the American Southwest: seemingly endless miles of sublime wilderness, interrupted by some of the most garish civilization on Earth, the sprawling Sunbelt cities of Las Vegas and Phoenix.

INCLUDING: Bonneville Speedway 199 • Cowboy Poetry Festival 200 • Million Dollar Courthouse 202 • The Extraterrestrial Highway ("Area 51") 205 • Las Vegas 207-209 • Hoover Dam 211-212 • Tom Mix Monument 220 • Biosphere II 221 • Titan Missile Museum 225 • Tumacacori 226

THE LONELIEST ROAD: US-50 .... 230~274

Following in the hoofsteps of riders on the Pony Express and Santa Fe Trail, this history-rich old road runs from the California coast, up and over the stunning Sierra Nevada Mountains, and across the existentially empty Great Basin. Continuing on its lonely way past the uninhabited alkaline wastes of the Great Salt Lake, US-50 touches on the wonderous landscape of Utah's Canyonlands before climbing up into the Colorado Rockies.

INCLUDING: Napa Valley Wine Country 234-236 • Gold Discovery State Historic Park 239 • Lake Tahoe 240-243 • Pony Express 249 • Great Basin National Park 251-253 • Butch Cassidy and the Hole-in-the-Wall Gang 258 • Colorado National Monument 261-262 • Crested Butte 266 • Royal Gorge 268 • Pike's Peak 269-270 • Santa Fe Trail 272-273

THE MOTHER ROAD: ROUTE 66 .... 276~319

The mystique of Route 66 draws people from around world. This legendary old road blazes across California and the Southwest on a diagonal trip that takes in some of the country's most archetypal roadside scenes, from the sand and sun of Southern California, past the Grand Canyon and the Native American communities of the Southwest, to the landmark Cadillac Ranch in the middle of the Texas Panhandle. Drive any or all of what John Steinbeck called the "Mother Road," past the array of neon-signed motels, funky roadside attractions, and homespun diners that give it life, and get your kicks on Route 66.

INCLUDING: Santa Monica 278-279 • Roy Rogers and Dale Evans Museum 283 • Exotic World 284 • London Bridge 288 • Flagstaff 296 • Grand Canyon National Park 297-300 • Sleep in a Teepee: Wigwam Village 306 • Petrified Forest National Park 307 • Sky City: Acoma Pueblo 310 • Cadillac Ranch 317

SOUTHERN PACIFIC: US-80 . . . . 322~351

Cruising along and occasionally crossing the Mexican border, US-80 races between the beaches of San Diego and the caverns of Carlsbad, deep in the bowels of the earth beneath the desert of New Mexico. Following US-80 and other scenic roads along what used to be called the Old Spanish Trail, this route takes you to some of the most important sites of the wild Wild West, and introduces the spicey food and spikey flora that typify the nation's southwestern borderlands.

INCLUDING: Cabrillo National Monument 323-324 • Tecate 324 • Desert View Tower 326-327 • "The Center of the World" Pyramid 328 • Organ Pipe Cactus National Monument 331-332 • Saguaro National Park 333-334 • The Thing! 336 • Tombstone, Arizona 336-337 • White Sands National Monument 343 • El Paso 345-347 • Ciudad Juárez 347-348 • Guadalupe Mountains National Park 348-349 • Carlsbad Caverns National Park 349-350 • Roswell: UFO Central 351

CANYONLANDS LOOP: THE GRAND CIRCLE. . . . . . . 354~395

A breathtaking desert vision of red rock sandstone spires and canyons awaits you. Nearly roadless and almost uninhabited just 50 years ago, the canyonlands area of southern Utah and northern Arizona holds some of the most eye-popping scenery you'll ever see, almost all of it protected in a huge swath of national parkland. And it's all yours to behold, from the comfort of your own front seat along this incredibly scenic loop tour, or better yet from the many great trails that lead away from the thin ribbon of asphalt.

INCLUDING: Canyonlands National Park: Island in the Sky 356 • Arches National Park 357-358 • Moab 358-362 • Hole 'N The Rock 363 • Canyonlands: The Needles 363-364 • Monument Valley 370 • Navajo National Monument 372-373 • Grand Canyon–North Rim 380-381 • Zion National Park 384-385 • Bryce Canyon National Park 387 • Grand Staircase– Escalante National Monument 389 • Capitol Reef National Park 392-393 • Canyonlands: The Maze 394

FOUR CORNERS LOOP: NATIVE AMERICA. . . . . 398~443

Overlapping the Canyonlands Loop, this road trip takes up where that one leaves off, circling through the heart of the Native American Southwest. Our Four Corners Loop travels from the sprawling Navajo Nation to the Hopi mesas and Pueblo villages, and back in time to explore the amazing Anasazi cliff palaces built here hundreds of years before Columbus. This tour takes you light years away from contemporary America, without ever leaving the country.

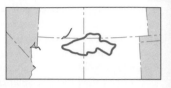

INCLUDING: Four Corners Monument 400 • Hopi Cultural Center 402 • Walpi 402-404 • Canyon de Chelley National Monument 404-406 • Hubbell Trading Post 406 • Chaco Canyon 408-409 • Bandelier National Monument 411 • Los Alamos National Laboratory 411 • Santa Fe 412-417 • The High Route 423-424 • Taos 427-431 • Taos Pueblo 431-432 • Durango 437 • Mesa Verde National Park 439-440

HOW TO USE THIS BOOK

Road Trip USA: California and the Southwest describes nine very different driving tours around seven states and parts of two countries, giving complete details for over 10,000 miles of generally scenic and frequently historic roads all across California and the Southwestern corner of the USA. The main aim of this book has been to establish a network of alternatives to the efficient but bland Interstate highway system, which, to paraphrase the late Charles Kuralt, have made it possible to drive all the way across the country without seeing anything. In parts of the Southwest, the Interstates are truly a blessing—especially at night, if you're doing a marathon drive to get somewhere by dawn—but generally I suggest following older, more scenic highways, and taking as many detours as you can along the way.

Out of the thousands and thousands of miles of highway crisscrossing California and the Southwest, I've selected these routes because they offer consistent peaks of driving pleasure. The chapters don't always follow a single numbered route, but frequently suggest more scenic or interesting alternatives or detours to visit significant sights: veering off old US-80 in Arizona to tour Organ Pipe National Monument (and maybe cruise south to the Sea of Cortez for an ultra-fresh shrimp taco or two), or detouring off my favorite unknown highway, US-395, to climb up into the wonderful wilderness of the eastern Sierra Nevada mountains.

Road Trip USA: California and the Southwest has been designed to work both as an entertaining armchair read, and as a helpful mile-by-mile guide when you're out on the road. Each of these routes has a distinctive character, so I've described them in separate **chapters**, starting with four north-to-south routes, then covering three west-east routes. (Though purists may say these roads should be covered east to west, following the course of historical events, going from the west to the east also means you never have to drive into the sunset.) Last, but certainly not least, are a pair of loop trips around some of the breathtaking scenery of the Southwest—the immense canyonlands of the Colorado Plateau, and the Native Americana of the Four Corners region.

The **table of contents** on the previous pages lists some of each chapter's highlights and gives page references, so you can jump in at any point along the way. Places where two routes intersect are clearly cross-referenced throughout the book, so you can organize an itinerary to suit yourself, following US-50 along the Santa Fe Trail, for example, then heading south along the Million

Dollar Highway to Durango, joining the Four Corners Loop south and east through Santa Fe before getting your kicks on Route 66.

Each of the nine highway-by-highway chapters begins with a keynote essay giving a brief overview of the road, and the chapters themselves are organized in geographical order, so that the words track the changing scene. Each chapter is sub-divided into small enough stretches that, with a little practice, it's easy to use even if you're traveling in the opposite direction to the flow of the text.

Along the way, I've also pointed out the best places to eat and sleep, with a definite focus on unique regional specialties, such as Tex-Mex joints in New Mexico or truck stops selling Navajo tacos in Arizona, and a full range of accommodations, from the many historic lodges of the national parks to the countless neon-signed motels along Route 66 in the Southwest. All of this background and practical information is woven together in each segment of text, so there's no need to flip through the pages to find a key piece of information.

Throughout each chapter we've included a series of detailed **maps**, all of which show the chosen route in a blue tint, so you can keep on track even when wandering the lonely roads of Nevada. Odds and ends of trivia, history and car culture memorabilia are given in the margins of the text; this is also where we've listed selected radio stations, short-but-scenic detours and other details of passing interest. Longer **special topic** essays are sprinkled throughout the main text, covering in greater detail some of the many fascinating aspects of each place's past—tracing the Space Race legacy across the Southern California desert, for example, or telling the story of the Pony Express.

As part of our effort to guide you along the roads less traveled, one of the most important ways in which this book differs from traditional travel guides is that, so we could have space to write about the roads, we have limited coverage of metropolitan areas to short **Survival Guides**. These two-or-three-page mini-guides are intended to give essential tips on what to see and where to eat and sleep in the handful of really big cities, so that you can make the most of a passing visit.

The final section of the book is called **Road Trip Resources**, where the Recommended Reading section describes dozens of great books to take with you on your travels. There's also a **Road Trip Timeline**, which marks historic milestones in the development of California and the Southwest. At the very end of the book, there is an extensive **index**, so you can quickly find what we have to say about a given place. Interspersed throughout the index are boxes giving the phone numbers for the different state tourism and road conditions information services, and thematic boxes, which highlight such special subjects as minor league baseball teams and significant annual events—and tell you where to find them in the book.

DID WE MISS SOMETHING?

Let us hear from you. We welcome comments from bikers, RVers, hikers, campers, and Net surfers, also hotel and restaurant proprietors, and anyone else who has something to say about this book. Please address your comments to:

Road Trip USA: California and the Southwest
5855 Beaudry Street
Emeryville, CA 94608, USA
e-mail: info@travelmatters.com

Short tidbits of text in the margins point out odd facts and interesting pieces of information about the area the route is passing through. Marginal comments throughout the book may recommend a local radio station, a nearby restaurant, or a scenic detour, or offer a piece of roadside trivia.

From Taos, our route heads into the mountains of Colorado, passing through the mining-camp-turned-mountain-bike-mecca of Durango on the way to Mesa Verde National Park, where the most stunningly sited Anasazi ruins anywhere are tucked into sheer cliffs at what feels like the top of the world. No matter how many—or how few—other Anasazi remnants you see here in the Southwest, Mesa Verde is a place you'll never forget.

By far the best map of the Four Corners area is the Automobile Club of Southern California's **Indian Country,** available from most AAA offices and just about everywhere on the route.

The term **Anasazi,** which means "ancient enemies" or "enemies of my ancestors" in Navajo, is coming under fire for its negative connotations by contemporary tribes who claim them as ancestors. Today, you'll often hear the term "ancestral Puebloans" used instead.

The Four Corners Monument

One of the better examples of Tourist Man's neverending search for novelty, the Four Corners Monument (daily 8 AM-5 PM, 7 AM-7 PM in summer; $1.50 per person) marks the only spot where four U.S. states meet. The borders of Colorado, New Mexico, Utah, and Arizona—and hundreds of eager visitors every day—all come together at this otherwise unremarkable spot, which is located at the north end of a short driveway, off US-160 from the New Mexico "corner." The actual convergence is surrounded by a circle of flagpoles and marked by a concrete slab in which are embedded the four state seals and the motto "Here Meet, Under God, Four States." Visitors take turns climbing up to a short platform to take pictures of their fellow travelers standing in four states at once, while dozens of Navajo souvenir, crafts, and fry bread stands form an outer wall around the monument.

The actual spot was established and mapped as the mutual border way back in 1875, but Four Corners only became the tourist attraction it is today after the US-160 highway was opened in 1962. The Four Corners Monument is operated as a Navajo tribal park; Golden Eagle and other park passes are not accepted, and there's no camping (or water) available. (There are some portable toilets, though, if you're desperate.)

FOUR CORNERS LOOP: NATIVE AMERICA 401

Teec Nos Pos and Mexican Water

South and west of the Four Corners Monument, US-160 runs across the Navajo Nation along the south side of the Utah-Arizona border. At Teec Nos Pos, where US-160 is joined by US-64 from Farmington, a pair of trading posts and gas stations stand astride the crossroads, while the impressive (and uranium-rich) Carrizo Mountains rise up to the south. Similarly small communities line the route west, past the bright red sandstone of Red Mesa to Mexican Water ("Home of the Red Mesa Redskins"), where another trading post and gas station combo is joined by the **Mexican Water Restaurant**, known for its very good Navajo Tacos.

South from Mexican Water, US-191 runs along Chinle Wash to the west end of Canyon de Chelly National Monument. Seven miles west of Mexican Water along US-160, the **Navajo Trails Motel** (520/674-3618) offers the only rooms for many miles; doubles cost around $60 a night.

Somewhat ironically, the Four Corners Monument is actually on Navajo Nation land, legally distinct from any of the four states that supposedly meet here. Adding to the nominal confusion, the Arizona corner is officially part of Apache County, though that tribe's reservation is hundreds of miles to the south.

From just north of the Four Corners Monument, you can turn west off US-160 onto Hwy-41, which leads across the northern Navajo Nation through the oil-drilling center of Aneth, then, via Hwy-262 and Hwy-163, to the Mormon town of Bluff and on to Monument Valley.

Former Navajo Nation chairman **Peter MacDonald**, who was sentenced to 14 years in prison for corruption in the early 1990s, grew up in the Teec Nos Pos community.

Kayenta marks the junction with our Canyonlands Loop, which heads 24 miles north to Monument Valley (and beyond) and west to Lake Powell, the North Rim of the Grand Canyon, and Zion and Bryce National Parks in southern Utah. The two routes run together between Kayenta and Tuba City; those two towns, and the stretch of US-160 between them, are covered on pages 372-374.

Third Mesa: Old Oraibi

Heading east from the mainly Navajo community of Tuba City, this is the first substantial Hopi community you encounter. It's also the oldest. In fact, Old Oraibi is considered to be one of the oldest inhabited places in North America, with signs of occupation dating to well before A.D. 1300. Located on top of what's known as Third Mesa, around 40 miles east of Tuba City, Old Oraibi

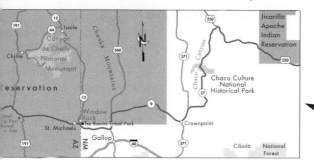

Right column marginal text:

To make it easy to find where you are, throughout *Road Trip California and the Southwest* the prose is broken up into blocks of text, describing a certain town, state park, section of highway or detour. Each of these segments tells you all you need to know: some history, something of the layout of the town, the main attractions, and necessary practicalities of where to eat, sleep, and find further information.

At points in the text where two routes intersect, a bold banner gives the cross-referenced pages for the other route, so you can easily switch from route to another.

For every hundred to two hundred miles of highway, we have included a detailed map. On these maps, which appear every few pages throughout the book, we have highlighted the route in a blue tint, to make it easy to follow. All the towns and points of interest described in the text are also printed on the maps in blue.

SEEING CALIFORNIA AND THE SOUTHWEST

Whether you're after wild beauty, a sense of history, cutting-edge culture and cuisine, or a mix of all three, California and the Southwest offers something for everyone. The natural landscape is definitely the main draw for most visitors, with so many natural wonders the whole region sometimes seems to merit protection as a national park. As it is, parks are plentiful and consistently amazing, whether you're gazing down into the great gorge of the Grand Canyon, staring up at the glaciated granite cliffs of Yosemite Valley, watching the waves break along the Big Sur coast, or standing at the foot of the mighty redwoods along the Avenue of the Giants. Wherever you go, the larger-than-life scale of the natural scene is frequently mind-boggling.

The relationship between man and nature here dates back many thousands of years, but signs can be few and far between. The past is most beautifully present in the awesome Anasazi cliff palaces and pueblos of the Four Corners region, where a series of intricately interconnected cities, on a par with those of the Inca and Maya civilizations, grew to a peak of achievement a millennium ago, then mysteriously disappeared, almost without a trace. Other signs of Native American presence do persist throughout the region, especially in New Mexico's vibrant Pueblo villages, but in most places signs of human history date to much more recent events—such as the establishment of Spanish Catholic missions in the mid-to-late 1700s. The missionaries were followed closely by miners and fur-trappers, ranchers and farmers, railroad builders and Mormons, all of whom had a major impact. Fortunately and surprisingly,

---

CONSIDERATIONS FOR INTERNATIONAL TRAVELERS

All the usual rules for the foreign traveler visiting the U.S. apply in California and the Southwest, with some specific regional additions. First among these is to realize just how truly wild and untamed great stretches of the Southwest in particular can be, with huge distances between even the most basic services— when the signs say Next Gas 200 Miles, it's no exaggeration. Carry some food and a couple of bottles of water (a gallon a day per person), especially if you want to explore the deserts.

In terms of starting and finishing points for your trip, most international airlines fly only to San Francisco and Los Angeles; fewer flights serve other cities, namely Las Vegas and Phoenix. Connecting flights to other cities in the Southwest are usually pretty inexpensive, so long as you book them when you buy the international ticket. Also, be aware that some major services, such as car rental companies and hotels, will expect you to pay using a credit card; so if you have one, bring it.

many of these mining camps, outposts, and homesteads haven't been torn down, built on, or even built around, but stand as vivid evocations of what life was like, not so very long ago, here on the most distant frontier of the New World.

Some of these early outposts dried up and disappeared, but a few grew to become modern big cities. The most history-rich cities and towns—like Santa Fe, San Francisco, and Monterey—have preserved their older quarters to such a degree that you can still get a strong sense of the past. But otherwise, especially in the sprawling Sunbelt cities of Los Angeles, Las Vegas, or Phoenix, very little of the contemporary world bears any real relation to anything that came before—natural or otherwise. Whatever their comparative paucity of cosmopolitan character or old-fashioned charm, the big cities do, however, have most of the big museums, the necessary services and facilities, and almost all of the entertainment. Added to the offerings of the dozens of small and not-so-small towns sprinkled around California, and to a lesser degree the Southwest, it makes for a great range of food, drink, and accommodation options. Thanks in part to the recent boom in adventure travel, which has brought espresso machines to just about every corner of the region, wherever you go you'll find local cafes, bijou restaurants, and all sorts of places to stay—from youth hostels in old lighthouses to homespun B&B inns in old farmhouses to roadside motels.

When to Go

There's no bad time of year to travel around California and the Southwest, but there's really no "best" time, either. The region is so vast and diverse that the climate varies from place to place nearly as much as it does from season to season—for example, winter in the Arizona deserts feels very similar to summer in the mountains—so no matter when you visit you can probably find the weather you want, if you go to the right places. On the other hand, this extreme regional variation also means that if you're planning to see a lot of different places, you should also be prepared for a lot of different weather—basically all four seasons, at any time of year. And if you include the extreme climates (winter in the mountains and summer in the deserts), you effectively have six seasons to deal with, adding "extremely cold" and "extremely hot" to the ends of the usual scale.

For most of the places covered in this book, the most popular time to visit is summer, when schools are out and all America hits the highways. But summer is by no means the best time to visit: the weather's too hot, the national parks are swarming with visitors, campgrounds and restaurants are full, and all but the most distant backroads are clogged with fellow travelers. That said, even in the middle of August you can still find a place of your own—you just have to hike a bit farther to get there.

In the desert regions, however, the opposite is true: summer is the low season, when it's 110° for weeks on end and anyone with the ability to be elsewhere usually is. During summer, some desert places shut down entirely, but others offer bargain rates to tempt travelers. For deluxe resorts, this is especially true—winter and spring are peak seasons for the dude ranches and desert golf resorts that dot the Southwest, but if you can stand the summer heat you can sometimes take advantage of these luxury facilities at discounts of more than 50% off the high season rates. Springtime in the desert is most remarkable for the wildflowers, whose fleeting blooms carpet the otherwise brown ground with a sparkling array of yellows, reds, and purples.

Winter, naturally, is also the prime time for the region's many ski resorts. There is great skiing all over California and the Southwest, from the Sierra Nevada centers of Mammoth and Tahoe (home of the 1960 Winter Olympics) to the Wasatch resorts above Salt Lake City (site of the 2002 Olympic games). Alpiners, Nordics, 'boarders—even snowshoers—can find terrain to suit their mood. All across California and the Southwest, the winter months also see other sorts of seasonal visitors: migratory

SAMPLE ITINERARIES

SEVEN DAYS FROM LAS VEGAS

Day 1: Leave the Strip behind and head over the hills to Death Valley.

Day 2: Watch the sunrise, then race across the desolate new Mojave National Preserve on your way to the boulders and forests of Joshua Tree National Park.

Day 3: Have a diner-style breakfast in the retro-desert resort of Palm Springs, then cruise along the shores of the Salton Sea on your way to Yuma, a historic crossing on the Colorado River.

Day 4: Cruise up the Colorado River to see London Bridge, then continue the nostalgic trip by following a magical stretch of old Route 66 east to Flagstaff.

Day 5: Hike or ride a mule down into the Grand Canyon.

Day 6: Loop around past bizarre Lake Powell to the redrock canyons of Zion National Park.

Day 7: Head back to Las Vegas, by way of Lake Mead, the Valley of Fire, and the Lost City.

SEVEN DAYS FROM SAN FRANCISCO

Day 1: Cruise up the coast through Point Reyes to Mendocino.

Day 2: Follow the Avenue of the Giants past the magnificent redwood trees, then head inland from Arcata to the historic gold mining town of Weaverville.

Day 3: Loop around volcanic Mount Lassen, then cruise south to Lake Tahoe.

Day 4: Head east into Nevada, then follow scenic US-395 south past the ghost town of Bodie and lunar Mono Lake to Tuolumne Meadows, high up in the backcountry of Yosemite National Park.

Day 5: Enjoy the granite cliffs and towering waterfalls of Yosemite Valley.

Day 6: After a quick tour of the historic Gold Country, head west to the vineyards of the Napa Valley wine country.

Day 7 Back to San Francisco, by way of Sonoma, Muir Woods, and the Golden Gate Bridge.

birds, escaping the arctic cold of the Midwest and Canada, and migratory "snowbirds"—Rvers, retirees, and others—doing the exact same thing. The former can be seen at the dozens of wildlife refuges along the region's rivers, the latter tend to congregate on the fringes of the deserts, in towns like Tecopa outside Death Valley, and anywhere along the Colorado River.

Fall is as close as it gets to an ideal time to travel, and especially in California, anywhere from the coastal areas to the deserts the weather is at or near peak form. In the mountains, the aspens turn gold against the evergreen forest backdrop, and an occasional light snow dusts the peaks. However, since so much of the Southwest is at high elevations—the South Rim of the Grand Canyon is 7,000 feet above sea level, and most of the Colorado Plateau Canyonlands are more than a mile high—sudden storms can be a real hindrance to safe travel.

Getting There

Since the area covered by this book is so large, you can't realistically expect to see all of it in a single tour. That said, you can definitely see a lot of very different places in a very short time, if you plan your trip efficiently. Anyone starting from outside the region, and people already there who don't thrill at the prospect of an all-night drive, should think about flying into one of the many big gateway cities and traveling from there. With a little advance notice, flights and car rentals don't have to cost very much—sometimes barely more than what it would cost for the gas, food, and lodging to get you from your home to the start of your trip. Las Vegas, for example, makes a great starting point for a tour of this vast region, and unless there's a big convention or boxing match going on, you can get cheap flights and $125-a-week car rentals—with unlimited miles, an essential for any road trip tour. Los Angeles and San Francisco, and to a lesser extent Phoenix and Salt Lake City, also make fine start and finish points, and if you're willing to do an all-night drive or two, you can get to and from just about anywhere in this book in less than 24 hours.

> Besides insisting on unlimited free miles, the keys to keeping rental car costs down are to rent and return your car from the same location, and to rent in weekly increments. Always ask for the best deals, and resist pressure to upgrade to a bigger (more expensive) car.

Getting Around

Having a car is definitely a key to happy traveling in California and the Southwest—as you probably guessed from the title of this book, driving is by far the best way to get a feel for the region. By all means ride a bike, paddle your kayak, and get out and hike, but since in some places public transit is nonexistent and even tiny towns can be a hundred miles or more apart, you definitely need a car to get around California and the Southwest.

Though the railroads, especially the Santa Fe and Union Pacific, which built many of the grand hotels in the national parks, were in many ways the creators of the tourism industry in the Southwest, rail travel these days is not a practical option. Amtrak offers very limited service, with maybe one train a day traveling between the big cities. This doesn't work very well on its own, but in conjunction with a rental car can be great if you want to do a multi-center tour: fly to L.A. and get a car for a few days to tour around, then hop on the overnight train to Salt Lake City to rent another car for your tour of the Canyonlands. Amtrak does run connecting bus tours to Yosemite, the Grand Canyon and other points of interest, so you can see something without being behind the wheel the whole time, but traveling in California and the Southwest really comes down to one word: drive.

As anyone who rides one will no doubt tell you, motorcycles are perhaps the ideal mode of traveling around California and the Southwest. Although I've pointed to a few stretches of highway that are most fun on a bike, I haven't made any great distinction between driving and motorcycle riding tours—though you will find herein various hangouts along the way that seem to cater to and attract the two-wheeled world. I've also mentioned the few places (Palm Springs, Las Vegas, and Los Angeles) where neophyte riders can rent a bike (usually a Harley-Davidson) and get a feel for motorcycle touring.

At the opposite end of the driving-pleasure spectrum from motorbikes are those lumbering multi-bedroom behemoths—recreational vehicles, which really come into their own when traveling in the wide open spaces of the Southwest. Though not exactly fun to drive, these machines make it possible to be comfortable for extended periods time in inhospitable places that otherwise would be off-limits to any but the hardiest travelers. Ideal for families or small groups, traveling in one of these self-contained cruisers can really build a sense of camaraderie, and best of all you have everything you need—beds, bathrooms, kitchens—under one roof, wherever you go. RVs come in all sizes, and are available for rent from companies all over California and the Southwest, including **Cruise America** (800/327-7799). Costs run $500-750 per week, plus mileage, which can add up pretty quickly if you do a fair amount of driving.

In addition to Amtrak, there are also a few historic railroads—Williams to the Grand Canyon, Chama, the Durango Skunk Train—which make a nice change of pace from being behind the wheel. These all travel through glorious scenery, but they all bring you back to where you began; all these and more are listed in the Index, under Historic Railroads.

Where to Eat

Apart from the superior driving pleasure, the real advantage of avoiding the freeways and following the roads described herein is clear: the food. From taco stands to four-star restaurants, the best food is almost always well away from the freeways, and usually along some scenic backroad like the ones in this book. I've listed the best of the bunch, but one of the greatest pleasures of traveling is discovering some great place all by yourself, so be adventurous—this is a land of good food, and you're unlikely to go wrong.

Eating options vary tremendously upon where you travel—in the wealthy, densely populated parts of coastal California, all kinds of good food can be found around every turn, but in the middle of the Nevada nowhere, your choices are not so plentiful. Even here, though, great meals can be found—usually at some nondescript-looking Basque hotel, where the same hearty, family-style meals have been served for most of a century. In the ranchlands of New Mexico, keep your nose attuned to the smell of smoke and chiles, and an eye out for a line of pickups outside some concrete block roadhouse; chances are, great food is on the menu inside. On the other hand, in Santa Fe, there are so many great restaurants you'd have to work hard *not* to eat well.

Where to Stay

Throughout this book, I've tried to recommend a range of quality accommodations in all price ranges, but when it comes down to it, I find there are basically two types of places to stay. The most common is the sort where you simply want a clean bed in a quiet room, so you can sleep soundly and get back on your way the next morning. This type of accommodation—copiously offered by that all-American roadside icon, the motel—is abundant throughout California and the Southwest, and unless there's some major event going on it's very rare that every room in a given town will be taken. Two people sharing a room should count on spending around $50 a night for a standard motel, including the usual array of taxes—much less in places, a little more in bigger cities or during peak season. I've listed a few favorite motels throughout this book (usually ones with a particularly fine neon sign in addition to the requisite clean bed), but the best guarantee of finding something to your liking is to stop driving when the sun goes down, and find a place to sleep then and there. The later you leave it, the less choice you will have.

The second type of place to stay is the one worth planning your trip around—a historic lodge in the National Park, a romantic Victorian-era B&B in some idyllic setting, that sort of thing. I recommend mixing in at least a few of these into your travel plans. Though many are often booked solid for months in advance, it never hurts to ask if they happen to have a vacancy.

Alternatively, I've also included hostels, which offer cheap but spartan accommodations, often in beautiful locales, like old lighthouses in California and mining cabins in Colorado. Not only can staying in hostels save you money, it's also a great way to meet fellow travelers.

Camping is the best way to experience the wide open spaces—you really haven't seen the desert until you've spent the night under the brilliant stars, and been awakened by the brightest sun you've ever seen. Along all the routes, especially in the prettiest places, I've pointed out the best campgrounds—mostly in national forests, but also on Bureau of Land Management lands, and in the national and state parks. Contact numbers are given throughout the book, but for more general information, call the state and national park numbers listed under Camping Information in the Index.

PACIFIC COAST HIGHWAY

PACIFIC COAST HIGHWAY

F or some reason, when people else-where in the country refer to Cali-fornia, they make it sound like a land of kooks and crazies, an overbuilt suburban desert supporting only shopping malls, freeways, and body-obsessed airheads. All of which may be true in small pockets, but the amazing thing about California, and the coast of California in particular—from the ancient green forests of Northern California to the gorgeous, golden-sand beaches of Southern California—is that despite its many millions of residents it is still mostly wild, open, and astoundingly beautiful country, where you can drive for miles and miles and miles, and have the scenery all to yourself.

Remaining within sight of the Pacific Ocean almost all the way from Oregon south to the Mexican border, this 1,000-mile, mostly two-lane route takes in everything from near-rainforest to near-desert. Most of the California coast is in the public domain, freely if not always easily accessible, and protected from exploitation and development within dozens of national, state, and local parks, which preserve the natural landscape and provide habitat for such rare creatures as mountain lions, condors, gray whales and spotted owls.

The cities and towns along the way are every bit as different from one another as the diverse landscapes. Besides passing through the seemingly polar-opposite cities of San Francisco and Los Angeles, this coastal route takes you to all manner of medium, small and very small towns, starting with the rough-and-tumble logging and fishing communities set amongst the great redwood forests of Northern California. Here, where the tallest and most majestic living things on earth line the "Avenue of the Giants," you'll also find some of the best (meaning gloriously kitschy) remnants of the golden age of car-borne tourism: drive-through trees, drive-on trees, houses carved out of trees, Paul Bunyan statues, and much more.

The far north coast is as wild as anywhere in the country, but the closer you get to San Francisco, the more civilized things become. From the B&B haven of picturesque Mendocino, to the rustic resorts lining the Russian River, and the gourmet delights of the expansive Wine Country—there is something to suit every taste, budget, or interest. South of San Francisco, the phenomenal beauty of the far north coast is rivaled only by the incredible land-and seascape of Big Sur, midway along the Pacific Coast Highway. Bookended by California's historic capital, Monterey, and by the amazing mountaintop estate of Citizen Kane (Hearst Castle), the central part of the route holds more fascinating if less famous attractions, including the best of California's many Spanish colonial missions, dating back over two centuries—an eternity by Golden State standards.

Continuing south stretch the beach fronts of Southern California—the land of palm trees, beach boys, and surfer girls of popular lore, which really does exist, though only in this southernmost quarter of the state. A pair of very pleasant small cities, Midwestern-feeling San Luis Obispo and ritzy Santa Barbara, make excellent stops in themselves, smoothing the transition from the lush and comparatively rural northern quarters of the state into the busy environs of Southern California. The unwieldy Los Angeles-to-San Diego megalopolis seems more and more like one monstrous, 100-mile-long exurbia, linked by an ever-tighter chain of freeways (I-5, I-15, I-215, I-405, I-705, I-805); but while it's true that the natural beauty that brought so many people to Southern California in the first place is increasingly endangered, some lovely, almost untouched places remain, hidden away but within easy access of the fast lane. I've pointed these out as best I can; enjoy them while they last.

Jedediah Smith Redwoods State Park

The northernmost of the great redwood groves, Jedediah Smith Redwoods State Park covers nearly 10,000 acres of virgin forest along the Oregon border and the banks of the Smith River. Stretching east of US-101, and most easily accessible

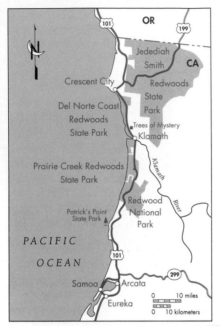

from scenic US-199, the park offers over 30 miles of usually uncrowded hiking trails through the pristine wilderness, and is considered by many to be the most perfect of all the redwood forests. At the southern end of the park, turn off US-199 onto Howland Hill Road, an incredibly scenic five-mile, one-lane, one-way loop which was once paved in redwood planks (it's now gravel). Howland Hill Road passes through grove after grove of stately redwoods, including **Stout Grove**, where trails lead past the park's tallest tree and a number of summertime swimming holes along the Smith River. There's also a nice **campground**, with hot showers ($16 in summer, $14 rest of year; 800/444-7275).

Crescent City

The county seat and largest city in Del Norte County, Crescent City (pop. 4,380) is best treated as a base from which to explore the surrounding wilderness. The foggy weather that helps the redwoods thrive makes the city fairly depressing and gray, and what character it developed since its founding in 1853 has been further eroded by storms; a giant tsunami, caused by the 1964 earthquake off Alaska, destroyed nearly the entire city.

Crescent City includes the usual motels (including a Travelodge and a Best Western) and restaurants, as well as one unique spot: the **Ship Ashore**, a gift shop, restaurant, and motel along US-101 about 10 miles north of town, marked by a grounded ship.

Crescent City is the headquarters for **Redwood National Park**; a block east of US-101 at 1111 2nd Street (707/464-6101), this is the best source of information for southbound travelers.

Del Norte Coast Redwoods State Park

Spreading south from the Jedediah Smith redwoods, Del Norte Coast Redwoods State Park runs alongside the Pacific Ocean (and US-101) for about 10 miles, containing more than 6,000 acres of first- and second-growth redwoods as well as brilliant blooms of rhododendrons, azaleas, and spring wildflowers. Del Norte also protects miles of untouched coastline, the best

The Smith River and Jedediah Smith parks were named in memory of the legendary fur-trapping mountain man, **Jedediah Strong Smith,** who in 1826 at the age of 27 led the first party of Americans overland to California. In 1828, after being arrested as a spy and jailed by the Mexican authorities, Smith was released and walked back east, heading inland along the river that now bears his name.

Outside Crescent City, California's most violent, long-term criminals are kept behind bars in the state-of-the-art **Pelican Bay State Prison,** built in 1990.

stretch of which is accessible from the end of **Enderts Beach Road**, which cuts west from US-101 just north of the park entrance. From here, a 30-mile trail follows the coast to Prairie Creek.

The state park area is bounded on the south by an undeveloped section of Redwood National Park. Amongst the trees, the **HI Redwood Hostel** (707/482-8265), 14480 US-101, 12 miles south of Crescent City and two miles north of the Trees of Mystery, is housed in a historic farmhouse and offers cozy dormitory accommodations and a few private rooms for about $12 per person for members, $15 non-members.

Much of the land along the Klamath and Trinity Rivers is part of the extensive **Yurok and Hoopa Valley Indian Reservations**, which stretch for over 30 miles upstream from the Pacific Ocean. Because there's no through road, however, the easiest access is via Willow Creek, from where Hwy-96 runs north to Hoopa, the main community here. For more on the Native American cultures, contact the Hoopa Tribal Museum (530/625-4110).

Trees of Mystery and Klamath

Hard to miss along US-101, thanks to the massive statues of Paul Bunyan and Babe the Blue Ox looming over the highway, the Trees of Mystery (daily 8 AM-dusk; $6.50) are literally and figuratively the biggest tourist draws on the Northern California coast. Along the Tall Tales Trail, chainsaw-cut figures, backed by audiotaped stories, stand in tableaux at the foot of towering redwoods; there's also a huge gift shop and the End of the Trail Museum, a small (and free!) collection of Native American art and artifacts. Across the highway, **Motel Trees** (707/482-3152) has standard rooms from $40 and a coffee shop.

Along the banks of the mighty Klamath River, four miles south of the Trees of Mystery, the town of Klamath is a brief burst of highway sprawl, supported by anglers who flock here for the annual salmon runs. At the south end of town, drive through the **Tour-Thru Tree** ($2), then cross the Klamath River on a historic bridge graced by a pair of gilded cement grizzly bears.

Prairie Creek Redwoods State Park

The largest of the trio of north coast redwood parks, Prairie Creek Redwoods State Park is best known for its large herd of endangered **Roosevelt elk**, which you can usually see grazing in the meadows along US-101 at the center of the park, next to the main **ranger station** (707/464-6101). A new freeway carries US-101 traffic around, rather than through, the Prairie Creek redwoods; to reach the best sights, detour along the well-signed Newton B. Drury Scenic Parkway, which follows Prairie Creek along the old highway alignment through the heart of the park.

Last of the Roosevelt Elk Prairie Creek Park

Though the Jedediah Smith, Del Norte Coast, and Prairie Creek redwoods are on state-owned land, they are managed jointly under the auspices of Redwood National Park.

Another elk herd can be spotted among the coastal dunes at **Gold Bluffs Beach**, which stretches for 11 miles through untouched wilderness; there's a primitive **campground** and trails leading from US-101, or you can follow Davison Road northwest from US-101, three miles south of the ranger station.

Apart from the elk, Prairie Creek offers the usual mix of old-growth redwood trees, which here more than in the other parks mingle with dense growths of Sitka spruce and Douglas firs to form a near rainforest of greenery.

REDWOOD
NATIONAL
PARK

Ft. Dick
Lake Earl
Point Saint George
Crescent City
Gasquet   199
Jedediah Smith
Redwoods
State Park

Redwood
National
Park

Del Norte Coast
Redwoods
State Park

Requa

Trees of
Mystery
Klamath
Klamath
River

Six
Rivers
National
Forest

PACIFIC

OCEAN

Yurok
Indian
Reservation

Prairie Creek Redwoods
State Park

Redwood

National

Park

101   Orick

Stone
Lagoon

Big
Lagoon

0   10 miles
0   10 kilometers

Redwood National Park

Established in 1968, and later enlarged at a total cost of over $500 million, Redwood National Park protects some 100,000 acres of redwood forest, including the 30,000 acres previously preserved in the adjacent Smith, Del Norte and Prairie Creek State Parks. To be honest, apart from the adjacent state parks, the trees preserved here aren't by any means the oldest, largest, or most beautiful; in fact, much of the federal park land is second- or third-growth timber, clear-cut as recently as the 1960s. Though redwoods are the fastest-growing softwoods on earth—growing three to five feet a year when young—the groves here are rather disappointing compared to those in nearby areas, and serve more as an environmental buffer zone than a tree-lover's pilgrimage site.

That said, Redwood National Park does hold two special sights. The **Lady Bird Johnson Grove**, a mile east of US-101 on Bald Hills Road, is where the National Park was dedicated in 1969, and it features a mile-long trail through an ancient-feeling old-growth redwood forest. Ten miles farther along the same steep, narrow and gated road (get the combination from one of the ranger stations), then a long hike over the hills, the Tall Trees Grove holds the **world's tallest tree**, the 368-foot Libbey Tree, whose trunk measures over 14-feet across.

The groves of giant trees in Redwood National Park were used as a location for the *Star Wars* film *Return of the Jedi*, in which the characters cruised through the forest on airborne cycles. More recently, Patrick's Point played a starring role in *Jurassic Park*.

At the south end of Redwood National Park, enjoy Teutonic breakfasts at the German-run **Rolf's Park Cafe**, attached to the fairly basic, $40-a-night **Prairie Creek Motel** (707/488-3841); for over 15 years, the pair have made a good budget base for exploring the park and environs. Four miles south of Rolf's, the roadside strip town of **Orick** stretches toward the coast, where the main Redwood National Park **visitors center** (707/464-6101 ext. 5265) stands at the mouth of Redwood Creek.

Patrick's Point State Park

If your idea of heaven is sitting on a rocky headland listening to the roar of the Pacific while watching the sunset or looking for passing gray whales, you won't want to pass by Patrick's Point State Park. Three different 200-foot-high promontories at the heart of the park provide panoramic views, while the surrounding acres hold cedar and spruce forests (but no redwoods), open pastures bright with wildflowers, great tidepools, a wide dark sand beach, and two **campgrounds** with hot showers (800/444-7275). Also here are the preserved and restored remnants of a Yurok village; for further information, contact the **visitors center** (707/677-3570).

Continuing south, US-101 becomes a four-lane freeway along the ocean to Arcata and Eureka, but the old US-101 alignment winds along the cliff tops between Patrick's Point and the small town of Trinidad. Along this road you'll find some nice older motels, like the **Patrick's Point Inn** at 3602 Patrick's Point Drive (707/677-3483 or 800/354-7006), which is just a half-mile from the park entrance, and has oceanside rooms from around $60 a night. Also here is the excellent **Larrupin Cafe**, 1658 Patrick's Point Drive (707/677-0230), which serves up bountiful portions of very fresh all-American food in a friendly, homey ambience—California cuisine without the snooty pretense you sometimes find farther south. It's open for dinner only, every day but Tuesday, and is cash-only; two can dine well for around $50.

The author **Bret Harte** was run out of Arcata by angry townspeople in 1860, after writing an editorial in the local paper criticizing the massacre of a local Wiyot tribe.

Bigfoot Country: US-299

North of Arcata, scenic US-299 runs inland from the coast for over 150 miles, cutting over the coastal mountains to the northern Central Valley. Following the Mad River through the logging and farming town of Blue Lake (where, alas, there is no lake), after 35 miles the road reaches the town of **Willow Creek**, which claims to be the heart of "Bigfoot Country." Along with boasting a large statue of the furry beast (who is said to inhabit the rugged mountains south of town), and a chance to sample "Bigfoot burgers" at the small cafe at the east end of town, Willow Creek offers whitewater rafting, swimmable beaches, and top-rated salmon fishing along the Trinity River. For further information, and details on the annual Bigfoot Days celebrations, contact the chamber of commerce (530/629-2693).

McKinleyville, where US-299 heads east from the coast, boasts the **"World's Tallest Single-Tree Totem Pole."** See it for yourself in the parking lot of the town's main shopping center, on City Center Road.

From Willow Creek, US-299 continues east along the Trinity River, eventually passing by the beautiful Trinity Alps to reach historic **Weaverville**, the well-preserved center of a mid-1850s gold rush area, before linking up with I-5 at Redding. Please see page 115 for details on the eastern section of US-299.

Arcata

The most attractive and enjoyable town on the far north coast of California, Arcata (pop. 15,197) makes a great base from which to explore the rivers and redwoods. The presence of

PLEASE
DO NOT CLIMB
ON ROCKS

Humboldt State University campus on the hills above US-101 accounts for the town's youthful, non-conformist energy, especially in the cafes, bookstores, and bars that surround the lively **Town Plaza**, two blocks west of US-101 at 9th and G Streets, incongruously graced by palm trees and a statue of President McKinley. The *Utne Reader* recently rated Arcata as "the most enlightened small town in California," and spending even a little time here in this vibrant, cooperative Ecotopia may make you wonder whether or not you really do have to race back to the big city 9-to-5 grind.

Around Arcata you can admire the areas's many elaborate Victorian-era cottages, listen to street musicians playing Bob Dylan and Grateful Dead tunes, hunt wild mushrooms, clamber over sand dunes or hike in the redwoods; afterwards relax with a cup of tea or, better yet, a soak in a hot tub at homey **Cafe Mokka**, the coast's only combo sauna and espresso bar at 5th and J Streets (707/822-2228). Lively cafes and restaurants surround the plaza, while microbrewed beers flow from the taps of the many amiable bars, most of which feature live music. For food, drink and entertainment all under one roof, head to the **Humboldt Brewery**, just

off the plaza at 856 10th Street; and for a complete selection of foodstuffs and supplies, and more insight into the local community, head to the large and stylish **Arcata Co-op**, at 8th and I Streets two blocks uphill from the plaza.

For a place to stay, the centrally located **Hotel Arcata** (707/826-0217 or 800/344-1221), on the plaza at 708 9th Street, has rooms from $60, or you can take your pick of the usual motels along US-101.

Eureka

Evolving into a lively artists colony from its roots as a fairly gritty and industrial port, Eureka was well known to fur trappers and traders long before it became a booming lumber and whaling port in the 1850s. Thanks to the lumber trade, Victorian Eureka grew prosperous, building elaborate homes including the oft-photographed but closed-to-the-public **Carson Mansion** along the waterfront at 2nd and M Streets, two blocks west of US-101.

Along with dozens of well-preserved Victorian houses, Eureka has done a fine job of finding new uses for its many ornate commercial buildings, which have been preserved to house a wonderful range of bookstores, art galleries, cafes and restaurants in what's now called Old Town, a half dozen blocks along the waterfront west of US-101. This historic downtown quarter also has a number of good places to eat and drink, including **Ramone's Bakery**, 209 E Street, the pub-like **Cafe Waterfront** at 1st and F Streets, and the popular **Sea Grill**, a block from US-101 at 316 E Street. Another good place is the no-frills **Seafood Grotto** ("We Catch 'em, Cook 'em, Serve 'em"), south of Old Town along US-101 at 6th and Broadway.

the Carson Mansion

Accommodation options range from roadside motels—including a handy Travelodge on US-101 downtown—to upscale places like the **Carter House Inn**, 1033 3rd Street (707/445-1390), a re-created Victorian manor with spacious rooms and a big breakfast for $125 and up. For a more authentic Victorian experience, stay at one of California's most delightful B&Bs, the **Elegant Victorian Mansion** at 1406 C Street (707/444-3144). A real treasure in a land of nice B&Bs, this magnificently restored 1888 Eastlake-style home has been opulently decorated with real antiques and Bradbury & Bradbury wallpapers by the hospitable Belgian-born innkeeper Lily Vieyra, and offers four nonsmoking rooms, ranging from $85 to $225 a night.

For further information, contact the **Eureka! Humboldt County Convention and Visitors' Bureau** at 1034 2nd Street (707/443-5097 or 800/338-7352).

In Eureka, check out the **Romano Gabriel Wooden Sculptures,** displayed in a plate-glass showcase at 315 2nd Street. This brilliantly colorful folk art extravaganza of faces and flowers originally stood in the front yard of local gardener Romano Gabriel, who made them out of discarded packing crates and other recycled materials over a period of some 30 years before his death in 1977.

Samoa

Even if you're just passing through, don't miss the chance to visit the busy mill town of Samoa, across the bay from Eureka but easily reachable via the Hwy-255 bridge. Follow the signs past the piles of logs and belching mill chimneys to the unique **Samoa Cookhouse** (707/442-1659), built at the turn of the century by the Louisiana Pacific lumber company, which still owns most of the peninsula. Inside the cookhouse, which is packed with logging memorabilia, take a seat at one of the 20-foot-long tables (redwood, of course, covered in checkered oilcloth) and dig into the family-style feast. There are no menus, just huge platters of food at ridiculously low prices—$6 for breakfast (from 6 AM, with great hash browns!) and $7 for lunch (served till 3 PM), $12 for a two-meat, four-course dinner (served 5-9 PM, 5-10 PM in summer).

Ferndale

Well worth the 10-mile detour west of US-101, the historic town of Ferndale (pop. 1,331) is an odd fish along the woodsy Northern California coast, a century-old dairy town that would look more at home in middle America. The three-block-

KINETIC SCULPTURE RACE

Arcata's creative community comes alive every Memorial Day weekend for the world-famous Kinetic Sculpture Race, in which participants pedal, paddle, and otherwise move themselves and their handmade vehicles across land and sea. Part art, part engineering and part athletic competition, the kinetic sculpture race is like nothing you've seen before. Beginning midday Saturday and running around the clock until Monday afternoon, a mind-boggling array of mobile contraptions—past winners have included everything from dragons and floating flying saucers to Egyptian Pyramids (named "Queen of Denial") and a Cadillac Coupe de Ville—make their way over land, sand and sea from the town square of Arcata to the main street of Ferndale, twice crossing chilly Humboldt Bay.

Rule Number One of the Kinetic Sculpture Race is that all of the "sculptures" must be people-powered; beyond that, imagination is the primary guide. Many "rules" that have developed over the years since the race was first run in 1969, including such pearls as "In the Event of Rain, the Race is Run In the Rain," but most of these emphasize the idea that maintaining style and a sense of humor are at least as important as finishing the fastest. Since the Grand Prizes are valued at somewhere around $14.98, racers take part solely "for the glory," but prizes are awarded in many categories: first- and last-place finishers are winners, and the racer who finishes in the exact middle of the pack gets the coveted Medio-Car Award—a broken-down old banger.

Spectators are expected to be active participants, too, so be prepared to shout and scream and applaud the competitors, or even jog or bike or kayak alongside them. There are many great vantage points along the route, but you have to be in the right place on the right day. The Kinetic Sculpture Race begins at noon on Saturday with a pre-race line-up around Arcata's Town Square, from where racers wind along country roads to the sandy Samoa Peninsula before spending the first night in downtown Eureka. Sunday morning the racers head across Humboldt Bay from Field's Landing, then camp out overnight along the ocean. Monday's trials include another water crossing and the muddy mess of the Slimey Slope, culminating in a mad dash down the Main Street of Ferndale surrounded by cheering multitudes. It's all good fun, and a great focus for a visit to this remarkable corner of the world.

For further information, call the race organizers (707/786-9259) or the Eureka visitors bureau (800/346-3482).

"Just for the Halibut" sculpture racing along Samoa Peninsula

long, franchise-free Main Street includes a fully stocked general store and the Golden Gait/Gate Mercantile, and whitewashed farmhouses dot the pastoral valleys nearby. Ferndale's diverse history is well documented inside the **Ferndale Museum**, off Main Street at Shaw and 3rd Streets (hours vary; 707/786-4466), and the wacky racers that take part in the annual Kinetic Sculpture Race are displayed in the center of town at 393 Main Street.

The fine food at **Curley's Grill**, 460 Main Street, has made it a popular place to eat, while *the* place to stay (or at least to see) in Ferndale is the lushly landscaped late-Victorian **Gingerbread Mansion**, 400 Berding Street (707/786-4000), with deluxe rooms from around $100 a night. Also nice is the **Shaw House**, an 1854 American Gothic masterpiece with B&B rooms and bikes for rent at 703 Main Street (707/786-9958).

Pick up free walking-tour maps and other visitor information at the **chamber of commerce** on Main Street (707/786-4477).

The area around Ferndale has been hit by numerous earthquakes, including a destructive tremor in April 1992 that registered 6.9 on the Richter scale.

*From early December until the end of the year, Ferndale's Main Street is graced by **"America's Tallest Living Christmas Tree,"** a 170-foot-tall Sitka Spruce draped in spectacular lights.*

The Lost Coast

Between Ferndale and Mendocino, the main US-101 highway heads inland along the Eel River, but if you have time and a taste for adventure, head west from Ferndale along the narrow, winding Mattole Road, which loops around Cape Mendocino through the northern reaches of the so-called Lost Coast, a 100-mile stretch of shoreline justly famous for its isolated beauty. By road, you can only get close to the ocean at a few points—the few miles south of Cape Mendocino, and again at the fishing resort of **Shelter Cove**, west of Garberville—but hikers can have a field day (or week) exploring the extensive coastal wilderness. Some 50 miles of rugged, untouched coastline, packed with tidal pools and driftwood-strewn beaches, have been preserved in a pair of parks, the Kings Range National Conservation Area in the north, and the Sinkyone Wilderness State Park farther south. The most popular hiking route starts in the north at the small **Mattole Campground**, west of Petrolia at the end of Lighthouse Road, then follows the coastline south for 25 miles to Black Sands Beach, near Shelter Cove; plan on three days for the whole trek, expect morning fogs (or worse!), and purify all water before drinking.

The Lost Coast area was the site of the first oil wells in California, which were drilled in the 1860s near the town of Petrolia but are long gone.

Besides the Mattole Road, which makes a 73-mile loop between Ferndale and the Rockefeller Forest section of Humboldt Redwoods State Park, a network of rougher and even more remote routes allow auto access to the Lost Coast, linking the hamlet of Honeydew with coastal Hwy-1 near Rockport. If you do explore this wild (and very rainy) region, take a good map and plenty of food and water, and be careful. For further information on the Lost Coast, contact the Bureau of Land Management office in Arcata (707/825-2300).

Scotia

Back along US-101, on the banks of the Eel River midway between the coast and Humboldt Redwoods State Park, Scotia is the only true company town left in California. The Pacific Lumber Company (PALCO) built it in the 1880s and still owns everything, from the two huge mills to the 10 blocks of white-painted houses, church, and schools that constitute this little community of about 1,000 people.

Stop first at the small **museum**, housed in the redwood-built Greek Revival former bank at the center of town, to pick up passes for self-guided **tours** (Mon.-Fri. 7:30-10:30 AM and 11:30 AM-2 PM; free) of the world's largest redwood mill. Following a yellow painted line through the mill at your own pace, you can gawk at (and listen to—it's a noisy business) every stage of the milling process. First, cut logs get de-barked by a powerful jet of water, then laser-guided band saws slice the logs into rough boards, which are turned into finished lumber. A raised catwalk runs through the center of the mill, and signs explain what's happening at each stage.

The one place to stay in town is the rustic **Scotia Inn** (707/764-5683), which has B&B rooms ($60-160 a night) and a very good restaurant; it's on Main Street, a block from the Scotia museum.

Humboldt Redwoods State Park: Avenue of the Giants

Sheltering the biggest and best collection of giant coastal redwoods anywhere in the world, Humboldt Redwoods State Park is an exceptionally breathtaking corner of an exceptionally beautiful region. Covering 50,000 acres along the Eel River, this is the true heart of redwood country, containing the largest and most pristine expanses of virgin forest as well as some of the largest, tallest, and most remarkable trees.

PALCO, the lumber company that owns and runs Scotia, used to own the hugely controversial **Headwaters Forest,** which at over 2,700 acres was the largest old-growth redwood grove still in private hands. After years of acrimony, in March 1999 the Headwaters Forest and the land around it was sold to the federal government for some $300 million. The purchase will enable scientists to study this extensive old-growth habitat in its primeval state. For up-to-date information on anything to do with the Headwaters Forest Reserve and to make reservations for hikes to the southern area of the forest, contact the very helpful, ever-friendly Bureau of Land Management office in Arcata (707/825-2300).

The well-graded fire roads through the Rockefeller Forest make excellent mountain bike routes.

Even if you're just passing through, be sure to turn onto the amazing Avenue of the Giants, 32 miles of old highway frontage between Jordan Creek and Phillipsville, parallel to the fast and busy US-101 freeway that runs on stilts through the park. If you just want a taste of the redwoods, there are seven exits off US-101 that lead right onto the Avenue of the Giants, but no matter how you get here, driving or riding along the Avenue of the Giants is a totally amazing experience, as you follow the thin ribbon of smooth blacktop past towering, arrow-straight redwoods, so close they seem about to step out across the road in front of you.

At the north end of the park you'll find an impressive collection of trees in the well-marked **Founders Grove**, where a half-mile nature trail leads past the 362-foot-tall, 1,600-year-old **Dyerville Giant**, lauded as the world's tallest tree before it fell during the winter of 1991. West of Founder's Grove, across US-101, the 13,000-acre **Rockefeller Forest** is one of the largest old-growth redwood forests in the world, and includes two of the park's champion trees, each over 360 feet tall and some 17 feet in diameter.

In and amongst the park's natural splendors, there are a number of unnatural attractions as well: the Eternal Treehouse in Redcrest and the Shrine Drive-Thru Tree in Myers Flat are just two of the many wacky-tacky tourist traps of Redwood Country. (See the special topic Redwood Country Roadside Attractions for more.)

The best source of information on the park is the **visitors center** (707/946-2263) in **Weott**, midway along the Avenue of the Giants; there's a pleasant **campground**

REDWOOD COUNTRY ROADSIDE ATTRACTIONS

The stretch of US-101 through the redwood country of Humboldt County is lined by pristine groves of massive trees, and provides boundless opportunities to come face-to-face with your own insignificance in nature's greater scheme of things. But if you ever tire of this display of natural majesty, or simply want to keep it in context with the modern "civilized" world, you're in luck: every few miles, amongst the stately trees, you'll come upon shameless souvenir stands selling redwood burl furniture and chainsaw sculptures—including one featuring Biblical figures, called "Carving for Christ"—as well as tacky tourist traps like the **World of Bigfoot,**" near Richardson Grove State Park, or "**Hobbittown USA,**" in Phillipsville. None of these is big or bold enough to detract from the main event—the big trees—and since they've been in operation since the earliest days of car-borne tourism, they're really as much a part of the Redwood Country experience as the trees themselves. In any case, since most charge only a couple of dollars' admission, there's not a lot to lose.

While you're encouraged to stop at any and all of them —at least long enough to buy a postcard or two—some of the more tried-and-true attractions are, in north to south order: the **Trees of Mystery,** marked by huge statues of Paul Bunyan and Babe the Blue Ox along US-101 in Klamath; the **Eternal Treehouse** in Redcrest; the **Shrine Drive-Thru Tree** in Myers Flat, which wagon-borne travelers drove through over a century ago; and the **One-Log House** in Phillipsville, a mobile home carved from a single, 32-foot redwood log. At the south end of Redwood Country, near the town of Leggett, are two more. **Confusion Hill** is one of those places where water runs uphill and the rules of physics seem not to apply. There's also a little railway train here that chugs uphill to a very nice grove of trees. **Chandelier Drive-Thru Tree,** south of Leggett off old US-101 on Drive-Thru Tree Road, allows you to drive your car through a 315-foot redwood tree.

The protection of the mighty redwood forests of Northern California was made possible not by the state or federal governments but primarily by the efforts of the **Save the Redwoods League,** a private organization that has raised, since its founding in 1918, millions of dollars to buy or preserve over 160,000 acres of redwood forest. To support these efforts, write to 114 Sansome Street, Room 605, San Francisco, CA 94104, or call 415/362-2352.

($14; 800/444-7275) with showers, right next door. You may have to drive a ways north (to Ferndale, Eureka, or Arcata) or south (to Garberville) from the park to find a really good meal, but there are a few nice places to stay in and amongst the Humboldt Redwoods. Across from the Eternal Treehouse, the **Redcrest Resort,** 26459 Avenue of the Giants (707/722-4208), offers old-fashioned cabins from around $50, and a pleasant campground. Midway along the Avenue of the Giants, the historic **Myers Inn** (707/943-3259) in Myers

Most of the old towns along the Eel River were destroyed by a terrible flood in 1964, when the river rose as high as 35 feet above the Avenue of the Giants.

Flat has comfy B&B rooms from around $125, while farther south the hamlet of Miranda holds the relaxing **Miranda Gardens Resort** (707/943-3011), with motel rooms and rustic cabins at $50-140 a night.

Garberville and Redway

Since its recurring presence in the national media during the U.S. government's high-profile, late 1980s raids on local marijuana plantations, Garberville has returned to its previous sleepy self. The US-101 freeway bypasses the town, which stretches for a half-dozen blocks along Redwood Drive, the well-signed business loop off the highway.

Enjoy an early morning breakfast with locals at the **Eel River Cafe**, 801 Redwood Avenue, or enjoy an espresso and healthy food at the **Woodrose Cafe**, a block south at 911 Redwood Avenue. Garberville also has all the motels you could want, including the $50-a-night **Motel Garberville**, 948 Redwood Drive (707/923-2422).

Just west of Garberville on the old highway, Redway is a small and usually quiet enclave that's worth the short sidetrip, if only for breakfast, lunch, or dinner at the **Mateel Cafe**, a health-conscious gourmet haunt along Redwood Avenue at the center of town.

Along US-101, four miles south of Garberville, one of the region's most characterful places is the **Benbow Inn** (707/923-2124), a circa 1926 mock Tudor hotel with 55 fairly pricey rooms (doubles run $90-190) and a nice restaurant offering afternoon tea and scones on a sunny terrace overlooking Lake Benbow. Another four miles south along US-101, **Richardson Grove State Park** (707/247-3318) has nearly 1,000 acres of redwoods plus a lodge, a restaurant, cabins and a campground; just north of the park is the **World of Bigfoot**, a wonderfully tacky roadside souvenir stand, selling everything from postcards and fridge magnets to giant redwood carvings of you-know-who.

From Redway, the well-maintained Briceland Road heads over the coast range to **Shelter Cove,** at the center of the wild Lost Coast.

The annual **Reggae on the River** festival, organized by the Mateel Community Center (707/923-3368), attracts top performers and thousands of fans to French's Campground near Piercy every August. Any time of year, you can hear some reggae grooves among the 1970s classic rock of **KHUM 104.7 FM.**

Leggett: the Drive-Thru Tree

No longer even a proverbial wide spot in the road since the US-101 freeway was diverted around it, Leggett marks the southern end of the Humboldt redwoods. At the south end of Leggett, a mile from the US-101/Hwy-1 junction along the old highway, stands one of the redwood region's most venerable and worthwhile roadside attractions, the "original" **Drive-Thru Tree** (daily 8 AM-dusk; $3). In addition to the famous tree, which had the hole cut through it in the 1930s, there's an above-average gift shop with a broad range of books, postcards, and schlocky souvenirs.

South of Leggett, US-101 runs inland through the heart of the Mendocino County wine country, while scenic Hwy-1 cuts west over the coastal mountains to the delightful little town of Mendocino, winding along the Pacific south to San Francisco.

US-101: Willits, Ukiah, Hopland, and Cloverdale

If you don't have enough time to follow the gorgeous coastal route along Hwy-1, don't despair: the much-faster inland route along US-101 is plenty pretty, passing through the heart of the Mendocino County wine country. Vineyards and tasting rooms line the roadside, extensive forests cover the surrounding hills and mountains, and amidst the scenery are a few diverse towns, ranging from quiet hamlets

At the south end of Leggett, the "original" Drive-Thru Tree

to fairly industrial milltowns. Most of the towns here are actually a mix of the two, with pleasant residential quarters and quaint downtowns coexisting with lumber mills belching out steam and the rich scent of wood pulp.

Though US-101 is more and more of a freeway, bypassing the towns and slowly losing what's left of its old road qualities, it's not hard to encounter the picturesque small-town scenery. In **Willits**, where the Skunk Train runs over the coast to Fort Bragg, the highway drops down to two lanes through the center of town, passing beneath a neon-lit welcome sign that arches over US-101 and reads Willits—Heart of Mendocino.

Midway between Eureka and San Francisco, the lumber mill town of **Ukiah** (pop. 14,600) is the region's biggest burg. The old US-101 route, State Street, is lined by the usual barrage of fast-food restaurants and one unique survivor from the early days of automobile tourism: the **World's Largest Redwood Tree Gas Station**, next to a Union 76 station at 859 N. State Street and hardly changed since 1936, when it was

carved from the trunk of a 1,500-year-old redwood tree. Ukiah also holds a very worthwhile collection of local Native American basketry and anthropological exhibits at the wonderful **Grace Hudson Museum**, 431 S. Main Street (Wed.-Sun. 10 AM-4:30 PM; donations; 707/467-2836).

The next city to the south, **Cloverdale**, has also been bypassed by the US-101 freeway, but the reasons for turning off here are both touristic and culinary. Cloverdale ("Where the Vineyards Meet the Redwoods") marks the junction with Hwy-128, a scenic route through the Anderson Valley, but more importantly for food fans it's home to two great places to eat. **World Famous Hamburger Ranch**, occupying the old Top of the Hill Texaco filling station on the north side of town at 31195 N. Redwood Highway (daily 7 AM-9 PM; 707/894-5616) is an excellent roadside cafe serving bountiful breakfasts and beefy burgers, plus pasta dishes (and great beers), inside or on a sunny terrace. In town, more burgers, plus root beers and ice cream cones, can be had at the 1940s classic **Pick's Drive In**, at 115 S. Redwood Highway.

Approaching the San Francisco Bay Area, US-101 passes through the famous wine-growing regions of Sonoma County.

Hippies, free-thinkers, and other independent spirits will want to stop at the **Real Goods** solar-powered sustainable-living store on the south side of Hopland, where you can check out or purchase everything you need to live "off the grid," from water heaters to windmills.

But if you only have time for one stop on this leg, make it **Hopland**, halfway between Ukiah and Cloverdale. As the name suggests, this is an old hop-growing district, birthplace of Red Tail Ale and other fine Mendocino brews, which are now made up in Ukiah. Hopland is also home to the excellent **Cheesecake Lady**, bakers of excellent desserts and snacks; across the highway, the **Bluebird Cafe** serves up delectable and plentiful meals all day long. Tiny Hopland (pop. 817) is also world headquarters for the huge Fetzer winery (samples available at the tasting room east of town).

Near where Hwy-1 reaches the Mendocino coast north of Rockport, a small county road (Hwy-431) cuts north to the remote reaches of the Sinkyone Wilderness State Park and the rugged Lost Coast.

Rockport and Westport

From US-101 at Leggett, Hwy-1 twists west over the rugged coastal mountains before hugging the coast through the weatherbeaten logging and fishing communities of Rockport and Westport. The small and informal **Howard Creek Ranch** (707/964-6725) in Westport offers comfortable B&B rooms, an outdoor hot tub, and easy access to the driftwood-laden beach.

From Fort Bragg, the California & Western Railroad runs a number of historic steam- and diesel-powered **Skunk Trains** over the mountains to Willits and back. Half-day and full-day trips ($27-35; 707/964-6372) run year-round.

Farther south, just north of Fort Bragg, MacKerricher State Park protects seven miles of rocky coast and black-sand beaches (all linked by a hiking trail), plus blufftop meadows and waterfront pine forest; the very nice **campground**, as in all California state parks, is reservable through the private concessionaire ReserveAmerica (800/444-7275).

Fort Bragg

Even if you could keep yourself from stopping along this beautiful stretch of highway, it would take more than an hour to cover the 44 miles between US-101 and the first real coastal town, Fort Bragg (pop. 6,100), whose burly, blue-collar edge comes as something of a shock on the otherwise undeveloped, touristy Mendocino coast. Home to a large Georgia Pacific lumber mill and the region's largest commercial fishing fleet, Fort Bragg takes a mostly no-frills approach to the tourist trade, leaving the dainty B&B scene to its upscale neighbor, Mendocino. However, there are a few down-to-earth places to eat: very good omelettes and other egg dishes are available at the appropriately named **Egghead Restaurant**, 326 N. Main Street, while **The Wharf**, along the Noyo River at 780 N. Harbor Drive, serves good value seafood dinners. Fort Bragg's many motels, including the **Fort Bragg Motel**, 763 N. Main Street (707/964-4787), are the coast's only cheap accommodation options, after camping.

For more complete information on the Fort Bragg/Mendocino area, contact the **North Coast Chamber of Commerce**, 332 N. Main Street (707/961-6300 or 800/726-2780).

On the north side of Fort Bragg, at the west end of Elm Street, **Glass Beach** is the new name for the old Fort Bragg trash dump, where ocean waves have polished thrown-away bottles so that at low tide the glass forms a colorful and truly sparkling strand. Visitors are allowed onto the beach for collecting treasures.

Mendocino

One of the prettiest towns on the California coast (as seen in TV shows like *Murder, She Wrote* and numerous movies), Mendocino (pop. 1,100) is an artists-and-writers community par excellence, and an upscale escape for wage-slaving visitors from San Francisco. Originally established as a logging port in the 1850s, Mendocino successfully preserved both its soft sandstone coastline—great for wintertime whalewatching—and its New England-style clapboard houses, many of which have been converted into luxurious B&B inns.

Mendocino is ideal for leisurely wandering. Hence, the main thing to do here is to meander through the heathers and other coastal flora that fill the **Mendocino Headlands State Park**, wrapping around the south, west and north edges of town and providing uninterrupted views over the restless Pacific shore. For field guides, maps, tips on whalewatching—or to see a model of what Mendocino looked like during its lumbering heyday—stop inside the park **visitors center**, overlooking the ocean from the historic Ford House at 735 Main Street (707/937-5397).

Just north of Mendocino along Hwy-1, **Russian Gulch State Park** (707/937-5804) has longer, wilder hiking trails; one runs inland through redwood forests up to a seasonal waterfall, and another winds along the shore, where the ocean waves have carved a blowhole that shoots water into the air during stormy weather.

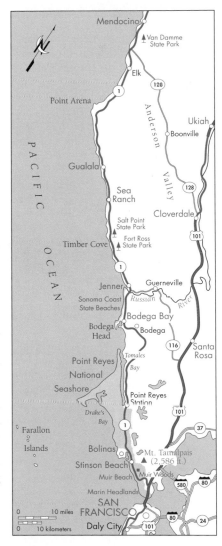

Mendocino Practicalities
Along with its many fine art galleries, boutiques and book shops, Mendocino has some of California's best restaurants—a wonderful treat before or after a day out appreciating the wonders of nature. If you're not being served a home-cooked "B" at your B&B, enjoy a breakfast of coffee and pastries at **Tote Fête Bakery,** 10450 Lansing Street (707/937-3383). For lunch, join what's left of Mendocino's hippies for salads, sandwiches, and veggie-and-tofu burritos at the **Mendocino Cafe,** 10451 Lansing at Albion Street (707/937-2422), or indulge your tastebuds at the **Moosse Café,** 390 Kasten at Albion Street (707/937-4323), which has great food and world famous desserts. For dinner, many Mendocino visitors plan their visits around a meal at **Cafe Beaujolais,** two blocks from the waterfront at 961 Ukiah Street (707/937-5614), which serves a prix fixe gourmet feast of California cuisine delicacies, nightly 6-9 PM.

Prettiest and most central of Mendocino's many lovely B&Bs, the historic **MacCallum House,** 45020 Albion Street (707/937-0289), includes a beautiful garden, good breakfasts, and a cozy nighttime bar and restaurant. Above the village, just west of Hwy-1 at 44800 Little Lake Road, the **Joshua Grindle Inn** (707/937-4143 or 800/474-6353) is a quiet B&B in a quaint 1870 farmhouse, with a wraparound porch overlooking two acres of gardens. About the only place to stay in Mendocino for under $100 is the circa 1858 **Mendocino Hotel,** on the downtown waterfront at 45080 Main Street (707/937-0511).

> Though Mendocino is tiny—maybe 10 full blocks altogether—its street numbers are huge, rising to five digits. Hwy-1 bypasses Mendocino, but the old road lives on as Lansing Street, east and north from the center of town.

> One place worth keeping an eye out for 15 miles south of Mendocino along Hwy-1 is the tiny roadside community of **Elk,** which has a good cafe, a general store, and a trail leading down to the Pacific at Greenwood Cove.

Van Damme State Park

> Driving through the Anderson Valley in summer, pick up picnic supplies at **Gowan's Oak Tree,** a wonderful roadside fruit-and-vegetable stand along Hwy-128, two miles west of Philo.

South of Mendocino at the mouth of the Little River, Van Damme State Park stretches for five miles along the coastal bluffs and beaches and includes some 1,800 acres of pine and redwood forest. The park's unique attribute is the oddly contorted **Pygmy Forest,** a natural bonsai-like grove of miniature pines, cypress, and manzanita, with a wheelchair-accessible nature trail explaining the unique ecology; the trailhead is four miles east of Hwy-1. There's also a small, very popular campground, and a **visitors center** (707/937-0851) housed in a New Deal-era recreation hall.

Detour: Anderson Valley

From Hwy-1 south of Mendocino, Hwy-128 cuts diagonally across to US-101 through the lovely Anderson Valley, home to numerous fine wineries (including Husch, Navarro, and Kendall-Jackson) and the *Anderson Valley Advertiser,* one of

California's most outspoken local newspapers. Anderson Valley also has its own regional dialect, called Boontling, combining English, Scots-Irish, Spanish, and Native American words into a lighthearted lingo created, some say, simply to befuddle outsiders—in Boontling, to "shark the bright-lighters."

To find out more, stop in the valley's tiny main town, **Boonville**, and peruse the book shop alongside the Horn of Zeese coffee shop. Another place to check out is next door's Anderson Valley Brewing Company, a pub-like restaurant and saloon that's the birthplace of delicious Boont Amber, the state's finest microbrew. And for a real treat, arrange to have a meal at the wonderful **Boonville Hotel** across the street (707/895-2210), where foodies from all over the country have been flocking for a taste of the eclectic, farm-fresh cuisine cooked up by John Schmitt, whose family used to run the legendary French Laundry in Yountville. Prices are high though not exorbitant (for example: pork tenderloin served with orange chutney and garlic mashed potatoes costs around $20), but it's a small place and reservations are strongly suggested. (There are also a few rooms for overnight guests.)

Heading southeast from Boonville, Hwy-128 joins up with US-101 at Cloverdale, then veers off east again from Geyserville on a lovely rural two-lane cruise through Knights Valley to Calistoga and the northern Napa Valley. The route through the famous Wine Country of the Napa Valley is described on pages 234-236.

Gualala

The southernmost 40 miles of Mendocino coastline are almost totally undeveloped and virtually uninhabited, with green forests and coastal coves as far as the eye can see. Situated at the very southern edge of the county, the old logging port of Gualala (pop. 950) has one truly remarkable feature: the Russian Orthodox domes of **St. Orres** (707/884-3303), a B&B inn and very expensive Francophile gourmet restaurant glowing with polished wood and stained glass, above Hwy-1 on the north side of town. You'll also find inexpensive lodging (rooms for less than $50 a night, a real rarity in these parts) and a locally popular restaurant right in town at the **Gualala Hotel** (707/884-3441).

At the north end of Gualala, be sure to stop at **The Food Company** deli and sample some of the world's finest ginger cookies, baked fresh daily and truly delicious. The deli also offers a full range of picnic foods – salads, dips, breads, beers, wines—and did we mention the ginger cookies?

Sea Ranch

Midway between Mendocino and the San Francisco Bay Area, the vacation home community of Sea Ranch was laid out in the mid-1960s by an enthusiastic group of then-young architects and planners, including Lawrence Halprin and the late Charles Moore, who hoped to show that development need not destroy or negatively impact the natural beauty of the California coast. Strict design guidelines, preserving over half the 5,000 acres as open space and requiring the use of muted natural wood cladding and other barn-like features, made it an aesthetic success, which you can appreciate for yourself at the **Sea Ranch Lodge** (707/785-2371). The lodge offers good meals and rooms from around $100 a night.

The rest of Sea Ranch, however, is strictly private, which has raised the hackles of area activists, who after years of lawsuits finally forced through a few coastal access trails in the mid-1980s; these are marked by turnouts (parking $2) along Hwy-1.

Salt Point State Park
The many sheltered rocky coves of Salt Point State Park make it ideal for undersea divers, who come to hunt the abundant abalone. Along the five miles of jagged shoreline, pines and redwoods clutch the water's edge, covering some 6,000 acres on both sides of Hwy-1. Though parts of the park were badly burned in a 1994 fire, Salt Point is still a prime place for hiking or camping. For more information, or for a guide to the many remnants of the Pomo tribal village that stood here until the 1850s, contact the **visitors center** (707/ 847-3221).

One of the few positive effects of cutting down the native redwood forests that once covered the Northern California coast has been the emergence of giant-sized rhododendrons in their place. You'll find the most impressive display at the **Kruse Rhododendron Preserve**, high above Hwy-1 at the center of Salt Point State Park, where some 350 acres of azaleas and rhododendrons, some reaching 15 feet in height, burst forth in late spring, usually peaking around the first week of May.

In between Salt Point and Fort Ross, Beniamo Bufano's 72-foot *Peace* statue looms alongside Hwy-1 above craggy **Timber Cove,** where there's also a nice restaurant and lodge.

Fort Ross State Historic Park
If you're captivated by California's lively history, one of the most evocative spots in the state is Fort Ross State Historic Park (daily 10 AM-4:30 PM; $5 per car; 707/847-3286), the well-restored remains of a Russian fur-trapping outpost built here in 1812. During a 30-year residency, the Russians farmed wheat and potatoes, traded with native tribes, and trapped local seals and sea otters for their furs, which commanded huge sums on the European market. The near destruction of the sea otter population by 1840 caused the company to shut down operations, and sell the fort to Sacramento's John Sutter, who went bankrupt to finance the purchase. Later, the abandoned fort was badly damaged by the 1906 San Francisco earthquake and a number of fires, but the state has completed a high-quality restoration and reconstruction project, using hand-hewn lumber and historically accurate building methods to replicate the original barracks and other buildings, including a luminous redwood chapel.

Outside the fort's walls, a modern **visitors center** traces the site's natural, native, and Russian history, and offers information on the park's small **campground** and many fine hiking trails.

Russian Orthodox Chapel at Fort Ross

South of Fort Ross, Hwy-1 climbs high above the rugged coastline, offering breathtaking vistas of the Pacific Ocean hundreds of feet below. Twelve miles south of Fort Ross, Hwy-1 reaches the resort community of **Jenner** (pop. 300), which stretches along the broad mouth of the Russian River.

the closing of the Russian River ferry, c. 1931

The Russian River: Guerneville

From Jenner, Hwy-116 runs east along the Russian River, passing through forests, vineyards, and popular summertime resort towns, most of which date back over 100 years to the heyday of the redwood logging industry. The first of these is **Duncan's Mills**, a wide spot in the road that hosts a summertime rodeo and has a great roadside restaurant, the **Blue Heron** (hours vary; 707/865-9135). Continuing east along the river, the next town you reach is quaint Monte Rio, a ramshackle little town that's the unlikely looking home to the world's most exclusive male-only power-broking summer camp, Bohemian Grove. South from Monte Rio, the narrow, winding **Bohemian Highway** wiggles south to the town of **Occidental**, where a number of Wild West-looking saloons and hotels double as very popular Italian restaurants.

The largest of the Russian River resort towns is Guerneville, on Hwy-116 a dozen miles east of the coast, with an alternative-minded (mostly gay and lesbian) summer population, a number of worthwhile cafes along Main Street, and, best of all, wonderful little Johnson's Beach, where a dam blocks the river, making for a great swimming hole. Canoes, kayaks, campsites and more are available from the family-friendly **Johnson's Beach Resort**, 16241 1st Street (707/869-2022); the main gay-and-lesbian-friendly resort on the river is **Fife's**, 16467 River Road (800/7-FIFES-1 or 800/734-3371).

Just three miles north of Guerneville, one of the last big stands of natural redwoods is preserved in the 750-acre **Armstrong Redwoods State Reserve** (707/869-2015), which has cool hiking trails and campsites among the massive trees.

After winding along the river, 35-odd miles from the Pacific, Hwy-116 eventually links up with the US-101 freeway to and from San Francisco, providing a faster alternative to coastal Hwy-1.

East of Guerneville along the Russian River, one of California's best known vineyards, **Korbel Champagne Cellars,** has been producing excellent sparkling wines for over 100 years. Tours and tasting are available (daily 10 AM-4 PM; free; 707/824-7000).

Sonoma Coast State Beaches

South of Jenner and the Russian River, Hwy-1 hugs the coast along 10 miles of rocky coves and sandy beaches, collectively protected as the Sonoma Coast State Beaches. Starting with Goat Rock at the southern lip of the Russian River mouth, a bluff-top trail leads past intriguingly named and usually unpopulated pocket strands like Blind Beach, Schoolhouse Beach, Shell Beach, and Salmon Creek Beach. Most of these

The **Russian River** has breached its banks many times in recent years, exceeding its usual level by some 25 feet or more. These floods have destroyed many riverfront businesses and houses, evident in the many abandoned buildings lining the roadside.

are day-use only, but at Wrights Beach midway along, there's a small and very attractive beachfront campground (800/444-7275).

At the southernmost end, the coastal park broadens to include the wildflower-covered granite promontory of **Bodega Head**, which juts into the Pacific and provides a great vantage point during the winter gray whale migrations. There's a large campground at the **Bodega Dunes** (800/444-7275), which stretch inland for nearly two miles from the ocean to Hwy-1.

While hiking along the Sonoma Coast, be careful: over 75 people have been drowned by sleeper waves, which rise unannounced and sweep people off the rocky shore.

US-101: Santa Rosa and the Sonoma Valley

Foggy weather, or a fondness for fine wine, may make you forsake the beautiful Sonoma County coastline in favor of the much warmer wine-growing regions of its inland valleys. The US-101 freeway cuts north-south across the heart of the region, passing through the Sonoma County seat, Santa Rosa (pop. 113,300). Now a fairly bustling big city, Santa Rosa is best known as the home of horticulturalist Luther Burbank, who settled here in 1875 and spent the next 50 years in his gardens, developing over 800 new varieties of flowers, fruits, and vegetables including the Shasta daisy, the perfect Santa Rosa plum, and the russet potato, all of which can be seen at the **Luther Burbank Home and Gardens** (daily 8 AM-5 PM; free; 707/524-5445), at the southeast edge of downtown.

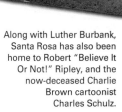

Santa Rosa also marks the northern turnoff from US-101 onto scenic Hwy-12, which heads east into the north end of wonderful Sonoma Valley. One of the prettiest wine-growing regions in the world, the Sonoma Valley is smaller and much more manageable than the bigger and busier Napa Valley, which is just east, over the steep Mayacamas Mountains. Vineyards line the roadside all the way down the Sonoma Valley's Hwy-12 to the hamlet of **Glen Ellen**, where the 800-acre ranch of author Jack London has been preserved as a state park, almost unchanged since his dream house burned to the ground the day London and his wife were due to move in. Hike among the oak trees along the short trails, one of which leads to London's sparsely-marked grave.

Along with Luther Burbank, Santa Rosa has also been home to Robert "Believe It Or Not!" Ripley, and the now-deceased Charlie Brown cartoonist Charles Schulz.

South of Glen Ellen, Hwy-12 runs for another 10 miles through a series of somewhat forlorn old hot springs resorts, before reaching the wonderful historic town of Sonoma.

Detour: Sonoma

One of the most picture-perfect historic towns in Northern California, Sonoma (pop. 8,100) is a must-see stop for anyone interested in almost any aspect of the Golden State. Founded in 1823 around the northernmost of the Franciscan missions, the town served as the sleepy capital of Mexican "Alta California" before being unceremoniously captured by a band of American frontiersmen in 1846. These freebooting Americans, aided and abetted by Col. John C. Frémont, proclaimed California an independent republic, which lasted for all of a month—though its emblem, the "Bear Flag," was retained as the state flag of California once the official American government took over for good.

A heroic statue on the spacious central square remembers the raising of the Bear Flag here in 1846, and buildings all around the square—including the old mission, and some barracks from the Mexican presidio—testify to Sonoma's rich heritage. Many of these historic structures now house delis, bakeries, wine stores and restaurants, ranging from the traditional Mexican fare of **La Casa**, 121 E. Spain Street (707/996-3406), to the upscale inventiveness of **Babette's** (707/939-8921), which serves delicious five-course prix-fixe nouvelle cuisine dinners plus less fancy lunches in the adjacent bar.

Places to stay in and around Sonoma are, not surprisingly, on the expensive side. The plentiful roadside motels start around $100, so you may feel it's worth spending a little more to enjoy the more inviting likes of the **Victorian Garden Inn**, a delightful B&B in an 1870s farmhouse, two blocks from the plaza at 316 E. Napa Street (707/996-5339). Also nice is the simple, Spanish colonial-style **El Dorado Hotel**, 405 W. 1st Street on the west side of the plaza (707/996-2351).

For more complete listings, winery maps, and other information, contact the Sonoma Valley **visitors bureau** on the plaza (707/996-1090). Heading south from Sonoma, or coming here from the Bay Area, Hwy-121 runs a dozen miles south to San Pablo Bay, along which Hwy-37 runs between US-101 (at Novato) and the I-80 freeway (at Vallejo).

Bodega Bay and Valley Ford

Protected by the massive bulk of Bodega Head, the fishing harbor of Bodega Bay has grown into an upscale vacation destination, with vacation homes lining the fairways of golf resorts, and $120-a-night hotels overlooking the still busy commercial wharves.

South of Bodega Bay, Hwy-1 cuts inland around the marshy coastal estuaries, passing a mile south of the lovely little town of **Bodega**, which Alfred Hitchcock used for many of the scariest scenes in his 1960 movie *The Birds*. The next town you pass through, Valley Ford, is a photogenic spot that holds a great old family-run roadhouse, **Dinucci's** (707/876-3260), serving huge portions of unreconstructed Italian food—minestrone, fresh bread, salad, and pasta—for around $10 per person.

Point Reyes Station

Between Bodega Bay and the Golden Gate Bridge, Hwy-1 slices through one of the country's most scenically and economically wealthy areas, **Marin County**. Though less than an hour from San Francisco, the northwestern reaches of the county are surprisingly rural, consisting of rolling dairylands and a few untouched small

Tomales Bay marks the rift zone formed by the **San Andreas Fault,** which runs parallel to Hwy-1 and divides Point Reyes from the rest of Northern California.

A sign outside the small white garage on Main Street in Point Reyes Station claims that it is the oldest Chevrolet dealer in California.

As you might have guessed, all the Drakes around Point Reyes refer to the English explorer and pirate Sir Francis Drake, who landed here in 1579.

towns; Hwy-1 follows a slow and curving route along the usually uncrowded two-lane blacktop.

After looping inland south of Bodega Bay, Hwy-1 reaches the shore again at oyster-rich Tomales Bay, around which it winds for 20 miles before reaching the earthy but erudite town of Point Reyes Station. At the center of the three-block Main Street, the excellent **Station House Cafe** (415/663-1515) serves incredibly good breakfasts (for a true taste of Marin, try the French toast made with challah bread), delicious lunches (sit on the patio and sample some great-tasting local oysters, on the half-shell or barbecued) and full dinners, featuring Marin's own Niman-Schell organic beef.

Point Reyes National Seashore

West from Hwy-1 and the town of Point Reyes Station, the 74,000-acre Point Reyes National Seashore offers an entire guidebook's worth of hiking and cycling trails, broad beaches, dense forests, and more. A good first stop is the Bear Valley **visitors center** (daily 9 AM-5 PM; free; 415/663-1092), two miles south of town via Hwy-1, then west on Bear Valley Road from the crossroads at Olema. The most popular trail leads three easy miles west from the visitors center, reaching the shore at Arch Rock and offering a great introduction to the Point Reyes area.

Three main roads lead into the Point Reyes National Seashore. The middle road, Sir Francis Drake Highway, is the longest, winding along Tomales Bay through the hamlet of Inverness, then bending west past the oyster-growing marshes of Drake's Estero to the far tip of Point Reyes, where a long stairway drops down to a lighthouse offering a sweeping panorama of the Pacific Ocean—and a great chance to catch a glimpse of migrating gray whales leaping offshore (Nov.-April only). From Olema, another road, Pierce Point Road, cuts off to the north, passing Tomales Bay State Park (which has the area's best swimming at Heart's Desire Beach) and continuing to McClure's Beach, at the far north tip of Point Reyes. The other option, Limantour Road, runs west from near the Bear Valley visitors center, reaching the coast at Limantour Beach, where coastal sand dunes and an estuary adjoin the long sandy strand.

Eight miles from the visitors center, the **HI Point Reyes Hostel**, 1380 Limantour Road (415/663-8811), has the only accommodations in the seashore: $12-15 dorm beds in an old farmhouse on the road to Drake's Bay. Dozens of backcountry campsites are open to backpackers, and if you can spare $150 or so a night, dozens of small but deluxe B&B inns operate in and around Point Reyes. Try for the tree-top Eagle's Nest room at the **Blackthorne Inn**, 266 Vallejo Avenue in Inverness Park (415/663-8621), or a bayfront cabin at **Manka's Inverness Lodge**, on Sir Francis Drake Highway in Inverness (415/669-1034). These are popular and often booked solid; if so, contact the **West Marin Chamber of Commerce** (415/663-9232) for more listings.

Bolinas and Stinson Beach

Sitting at the southern end of the Point Reyes peninsula, Bolinas is a small town with a well-earned reputation for discouraging tourists; the signs leading you here from Hwy-1 are regularly torn down by locals bent on keeping the place—little more than a general store, a bakery, and a bar—for themselves. Another secret locals try to keep to themselves is that Bolinas has one of the coast's best tidepool areas at Duxbury Reef, just west of town. It is the largest temperate-water reef (as opposed to tropical coral reef) in North America. Some of its specialties are nudibranchs, including the rare Chan's dorid, the southern-dwelling Hilton's aeolid, and the common, yet very beautiful Hopkin's rose. Seastars, sea snails, chitons, piddock clams, and various crabs and fish are found in greater abundance here than most anywhere else, mainly because Duxbury Reef receives so few visitors.

The marshes of Drake's Estero, six miles west of Inverness, are one of California's prime oyster-growing habitats. In season (Sept.-April or longer), you can buy them fresh from the water at **Johnson's Oyster Farms** (415/669-1149).

In contrast, the broad strands of Stinson Beach, four miles south along Hwy-1, are the Bay Area's most popular summertime suntanning spots. A grocery store and deli, the **Livewater Surf Shop** (which rents boards and the essential wetsuits), and a couple of outdoor bar-and-grills along Hwy-1 form a short parade at the entrance to the beach. For a hearty breakfast, lunch, or dinner, stop at the homey **Parkside Cafe** (415/868-1272), nestled between the beach and Hwy-1 at 43 Arenal Avenue; if you want to stay overnight, make friends with someone who owns a beach house, or try the basic but cheap **Stinson Beach Motel**, 3416 Hwy-1 (415/868-1712).

If you have the chance to plan ahead, try to book a night at the **Steep Ravine Cabins**, just over a mile south of Stinson Beach on the ocean side of Hwy-1. Now part of Mount Tamalpais State Park, these 10 rustic redwood cabins are very basic roofs-over-the-head (bring sleeping bags and food; water faucets are just outside the door) in an absolutely beautiful coastal chasm. The cabins cost $30 a night, and reservations are handled by ReserveAmerica (800/444-7275).

The all-terrain mountain bike, which now accounts for half of all bikes on (and off) the roads, was invented in the late 1970s by a group of daredevil Marin cyclists intent on cruising down the fire roads of Mount Tamalpais at the highest possible speed.

Mount Tamalpais, Muir Woods, and Muir Beach

From the coast, a pair of roads, Panoramic Highway and the Shoreline Highway (Hwy-1), twist up and over the slopes of Mount Tamalpais (elev. 2,586 feet), the signature peak of the San Francisco Bay Area. Known usually as "Mount Tam," the whole mountain has been protected in semi-natural state within a series of state and national parks, and its voluptuous slopes offer

incredible views of the urbanized Bay Area and the untouched coastline; drive to within 100 yards of the top for a 360-degree panorama, or stop at the Pan Toll **ranger station** (415/388-2070) for a map of Mount Tam's hiking trails and fire roads—many of which are excellent mountain bike routes.

At the Mill Valley junction of Hwy-1 and the US-101 freeway, a historic roadside restaurant has been resurrected as the **Buckeye Roadhouse,** 15 Shoreline Highway (415/331-2600), where you can feast on fine BBQ, great steaks, and burgers, and delicious desserts in a lively, retro-Route 66 atmosphere.

Every August since 1904, one of the country's wildest foot races, the **Dipsea,** has followed a rugged trail from the town of Mill Valley over Mount Tamalpais to Stinson Beach.

Only a dozen miles from the Golden Gate Bridge, a deep, dark valley between the coast and Mount Tamalpais holds the last surviving stand of Marin County redwoods, preserved for future generations as the Muir Woods National Monument (daily 8 AM-dusk; $2; 415/388-2595), and named in honor of turn-of-the-century naturalist John Muir. A paved, mile-long trail takes in the biggest trees, but since the park is often crowded with busloads of sightseeing hordes making the tour from San Francisco, you may want to explore the farther-flung areas, climbing up Mount Tamalpais or following Muir Creek two miles downstream to the crescent-shaped cove of Muir Beach, along Hwy-1.

Marin Headlands

If you can avoid the magnetic pull of the Golden Gate Bridge and San Francisco, take the very last turnoff from US-101 (northbound drivers, take the second turnoff after crossing the bridge) and head west to the Marin Headlands, a former military base that's been turned back into coastal semi-wilderness. A tortuous road twists along the face of 300-foot cliffs, giving incredible views of the bridge and the city behind it. The road continues west and north to the **visitors center** (415/331-1450), housed in an old chapel, with a reconstructed Miwok shelter and details on hiking and biking routes.

Nearby, the barracks of old Fort Barry have been converted into the very peaceful **HI Marin Headlands Hostel** (415/331-2777), which has dorm beds and private rooms for $13 per person, $39 for family rooms.

The Farallone Islands

Thirty-two miles west of the Golden Gate Bridge, the Gulf of the Farallones National Marine Sanctuary is named for the Farallones, a rugged cluster of rocky islands that on a clear day rise up like sharp spikes on the western horizon. The Farallones are said to be the only place on the Pacific coast south of Alaska where the wild animal population is as great today as it was when Europeans made first landfall in California, over 400 years ago. Because no one but a handful of scientists on any given day are allowed to land on the islands, shoreline rocks are home to dense colonies of baying northern sea elephants and other pinnipeds, while the rugged, steep bluffs and ledges, covered in guano, make exceptional breeding grounds for many species of birds. Brandt's cormorants, western gulls, common murres, pigeon guillemots and Cassin's auklets are abundant nesters; during courtship season (Feb.-May) the Cassin's auklets haunt the islands with their macabre mating, greeting, and calling shrieks. So ghastly are these wild choruses that the native Ohlone people believed that the Farallones were the domain of dead souls. Puffins, kittiwakes, phalaropes, Leach's petrels and ashy storm-petrels can be seen on or around the islands, and albatrosses and shearwaters

The most northerly of California's offshore preserves, off the coast 60 miles northwest of San Francisco, the **Cordell Bank National Marine Sanctuary** protects an underwater mountain where thousands of diverse sea creature species congregate. The California current flows along the south side of banks, bringing nutrient-rich water, which makes Cordell Bank a fine place to see marine mammals and birds.

may also be found here. Elephant seals come in autumn, but the whales (which are more sporadic) pass on their migrations from January to May.

Boats to the waters off the Farallon Islands offer some of the continent's most exciting opportunities for birding and watching ocean mammals (including blue whales), but for the most part wildlife watchers can approach these exciting shores only on scheduled tours, such as those offered by the nonprofit **Oceanic Society Expeditions**, based at Fort Mason Center, Building E, in San Francisco (415/474-3385). The headquarters of the Farallones National Marine Sanctuary is also located at Fort Mason (415/561-6622).

Across San Francisco

From the north, Hwy-1 enters San Francisco across the glorious Golden Gate Bridge, where parking areas at both ends let you ditch the car and walk across the elegant two-mile-long span. South from the bridge, Hwy-1 follows 19th Avenue across Golden Gate Park, then runs due south through the outer reaches of San Francisco, finally reaching the coast again at the often foggy town of Pacifica.

The most scenic alternate to Hwy-1 is the **49 Mile Drive**, the best part of which heads west from the bridge through Presidio National Park, along Lincoln Boulevard and Camino del Mar, following the rugged coastline to Lands End, where you can hike around and explore the remains of Sutro Baths, play the old-time arcade games at the Musee Mechanique, or experience the wonders of the Camera Obscura. (See the San Francisco Survival Guide for details.) From Land's End, this scenic route runs south along the oceanfront Great Highway, which eventually links back up with Hwy-1.

Since driving and parking in San Francisco can be frustrating and expensive (Steve McQueen could never make *Bullitt* in today's traffic!), consider parking out here in the suburbs and taking public transportation into the center of town. Two of the main **Muni** trolley lines (the N-Judah, along Judah Street, and the L-Taraval, along Taraval Street; fare $1) run between downtown and the coast south of Golden Gate Park, where parking is (comparatively) plentiful.

San Francisco is the start of our road trip along US-50, beginning on page 230.

SAN FRANCISCO SURVIVAL GUIDE

SAN FRANCISCO IS EASILY THE MOST ENJOYABLE CITY IN THE U.S. Its undulating topography turns every other corner into a scenic vista, while its many engaging neighborhoods are perfect for aimless wandering. Check out the exotic shops of Chinatown, the corridors of power in the Financial District, the Italian cafes of North Beach, the hippie holdouts of Haight-Ashbury, or the brilliant murals of the latino Mission District. Museums document everything from Gold Rush history to cutting edge modern art, while stellar restaurants offer the chance to sample gourmet food from around the world-all in an easily manageable, densely compact small city.

(continues)

If there's one place in the city you should stop to get your bearings, it's **Fort Point**, a massive, photogenic Civil War fort standing along the bay, directly beneath the Golden Gate Bridge. You can wander at will through the honeycomb of corridors, staircases, and gun ports, watch the fearless surfers and windsurfers offshore, and take in a panoramic view of the City by the Bay. From here you can walk up to and across the Golden Gate Bridge, or east along the bay to the heart of the city (about two miles one-way), or follow the numerous walking and cycling trails that wind through the surrounding **Presidio National Park**.

If there's one other place that should be on your S.F. itinerary, it's **Alcatraz**. Aptly known as The Rock, from 1934 until 1963 this was America's most notorious prison. Now preserved as a historical park, the island is worth a visit as much for the views of the city and the bay as for its grim past. In the cell house, audio-guided walking tours, narrated by former prisoners and prison guards, recount what it was like to be locked up with the likes of Al Capone, George "Machine Gun" Kelley, and the psychopathic "Birdman" Robert Stroud, who spent 17 years here. To reach Alcatraz, take one of the **Red & White Fleet** ferries which leave throughout the day from Pier 41 at Fisherman's Wharf. Alcatraz is one of the city's prime tourist destinations, so buy your tickets as far in advance as possible (800/229-2784).

Speaking of tickets, Barry Bonds and the rest of the **San Francisco Giants** (415/467-8000) play at their new downtown stadium, south of Market Street, while the **Oakland A's** (510/638-5100) play across the bay at Oakland-Alameda County Stadium, off I-880 near the Oakland Airport.

Practicalities

San Francisco International Airport (SFO) lies 15 miles south of the city, and handles the great majority of domestic and almost all international flights. It's an easy airport to navigate and offers a wide range of car rental and shuttle bus services. There's also an airport in **Oakland** across the bay, which handles a few domestic flights, mostly cheap **Southwest Airlines** flights from the western U.S.; it too has shuttles and rental car offices. The main routes into San Francisco by road are **US-101**, which runs from San Jose in the south and across the Golden Gate Bridge from the north, and **I-80**, which heads in from the east via the Bay Bridge.

San Francisco is one of the few West Coast cities where you really don't need a car, since distances are short and public transportation quite extensive; the gridded street plan makes it easy to find your way around. San Francis-

co's Municipal Railway (Muni; 415/673-6864) network of public transit buses, trams, and cable cars will take you all over the city. Park at the west end of one of the transit lines and ride into town.

Knowing how popular San Francisco is, it's no surprise that room rates are pretty high-the average is about $150 a night. The best budget options are the two III hostels, one on the bay at Fort Mason (415/771-7277), another downtown at 312 Mason Street (415/788-5604); both cost about $18 a night. There are some nice motels on the outskirts of downtown, like the nouveau retro **Hotel del Sol**, in the Marina District at 3100 Webster Street, (415/921-5520), with stylish rooms, a pool, and free parking, and doubles from around $95. Most of the older downtown hotels have been gussied up for expense-account visitors, but one friendly, family-owned survivor is the **San Remo Hotel**, 2337 Mason Street (415/776-8688), in between North Beach and Fisherman's Wharf, where nice rooms with shared bathrooms cost around $60. And if you're lucky enough to have someone else paying your hotel bills, consider a stay at the **Mandarin Oriental**, 222 Sansome Street (415/885-0999 or 800/622-0404), the only hotel where you see both the Golden Gate and the Bay Bridge while soaking in your bathtub, 45 floors above the madding crowd; doubles start around $300.

The only problem for visitors eating out in San Francisco is deciding where to go-there are so many great places that choosing among them can be a painful process. For breakfast, **Sears Fine Foods**, 439 Powell Street on Union Square, and **The Grubstake**, an old trolley car diner at 1525 Pine Street, are both local institutions. Two more culinary landmarks are the **Swan Oyster Depot**, near City Hall at 1517 Polk Street, a simple oyster bar, serving the city's freshest shellfish (Mon.-Fri. till 6 PM only), and **Sam's Grill**, downtown at 374 Bush Street, with incredible grilled meat and fish dishes, melt-in-your-mouth shoestring fries, and ancient-looking wooden booths that seem like set pieces from a Sam Spade mystery.

For other-than-American food, San Francisco has what might be the country's best cheap Chinese place: the **House of Nan King** at 919 Kearny Street, between Chinatown and North Beach. In North Beach proper, Italian food is the order of the day, served up at family-style places like **Capp's Corner**, 1600 Powell Street, or any of the many lined up along Green Street.

The **San Francisco Convention and Visitors Bureau** (415/974-6900) publishes a good free street map and offers extensive listings of attractions, accommodations, and restaurants, available from the visitors center at Hallidie Plaza, next to the Muni station and cable car turntable at Powell and Market Streets downtown. San Francisco's main daily **newspaper**, the morning *Chronicle*, and multitude of free papers like the *Bay Guardian* and the *SF Weekly*, are available on the streets and at cafes and book stores throughout the Bay Area.

For a memorable first or last look at San Francisco, from Pacifica follow the signs to **Sweeney Ridge,** the grass and wildflower-covered coastal summit from which, on November 4, 1769, the Portolá expedition first laid European eyes on the great bay.

Looking for the world's biggest waves? Head down to **Maverick's,** an offshore reef area a half-mile off Pillar Point, three miles north of Half Moon Bay. In winter, when conditions are right, 35-foot waves draw expert surfers from all over the world. For a report, call Maverick's Surf Shop, 530 Main Street in Half Moon Bay (650/726-0469).

The San Mateo Coast

From the San Francisco city limits, Hwy-1 runs along the Pacific Ocean through the rural and almost totally undeveloped coastline of San Mateo County. The first eight miles or so are high-speed freeway, but after passing through the suburban communities of Daly City and Pacifica, the pace abruptly slows to a scenic cruise. The highway hugs the decomposing cliff tops for the next few miles before reaching **Montara,** where the old but still functioning lighthouse has been partly converted into the **HI Point Montara Hostel** (650/728-7177).

South of Montara, Hwy-1 bends inland around the rocky shores of the **James V. Fitzgerald Marine Preserve** (650/728-3584), a wonderful tidepool area that's best known for its marine snails (having over 77% of the species found from Alaska to Baja) and for being the northernmost and southernmost range of more than 50 different plants and animals. The three-mile-long preserve, stretching south to Pillar Point is an excellent place to find monkey eels, cabezon, sea urchins, seastars, anenomes, annelids (sea worms) and many more creatures. However, the tidepool ecosystem is extremely fragile, so always treat everything you find with great care and remember to put everything back in its exact spot after you have examined it.

South of Pillar Point and the Fitzgerald Reserve is the small fishing harbor at Princeton, where you can appreciate other aspects of local sea life by enjoying a variety of grilled fresh fish at **Barbara's Fish Trap,** an inexpensive, family-friendly restaurant on the waterfront at 281 Capistrano Road (650/728-7049).

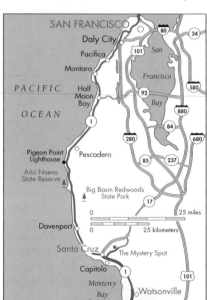

The first sizeable coastal town is **Half Moon Bay,** 25 miles south of San Francisco, but seemingly much more distant. A quiet farming community that's slowly but surely changing into a Silicon Valley suburb, Half Moon Bay still has an all-American Main Street, a block east of Hwy-1, lined by hardware stores, cafes, bakeries, and the inevitable art galleries and B&Bs housed in 100-year-old farmhouses. A good B&B to choose is **Zaballa House,** at the north end of town at 324 Main Street (650/726-9123), which has comfortable, $75-a-night rooms in the town's oldest building. The main event here is the annual, mid-October **Pumpkin Festival,** which celebrates the coming of Halloween with a competition to determine the world's largest pumpkin—winning gourds weigh as much as a half-ton!

For further information, call the Half Moon Bay visitors center (650/726-5202).

Pescadero and Pigeon Point Lighthouse

The 50 miles of coastline between Half Moon Bay and Santa Cruz are one of the great surprises of the California coast: the virtually unspoiled miles offer rocky tidepools and driftwood-strewn beaches beneath sculpted bluffs topped by rolling green fields of Brussels sprouts, pumpkins, cabbages, and artichokes. The biggest town hereabouts, Pescadero (pop. 500) is a mile or so inland from Hwy-1, well worth the short detour for a chance to sample the fresh fish, great pies, and other home-cooked treats at **Duarte's Tavern**, 202 Stage Road (650/ 879-0464), open daily for breakfast, lunch, and dinner at the center of the block-long downtown.

Ten miles south of Pescadero, the photogenic beacon of Pigeon Point Lighthouse has appeared in innumerable TV and print commercials; the graceful, 150-foot-tall brick tower is open for tours (Sunday 10 AM-3 PM; $2 donation), and the adjacent lighthouse quarters function as the very popular **HI Pigeon Point Hostel** (650/879-0633), with a hot tub perched above the crashing surf.

Año Nuevo State Reserve

One of nature's more bizarre spectacles takes place annually at Año Nuevo State Reserve (8 AM-dusk daily; $5 per car), where each winter hundreds of humongous northern elephant seals come ashore to give birth and mate. The males reach up to 20 feet head-to-tail, weigh as much as three tons, and feature the dangling proboscises that inspired their name. These blubbery creatures were hunted almost to extinction for their oil-rich flesh. In 1920, fewer than 100 were left in the world; their resurgence to a current estimated population of 80,000 has proved that protection does work.

Every December hordes of male elephant seals arrive at Año Nuevo, the seals' primary onshore rookery, after spending the summer at sea, ready to do battle with each other for the right to procreate. It's an incredible show: the bulls bellowing, barking, and biting at each other to establish dominance—the alpha male mates with most of the females, and the rest must wait until next year. Pups conceived the previous year are born in January, and mating goes on through March. During the mating season, ranger-led tours ($4; 800/444-4445) are the only way to see the seals; these tours are very popular, so plan ahead and try to come midweek.

Big Basin Redwoods State Park

The oldest and largest of California's state parks, Big Basin Redwoods State Park (831/338-8860; $6 per car) protects some 18,000 acres of giant coastal redwoods. Established in 1902, the park has many miles of hiking and cycling trails, high up in the mountains. The heart of the park, nine miles up Hwy-236 from Boulder

Though the San Mateo coastline is quite beautiful, the waters are very cold—and home to a hungry population of **great white sharks,** which have been known to attack surfers as well as seals.

Midway between Año Nuevo State Reserve and Santa Cruz, the **Davenport Cash Store,** on the east side of Hwy-1 in the village of Davenport, serves hearty breakfasts and lunches. Tiny Davenport is also the birthplace of the Odwalla fresh fruit juice company.

Natural Bridges State Park, two miles north of Santa Cruz via West Cliff Drive, has a natural wave-carved archway and, in winter, swarms of monarch butterflies.

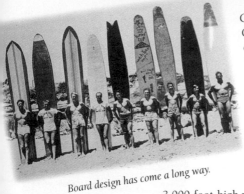

Board design has come a long way.

Creek, is most easily accessible from Santa Cruz, but a popular trail winds up from the coast to the crest, starting from Hwy-1 at Waddell Creek Beach, a popular haunt for sail boarders, who sometimes do flips and loops in the wind-whipped waves.

Santa Cruz

The popular beach resort and college town of Santa Cruz (pop. 51,500) sits at the north end of Monterey Bay, an hour's drive from San Francisco, at the foot of a 3,000-foot-high ridge of mountains. Best known for its Boardwalk amusement park, which holds the only surviving wooden roller coaster on the West Coast, and for the large University of California campus in the redwoods above, Santa Cruz takes its name from the ill-fated mission settlement begun here in 1777 but wiped out by an earthquake and tidal wave in 1840. Modern Santa Cruz was all but leveled by another earthquake in 1989, but has since recovered its stature as one of the most diverting stops on the California coast.

The downtown area lies a mile inland, so from Hwy-1 follow the many signs pointing visitors toward the wharf and the beach, where plentiful parking is available. Walk, rent a bike, or drive along the coastal Cliff Drive to the world's first **Surfing Museum** (Wed.-Mon. noon-4 PM; donations), which is packed with giant old redwood boards and newer high-tech cutters, as well as odds and ends tracing the development of West Coast surfing. Housed in an old lighthouse, the Surfing Museum overlooks one of the state's prime surfing spots, Steamer Lane, named for the steamships that once brought day-tripping San Franciscans to the wharf.

A large part of the Santa Cruz economy still depends upon visitors, and there are plenty of cafes, restaurants, and accommodations options. Eating and drinking places congregate west of Hwy-1 along Front Street and Pacific Avenue in downtown Santa Cruz, which has a number of engaging, somewhat countercultural book and record shops along with cafes like **Zoccoli's**, 1534 Pacific Avenue (831/423-1711), which has great soups and sandwiches. Vegetarians will enjoy the lively **Saturn Cafe**, open all day at 1230 Mission Street (831/429-8505), along Hwy-1 on the north side of town, at the foot of the UC Santa Cruz campus.

Motels line Hwy-1, and cheaper ones huddle around the waterfront area, with rates ranging $30-100 a night depending upon location and time of year; the oldest (and funkiest) ones stand atop Beach Hill, between the Boardwalk and downtown. You can also avail yourself of the **HI Santa Cruz Hostel**, 321 Main Street (831/423-8304), with dorm beds in an immaculate 1870s cottage for just $13-15 per person. Another characterful old place is the **Capitola Venetian Hotel** (831/476-6471), a 1920s mission-style complex right on the beach at 1500 Wharf Road in Capitola, three miles east of Santa Cruz. Among the many nice B&Bs is the rustic **Babbling Brook**, 1025 Laurel Street (831/427-2437 or 800/866-1131).

For more complete listings or other information, contact the **Santa Cruz Visitors Council**, 701 Front Street (831/425-1234 or 800/833-3494).

Santa Cruz Boardwalk

The bayfront Santa Cruz Boardwalk should really be your main stop; besides the dozens of thrill rides and midway games, it boasts the art deco Cocoanut Grove ballroom, where throughout the summer swing bands still play the sounds of the 1930s and 1940s, and two rides that are such classics of the genre they've been listed as national historic landmarks. The biggest thrill is the **Giant Dipper** roller coaster, open since 1924, a senior citizen compared to modern rides but still one of the top 10 coasters in the country—the clattering, half-mile-long tracks make it seem far faster than the 40 mph maximum it reaches. Near the roller coaster is the beautiful Charles Looff **carousel**, one of only six left in the country, with 70 handcarved wooden horses doing the same circuit they've followed since 1911; grab for the brass rings while listening to music pumped out by the 342-pipe organ, imported from Germany and over 100 years old.

the roller coaster at Santa Cruz

Santa Cruz has just about fully recovered from the 1989 Loma Prieta earthquake, which had its epicenter in the hills southeast of the city.

Along with these and many other vintage arcade attractions, the amusement park also features a log flume ride, a sky ride, a two-story miniature golf course installed inside the old bathhouse, plus a bowling alley and all the shooting galleries, laser tag, and virtual reality machines you could want. The Boardwalk, which has been paved but retains a great deal of charm and character, is open daily in summer, and weekends only during the rest of the year. Admission is free and individual rides vary in price, with the Giant Dipper costing $3 a trip and all-day passes priced about $20. For more information, call 831/423-5590.

Coastal farms along the Monterey Bay grow nearly 85% of the nation's **artichokes**, which you can sample along with other produce at stands along Hwy-1.

The Mystery Spot

In the hills above Santa Cruz, east of Hwy-1 at 1953 Branciforte Drive, the Mystery Spot (daily 9:30 AM-5 PM; $4) is one of those fortunate few tourist traps that actually gets people to come back again. Like similar places along the Pacific coast, the Mystery Spot is a section of redwood forest where the usual laws of physics seem not to apply (trees grow in oddly contorted corkscrew shapes, and balls roll uphill). Among those who study vortexes and other odd geomantic places, the Mystery Spot is considered to be the real thing, but you don't have to take it seriously to enjoy yourself.

Watsonville, Castroville, and Moss Landing

Between Santa Cruz and Monterey, Hwy-1 loops inland through the farmlands fronting Monterey Bay. Part freeway, part winding two-lane, Hwy-1 races through, and to be honest there's not a lot worth stopping for: the beaches can be dreary, and the two main towns, Watsonville and Castroville, are little more than service centers for the local fruit and vegetable packers. Watsonville is still reeling from the 1989 Loma Prieta earthquake, which destroyed half of the downtown area, though Castroville—where in 1947, then-unknown **Marilyn Monroe** reigned as "Miss Artichoke" during Castroville's Artichoke Festival, still celebrated each September—

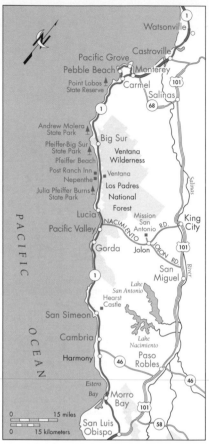

does have one odd sight: the "World's Largest Artichoke," a concrete statue outside a very large fruit stand at the center of town.

Back on the coast, midway along Monterey Bay, the port community of Moss Landing is a busy commercial fishery, with pelicans aplenty. Moss Landing is also home to the research arm of the Monterey Bay Aquarium, to an obtrusively huge electricity generating plant, and to a handful of oyster bars and restaurants like **The Whole Enchilada** (right on Hwy-1 just south of the power plant), which has spicy seafood and a popular Sunday jazz brunch.

On the inland side of Moss Landing, **Elkhorn Slough** (831/728-0560) is Monterey Bay's largest protected estaurine marsh, and a prime breeding ground and birdwatching refuge. In summer, from trails through the marsh, visitors can also see watch leopard sharks swimming through the shallow water, their dorsal fins cutting the surface, just like in the movie *Jaws.* (To be accurate, the sort of sharks seen in that movie were great whites, which aren't found in Elkhorn Slough, though they are numerous off the coast.) That said, this is probably the easiest place on the California coast to get within a few feet of wild sharks, which come here to give birth to their young.

Continuing south, much of the bayfront between Moss Landing and Monterey formerly belonged to the U.S. Marine Corps base at Fort Ord. Almost the entire parcel was turned over to the state of California to house the **California State University at Monterey Bay**, which opened its doors in 1995.

Detour: San Juan Bautista

Away from the coast, 15 miles inland from Monterey Bay via Hwy-129 or Hwy-156, stands one of California's most idyllic small towns, San Juan Bautista. It centers upon a grassy town square bordered by a well-preserved mission complex, complete with a large church and monastery standing since 1812. Two other sides of the square are lined by hotels, stables, and houses dating from the 1840s through the 1860s, preserved in their entirety within a state historic park (daily 10 AM-4:30 PM; $2; 831/623-4881).

Completing the living history lesson, the east edge of the square is formed by one of the state's few preserved stretches of El Camino Real, the 200-year-old Spanish colonial trail that linked all the California missions with Mexico. Adding to the interest, the trail runs right along the rift zone of the San Andreas Fault, and a small seismograph registers tectonic activity. (Incidentally, San Juan Bautista was where the climactic final scenes of Alfred Hitchcock's *Vertigo* were filmed—though in the movie, they added a much more prominent bell tower with a seemingly endless staircase.)

The town's Main Street is a block from the mission, and is lined by a handful of antique shops, Mexican restaurants, and cafes such as the **Mission Cafe**, 300 3rd Street.

Monterey

The historic capital of California under the Spanish and Mexican regimes, Monterey (pop. 31,954), along with its peninsular neighbors Carmel and Pacific Grove, is one of the most satisfying stops in California. Dozens of significant historical sites have been well preserved, most of them concentrated within a mile-long walk called the Path of History that loops through the compact downtown area. Park in the lots at the foot of Alvarado Street, Monterey's main drag, and start your tour at **Fisherman's Wharf**, where bellowing sea lions wallow in the water, begging for popcorn from tourists. Next stop should be the adjacent **Custom House**, the oldest governmental building in the state, recently restored as the Monterey State Historic Park **visitors center** (10 AM-5 PM; 831/649-2836); here you can pick up maps or join Path of History walking tours of old town Monterey.

One of the other landmarks you should look for on a walking tour, whether guided or self-guided, is the **Larkin House**, on Jefferson Street three blocks up Alvarado Street. Built in 1835 by New England-born merchant Thomas Larkin, who went on to serve as the American consul in Monterey, this house—with its adobe walls and wooden balconies—served as the model for millions of "Monterey style" suburban houses.

West from the Custom House, which is now surrounded by the modern Doubletree Hotel complex, you can follow the old railroad right-of-way along the water to **Cannery Row**, where abandoned fish canneries have been gussied up into upscale bars and restaurants—most of them capitalizing on ersatz Steinbeckian themes. The one real attraction here is the excellent **Monterey Bay Aquarium** (daily 10 AM-6 PM; $15.95; 800/756-3737), 886 Cannery Row, housed in a spacious modern building and loaded with state-of-the-art tanks filled with over 500 species of local sea life. The aquarium is rated by many as the best in the world, so plan on spending half a day at least (and try to come midweek to avoid the crowds). The as-natural-looking-as-possible displays let visitors

Author John Steinbeck lived in and around the Monterey Peninsula for many years, and set many of his stories here, though things have changed so much in recent years that his beloved Cannery Row is hard to recognize. Steinbeck was born and is buried in Salinas, east of Monterey on US-101; for more on him, see pages 74-77.

Along Hwy-1 on the northwest edge of town, the elegant **Hotel del Monte**, a grand resort that attracted the first wealthy tourists to Monterey beginning in 1880, is now surrounded by the large U.S. Navy Postgraduate School.

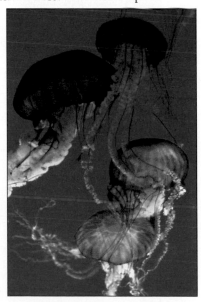

sea nettles , Monterey Bay Aquarium

The internationally famous **Monterey Jazz Festival** is held every year at the end of summer. For performers, dates, and other information, phone 800/307-3378.

touch tidepool denizens, watch playful sea otters (who are fed by hand three times daily), gaze into the gently swaying stalks of a three-story-tall kelp forest, or stare into dimly lit tanks full of the truly weird creatures that live thousands of feet below the bay. Some of the most popular creatures are the hypnotically bizarre jellyfish, lit by psychedelic black-lights to show off their brilliant

MONTEREY BAY NATIONAL MARINE SANCTUARY

The coastal waters of Northern California offer some of the greatest biodiversity in North America, thanks largely to Monterey Bay, and specifically to Monterey Bay canyon. Dropping steeply from near sea level at the coast to about 12,000 feet below sea level, the canyon is home to hundreds of deep-sea species rarely found so close to shore, giving a variety and richness to the bay's sealife that attracts marine biologists from all over the world. Recognizing this, the federal government has mandated an unusual degree of protection to Monterey Bay and the ocean waters both north and south.

The Monterey Bay Aquarium, which collects all its specimens from Monterey Bay, provides an excellent public window on this cornucopia of offshore life. Researchers and tourists alike can view more than 300,000 examples of nearly 600 species of plants and animals from all Monterey Bay habitats, from tidepools and estaurine marsh to the deep ocean. Still, the aquarium's tanks offer only a glimpse of the region's richness.

Covering more than 5,000 square miles, Monterey Bay National Marine Sanctuary is the largest marine sanctuary off the coast of North America, extending about 400 miles from Marin County to San Luis Obisbo County. The area is famous for its excellent opportunities to view seabirds and whales, as well as hundreds of fish species and sundry phyla of invertebrates. More than a hundred conspicuous species (those that can be seen by the naked eye) are indigenous to Monterey Bay and found nowhere else.

Practically speaking, only scientists, anglers, and deep-sea divers have much opportunity to view the region's marine life *in situ*, but there are many opportunities to get out on the surface for whalewatching, birdwatching, kayaking, fishing, or cruising. Many whalewatching and other cruises leave from Fisherman's Wharf in Monterey, but for a more up-close and personal encounter, contact specialist wildlife outfitters like the **Sea Kayak Center** (831/373-5357) or **Sea Life Tours** (831/372-7150). For more information, contact the headquarters of the Monterey Bay National Marine Sanctuary at 299 Foam Street in Monterey (831/647-4201).

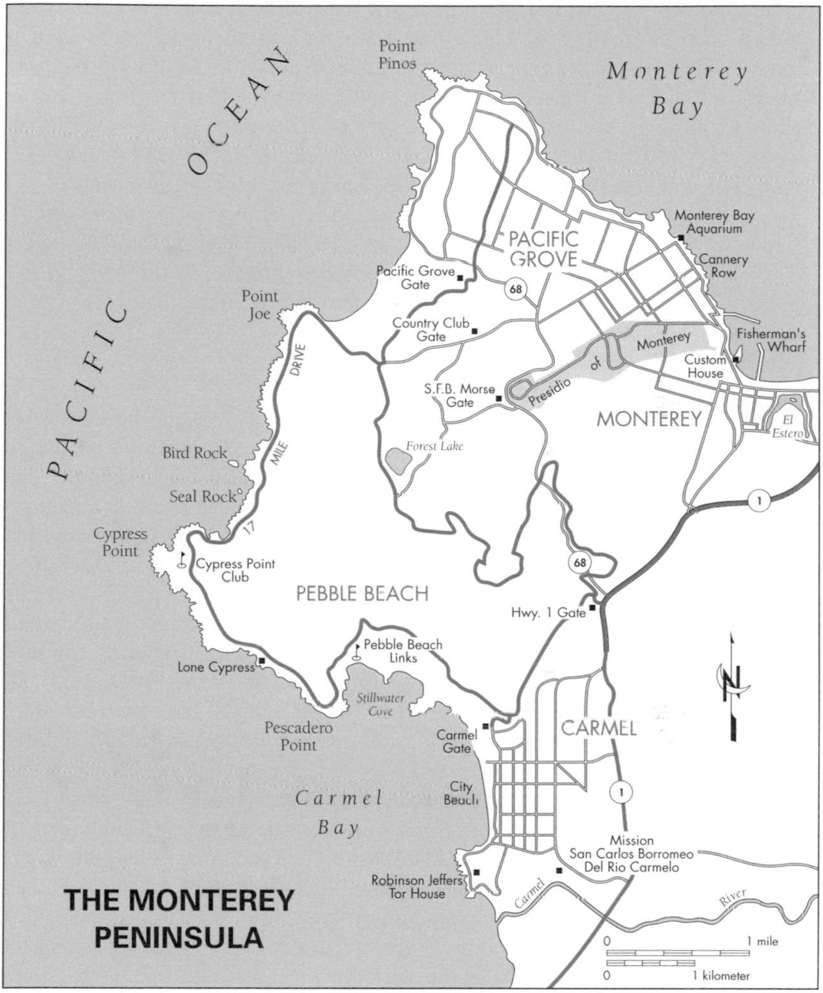

O C E A N

P A C I F I C

Point Pinos

Monterey Bay

Monterey Bay Aquarium

PACIFIC GROVE

Cannery Row

Pacific Grove Gate

68

Point Joe

Country Club Gate

Presidio of Monterey

Fisherman's Wharf

Custom House

S.F.B. Morse Gate

MONTEREY

El Estero

Bird Rock

Forest Lake

MILE DRIVE

Seal Rock

1

Cypress Point

17

Cypress Point Club

PEBBLE BEACH

68

Hwy. 1 Gate

Pebble Beach Links

Lone Cypress

Stillwater Cove

N

Pescadero Point

Carmel Gate

CARMEL

City Beach

1

Carmel Bay

Mission San Carlos Borromeo Del Rio Carmelo

THE MONTEREY PENINSULA

Robinson Jeffers Tor House

Carmel River

| 0 | | 1 mile |
| 0 | | 1 kilometer |

florescent colors, and the swirling schools of tuna and sardines—plus the odd shark and barracuda—in the amazing Outer Bay exhibit.

Monterey Practicalities

Because Monterey gets a considerable tourist trade, there's no shortage of restaurants, though good food at reasonable prices can be hard to find. One good bet is the **Old Monterey Cafe**, 489 Alvarado Street, serving large portions at breakfast and lunch. For seafood, catch an early-bird special (before 6 PM) at one of the dozen restaurants on the wharf—**Cafe Fina** (831/372-5200) does great wood-oven pizzas as well. Top of the scale is flashy **Montrio**, 414 Calle Principal (831/648-8880), which serves San Francisco-style grilled chicken and fish dishes in a converted fire station; reservations are essential, ever since *Esquire* magazine rated it restaurant of the year in 1995.

Places to stay vary widely, starting with a slew of budget motels such as the **Motel 6** at 2124 Fremont Street (831/646-8585) in Seaside, on the north edge of Monterey. Other moderate motels line Munras Street along the old US-101 highway frontage south toward Carmel, while prices in downtown Monterey hover in the $120-a-night range. One exception to the generally high prices is the refurbished and centrally located **Monterey Hotel**, 406 Alvarado (831/375-3184 or 800/727-0960), which offers exceptionally good deals, from $50 a night for two people.

One of Monterey's many intriguing historical sites is the whalebone pavement inlaid into the sidewalk in front of California's First Theater, near the waterfront at the foot of Pacific Street.

For additional information, or listings of the many restaurants and hotels in Monterey, Pacific Grove and Carmel, contact the **Monterey Peninsula Visitors Bureau**, in the lobby of the Maritime Museum on Custom House Plaza (daily 9 AM-5 PM; 831/649-1770).

Pacific Grove is the best known of about 20 places in California where millions of monarch butterflies spend the winter months. From October until March, the butterflies congregate on the "Butterfly Trees," a grove of pines on Ridge Road off Lighthouse Avenue, well signed from downtown.

Pacific Grove

Perched at the tip of the Monterey Peninsula, Pacific Grove (pop. 16,117) is a quiet throwback to old-time tourism, dating from the late 1880s when the area was used for summertime Methodist revival meetings. The revivalists' tents and camps later grew into the West Coast headquarters of the populist Chautauqua educational movement, based in upstate New York. The town still has a curiously Midwestern feel, from its many small churches to the rows of well-maintained Victorian cottages lining its quiet streets. Besides the many fine old buildings, the best reason to come here is the beautiful, fully accessible shoreline, which boasts some of the coast's best tidepools, sunset views, and endless opportunities for winter whalewatching.

Biologists favor Pacific Grove's shoreline over any other California rocky coast, not only because of the sheer numbers of rare species, but also because of the variations among the species. Food nutrients are so rich that animals are able to grow much larger than at a colder or surf-protected shore. Looking into deep pools, kelp masses, or just beyond shore, you may see schools of opalescent squid, giant Pacific octopuses (which exceed 16 feet in length) or the black seahare, a mollusk that weighs up to 40 pounds. There are many tidepool areas all along Pacific Grove's rocky headlands; following Ocean View Boulevard counterclockwise from the Monterey Bay Aquarium, some superb stretches can be enjoyed at Point Cabrillo, Shoreline Park, Berwick Park, Lover's Point, Perkins Park and around the tip of Point Pinos at Asilomar State Beach.

These tidepools are deservedly popular, but visitors should always remember that the rocky shore ecosystem is extremely fragile. It may take several years for a square foot of land to recover after certain plants or animals have been removed. The most important tidepool law is to put everything back in its exact spot after you have examined it.

A quarter-mile inland from the shore, Pacific Grove's main street, Lighthouse Avenue, runs through the 15-mph commercial district of galleries, movie theaters, and cafes like **Toastie's**, a comfy breakfast and lunch place at 702 Lighthouse

Avenue. Nearby **Pepper's**, 170 Forest Avenue (831/373-6892), serves very good, fresh Mexican food. A range of fairly priced fish dishes are on the menu at **The Fishwife** (831/375-7107), overlooking the ocean on Sunset Drive at the north end of the Seventeen Mile Drive.

Until 1969, Pacific Grove's Methodist antecedents prevailed, and drinking alcoholic beverages was banned—as was reading Sunday newspapers— within the city limits.

Places to stay in Pacific Grove seem to be more reasonably priced than in Monterey or Carmel, with summer rates in the $75-a-night range. At the lower end of the scale, the **Bide-a-Wee Motel**, 221 Asilomar Boulevard (831/372-2330), is an old-fashioned motor court two blocks from the ocean. Rustic **Asilomar Conference Center**, 800 Asilomar Boulevard (831/372-8016), has woodsy, Julia Morgan-designed cabins and spacious grounds, but is often filled with church groups or convention-goers. Pacific Grove also offers a bumper crop of Victorian B&Bs, like the pair of neighboring inns near Lover's Point at 555-557 Ocean View Boulevard, the **Grand View** and the **Seven Gables**. The two share a flower garden as well as a phone number (831/372-4341). Rooms here start around $150 a night.

The Seventeen Mile Drive and Pebble Beach
Stretching along the coast between Pacific Grove and Carmel, the Seventeen Mile Drive is one of the most famous toll roads in the nation. Opened in the 1880s, the route initially took guests at Monterey's posh Del Monte Hotel on a scenic carriage ride along the coast through the newly planted Del Monte Forest between Carmel and Pacific Grove. Guided by Samuel F. B. Morse, son of the inventor, the formerly wild area underwent development beginning in the 1920s, first with golf courses like Pebble Beach and Cypress Point, and since then with resort hotels and posh homes.

Enter the drive at any of the gates, where you'll pay the toll ($7.25 at time of writing) and be given a map and guide to the route, pointing out all the scenic highlights, especially the trussed-up old **Lone Cypress**, sub

Lone Cypress

ject of so many Carmel postcards. It's definitely worth doing, if only to say you have; to be honest however, the views from the drive are no more or less splendid than they are from the toll-free drives, like Ocean View Boulevard in Pacific Grove, Scenic Drive in Carmel, or the more distant Hwy-1 through Big Sur.

If you're in the mood to splurge on wanton luxury, you can also stay overnight at either of two extremely plush golf and tennis resorts along the Seventeen Mile Drive: the modern, suburban-style country club of the **Inn at Spanish Bay**, which is also home to an Ansel Adams photography gallery; or the stately, old-money **Lodge at Pebble Beach**. Both resorts charge upwards of $300 a day; for details on accommodations (or golfing fees and tee times), call 831/647-7500.

One event that brought Pebble Beach to national attention was the annual golf tournament hosted by Bing Crosby. Originally an informal celebrity get-together, it grew into one of the main events of the professional circuit and is now the **AT&T-Pebble Beach Pro-Am,** held each winter. Every August for nearly 50 years, classic car collectors from around the world have flocked to Pebble Beach for the annual Concours d' Elegance, showing off their immaculately restored luxury automobiles.

Carmel

The exclusive enclave of Carmel-by-the-Sea (to give its complete name) began life in the early years of the 20th century as a small but lively bohemian colony inhabited by the literary likes of Sinclair Lewis, Mary Austin, and Upton Sinclair. However, with a few arts-and-craftsy exceptions, by the 1950s Carmel had turned into the archly conservative and contrivedly quaint community it is today—a place where Marie Antoinette would no doubt feel at home, dressing down as a peasant, albeit in Chaps by Ralph Lauren. Preserving its rural feel by banning street addresses (and skateboards, and home mail delivery), Carmel simultaneously loves and abhors the many thousands of tourists who descend on it every weekend to windowshop its many designer boutiques and galleries filling the few blocks off Ocean Avenue, the main drag through town.

Though it's easy to be put off by the surface glitz, Carmel does have a lot going for it. The water is too cold and treacherous for swimming, but broad **City Beach** at the foot of Ocean Avenue gleams white against a truly azure cove. To the south, aptly named **Scenic Drive** winds along the rocky coast, past **Tor House** (hour-long tours Fri. and Sat. 10 AM-3 PM; $7; 831/624-1840), rustic home of the great nature poet Robinson Jeffers. One of the literary figures who established Carmel as a bohemian artists colony, Jeffers lived here from 1914 until 1962. Next to Tor House, using boulders he and his helpers carried up from the beach, he hand-built the impressive Hawk Tower, where he wrote many of his wonderful poems, like this one about pictographs along the Carmel River, published in 1929:

✺ HANDS ✺

Inside a cave in a narrow canyon near Tassajara
The vault of rock is painted with hands,
A multitude of hands in the twilight, a cloud of men's palms,
no more,
No other picture. Ther's no one to say
Whether the brown shy quiet people who are dead intended
Religion or magic, or made their tracings
In the idleness of art; but over the division of years these careful
Signs-manual are now like a sealed message
Saying: "Look: we also were human; we had hands, not paws.
All hail
You people with the cleverer hands, our supplanters
In the beautiful country; enjoy her a season, her beauty, and come down
And be supplanted; for you also are human."

Tor House is still home to Jeffers' descendants, who preserve the home as a memorial and museum. A quarter-mile south of Tor House, another broad beach stretches around the mouth of Carmel River at the usually un-populated Carmel River State Park, a favorite spot for scuba divers exploring the deep undersea canyon.

Above the beach, just west of Hwy-1 a mile south of central Carmel, **Carmel Mission** (daily 9:30 AM-4:30 PM; donations) was the most important of all the California missions, serving as home, headquarters, and final resting place of Father Junipero Serra, the Franciscan priest who established Carmel and many of the 20 other California missions, and who is entombed under the chapel floor. The gardens—where on weekends wedding parties alight from limos to take family photos—are beautiful, as is the facade with its photogenic bell tower; this is the mission to visit if you visit only one.

Though most of Carmel's many art galleries seem directed at interior decorators, a few are worth searching out, including the **Photography West Gallery** on the southeast corner of Dolores and Ocean Streets, and the **Weston Gallery** on Sixth Avenue near Dolores Street, featuring the works of Edward Weston, Ansel Adams, and other Carmel-based photographers.

Carmel Practicalities

Dozens of good and usually expensive restaurants thrive in Carmel, but one place to see, even if you don't eat there, is the tiny, mock-Tudoresque **Tuck Box Tea Room** on Dolores Street near 7th Avenue. Rebuilt after a fire but still dolls'-house cute, it serves up bacon-and-eggs breakfasts and dainty plates of shepherd's pie and Welsh rarebit for lunch; closed Monday and Tuesday. If you'd rather join locals than mingle with your fellow tourists, head to **Katy's Place**, on Mission Street between 5th and 6th, serving some of the world's best eggs Benedict.

Carmel has only one place approximating a budget option, the very pleasant **Carmel River Inn** (831/624-1575 or 800/882-8142) just west of Hwy-1 near the Carmel Mission, but even here peak season rates average $100 a night. However, if you want to splurge on a bit of luxury, Carmel is a good place to do it. Besides the golf course resorts of nearby Pebble Beach, Carmel also has the commodious, 1920s-era, mission-style **Cypress Inn** at Lincoln and 7th (831/624-3871 or 800/443-7443), partly owned by dog-loving Doris Day (and featuring posters of her movies in the small bar off the lobby), with rooms from under $150. A relaxing spot away from downtown is the **Carmel Mission Ranch**, at 26270 Dolores Street (831/624-6436 or 800/538-8221), a short walk from the beach and the mission, and offering resort-level facilities at room rates that run close to $250 a night. At all of these places we quote peak-season rates; off-season rates will be much lower, so be sure to ask about any special deals that might be on offer.

Carmel's leading light, **Clint Eastwood,** seems ever-present: besides serving as mayor for many years, he owns the Mission Ranch resort. As a filmmaker, he used Carmel as the location for one of his most disturbing movies, the psychopathic 1970s film *Play Misty for Me.*

The photogenic **Bixby Creek Bridge,** 15 miles south of Carmel, was the largest concrete bridge in the world when built in 1932. The old coast road runs along the north bank of the creek, linking up again with Hwy-1 near Andrew Molera State Park.

The northern extent of Big Sur is marked by the volcanic hump of **Point Sur,** 19 miles south of Carmel, a symmetrical dome capped by a 100-year-old lighthouse.

Point Lobos State Reserve

The sculpted headland south of Carmel Bay, now protected as Point Lobos State Reserve (daily 9 AM-5 PM, till 6:30 PM in summer; $7 per car), holds one of the few remaining groves of native Monterey cypress, gnarled and bent by the often stormy coastal weather. The name comes from the barking sea lions (*lobos del mar*) found here by early Spanish explorers; sea lions, otters, and—in winter— whales are often seen offshore or in the many picturesque coves.

The entrance to the reserve is along Hwy-1, three miles south of Carmel Mission, but in summer the park is so popular that visitors sometimes have to wait in line outside the gates. If possible, plan to come early or during the week.

Andrew Molera State Park

Spreading along the coast at the mouth of the Big Sur River, 21 miles south of Carmel, Andrew Molera State Park is a grassy former cattle ranch on the site of one of Big Sur's oldest homesteads. In the 1850s, immigrant John "Juan Bautista" Roger Cooper bought the land and built a cabin, which still stands along Hwy-1 near the park entrance. Well-blazed trails wind along both banks of the river down to the small beach, horses are available for hire, and there are quite a few nice places to **camp** (walk-in only, $3 per person).

Big Sur Village

South of Andrew Molera, Hwy-1 cuts inland toward the heart of Big Sur, the deep and densely forested valley carved by the Big Sur River. Consisting of little more than three gas stations, a couple of roadside markets, and a number of lodges and restaurants, the mile-long village of Big Sur (pop. 950) represents the only real settlement between Carmel and Hearst Castle.

At the north end of town, the **Big Sur River Inn** (831/625-5255 or 800/548-3610) has moderately priced, rustic rooms in the lodge and in the motel across the highway; it also has a woodsy, warm, and unpretentious restaurant overlooking the river. A half-mile south, on the river side of the highway, is a small complex that includes crafts galleries, a grocery store, and the homey **Big Sur Village Pub,** which features good beers, pizzas, and pub grub. Continuing south, the next mile of Hwy-1 holds Big Sur's main family-oriented resorts, all offering rustic cabins and campgrounds along the river: **Riverside** (831/667-2414); **Ripplewood** (831/667-2242); and **Fernwood** (831/667-2422).

BIG SUR

Big Sur, the 90 miles of coastline south of Carmel from Point Sur Lighthouse all the way to Hearst Castle, is one of the most memorable stretches of coastline on the planet, with 5,000-foot-tall mountains rising straight up from the Pacific Ocean. Early Spanish missionaries dubbed it *El País Grande del Sur,* the "Big Country of the South," as it was south of their colony at Carmel, and the rugged land has resisted development or even much of a population—the current total of around 1,500 is roughly the same as it was in 1900, and for the 3,000 years before that.

Highway 1, the breathtaking drive through Big Sur, was finally cut across the very steep cliffs in 1937, requiring 20 years of convict labor and several fatalities. Named the state's first scenic route, so dedicated by Lady Bird Johnson in 1966, it's an incredible trip. Like the Grand Canyon and other larger-than-life natural wonders, Big Sur boggles the mind and, in an odd way, can be hard to handle; you have to content yourself with staring in awestruck appreciation, taking pictures, or maybe toasting the natural handiwork with a cold beer or glass of wine at one of the few but unforgettable cafes and restaurants along the way.

However beautiful the drive along Hwy-1, it's also narrow, twisting, packed with sluggish RVers on holiday weekends, and often closed by mudslides and washouts during torrential winter storms. In 1983, the biggest storm in recent memory closed the road for over a year, and in 1998 70 miles of it were blocked for over 4 months; sections of it are closed almost every year.

There are also very few services, and most of the overnight accommodations are booked solidly during the peak summer season. Spring brings wildflowers, while fall gets the most reliably good weather. No matter when you come, even if you just drive through in an afternoon, be sure to stop whenever possible and get out of the car; scenic viewpoints line the roadside, and dozens of trails lead off into the wilds.

Pfeiffer–Big Sur State Park

Roughly a half-mile south of Big Sur village, Pfeiffer–Big Sur State Park is the region's main event, an 810-acre riverside forest that's one of the most pleasant (and popular) parks in the state. Besides offering a full range of visitor services—restaurant, lodge, campground, and grocery store—the park includes one of the Big Sur's best short hikes, a two-mile loop on the Valley View trail that takes in stately redwoods as well as oak and madrone groves, a 40-foot waterfall, and a grand vista down the Big Sur valley to the coast. Campsites cost $15-20 (800/444-7275); for cabins or rooms at the lodge, call 800/424-4787.

The best basic guide to Big Sur is an annual free newspaper, *El Sur Grande,* published by Monterey County and available at ranger stations and many other locations in and around Big Sur.

The park also has the main **ranger station** (831/667-2315) for all the state parks in the Big Sur area. Just south of the park entrance, a U.S. Forest Service **ranger station** (831/667-2423) on the east side of Hwy-1 has information on hiking and camping opportunities in the mountains above Big Sur, including the isolated (but poison-oak-ridden) Ventana Wilderness.

Pfeiffer Beach

South of Pfeiffer–Big Sur State Park, halfway up a long, steep incline, a small road turns west and leads down through dark and heavily overgrown Sycamore Canyon, eventually winding up at Big Sur's best beach, Pfeiffer Beach. From the lot at the end of the road, a short trail runs through a grove of trees before opening onto the broad white sands, loomed over by a pair of hulking offshore rocks. The water's way too cold for swimming, but the half-mile strand is one of the few places in Big Sur where you can enjoy extended beachcombing strolls. The beach's northern half attracts a clothing-optional crew, even on cool gray days.

The landmark **red farmhouse** along Hwy-1 at the entrance to Ventana was built in 1877 by pioneer rancher W.B. Post, whose descendants developed the Post Ranch Inn.

Ventana and the Post Ranch Inn

South of Sycamore Canyon, roughly three miles from the heart of Big Sur village, Hwy-1 passes between two of California's most deluxe small resorts. The larger of the two, Ventana (831/667-2331 or 800/628-6500), covers 1,000 acres of Big Sur foothills and offers saunas, swimming pools, and four-star accommodations in 1970s-style cedar-paneled rooms and cabins. Rates range $200-800 a night, and there's also a very fine restaurant with incredible views and reasonable prices, to which guests are ferried in a fleet of golf carts.

Completed in 1992 and directly across Hwy-1 from Ventana, the Post Ranch Inn (831/667-2200 or 800/527-2200) is at the forefront of ecotourism, a low-impact but ultra high-style luxury resort hanging high above the Big Sur coast. In order to preserve Big Sur's untarnished natural beauty, the Post Ranch Inn is designed to be virtually invisible from land or sea: the 24 accommodations—all featuring a king-sized bedroom and a Jacuzzi bath with built-in massage table—blend in with the landscape, disguised either as playful tree houses raised up in the branches of the oaks and pines, or as underground cabins carved into the cliff top. Rates start at $300 a night, but if you want to have a look and plan for a future escape, tours of the resort are given Mon.-Fri. at 2 PM.

Nepenthe

One of the most popular and long-lived stopping points along the Big Sur coast, Nepenthe is a rustic bar and restaurant offering good food and great views from atop a rocky headland, a thousand feet above the Pacific. Named for the mythical drug that causes one to forget all sorrows, Nepenthe looks like something out of a 1960s James Bond movie, built of huge boulders and walls of plate glass. The menu too is somewhat dated; burgers, steaks, and fried fish predominate.

The hilltop where Nepenthe now stands was previously the site of a rustic cabin that **Orson Welles** bought for his wife **Rita Hayworth** in 1944.

Sharing a parking lot, and taking advantage of similar views, the neighboring **Cafe Kevah** serves a veggie-friendly range of soups, salads, and quesadillas, plus good teas and coffees and microbrewed beers on a rooftop deck; you'll find a gift shop downstairs selling top-quality arts and crafts and knitwear by Kaffe Fassett, who grew up here and whose family owns the place.

Right along Hwy-1, at a sharp bend in the road just south of Nepenthe, the **Henry Miller Memorial Library** (irregular hours, usually daily 11 AM-5 PM in summer; 831/667-2574) carries an erratic but engaging collection of books by and about the author, who lived in Big Sur for many years in the 1950s.

About six miles south of Nepenthe, or a mile from the parking area at Julia Pfeiffer Burns State Park, a steep trail drops down to Partington Cove, where ships used to moor in the protected anchorage. The last stretch of the trail passes through a 100-foot-long tunnel hewn out of solid rock.

A half-mile south of Nepenthe on the east side of the highway, one of the oldest and most atmospheric places to stay is **Deetjen's Big Sur Inn** (831/667-2377), a rambling and rustic redwood lodge built by a Norwegian immigrant in the 1930s and now a nonprofit operation offering comfortable rooms for $75-150 a night. Deetjen's also serves Big Sur's best breakfasts (8-11 AM) and hearty dinners.

Julia Pfeiffer Burns State Park

If for some untenable reason you only have time to stop once along the Big Sur coast, Julia Pfeiffer Burns State Park (dawn-dusk daily) should be the place. Spreading along both sides of Hwy-1, about 14 miles south of Big Sur village, the park includes one truly beautiful sight, a slender waterfall that drops crisply down into a nearly circular turquoise-blue cove. This is the only waterfall in California that plunges directly into the Pacific.

Three miles south of Julia Pfeiffer Burns State Park, the New Age **Esalen Institute** offers a variety of "Human Potential" workshops; they also have an incredible set of natural hot springs, right above the ocean and sometimes open to the public midnight-5 AM. For information or reservations, phone 831/667-3000.

From the parking area, east of the highway, a short trail leads under the road to a fine view of the waterfall, while another leads to the remnants of a pioneer mill, complete with a preserved Pelton wheel. Other routes climb through redwood groves up to the chaparral-covered slopes of the Santa Lucia Mountains.

Lucia, Pacific Valley, and Gorda

The southern reaches of the Big Sur coast are drier and more rugged, offering bigger vistas but fewer stopping places than the northern half. The road winds along the cliffs, slowing down every 10 miles or so for each of three gas station/cafe/motel complexes, which pass for towns on the otherwise uninhabited coast. The first of these, 25 miles south of Big Sur village, is Lucia, which has a very good restaurant and lantern-lit cabins. High on a hill just south of Lucia, marked by a slender black cross, is the Benedictine **New Camaldoli Hermitage**, open to interested outsiders as a silent retreat. For details, phone 831/667-2456.

Kirk Creek Campground (831/667-2423), operated by the U.S. Forest Service at the foot of scenic Nacimiento Road, has the most accessible oceanside campsites in Big Sur.

Continuing south, Hwy-1 runs through Pacific Valley, the hills above which are a popular hang-gliding spot, then passes by a number of small but pretty beaches and coves before reaching Gorda, the southernmost stop on the Big Sur coast. Beyond here, a series of small state parks lines the highway, but the next services are 25 miles farther south in San Simeon, at the entrance to Hearst Castle.

Steinbeck Country: The Salinas Valley

For any number of reasons—bad weather, lack of time, or an abiding interest in American literature—you may opt to bypass the lengthy drive along the coast and follow much-faster US-101 through the Salinas Valley instead. Though nowhere near as scenic as the coastal route through Big Sur, the drive through the Salinas Valley does have its have its fair share of interest, thanks to a string of Spanish colonial missions, and the life and work of California's preeminent novelist, John Steinbeck. The two attractions are closely intertwined, and since Steinbeck's work is so closely linked with the natural and cultural history of his native land, traveling

EL CAMINO REAL AND THE CALIFORNIA MISSIONS

While the American colonies were busy rebelling against the English Crown, a handful of Spaniards and Mexicans were establishing outposts and blazing an overland route up the California coast, along the New World's most distant frontier. Beginning in 1769 with the founding of a fortress and a Franciscan mission at San Diego, and culminating in 1776 with the founding of another outpost at what is now San Francisco, a series of small but self-reliant religious colonies was established, each a day's travel apart and linked by El Camino Real, "The King's Highway," a route followed roughly by today's US-101.

2527. EL CAMINO "REAL" BELL. SAN GABRIEL MISSION, CAL.

Many of the colonies grew to become the state's largest cities; others were abandoned and all but disappeared. Some of the missions have been preserved, others restored in varying degrees of authenticity and apocryphal romance, and the route itself is in the process of being declared a national historic trail. Some of the most interesting missions are listed below, north to south, followed by the dates of founding.

San Francisco Solano de Sonoma (1823). The only mission built under Mexican rule stands at the heart of this history-rich Wine Country town.

San Juan Bautista (1797). This lovely church forms the heart of an extensive historic park, in the town of the same name. See page 62.

San Carlos Borromeo (1770). Also known as Carmel Mission, this was the most important of the California missions. See page 69.

San Antonio de Padua (1771). This reconstructed church, still in use as a monastery, stands in an undeveloped valley, inland from Big Sur in the middle of Hunter-Leggett Army base. Monks still live, work and pray here, making for a marvelously evocative visit. See page 76.

San Miguel Arcangel (1797). The only mission not to have undergone extensive renovations and restorations—almost everything, notably the vibrantly colorful interior murals, is as it was. See page 76.

San Luis Obispo de Tolosa (1772). It's the centerpiece of this small central coast city. See page 78.

La Purisima Concepcion (1787). A quiet coastal valley is home to this church, which was restored in the 1930s using traditonal methods as part of a New Deal employment and training project. See page 80.

Santa Barbara (1782). Called the "Queen of the Missions," this lovely church stands in lush gardens above the upscale coastal resort city. See page 82.

San Gabriel Arcangel (1771). Once the most prosperous of the California missions, it now stands quietly and all but forgotten off old Route 66 east of Los Angeles. See page 280.

San Juan Capistrano (1776). Known for the swallows that return here each year, this mission has lovely gardens but the buildings have been badly damaged by earthquakes and the elements, meaning they've been under scaffolding for years. See page 96.

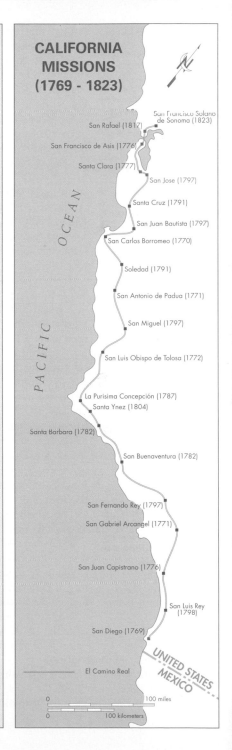

CALIFORNIA MISSIONS (1769 - 1823)

San Francisco Solano de Sonoma (1823)
San Rafael (1817)
San Francisco de Asis (1776)
Santa Clara (1777)
San Jose (1797)
Santa Cruz (1791)
San Juan Bautista (1797)
San Carlos Borromeo (1770)
Soledad (1791)
San Antonio de Padua (1771)
San Miguel (1797)
San Luis Obispo de Tolosa (1772)
La Purisima Concepción (1787)
Santa Ynez (1804)
Santa Barbara (1782)
San Buenaventura (1782)
San Fernando Rey (1797)
San Gabriel Arcangel (1771)
San Juan Capistrano (1776)
San Luis Rey (1798)
San Diego (1769)

PACIFIC OCEAN

UNITED STATES
MEXICO

El Camino Real

0   100 miles
0   100 kilometers

From Hwy-1 at Kirk Creek, five miles south of Lucia, the narrow **Nacimiento Road** makes an unforgettable climb over the coastal mountains past Mission San Antonio de Padua, linking up with US-101 at King City in the Salinas Valley. Because the road passes through sections of Hunter Ligget Army Base, you may need to show valid car registration and proof of insurance, but it's a wonderful drive, in either direction. Unfortunately, this part of Big Sur was badly burned in 1999 fires, so be prepared for some less-than-pristine vistas.

In order to help prevent erosion and mud slides, the roadside along Hwy-1 in the southern half of Big Sur has been planted with odd-looking bunches of pampas grass, which help keep the hills from washing away but have become a intrusive pest, crowding out local flora. The most extreme example of this is at Kirk Creek campground, where the formerly open pastures have changed into a veritable pampas forest.

If you're interested in the larger-than-life work of Pop Art maestro Claes Oldenburg, you'll want to stop and see his mammoth *Hat in Three Stages of Landing,* a trio of giant yellow steel cowboy hats hovering next to the rodeo grounds at 940 N. Main Street in Salinas.

through this rural region is all the more satisfying if you know a little about them both.

First, the missions, which range from the nearly invisible to the most evocative of any in California. From Carmel, El Camino Real, the old road linking the missions, bent inland and then south to the **Mission Maria Santisima Nuestra Señora Dolorisisima de la Soledad**, the remains of which are a mile west of US-101 from the town of **Soledad**. A whitewashed chapel has been reconstructed, and there's a small museum (daily 10 AM-4 PM, closed Tues.; donations), but the mission was flooded repeatedly after construction in 1791, and abandoned for 120 years until restoration efforts began in the 1950s.

The next mission to the south, **Mission San Antonio de Padua** (daily 10 AM-4 PM; donations; 831/385-4478), was the first one built in the Salinas Valley; third oldest of all the California missions, it is still in primary use as a monastery, run by robed Franciscan brothers. Though the mission itself, and the extensive grounds around it, are in excellent shape (the fields, wells, aqueducts and farming equipment have hardly changed in 200 years), it is surrounded on all sides by the sprawling (but mostly disused) Fort Hunter Ligget U.S. Army base, so you may need to show ID and proof of car insurance (or a rental car contract) to armed guards at the gates. If you visit the mission, consider staying the night at the nearby **Hacienda** (831/386-2446), a rustic hunting lodge, built by William Randolph Hearst in 1930, that now offers rooms ($30-50) as well as lunch and dinner. Guests at the Hacienda get access to all the facilities on the base—gyms, movie theater, and more—and since the military is hardly here any more, you can pretty much hike or bike around at will. Mission San Antonio is well-signed, 26 miles southwest of US-101 from King City; the road continues west over the Santa Lucia mountains to the southern edge of Big Sur, through the heart of the forested area that burned in 1999 fires.

The southernmost Salinas Valley mission, **Mission San Miguel Arcangel** (daily 9:30 AM-4:30 PM; donations; 805/467-3256), is right off US-101 in the small town of San Miguel, but despite its proximity to the freeway it feels as old and intact as any of the California missions. Still home to a resident community of Franciscan monks, San Miguel Mission is perhaps most memorable for the well-preserved interior of the mission chuch, which features brilliantly colored fresco murals of trompe l'oeil arches, unchanged since the 1820s, along with stunning starburst reredos. (See the special topic El Camino Real and the California Missions, including a map, for more on California's missions.)

Along with this trio of Spanish colonial missions, the other main figure in Salinas Valley history was the Nobel Prize-winning writer John Steinbeck. Born in Salinas in 1902, he grew up in an ornate Victorian home that stands at 132 Central

Avenue, very near the new **National Steinbeck Center**, 1 Main Street (daily 10 AM-
5 PM; $7; 831/775-4720), which dedicates thousands of square feet to the life and
work of a man who was effectively run out of town after the publication of his
breakthrough novel, *The Grapes of Wrath*, which won a Pulitzer
Prize in 1939. His previous book, *Of Mice and Men*, and his later
works *Cannery Row* and *East of Eden*, were all set in and around
the Salinas Valley and nearby Monterey Peninsula, but Steinbeck himself spent most of his adult life in New York. He returned briefly while writing the wonderful road trip tale *Travels
With Charley*, then came home for good after his death in 1968.
Steinbeck is buried in Salinas at the Garden of Memories, 768
Abbott Street.

The **James Dean**
memorial, 27 miles east of
Paso Robles near the
junction of Highways 46 and
41, is next to the site where
the talented and rebellious
actor (who, coincidentally,
starred in the film version of
John Steinbeck's *East of
Eden)*, crashed his silver
Porsche and died on Sept.
30, 1955.

San Simeon: Hearst Castle

At the south end of rugged Big Sur, the mountains flatten out and turn inland, and the coastline becomes rolling, open range ranch land.
High on a hill above Hwy-1 stands the coast's
one totally unique attraction, Hearst Castle. Located 65 miles south of Big Sur village and 43
miles northwest of San Luis Obispo, Hearst
Castle is the sort of place that you really have to
see to believe, though simple numbers—144
rooms, including 36 bedrooms—do give a
sense of its scale.

Even if Hearst's taste in interior design (or
his megalomania, which by all accounts was
understated by his fictional portrayal in Orson
Welles's *Citizen Kane*) doesn't appeal, Hearst
Castle cries out to be seen, if only as a reveal-
ing landmark to one of this century's most
powerful and influential Americans. Hearst in-
herited the land, and most of his fortune, from
his father George Hearst, a mining mogul, and
began work on his castle following the death of his mother in 1919. With the help
of the great California architect Julia Morgan, who designed the complex to look
like a Mediterranean hill town with Hearst's house as the cathedral at its center,
Hearst spent 25 years working on his "castle"—building, rebuilding, and filling
room after room with furniture, all the while entertaining the great and powerful
of the era, from Charlie Chaplin to Winston Churchill.

A small **museum** (daily 9 AM-5 PM; free) in the visitors center, next to where
you board the trams that carry you up to the house, details Hearst's life and times.
If you want to go on a **tour**, the Introductory Tour gives the best first-time
overview, taking in the main house and the two swimming pools. Other tours
specialize in different aspects of the house and gardens; each one costs $14 and
takes around two hours. Advance reservations (800/444-4445) are all but essential, especially in summer.

Cambria

Without Hearst Castle, Cambria would be just another farming town, but being next to the state's number-two tourist attraction (after Disneyland) has turned Cambria into quite a busy little burg. Apart from a few hokey, tourist-trapping souvenir shops at the north end of town, it's a casual, walkable, and franchise-free community of arts and crafts galleries, boutiques, and good restaurants; from Hwy-1, Main Street makes a three-mile loop around to the east, running through the heart of town.

Hearty breakfasts are available at the **Redwood Cafe**, 2094 Main Street. Well-prepared multiethnic and vegetarian food is on the menu at **Robin's**, a half-block off Main Street at 4095 Burton Drive. Places to stay range from standard motels like the **Bluebird Motel**, 1880 Main Street (805/927-4634), to the rustic **Cambria Pines Lodge** (805/927-4200), on a hill above Hwy-1 at 2905 Burton Drive.

The coastal coves just north of San Simeon have become a favored rookery of California's ever-expanding population of northern elephant seals. No Parking signs have been posted along Hwy-1 to protect the animals' privacy, but during mating season people still park and walk down to the shore to see them up close and personal. The only officially sanctioned place to see the elephant seals is at Año Nuevo State Reserve, north of Santa Cruz.

Five miles south of Cambria, **Harmony** (pop. 18) is a former dairy town turned arts-and-crafts colony, with a range of galleries and a small wedding chapel. The region's other flyspeck town, Cayucos, sits along the coast 10 miles farther south.

From Main Street in Morro Bay, Hwy-41 is a wonderful drive up and over the coastal mountains to Atascadero on US-101. Passing through farms and the top end of the **Los Padres National Forest,** the road gives some great coastal panoramas, but the best views are from the top of 2,620-foot Cerro Alto, a volcanic cone that stands just south of Hwy-41, eight miles east of Morro Bay.

Morro Bay

Marked by the Gibraltar-like monolith of Morro Rock, which was noted by Juan Cabrillo in 1542 and now serves as a peregrine falcon preserve and nesting site, the busy commercial fishing harbor of Morro Bay (pop. 9,950) is lined by seafood restaurants like **The Galley**, 899 Embarcadero, a half-mile west of Hwy-1. A thin, six-mile-long strip of sand protects the bay from the Pacific Ocean, forming a seabird-rich lagoon that's included within Morro Bay State Park, a mile southeast of the harbor. There's an informative museum with displays on local wildlife, and just down Hwy-1 at the edge of the park the friendly **Bayside Cafe** (805/772-1465) serves lunch daily and dinner Thurs.-Sat. Next door, when the weather's nice, you can rent **kayaks** ($6 an hour) and paddle around the estuary.

The rest of Morro Bay is pretty quiet; one unusual sight is the giant **outdoor chessboard** on the waterfront in City Park, along the Embarcadero at the foot of Morro Bay Boulevard. For details, or to reserve the waist-high playing pieces, call 805/772-6278.

San Luis Obispo

Located midway between San Francisco and Los Angeles at the junction of Hwy-1 and US-101, San Luis Obispo (pop. 43,000) makes a good stopping-off point, at least for lunch if not for a lengthier stay. Like most of the towns along this route, San Luis, as it's almost always called, revolves around an 18th-century mission, here named **Mission San Luis Obispo de Tolosa,** which is said to be the place where Franciscan missionaries first developed California's traditional red-tiled roofs. Standing at the heart of town, at Chorro and Monterey Streets, the mission overlooks one of the state's liveliest downtown districts, with dozens of shops and restaurants backing onto Mission Plaza, a two-block park on the banks of Mission Creek.

Besides the mission and the lively downtown commercial district that surrounds it, San Luis holds a singular roadside attraction, the **Madonna Inn**, which stands just west of US-101 at the foot of town. One of California's most noteworthy pop culture landmarks, the Madonna Inn is a remarkable example of what architecturally minded academic types like to call vernacular kitsch, decorated in a wild barrage of fantasy motifs: the bright pink honeymoon suites, known as "Just Heaven" and "Love Nest"; the "Safari Room" covered in fake zebra skins with a jungle-green shag carpet; the cavelike "Cave Man Room"; or over 100 others, of which no two are alike. *Roadside America* rated the Madonna Inn as "the best place to spend a vacation night in America," but if you can't stay the night, at least stop for a look at the gift shop, which sells postcards of the different rooms. Guys should head down to the men's room, where the urinal trough is flushed by a waterfall. Room rates run $80-150 a night; for reservations or more information, call 805/543-3000 or 800/543-9666.

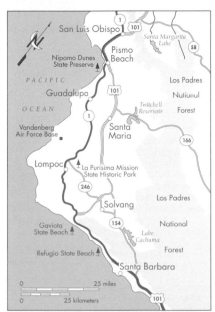

Though the Madonna Inn has a huge, banquet-ready restaurant—done up in white lace and varying hues of pink—the best places to eat are located downtown, near the mission. For healthy food in a friendly, sunny space, try the **Rhythm Cafe** overlooking Mission Creek at 1040

Broad Street. For an outstanding Italian meal, head to **Buona Tavola**, 1037 Monterey Street. **Linnaea's Cafe**, 1110 Garden Street off Higuera, serves coffee and tea and sundry snack items all day and night; there's also the lively, multi-culti **Big Sky Cafe**, 1121 Broad Street, and the usual range of beer-and-burger bars you'd expect from a college town (San Luis is the home of California Polytechnic State University, aka Cal Poly).

Along with the Madonna Inn, San Luis has a number of good places to stay, with reasonable rates that drop considerably after the summertime peak season. Besides the national chains—Embassy Suites, Howard Johnson's, Super 8, two Travelodges and three Best Westerns—try the **Adobe Inn**, 1473 Monterey Street (805/549-0321), or **La Cuesta Motor Inn**, 2074 Monterey Street (805/543-2777 or 800/543-2777). There's also the **HI San Luis Obispo Hostel**, 1617 Santa Rosa Street (805/544-4678) near downtown and the Amtrak station.

Another San Luis landmark, the **world's first motel,** opened at 2223 Monterey Street in 1925. Originally called the Milestone Motel, the Spanish revival structure was later renamed the Motel Inn but went out of business long ago and now stands, forlorn but not forgotten, next to US-101 on the grounds of the Apple Farm restaurant and motel.

Every Thursday evening, the main drag of San Luis Obispo, **Higuera Street,** is closed to cars and converted into a very lively farmer's market and block party—with stands selling fresh food and good live bands providing entertainment.

A pedestrian walkway in downtown San Luis Obispo, off Higuera Street between Garden and Broad Streets, has become known around the world as **Bubble Gum Alley.** Since the 1950s, local kids have written their names and allegiances on the brick walls, using chewing gum rather than the more contemporary spray paint.

At the south end of Pismo Beach, **Nipomo Dunes State Preserve** holds endless acres of sand dunes and marshlands, as well as the buried remains of a movie set used in C.B. DeMille's *The Ten Commandments.*

In the late 1930s, Nipomo was the place where **Dorothea Lange** took that famous photograph of a migrant mother huddling with her children in a farm workers camp. It's also home to **Jocko's** (805/929-3686), a popular steakhouse and cocktail bar right off US-101 on Thompson Road, the old highway.

For more information, contact the San Luis Obispo Chamber of Commerce (805/781-2777), and pick up a copy of the free weekly *New Times.*

Pismo Beach

South of San Luis Obispo, Hwy-1 and US-101 run along the ocean past Pismo Beach (pop. 7,800), a family-oriented beach resort where the main attraction is driving or dune-buggying along the sands. Pismo was once famous for its clams, now overharvested to the point of oblivion, but you may still see people pitchforking a few small ones out of the surf. The area has grown significantly in the past decade, thanks mainly to an influx of retired people housed in red-roofed townhouses, but Price Street, the old road frontage, offers a wide range of motels and fast-food restaurants—nothing very special, but handy.

Guadalupe and Santa Maria

South of Pismo Beach, the highways diverge. Hwy-1 cuts off west through the still agricultural areas around sleepy Guadalupe (pop. 5,479), where produce stands sell cabbages, broccoli, and leafy green vegetables fresh from the fields. The town itself feels miles away from modern California, with a four-block Main Street lined by Mexican cafes, bars, banks, and grocery stores. A great place to get a feel for Guadalupe is at the **Far Western Tavern,** open daily for lunch and dinner at 899 Guadalupe Street (805/343-2211). Try the steaks, which are awesome.

If you opt to follow US-101, shopping malls and tract-house suburbs fill the inland valleys through Santa Maria, a town best known for its thick cuts of barbecued beef, which can be sampled at the large and historic **Santa Maria Inn,** a half-mile west of US-101 at 801 S. Broadway (805/928-7777).

Lompoc and La Purisima Mission State Historic Park

The rolling valleys around Lompoc are famed for their production of flower seeds, and consequently the fields along Hwy-1 are often ablaze in brilliant colors. Apart from colorful murals adorning downtown buildings, Lompoc as a town is not up to much, despite the unusual nature of the area's two main nonagricultural employers: a minimum-security federal prison and the Vandenburg Air Force Base, site of numerous missile tests and the aborted West Coast space shuttle port.

With its long arcade reaching across the floor of a shallow, grassy valley, Mission La Purisima (daily 10 AM-5 PM; $5 per car) gives a strong first impression of what the missions may have looked like in their prime. Four miles northeast of Lompoc, between Hwy-1 and US-101 on Hwy-246, the mission here was originally built in 1812 but fell to ruin before being totally reconstructed as part of a WPA make-work scheme in the New Deal 1930s. During the restoration, workers used period techniques wherever possible, hewing logs with hand tools and stomping mud and straw with their bare feet to mix it for adobe bricks. Workers also built most of the mission-style furniture that fills the chapel and the other rooms in the complex. Also here: a functioning aqueduct, many miles of hiking trails, and a small museum.

Solvang

America's most famous mock-European tourist trap, the Danish-style town of Solvang was founded in 1911. Set up by a group of Danish immigrants as a cooperative agricultural community, Solvang found its calling catering to passing travelers, and the compact blocks of cobblestoned streets and Olde Worlde architecture, highlighted by a few windmills and signs advertising the Hamlet Motel among many more suspicious claims to Danishness, now attract tourists by the busload. Many other U.S. towns (Leavenworth, Washington, and Helen, Georgia, to name two) have been inspired by Solvang's success, but to be honest there's nothing much to do here apart from walking, gawking, and shopping for pastries.

Just east of Solvang's windmills and gables, the brooding hulk of **Mission Santa Ynez** stands as a sober reminder of the region's Spanish colonial past. Built in 1804, it was once among the more prosperous of the California missions, but now is worth a visit mainly for the gift shop selling all manner of devotional ornaments.

Hwy-154: Santa Ynez Valley

Pop singer Michael Jackson's **Neverland Ranch** lies in the foothills of the Santa Ynez Valley, southeast of Solvang via the truly scenic Hwy-154, which loops inland south to Santa Barbara. Starting in the north off US-101, Hwy-154 winds through the wine-growing regions around Los Olivos, past the horse ranches that surround Lake Cachuma (the main reservoir for Santa Barbara), then approaches the coast after a breathtaking trip up and over San Marcos Pass, dropping 2,000 feet in little more than four miles. On the valley side of the summit, the **Cold Spring Tavern**, 5995 Stagecoach Road (805/967-0066), is the best place to break your journey.

Gaviota and Refugio State Beaches

Between Solvang and Santa Barbara, US-101 follows the coast past some of California's most beautiful beaches. Dropping through a steep-sided canyon, US-101 reaches the coast at Gaviota State Beach, where a small fishing pier and camp-

Between San Luis Obispo and Santa Barbara, US-101 turns inland from the coast around Point Conception, the traditional dividing line between central and Southern California. Nearly roadless and generally hard to reach, this untouched stretch of California coast is best seen from Amtrak's **Coast Starlight train,** which runs once daily in each direction (800/USA-RAIL for details). Whales, dolphins, and other wildlife, along with the launching pads of the aborted space shuttle port of Vandenburg Air Force Base, are just a few of the attractions of this lovely coastal cruise. To do it in a day, you have to return by Amtrak bus.

The town of Buellton, a block west of US-101 at the Solvang exit, holds one of California's classic roadside landmarks, **Andersen's Pea Soup Restaurant,** advertised up and down the coast.

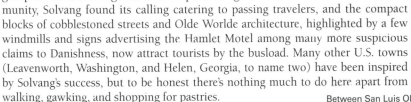

Local sybarites love to soak in the naturally hot waters of **Las Cruces hot spring,** tucked away up a canyon just south of the US-101/Hwy-1 junction.

Rancho del Cielo, the ranch of former President **Ronald Reagan** spreads along the crest of the coastal hills above Refugio State Beach.

ground are overwhelmed by the massive train trestle that runs overhead. Continuing south, US-101 runs atop coastal bluffs past prime surfing beaches, usually marked by a few VWs pulled out along the west side of the highway. Midway along this stretch of coast, some 22 miles north of Santa Barbara, Refugio State Beach has groves of palm tress backing a clear white strand. There's also a small, summer-only store, and a number of attractive campsites with hot showers.

Reservations for camping at Gaviota or Refugio, or at any California state beach, must be made through ReserveAmerica.

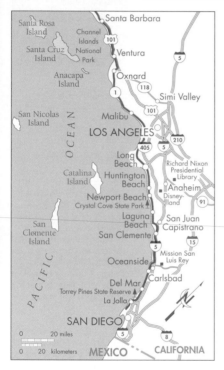

Santa Barbara

The geographical midpoint of California may well be somewhere near San Francisco, but the Southern California of popular imagination—golden beaches washed by waves and peopled by blond-haired surfer gods—has its start, and perhaps best expression, in Santa Barbara. Just over 100 miles north of Los Angeles, Santa Barbara has grown threefold in the last 50 years, but for the moment at least it manages to retain its sleepy seaside charm. Much of its character comes from the fact that, following a sizeable earthquake in 1929, the town fathers—caught up in the contemporary craze for anything Spanish revival—required that all buildings in the downtown area exude a mission-era feel, mandating red-tile roofs, adobe-colored stucco, and rounded arcades wherever practicable. The resulting architectural consistency gives Santa Barbara an un-American charm; it looks more like a Mediterranean village than the modern city that, beneath the surface, it really is.

For a good first look at the city head down to the water, where **Stearns Wharf** sticks out into the bay, bordered by palm tree-lined beaches populated by joggers, inline skaters, and volleyball players. From the wharf area, follow State Street away from the sands to the downtown district, where Santa Barbarans parade among the numerous cafes, bars, and boutiques. At the north end of downtown, don't miss the excellent **Museum of Art** (Tues.-Sat. 11 AM-5 PM, Sunday noon-5 PM; $3), at 1130 State Street. A block east on Anacapa Street, the **county courthouse** is one of the finest public buildings in the state, a hand-crafted Spanish revival monument set in lush semitropical gardens, with an observation tower (daily 9 AM-5 PM; free) giving a fine view over the red-tiled cityscape.

Santa Barbara's reigning attraction, **Mission Santa Barbara** (daily 9 AM-5 PM; $2) stands atop a shallow hill a well-posted mile up from State Street, looking out over the city and shoreline below. Called the "Queen of the Missions" by the local

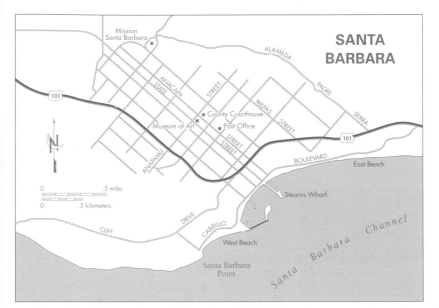

tourist scribes, Mission Santa Barbara is undeniably lovely to look at, its rose-hued stone facade perfectly complemented by the roses and bougainvillea that frame the well-maintained gardens and lawns.

Santa Barbara has perhaps the coast's best variety of places to eat. Early risers can enjoy the greasy spoon breakfasts (daily 6 AM-1 PM, Sunday from 7 AM) at **Esau's Coffee Shop**, 403 State Street, a block north of US-101. State Street holds most of the lunch and dinner places, too, including the old-fashioned burgers and beers on tap in the dark wood dining room of **Joe's Cafe**, 536 State Street (805/966-4638). Finally, some of the world's best hole-in-the-wall Mexican food is served a half-mile east of State Street at **La Super-Rica**, 622 N. Milpas Street (805/963-4940), where such distinguished foodies as Julia Child have come to chow down on freshly made soft tacos and delicious seafood tamales—all at bargain basement prices.

Santa Barbara is one of many great places along the coast to go on a whale-watching cruise, such as on the *Condor* or other boats. Trips take a half-day or full day, and some head out to the Channel Islands. Call 805/963-3564 or 888/779-4253 for details or reservations.

The city's accommodations, however, are among the central coast's most expensive, especially in summer when even the most basic motel can charge as much as $100 a night. One of the nicest of the many motels is the **Franciscan Inn**, 10 Bath Street (805/963-8845), just a short walk from the beach and wharf. At the top of the scale, the **Simpson House**, 121 E.

SANTA BARBARA MISSION. CAL.

The national budget chain Motel 6 got its start in Santa Barbara, where they now have five properties, including one near the beach at 443 Corona Del Mar (805/564-1392).

Former congressman (and wannabee U.S. senator) **Michael Huffington** lives in the wealthy enclave of Montecito, just south of Santa Barbara.

In the beach resort of **Summerland,** the Nugget Restaurant along the old US-101 highway at 2318 Lillie Avenue (805/969-6135) has a saxophone that President Clinton plays whenever he's vacationing here. The next exit to the south takes you to Santa Claus Lane, a seasonal shopping street with a giant-sized statue of St. Nick.

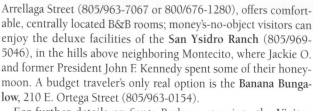

Arrellaga Street (805/963-7067 or 800/676-1280), offers comfortable, centrally located B&B rooms; money's-no-object visitors can enjoy the deluxe facilities of the **San Ysidro Ranch** (805/969-5046), in the hills above neighboring Montecito, where Jackie O. and former President John F. Kennedy spent some of their honeymoon. A budget traveler's only real option is the **Banana Bungalow,** 210 E. Ortega Street (805/963-0154).

For further details on Santa Barbara, stop into the **Visitor Information Center** near Stearns Wharf at 1 Santa Barbara Street (805/966-9222 or 800/676-1266).

Channel Islands National Park

South of Santa Barbara, US-101 widens into an eight-lane freeway along the coast. Looking out beyond the partially disguised offshore oil wells, on a clear day you can't miss the outlines of the Channel Islands, whose rocky shores are protected as a national park. Consisting of eight islands altogether, they sit from 12 to nearly 50 miles off the mainland, but only the smallest and closest, Anacapa Island, is easily accessible to the public; daily charters from Ventura Harbor are offered by **Island Packers** (805/642-1393).

Detour: Ojai and Highway 33

Above Ventura, in the rolling foothills of the Santa Ynez Mountains, the hideaway community of Ojai (pop. 7,613; pronounced "O-hi") has an easy-going, artsy-craftsy feel that belies its wealthy demographics. Talk of the New Age is old hat in Ojai, which has been spiritually minded since the theosophist Krisnamurti gave a series of lectures here in the 1920s, resulting in the establishment of the Krishnamurti Society and Library (805/646-4948), northeast of town. *Doors of Perception* author Aldous Huxley also spent time here, and though Ojai has grown considerably since then, the setting is still superb, especially if can time your travels to be here around sunset, when the entire valley hums with a vibrant pink glow.

Apart from appreciating the sunset, or contemplating the nature of existence, there's not a lot to *do* in Ojai. Though after a quick ramble around town, and perhaps a bite to eat at the veggie-friendly **Ojai Cafe Emporium,** 108 S. Montgomery Street (805/646-2733), you can head west along Hwy-150 to lovely Lake Casitas (site of the 1984 Olympics rowing competitions), or better yet, head north along Hwy-33, which winds up into the chapparal-covered **Los Padres National Forest** through scenic Wheeler Gorge. The drive—which switchbacks smoothly up to a peak of 5,084 feet, 30 miles above Ojai, before winding back down into the agricultural Central Valley—is a thrill in itself, and best finished off with a soak at the historic **Wheeler Hot Springs,** six miles north of Ojai at 16825 Maricopa Highway (805/646-8131 or 800/994-3353). Here you'll find a nice restaurant in addition to the naturally heated mineral water hot tubs.

Ventura

Midway between Malibu and Santa Barbara, Ventura (pop. 95,000) is an offbeat little place, its three-block Main Street lined by enough thrift shops (seven at last count) to clothe a destitute retro-minded army. Apart from searching out vintage couture, the main reason to stop is the small and much-reconstructed **Mission San Buenaventura** (Mon.-Sat. 10 AM-5 PM, Sunday 10 AM-4 PM; $1), standing at the center of Ventura at 225 E. Main Street, just east of the US-101 freeway. This was the ninth in the California mission chain, and the last one founded by Father Serra, in 1782. A block from the mission at 113 E. Main Street, the **Albinger Archaeological Museum** (Tues.-Sun. 10 AM-4 PM; free) collects a wide range of artifacts—the oldest from 1500 B.C, the most recent from early American settlers— all excavated from a single city-block-sized site alongside the mission.

The mountains above Ojai are the last remaining breeding ground for the **California condor,** a huge vulture of a bird whose wingspans can reach over nine feet across.

Ventura is the birthplace and headquarters of the outdoor equipment and fashion company **Patagonia,** started and still owned by legendary rock climber Yvon Chouinard.

Ventura doesn't get anything like the tourist trade that Santa Barbara draws, but it does have the very pleasant **Bella Magiore Inn**, offering good-value B&B rooms in a nicely restored 1920s courtyard house at 67 S. California Street (805/652-0277 or 800523-8479), between downtown and US-101.

South of Ventura, US-101 heads inland through the San Fernando Valley to Hollywood and downtown Los Angeles, while Hwy-1 heads south through the 10 miles of stop-and-go sprawl that make up the farming community of **Oxnard** (pop. 149,457), then continues right along the coast through Malibu and West Los Angeles.

Detour: Simi Valley

If you opt to follow US-101 rather than coastal Hwy-1 into Los Angeles, be sure to check out the somnolent suburb of Simi Valley, 20 miles east of Ventura. Home to the jury that acquitted the LAPD officers who beat Rodney King, it's also where the hilltop **Ronald Reagan Presidential Library** (daily 10 AM-5 PM; $4; 805/522-8444) fills 150,000 square feet of Spanish-style stucco; to get there, take US-101 to Hwy-23 North, exit at Olsen Road, and follow the signs.

The other Simi Valley sight to see is **Bottle Village**, a complex of small buildings and sculptures built out of glass bottles, TV sets, hubcaps and assorted other recycled refuse in the 1940s and 1950s by the late Tressa Prisbey. Badly damaged in the 1992 North-ridge earthquake, and subject of a heated battle between preservationists and those who think it's a pile of junk, the village can be viewed from the road or by occasional guided tours; it's at 4595 Cochrane Street (donations; 805/583-1627), a mile south of the Hwy-118/210 freeway, between the Tapo Canyon and Sterns Road exits.

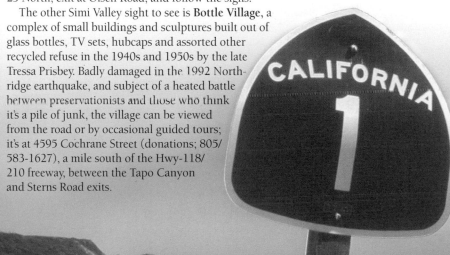

Mulholland Drive
From Hwy-1 at Leo Carrillo State Beach, legendary Mulholland Drive begins its epic 55-mile journey along the crest of the Santa Monica Mountains, from the Pacific shore all the way to the Hollywood Bowl. The western half, parts of which aren't even paved, is by far the wildest section of the drive, passing by a series of state and county parks that preserve everything from old movie and TV show sets (including those used by *M.A.S.H.* at Malibu Creek State Park, and ones used in *Dr. Quinn: Medicine Woman* at Paramount Ranch), to Cold War-era ballistic missile sites. The eastern half, running between the San Diego and Hollywood freeways and overlooking the bright lights of Beverly Hills and the San Fernando Valley, is a totally different animal. For further information, contact the Santa Monica Mountains Conservancy (310/858-7272).

Pacific Coast Highway Beaches
Running right along the beach, the Pacific Coast Highway (Hwy-1) heads south from Oxnard around the rocky headland of Point Mugu (ma-GOO), where the U.S. Navy operates a missile testing center and the Santa Monica Mountains rise steeply out of the Pacific Ocean. Most of these chaparral-covered granite mountains have been protected as park land, with hiking, cycling, and riding trails offering grand views and a surprising amount of solitude. A series of state-owned beaches mark your progress along the coastal road, but this stretch is basically natural wilderness —apart from the highway, of course. Biggest and best of the beaches hereabouts is the lovely **Leo Carrillo State Beach**, which has a sandy strand, some great tidepools, and a sycamore-shaded campground (310/457-6589 or 800-444-7275).

South of Leo Carrillo, which marks the Los Angeles County line, heading toward Malibu, there are many more public beach areas, including (in roughly north-to-south order) Nicholas Canyon County Beach, El Pescador, El Matador (where episodes of TV's *Baywatch* have been filmed), and big brash Zuma Beach, where the highway bends inland.

The main route inland from the coast, Malibu Canyon Road, was the site of the key murder scene in James M. Cain's thriller *The Postman Always Rings Twice.*

Malibu
South of Zuma Beach, houses begin popping up along Hwy-1 to block the oceanfront views, and more elaborate multi-million-dollar homes dot the canyons above as well, forming the sprawling exurbia and movie star playground of Malibu, which stretches along Hwy-1 for the next 27 miles into Santa Monica and metropolitan L.A. It's hard to get more than a glimpse of the garage doors or wrought iron gates of these palaces, but this is the address of choice for the movers and shakers of the entertainment world: if you can name them, they probably own property here. Most of the truly huge estates are hidden away on ranches high up in the mountains. One of the few accessible hideaways has been evolving since 1993, when Barbra Streisand donated her 22-acre ranch in Ramirez Canyon for use as a botanical preserve. It's managed by the Santa Monica Mountains Conservancy and is open to visitors on guided tours only ($30; 310/589-3200 or 589-2850).

From Hwy-1, the most prominent sight is the Pepperdine University campus, which was described by the late great architect Charles Moore as "an overscaled motel set in obscenely vivid emerald lawns." Better known for its volleyball teams than its academic rigor, Pepperdine is the place Clinton-chasing Special Prosecutor Kenneth Starr agreed to be Dean of the Law School, only to quit in continuing pursuit of Monica Lewinsky a few days later. Below the bluff-top campus, the legendary Malibu Colony stretches along the coast in high-security splendor. About the only place in Malibu where it's fun (and legal) to explore is the area around the landmark **Malibu Pier**, which juts into the ocean at the heart of Malibu's short and rather scruffy commercial strip. North of the pier, which was used most famously in TV's *The Rockford Files*, stretches Surfrider Beach, site of most of those Frankie Avalon and Annette Funicello beach blanket babylon movies made during the 1950s. The pier and the beach are part of **Malibu Lagoon State Park**, which also protects the historic **Adamson House**, 23200 Pacific Coast Highway (Wed.-Sat. 11 AM-2 PM; $2; 310/456-8432), a lovely old circa 1929 Spanish revival courtyard home, right on the beach and full of gorgeous tile work and other architectural features. Tours of the house are given throughout the day, and fascinating exhibits portray Malibu history and the Rindge family who once owned the entire region.

At the far north end of Malibu, the ramshackle **Neptune's Net** restaurant at 42505 Pacific Coast Highway is a great place to hang out and star-gaze while enjoying fresh seafood, served up on paper plates for that down-home Hollywood feel.

Between Malibu and Santa Monica, Topanga Canyon is home to an alternative community of hippies and New Agers; nearby, but closed until 2001, is the original **J. Paul Getty Museum**, which displayed the oil magnate's art collection prior to the opening of the massive Getty Center above Brentwood. To reach the new Getty Center from the shore, follow winding Sunset Boulevard 10 miles east to the San Diego freeway, but call first for parking reservations (310/440-7300), which are essential. From Sunset Boulevard south to Santa Monica, Hwy-1 runs along the wide-open sands of Will Rogers State Beach, gifted to the public by the Depression-era humorist.

Santa Monica marks the western start of legendary Route 66, which is described beginning on page 276.

Crossing Los Angeles

From Malibu and Topanga Canyon, Hwy-1 swoops along the shore, running along the beach as far as the landmark Santa Monica Pier before bending inland through a tunnel and metamorphosing quite unexpectedly into the I-10 Santa Monica Freeway. The second exit off this freeway (which has been officially dubbed the Christopher Columbus Transcontinental Highway, running all the way east to Jacksonville, FL) lets you off at Lincoln Boulevard, which carries the Hwy-1 moniker south through Venice and Marina Del Rey to Los Angeles International Airport (LAX), where it runs into Sepulveda Boulevard.

After passing through a tunnel under the airport runways—worth the drive just for the experience of seeing 747s taxiing over your head—Sepulveda emerges in the Tarantino-esque communities of LA's "South Bay," which lack the glamour of chi-chi Santa Monica and Malibu. At the south end of Manhattan Beach, one of a trio of pleasant if surprisingly blue-collar beach towns (the others are Hermosa Beach and Redondo Beach), Sepulveda Boulevard changes its name to Pacific Coast Highway, then bends inland to bypass the ritzy communities of the Palos Verdes

Peninsula. A series of coastal parks (especially the blufftop park at Point Vicente, the southwesternmost tip of Los Angeles County) definitely make the detour around the peninsula along Palos Verdes Drive worth the while. Either way you go, you eventually end up in the industrial precincts of San Pedro and Wilmington that border the absolutely massive Los Angeles/Long Beach harbor, the busiest on the West Coast.

LOS ANGELES SURVIVAL GUIDE

LOVE IT OR HATE IT, one thing you can't do about L.A. is ignore it. Thanks to Hollywood in all its many guises (movies, television, the music industry), and a recent spate of natural and unnatural disasters, beginning with Rodney King, and continuing through earthquakes, fires, floods, and high-profile murder trials—O.J. and the Menendez Brothers to name the most notorious two-the city is always rearing its head.

Without falling too deeply under the spell of its hyperbole-fueled image-making machinery, it's safe to say that L.A. definitely has something for everyone, though a guide as brief as this can only help to point you in the right direction through its multicultural myriad of attractions. In keeping with its car-centered culture, however, our suggested tour ignores the many individual attractions and focuses instead on a trio of recommended tours.

Cruising L.A.
Mulholland Drive: Winding along the crest of the Hollywood Hills, Mulholland Drive is the classic L.A. cruise. Starting in the east within sight of the Hollywood Sign and the Hollywood Bowl, this ribbon of two-lane blacktop passes by the city's most valuable real estate, giving great views on both sides, both by day and after dark, ending up eventually at the north end of Malibu on Hwy-1. See page 86 for more.

    Sunset Boulevard: Another classic L.A. cruise, running from the scruffy fringes of downtown all the way west to the coast, Sunset Boulevard gives glimpses into almost every conceivable aspect of Los Angeles life. Starting at Olvera Street, the historic core of colonial Los Angeles, Sunset Boulevard's 27-mile course then winds west past Gower Gulch, site of the first Hollywood movie studios. In West Hollywood it gets re-named the "Sunset Strip," still the liveliest nightclub district in town. Further along, through Beverly Hills and Bel-Air, Sunset is lined by the largest mansions you're likely to see. After passing beneath the new **Getty Center** (free, but parking reservations are required; 310/440-7300), it continues through Brentwood and Pacific Palisades, then finally hits the beach.

Long Beach

Directly south of downtown Los Angeles, the city of Long Beach (pop. 429,433) is the second-largest of L.A.'s constituent cities, but in many ways it feels more like the Midwest than it does like Southern California. Long Beach is probably best known as the home of the cruise ship RMS *Queen Mary*, one of the largest and most luxurious liners ever to set sail. Impossible to miss as it looms over Long Beach

Wilshire Boulevard: Wilshire is L.A.'s main commercial artery, starting at the heart of downtown. After cutting through MacArthur Park, where someone really ought to sculpt a giant cake and leave it out in the rain, it runs west to the "Miracle Mile," a bustling business district of the art deco 1930s that is now home to a collection of diverse museums: the mastodons and saber-toothed tigers of the La Brea Tar Pits and the George C. Page Natural History Musem, the huge L.A. County Museum of Art, and the not-to-be-missed **Petersen Automotive Museum**, 6060 Wilshire Boulevard (daily 10 AM-6 PM; $7; 323/930-2277). Wilshire then races west through Beverly Hills past the foot of Rodeo Drive before winding up at the bluffs above Santa Monica Bay.

Practicalities

Most flights into Los Angeles arrive at LAX, on the coast southwest of downtown, where you'll find all the usual shuttles and rental car agencies. Other airports, served primarily by short-haul airlines from other West Coast cities, include Hollywood/Burbank, Long Beach, Ontario, and John Wayne, in Orange County.

The Los Angeles Dodgers (323/224-1448) play at beautiful Dodger Stadium, on a hill above downtown.

Arriving by land, the outskirts of Los Angeles stretch for so many miles in all directions that it is truly impossible to tell where it begins or ends. The sprawl sprawls much farther than the eye can see (even on the rare clear days): south as far as San Diego, north nearly to Santa Barbara, and east across the desert toward Palm Springs. However, considering it has a population of nearly 10 million people, and at least as many cars as humans, getting around the 1,000-plus square miles of Los Angeles is not always the nightmare it may at first seem to be. So long as you can avoid "rush hour" traffic (i.e., stay off 7 AM-10 AM, and again 3-8 PM), the freeways are very handy, but visitors see a lot more by following the surface streets to get places.

Before choosing a place to stay, think about where you want to spend your time, and settle near there. Beachfront accommodations range from the handy and cheap **Santa Monica HI Hostel**, 1436 2nd Street, Santa Monica (310/392-0325), to the **Hotel Queen Mary**, Pier J, Long Beach (800/437-2934), offering somewhat cramped quarters in this minimally converted old luxury liner; rooms $120-250. High-end places abound, but few are more comfortable, atmospheric or conveniently located than the legendary **Beverly Hills Hotel**, 9641 Sunset Boulevard, Beverly Hills (310/276-2251 or 800/283-8885). This is the grande dame of L.A. hotels, and one of the classiest in the world; stop in

(continues)

A half-mile north of the LAX airport, a block west of the I-405 San Diego Freeway at 805 W. Manchester Boulevard, there is one must-see road trip stop: **Randy's Donuts,** a round-the-clock doughnut shop topped by a photogenic, three-story-tall doughnut.

Los Angeles has been fodder for more essayists and authors than any other American city, but two books stand out from the crowd: the late Charles Moore's *Los Angeles, A City Observed* is the most eye-opening and easy-to-use guide to the city's architecture and history, while Mike Davis's thought-provoking collection of essays *City of Quartz* treats the city as postmodern disaster-in-progress.

for breakfast or a late-night drink at the legendary Polo Lounge if you can't manage the $350-a-night (and up) room rates.

For food, one place I always try to stop is the **Apple Pan**, 10801 W. Pico Boulevard (310/475-3585), an ancient (since 1947) landmark on the West L.A. landscape, serving the best hamburgers on the planet—though I'll admit to being biased, since I grew up eating them. Take a seat at the counter and dive into a pile of chunky fresh-fried french fries, but be sure to save room for a slice of their wonderful fruit pies. On old Route 66, in the heart of trendy West Hollywood, **Barney's Beanery**, 8447 W. Santa Monica Boulevard (323/654-2287), is a crusty old roadhouse, with famous chili and lots of good, inexpensive food, plus a great selection of beers, and plenty of pool tables. Late at night, the huge sandwiches and heart-warming soups at **Canter's Deli**, 419 N. Fairfax Avenue (323/651-2030), draws all kinds of night owls to a lively New York-style deli in the heart of the predominantly Jewish Fairfax District, open 24 hours every day. Downtown, tucked away between Union Station and Olvera Street in the old heart of L.A., **Philippe's French Dip Sandwiches**, 1001 Alameda (213/628-3781), is a classic workingman's cafeteria, offering good food at impossibly low prices, with character to spare.

The usual array of information about hotels, restaurants, and attractions is available through the **Los Angeles Convention and Visitors Bureau**, 695 S. Figueroa Street (213/689-8822 or 800/228-2452). To find out about current events and issues, read the mammoth *Los Angeles Times*, the biggest and best daily newspaper in the state. For articles with attitude and the best listings of events and activities, pick up a copy of the free *L.A. Weekly*, available (along with dozens of similar publications) at cafes, bars, and bookstores all over Southern California.

Los Angeles has a half-dozen different **area codes** to cover its metropolitan area, so to minimize confusion we have included the appropriate prefix in all the phone numbers we've given in this book.

harbor, the stately ship is open for self-guided tours (daily 10 AM-6 PM, 9 AM-9 PM in summer; $13; 562/435-3511).

In place of Howard Hughes's famous "Spruce Goose" airplane, which used to stand next door, there's now a Cold War-era Soviet submarine, and across the bay on the main downtown Long Beach waterfront, the new **Aquarium of the Pacific** (daily 10 AM-6 PM; $14; 562/590-3100) explores the diverse ecosystems of the Pacific Ocean, from tropical coral reefs (shown off in an amazing 360,000-gallon display) to the frigid waters of the Bering Sea.

Along with the annual Toyota Long Beach Grand Prix, an Indy Car race held on the city streets every April, other Long Beach attractions include the **world's largest mural**, a 115,000-square-foot painting of whales on the outside of the Long Beach Arena; the self-proclaimed **Skinniest House in the USA**, at 708 Gladys Avenue (562/436-3645); and the usually interesting **Long Beach Museum of Art**, housed in a 1912 Craftsman house at 2300 E. Ocean Boulevard (Wed.-Sun. 10 AM-5 PM; $2; 562/439-2119), with cutting-edge modern art displayed in galleries designed by architect Frederick Fisher.

Long Beach also marks the southern end of L.A.'s reborn streetcar and subway system, and you can ride the Blue Line north to downtown. It's a neat little city that can make an inexpensive and less stressful base for exploring the greater Los Angeles area, especially Disneyland. The most interesting neighborhood of cafes and shops lines 2nd Street near the campus of Cal State Long Beach, which is semi-famous for its most successful drop-out, director Steven Spielberg. For a handy bed in the downtown area, there's a **Best Western** at 1725 Long Beach Boulevard (562/599-5555), directly across from a Blue Line train stop, with rooms for $60 a night.

For more information, contact the Long Beach **visitors bureau** (562/436-3645 or 800/452-7829).

Since Hwy-1 follows slow-moving Lincoln Boulevard and other surface streets across L.A., if you are in any sort of hurry stay on the Santa Monica Freeway (I-10) east to the San Diego Freeway (I-405), and follow that south as far as you're going. Coming from the south, follow the freeways in reverse order—or risk the time-consuming consequences.

One of the least expensive lodging options in L.A. is the $15-a-night **HI South Bay Hostel,** 3601 S. Gaffey Street (310/831-8109), on a hill overlooking the harbor area.

One of the country's top jazz stations, **KLON 88.1 FM,** broadcasts commercial-free music all over the Southern California region.

Huntington Beach

Winding south and east from Long Beach, Hwy-1 continues along the coast past a series of marshlands and small-craft marinas. After leaving Los Angeles County at **Seal Beach**, where a big U.S. Navy base has preserved the largest remaining natural estuary in Southern California, the first real point of interest is the town of Huntington Beach (pop. 181,519), one of the largest communities in Orange County. Founded in 1909 by Henry Huntington as a stop along his legendary Pacific Electric "Red Car" interurban railway network, Huntington Beach is best known as the place where **surfing** was first introduced to the U.S. mainland. To attract Angelenos down to his new town, Huntington hired Hawaiians to demonstrate the sport, which at the time made use of huge solid wooden boards, 15 feet long and weighing around 150 pounds. Huntington Beach, especially around the pier, is still

A well maintained and usually uncrowded bike path winds along the oceanfront between Long Beach and Newport Beach, with only occasional detours along traffic-filled inland streets.

Though Orange County still has a national reputation for being wealthy and mostly white, there are many pockets of diversity, including the country's largest Vietnamese community—known as Little Saigon, along the I-405 San Diego Freeway in Westminster.

a very popular surfing spot—though contemporary surfers slice through the waves on high-tech foam-core boards, a third the size of the original Hawaiian long boards and weighing under 10 pounds. The history and culture of West Coast surfing, with examples of boards then and now (plus special collections documenting surf movies of the early 1960s, and the invention of surf music by local heros Leo Fender and Dick Dale) is recounted in the small but enthusiastic **International Surfing Museum**, two blocks from the pier at 411 Olive Avenue (daily noon-5 PM) in the heart of the renovated beachfront business district of bars and surfboard shops.

At the end of the pier, which is almost always surrounded by surfers fighting for the next ride, enjoy a burger and a 270-degree ocean view at **Ruby's Diner**. Also fun, especially if you like old airplanes, is the **Glide 'er Inn**, in Seal Beach at 1400 Pacific Coast Highway. For a cheap place to stay, try the handy **Colonial Inn Youth Hostel**, 421 8th Street (949/536-3315), with dorm beds for $13 and double rooms for $30, or the handy **Ramada Sunset Beach Motel**, 17205 Pacific Coast Highway (714/840-2431), where doubles go for around $85. Campers will appreciate **Bolsa Chica State Beach**, on the coast just north of Huntington Beach; the 50 RV sites require advance reservations (800/444-7275).

Disneyland

Like a little bit of Middle America grafted onto the southern edge of Los Angeles, Orange County is a totally different world. In contrast to L.A.'s fast-paced, edgily creative multiethnic stew, much of Orange County is suburban America writ large—in short, a perfect place to build the ultimate escapist fantasy, the self-proclaimed "Happiest Place on Earth," Disneyland.

If you haven't been before, or not for a while at any rate, here are some useful tidbits of information: Disneyland is 20 miles south of downtown L.A., right off I-5 in the city of Anaheim—you can see the Matterhorn from the freeway. The park is open daily at least 10 AM-6 PM, including winter weekends; in summer, it remains open until midnight. Admission to the park, which includes all rides, costs around $39 for one day, $68 for any two out of five days; kids under 12 save 20%.

The phenomenon of Disneyland has been done to death by all sorts of social critics but the truth is, it can be great fun—provided you visit out of season and get there early to avoid the crowds, and really immerse yourself in the extroverted, mindless joy of it all. Most of the rides are great, each in different ways (I like

"Pirates of the Caribbean" best), but there can be little forgiveness for "It's a Small World." Avoid it like the plague, or risk having the insipid song ringing in your head for days afterward.

Disneyland opened in 1955, when there was nothing around; now it's surrounded by motels, where it's well worth staying overnight so you can get an early start, go back to your accommodation for a while, and come back for the nightly fireworks show. A highly recommended place to stay is the **West Coast Anaheim Hotel**, a block from Disneyland at 1855 S. Harbor Boulevard (714/750-1811), offering spacious modern rooms (and a nice pool) from $65 per night, with free parking and free shuttles every half-hour to and from Disneyland.

For further park details, including opening hours, call Disneyland (714/781-4565); for lodging and other information, call the **Anaheim Convention and Visitors Bureau** (714/758-0222).

Richard Nixon Presidential Library

If you've already done the Disneyland thing, there is one other Orange County attraction you really shouldn't miss: the Richard Nixon Presidential Library (Mon.-Sat. 10 AM-5 PM, Sunday 11 AM-5 PM; $4.95; 714/993-3393), 18001 Yorba Linda Boulevard, 10 miles northeast of Disneyland off Hwy-91. The library is built on the very ground where the former president was born in 1914; it's also where he and his wife Pat are buried, side by side next to the restored Craftsman-style bungalow where Nixon grew up. No matter what your feelings toward him, the spare-no-expense displays do a fascinating job of putting his long career into the distorted perspective you'd expect from the only president ever forced to resign from office. (If you've been to other presidential libraries, you may have noticed that not all are as well funded as this one. That's because the library was paid for by Nixon's friends and receives no federal money—no doubt this is how it gets away with presenting Watergate as a liberal plot to take over the country.) If you can take the show at face value, highlights are many, such as the grainy pictures of the pumpkin patch where Alger Hiss supposedly concealed the microfilm that Nixon and Joe McCarthy used to put him in prison as a Communist spy, next to photos of Nixon and JFK as chummy freshman U.S. senators sharing sleeping compartments on a train. Particularly intriguing is the grand display of Christmas cards, exchanged by the Nixons with some very unlikely figures: Khrushchev and sundry Soviets, as well as every king, queen, and tinpot dictator you could name. The best-selling item in the gift shop? Postcards of Nixon greeting Elvis Presley, also available as place mats, china, and fridge magnets.

Visiting the Nixon Library also gives you a chance to have a look at one of nation's newest and most high-tech toll roads. Inaugurated in late 1995 along the median strip of the Riverside Freeway (Hwy-91), a new lane was added for drivers willing to pay a variable toll (25 cents to $2.50, depending upon time of day), which is charged through the use of radio transponders affixed to the windshield. But be warned: driving in the toll lanes *without* one of these transponders can get you a ticket very quickly.

Detour: Catalina Island

It might seem odd for a book about the open road to suggest trading in your car for a boat, but if you do you can enjoy one of the less-hyped gems of Southern California: lovely Catalina Island, which sits about 25 miles off the coast of Los Angeles.

Accessible by ferry from Newport Beach, Long Beach and Los Angeles harbors, Catalina Island offers a quick yet unforgettable escape from the high-speed frenzy of the rest of Southern California.

C-26—Steamers "Catalina" and "Avalon" at Pier, and Casino.

Avalon Bay, Santa Catalina, California

Once owned by chewing gum magnate William Wrigley, the island was developed for visitors during the 1920s, and still retains its Roaring Twenties feel. The only real town on the island, which is over 20 miles long and up to 8 miles wide, is at Avalon (pop. 2,950), where a large art deco ballroom, now known as the **Casino**, drew Benny Goodman and other big bands with its circular, 10,000-square-foot dance floor. Guided tours of the waterfront Casino, which also includes a stylish movie theater, beautiful tile work and several wonderful murals, are offered by reservation ($8; 310/510-2500).

From 1921 to 1951, the Chicago Cubs baseball team, which William Wrigley also owned, came to Catalina Island for their annual spring training.

The rest of Avalon consists of brightly colored small vacation houses, climbing the steep hills like some Mediterranean hill town. To immerse yourself in the Avalon ambience, stay the night at the historic **Zane Grey Pueblo Hotel** (310/510-0966 or 800/378-3256), built and lived in for many years by the eponymous author of all those romantic Western novels. Bed and breakfast rooms, and use of the arrow-shaped swimming pool, start at around $90 a night.

Away from Avalon, almost the entire island has been preserved as a nature reserve, with miles of fine hiking trails, camping, and endless ocean views. For more on any of these, contact the **visitors bureau** (310/510-1520). To get to Catalina from the mainland, ferries operated by **Catalina Express** (310/519-1212) leave from Long Beach and Los Angeles harbors; boats from Newport Beach are operated by **Catalina Passenger Service** (714/673-5245). All of these ferries cost around $30 roundtrip, and take about an hour each way. If you have any predilection for travel sickness, take medication before boarding the ferry—the long journey on these high-speed boats can be unexpectedly rough at times. Another good trick to reduce seasickness is to fix your gaze on the horizon or some other stationary point.

Newport Beach

Back on the coast, if you want to get a sense of what wealthy Orange Countians do to enjoy themselves, spend some time along the clean white strands of Newport Beach. Located at the southern edge of the Los Angeles suburban sprawl, Newport started life as an amusement park and beach resort at the southern end of the L.A. streetcar lines. In the 1930s and 1940s, thousands of Angelenos spent summer weekends at the **Balboa Pavilion**, at the southern tip of the slender Balboa peninsula, where a few remnants of the pre-video game amusements survive—a Ferris wheel, a merry-go-round, and those Pokerino games in which you win prizes by rolling rubber balls into a series of numbered holes.

Midway along the peninsula, near 23rd Street, Newport Pier is flanked by another holdout from the old days: the **dory fleet**, where almost every day small boats set off to catch rock cod and more exotic fish that, starting around noon, are sold straight from the boats at an outdoor market right on the sands.

To return to Hwy-1 from Balboa peninsula, you can either backtrack around the harbor or ride the **Balboa Ferry,** which shuttles you and your car from the Pavilion across the harbor past an amazing array of sailboats, power cruisers, and waterfront homes.

A mile south of Balboa Pavilion, next to the breakwater at the very southern end of Balboa peninsula, **The Wedge** is one of the world's most popular and challenging bodysurfing spots, with well-formed waves often twice as high as anywhere else on the coast.

Crystal Cove State Park

Midway between Newport and Laguna Beaches, amidst the ever-encroaching Orange County sprawl, Crystal Cove State Park (daily dawn-dusk; $6 per car; 949/494-3539) protects one of Southern California's finest chunks of coastline. With three miles of sandy beaches and chaparral-covered bluff lined by well-marked walking trails, it's a fine place to enjoy the shoreline without the commercial trappings. Originally home to Native Americans, the land here was later part of Mission San Juan Capistrano and, until 1979 when the state bought it, the massive Irvine Ranch, which once covered most of Orange County.

The main parking area for Crystal Cove is at **Reef Point**, a mile north of Laguna Beach near the south end of the park, where there are bathrooms and showers plus excellent tidepools, a fine beach, and a well-preserved collection of 1930s beach cottages. There is also a large section inland from Hwy-1, the sage and thistle glade of **El Moro Canyon**, which (despite being singed in a 1993 wildfire) gives a vivid sense of Orange County's rapidly vanishing natural landscape. Come in spring for a nine-mile full-circle hike through a vibrant display of wildflowers.

Laguna Beach

Compared with the rest of Orange County, Laguna Beach (pop. 23,200) is a relaxed and enjoyable place. Bookstores, cafes, and galleries reflect the town's beginnings as an artists' colony, but while the beach and downtown area are still very attractive, the surrounding hills have been covered by some of the world's ugliest tracts of "executive homes."

Right across Hwy-1 from the downtown shopping district, which is full of pleasant cafes and a wide range of art galleries, Laguna's main beach (called simply Main Beach) is still the town's main draw, with a boardwalk, some volleyball courts where the standard of play is very high, and a guarded swimming beach with showers.

Many other fine but usually less crowded and quieter beaches are reachable from Cliff Drive, which winds north of downtown Laguna past cove after untouched cove; follow the signs reading Beach Access.

Adjacent to the beach, right on Hwy-1, is **Greeter's Corner Cafe,** locally famous thanks to an elderly gentleman named Eiler Larsen,

During the annual **"Pageant of the Masters,"** Laguna Beach residents re-create scenes from classical and modern art by forming living tableaux, standing still as statues in front of painted backdrops. Held every summer, it's a popular event and proceeds go to good causes, so get tickets ($10-40; 949/494-1145 or 800/487-3378) well in advance.

South of Laguna Beach, the harbor town of **Dana Point** takes its name from author Richard Henry Dana, whose book *Two Years Before the Mast* documented time spent on a ship sailing up and down the California coast back in the 1820s. One of Dana Point's more recent locals was one Hobie Alter, inventor of the foam core surfboard and the twin-hulled Hobie Cat catamaran.

Many visitors to the chapel at San Juan Capistrano are terminally ill patients saying prayers to **St. Pereguin,** the patron saint of medical miracles.

now deceased, who for 30 years used to stand out front and wave at the passing traffic. The food is fine, and you can eat outside on the broad deck overlooking the beach. Another place worth searching out is the small **Taco Loco,** 640 S. Hwy-1 at the south end of the downtown strip, where the ultra-fresh Mexican food includes your choice of three or four different seafood tacos, from shark to swordfish, in daily-changing specials from about $1.50 each.

Places to stay are expensive, starting at around $100 a night, and include the centrally located, somewhat older **Hotel Laguna,** 425 S. Hwy-1 (949/494-1151), and the beachfront **Laguna Riviera Hotel and Spa,** 825 S. Hwy-1 (949/494-1196). On an oceanside bluff six miles south of Laguna Beach, the **Ritz Carlton Laguna Niguel** (949/240-2000 or 800/241-3333) is California's only Mobil five-star rated resort, with everything you could want from a hotel—all yours for $350 a day.

South of Laguna Beach, Hwy-1 follows the coast for a final few miles before joining up with the I-5 freeway for the 40-mile drive into San Diego.

San Juan Capistrano

Of the 21 missions along the California coast, **Mission San Juan Capistrano** (daily 8:30 AM-5 PM; $5; 949/248-2049) has been the most romanticized. When the movement to restore the missions and preserve California's Spanish colonial past was at its apogee in the late 1930s, its main theme song was Leon Rene's "When the Swallows Come Back to Capistrano," popularizing the legend that these birds return from their winter migration every St. Joseph's Day, March 19th. After wintering in Goya, Argentina, they do come back to Capistrano, along with several thousand tourists, but the swallows are just as likely to reappear a week before or a week after— whenever the weather warms up, really.

The mission, which has lovely, bougainvillea-filled gardens, stands at the center of the small, eponymously named town, a short detour inland along I-5 from the coast. Besides the birds, the main attractions include the small **chapel,** the last surviving church where the beatified Father Serra said Mass, widely considered to be the oldest intact church and perhaps the oldest building of any kind in California; and the ruins of the massive **Stone Church,** a finely carved limestone structure that collapsed in an earthquake in 1812, just six years after its completion.

To get a sense of the huge scale of the Stone Church, a full-sized replica called the New Church has been constructed behind the mission, and now serves as the official mission church, open to visitors except during religious services. Across the street from the New Church, the Michael Graves-designed local **library** gives an intriguing postmodern take on the mission style.

In the block between the Mission and the I-5 freeway, the **Walnut Grove Restaurant** and **Mission Inn Motel** are two of the few survivors of old-style San Juan Capistrano, holding out against the relentless suburbanizing that has leveled many of the surrounding historic commercial structures. Another unique spot is the **Coach House**, 33157 Camino Capistrano (949/496-8930), one of Southern California's best small clubs for listening to live music.

San Clemente

At the southern tip of coastal Orange County, San Clemente marks the midway point between San Diego and Los Angeles. A sleepy little community, San Clemente is probably best known as the site of **Casa Pacifica**, the one-time "western White House" of former president Richard Nixon, who lived here following his election in 1968 until after his resignation in the mid-1970s. The white-walled, mission-style house at the south end of Avenida del Presidente (the western frontage road to the I-5 freeway) is more easily visible from the beach below, though the 25 acres of trees have grown up to obscure it fairly completely.

San Clemente is also the site of "La Christianita," which in 1769 was the first baptism in Alta California. The event is remembered by a plaque in the civic center parking lot, a block east of I-5.

Regular trains run from here along the coast north to L.A. and south to San Diego, making it a handy midway base if you'd rather not fight the terrible commuter traffic. Even if you're just passing through, you can enjoy a walk on the long pier at the center of town, get a drink or a bite to eat at the many cafes along the beachfront Avenida del Mar, or amble south to **San Clemente State Beach** (949/492-3156), which has three miles of nice white sands backed by bluffs and over 150 campsites, half of them with RV hookups. San Clemente also has a handy HI **hostel**, in an old library just a short walk from the beach at 233 Avenida Granada (949/492-2848).

Mission San Luis Rey de Francia

In the sun-bleached hills above the blue Pacific, four miles east of the ocean off the I-5 freeway along Hwy-76, Mission San Luis Rey de Francia (Mon.-Sat. 10 AM-4:30 PM, Sunday noon-4:30 PM; $3) was among the largest and most successful of the California missions. Its lands have been taken over by Camp Pendleton, and most of the outbuildings have disappeared, but the stately church at the heart of the complex survives in fine condition, worth a look for the blue-tinted dome atop the bell tower and for the haunting carved stone skull that looks down from the cemetery gate.

The northwest corner of San Diego County is taken up by the U.S. Marine Corps' massive **Camp Pendleton** training base, which fills 125,000 acres, running for 20 miles along the coast and 15 miles inland.

Alongside the prominent nuclear power plant at **San Onofre**, one of Southern California's better surfing beaches has been home to the friendly, family-run **Pascowitz Surf Camp** (949/361-9283), every summer since 1972.

Oceanside

At the southern edge of 125,000-acre Camp Pendleton Marine Corps Base, Oceanside (pop. 130,000) is the largest city between Los Angeles and San Diego but offers little to attract the casual visitor—apart from guided tours of Camp Pendleton's amphibious-assault training exercises, and the state's longest fishing pier. But if you're in the mood to shop for camouflage gear, watch the muscle cars cruise Hill Street, get a $3 G.I. Joe haircut, or drink beer with a gang of young recruits, this is the right place.

South from Oceanside, all the way to San Diego, a very pleasant alternative to the often-clogged I-5 freeway is the old alignment of US-101, now signed as County Road S21 (and occasionally, Coast Highway 101). Slower than the freeway but

A long but worthwhile detour inland from San Luis Rey brings you to the least visited but perhaps most evocative of all the California missions, **Mission San Antonio de Pala.** Located on the Pala Indian Reservation, 20 miles east of San Luis Rey along Hwy-76, then another 100 yards north along a well-marked side road, Mission San Antonio de Pala is the only California mission still serving its original role of preaching to the native people, and gives an unforgettable impression of what California's mission era might have been like.

Some of the best views of the Southern California coastline can be had from the windows of the frequent **Coaster** commuter trains, which run right along the shore between San Juan Capistrano and Del Mar. The full trip between San Diego and Los Angeles takes about two hours; for details, call MetroLink (213/808-5465).

One of the nicest beaches in Southern California is tucked away west of historic Coast Hwy-101 between Carlsbad and Del Mar. **San Elijo State Beach,** just south of Encinitas at Chesterfield Drive (760/753-5091), is almost invisible from the highway, but opens onto a long golden strand backed by cliffs, and offers camping, BBQ grills, and everything else you could want from a beach.

still in regular use, the old road is now the main drag of quaint beachfront towns like Carlsbad, Leucadia, Encinitas and Del Mar. If you have the time, it's a great drive, in sight of the ocean for most of the way.

Carlsbad: La Costa and Legoland

Named for the European spa town of Karlsbad, in what's now the Czech Republic, Carlsbad (pop. 65,000) was established in the 1880s and had a brief heyday as a spa town until the 1930s. A few remnants of the historic resort area, including the circa 1887 landmark **Neiman's Restaurant,** still survive along old US-101 in the center of town, but these days Carlsbad is best known as the home of **La Costa Resort and Spa,** (760/438-9111 or 800/854-5000), a 500-room complex of luxurious rooms, health spas, golf courses and tennis courts covering 400 acres of hills on the inland side of I-5.

Carlsbad's other main attraction, from its opening in early 1999, is the first American outpost of the popular European children's theme park **Legoland** ($32 adults, $25 children; 760/438-5346). Built out of more than 30 million Lego bricks, and covering 128 acres above the Pacific Ocean, the park is divided up into three main areas, including MiniLand, where miniature landscapes modeled on New York, New Orleans, New England and the Northern California coast have all been constructed using the trademark plastic bricks.

For information on visiting Carlsbad, contact the **visitors bureau** (760/434-6093 or 800/227-5722).

South Carlsbad State Park, three miles south of town, is one of the nicest and most popular places to camp on the Southern California coast, its spacious campsites (with hot showers) spread out along a sandstone bluff above a broad beach. However-er, swimming can be dangerous, because of strong riptides. If you don't want to camp, or pay the $6-a-day parking fee, leave your car at the park entrance, which is well-marked on a surviving stretch of the old US-101 highway.

Del Mar and Torrey Pines

Most of the time Del Mar (pop. 4,860) is a sleepy little upscale suburb of San Diego, with big houses backing onto a fine, four-mile-long beach. The waves here are well suited to bodysurfing, but the sands can be hard to reach in summer because of a lack of parking—weekdays it's less of a problem. In late summer, the town comes to life for the late summer thoroughbred racing season at beautiful **Del Mar Racetrack** (built by Hollywood types like Bing Crosby, and seen in *The Grifters* and many other Hollywood movies); call for details (858/755-1141).

South along the Camino Del Mar coast road from Del Mar, hang gliders, tide-poolers, surfers, and beachcombers flock to the nearly 2,000 acres of bluffs and beaches protected in Torrey Pines State Reserve (daily 9 AM-dusk; $4). Named for the long-needled pines that grow naturally only here, the reserve is crisscrossed by hiking trails leading down steep ravines between the bluffs and the sands. The old Coast Highway through the park is popular with cyclists and inline skaters, and a short hike along the Broken Hill Trail leads to a ruddy brown cliff that looks out over the water to La Jolla—seven miles away.

Overlooking the Pacific from atop a bluff at the south end of the reserve, the **Salk Institute** is one of the world's most important centers for research in the life sciences. Founded by the late Jonas Salk, designed by Louis Kahn, and modeled in part on the gardens of the Alhambra in Granada, the institute is open for **tours** (Mon.-Fri. 10 AM, 11 AM, and noon; free; 858/453-4100).

Stretching inland and south from the Salk Institute the hills are covered with faceless business parks around the spacious campus of the **University of California at San Diego** (UCSD), beyond which spreads La Jolla and the greater San Diego area.

San Diego is also the beginning of our Southern Pacific route along US-80, described beginning on page 322, which runs east across Arizona, New Mexico, and western Texas.

Driving San Diego

South from La Jolla, the US-101 highway is buried by the I-5 freeway. Old US-101 can still be followed, however, by following Pacific Highway past Mission Bay and Lindbergh Field toward San Diego Bay, where it becomes Harbor Drive—where the Tijuana Trolley now runs. Southbound automobile travelers must take I-5 in order to pass through the official border crossing at San Ysidro/Tijuana.

Besides hang gliders, Torrey Pines is prime air space for remote-controlled **model gliders,** which float gracefully in the nearly constant onshore breeze. The primary launching spot is the small city park at the south end of Torrey Pines State Reserve.

La Jolla's coastal coves and caves are best appreciated by snorkelers and kayakers, but pedestrians can get a glimpse by clambering down a hand-dug stairway to Sunny Jim Cave, at the western edge of the waterfront. The stairs start at the **Cave Store,** 1325 Cave Street ($2; 858/459-0746).

Between La Jolla and San Diego, at **Belmont Park** (619/491-2988), the Giant Dipper wooden roller coaster survives as the sole remnant of a 1920s beachfront amusement park.

SAN DIEGO SURVIVAL GUIDE

SET ALONG A HUGE PACIFIC OCEAN HARBOR at the southwestern corner of the country, just a few miles from the Mexican border, San Diego embodies the Southern California ideal. Like most of California, San Diego was first settled by Spanish missionary Franciscan friars in the late 1700s, but it remained a small village of farmers and ranchers until the arrival of the transcontinental Southern Pacific Railroad in 1882, which brought middle-class Midwestern masses to the coast by the thousand. For a while, around the turn of the century, it rivaled Los Angeles as a boomtown based on wild real estate speculation, but while L.A. continued to expand by leaps and bounds San Diego grew

(continues)

more slowly. San Diego's economy has long been based around the U.S. Navy, and as recently as the 1960s extensive tuna-fishing fleets filled the rest of the busy harbor, which even more recently hosted the America's Cup yacht races.

Despite a metropolitan population of two and a half million people, San Diego (which is California's second-largest city) still feels very small and anything but urban. For visitors and residents alike, the main attractions of San Diego are the city's usually sunny climate and its miles of clean and uncrowded beaches, such as Pacific, Mission and Ocean Beaches, rather than any great historic or cultural sights. The main things to see in San Diego are in **Balboa Park,** a lushly landscaped 1,150-acre spread on downtown San Diego's northwest edge, which was laid out and constructed as part of the 1915 International Exposition celebrating the completion of the Panama Canal. The many grand buildings, all built in gorgeous Spanish Revival style by architect Bertram Goodhue, have been preserved in marvelous condition, and now house sundry museums, ranging from automobiles to fine art to a functioning replica of Shakespeare's Globe Theatre. A passport ($21), available from the **visitors center** (619/239-0512), allows entrance to any eight of the park's dozen museums within a week of purchase. Balboa Park is also the location of the **San Diego Zoo** ($16 admission, plus $6 for tram tour and aerial ride; 619/231-3153), one of the largest and most popular menageries in the world.

To see the different sides of San Diego, head to its contrasting corners. The richest district, La Jolla, is on the coast northwest of the city proper. The recently renovated **Museum of Contemporary Art** (Tues.-Sat. 10 AM-5 PM; $4), overlooking the ocean at 700 Prospect Avenue, plus great surfing (head to Windansea for the best waves), beachcombing and skin diving in the famous coves, not to mention the tons of good cafes, restaurants, and art galleries, have long made La Jolla an all-around great day-trip. Another side of San Diego is revealed by a trip south of the Mexico border to lively **Tijuana**, easily reachable via the Tijuana Trolley from downtown.

The **San Diego Padres** (619/283-4494) play at concrete Qualcomm Stadium, off I-15 at the Friars Road exit.

Practicalities

The city of San Diego bends diagonally around its natural harbor, which makes orientation occasionally confusing. The main airport, Lindbergh Field, is on the waterfront just north of downtown—and has one of the swiftest final approaches of any American airport. By road, the I-5 freeway runs right through downtown San Diego, between Mission Bay and the Mexican border, while the I-8 freeway comes in from the east via Mission Valley.

Because it is small and relatively compact, San Diego is easy to get around. Downtown is walkable, and on a bike you could see most everything in a day. Buses operated by San Diego Transit ($1; 619/234-1060) fan out from downtown, while the light rail Tijuana Trolley ($2) runs south from downtown to the Mexico border.

Places to stay are generally modern, clean, and comfortable, though rates vary with seasons and conventions. The cheapest beds are at the **HI San Diego Hostel**, in the historic downtown Gaslamp District at 521 Market Street ($20; 619/525-1531); there's a second **HI Point Loma Hostel** northwest of downtown, near Sea World at 3790 Udall Street (619/223-4778). Near the beach and Point Loma, the **Ocean Villa Motel**, 5142 W. Point Loma Boulevard (619/224-3481), has ocean-view rooms for around $60. For top-of-the-line accommodations, or just to appreciate the historic architecture, head to the wonderful old **Hotel Del Coronado**, across the bridge from downtown at 1500 Orange Avenue (619/522-8000). Rising up in turreted glory, this fabulously grand Victorian-era resort hotel still caters, as it always has, to the four-star trade. (It's also where the Man Who Would Be King, England's Edward VIII, first met his femme fatale Mrs. Simpson, whose husband was commander of the local navy base.) Rooms from under $200.

Though you may feel the need to duck when planes land at nearby Lindbergh Field, for breakfast there's the **Hob Nob Hill**, 2271 First Avenue (619/239-8176), a classic old coffee shop, with pecan waffles worth driving all night for. In La Jolla, **The Spot**, 1005 Prospect Avenue, two blocks from La Jolla Cove, is a longtime local favorite that serves hefty portions of burgers, BBQ ribs and chicken, plus pizzas, at moderate prices. San Diego's most popular old-style Mexican place is, appropriately enough, the **Old Town Cantina**, 2489 San Diego Avenue (619/297-4330), near the Old Town historic park.

The best range of information is available from the **San Diego International Visitors Center**, 11 Horton Plaza (619/236-1212), downtown at 1st and F Streets. The main daily paper is the *San Diego Union-Tribune*, and local issues and events are covered in the *Reader* and other free weekly papers.

CENTRAL VALLEY AND NATIONAL PARKS: HWY-99

CENTRAL VALLEY AND NATIONAL PARKS: HWY-99

When people think of California, many conjure up images of an imagined good life: healthy, ever-youthful people enjoying themselves on sandy beaches that stretch for miles along the gentle Pacific Ocean, living in spacious houses and working as movie stars or TV personalities; the whole scene is drenched in sunlight, bordered by palm trees and lush gardens producing flowers and fruit all year round, against a background of snow-capped mountains covered in pines. These are images of California you might get from travel brochures—or from watching too much *Baywatch* or *Beverley Hills 90210*. But they paint only a partial picture, one that leaves out the very heart of the state: the Central Valley.

Stretching the entire length of California along its two main rivers—the Sacramento in the north and the San Joaquin in the south—the Central Valley is the hard-working, anything-but-glamorous sibling to the upscale coast. Though famed for producing fine wines, Silicon Valley technology, and Hollywood blockbusters, California is also by far the biggest agricultural producer in the U.S. And it's here in the Central Valley that most of this farming and ranching goes on. The Central Valley is also a place people are born, get married, settle down, and raise families in the sorts of small towns—like Visalia, Chowchilla, and Red Bluff—that you probably thought had vanished a generation ago. Though not fancy, these towns are welcoming, and as you travel through Lodi, or Modesto, or Yreka, or a score of others, you'll be greeted by giant arches spanning a Main Street business district that, if you put different cars on the road, could easily pass for Andy Griffith's Mayberry.

Highway 99, eclipsed in many places by Interstate 5, runs through the heart of this frequently overlooked, underappreciated, and raced-through region and lets you sample a side of California that, while it doesn't pretend to offer pleasures comparable to those in the rest of the state, definitely paints a fuller picture. More appealingly, there are dozens of scenic detours off Highway 99 that take you away up into the many picturesque towns of the Gold Country, where the original '49ers flocked in search of gold, over 150 years ago. Though most frequently identified with the Mother Lode—the fairly short but crowded band of gold mines, ghost towns, and weekend getaways that dot the forested foothills above the historic state capital, Sacramento— California's gold-mining country actually starts much farther north, at the historic hamlets of Weaverville and Shasta, and stretches south nearly to Los Angeles, where the very first gold mines were opened as early as 1842 at Placerita Canyon.

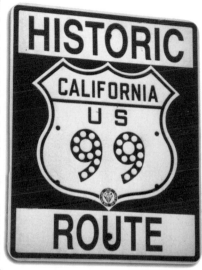

History aside, the reason most travelers find themselves on Hwy-99 is that they are bound somewhere else—racing between the coast and the many national and state parks that fill the mountains on the Central Valley's eastern boundary. From Mount Shasta and the volcanic wonderland of Mount Lassen in the far north, to the humongous giant Sequoia trees of Kings Canyon/Sequoia National Park, and centered in the glaciated spectacle of one of the true wonders of the natural world, Yosemite Valley, Hwy-99 is the main gateway to many of California's most captivating spots. South of Los Angeles, Hwy-99 has been wiped off the maps, replaced by faster freeways, but you can still follow traces of the old highway through the desert oasis of Palm Springs, detouring to Joshua Tree National Park or continuing along the shores of the bizarre Salton Sea, all the way south to Mexico.

Yreka

Founded back in 1851, after gold was discovered by a prospector's mule, Yreka (pop. 7,500; pronounced "wy-REE-ka") is the largest town between Redding and the Oregon border. Seat of sprawling Siskiyou County and one-time capital of the short-lived State of Jefferson, Yreka has a full range of visitor services. Enough of its historic core survives to tempt travelers off the I-5 freeway, which passes just a block east of downtown. The entrance to "Old Town" Yreka from I-5 is marked by a statue of a miner and a recently refurbished arch, now stranded on a traffic island after spending most of its life spanning the intersection of Miner Street and Main Street (the old Hwy-99 route through town).

Yreka is more a service center for the surrounding region than it is a destination in itself. The main attractions in town include a display of gold nuggets in the **Siskiyou County Courthouse**, 311 4th Street (Mon.-Fri. 8 AM-5 PM; free); historic artifacts and preserved buildings at the **Siskiyou County Historical Museum**, 910 S. Main Street (Tues.-Sat. 9 AM-5 PM; $2); and the chance to take a ride on the historic

Blue Goose, a circa-1915 steam train operated by the Yreka Western Railroad, 300 E. Miner Street (summer only Wed.-Sun. at 10 AM; $9; 530/842-4146).

Downtown Yreka, along Miner Street west from the welcoming arch, holds a handful of places to eat, many housed in turn-of-the-century brick buildings. For a place to stay, try the **Wayside Inn**, 1235 S. Main Street (530/842-4412 or 800/795-7974), a clean and tidy motel with double rooms for around $40.

Old US-99: State of Jefferson National Scenic Byway

North of Yreka, old US-99 is still in use as Hwy-263, winding along the west side of the freeway and offering a much more scenic alternative. Part of the State of Jefferson Nation-

---

WELCOME TO THE CENTRAL VALLEY!

Stretching from Oregon south to the Tehachapi Mountains, the Sacramento and San Joaquin Valleys in the center of California has long been derided by coast dwellers, but it's a proud and welcoming place. The most obvious proof of this regional hospitality can be seen in the many Welcome signs that greet visitors up and down the state. Most of these date from the 1920s and are fairly simple, with the name of the town emblazoned on a large arch spanning what used to be the main route—usually old US-99. Modern freeways have bypassed these quaint relics, but most still stand as monuments to civic pride.

North to south, some of the most prominent and picturesque can be seen in:

- Yreka (see page 105)
- Weed (see page 108)
- Lodi (see page 130)
- Modesto (see page 131)
- Fresno (see page 139)

al Scenic Byway, which continues west along the banks of the Klamath River, the drive is far more interesting than the trek along I-5, which climbs high above the river, missing out on all the trees and gorges. Highlights along Hwy-263 include the sculpted concrete arches of the Dry Gulch Bridge and the green steel span of the Pioneer Bridge, built in 1931 and rising 231 feet above the Shasta River. In places all along Hwy-263, you can easily see the remains of the earliest paved road through here, dating back to 1914 and barely eight feet wide. Hwy-263 merges into I-5 at the junction with Hwy-96, 10 miles north of Yreka.

I-5 SURVIVAL GUIDE: YREKA TO SACRAMENTO

ACROSS NORTHERN CALIFORNIA, most of old US-99 has been bypassed and re-placed by the I-5 freeway, which bombs along at 70 mph on its international journey between Canada and Mexico. Places where the two routes coincide, such as the beautiful drive from Lake Shasta to the Oregon border, are covered more fully in the main text, but for those who don't have time to savour the old road, here are a few of the more interesting stops along I-5.

Between the Oregon border and the city of Sacramento, consider pulling off at:

MM 801: State of Jefferson Scenic Byway (see pages 106-107)

MM 788: Hwy-3 to Etna and the Trinity Alps (see page 114)

MM 752: Mount Shasta City (see page 109)

MM 743: Dunsmuir (see page 111)

MM 738: Castle Crags State Park (see page 112)

MM 697: Shasta Dam (see page 112)

MM 629: The entrance to **Orland** is marked by a massive Spanish Revival style concrete arch.

MM 613: South of **Willows** and just east of I-5, the Sacramento National Wildlife Refuge is a 10,776-acre marshland that hosts more than two million waterfowl during winter, including abundant populations of the otherwise rare Ross' geese and greater white-fronted geese. Willows also has a great Asian restaurant, **Fu Hing** at 100 S. Tahama Street (530/934-8922), which beats the pants off the standard roadside fast food options.

MM 586: On the south side of the town of **Williams**, the abandoned Mammoth Orange was once a roadside stand selling orange juice to passing travelers.

MM 562: Junction with I-505 to and from San Francisco.

MM 546: The historic city of **Woodland** has the Hays Antique Truck Museum (daily 10 AM-5 PM; $6; 530/666-1044), stocked with a fascinating collection of antique trucks, one of California oldest opera houses. Right next door you'll find the friendly BBQ and burger place **Ludy's**, 667 Main Street (530/666-4400).

Yreka marks the northern end of Hwy-3, the official Trinity Heritage Scenic Byway, which runs south through the Trinity Alps all the way to the historic gold-mining camp of Weaverville.

Along US-97, about a dozen miles northeast of Weed, 32 acres of metal sculptures at the **Living Memorial Sculpture Garden** (daily dawn-dusk; free) honor soldiers, nurses, refugees, and prisoners of war. Farther north, approaching Oregon, US-97 runs through Butte Valley, home to numerous wildlife refuges and the largest concentrations of **bald eagles** outside Alaska.

Heading west from the I-5 junction, the State of Jefferson National Scenic Byway follows Hwy-96 along the banks of the Klamath River. The "State of Jefferson" refers to a short-lived independence movement by counties on both sides of the Oregon-California border, who thought they could improve public facilities, especially roads, by establishing a new state—or at least by taking advantage of the publicity such a movement would garner. The secession effort began November 27, 1941, with the blocking of US-99 and other main roads, but came to a swift end two weeks later, following the bombing of Pearl Harbor and America's entry into World War II.

Old US-99: Gazelle

Between Yreka and Weed, old US-99 bends west from the I-5 freeway, offering a 20-mile-long, two-lane side trip through the ranch lands and walnut groves of the Shasta Valley. The biggest town hereabouts is tiny Gazelle, south of which a small but photogenic billboard (complete with a dancing bear) advertises "Roadside Rest Ahead." Gazelle also boasts the cozy **Hollyhock Farm B&B**, 18705 Old US-99 (530/435-2627), where you can get away from it all, enjoy a stunning Mount Shasta view—and bring your dogs (or horses), too.

Facing Mount Shasta from an idyllic spot four miles west of old US-99, on a country road that turns off just north of the I-5 Gazelle exit, **Stewart Mineral Springs** (530/938-2222) has spring-fed natural hot tubs, a sauna, and a creek, plus camping, tepees, cabins, and motel-type rooms—all for very reasonable prices.

Weed

Located at the junction of I-5, old US-99, and busy US-97, which runs north through Oregon and Washington along the eastern side of the Cascade mountain range, Weed (pop. 3,100) is a rough-and-tumble town that seems more interested in sawing logs than catering to tourists. (There's a *big* lumber mill at the east edge of town.) Described in the New Deal-era *WPA Guide to California* as "a lumber town, bleak and raw-looking," Weed hasn't changed all that much in the intervening 60-odd years. Weed Boulevard, the main street through town, has a set of old

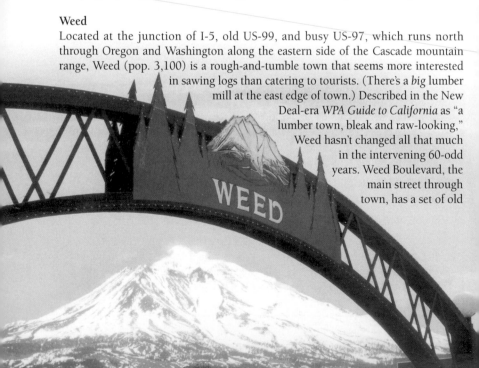

buildings fronted by elaborate wrought-iron balconies; one of these holds the amiable **Black Butte Saloon**, a popular watering hole. For an all-in-one place to eat and sleep, try the **Hi-Lo Motel and Cafe**, 88 S. Weed Boulevard (530/938-2904), fronted by a nifty neon sign. Rooms go for around $35. The Hi-Lo is also an RV park.

Like Yreka and many other old US-99 towns, Weed has a large arch spanning the old highway. Unlike the others, though, this arch also frames a magnificent view of Mount Shasta, rearing up south of town.

Mount Shasta

A truly magical mountain, visible from 150 miles away, Mount Shasta dominates the skyline of north-central California. "Lonely as God and white as a winter moon," as frontier poet Joaquin Miller put it, Mount Shasta stands aloof from the surrounding valleys, rising to 10,000 feet from its base to a summit 14,162 feet above sea level. This massive dormant volcano (the largest in the lower 48 states) exerts a powerful presence over the entire region. But if you're tempted to try to climb to the top, take care: it's a demanding climb, and the altitude, the difficult terrain, and unpredictable weather make it unsafe for casual trekkers. That said, hundreds do make the climb every year. For the required permits and information on routes, contact the Shasta National Forest **ranger station**, 204 W. Alma Street (530/926-4511), in Mount Shasta City.

In winter, snow chains for tires may be required along I-5 from the Oregon border south to Dunsmuir.

To get as close as you can by road, follow the 12-mile-long Mount Shasta Scenic Drive, officially known as the **Everitt Memorial Highway**, which climbs nearly 5,000 feet up the southern flank of the mountain, starting in the center of Mount Shasta City. There are campgrounds along the route and another at the end of the road—**Panther Meadows**, around 8,000 feet in elevation and often packed full of summer wildflowers. **Bunny Flat**, 1.8 miles from the end of the road, is a popular winter sports area and also marks the most popular trailhead for climbers heading to the summit. First stop on this summit route is a rustic stone lodge, built by the Sierra Club in 1923; even if you don't plan to tackle the climb to the top, the lodge makes a great day-hike destination.

Mount Shasta City

Sitting at the southern foot of Mount Shasta, Mount Shasta City (pop. 3,460, elev. 3,554 feet) in recent years has evolved into a uniquely Northern California ensemble of New Age bookstores, organic produce markets, outdoor recreation shops, and superb restaurants—clearly catering to city folks and urban escapees. Originally called Sisson (after J. H. Sisson, local postmaster and mountain-climbing friend of John Muir), Mount Shasta City stretches for some three miles along Mount Shasta Boulevard, which follows the railroad tracks and the old Hwy-99, east of the I-5 freeway.

In 1987, Mount Shasta found its way into the international spotlight thanks to the much-hyped **Harmonic Convergence,** during which hundreds of New Age believers came here to welcome the advent of the Aquarian Age.

On the north side of Mount Shasta City, a half-mile west of I-5 at 1 Old Stage Road, stop by the historic **Sisson Fish Hatchery,** the oldest west of the Mississippi. In the open ponds, you can see (and feed, for 25 cents) some three million brown and rainbow trout being raised. A small museum here traces local history.

Though it marks the start of the main road up the mountain, there's not much to do in town, so apart from the splendid high mountain setting, what draws visitors to Mount Shasta City must be the food: this small town has more good restaurants than many places 10 times its size. For a hearty breakfast, head to the **Black Bear Diner**, near I-5 at 401 W. Lake Street; for breakfast, lunch, or dinner, don't miss **Lily's**, 1013 S. Mount Shasta Boulevard (530/926-3372), which serves a Mexican-flavored range of healthy pasta and meat dishes all day, every day. Next door, the **Has Beans** coffeehouse has the best cup of java in town, served in a historic rock-faced building. In the center of town, another reliable haunt is the international-minded **Willy's Bavarian Kitchen**, 107 Chestnut Street, offering what the restaurant describes broadly as German-American diner food, with many vegetarian dishes and excellent smoothies—in a rustic log cabin, no less. For a quick junk-food fix, it's hard to beat **Dominic's Dog House**, 321A N. Mount Shasta Boulevard.

At the south edge of Mount Shasta City, along old US-99 at the Hwy-89 junction, a picturesque old gas station survives as a fine example of classic roadside Americana. This particular one was built in 1930 as a Richfield station. It now serves as studios for radio station KWHO.

The most comfortable place to stay is probably the **Best Western Tree House Inn**, right off the central I-5 exit at 111 Morgan Way (530/926-3101 or 800/528-1234), with a woodsy feel, a restaurant and bar, and a big indoor swimming pool. The nicest B&B around has to be the 1920s farmhouse that's been converted into the **Mount Shasta Ranch**, west of I-5 and south of the fish hatchery at 1008 W. A. Barr Road (530/926-3870). Sleep cheap at the **Alpenrose Hostel**, 204 E. Hickey (530/926-6724), on the north edge of town next to the **KOA Kampground**, 900 Mount Shasta Boulevard (530/926-4029), which has RV sites for around $20 a night, plus a few small cabins and tent sites.

For hiking, camping, and other outdoor equipment, stop at **Fifth Season Sports**, 300 N. Mount Shasta Boulevard (530/926-3606). It's also a good spot to tap into local knowledge of the Mount Shasta area, as is the ranger station. For more general information, stop by the Mount Shasta **visitors bureau**, right off I-5 at 300 Pine Street (530/926-4865 or 800/397-1519).

Fly-fishing devotees probably already know about Cassel, a tiny town on Hat Creek just south of McArthur Burney Falls; it's home to **Clearwater House** (415/381-1173 or 530/335-5500), one of the West Coast's top fishing camps, with seven anglophilic rooms (about $165 per person per day, including three full meals) and all the trout you can handle.

Detour: Hwy-89 to McArthur Burney Falls State Park

Cutting east from I-5 at the south edge of Mount Shasta City, Hwy-89 is one of many great scenic drives in Northern California. Winding around the foot of Mount Shasta—and past the entrance to **Mount Shasta Ski Park** (530/926-8610), the region's low-cost but primo alpine ski and snowboarding area (1,400-foot vertical drop, 425 skiable acres)—Hwy-89 passes one-time lumber camp and company town of **McCloud**, 10 miles east of I-5. There, the circa-1916 **McCloud Hotel**, in the center of town at 408 Main Street (530/964-2822), offers renovated rooms with private baths from around $90. (If you arrive in a pre-WWII automobile, you get a 20% discount on the room rate.)

East of McCloud, Hwy-89 climbs steeply up and over Dead Horse Summit (elev. 4,533 feet) on its way to McArthur Burney Falls State Park (daily 9 AM-5 PM; $5 per car), 60 miles southeast of Mount Shasta. Here, amid dense forest, a powerful torrent in the Pit River cascades 130 feet over a series of volcanic terraces. A pair of trails gives up-close views of the falls. One trail leads down into the gorge, while another climbs to an overlook above the falls.

Continuing east and south, Hwy-89 curves through Mount Lassen Volcanic National Park and along the crest of the Sierra Nevada Mountains toward Lake Tahoe and beyond—a wonderful alpine cruise.

Dunsmuir

Located midway between Mount Shasta and Castle Crags State Park and bypassed by the oldest intact section of the I-5 freeway, the small town of Dunsmuir (pop. 2,129) is easy to miss— but well worth taking the time to visit. Rising above the Sacramento River, which here still tumbles and roars more like a mountain stream than the placid aqueduct it becomes farther south, Dunsmuir is among the more historic and characterful places in Northern California. Passing through it is like stepping back into a sepia-toned postcard of a vanished America. The old US-99 route rolls (at 25 mph!) along Dunsmuir Avenue through the photogenic center of town, passing tin-roofed filling stations, 1930s-era motor courts such as the old Oak Tree Inn, and dozens of dainty, gable-roofed houses with broad front porches stacked with firewood. The compact business district is dominated by the marquee of the California Theatre (which is still in business, showing the latest Hollywood hits). Perhaps best of all, there's not a franchise in sight.

Originally named Pusher, because of the extra locomotives added to help push trains over the high passes to the north, Dunsmuir was renamed in honor of a Canadian visitor who built the fountain in City Park, still bubbling with crystal-clear natural spring water from the nearby source of the Sacramento River.

A block downhill from Dunsmuir Avenue, the west bank of the Sacramento River is lined with busy Union Pacific switching yards (Amtrak passes through twice a day, at ungodly hours), and two blocks of old brick buildings housing art galleries, a natural foods store, a nursery, and the **Upper Sacramento River Exchange Center**, 5819 Sacramento Avenue (530/235-2012), home offices of the environmental watchdogs who have been acting as stewards of the Sacramento River since a disastrous chemical spill of 1991.

The riverside strip is also home to one of the best restaurants in the Mount Shasta region: **Cafe Maddalena**, 5801 Sacramento Avenue (530/235-2725), a wonderful little cafe, with white linen tablecloths and delicious country Italian delicacies prepared by the Sardinia-born chef, eponymous Maddalena Sera. The cafe is open for dinner only, Thurs.-Sun. only, May-Dec. only—but is so good it's worth planning your trip around. If the Maddalena is not open, try the excellent **Burger Barn**, regularly voted among the best for miles, or **Cindy's Place**, open 24 hours at the center of town.

Though it's one of the prettiest and most pleasant small towns anywhere in the state, the picturesque town of Dunsmuir is, unfortunately, probably best known for the railroad tank cars full of agricultural pesticide that spilled into the Sacramento River here in 1991, killing all life along the river for 50 miles downstream. The river has recovered, and things have pretty much returned to normal. In fact, if anything, the long-term effects have been positive—the catastrophe galvanized local efforts to protect the river and the entire watershed ecosystem. Those efforts have brought some truth back to the town's longtime slogan: "Dunsmuir—Best Water on Earth."

One reliable Dunsmuir-area river-rafting outfitter is **River Dancers Rafting Company** (800/926-5002); prices for a day trip start at $70, $50 for ages 4-17. Season for the upper Sacramento River is generally May and June, but you can run the Klamath and Trinity Rivers all summer long.

Dunsmuir also has some nice places to stay, ranging from a pleasantly rustic **Travelodge**, downtown at 5400 Dunsmuir Avenue (530/235-4395), to the historic **Cave Springs Motel**, along old US-99 on the north side of town at 4727 Dunsmuir Avenue (530/235-2721). The Cave Springs opened as a motor court back in 1922 (before US-99 was US-99) and has stayed in business ever since; rustic cabins and motel rooms, set back from the road and well out of range of freeway noise—with a pool, horseshoes, and bocce ball courts—range $40-75 a night.

Castle Crags State Park

Rising more than 3,500 feet above I-5, six miles south of Dunsmuir, Castle Crags State Park (530/235-2684; daily 7:30 AM-10 PM; $5 per car) takes its name from the silvery forest of towering granite pinnacles that dominate the western skyline. A strenuous three-mile hike from the parking lot brings you to the foot of the crags and a grand panorama dominated by Mount Shasta. Other, easier trails crisscross the park, leading from the Sacramento River through dense stands of fir and Jeffrey pine. Camping (for tents and RVs) is reservable through ParkNet (800/444-7275).

North of the park, one of the best views of Castle Crags can be had from a room (perhaps even your own caboose) at the **Railroad Park Resort**, 100 Railroad Park Road (530/235-4440), west of I-5 at the Railroad Park exit. Dozens of historic train carriages and cabooses have been converted into $70-a-night motel rooms, and there's a very good on-site restaurant—in an old dining car, naturally—and RV and camping sites, too.

Lake Shasta

One of the great engineering feats of the Depression-era New Deal, the massive 602-foot-tall concrete wall of **Shasta Dam** blocks the Sacramento River to form Lake Shasta. Lake Shasta was the key element in the ambitious Central Valley Project, which harnessed theSacramento, McCloud, and Pit Rivers to irrigate fields and supply power to cities throughout California. In case mere numbers don't give a fair picture of the scale of the enterprise, Shasta Dam is taller than the Washington Monument, its spillway is more than twice as tall as Niagara Falls, and the water impounded here is diverted through a series of canals and aqueducts to raise crops as far away as Bakersfield.

Essential as it is to agriculture in the Sacramento Valley, Lake Shasta is also a key feature of the regional tourism industry, providing a summer playground for camping, fishing, water-skiing, and, especially, houseboating; for details, contact the **Shasta-**

Cascade Wonderland Association (530/243-2643 or 800/326-6944).

Shasta Dam itself, which is open for hour-long guided tours (daily 9 AM-4 PM; free; 530/275-4463) is three miles west of I-5 and can be reached by taking Shasta Dam Boulevard (Hwy-151), off I-5 about 10 miles north of Redding. I-5 runs right over the waters of Lake Shasta on a series of bridges, and during drought years you can sometimes spy the remnants of old US-99 bridges, which usually lie beneath the reservoir.

Redding

Located at the foot of the Cascade Mountains, at the point where they begin to fade into the flat expanse of the Sacramento Valley, Redding (pop. 66,462) is a sprawling big city and the commercial heart of vast inland reaches of Northern California. Redding is definitely more of a service center for the surrounding countryside than it is an attraction in itself, but it's a pleasant enough place—certainly worth the quick detour off the freeway.

If you've been bombing along I-5, get out and stretch your legs along the Sacramento River, following the six-mile trail that wraps around the east side of the downtown area. Or search out photogenic remnants of old US-99 along Market Street (known as "Miracle Mile" north of downtown), lined by classic motor courts and motels of the 1920s through 1940s.

For something more than the fast food whose purveyors line the freeway offramps, head to the south side of downtown, where a pair of characterful haunts have been making locals happy for eons. Tucked away next to a Safeway store, funky **Buz's Crab**, 2159 East Street (530/243-2120), is a surprising find here, so far from the sea, but it has one of the largest menus of fresh seafood anywhere—everything from fish and chips to charbroiled snapper, cod, mahi mahi, halibut, salmon, shark, swordfish, catfish, and sea bass. Sound like a fishmonger's more than a restaurant? Okay, that's correct; Buz's is both, operating its own (small) fleet of trucks to haul in the daily fresh catch from port. For beef, the best steaks in town are at **Jack's Grill**, 1743 California Street (dinner only, closed Sunday; 530/241-9705), a 1930s tavern that retains its old-fashioned character.

The usual barrage of motels line the I-5 frontage, though a steady convention trade supports some more upscale places, like the large **Doubletree Hotel**, 1830 Hilltop Drive (530/221-8700).

Shasta State Historic Park

There may not be all that much to keep you in Redding, but five miles west of town on US-299—which cuts across the mountains all the way to Arcata on the coast—the remnants of an early California gold mining camp have been partly restored

I-5 crosses high above Lake Shasta on the **Pit River Bridge,** a double-decker (highway on the upper level, railroad below) that opened in 1942 as one of the world's largest: 3,200 feet long, with piers nearly 400 feet tall.

Rock climber and clothing manufacturer **Royal Robbins** honed his skills climbing at Castle Crags during the 1940s and 1950s.

North of Lake Shasta, all the way to Weed, I-5 follows a sinuous route through the mountainous landscape of Northern California, attracting motorcyclists and would-be Formula 1 racers with miles and miles of twisting, G-force-inducing chicanes—though the legal top speed is 55 mph.

Roughly midway between Dunsmuir and Redding, get off I-5 at Vollmers to get a close-up view of one of the most beautiful **old highway bridges** anywhere. Arching high above Dog Creek, barely 100 yards east of the freeway, this delicately sculpted masterpiece was completed in 1928 and remained in use until 1955. From the freeway exit, a dirt road (signed Not a Through Street) leads downhill through the overgrowing brush to the bridge, which you can still walk or drive across.

Between Redding and Lake Shasta, west of the Pine Grove exit off I-5, if you're lucky you may be able to enjoy a burger or a drink at one the last surviving emblems of classic California roadside schlock: orange-shaped **Giant Orange** fast-food stand. At time of writing, the Giant Orange had recently closed, but it may be open again by the time you read this.

and preserved as Shasta State Historic Park (Wed.-Sun. 10 AM-5 PM; $2; 530/243-8194). The old courthouse has been gussied up as a visitors center, with displays on the town of Shasta City, which in 1850 had a population of over 2,500 but which slowly died starting in the 1880s, after the gold ran out and the railroad located its route through what's now Redding.

Detour: Hwy-3 through the Trinity Alps

If you really want to get a feel for far northern Northern California, turn well off the fast lane and cruise along Hwy-3, the official **Trinity Heritage Scenic Byway**, which winds through the mountains west of I-5 between Yreka and Weaverville. If raging rivers, dense groves of conifers, wide cattle-ranching valleys and occasional backcountry towns are your cup of tea, this is one of the state's great drives.

Starting in the north near Yreka, Hwy-3 lopes across the Scott River Valley, passing a few churches and vacation cabins through the historic town of Fort Jones (pop. 550), which serves as gateway to the extensive backcountry of the Marble Mountains Wilderness farther west. The highway then curves south and slightly east, just bypassing one of the more photogenic towns out here, tiny **Etna** (pop. 835). Turn off Hwy-3 onto Etna's Main Street, which is dominated by a massive flagpole standing in front of the circa-1894 red metal former firehouse, now a small museum and local library, at 520 Main Street. Before or after wandering around town, stop for a shake at the soda fountain inside the circa-1880 Scott Valley Drug, across the street, or a meal at Etna's best surprise, a wonderful little Southeast Asian place, **Sengthong's**, a block away at 434 Main Street (530/467-5668), serving up freshly made and totally authentic versions of Vietnamese and Thai food.

Midway between Weaverville and Yreka, at the south end of the Scott River Valley, the near-ghost town of **Callahan** has a pair of photogenic old hotels, a pool hall, a post office, and one of the state's oldest general stores, Farrington's, all lined up along the highway. South of here, Hwy-3 climbs up and over 5,401-foot Scott Pass, then twists steeply back down, entering the Trinity River watershed and running along the eastern edge of the Trinity Alps. There are campgrounds aplenty here, like the Trinity River Campground, 10 miles north of Trinity Center. For details, and information on exploring the Trinity Alps Wilderness (second largest in California), contact the main U.S. Forest Service **ranger station** in Redding (530/246-5222).

If you're not inclined to backpack or camp, you can spend the night in one of California's most attractive country B&Bs, the **Carrville Inn** (530/266-3511), a half-mile west of Hwy-3 near the north shore of Trinity Lake. Surrounded by apple and cherry groves and stately oaks and located on what used to be the main stagecoach route between California and Oregon, the inn was established back in 1854 and now provides all the modern creature comforts in truly Victorian ambience.

South from the Carville Inn, Hwy-3 winds along the red earth shoreline of Trinity Lake for about 25 miles before reaching historic Weaverville.

US-299: Weaverville and the Trinity River Scenic Byway

The only main highway linking the upper Sacramento Valley with the coast, US-299 is not only a handy route but also an enjoyable drive packed full of touring pleasure and scenic delights of both natural and man-made varieties. Starting from Redding, US-299 (which has been officially dubbed the Trinity River Scenic Byway) passes through the remnants of historic Shasta, then along the north shore of Whiskeytown Lake (the best-looking reservoir anywhere), before climbing deep into the mountains. Heading up from the often baking-hot environs of Redding, the shift from valley to mountain is as sudden as the road is steep and snaking, making its way up and over 3,215-foot Buckhorn Summit and into the dense green of Shasta-Trinity National Forest.

The road is fun to drive, and all the better for its first destination: Weaverville, a truly quaint little town that looks much as it did over a century ago, when it was first settled by gold miners. Through Weaverville, US-299 is Main Street, lined by a few blocks of picturesque buildings, some of which still have external balconies and spiral staircases. Most of the businesses preserve the old Gold Rush appearance (one at 219 Main Street boasts "California's Oldest Living Pharmacy," an odd mix of 1950s Rexall and 1850s pharmacopoeia). Side streets hold Victorian-era cottages fronted by picket fences and tidy gardens, and there's one truly historic site: the **Weaverville Joss House**, a block west of downtown, constructed in 1874 and now preserved as a state park (daily 10 AM-4 PM; $2; 530/623-5284). Set along a creek in a pleasant little park, the brightly colored building seems to be made of tiles and other traditional materials, but it's all wood. The interior, which is still sometimes used for worship, holds a 3,000-year-old Taoist altar and an array of candles and incense.

On Main Street, a block up from the Joss House, **Noelle's Garden Cafe** is a reliable place to eat, with a range of eclectic veggie-friendly dishes, served in summer on a nice terrace. Fans of roadside architecture will want to stay at the historic **Red Hill Motel**, at the north end of Main Street (530/623-4331).

North and especially south from Redding, old Hwy-99 is still in use as Market Street (Hwy-273), lined by some nifty old neon-signed motels. The best stretch runs for 15 miles south from Redding to Anderson, where it rejoins the I-5 freeway in a flurry of factory outlet shopping malls.

West from Weaverville, US-299 is a slow but very scenic drive along the Trinity River, eventually reaching the coast near Arcata. About 10 miles west of Weaverville, at the ghost town of Junction City, US-299 links up with the wild and scenic Trinity River, which it follows for some 55 miles west through gorgeous mountain forest all the way to Willow Creek.

For details on the section of US-299 between Willow Creek and the coast, see page 35.

Red Bluff

Located along the Sacramento River at the junction of I-5 and Hwy-99, Red Bluff takes its name from the colored cliffs that rise from the green waters of the Sacramento River. The northernmost navigable point in the Sacramento Valley, over 200 miles from San Francisco Bay, Red Bluff has long been an important stopping point

In summer, Red Bluff is frequently among the hottest spots in the U.S., with an all time high of 121° F, recorded in 1981.

The annual **Red Bluff Rodeo,** held over two days every April, is one of the largest in the world, drawing participants and spectators from all over the western U.S. For details, call 530/527-8700.

for travelers—and the flurry of fast-food franchises that greets visitors shows that that, at least, hasn't changed.

The downtown area along Main Street (old US-99) is quaint and full of local shops and restaurants, but the main attraction in Red Bluff is a well-preserved adobe house, built around 1850 along the west bank of the Sacramento River by William B. Ide, founder and only president of the short-lived California Republic. Shaded by one of the biggest oak trees you'll ever see, the **Ide Adobe** (daily 8 AM-dusk; free, parking $3), a mile north of downtown Red Bluff, then a mile east along Adobe Road, is furnished as it might have been back in frontier times; restored stables, a working forge, and vegetable gardens offer an evocative look back into California history.

South from Red Bluff, old US-99 splits into two branches. The quicker but duller western route is now the I-5 freeway, while the eastern branch retains the number 99, running as Hwy-99 along the foot of the Sierra Nevada mountains through Chico, Oroville, and Yuba City. The two branches rejoin at Sacramento, 130-odd miles away.

LASSEN VOLCANIC NATIONAL PARK

The unique landscape of Lassen park—rolling mountains, meadows, forests, and lakes, plus volcanic fumaroles and steaming mud pots as bizarre as those in Yellowstone—is undeniably beautiful, but the place had to be blown to smithereens for anyone to notice. Only in 1916, after two years of watching Mount Lassen explode over a course of nearly 300 distinct volcanic explosions, did the government grant national park status to the area.

Though the Lassen landscape is very young in geological terms, the volcano underlying it is quite a survivor, a remnant of a 600,000-year-old volcanic behemoth called Mt. Tehama, which grew to a height of 11,500 feet and a diameter of 11 miles. As Tehama wore down over subsequent centuries, a minor volcanic dome on its western flank continued to grow, eventually towering over all the other remnants of old Tehama; Lassen Peak is that volcanic dome, one of the largest on earth. Until another Cascade Range volcano, Mount St. Helens, blew up in 1980, Lassen was the only volcano in the contiguous United States to erupt in the 20th century.

Though born from devastation, the national park today is more a monument to rejuvenation, for the forests and meadows are again reclaiming the devastated areas, slowly eradicating the awesome desolation with an exquisite carpet of cosmic justice. But the game's not over: Lassen's magma chamber is still loaded, still alive, still restless. The steam vents and mud pots on its flanks hiss and sputter, warning of the undiminished heat beneath the surface. That, in a way, is what makes a visit to Lassen so dramatic: it could blow again—tomorrow. (On the other hand, scientists have a much better understanding of volcanism than they did a hundred years ago, and most agree that Lassen's next tantrum won't come without ample warning.)

Mount Lassen is about 50 miles east of I-5, linked to Redding by Hwy-44 and to Red Bluff by Hwy-36. Both these roads connect up with Hwy-89, the scenic main route through the park. Starting in the north, Hwy-89 (which has been officially dubbed the **Lassen National Scenic Byway**) enters the park

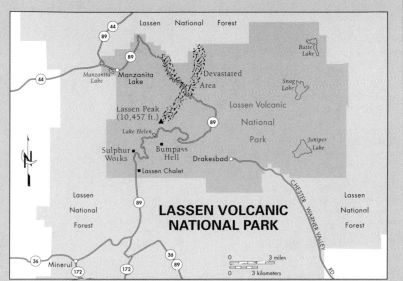

near lovely **Manzanita Lake**, which was formed a thousand years ago when talus rockfall dammed Manzanita Creek. The lake is encircled by a popular two-mile hiking trail, and along its eastern shores are a nice campground, a visitors center and store, and the fascinating **Loomis Museum** (daily 9 AM-5 PM in summer only; free), which displays a photographic record of the mountain's most impressive eruptions, along with collections of local Native American artifacts. The main park **visitors center** is also here.

Most of Mount Lassen is closed by snow from November to May, but the roads are plowed to the park entrances, from where you can explore the backcountry on cross-country skis or snowshoes. The geothermal areas of Bumpass Hell, two miles from the southwest entrance, are all the more steamy and impressive against a backdrop of sparkling snow.

As the park road (Hwy-89) winds east and then south around Mount Lassen, it passes the extensive "devastated area" obliterated by mudflows and superheated air during the 1915 eruption. At roughly its midpoint, the park road passes **Summit Lake**, then bends back west, winding along **Kings Creek**, where one of the prettiest of the park's trails dips a mile and a half downhill through forest and meadow, past steep and treacherous waterfalls cascading over slickly polished stone terraces. Another six miles beyond the waterfalls, this trail ends up in Warner Valley, site of Lassen's only in-park accommodations. The road climbs west to a 8,512-foot crest, where a strenuous five-mile roundtrip path climbs north to the 10,457-foot summit of Lassen Peak; the climb and the vista are equally breathtaking.

The sights most visitors come to see, however, are concentrated in the southwest corner of the park. Just downhill from the Lassen Peak trailhead, the park's most fascinating trail heads south from Lake Helen down to **Bumpass Hell**, where a boardwalk carries visitors through a valley of steaming, stinking fumaroles, boiling springs, and bubbling mud pots. A little farther south on

(continues)

Bumpass Hell was named for its discoverer, Kendall Vanhook Bumpass, a German-born explorer, guide and Mt. Lassen promoter who lost the use of his leg after falling into one of the boiling mudpots here.

Though "Almanor" sounds vaguely Spanish, the word comes from a combination of the names Alice, Martha and Elinore—daughters of the president of the Great Western Electric Company, which developed the "lake" out of what was previously known as Big Meadows.

Hwy-89, the road passes close to a smelly, steaming mountainside known as **Sulphur Works**, then a mile later leaves the park after passing the old ski area at Lassen Chalet.

Practicalities

The Lassen area, and the park in particular, is lean on "civilized" amenities, though gas, food, and lodging are all available in nearby towns—of which **Chester**, 30 miles southeast of the park on the shores of Lake Almanor, wins accolades for fishing, fine scenery, and friendliness. Mountain resorts along the lake's eastern shore include the **Dorado Inn**, 4379 Hwy-147 (530/284-7790), while on the southwest shore nothing beats old-fashioned **Camp Prattville**, off Hwy-89 at 2932 W. Almanor Drive (530/259-2464), which boasts a very popular restaurant famous for french fries, bread pudding, and great pies. Right in the center of Chester, the **Timber House Lodge**, on Hwy-36 at First Street (530/258-2729), is a see-it-to-believe-it restaurant featuring a hand-hewn interior constructed of massive timbers, while the **Bidwell House**, 1 Main Street (530/258-3338), is a lovely, mid-sized B&B in the former summer home of Sacramento Valley pioneer John Bidwell.

From Chester, the Warner Valley Road leads north for 17 miles, reaching into the Lassen park backcountry at Warner Valley, home of the **Drakesbad Guest Ranch** (530/529-9820), a rustic resort that has grown from its beginnings as an 1880s sheep ranch. The only place to stay inside Lassen Park that offers a roof over your head, Drakesbad is very small (around 20 rooms and cabins), very comfortable, and quite expensive (doubles start around $200 a night), but the food (included in the price) is great and the location (complete with on-site natural hot spring) unbeatable.

Closer to the park's southern entrance, three miles southeast of Mineral on Hwy-172, the old-fashioned **Mill Creek Resort** (530/595-4449) has quiet, 1940s-era cabins with kitchenettes for around $75 a night.

For more information on camping, hiking, or exploring Lassen National Volcanic Park, ask at the entrance stations (where you have to pay the $10 per car fee), or contact the Lassen **park headquarters**, a mile west of Mineral on Hwy-36 (530/595-4444).

Chico

Home to a major campus of California State University and offering easy access to the nearby mountains, Chico (pop. 54,100) is one of the more charming and live-able small cities in California. Chico is also among the oldest places in the state, having grown up around the stately Victorian palace of its founding father, John Bidwell. The house is now preserved as the **Bidwell Mansion State Historic Park** (daily 10 AM-5 PM; $2), a local history museum at 525 Esplanade, just north of downtown. Downtown Chico is compact and walkable, combining college-town standards (coffeehouses, pizza-slice joints, and book and bike shops) with older, more long-established businesses that hark back to the city's past as a farm-community hub.

Hwy-99, which is a 25-mile-long, four-lane freeway north and south of Chico, bypasses the downtown area and pretty much misses out on the local landscape of oak trees and fruit and nut orchards. The old US-99 route is slower, but gives a much better sense of the area. North of Chico, this older route followed Esplanade Boulevard; south of town, old US-99 followed the railroad tracks along Park Avenue and Midway Road, rejoining the present Hwy-99 at Gridley.

When you think of Sherwood Forest, you probably don't visualize California's Central Valley, so you may be surprised to learn that exterior scenes from the famous 1937 Errol Flynn movie *Robin Hood* were filmed in and around the oak groves of Chico's **Bidwell Park,** a 2,250-acre spread stretching along Chico Creek east from Bidwell Mansion.

Detour: Feather River National Scenic Byway

When residents of the northern Sacramento Valley want to re-visit the good ol' days, they head northeast along the Feather River Highway (Hwy-70), a scenic drive that seems to travel back in time as it moves from the flatlands surrounding Chico and Oroville, up into the mountains along a deep, alpine canyon. When the distant ridges of the plunging, V-shaped gorge are shrouded in misty clouds, the upper canyon in particular exudes an almost primordial presence, while the many towns and resorts along the river seem unchanged since the

Chico is best-known to beer drinkers as the source of **Sierra Nevada Pale Ale,** a rich and hoppy brew cooked up at Sierra Nevada's state-of-the-art brewery, located just west of Hwy-99 at 1075 E. 20th Street (530/893-3520); the on-site taproom and restaurant is one of the town's most popular eateries.

THE ISHI WILDERNESS—STOMPING GROUNDS OF THE LAST YAHI

In the rugged foothills where the Cascades and Sierra Nevada collide, east of Hwy-99 between Red Bluff and Chico, a section of the Lassen National Forest has been set aside as the **Ishi Wilderness Area,** a living memorial to Ishi, "The Last Wild Indian." Ishi (which simply means "man" in his native language) was the last surviving member of the Yahi Yani Indians. In 1911, he walked out of the woods into the town of Oroville. Ishi was taken to the Bay Area, where he worked with anthropologist Alfred Kroeber, who set about documenting Ishi's vanished way of life. Ishi became something of a one-man freak show before dying of tuberculosis in 1916. Kroeber wrote a bestselling book about Ishi, but to get an appreciation of Ishi's way of life, pay a visit to his foothills homeland; information, maps, and trail guides are available from the Lassen National Forest ranger station in Chester (530/258-2141).

In 1846, during what was known as the Bear Flag Revolt, William B. Ide and a handful of other American settlers in what was then still Mexican territory forcibly declared independence for California, planting a flag in Sonoma Plaza that featured a prowling grizzly bear and the words "California Republic." Though that "bear flag" is still the official state flag of California, the republic lasted only 24 days, until American military forces took control of California at the start of the Mexican-American War.

The time-warp atmosphere of the Feather River canyon is enhanced by the Western Pacific railroad line that leapfrogs alongside the highway on erector-set bridges, playing hide-and-seek with passing cars through mountain tunnels.

1950s—or even the 1850s, in the case of the many Gold Rush mining camps whose remains haunt the roadside. Even in the settlements of the lower canyon—the miniature hydroelectric dams, the vintage powerhouses, the rambling old hotel that virtually constitutes the entire town of Belden—it all seems to have been designed to evoke a sense of Brigadoon.

Before it became vacation country, the Feather River was Gold Country, as readers familiar with Dame Shirley will recall when they come to Rich Bar, just upriver from Belden. Louise Amelia Knapp Smith Clappe (pen name Dame Shirley) arrived here in 1851, riding a horse down the precipitous canyon wall and taking up residence for a year with her husband, a doctor. Her colorful descriptions of life in a mining community were published in a Marysville newspaper and later compiled into one of the more entertaining firsthand accounts of the Gold Rush, *The Letters of Dame Shirley*. More substantial but less populous than in Dame Shirley's day, Rich Bar basks in quiet almost as intense as the silence that prevails in its cemetery on the hillside.

The towns of the upper Feather River are by far the largest, and yet they still manage to evoke the hazy, halcyon past. **Quincy**, the somewhat sprawling Plumas County seat, generates nostalgia even for people who didn't live through the Eisenhower years, with a Main Street that looks like a Wild West film set. From Quincy, Hwy-70/89 heads south, climbing over 4,439-foot Lee Summit before rejoining the Feather River, this time along its Middle Fork. Hwy-70 splits off from Hwy-89 at Blairsden; Hwy-89 continues south toward Lake Tahoe, while Hwy-70 sticks with the Feather River, running east through **Portola**, home of the Portola Railroad Museum (daily 10 AM-5 PM; $2 donation requested; 530/832-4131), whose collection of working locomotives is used for rides during summer weekends.

Finally, as it winds its way toward the Nevada border, Hwy-70 crosses over mile-high Beckwourth Pass, the lowest and easiest of all Sierra passes. The pass is named for the African-American mountain man who scouted the route, Jim Beckwourth, son of a planter and a slave, and an honorary chief of the Crow tribe.

Oroville

South of Chico, you have another choice of highways: you can follow Hwy-99 through the valley, or edge slightly east and south through the foothills along Hwy-70, a much more scenic route that adds only a single mile to the trip. The first place you come to on the Hwy-70 foothill route is Oroville (pop. 13,000), which (as you might have guessed from the name) dates back to the Gold Rush years. A few historic buildings survive around the town, including the ornate **Chinese Temple**, 1500 Broderick Street (Tues.-Wed. 1-4 PM, Thurs.-Mon 11 AM-4:30 PM; $2;

Jim Beckwourth

530/538-2496), an 1863 structure that houses Buddhist and Taoist shrines.

Contemporary Oroville owes its existence to the massive Oroville Dam, at 770 feet the tallest earthen dam in the country, which blocks the Feather River east of town. A visitors center (daily 9 AM-5 PM; free; 530/538-2219) tells about the dam's construction and gives grand views of the huge lake behind it, which is popular with anglers and houseboaters. Tours of the dam's power-generating plant are also available.

Hwy 99: Chico to Marysville-Yuba City

Birdwatchers have good reason to follow Hwy-99 between Chico and Sacramento—or rather, they have a million good reasons, since that's the approximate number of migrating birds that pass through the Gray Lodge Wildlife Management Area every winter. This state-owned refuge ($2.50 per car), about six miles west of Hwy-99 from the town of Gridley, comprises more than 9,000 acres of marshes and levees on the north side of the Sutter Buttes, a dramatic cluster of three-million-year-old volcanoes that rise sharply above the surrounding orchards and wetlands. During winter, migrating pintails, green-winged teal, American widgeon, and snow geese are especially common. Wood ducks can be seen all year, along with Virginia rails, coyote, beaver, and numerous hawks. More than 60 miles of levee roads and trails are open to the public—including duck hunters, so avoid the refuge during hunting season (mid-October to mid-January). For more information, contact the visitors center, which is located in Gridley at 3207 Rutherford Road (530/846-5176).

Backroad botanists will want to explore the Butterfly Valley Botanical Area, on a dirt road off Hwy-70/89 near the vintage resort of Keddie. The preserve was formed to protect the **sundew,** a pinkish-flowered plant that eats insects. Hapless victims get stuck in sticky drops that the plant oozes on its leaves, whereupon the leaf bends inward slowly, moving its meal to digestive glands. You can find the carnivorous sundew in boggy meadows along the road.

If you want to travel between the Gray Lodge refuge on Hwy-99 and the even larger Sacramento National Wildlife refuge along I-5, you can cross the Sacramento River on its last remaining **ferry,** which crosses the river between the tiny towns of Princeton and Afton.

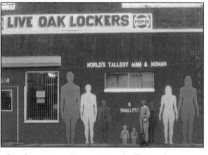

The town of **Gridley** itself (pop. 4,631), where Hwy-99 slows to a 35-mph speed limit, is quite a nice place. West of the highway and its gauntlet of franchised fast-fooderies (though it's also home to Casa Lupe, hallowed longtime local favorite for Mexican food, and recently expanded to add a Mexican food grocery), over a dozen well-shaded downtown blocks hold well-preserved, well-used banks, hardware stores, churches, and more, all surrounding the pink and grey art deco spire of the Butte Theater (which, alas, no longer shows movies).

Wildlife aside, another good reason to take the Hwy-99 route is the chance to dine at a classic old Californian roadhouse, **Pasquini's** (Mon.-Sat. 5-10 PM; 530/695-3384), right on Hwy-99 in the hamlet of Live Oak, five miles north of Yuba City. Meat is the specialty of this family-friendly dinner house—try the Basque-style grilled lamb—though fish and pasta are also superb, and very reasonably priced. Hwy-99's route through Live Oak also holds another throwback: **McDevitt's Penny Candy Store,** a candy cane-striped roadside stand packed full of stuffed animals, cheap toys, and bin after bin of 1¢ candies.

The angular peaks rising to the west of Hwy-99 between Gridley and Yuba City are known as the **Sutter Buttes,** a 2,000-foot-high volcanic upthrust that's sometimes classified as the world's smallest mountain range. Unfortunately, the entire range is private property, and access is difficult.

After John Sutter lost his fortune following the Gold Rush of 1849, he and his wife retired to a small farm along the banks of the Feather River in what's now Sutter County.

Marysville's Riverfront Park is the location of one of California's premier music events, the open-air **Sierra Nevada World Music Festival,** three days of reggae and other roots music held every June. For details, phone 415/472-5550.

From Marysville and Yuba City, scenic Hwy-20 climbs east into the Gold Country foothills to the towns of Grass Valley and Nevada City, and continues climbing, joining I-80 at Emigrant Gap for the ride up and over Donner Pass. Hwy-20 also runs west across the Central Valley, eventually ending up on the coast at Fort Bragg.

South of Live Oak, Hwy-99 briefly turns into oleander-lined freeway as it approaches Yuba City.

Marysville and Yuba City

It's hard to pinpoint what makes Marysville (pop. 12,300) feel special, but it does have a sense of place that's sorely lacking from many other Sacramento Valley towns. Hwy-70 slows to a crawl through the historic downtown, winding around a large lake and park that spreads along the banks of the Yuba River, just upstream from its confluence with the Feather River. The nearby levee holds the unique **Bok Kai Temple,** dedicated to the Chinese river god. Also here is the historic-feeling **Silver Dollar Saloon,** 330 1st Street (530/743-0507), where more hedonistic worshippers give thanks for cold beers, BBQ ribs and chicken, and live country and rock music on weekends.

Just across the Feather River, three miles west of Marysville, Yuba City (pop. 27,400) is an agricultural market town that Rand McNally has frequently rated as among the least-pleasant places to live in the U.S. There's nothing obviously horrible about it, but nothing especially charming either; for relief from the mini-mall sprawl, head to the historic downtown district and get a bite to eat at the sophisticated **City Cafe,** 667 Plumas Street (530/671-1501).

South from Marysville and Yuba City, Hwy-70 and Hwy-99 run parallel to each other on opposite sides of the Feather River, coming together some 20 miles north of Sacramento. The old US-99 route, however, angled east along what's now Hwy-65, running through the towns of Lincoln and Roseville before joining up with old US-40 for the final run into Sacramento.

Gold Country Detour: Nevada City and Grass Valley

Just a half-hour east of Marysville via Hwy-20, the scenic community of Nevada City (pop. 2,900; elev. 2,525 feet) boasts more Gold Rush architecture in its downtown district than any other town in the Sierra foothills. Called the Queen City of the Gold Country, Nevada City has dozens of elaborately ornamented Victorian-era houses and businesses crowding the main thoroughfare, Broad Street, for the better part of a mile above Deer Creek. Dating from 1856, the National Hotel near the foot of Broad Street has been in operation longer than any other

CENTRAL VALLEY WILDLIFE REFUGES

The Central Valley is a major conduit of the Pacific Flyway, the route of millions of migrating birds who breed in Canada and winter in California, Mexico and Central and South America. Some birds, such as Ross's geese, live nowhere else but along the flyway, nesting in Canada and wintering here in the Central Valley. To protect the wetlands crucial to this epic migration, many refuges have been established among the bottomlands of the Sacramento and San Joaquin Rivers, and their tributaries, by the various governments as well as by private organizations including the Nature Conservancy and Ducks Unlimited. From north to south, some of the largest and most visitor-friendly wildlife refuges include:

• **Sacramento National Wildlife Refuge:** This 10,776-acre marsh complex near Willows (on I-5) hosts more than two million waterfowl during winter, including abundant populations of the otherwise-rare Ross's geese and greater white-fronted geese. Eurasian widgeon, blue-winged teal, and other genuinely rare or uncommon species may also be present. This refuge is also a haven for the secretive American bittern and local white-faced ibis. Beavers are common here, too. The endangered elderberry longhorn beetle may be spotted here, as well as the giant garter snake. Birdwatching is best November through March, with peak season in December. A short loop hike leads from the excellent visitors center ($2; 530/934-2801), but an unpaved vehicular loop covers more territory and visits a greater variety of habitats. Besides, birds are less fearful of automobiles than of pedestrians, so an observer using a car as a blind often has better luck than a hiker.

• **Gray Lodge Wildlife Management Area:** Hosting an annual population of one million waterfowl, this unit of the Sacramento National Wildlife Refuge, off Hwy-99 near Gridley, comprises more than 9,000 acres of marshes and levees on the north side of the Sutter Buttes, a dramatic cluster of three-million-year-old volcanoes that rise sharply to 2,117 feet above the surrounding orchards and wetlands. See page 121 for more.

• **Consumnes River Preserve:** Managed by the Nature Conservancy, the brackish marshes and freshwater ponds of the Consumnes River Preserve sit on the edge of the delta, straddling Route 99 and providing rest stops for migratory sandhill cranes and hundreds of other birds. See page 127 for more.

• **Los Banos Wildlife Area:** This San Joaquin Valley refuge (209/826-0463) is a paradise to shorebirds. Yellowlegs, sandpipers, and even a casual ruff may be spotted here. It is also noted for long-eared owls, herons, bitterns, and moorhens. Black terns and merlins are not uncommon. The reserve is on Henry Miller Avenue, east of I-5 about five miles north of Los Banos on Hwy-165.

hotel west of the Mississippi; at the foot of town, just west of the Hwy-49 freeway that was unfortunately bulldozed through in the 1960s, another interesting spot is the old **Firehouse #1**, 214 Main Street (530/265-5468), a fine historical museum containing an altar from a Chinese temple, Donner Party relics, and hundreds of Gold Rush artifacts.

Nevada City is famously dainty and easy to browse; its next door neighbor, Grass Valley (pop. 9,000; elev. 2,420 feet) is bigger and brawnier, home to what once was the biggest and brawniest gold mine of them all, the Empire Mine. A generation ago, the round-the-clock rumble of its stamp mills could be heard for miles; closed in 1956, it's been preserved as the **Empire Mine State Historic Park** (daily 10 AM-5 PM; $3; 530/273-8522). You can tour the impressive mansion of the mine's owner, peer into the seemingly bottomless shaft down which miners rode railcars on their way to work the 367 miles of underground tunnels, or study the rusting array of massive machinery that turned solid rock into some six million ounces of precious gold.

South from Grass Valley and Nevada City, Hwy-49 runs across the foothills to Auburn, where it links up with the I-80 freeway. A much more interesting drive heads north from Nevada City along Hwy-49, which twists and turns steadily up into the mountains, past the numerous old gold mines (including the mini-Grand Canyon carved by miners at Malakoff Diggins, another state historic park) before

reaching one of the prettiest little towns in the western U.S., **Downieville**. Beyond Downieville—which has a great little cafe-bakery, the **Downieville Cafe Bakery** (530/289-0108) on Hwy-49 in the center of town—scenic Hwy-49 continues to climb, winding beneath the volcanic Sierra Buttes before hitting the Sierra crest at Yuba Pass, where it links up with Hwy-89, looping south to I-80, Truckee, and Lake Tahoe.

Nevada City and Grass Valley Practicalities

Grass Valley, and especially Nevada City, are deservedly popular tourist destinations, but unless you're here on a busy weekend they're usually fairly quiet and peaceful places, with more nice cafes, unique boutiques, and especially quaint B&Bs than most towns 10 times their size. Nevada City has the best range of both, with good restaurants and arts and crafts galleries filling the historic downtown blocks of Broad Street and Commercial Street. The best place to get a feel for what makes Nevada City special is the very inviting **Broad Street Books & Cafe**, at the top of downtown at 426 Broad Street (530/265-4204), where you can enjoy a sandwich or sip an espresso on the front patio and watch the world go by. Within two blocks are the bistro-style **Posh Nosh**, 318 Broad Street (530/265-6064), the downhome diner **Moore's**, 216 Broad Street (530/265-9440), and **Cousin Jack Pasties**, 220 Broad Street (530/265-4260). The last is the best chance to sample a local specialty, Cornish pasties, imported here a century ago by hard-rock miners from

Cornwall, England. There are yet more pastie places in Grass Valley, plus the very popular **Main Street Bar & Grill**, 213 W. Main Street (530/477-6000).

Grass Valley, right off the Hwy-49 freeway at the Hwy-20 junction, also holds the area's most unusual motel: the **Northern Queen**, 400 Railroad Avenue (530/265-5824), which stands on the site of an old narrow gauge railroad depot, next to a well preserved Chinese cemetery. The owners tend the graves and run a replica train that guests can ride free; the rooms are the least interesting thing about the motel but are clean and fairly quiet and cost around $60. There are also some cottages and large chalets on the property; these cost about $100. Another outstanding place to stay, especially if you're oriented toward the outdoors, is the **Outside Inn**, 575 E. Broad Street (530/265-2233), in Nevada City. The owners recently upgraded this classic, old 1940s motor court, which offers a full range of rooms, kitchenettes and suites, plus secure storage for your gear (saves hauling your kayaks into the bedrooms!) and a wealth of expertise on the area. The real accommodation draws here are Nevada City's many fine B&B inns, which fill some of the town's most elaborate Victorian homes. A perennial favorite is **Grandmere's Inn**, 449 Broad Street (530/265-4660), which has lovely terraced gardens and excellent breakfasts.

For complete visitor information on both towns, contact the **Grass Valley-Nevada County Visitors Bureau**, 248 Mill Street in Grass Valley (530/273-4667).

In and around Nevada City, tune to community radio station **KVMR 89.5 FM** to get an aural sense of the diversity and energy of this Gold Country enclave.

In Grass Valley, right off the Hwy-20 junction, the area's most unusual motel has to be the **Northern Queen,** 400 Railroad Avenue (530/265-5824), which stands on the site of an old narrow gauge railroad depot, next to a well-preserved Chinese cemetery. The owners tend the graves and run a replica train that guests can ride for free; the rooms are the least-interesting aspect of the place but are clean and fairly quiet and cost around $60. There are also some cottages and large chalets on the property; these cost around $100

Sacramento

Spreading for miles at the heart of California's 500-mile-long, agriculturally rich Central Valley, Sacramento (pop. 369,400) is not what most would expect of the capital of the Golden State. Green and suburban, with only the state capitol and a few modern towers rising over fine Victorian houses that line the leafy downtown streets, Sacramento is a relatively quiet backwater that effectively embodies California's bipolar politics. It forms a sort of neutral ground between the liberal urban centers, which contain 90% of the state's population, and the conservative, rural rest, which covers 90% of the land.

Now scythed by freeways—Hwy-99, I-5, I-80, and US-50 all come together here—and stretching for miles along the banks of the Sacramento and American Rivers, the city was chosen as the state capital during the Gold Rush era, when Sacramento was the main jumping-off point for anyone headed to the Sierra Nevada mines. Dozens of buildings dating from that era have been restored in **Old Sacramento**, a diverting shopping complex

The old US-99 bridge into Sacramento across the American River is still in use (for cyclists and rollerbladers) alongside the I-5 freeway at Discovery Park, a mile north of Old Sacramento. The bridge is part of the 30-mile **Jedediah Smith Trail,** which follows the river between Sacramento and Folsom.

and tourist trap along the riverfront, where ersatz paddle-wheel steamboats offer sightseeing cruises and the excellent **California State Railroad Museum** (daily 10 AM-5 PM; $5) documents the history of western railroads. Along with the wealth of Gold Rush architecture, there are memorials to the Pony Express and the transcontinental railroad, both of which had stations here. During Memorial Day weekend, Old Sacramento hosts the **Sacramento Jazz Jubilee** (916/372-5277), which draws an enormous crowd intent on hearing 100 or so mostly Dixieland bands.

California's capitol as it appeared in the early 1900s. A 40-acre park surrounds the building; guided tours of both are offered in spring, summer, and fall. Call 916/324-0333 for details.

Away from the riverfront, and under the unforgivably ugly I-5 freeway, "Old Sac" connects up with the wanderable Downtown Plaza shopping mall, which has all the fast-food and upscale boutiques you could want, plus a branch of the Hard Rock Cafe chain. Two blocks south, standing at the west end of a pleasantly landscaped park, the impressive **California State Capitol** (daily 9 AM-5 PM; free) has publicly accessible legislative chambers of the state's Senate and Assembly, a small museum, and hallways full of exhibits on the Golden State's diverse counties. A block south of the capitol, the brand-new **Golden State Museum** (Wed.-Sat. 10 AM-5 PM; $6.50; 916/653-7524), at 1020 O Street, is a multimedia extravaganza that recounts many stories of California's past, present, and possible future. Paid for by the state but run by an independent non-profit group, the 35,000-square-foot museum opened late in 1998 and touches on everything from natural resources to the impact of roads on the landscape, involving the visitor through a variety of interactive displays—a sit-down diner has a jukebox on which you can call up conversations between deal-making politicos, and a 1960s vintage bus tells the tales of California's many immigrants, from Dust Bowl refugees to migrant farm workers.

Two miles east of the waterfront, at 27th and L Streets, Sacramento's main historic attraction is **Sutter's Fort** (daily 10 AM-5 PM; $2), a reconstruction of the frontier outpost established here in 1839 by Swiss settler Johannes Sutter. The first commercial—as opposed to religious—settlement in Alta California, Sutter's Fort played a vital role in early West Coast history. This was the intended destination of the Donner Party. And it was one of Sutter's employees, James Marshall, who launched the Gold Rush when he discovered flakes of gold at Sutter's Mill in the Sierra Nevada foothills above Sacramento. The grounds of Sutter's Fort also hold the small but interesting **California State Indian Museum**, which has displays of baskets and other Native American handicrafts.

Sacramento Practicalities
The Old Sacramento area, along the downtown waterfront, has some good but painfully touristy restaurants and bars. The Midtown neighborhood south of Sutter's Fort holds Sacramento's best range of restaurants, including the tasty but inexpensive **Cafe Bernardo**, at 2726 Capitol Avenue, with fresh salads, pizza and pasta dishes, and great fruit smoothies or cocktails from the Monkey Bar next

door. On the opposite corner stands **Biba**, perhaps the city's best (and most expensive) restaurant. Another good bet nearby is **Paragary's**.

Another lively spot is the **Tower Cafe**, attached to the landmark 1920s Tower Theater (which plays art-house features), at 1518 Broadway, and serving healthy, multi-ethnic food with a world-beat attitude. (The cafe is where the Sacramento-based **Tower Records** CD- and bookstore company got its start; both have stores across the street, open till midnight every night.)

Though Sacramento can't compete with San Francisco for cutting-edge cuisine, it does excel in one culinary niche: **hamburgers**. There are some truly great old burger places in and around downtown Sacramento, including **Ford's Real Hamburgers**, at 1948 Sutterville Road, on the south side of expansive Land Park, **Nationwide Meats**, 1015 24th Street in Midtown, and funky little **Jim Denny's**, a 1930s burger stand at 816 12th Street, downtown between H & I.

Places to stay include the wonderful **HI Sacramento International Hostel**, in a fabulous Victorian mansion right downtown at 900 H Street (916/443-1691), with beds from $13/night for members, $16/night nonmembers, and **Motel 6**, along the river near Old Sacramento at 227 Jibboom Street (916/441-0733). For a more unusual experience, how about staying the night in a 1920s paddlewheel riverboat? The **Delta King** (916/444-5464) is permanently moored off Old Sacramento and has rooms in the $100-150 range. There are many B&Bs in the historic Midtown residential district, including the **Hartley House**, 700 22nd Street (916/448-5417), and **Abigail's**, 2120 G Street (916/441-5007).

For further information, contact the Sacramento **visitors** bureau, 1421 K Street (916/264-7777).

Sacramento marks the junction of old US-99 with I-80 and historic US-50, which are covered in the Loneliest Road chapter that begins on page 230.

The Lincoln Highway: Galt and Woodbridge

South from Sacramento, Hwy-99 is a very busy and unattractive freeway, so if you have the time you may prefer to trace the old route, which follows Stockton Boulevard south and somewhat east from downtown. The start of the route is not what most people would consider scenic, but it does offer sharp insight into rural California's multicultural present, with a multitude of Vietnamese, Cambodian and other Southeast Asian markets packing the roadside mini-malls, especially around Florin Road.

Stockton Boulevard merges back into the Hwy-99 freeway about five miles south of Sacramento, and the historic route runs alongside (or underneath) the freeway for some 15 miles before it reemerges as the main street (Lincoln Way) through the town of Galt. From here south, the old Lincoln

---

Sidebar:

Finding your way around Sacramento is pretty easy: north-south streets are numbered starting in the west at the riverfront, while east-west ones are in alphabetical order. Capitol Avenue, at the center, takes the place of M Street, and Broadway should have been Y Street.

After 30 years of trying, Sacramento finally managed to snag a professional baseball team in 1999, bringing Triple A champions down from Vancouver, BC. Renamed the **Sacramento River Cats**, they play at brand new Raley Stadium across the river from Old Sacramento; for schedules or tickets, call 916/319-4700.

Straddling Hwy-99 between Sacramento and Galt, and managed by the Nature Conservancy, the **Consumnes River Preserve** sits on the eastern edge of the Sacramento Delta. Its brackish marshes, freshwater ponds, and riparian habitats provide wintering stations for herons, woodpeckers, pheasants, and sandpipers. Most spectacular are its flocks of sandhill cranes and tundra swans. Occasionally, a Bewick's swan turns up, too. The reserve visitors center (916/684-2816) is on Franklin Boulevard, north of Galt.

I-5 SURVIVAL GUIDE: SACRAMENTO TO LOS ANGELES

WHEN INTERSTATE 5 WAS FIRST OPENED IN THE EARLY 1970s, it passed through such a no man's land that there were no services of any kind for over 200 miles; so many cars were running out of gas that the state highway department had to run round-the-clock emergency services, providing motorists with apologies and enough fuel to get them to safety. Nowadays there are plenty of gas stations and a few other sights, including the sinuous California Aqueduct which winds along parallel to the freeway almost the entire way.

Between Sacramento and Los Angeles, here are some things to see:

MM 468: North of the junction between I-5 and Hwy-120, near **Tracy**, a trio of burly old bridges cross the San Joaquin River; a couple of these used to carry the historic Lincoln Highway, on its way west to San Francisco.

MM 447: At **Westley**, one of the biggest environmental disasters in California is waiting to happen, thanks to the millions and millions of junked tires that have ended up here. No one knows what to do with them, but someone better act fast; in 1999, the tires were struck by lightning and burned for months, spewing thick toxic smoke all over the Central Valley.

MM 422: A few miles northeast of **Gustine** on Hwy-33, hungry, thirsty travelers head to the hamlet of Newman for the steak sandwiches and frosty magaritas at **Marty's**, 29030 Hwy-33 (209/862-1323).

MM 408: Just east of I-5 via Hwy-152, the town of **Los Banos** has two star attractions: **Los Banos Drugs**, 601 J Street (209/826-5834), a perfectly preserved 1950s drug store with a soda fountain dishing up thick shakes and creamy sundaes; and the family-style Basque food served at the **Wool Growers Restaurant**, 609 H Street (209/826-4593).

MM 339: In the middle of nowhere, surrounded by acres and acres of smelly feed lots, beef eaters head to the source for some of the state's finest steaks, dining at **Harris Ranch**.

MM 282: The pair of gas stations and convenience stores at **Lost Hills** marks the junction with Hwy-46, formerly known as US-466, along which actor James Dean drove west from old US-99 on his way to Monterey—before dying in a collision near Cholame, 38 miles west of I-5.

MM 215: At **Grapevine**, the ghostly remnants of a motel and gas station sit at the northern foot of the Tehachapi Mountains. The mountains are still a formidable obstacle for travelers, but not so long ago they were passable only by an all-day drive along what's now one of California's oldest highways, the Old Ridge Route.

Highway route really comes into its own, following what's now the Lower Sacramento Road (County Road J10) south to Woodbridge, a quiet hamlet at the center of expansive vineyards, with a number of very well-preserved buildings dating from the 1860s and 1870s. With a couple of nice restaurants and a walkably compact center, Woodbridge is one of the few pleasant little towns left in this part of the Central Valley.

Continuing south, following the old Lincoln Highway route is about the only way to avoid the roadside sprawl that spreads between the two busy freeways Hwy-99 and I-5.

Detour: Sutter Creek and Jackson

One of the few new mines in California's Gold Country recently opened along Hwy-49, just north of Sutter Creek.

A 45-minute drive along Hwy-16 southeast from Sacramento, or an equivalent trip along Hwy-88 from Stockton, brings you to two of the most popular weekend getaways in the Gold Country. The more northerly of these anything-but-identical twin towns, Sutter Creek (pop. 1,800; elev. 1,198 feet) offers a charming, walkable Main Street lined with handsome old balconied structures, many now converted to antiques dealers, art galleries, boutiques, restaurants, knick-knackeries and bed and breakfasts. Despite the fact that Sutter Creek seems determinedly set in the nostalgic past, there are some fascinating corners, not least of them the Dickensian wonderland of **Knight Foundry**, at 81 Eureka Street, two blocks east of Hwy-49. Hardly changed since it opened in 1873, the foundry is in the process of being re-opened as a state historic park. Another evocative historic sight is the circa-1898 interior of the **Monteverde General Store**, on Randolph Street a block east of Hwy-49; the store is kept as it was a century ago, merchandise and all.

Just north of Sutter Creek along Hwy-49, and little more than a wide spot in the road, California's smallest incorporated city is tiny **Amador City**. With barely 200 residents, Amador City is home to one of the nicest places to stay or eat in the entire Gold Country region: the 1879 **Imperial Hotel** (209/267-9172), which offers B&B rooms and elegant, ultra-fresh California cuisine (dinner only) at the north end of town (at a *very* sharp bend in Hwy-49).

Amidst Jackson's Gold Rush heritage is a fine piece of Art Deco architecture: the 1939 **Amador County Courthouse**, *hard to miss at the top of the hill, a block south of the museum.*

Five miles south of Sutter Creek, the bigger and busier city of Jackson (pop. 3,500) stakes its claims to travelers' interest by virtue of an old meat-and-potatoes downtown commercial district along Main and Water Streets. Redolent of the hardworking 1930s, Jackson evolved around the **Kennedy Mine**, northeast of town on Jackson Gate Road. The Kennedy Mine, which was worked until 1942, had the deepest vertical shaft in the United States, at 5,912 feet; the star of the Kennedy's industrial remnants is a system of enormous tailing wheels, which carried the waste rock away from the mines—the wheels were balanced so precisely that

you could move them with a finger. Built in 1905, they can be seen from the highway—or up-close on a tour (Saturday and Sunday mid-March to mid-October only; 209/223-9542), which also visits the extensive headframe and out-buildings of the

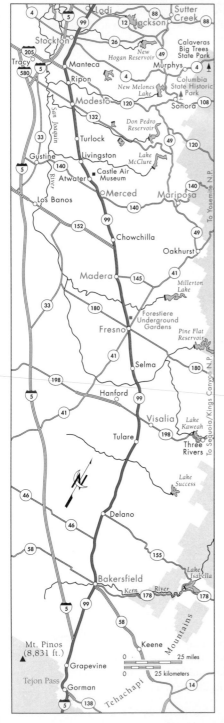

mine. You can also see a working model of this engineering marvel at the **Amador County Museum**, 225 Church Street (Wed.-Sun. 10 AM-4 PM; donations; 209/223-6386), on a hill overlooking downtown. The museum celebrated its 50th anniversary in 1999.

Jackson's Main Street, with its antique shops, biker-friendly bars, and cafes (try **Fat Freddy's**, in the old Wells Fargo office) has the great advantage of being bypassed by Hwy-49. Hwy-49, on the other hand, has one great attraction: **Mel's and Faye's Diner**, 205 Hwy-49, at the corner of Main Street (209/223-0853), open daily since 1956 for big breakfasts, great burgers (including the famous "Mooburger," with gobs of cheese and grilled onions), and milk shakes that make a meal by themselves.

Lodi and Stockton

Despite having a nice old Spanish Revival arch—the oldest in the country, built in 1907, with three bells and a bear, located on Pine Street near the downtown railroad tracks—and a water tower shaped like fluted Doric column, the Hwy-99 town of Lodi (pop. 51,900; elev. 54 feet) is perhaps best known from the Creedence Clearwater Revival song whose mournful refrain ran, "Oh Lord, stuck in Lodi again." On the east side of Hwy-99, midway between Lodi and Stockton, look out for **Pollardville**, an old-fashioned roadside attraction that seems more than a little forlorn. In business "since 1944," when it started as a restaurant famous for its chicken dinners, Pollardville is basically still a restaurant, with a tall tower of a sign and a ton of old mining and farm equipment, plus what looks like an old paddlewheel steamboat, stashed in the ersatz "ghost town" alongside.

A dozen miles south of Lodi, Hwy-99 reaches Stockton (pop. 211,000; elev. 14 feet), a major Central Valley city with a surprising feature: California's farthest-inland oceangoing port, from which much of the Central Valley's agricultural produce gets shipped around the world. Running midway between the Hwy-99 and I-5 freeways, Wilson Way is the old US-99 route, but little remains of its old road character. Stockton doesn't look like much these days, but it has a rich history going back to the time of the Hudson's Bay Company. All this and more is well documented at the **Haggin Museum**, 1201 N. Pershing Avenue (Tues.-Sun. 1-5 PM; donations; 209/462-4116), where displays include dozens of historic vehicles (inlcuding the earliest "Caterpillar"-type tractors, invented here by Benjamin Holt in the 1870s), a re-creation of a Gold Rush Main Street, and some above-average paintings by the likes of Thomas Moran and Albert Bierstadt.

Modesto

Modesto (pop. 179,000; elev. 88 feet) is the base of operations for the massive but still family-owned **Gallo** wineries, which

produce a whopping 115 million gallons annually—something like one-third of all the wine drunk in the U.S. But the city is perhaps better known in car-culture circles as the hometown of *American Graffiti* filmmaker George Lucas. Though the movie was shot primarily in Petaluma, not Modesto, the cruising culture it depicts is memorialized in a statue of two teenagers lounging on the fender of a 1957 Chevy, east of downtown where J Street bends into McHenry Street. The most famous Modesto monument is the large arch—emblazoned with the town slogan, "Water, Wealth, Contentment, Health"—that stretches over I Street just west of 9th Street. (9th Street is the old US-99 route).

For good Mexican food stop south of Modesto in the hamlet of Ceres and head to **La Morenita**, 1410 E. Hatch Road (209/537-7900), east of Hwy-99. Farther south, another good Mexican place is **El Jardin**, in Turlock, two blocks east of Golden State Boulevard (old US-99), at 409 E. Olive Street (209/632-0932).

Running up into the Sierra Nevada mountains from Jackson over Carson Pass, Hwy-88 is one of California's great scenic drives. See pages 164-165 for full coverage.

South of Stockton, Manteca marks the junction of Hwy-99 with Hwy-120, which runs east to the Gold Country town of Mariposa and on to Yosemite National Park. Heading west, via I-205 and I-580, Hwy-120 follows the old Lincoln Highway route to the San Francisco Bay Area, through Tracy, Livermore, and Dublin.

In the town of Ripon, along Hwy-99 midway between Stockton and Modesto, the historic building that houses the region's greatest Italian restaurant, **Christapaolo's**, 125 E. Main Street (209/599-2030), dates back to 1886.

Modesto was originally going to be called Ralston, after prominent San Francisco banker William Ralston, but he declined the honor. Hence the city's self-effacing name.

YOSEMITE NATIONAL PARK

Covering a huge expanse of the Sierra Nevada mountains, from the rolling foothills up to the serrated crest, Yosemite National Park is one of the wild wonders of the western U.S., with stupendous waterfalls, glacier-carved cliffs, and all the flora and fauna you could want. Over 840 miles of hiking trails crisscross the park terrain, which ranges from dense forest to silvery granite moonscapes high above timberline. But the main event here is the incredible granite gorge of **Yosemite Valley**. Seven miles long and more than 4,000 feet deep in places, the valley comprises only about 6% of this 1,170-square-mile national park, but its towering waterfalls, granite cliffs, and enchanting meadows draw visitors from around the world.

Most of the roads within Yosemite Valley have been closed to cars since 1967, and shuttle buses and bicycles have been the only way to get around, so serenity is easily found, despite the usual summer crowds. Everywhere you look is a beautiful sight, and the list of must-sees (Half Dome, Yosemite Falls, the great cliff of El Capitan, Vernal and Nevada Falls, not to mention the high country of Tuolumne Meadows or the park's extensive backcountry areas) is virtually endless. Just take your time to admire what you see, and don't worry too much about seeing it all—it'll be here when you come back.

Though hiking and gaping are the main Yosemite visitor activities, there are other options. In the main Yosemite Village visitors center, the **Yosemite Museum** (daily 9:30 AM-noon & 1-4 PM), holds a collection of native Ahwahneechee tools, baskets, and handicrafts; the reconstructed Ahwahneechee Village is out back. Yosemite aficionados will love the little Yosemite Library on the museum's second floor, a rainy-afternoon sort of place. Another quiet spot is the adjacent **Yosemite Cemetery**, where history buffs can search out pioneer graves, including that of Galen Clark, first park superintendent and a man whom John Muir called "the finest mountaineer I've ever known."

Yosemite Day-Hikes
Starting from the Ahwahnee Hotel (Shuttle Bus stop 4)—Yosemite's most prestigious hostelry, and a magnificent structure in its own right—an easy, one-

mile walk leads to Indian Caves, where you can climb and play in the jumble of huge talus boulders. Longer, but still level, is the 3.5-mile loop around what used to be known as Mirror Lake, now more correctly called Mirror Meadow. The big draws here are solitude and stupendous views of **Half Dome**, the distinctive rounded granite monolith rising 4,800 feet above the valley floor, its massive vertical face sheered off by Ice Age glaciers.

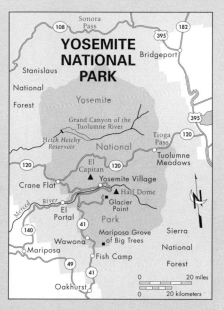

More strenuous trails leave from Happy Isles (Shuttle Bus Stop 16). This delightful spot at the mouth of the Merced River Canyon marks the start of the John Muir Trail, which runs 184 miles south to the summit of Mount Whitney. Day-hikes from Happy Isles lead up the famous Mist Trail steps to the lip of Vernal Fall (1.5 miles each way). Your thousand-foot gain in elevation may leave you puffing, and the mist thrown up by the falls' 315-foot plunge can soak you to the skin, but this trail is unparalleled anywhere for sheer spectacle. From the top of Vernal you can hike another 1.5 miles to the brink of Nevada Fall, where the Merced River drops 594 feet in a single bound. Adventurous hikers who start before sunrise can reach the 8,842-foot summit of Half Dome, 8.2 miles from Happy Isles. The final assault entails an 800-foot climb up its polished granite shoulder on a cable ladder. (Needless to say, if you fear heights or your lungs and legs aren't in tip-top condition, give the climb up Half Dome a miss.)

About the only radio station you can get in and around Yosemite is **KNBR AM 680**, all the way from San Francisco, which makes for some surreal contrasts— listening to reports of urban traffic jams while cruising the High Sierra (or stuck in vacation traffic in beautiful but often crowded Yosemite Valley).

When waterfalls flow swollen with snowmelt in spring, don't miss a close-up of **Yosemite Falls**, North America's highest waterfall, which plummets 2,425 feet in two spectacular leaps, with a connecting section of cascades between them. A paved path goes to the base of the 320-foot lower fall from a parking lot (Shuttle Bus stop 7) on Northside Drive, near Yosemite Lodge. A more ambitious 3.5-mile trail climbs up from the Sunnyside Campground (Shuttle Bus stop 8) to the top of the waterfall by way of wooded shelves and a talus-choked ravine in the north wall. Views of the middle cascades (675 feet) and the upper fall (1,430 feet) somewhat alleviate the relentless switchbacks to the narrow ledge where Yosemite Creek roars through its notch into gaping oblivion. *(continues)*

1300   YOSEMITE FALLS, YOSEMITE VALLEY, CALIFORNIA

Not just hikers get to peer from atop the valley rim; the Glacier Point Road winds some 30 miles from the valley to a sublime viewpoint atop Glacier Point, on the southern wall. From the fenced precipice, the valley floor seems a toy train set, minus the tracks, while Half Dome looms in profile, like a hooded monk pointing one shrouded arm up Tenaya Canyon toward the Yosemite high country. Hikers who prefer their views unhindered by walls and crowds might prefer to hike to Taft Point and the Fissures, an easy 1.2-mile trail that starts from the Sentinel Dome parking area, on the Glacier Point Road. Although Glacier Point's vistas are more comprehensive, the view from Taft Point is more exciting.

Practicalities

There are three highway routes into Yosemite Valley, and each one is unique. Certainly all romantic poets, landscape painters, and tour-bus operators should orchestrate their grand entrance by way of the Wawona Tunnel (Hwy-41 from Fresno), whose eastern portal exquisitely frames Bridalveil Fall and the 3,593-foot wall of El Capitan, the world's largest unbroken cliff. Thrill seekers and tailgating SUV-drivers will appreciate the steep, cliffhanging road from the San Francisco Bay Area—Hwy-120 via pictureque Groveland and Big Oak Flat—which darts in and out of tunnels with the Merced Canyon yawning at their elbows behind a little stone wall. (Hwy-120 also continues east through the Yosemite backcountry over Tioga Pass.) Geologists, historians, and other sensible folks might prefer the All-Weather Highway, the newly reconstructed Hwy-140 from Mariposa, which reveals Yosemite's geologic and human history while winding leisurely up the canyon of the Merced River, following the crashing waters upstream under Arch Rock and past Wildcat Falls and the Cascades.

Whichever route you take, everyone converges on the two-lane, one-way Southside Drive at Yosemite Valley's placid western end, creating interminable summer traffic jams.

When coming back from Glacier Point, consider turning south on Hwy-41 to Wawona and the **Mariposa Grove** of Giant Sequoias, 17 miles from Yosemite Valley. The highlight of this 250-acre grove, which can be toured on foot or by tram (May-Oct.; $7.50), is the truly massive, 2,700-year-old Grizzly Giant, whose circumference at the base measures 96 feet. Fifty yards away is the smaller California Tunnel Tree, with a hole cut so stagecoaches and, later, cars could pass through it. Complete your visit with a stay or a meal at the historic **Wawona Hotel** (209/375-6556), the oldest and most photogenic accommodation in the park, or by renting a cozy cabin at the rustic **Redwoods resort** (209/375-6666).

Once you've paid the entrance fee (Golden Eagle passes accepted) and made your way to Yosemite Valley, the first thing to do is to get out of the car. Parking at Camp Curry, Yosemite Lodge, or Yosemite Village may not be easy, but once accomplished, you can ride a free shuttle bus between all the primary points of interest—trailheads, lodges, and campgrounds. Once parked, orient yourself at Yosemite Village, the park's administrative and commercial center. Along with stores, restaurants, an ATM, and a post office, here you'll find the **Yosemite Valley Visitors Center** (209/372-0200), where you can buy books and maps and get your questions answered. The visitors center is also home to the Wilderness Office, where you can obtain the required wilderness permits for overnight trips (209/372-0740).

Whether you intend to camp or stay in the hotel, lodge, or tent-cabins, you'll need advance reservations. For campgrounds, phone the **Yosemite Reservation Service** (800/436-7275) from two weeks to five months in advance. Anywhere indoors—the tent cabins at Camp Curry, the motel rooms at Yosemite Lodge, or the historic Ahwahnee Hotel—often requires reservations for the summer high season to be made a year in advance; phone 559/252-4848. However, the front desks at each property do sometimes have same-day availability, and it doesn't hurt to ask about cancellations.

Because of the high demand for in-park lodging, you may find it necessary to overnight outside the park come in on day-trips. To the south, along Hwy-41, the town of **Fish Camp** is home to the plush characterful **Narrow Gauge Inn** (closed Nov.-March; 559/683-7720), which also has the best restaurant for miles. Near the west entrance, **El Portal**, on Hwy-140 and the Merced River, has the **Yosemite View Lodge** (209/379-2681) and the **Cedar Lodge** 9966 Hwy-140 (209/379-2612), the latter unfortunately associated with the horrific murders of Yosemite sightseers in 1999.

For up-to-date information about road and weather conditions around Yosemite, call 209/372-0200.

It's hard to be in Yosemite without thinking of **John Muir**, the pioneer preservationist who fought to protect the park from development over a century ago. You can still "meet" John Muir most evenings at the Yosemite Theater, behind the Yosemite Village visitors center and museum, when El Portal resident and Yosemite institution Lee Stetson presents a theatrical reincarnation.

In the 1980s, the Class-A **Modesto A's** had sluggers Mark McGwire and Jose Canseco on the same roster; they're both long gone, but the team still plays April-Aug. at Thurman Field (209/572-4487), southwest of downtown.

Ten miles east of Modesto on Hwy-132, **Miller's California Ranch**, at 9425 Yosemite Boulevard (209/522-1781), has old cars and carriages, plus a general store.

Detour: Columbia State Historic Park

The most popular destination in the Gold Country, Columbia State Historic Park (always open; free; 209/532-0150) is only 50 miles by road from Stockton, Modesto, and Yosemite National Park, but it feels a century or more removed in time. A place that tries to capture the flavor, sights, and smells—as well as the architecture—of the Gold Rush, Columbia is part living history, part real history, and part just plain fun. Within the 12-square-block area that has been preserved as a state park, cars are banned in favor of horses, and antique Wells Fargo stagecoaches still roll down Main Street—on a rattling ride around the nearby countryside, where they are frequently held up by performing bandits.

Historical exhibits in original and replica buildings all around Columbia show you how 19th-century Californians printed their newspapers and WANTED posters, drilled teeth for cavities (with an audio tape dramatizing the use of whiskey as an anesthetic!), taught school, fought fires, fixed wagons, and jailed desperadoes. Best of all is the opportunity to pan for gold in the sluice box in Matelock Gulch; the flume is "salted" with gold dust, so you have to pay $3-5 for the opportunity, but it is a fine way to learn the art of panning—and a blast for kids.

Columbia's pair of historic hotels—the jointly run **City Hotel** and **Fallon Hotel** (209/532-1479)—retain an old-time ambience (with the added comfort of electricity), the town's candy store still makes its own sweets, and sarsaparilla is still served at the Douglas Saloon. (For a cold beer—or a play on a "First-Rate Billiard Table"—you'll have to head to the equally historic **St. Charles Saloon**, just north of the state park boundary.) Located at the center of the southern Gold Country, off Hwy-49 near the three main historic and contemporary routes over the High Sierra crest (Hwys-4, 108, and 120, over Ebbetts, Sonora, and Tioga passes, respectively), Columbia is easily reachable and well worth the detour. Nearby towns offer more attractions. The quiet hamlet of **Murphys** (pop. 1,850; elev. 2,170 feet), just 10 miles north off Hwy-4, is one example. Birthplace of the tongue-in-cheek fraternity E Clampus Vitus, Murphys still maintains a streetside memorial to the organization, which was founded during the Gold Rush to preserve California history, drink beer, and make fun of self-important fraternal organizations such as the Masons and the International Order of Odd Fellows (I.O.O.F.), whose fraternal halls still pepper the Gold Country. The **Murphy's Hotel**, 457 Main Street (209/728-3444), has entertained a number of famous guests through the years, among them Black Bart, Ulysses Grant, and Mark Twain, who stayed here on his way to see the famous Big Trees at Calaveras Big Trees State Park.

Just three miles south of Columbia, **Sonora** is a busy little city with some splendid old architecture along Hwy-49, most notably the deep red St. James Episcopal Church, on the corner of Washington and Elkin Streets. The oldest of that denomination in the state, having held its first service in 1859, it is also probably among the most photographed churches in California. Above Sonora, **Hwy-108** climbs up and over Sonora Pass.

West of Sonora, Hwy-49, Hwy-108, and Hwy-120 all come together at historic **Jamestown**, one of the select Gold Country towns that still make their living largely by mining gold (at the large Homestake mine, west of town). Known locally as Jimtown, the city has a Main Street business district that sidesteps the busy highways and boasts a trio of good places to eat and drink: the Wild West-themed **Willow Steakhouse**, the Mexican-spiced **Smoke Cafe**, and the urbane **Michaelangelo**, all within 100 feet of each other. On a hill above downtown, **Railtown 1897 State Historic Park** (train rides on the hour, Sat. and Sun. 11 AM-3 PM; $6; 209/984-3953) offers a glimpse at a vintage roundhouse, workshop, and rail stock, as well as rides on the vintage Sierra Railway. If you get a sense of deja vu from the train and surrounding countryside, restrain yourself or risk being publicly identified as a fan of the old TV show *Petticoat Junction*, which featured the train here in its opening credits. (The train also, however, appeared in the Western classic *High Noon*.)

Livingston, a dozen miles north of Merced, had "the last stoplight on Hwy-99" before the freeway bypass was completed in 1997.

Along Hwy-99 at Atwater, just north of Merced, the **Castle Air Museum** outside former Castle Air Force Base has a collection of surplus warplanes that includes the fastest aircraft ever built, the Lockheed SR-71 Blackbird high-altitude spy plane.

Merced to Madera: The Mammoth Orange

The long straight stretch of Hwy-99 north of Fresno doesn't offer much to tempt travelers off the freeway, but the many small and medium-sized towns along here do have some oddities. Life in Merced, the main gateway to Yosemite National Park, no longer revolves around the magnificent old **Merced County Courthouse**, 2222 N Street, but the imposing structure, built in 1875, still dominates the town.

Chowchilla, 20 miles south of Merced, is infamous as the place where, on July 15, 1976, a schoolbus full of children was kidnapped, buried in a disused gravel quarry, and held for $5 million ransom. All 26 schoolchildren—who ranged in age from 5 to 14—managed to escape along with the bus driver, and three wealthy young wackos from San Francisco were convicted and jailed for life; a block south of the main street (Robertson Boulevard), in front of Chowchilla's courthouse, a plaque with a bronze bas-relief schoolbus commemorates the event. Chowchilla is also home to the semi-famous **Mammoth Orange**, along old US-99 four miles south of town. Opened along old US-99 in 1954 as one of 17 in a chain, this is the only Mammoth Orange still in business. Now selling excellent "Alaska-Size" burgers as well as the freshly squeezed orange juice it did during its heyday, this survivor from the late-classic period of roadside Americana even has its own exit off the northbound side of the freeway, at Road 22½.

Another 15 miles south, the old highway frontage through Madera, Gateway Road, is better preserved than in most of the Central Valley—many old motels and gas stations still stand, albeit in semi-abandoned states. If you're hungry, stop at **The Fruit Basket Family Restaurant**, in business since 1945 at the center of town, across from a pleasant park. About a mile south of Madera, the midpoint of old US-99's run across California is marked by a pair of trees, nicknamed **"The Pine and the Palm,"** which still stand in the median strip of the Hwy-99 freeway, a mile south of the Avenue 12 exit. Representing the two halves of the Golden State—the pine for the forests of the north, the palm for the sunny south—the trees were originally planted as part of a roadside park, but freeway expansion has isolated them in the central divider, with no safe access for pedestrians or passing drivers.

Detour: Mariposa

East of Merced along Hwy-140, the central route to Yosemite National Park, the town of Mariposa (pop. 1,200; elev. 1,953 feet) marks the southern end of the Mother Lode, the gold-bearing vein of quartz that forms the backbone of California's Gold Country. It's hard to persuade travelers bound for Half Dome to stop a while and check out the place, but there are at least two attractions that merit your time and attention. First of these is the dainty **Mariposa County Courthouse**, built in 1854 in the Greek Revival style and still in use—California's oldest court of law. It's a great place to get married, too. (Congratulations, Weyman and Lily!)

The other spot, two miles south via Hwy-49, is simply the best geology museum in a region born and raised on rocks. The **California State Mining and Mineral Museum** (in summer, daily except Tues. 10 AM-6 PM, rest of year Wed.-Sun. 10 AM-4 PM; $2; 209/742-7625) shows off some 20,000 specimens of crystals, gemstones, ores, minerals and just plain rocks—a beautiful array. There's also a tour through a simulated mine that's informative—and fun for kids.

Forestiere Underground Gardens

It's hard to imagine a less appropriate location for one of the more wonderful folk art environments in the country, but the unprepossessing northern outskirts of Fresno known as "Highway City" are home to the Forestiere Underground Gardens, 5021 W. Shaw Avenue (tour hours vary, usually every two hours Wed.-Sun. 10 AM-4 PM in summer, noon and 2 PM on weekends the rest of the year; $6; 559/ 271-0734), an amazing underground world carved out of the Central Valley floor by an enigmatic Sicilian immigrant, Baldasare Forestiere, who had learned to dig while working to build the Croton Aqueduct in New York City. Not at all claustrophibic or catacomb-like, his "gardens" are a carefully crafted, architecturally compelling series of subterranean spaces that provide all the comforts of home—10 feet below the surface.

Located just east of the current Hwy-99 freeway, this oddly spiritual labyrinth was created through half a lifetime of labor, from around 1905 to 1945. After being sold a piece of land that turned out to be underlain by a solid shelf of sedimentary hardpan, Forestiere decided to make the most of his misfortune by digging down to better soil, which lay 10 feet or more beneath the surface. Cutting the rock-hard hardpan with a pick, he used the pieces like stones, stacking and mortaring them into place to turn his trenches into courtyards, where he planted orange, lemon, grapefruit, pomegranate, and other trees, along with grapevines. Using only hand tools, over the years Forestiere connected the courtyards with vaulted hallways, and eventually the five-acre complex had grown to include a kitchen, a pair of bedrooms (one for winter, one for summer), a solar-heated bathroom, even a glass-bottomed aquarium, all well ventilated and well lit, keeping cool in summer and avoiding winter frosts.

When Baldasare died, childless, in 1946, he left the gardens to his brother Giuseppe, whose children and grandchildren have struggled to preserve it. Though the gardens are an official State Historical Landmark ("preserved as a living monument to a creative and individualistic spirit unbounded by conventionality," according to a nearby plaque), the surrounding land has been bulldozed to build motels and the nearby Hwy-99 freeway—and only about half of the original construction is open to the public. The gardens, now supported by a chairtable conservancy, are not at all commercialized (you can't even buy a postcard). But they've been feted as a work of visionary genius by art and architecture magazines around the world and are absolutely worth setting aside an afternoon to enjoy.

Fresno

Variously known as the "Raisin Capital" and "Turkey Capital" of the U.S., Fresno (pop. 406,900) is one of largest cities in the state, but there's little there there. Hometown of Armenian author William Saroyan, the city of Fresno covers a flat expanse of some of the state's finest farmland, and as it expands it's swallowing up more and more vineyards, orchards, and cotton fields and turning them into tract houses, tract houses, and more tract houses. There are big buildings downtown, and parks aplenty, but it's hard to see what might tempt a visitor bound for Yosemite (via Hwy-41) or Kings Canyon (via Hwy-180) to stop and spend some time here.

Fresno's nifty old welcome sign (with the slogan "Best Little City in the USA") is in a warehouse district on Van Ness Avenue, a mile south of downtown, and dates from 1925. The town's landmark old brick water tower, on Fresno Avenue at O Street downtown, dates from 1894 and now houses a visitors center (559/233-0836).

South of Fresno, Golden State Boulevard is an intact stretch of old US-99, running as frontage road along the east side of the Hwy-99 freeway for around 15 miles. Just east of the Hwy 99 freeway on Bethel Road in **Selma**, which has a nice, quiet downtown area complete with old-fashioned streetlamps, you can tour the world headqaurters of Sun-Maid Raisins, and maybe buy a box or two for the road.

The Giants-affiliated **Fresno Grizzlies** (559/442-1994) play Triple A baseball in the Pacific Coast League all summer long. Most games are broadcast on KYNO 1300 AM.

Visalia

By California standards, Visalia is almost ancient, having been founded way back in 1852, toward the end of the Gold Rush, as the first community in the San Joaquin Valley. Unlike many mining camps, however, Visalia has survived very well, and its well preserved buildings offer a glimpse of a rural idyll that's hard to imagine in the rest of the overcrowded, overamped state. The five miles of Hwy-198 that link Visalia with Hwy-99 are increasingly freeway-like, and east of town, Hwy-198 is four lanes all the way to the foothills, but to a great extent Visalia still *feels* like the small town it considers itself.

SEQUOIA AND KINGS CANYON NATIONAL PARKS

Adjacent to one another, jointly administered, sharing main access roads, and similarly endowed with the Sierra's largest forests of giant sequoias, deepest canyons, and highest mountains, these two parks are fraternal twins. Casual travelers, especially hasty ones, needn't worry about seeing both if time is limited; it's better to spend more time in one than to divide a short visit between them. Connoisseurs of fine mountain scenery, however, will find the pair unparalleled in California for extensive forest solitude, majestic gorges, and grand alpine scenery.

Combined with adjoining forests, the twin parks embrace the second-largest wilderness region in the continental United States, including several mountains exceeding 14,000 feet, the chief being **Mount Whitney** (14,495 feet), highest point in the contiguous U.S. In contrast, Kings Canyon is technically the nation's deepest gorge, though its deepest point—8,200 feet between the river and the 10,051-foot summit of Spanish Mountain—lies about 11 miles downstream from the park boundary. Hundreds of miles of trails wend through boreal forests and lace the high country canyons, meadows, passes, and plateaus, including the John Muir Trail, the Pacific Crest Trail, and the High Sierra Trail, which saunters 62 miles from the Giant Forest to the top of Mt. Whitney. This vast backcountry is open only to hikers, backpackers, or pack trains, preserving pristine solitude and rich wildlife; all backcountry campers are required to obtain a wilderness permit before starting their trips (559/565-3775).

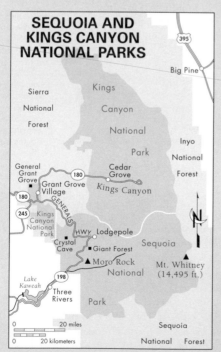

SEQUOIA AND KINGS CANYON NATIONAL PARKS

Sierra National Forest

Kings Canyon National Park

Big Pine

Inyo National Forest

General Grant Grove
Grant Grove Village
Cedar Grove
Kings Canyon

Kings Canyon National Park
Crystal Cave
HWY Lodgepole
Giant Forest
Sequoia
Moro Rock
National
Mt. Whitney (14,495 ft.)

Lake Kaweah
Three Rivers
Park

0   20 miles
0   20 kilometers

Sequoia National Forest

Even if you don't have the time, equipment, or inclination to head off into the wilds, you can still get an unforgettable glimpse of Mother Nature at her best. Though the road system thankfully does not traverse the high country, as it does in Yosemite, the highway is still richly endowed with extraordinary scenery. Most extraordinary by far are the great forests of giant sequoias, particularly the Giant Forest (Sequoia) and Grant Grove (Kings Canyon), an hour apart and both readily accessible by car.

The **Giant Forest** is home to the General Sherman Tree, a 275-

foot-tall monstrosity with a circumference of nearly 103 feet. Trails, as short or as long as you wish, wind through the forest visiting some of the thickest groves of giants, such as the House and Senate Groups. The Giant Forest contains its share of specimens remarkable for shape as well as girth—sundered, hollowed, fused, or deformed (but perfectly healthy) giants with names like Clothespin Tree, Buttress Tree, Telescope Tree, and Bear's Bathtub (actually filled with water, which you can see through a natural aperture about six feet above the ground). Another not-so-natural aperture cuts through the **Tunnel Log,** which you can drive a car through. (Not an RV, though—maximum clearance is eight feet.) A mile from the road, near lovely Crescent Meadow, a 19th-century rancher converted a single sequoia log into a snug cabin, walling off the open end, hanging it with a door and fitting it with bed, table, bench, fireplace, and window. Known as **Tharps Log,** this stands about eight feet tall at its entrance and tapers to about four feet at the far end, some 60 feet away.

Beds and meals are available at rustic **Bearpaw Meadow High Sierra Camp,** perched on a forested bench overlooking the granite cliffs of the Great Western Divide. This friendly outpost, reached by an 11-mile trek over the High Sierra Trail, is a perfect base of operations for day-hikes to Upper Hamilton Lake, Tamarack Lake, Redwood Meadow, and a score of other extraordinary places. Its creaking beds, canvas tents, warm showers, and excellent meals are extremely popular, so reserve your stay as early as possible in January (559/335-5500 or 888/252-5757).

Two other special sights near Giant Forest are **Crystal Cave,** where hour-long tours ($6; reserve at Lodgepole visitors center, 559/565-3782), are given throughout the summer months, and **Moro Rock,** a granite dome overlooking the 4,000-foot canyon of the Kaweah River. You scale the latter by means of a solid stairway that climbs through natural clefts in the rock—safe enough, but absolutely exposed to some severe cliffs. The view from the narrow, railed summit extends some 12 miles east to the ragged wall of the Great Western Divide.

Grant Grove (which was originally set aside in 1890 as General Grant National Park) does not offer the topographical variety of Giant Forest, but it does nurse its own bumper crop of gargantuan trees, among them the sublime General Grant Tree, which, at 40 feet in diameter, is about four feet thicker at its base than the Sherman tree. Also here, the grimly impressive Big Stump Trail tours a logged sequoia grove, with second-growth youngsters standing up amidst the detritus of chopped-down elders.

North and east from Grant Grove, the **Kings Canyon Scenic Byway,** Hwy-180, begins its 30-mile, 2,000-foot descent down the south wall of Kings Canyon to Cedar Grove. Like Yosemite Valley, the canyon of the Kings River was carved by glaciers and has sheer cliffs and a park-like floor. However, it lacks the waterfalls and dramatic juxtaposition of monumental rock formations of its more famous sister, so receives only a tiny fraction of Yosemite's visitors. The scenic highway ends five miles beyond Cedar Grove near lush **Zumwalt Meadows,** 3,500 feet beneath the rim of the valley. Trailhead for many spectacular backcountry journeys, Zumwalt Meadows also provides an idyllic setting for picnicking amid forest and flowery glades on the banks of the roaring Kings River.

(continues)

Practicalities

Despite the existence of many dead-end spurs that probe canyons on the west and east sides of the parks (see the High Sierra and Death Valley: US-395 chapter), no road crosses the Sierra Nevada through either park, so most people tend to confine their visits to the narrow corridor of main roads on the western side of the parks. A good two-lane highway makes a loop from the San Joaquin Valley, climbing as Hwy-180 from Fresno to the Grant Grove Junction, then cruising south through sections of both parks as Hwy-198, the historic (circa 1926) **Generals Highway**, before descending by way of Three Rivers (still Hwy-198) back down to Visalia. For a great side trip, take Hwy-180 east from Grant Grove along the "Kings Canyon Scenic Byway" to Cedar Grove and Zumwalt Meadows.

The great forests and high backcountry in both parks experience heavy snows, typically from November through early May, but sections do remain open to visitors in winter. Hwy-180 into Kings Canyon is closed for the winter, but the Generals Highway from Fresno to Wolverton is kept plowed so that cross-country skiers and snowshoers can explore the Christmas-card scenery of the snow-blanketed groves.

Until 1999, there was an entire village of tourist amenities nestling amidst the trees of Sequoia's Giant Forest; now all that remains is a small museum—and the trees themselves.

The principal visitors center of Kings Canyon National Park (559/565-4307) is at Grant Grove, where there's also a lodge, some lovely rustic cabins, a store, restaurants, campgrounds, and a museum; for lodging reservations in Kings Canyon, call 559/335-5500. Amenities in Sequoia National Park are grouped at plush new **Wuksachi Village and Lodgepole**, where there's another visitors center (559/565-3782). For Sequoia lodging, call 559/565-3301 or 888/252-5757. Campsites within both parks can be reserved six months in advance (800/365-2267).

At press time, **gasoline** was not available in either park, though there is a gas station northeast of Grant Grove at Hume Lake. To be safe, fill up in Fresno or Visalia before setting off into the mountains.

Sequoia National Forest, which envelops the western foothills of both parks, also harbors campgrounds and a handful of low-key, privately operated resort areas. The town of **Three Rivers**, between the parks and Visalia, contains several motels, stores, gas stations, and restaurants.

Two great ways to get a feel for Visalia life are to catch a Class A California League baseball game of the **Visalia Oaks**, who play April-Sept. at tiny Recreation Park, off Mooney Boulevard at 440 N. Giddings Avenue (tickets $6-8; 559/625-0480), or enjoy a burger and a shake at **Mearle's Drive-In**, 604 S. Mooney Boulevard. If you'd rather dine in a swankier ambience (and on more sophisticated food), **The Depot**, 207 E. Oak Street (559/732-8611), operates in Visalia's 100-year-old train depot.

South of Visalia, a few stretches of the old US-99 frontage still survive in towns like Tulare and Delano, but there's not a lot between here and Bakersfield, 50 miles away.

Bakersfield

If you know anything about Bakersfield, it's likely to be that it's a burly oil town, or that it's the heartland of California's country music scene. Think Steinbeck's *Grapes of Wrath*, or just about any Merle Haggard tune, and you can picture the scene: hardworking, hard-drinking men and women, struggling to make ends

Overpass - Bakersfield Inn - Bakersfield, Calif.

meet. For better or worse, the actual place never really seems to live up to its legend, but if you spend any time here you'll get plenty of glimpses of lives that seem far removed from most outsiders' images of California.

Old road fans will be able to see the big **Bakersfield Arch**, which had been removed and was being refurbished at press time. Once completed, the arch will span Buck Owens Boulevard (formerly Pierce Road). Another interesting old survivor is the landmark **Fox Theater**, in the heart of the down-at-heel downtown at 2001 H Street. Among many junk shops, downtown also holds the **Five and Dime Luncheonette**, still in business inside the old Woolworth's at 1400 19th Street (661/323-8222). Bakersfield's tradition of sheep-rearing also means it's rich in Basque eateries, such as the ever-popular **Wool Growers Restaurant**, 620 E. 19th Street (661/327-9584). For a burger or a slice of pie, go to **Happy Jack's Pie 'N' Burger**, 1800 20th Street (661/323-1661).

Places to stay, especially along the old US-99 route, all seem pretty dire. If you want help with lodging and other information, contact the **Bakersfield Convention and Visitors Bureau**, 1325 P Street (800/325-6001).

The Ridge Route

After the flatness of the Central Valley, the great Tehachapi Mountains loom up to offer a sudden change of scenery—and driving conditions. This contrast was even more evident in the years before the current I-5 freeway was blasted through. To get a sense of just what an obstacle these 8,000-foot peaks were to travelers, take a drive on one of the historic highways that remain—much slower than the freeway, but offering a much greater sense of adventure.

The first main automobile route up and over these mountains was known as the Ridge Route. Opened in 1915, it wasn't paved until 1919; it remained in use until 1933. At a legal maximum speed of 15 mph, the 75-mile trip took most of a day but was seen as a great advance over the nearest alternative, a 170-mile detour

Surrounded by alfalfa fields and dairy farms 14 miles west of Visalia, another well-preserved Central Valley place is **Hanford,** a historic Southern Pacific Railroad town that boasts a large Chinatown, with a Taoist temple dating from the 1890s, four blocks east of the central courthouse square.

Country music legend Buck Owens owns Bakersfield radio station **KUZZ 107.9 FM** and the **Crystal Palace** music club, 2800 Buck Owens Boulevard (admission usually $5; 661/328-7560), where 70+-year-old Buck and his band, The Buckaroos, still perform most weekend nights.

The Hwy-99 freeway officially ends at the I-5 junction south of Bakersfield, and no portion of the old US-99 route retains the "99" from here south, though it used to run all the way to the Mexican border.

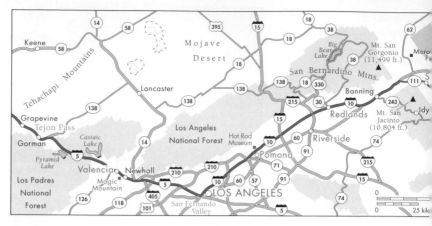

Tumbling down from the High Sierra into Bakersfield, by way of Lake Isabella, the **Kern River** is one of steepest rivers in California, which makes it popular with whitewater rafters and kayakers. The water varies from Class II (easy) to Class V (wild and dangerous), and trips cost anywhere from $20-120; for details, contact operators such as Sierra South (760/376-3745 or 800/457-2082).

Surviving sections of the original 1915 Ridge Route over the mountains were added to the National Register of Historic Places in 1997. A short but atmospheric stretch, and the ruins of an old motor court, survive in the hamlet of **Grapevine**, at the northern foot of the mountains in between the lanes of the I-5 freeway.

One of the high points, literally and figuratively, of the Tehachapi Mountains is 8,831-foot **Mount Pinos**, where miles of hiking and cross-country ski trails wind through the Los Padres National Forest, 11 miles west of I-5 from the Frazier Park exit. For information on camping, call 805/683-6711.

through the Mojave Desert. None of the many businesses that once stood along the old route survive, and you're likely to be the only person out here, but if you're feeling brave you can still travel back in time by driving considerable portions of this historic highway.

The Ridge Route followed the same path as today's I-5 from the foot of the mountains as far south as Gorman (which happens to lie astride the San Andreas Fault). From Gorman, the old Ridge Route runs southeast as Hwy-138 for about five miles past the Quail Lake reservoir, then veers south, as the Old Ridge Road. From here the road climbs swiftly, narrows considerably —feeling at times more like a flood-control ditch than a highway—and continues on its sinuous way for some 21 miles, rejoining I-5 near Castaic Lake via the Templin Highway.

Tejon Pass: I-5 and the Grapevine

In the 1930s, the historic Ridge Route was abandoned in favor of a much speedier alternative, which survives as frontage roads all along I-5. It's a frustrating task trying to follow this old US-99 route for any distance, but it does give access to most of the towns and historic sites along this stretch, starting with old Fort Tejon, which served as a US Army outpost from 1854 to 1864 and now has some lovely springtime wildflower displays. The towns here, not surprisingly, cater primarily to through-travelers, with plenty of gas stations and fast food, but not many reasons to linger. A pair of reservoirs, Pyramid Lake and Castaic Lake, hold L.A.-bound drinking water (transported 450-miles from the Feather River, through the California Aqueduct) and provide some scenic distraction from the busy freeway.

Valencia: Magic Mountain

Los Angeles County officially stretches all the way north to Gorman, but the suburban sprawl for which it is deservedly infamous

only makes it as far north as Valencia, a mere 40 miles from downtown. The one attraction here is a big one: **Six Flags Magic Mountain** (daily in summer, weekends only rest of year; $35; 818/367-5965), where more than 100 truly thrilling thrill rides are packed into a 260-acre amusement park. The coasters here cater to all tastes, from the old-fashioned wooden Psyclone to The Viper, with a 200-foot drop, plus the 10-story Freefall and various Batman-and-Robin-themed adventures. Arrive early to be sure you get your money's worth.

The Sierra Highway

The Sierra Highway, running north of and parallel to Hwy-14 between Newhall and Lancaster, used to form part of US-6, which at one time was the nation's longest highway, linking Long Beach with the tip of Cape Cod. The name is a bit misleading, since the road crosses the San Gabriel Mountains rather than the Sierra Nevadas, but if you like driving historic highways, you'll want to check this one out. A number of faded old gas stations and roadside cafes line the route, and midway along, the friendly and inviting **Halfway Cafe**, 15564 Sierra Highway (805/251-0102), is open 6 AM-3 PM every day, for great breakfasts and lunches. (Dinners are served Friday only.)

Walt Disney founded Valencia's California Institute for the Arts, better known as **Cal-Arts,** which has since grown into one of California's top art schools.

Old US-99 reappears briefly around Calgrove, which was fortunate, since this section, known officially as "The Old Road," became the only through route when the I-5 and Hwy-14 freeway bridges collapsed in the 1992 Northridge earthquake.

San Fernando Valley

What New Jersey is to New York City, the San Fernando Valley is to Los Angeles—a seemingly endless suburban sprawl, some 150 square miles of burger stands, car dealers, car washes, wrecking yards, and dingy roadside mini-malls. If you like this kind of thing, old US-99 offers one of the most direct non-freeway routes across it, following San Fernando Road from the foothills of the Tehachapis all the way to the edge of downtown.

The two real places of interest along this route are way out at the north edge of the valley. The older of the two is **The Cascades**, a man-made waterfall where, since 1913—when the 338-mile Los Angeles Aqueduct was completed—thousands of gallons of fresh water have tumbled down to make their splashy entrance into Los Angeles. Now frequently turned off, The Cascades are located along the east side of the I-5 freeway, near the intersection of Balboa Boulevard and Foothill

Between Newhall and Lancaster, Hwy-14 and the historic Sierra Highway both pass by **Vasquez Rocks,** which may look familiar since they were used as backdrop for numerous early Hollywood westerns and many episodes of The Lone Ranger TV show.

Boulevard (adjacent to the new Cascades Business Park). Also worth a look is the nearby **Mission San Fernando** (daily 9 AM-4 PM; $4; 818/361-0186), in between the I-5 and I-405 freeways at 15151 San Fernando Mission Road. Founded in 1797 and fully reconstructed following the 1971 Sylmar earthquake, the bougainvillea-covered walls, adobe arcades, and red-tiled roofs of the mission go a long way toward evoking a sense of colonial-era California, despite its present sub-suburban setting.

Crossing Los Angeles

Until 1962, when the Golden State Freeway was completed, US-99 followed San Fernando Road across the San Fernando Valley through Burbank and Glendale before entering downtown Los Angeles on Broadway. The route followed the Los Angeles River, cutting back and forth on a series of ornate concrete bridges, many of which still survive to be featured in many a low-budget movie. (The bridges appear in many big budget ones, too, including Terminator 2).

From downtown, the old US-99 route veered to the east through the San Gabriel Valley, first along Valley Boulevard and, after World War II, along the Ramona Parkway, which is now the San Bernardino Freeway (I-10). There's very little of the old route, or old roadside architecture, left in the greater Los Angeles area, so I don't suggest trying to follow the old road. If you want a scenic alternate across the San Gabriel Valley, follow old Route 66, which runs parallel to old 99 just a mile or so to the north. Route 66 across Los Angeles is described beginning on page 279.

The sights and sounds of Los Angeles are covered in a Survival Guide that appears in the Pacifc Coast Highway chapter, on pages 88-90.

Pomona: Hot Rod Museum!

In Pomona, at the far eastern edge of Los Angeles, between old Route 66 and old US-99, the "Fairplex" grounds where the Los Angeles County Fair is held each year are also home to the **National Hot Rod Association Motorsports Museum,** 1101 W. McKinley Avenue (Wed.-Sun. 10 AM-5 PM; $5; 909/622-2133). Tracing the history of drag racing from its early outlaw period to the glory days of the 1960s—when the likes of Don "Big Daddy" Garlits and Don "The Snake" Prudhomme thrilled a certain sector of the nation—the museum is a must-see for anyone who ever cared to see what a car could be made to do in a quarter-mile.

Detour: Riverside

Not so long ago, there was nothing but vineyards and orange groves between Los Angeles and the desert; now, there are no orange groves left at all. But if you manage to miss the worst rush-hour traffic imaginable and can close your eyes to some of the ugliest sprawl anywhere, you might enjoy a little detour south to Riverside, which, a mere century ago, was the economic and social center of Southern California. The lifestyle of a well-to-do orange grower has been re-created here at the **California Citrus State Historic Park,** on Van Buren Boulevard (daily 8 AM-5 PM; free; 909/780-6222), where hundreds of orange trees and a variety of other citrus have been preserved as a reminder of an earlier era.

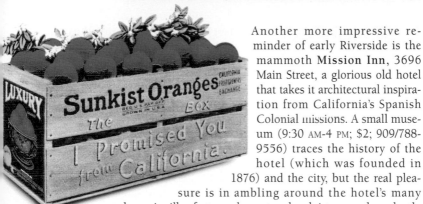

Another more impressive reminder of early Riverside is the mammoth **Mission Inn**, 3696 Main Street, a glorious old hotel that takes it architectural inspiration from California's Spanish Colonial missions. A small museum (9:30 AM-4 PM; $2; 909/788-9556) traces the history of the hotel (which was founded in 1876) and the city, but the real pleasure is in ambling around the hotel's many bougainvillea-festooned courtyards, cloisters, and opulently detailed public areas.

Redlands and the Rim of the World Scenic Byway

Like Riverside, Redlands was a vital force in the early history of Southern California. And, as with Riverside, most of its proudest moments are well in the past. Ornate Victorian houses line the quiet streets, and a few citrus groves still manage to survive on the outskirts, but there's not a great deal to see or do.

That said, the San Bernardino Mountains that rise above Redlands bring some splendid natural scenery right to its doorstep. Following Hwy-38 east and north from Redlands, along what is sometimes called the Rim of the World Scenic Byway, brings you swiftly up to the fringes of the 60,000-acre San Gorgonio Wilderness, which spreads around the 11,499-foot summit of Mount San Gorgonio, the tallest peak in Southern California. Hwy-38 bends back west, passing Big Bear Lake, then joins a series of other mountain highways to form a 110-mile loop, returning to Redlands via Hwy-18.

East of Redlands, old Hwy-99 is basically submerged beneath the I-10 freeway all the way to the edge of the desert.

From Banning, on I-10 just west of where it drops down San Gorgonio Pass into Palm Springs, a turnoff south onto scenic Hwy-243 takes you up to the hamlet of Idyllwild on the slopes of **Mount San Jacinto.** If you want to make a complete loop, continue south from Mount San Jacinto onto Hwy-74, the Palms to Pines Scenic Byway, which drops steeply down through the Santa Rosa Mountains, then enters the Palm Springs area at Rancho Mirage.

Detour: Joshua Tree National Park

At the north end of the Coachella Valley, where hundreds of windmills cover San Gorgonio Pass, you have three choices. You can stay on I-10 and bomb across the desert; you can turn off south onto Hwy-111, toward the resorts of Palm Springs, or you can veer off to the north, taking Hwy-62 on a wild ride to the north entrance of Joshua Tree National Park, one of the most beautiful bits of desert in the American southwest. The

Ten miles north of I-10 and a quarter-mile south of Hwy-62 (there's no sign—turn at Rocky's Italian Restaurant), the spring-fed stream at **Big Morongo Valley Preserve** (760/363-7190) makes it one of the desert's best birdwatching spots.

1,250-square-mile park is dominated by two striking features: dense forests of **Joshua trees**, a tall yucca (some grow to 40 feet) with multiple arm-like branches, and huge outcrops of quartz-veined pink granite known as **monzogranite**, which (along with the warm winter weather) attracts rock climbers from all over the world. And at night, the near-total absence of city lights makes the profusion of stars shine bright.

The best first stop on a visit to Joshua Tree is the main **visitors center** (daily 8 AM-5 PM; 760/367-5500), at the north entrance, where you can pick up maps and information on flora and fauna, scenic drives, camping, hikes, and historical tours of the park's many old mines and ranches.

Apart from plentiful—if primitive—camping, there are no accommodations in the park, but there is a marvelous (and fairly inexpensive) place to stay just outside the northern boundary: the **29 Palms Inn** (760/367-3505), which has a handful of humble adobe cabins, a swimming pool, and a nice cafe, in a palm-shaded natural oasis. Their motto says it all: "We discourage misery and offer alternatives."

In sharp contrast to the desert tranquillity of Joshua Tree National Park, the expansive Marine Corps Air-to-Ground Combat Training Center at **Twentynine Palms**, just north of the park, is often busy with simulated battles, so don't be too worried if you see tanks, fighters, and helicopter gunships on the horizon.

Palm Springs

If you believe the 1970s pop song, you may think it never rains in Southern California, but locals know better. When the winter glooms hit Hollywood, Hollywood flees inland to Palm Springs, an occasionally glitzy but surprisingly low-key resort community that has covered the upper Coachella Valley with miles and miles of golf courses, tennis courts, and swimming pools. Set at the foot of snow-capped mountains and stretching for nearly 30 miles between exits off I-10, four different communities (Cathedral City, Rancho Mirage, Palm Desert, and Palm Springs itself) merge into one another along Palm Canyon Drive (Hwy-111) and offer just about anything you could want from a vacation escape.

Starting in the north, Palm Springs (half of which is owned by the native Cahuilla Indians) is the oldest and most settled of these desert towns—it's been here long enough for there to be a strong "preservationist" movement, aimed at keeping the 1920s-1950s retro-chic character from being erased by larger-scale development. The beige stucco Spanish Revival heart of Palm Springs is about the only pedestrian-friendly space for miles—park here and amble among boutiques, galleries, and the history, art, and Native American exhibits at the 100,000-square-foot **Palm Springs Desert Museum**, a block west at 101 Museum Drive (Tues.-Sat. 10 AM-5 PM, Sun. noon-5 PM; $7.50; 760/325-0189).

Apart from window shopping or lying poolside nursing a cold drink, the other popular thing to do in Palm Springs is ride the **Aerial Tram** (daily 9 AM-8 PM; $18; 760/325-1391), which ferries people over a mile up Mount San Jacinto, from the desert floor to the pines in just a few minutes. In spring, you can even rent a pair of cross-country skis from the Mountain Station and set off on a backcountry tour, coming home for a swim in the evening.

I-10 SURVIVAL GUIDE: SOUTHERN CALIFORNIA

RUNNING FROM THE BEACHES OF SANTA MONICA all the way across the deserts of Arizona and New Mexico, the I-10 freeway overlays quite a few of the more scenic routes covered in this book, but generally goes its own way. I-10 is by far the quickest way to travel, and it does have a few attractions of its own, so if you're racing across the Southwest deserts don't miss these places, listed west to east, from Santa Monica to El Paso:

MM 0: I-10, the Christopher Columbus Transcontinental Highway, has its western end at **Santa Monica**, in a tunnel that links it with the beachfront Pacific Coast Highway.

MM 109: At **Cabazon**, don't miss the Wheel Inn restaurant, open 24 hours a day for over 40 years. Besides serving fresh pies and all-American road food, the Wheel Inn is best known for the giant steel-and-concrete dinosaurs that stand over the place, in a nice park just behind the restaurant. Built by Claude Bell, who owned the restaurant, the dinosaurs now contain a souvenir store.

MM 159: Southern entrance to Joshua Tree National Park.

MM 175: Near where General George S. Patton trained tank battalions for battle during WWII, the **General Patton Memorial Museum** (daily 9:30 AM-4:30 PM; $4; 760/227-3483) documents that era as well as the general history of the desert—exhibits on railroads, aqueducts, and more.

MM 242: The historic Colorado River town of **Blythe** has a few older motels and doughnut shops along Hobsonway, the old US-60 main drag north of I-10, but the real draw is 15 miles north of town along US-95, where a series of intaglios known as the **Giant Desert Figures**—ranging from 95 to 165 feet tall—were scratched into a bluff by ancient Native American people.

MM 244: Colorado River, the California-Arizona state line.

However much luxury they wrap their residents and invited guests in, the other towns offer very little to the casual visitor. Next door to Palm Springs, Cathedral City was long a desert gay and lesbian refuge but recently has become more "family oriented," with miniature golf courses and an IMAX theater. Next along is Rancho Mirage, home to former President Jerry Ford and his wife's world famous $500-a-day celebrity detox center. Especially in spring, when the desert blooms, the 1,200-acre **Living Desert** (Sept.-April 9 AM-4 PM, hours vary the rest of the year; $7.50; 760/346-5694) in Palm Desert is a wildlife park and botanical garden with representative species from all the world's deserts: bighorn sheep, birds of prey, mountains lions, even zebras.

Palm Springs Practicalities
The Palm Springs area is packed with destination resorts, where you can indulge yourself morning, noon, and night without ever having to leave the property. Each

of the big names (Ritz-Carlton, Westin, Hyatt, Marriott, and more) has gone all-out to make its resort the one you choose; older, more characterful escapes include the original, late-1920s **La Quinta** (800/854-1271), much expanded from the time when Frank Capra lived here, but still nice (of course, at $250 or so a night, it should be), with adobe casitas spread around lush gardens.

For mere mortals, there are also hundreds of fairly standard motels and hotels, usually with big swimming pools and other desert essentials. Rates vary tremendously, from dead cheap in the heat of summer (when many places close) to Las Vegas outrageous in winter and spring when a big golf tournament hits town.

Dining options vary from a few good, basic cafe-type places to many swanky, stylish, and very expensive restaurants. Of the former, the local champion is **Louise's Pantry**, 124 S. Palm Canyon Drive (760/325-5124), a classic late-1940s coffee shop (comfy booths, Formica counters, milk shakes, meatloaf, and more—including great pies) with the added advantage of being right at the historic heart of Palm Springs. Mexican places, pizza joints, and other standard options abound in mini-malls up and down Hwy-111.

For complete details on anything to do with Palm Springs, contact the **visitors center**, 2781 N. Palm Canyon Drive (760/778-8415 or 800/347-7746), on Hwy-111 at the north edge of Palm Springs.

Fans of minimalist Modernist architecture flock to Palm Springs to ogle landmark homes by the likes of Richard Neutra and John Lautner; for a handy guide, pick up the free Palm Springs Historic Architectural Highlights *pamphlet from the main Palm Springs visitors center.*

The town of Palm Desert, 10 miles south of Palm Springs, is the site of the nation's only **golf cart parade,** *held every November. Customized carts (from mock Humvees to replica Rolls-Royces) cruise the main drag, kicking off the start of the main winter season; for dates and other details, call 760/346-6111.*

Indio

The ritziness of the Palm Springs area is a distant memory by the time you reach Indio (pop. 36,800), which is only a marathon run to the southeast but feels a universe away. A commercial center, rather than a vacation destination, Indio is the hub of the working desert; despite being 22 feet below sea level, with an average summer temperature well up in the triple digits, this is where most of the millions of dollars worth of melons, dates, grapefruit, and other produce of the Coachella Valley gets shipped off to markets around the world.

The best place to get a literal taste of some of what goes on in and around Indio is **Shields Date Gardens** (daily 8 AM-6 PM; free; 760/347-0996), on Hwy-111 at the north end of town. A thick grove of date palms—most with built-in ladders for workers to pollinate and pick the fruit—surrounds the building. Inside, you can watch the funky old multimedia presentation *Sex Life of the Date,* which tells you all you ever wanted to know about the life cycle of these deliciously meaty treats. There's a store (with fresh dates at fairly low prices) and, best of all, a soda fountain (unchanged since 1950), where you can buy a cone or a

SHIELDS

Since 1924

DON'T MISS **IT!**

OPEN ALL YEAR

milk shake made with date ice cream—an ideal thirst quencher on a hot afternoon.

Indio also marks the spot where our route rejoins the old US-99 highway, which bypassed Palm Springs along what's now the I-10 freeway. Following Indio Boulevard—the main road—you pass many reminders of the old road, most notably **Clark's Auto-Truck Stop**, open 24 hours at 82173 Indio Boulevard (760/342-4776), decorated with a fine mural celebrating the old highway. Inside, there's a small "museum" of old US-99 memorabilia.

Salton Sea

South of Indio, old US-99 veered off south along today's Hwy-86, running along the western shore of the bizarre Salton Sea, one of the world's most unusual bodies of water. Recently famous for fish kills and bird poisonings thought to be caused by agricultural runoff, the so-called "sea" is actually the result of a big mistake: back in 1905, when engineers were improving a canal from the Colorado River, levees broke and the entire river was effectively diverted to the Imperial Valley. For two years, the entire flow of the Colorado River poured into this desert valley (which is 250 feet below sea level, and separated from the Gulf of California by a dry delta), before the riverbanks were eventually fixed. Land north and south of the "sea" is highly productive, but the shores are bone-dry and not exactly inviting; the water, however, is salty enough to make brave swimmers much more buoyant. Irrigation runoff has stabilized the Salton Sea at roughly its present 500-square-mile-size, but it's still a strange sight—a mirage that turns out to be real.

There's very little to look for along the shores, apart from a couple of desiccated campgrounds and trailer parks. If you want to explore a little, make your way along Hwy-111, through the flyspeck towns of Thermal and Mecca, down to **Niland** on the far east shore. Three miles east of town, at the far end of Main Street, you'll come to another strange place: Slab City, an itinerant RV community (see special topic).

South of the Salton Sea, Hwy-86 runs across the low, dry lands of the agricultural Imperial Valley, rambling through a series of dusty towns such as Brawley and El Centro, before hitting the Mexican border at Calexico, the U.S. equivalent of Mexico's much larger Mexicali. There's little to stop and see, but a couple of detours—west to Anza Borrego Desert State Park or east to the magical sands of the Algodones Dunes—are worth the trip (if you're here in spring, that is. In summer, it's hotter than blazes, and anyone with a choice is somewhere far away).

The **National Date Festival,** part of the Riverside County Fair, is held in Indio every February and features many unique pleasures, from camel racing to date milk shakes. For dates (of the calendar variety) and details, call 760/347-0676.

Dates make excellent in-car treats: no mess (apart from the pit), no wrappers, and they're moist and sweet and totally fat-free. Date stands up and down the Coachella Valley sell them by the pound, but some of the very best come through the mail from Howard's Choice (888/765-7667).

If you want to cruise the desert in true *Easy Rider* style (and have a valid motorcycle license), rent a Harley-Davidson from **Route 66 Harley Rental** (800/567-HAWG or 800/567-4294), off I-10 at Indian Canyon Road.

For a break from the usually searing heat of the desert, climb up west from Anza Borrego on Hwy-78 into the dense pine forests that surround the historic town of **Julian.** Along with a quaint Main Street, Julian also has another famous attraction: **apple pie,** available at places including the Julian Pie Company and the essential Mom's Pie's, 2119 Main Street.

Detour: Anza Borrego State Park

The largest state park in California, covering some 600,000 acres between the Salton Sea and the Southern California mountains, Anza-Borrego State Park protects a huge expanse of semi-wild desert in all its natural inhospitality. Named for both Spanish trailblazer Juan Bautista de Anza, who passed through on his way from Mexico to found San Francisco in 1774 and the native Bighorn sheep (*borregos*), the park revolves around the town of Borrego Springs (pop. 2,244), 30 miles west of the Salton Sea via County Road S-22.

Areas of historical and scenic interest, some accessible only via rough backcountry roads, are spread all around the park. Everything is at its best during the spring wildflower season. Find out about the status of the ocotillos, poppies, and other blooms by calling the wildflower hotline (760/767-4684); find out about everthing else the park has to offer from the visi-

SLAB CITY AND SALVATION MOUNTAIN

Points of interest around the Salton Sea are few and far between, but one must-see spot—especially for anyone interested in the more distant corners of the American psyche—is Slab City, also known as "The Slabs," an itinerant community of desert dwellers, three miles east of Niland via Main Street. Since the late 1950s, as many as 6,000 RV-driving squatters have been settling here, mainly for the winter months. There's no water and no electricity—just 640 acres of flat concrete slabs (hence the name), left over from a WWII-era U.S. Navy base—but there is a makeshift golf course, a pipe that delivers hot-springs water for alfresco showers, and a feisty population of leave-us-aloners.

Marking the main entrance to Slab City is Salvation Mountain, an eye-catching work of art painted on a series of hillsides by 70-odd-year-old Leonard Knight, who's been hard at work for 15 years. Knight lives on-site and often hands out free postcards of his three-story-tall icon, which is capped by a cross and the words "God is Love."

tors center (daily 9 AM-5 PM; $5 per car; 760/767-4205), on Palm Canyon Drive. Then head two miles north to Palm Canyon, where a two-mile trail leads to a lush green oasis. Accommodations range from a popular campground at Palm Canyon (reserve through ParkNet, 800/444-7275) to more luxurious Borrego Springs resorts such as **La Casa del Zorro**, 3845 Yaqui Pass Road (800/824-1884)

Detour: Algodones Dunes

A different sort of desert experience can be had at the Algodones Dunes, stretching south of Hwy-78 at the east edge of the Imperial Valley. Sahara-like expanses of sand—40 miles long and upward of 300 feet tall—are regularly overrun by all manner of dune buggies and off-road vehicles—two-, three-, and four-wheel-drives, some jacked up five to 10 feet in the air, riding high on massive tires. This is one the biggest and most popular off-road areas in the country, drawing people from all over Southern California as well as Arizona and Las Vegas, creating a surreal spectacle straight out of a Mad Max movie.

"Readily accessible from anywhere," according to their advertising copy, the very large and very friendly **Fountain of Youth Spa** (760/354-1340) is located on the eastern shore of the Salton Sea, midway along Hwy-11 at Hot Mineral Springs Road. Since the 1950s, RVers by the hundred have been wintering here, enjoying the healing waters as well as casual restaurants, massage treatments, horseshoe tournaments, and Sunday-night talent shows. Sites with full hookups go for $25/night, $140/week (discounts for longer stays).

The Algodones Dunes, also known as the Imperial Dunes, cover nearly a thousand square miles and were formed from a remnant shore of what's now the Sea of Cortez. Fortunately for those of a contemplative disposition, the dune buggy crowd has dominion only over the southern half of the dunes; in 1994, thanks to the same Desert Protection Act that established the Mojave National Preserve, the northern expanses were set aside as the 32,000-acre **North Algodones Dunes Wilderness,** which is administered by the local Bureau of Land Management office (760/337-4400). For information on anything to do in the dunes, from dune buggying to barefoot backpacking, stop by the Glamis Beach Store, the area's informal headquarters, right on Hwy-78 at the heart of the dunes. The main access to the wilderness is via the two-mile road that leads north from the Glamis Beach Store to a small parking area.

El Centro, at the heart of the Imperial Valley, marks the spot where old US-99 crosses the I-8 freeway and our east-west route along old US-80, which is described beginning on page 322.

HIGH SIERRA AND DEATH VALLEY: US-395

HIGH SIERRA AND DEATH VALLEY: US-395

Though it doesn't look like much on a map, or ring any bells with most travelers, the route between Reno and Los Angeles along US-395 takes in some of the greatest extremes in the lower 48 states, including the highest point (Mt. Whitney), the hottest place (Death Valley), the hottest hot springs (Hot Creek, near Mammoth Lakes), the southernmost glacier (Palisade Glacier), the ghostliest ghost town (Bodie, a state historical park north of Mono Lake), and the oldest living things on earth (the White Mountains's ancient bristlecone pine trees). The route also takes you to some of the lowest points: not only the geographical one (Badwater in Death Valley, at 282 feet below sea level is the lowest point in the U.S.), but historical ones as well, such as Manzanar National Monument, deserted remains of the internment camp where 10,000 Japanese-Americans were imprisoned during WWII, and the still-controversial Los Angeles Aqueduct, which effectively (if not always legally) siphons off the water supply of a quarter of California to satisfy the needs of that ever-growing metropolis.

Hyperbole aside, the road itself is truly amazing, running through undeveloped forest, rangeland, and desert at the foot of one sharply serrated mountain range after another. At the heart of the route, through the Owens Valley, US-395 is bordered by the two highest ranges west of the Rockies, rising up in snow-capped splendor on either side of the road, and beckoning anyone with a sense of adventure to turn off and explore the millions of acres of roadless wilderness that covers the High Sierra crest.

Starting at the top, north of Reno, our route begins in the Black Rock Desert of northwest Nevada on Hwy-445/447—one of the loneliest places on the planet, so flat and wide open that racers come here to set land speed records. From here, driving south around the shores of Pyramid Lake, is Reno, the "Biggest Little City in the World," according to the welcome sign that has stood there since the days when Reno was the Las Vegas of its day. High up in the mountains south of Reno sits one of the most significant old towns of the Wild West: Virginia City, where the biggest mining boom in American history, the Comstock Lode of the 1860s, created the wealth that built San Francisco, and where a young journalist who came to be known as Mark Twain made his name.

Next stop to the south is Carson City, quiet capital of the Silver State, beyond which US-395 soon drifts into California. Along this 100-mile stretch of US-395, so many side roads climb over 10,000-foot-high mountain passes—bound for Lake Tahoe, numerous wilderness areas, and the backcountry of Yosemite National Park—that you could spend a summer exploring the region without retracing your steps. Tioga Pass Road, the breathtaking route to Yosemite, is the last trans-Sierra pass for 200 miles, but from this pass south many other roads climb up to campgrounds and trailheads high in the mountains, bringing some of the wildest areas in the West within a day's hike from the end of the road.

From the foot of Tioga Pass, US-395 runs past the lunar-looking volcanic landscape around Mono Lake, and continues south past the eastern Sierra Nevada's only real resort area, Mammoth Lakes. Though home to the state's largest ski area, and some of its most

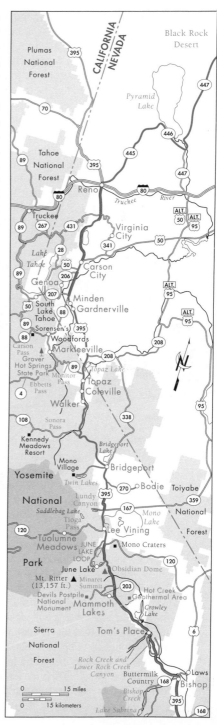

popular spots for fishing and mountain biking, even here the backcountry wilderness is close at hand. Access to outdoor recreation is the order of the day here and at the largest town we pass through on US-395, mighty Bishop, at the north end of the Owens Valley. The biggest city between Nevada and Los Angeles—pop. 8,000 —Bishop marks the start of the route through the Owens Valley, a long narrow cleft cutting between the High Sierra and the White Mountains to the east. Both ranges reach to over 14,000 feet, but apart from that have little in common: the High Sierra range is dotted with glacial lakes and alpine meadows, while the Whites are the desiccated home of gnarled, bristlecone pines, the oldest living things on earth.

South and east of the White Mountains stretches the only place in the world that makes them seem hospitable: Death Valley, the hottest, driest, and most desolate place imaginable. The spare beauty of the sun-baked geology of Death Valley more than makes up for its apparent lack of vitality, with miles and miles of expansive sand dunes, multi-colored hillsides covered in mineral-tinged rainbows, and sunsets and starry nights that make the long, hot days more than worthwhile.

Virginia Street, Looking South, Reno, Nevada

Reno's famous arch, which spans Virginia Street at 3rd Street downtown, was first erected in 1926 to mark the Lincoln Highway route through town. The current arch, the fourth to stand on the site, was built in 1987.

Reno

Short of spending time in Las Vegas, nothing heightens the contrast between natural and manmade Nevada than a stop in Reno, "The Biggest Little City in the World," as the bold archway over Virginia Street downtown proclaims. An ancient city by Nevada standards, dating back to pioneer days (the Donner Party camped here on their ill-fated way west), Reno first came to national prominence in the 1930s as a center for quickie divorces, and now has all the gambling of its larger sibling, Las Vegas, but with a pleasantly homey, settled-down feel.

Besides taking advantage of Reno's cheap hotel rooms and 24-hour casino-fueled fun, you should also pay homage to the seductive device that makes it all possible: the slot machine. Though it's not exactly a museum, the **Liberty Belle Casino**, near the Convention Center at 4250 S. Virginia Street (775/825-1776) tells the whole story of automated gambling, starting with the invention of the three-reel slot machine by immigrant Charlie Fey in San Francisco in 1885. (Fey's descendants now own the Liberty Belle.) Walk through the brass doors (salvaged from ruins of San Francisco's luxurious Palace Hotel, which was destroyed in the 1906 earthquake), and wander around the many old slot machines, fortune-telling machines, and penny arcade movies. Car culture fans will want to visit the $10 million, 100,000-square foot **National Automobile Museum**, on the south bank of the Truckee River at 10 S. Lake Street (Mon.-Sat. 9:30 AM-5:30 PM, Sunday 10 AM-4 PM; $7.50; 775/333-9300), perhaps the best and probably the most extensive car collection in the country. Styled like a classic late-1940s Chrysler, the very cool building displays just about every cool car you've ever heard of, and more, mostly in stage-set "streets" that provid evocative period background; there's a great gift shop, too. Don't forget to check out Reno's other national attraction: the **National Bowling Stadium**, a state-of-the-art 80-lane extravaganza, at Center and 4th Streets.

Reno Practicalities

Reno is located at the eastern foot of the Sierra Nevada mountains, on I-80 about 35 miles northeast of Lake Tahoe, and 30 miles north of the state capital, Carson City. The Reno airport often has cheap flights, thanks to Southwest Airlines in particular; it's the closest main airport to Lake Tahoe and handles flights from all over the western U.S. Shuttles into town cost a pittance (around $3), and all the usual rental car companies have airport offices.

Like anywhere in Nevada, getting **married** in Reno is easy: all you need is to be at least 18 years old (and not already married to someone else!). No blood tests, no waiting period—just a $35 fee for a license, payable at the Washoe County Courthouse, on Virginia Street just south of the river (daily 8 AM–midnight; 775/328-3275). To get **divorced**, however, you need to reside in Nevada for at least six weeks.

Like its brasher sibling to the south, Reno has a huge variety of rooms, nearly 25,000 of them, from spartan motels to sky's-the-limit resort hotels. The standard-bearer for Reno is **Harrah's**, 219 N. Center (775/788-3773 or 800/648-3773), with top-end rooms running from $100 and up. On the north edge of downtown, **Circus Circus**, at 500 N. Sierra Street (775/329-0711 or 800/648-5010), offers the cheapest big casino rooms—$25-a-night weekday specials. There are also tons of chain and local motels, plus the exotic **Adventure Inn**, 3575 S. Virginia Street (775/828-9000), where the honeymoon-ready rooms are all decorated with different themes: Jungle Room, Roman Room, Cave Room, Bordello Room, Tropical Room, ad nauseam.

Reno's casinos have a good selection of that Nevada specialty, the all-you-can-eat buffet. Our intrepid critic Deke Castleman (Reno resident and author of the dollar-and sense-saving *Nevada Handbook*) says the **Atlantis**, 3800 S. Virginia Street (775/825-4700) is the best. Another worthwhile local specialty is Basque cuisine, a reminder of the historical role of Basque sheepherders working on ranches all over Nevada's Great Basin. **Louis's Basque Corner**, 301 E. 4th Street (775/323-7203), serves some of the biggest and best meals you'll have anywhere—main dishes of lamb or other meat, joined by hearty soups, salads, french fries, and other goodies, all served up family style at big communal tables. Just down the street is another Basque winner, the **Santa Fe Hotel**, 235 Lake Street (775/323-1891), in business since 1949.

For more information, or for tips on midweek accommodation deals at a dozen or more casinos, contact the Reno **visitors bureau**, 4590 S. Virginia Street (775/827-7366 or 800/367-7366).

Though US-395 starts in the north up at the Canadian border, our trip starts at Reno and follows US-395 south to Los Angeles. The southern half of US-395 is a lovely drive and is covered in detail; the northern half is nice enough, but not nearly as feature-packed. North from Reno, the highway edges west into California, winding across the rim of the Great Basin along the eastern foot of the Sierra and Cascade mountain ranges.

Heading North: Pyramid Lake and the Black Rock Desert

Northeast of Reno, beyond ever-expanding suburbs, Pyramid Lake is an astounding sight: a big blue mirage that turns out to be the real thing. A triangular tufa formation rising out of the waters inspired John C. Frémont to name the lake back in 1844; nowadays this "pyramid" is even taller than it was then, since the level of the lake has dropped considerably, thanks to agricultural diversions. The Truckee River, which originates as

an outflow from alpine Lake Tahoe, ends its mountain ramblings in the waters of Pyramid Lake—the two lakes could hardly be more different, and each is unforgettable. The sight of Pyramid Lake is definitely worth the thirty-mile drive north from Reno on Hwy-445/447.

Continuing north from the eastern shore of Pyramid Lake, scenic Hwy-447 runs across a series of bone-dry lake beds toward **Gerlach**. Home to a huge Sheetrock factory, five bars, and at least one gas station, Gerlach (pop. 100 or so), "Where the Pavement Ends and the West Begins," is gateway to the moody and expansive Black Rock Desert. Best known in most circles as the location for the rocket-powered land speed record efforts of Richard "Thrust" Noble and Craig "Spirit of America" Breedlove, the million-acre Black Rock Desert is also the site of the annual post-bohemian Labor Day BBQ known as **Burning Man**.

Virginia City

In 1859, prospectors following the gold deposits up the slopes of Mt. Davidson discovered one of the richest strikes in world history: the **Comstock Lode**. Almost overnight, the bustling camp of Virginia City, high up in the mountains between present-day Reno and Carson City, grew into the largest settlement between Chicago and San Francisco, and over the next 20 years nearly a billion dollars in gold and silver (in 19th-century money!) was grubbed from deep underground. Afterward the town very nearly dried up and blew away, but thanks in part to the 1960s TV show *Bonanza*, in which Hoss and company were always heading over to Virginia City for supplies or to fetch the sheriff, tourists discovered the town and gave it a new lease on life.

These days Virginia City (pop. 1,500; elev. 6,220 feet) is both a tacky tourist trap and one of the most satisfying destinations in the state. Ten miles south of Reno via US-395, then east up scenic Hwy-341 over 6,799-foot Geiger Summit, or eight

The Castle, Virginia City's elegant 1868 mansion, was built by the superintendent of the Empire Mine.

miles via a very steep (grades in excess of 15%) drive up Hwy-341 from Carson City, Virginia City has an old main drag, C Street, that is packed with dozens of hokey but enjoyable attractions—like the amiable **Bucket of Blood Saloon**, which offers a panoramic view over the surrounding mountains. The streets above and below—and I do mean above and below: the town clings to such a steep slope that C Street is a good three stories higher than neighboring D Street—hold some of the most authentic sites. B Street, for example, has the elegant **Castle**, Nevada's premier mansion, with all the original furnishings and fittings, a block south of the ornate Victorian **Storey County Courthouse** and the landmark **Piper's Opera House**. Down the hill on D Street was once a more raucous quarter, where brothels and opium dens shared space with railroad tracks, cemeteries, and the mines themselves, such as Gold & Curry, Ophir, and Consolidated Virginia.

Before or after a wander around town, be sure to visit the excellent museum on the ground floor of the **Fourth Ward School** (daily 10 AM-5 PM, May-Nov.; $2), the Victorian gothic landmark at the south end of C Street. Exhibits inside recount the lively history of Virginia City, from mining technology to Mark Twain, who made his start as a journalist at Virginia City's *Territorial Enterprise*. An intact classroom is preserved as it was in 1936 when the last class graduated. Another not-to-be-missed spot is the **Red Light Museum** (daily 11 AM- 5 PM; $1), in the basement of the Julia C. Bulette Saloon on C and Union Streets, which displays an amazing barrage of antique condoms, pornographic postcards, opium pipes, and other sexually explicit oddities, impossible to describe.

In 1861, Orion Clemens was appointed secretary to the governor of what was then known as the Nevada Territory, and his younger brother Sam came with him to Nevada. Sam submitted dispatches of his mining and travel adventures around the territory to Virginia City's largest daily newspaper, the *Territorial Enterprise*. Sam eventually accepted a reporter's position on the newspaper and began perfecting his unique brand of Western frontier humor under the pen name **Mark Twain.**

Unless you're tempted by the many places to eat hot dogs and drink sarsaparilla along C Street, food options in Virginia City are very limited, though the **Brass Rail** and the **Delta Saloon** are both above par. The **Chollar Mansion B&B**, 565 D Street (775/847-9777) is a characterful place to stay, with three rooms in an old (circa 1861) mine-owner's mansion.

To get your bearings, stop by the historic railroad car that now houses the **Virginia City Chamber of Commerce** (775/847-0311); it's parked at the south end of C Street, between the Firehouse Museum and Wagon Wheel restaurant.

Carson City

Nevada's state capital and third largest city, Carson City (pop. 40,443) was named in honor of Wild West explorer Kit Carson. Nestled at the base of the sheer eastern scarp of the Sierra Nevada, the city was founded in 1858—a year before the discovery of the Comstock Lode riches, and six years before Nevada became a state.

Carson City is a hard place to characterize. Considering it's the capital, life is rather slow, with the main buzz being a few casinos. The **Carson Nugget** at 507 N. Carson Street (775/882-1626) on the main US-50/395 route through town, has a million-dollar collection of raw, unprocessed gold on display, along with

roulette, craps, and blackjack tables and the usual army of old ladies feeding banks of slot machines.

Gambling aside, the one place to stop in Carson City is the excellent **Nevada State Museum** (daily 8:30 AM-4:30 PM; $3; 775/687-4810), at 600 N. Carson Street, near the stately capitol—and cater-corner from the Nugget. Housed inside the solid old U.S. Mint building, built in 1870 to make coins from Comstock silver, are displays on mining (including a full-scale mock-up of a working mine), as well as displays describing the natural history of Nevada and the Great Basin. Also worth a look are the Stewart Indian Museum and the Nevada State Railroad Museum. The **Stewart Indian Museum** (daily 9 AM-5:30 PM; donations; 775/882-1808), offers displays of Native American artifacts and a great collection of Edward Curtis's anthropological photography. The museum is located on the former campus of a Bureau of Indian Affairs school, off US-395 south of town at 5366 Snyder Avenue. Also of note are the old Virginia & Truckee steam engines on display at the **Nevada State Railroad Museum**, farther south along US-50/395.

Good Mexican meals are the order of the day at **El Charro Avitia**, south of town at 4389 S. Carson Street, and the specials at the **Carson Nugget** can be incredibly cheap ($2 steak sandwiches). However, the best and most expensive fare is served at **Adele's**, where power brokers broker their power at 1112 N. Carson Street (775/882-3353). Motels line Carson Street north and south of the capitol; try the classic 1950s-style **Frontier** at 1718 N. Carson (775/882-1377), the **Motel Orleans** at 2731 S. Carson (775/882-2007), or **Motel 6** at 2749 S. Carson (775/885-7710).

For more complete visitor information, contact the **Carson City Convention and Visitors Bureau**, 1900 S. Carson Street (800/638-2321).

Carson City marks the junction between US-395 and our east-west trip along US-50, the "Loneliest Road in America." For details on the US-50 trip, see page 230.

Detour: Genoa

Just south of Carson City, at the foot of the Kingsbury Grade, a delightful little detour off US-395 takes you through Genoa, the oldest city in Nevada. In 1851 Mormon settlers chose this bucolic spot, where the Carson River meanders along the foothills of the Sierra Nevada, to build an outpost known as Mormon Station. The ranching and trading post settlement prospered, and was soon renamed Genoa (pronounced "Juh-NO-ah" by locals) for its mountain backdrop, which reminded one settler of mountains near the famous Italian port city. Brigham Young undercut the outpost's fortunes by recalling all Mormon settlers to Salt Lake City during a crisis with the U.S. Army in 1857, and though the town hosted Nevada's first territorial legislature in 1859, the Comstock mining frenzy to the north stole its financial thunder, much as Carson City did its political aspirations. US-395, which bypassed Genoa and instead went through nearby Minden and Gardnerville, stole its traffic. For more than a century, Genoa seemed doomed to have a backwater role; for better or worse, however, the 1990s brought a population boom to the Carson Valley, with a new breed of suburban settler who values the town's backwater status at a premium. For the moment, Genoa still retains its rural frontier feel, though new houses (tastefully old-looking, but clearly new) for Carson City commuters have been springing up in and around the historic downtown.

At the center of town is **Mormon Station State Park** (daily 10 AM-5 PM; 775/782-2590), which has a small museum and a stockade dating back to the 1850s. At Main and 5th Streets, the **Genoa Courthouse Museum** (daily 10 AM-4:30 PM; donations; 775/ 782-4325) has more comprehensive displays of historical items—everything from Native American baskets to the keys of the old jail, with an especially interesting exhibition on Wild West legend John A. "Snowshoe" Thompson, who carried the mail over the mountains between Genoa and Sacramento. The museum also offers a little tidbit on mining engineer and native son George Ferris, who designed and built the first of his namesake Ferris wheels for the 1893 World's Fair in Chicago.

A mile south of town via Foothill Road, Genoa's other great attraction is **Walley's Hot Springs** (775/782-8155), a modern resort hotel complex built around natural 160° F hot springs. Another nice place to stay is the **Genoa House Inn,** 180 Nixon Street (775/782-7075), a quaint historical B&B. Thriving on the tourism Genoa's charm generates, there are also some good shops and restaurants around town.

To get to Genoa from Carson City, turn off US-395 south of the US-50 junction onto Jack's Valley Road (Hwy-206), and follow that for 12 miles. From Stateline and Lake Tahoe, go east on Hwy-207, the very steep Kingsbury Grade (and also the most direct route between Carson City and Lake Tahoe), then turn north on Hwy-206.

Minden and Gardnerville

East of Genoa, Minden and Gardnerville, a seamless pair of Carson River Valley agricultural towns, straddle US-395 for miles. Though pleasant enough places, and famous for their Basque restaurants, both towns are suffering the effects of suburban sprawl disease, which is affecting the Carson Valley in the same ways it does many other fine places of once-distinctive character and vigorous mien—leaving them looking strung out, bloated, and disfigured by fast-food joints. By ducking west from the main drag (US-395) in Minden, however, you can still find Minden's fine grassy square, fronted by pleasant houses. Along Esmerelda Street, there's even a small, untouched piece of the old town: across from the Minden Hotel, the gas pumps of an ancient-looking Union 76 station still sit right out on the sidewalk. Around the corner, back on US-395, stop for food and drink at the popular **Pony Express Cafe.**

Continuing south along US-395, the more dynamic center of Gardnerville harbors **Sharkey's Nugget** (775/782-3133), a homespun, family-owned and -operated

The **Genoa Bar,** a block south of the courthouse at 2282 Foothill Road, is the oldest licensed premises in the state, in operation since 1863.

In Genoa's evocative cemetery, just north of town, look for the headstone (it's carved with crossed skis) of **John "Snowshoe" Thompson,** probably the nation's most heroic early mail carrier. For 20 winters, starting in January 1856, this tough Norwegian carried the mail 100 miles between Genoa and Placerville over the snow-bound Sierras. Taking as long as a week in each direction, using homemade skis and carrying 50 to 80 pounds of mail on his back, he never postponed his journey for storms or blizzards, and never lost his way. Thompson received scant remuneration for his services, performing the work largely for the sheer adventure of it.

casino and restaurant that's one of the more surreal sights in this often odd state. A sign outside advertises "Harley-Davidson and Other Bikers Welcome"—inside, the flashy decor of the standard modern casino is turned topsy-turvy in favor of a wonderfully eclectic collection of Western art (Cowboys and Indians aplenty), and more boxing memorabilia than you could possibly take in. (The boxing connection comes from the owner and founder, Milos "Sharkey" Begovich, whose nickname was borrowed from the 1932 World Heavyweight Boxing Champion, Jack Sharkey.) The Begovich family has been in the hospitality trade for parts of the past three centuries, and you'll definitely feel welcome here. They don't have rooms, but they do have a 24-hour coffee shop and some of the best prime rib dinners you'll ever have the chance to eat.

Across from Sharkey's on US-395 is one of Nevada's great Basque places, the **Overland Hotel**, 691 Main Street (775/782-2138), which is famous for massive portions of family-style food.

Hwy-88: Carson Pass

California's Alpine County, with only 1,200 residents, is one of the least populated of any county in the nation; it also has to rate among the most unspoiled and beautiful places on the planet. South of Lake Tahoe, adjoining Nevada and bisected by Hwy-88, this largely volcanic part of the Sierra Nevada is extraordinarily colorful, with reddish and black mountains patched with snow, green forests and meadows ablaze with wildflowers in spring and early summer; in fall the cottonwood and aspen leaves flame up in yellow.

Heading due south from Genoa, connected by a short spur from Gardnerville and US-395, Hwy-88 climbs west past the historic crossroads of Woodfords, up the rugged canyon of the West Carson River to the sudden lushness of Hope Valley. The name "Hope Valley," bestowed by Mormons in 1848, inspired later surveyors to christen the adjacent valleys as Faith and Charity. Along the highway at the heart of Hope Valley stands **Sorensen's**, 14255 Highway 88; 530/694-2203 or 800/423-9949), a wonderfully rustic (and surprisingly low-priced) getaway. Founded in 1926, this family-run four-season resort comes complete with cozy log cabins, a sauna, and a fine little restaurant.

Kit Carson and John C. Frémont crossed over the ridge west of Hope Valley—a saddle later called Carson Pass—in February of 1844. Battling deep snows and having scant supplies, Frémont climbed at least part way up Red Lake Peak, north of Carson Pass, to get his bearings. It was there that he became the first non-Native American to see Lake Tahoe. Today the saddle is marked by a pair of monuments commemorating "Snowshoe" Thompson and Kit Carson. Hikers can access a short and fairly level trail from behind the small Carson Pass **visitors center** (summer only; 209/258-8606) up to idyllic Frog Lake, and continue on to Winnemucca Lake, an easy jaunt (two miles each way) featuring copious summer wildflowers and rolling views of the volcanic valleys westward to Caples Lake.

Hwy-88 continues west from Carson Pass to the ski resort at Kirkwood, which receives some of the deepest snowfall of any spot in the Sierra Nevada and sometimes in the whole U.S., but the highway is kept open throughout the winter. Hwy-88 then passes through the resort community at Silver Lake and makes its way through the broad forest belt of the west slope of the Sierra Nevada range down to the Gold Country foothills. One of the highlights of this area is the hamlet of **Volcano**, which lies north of Hwy-88, some 15 miles east of the town of Jackson. Though now home to only about 100 people, Volcano once had dozens of hotels and dozens more saloons; all that's left for visitors today is the evocative old St. George Hotel (209/296-4458), which dates from 1862. The bar here is a venerable institution in its own right, the B&B rooms aren't expensive, and the food is plenty good.

From Volcano, you can head back to Hwy-88 and follow it down to Jackson, or wind along a much more scenic back road down to Sutter Creek.

Between Volcano and Jackson, be sure to stop at **Indian Grinding Rock State Historic Park** (daily 10 AM-4 PM; $5 per car; 209/296-7488), which has a ceremonial roundhouse, some cedar bark dwellings, one of the finest Native American museums in California, and a huge, flat stone slab peppered with over a thousand acorn-grinding mortar recesses. In spring, make your way from Volcano to the well-signed garden known as **Daffodil Hill**, where more than 300,000 bulbs bloom from mid-March to mid-April.

Markleeville: Grover Hot Springs

The drive along US-395 between Gardnerville and the California border is not especially thrilling, but a nearby detour definitely is. Head south from Gardnerville along Hwy-88, then cut off at Woodfords onto Hwy-89 to the Alpine County seat of Markleeville (pop. 165, elev. 5,525 feet), whose block-long main street contains a U.S. Forest Service **ranger station** (530/694-2911) and the venerable **Alpine Hotel** (530/694-2150), a century-old former inn offering full meals at the Alpine Restaurant, and the wonderfully rough-hewn watering hole called the Cutthroat Saloon. The town's two stores and deli are noteworthy landmarks in this sparsely settled country, as is the intimate **Villa Gigli**, west of town at 145 Hot Springs Road (530/694-2253), where all the pastas, sauces, breads—everything except the wines and cheeses—is cooked up fresh daily by Tuscany native Ruggero Gigli and his wife, who live next door. It's very popular, drawing fans from Lake Tahoe and Carson City, so book as early as you can to avoid disappointment.

In their trek across the Sierra Nevada, Pony Express riders followed the Carson River up West Carson Canyon, where the historic **Woodfords Store** at the Hwy-88/89 junction was once the local remount station. The store still serves travelers.

Markleeville's other main attention grabber is **Grover Hot Springs State Park** (hours vary; 530/694-2248), four miles west of town at the end of Hot Springs Road, where springs naturally heated to 148°F trickle from a grassy bank above wide meadows, heating two swimming pools. It's a little too institutional-feeling to be perfect (the pools are concrete, and bathing suits are required), but on a cool spring or autumn day, it's hard to beat the feeling of relaxing in hot water while soaking up the High Sierra views. There's a nearby campground, too, with showers but no hookups.

South of Markleeville, Hwy-89 continues on its stunning way, rejoining US-395 on the California side of the border, 27 miles south of Gardnerville. The beautiful drive along Hwy-89 is even more scenic traveling in the opposite direction, coming north from Topaz Lake and the junction with US-395. The incline of Hwy-89, west from Slinkard Valley to 8,314-foot Monitor Pass is rated by many road warriors as one of the most spectacular two-lane roads through the Sierra, for it clings close to the edge of the slope and just keeps rising to view upon view of mountains and desert.

One of the biggest events of Markleeville's year is the summer **Death Ride,** a grueling 128-mile bicycle marathon that starts at Turtle Rock Park, just north of town, and negotiates Carson, Ebbetts and Monitor Passes—a net gain of 15,000 feet—before finishing back in town. There are shorter versions of the ride suitable for mere mortals, phone the Markleeville chamber of commerce (530/694-2475) for dates and details.

Topaz Lake

The high desert reservoir of Topaz Lake, impounding the waters of the Walker River, straddles the Nevada-California border, and thereby ensuring that it would become a first-and-last chance gambling center for border-crossers. It's fairly low-key affair, and the setting is a million times more scenic than any of the big gambling towns; the 24-hour **Topaz Lake Lodge** (775/266-3338 or 800/962-0732) has a nice cafe, a lake-view bar, $45-a-night rooms, and an RV park.

From Topaz Lake south to Little Lake, US-395 is an official National Scenic Byway.

Crossing into California and continuing south from Topaz Lake, US-395 soon crosses scenic Hwy-89, which runs west and north over a series of High Sierra passes—following the crest all the way to distant Mt. Lassen, eventually.

Hwy-4/89: Monitor Pass and Ebbetts Pass

Pressing right against the foothills of the Carson Range, US-395 is intersected by yet another scenic detour, Hwy-89, which cuts a sharp right angle west into the canyon of Slinkard Creek. After twisting through the close quarters of the gorge, the road emerges in the high, dry sagebrush-covered Slinkard Valley, so broad and open that it distorts perspective, and makes the mountains seem closer than they are. From the crest of 8,314-foot Monitor Pass, we follow Monitor Creek through the highlands, with stupendous views westward of jumbled Raymond Peak (10,011 feet) and other summits of the Carson Range. Descending to the canyon of the East Fork Carson River, you have a choice: continue north along Hwy-89 to go to Markleeville (see above for details), or go west along wonderful Hwy-4, over Ebbetts Pass.

Ebbetts Pass is the least utilitarian of trans-Sierra highways, since it doesn't connect with any settlement on the eastern side, save for tiny Markleeville, which is better served by Hwy-88 over Carson Pass. Consequently, Hwy-4 closes in winter, receives only moderate usage during summer, and even then occasionally narrows to a single, though wide, paved and perfectly adequate lane. Meeting the Pacific Crest Trail at the 8,732-foot pass, park for a spell to sample either or both of two superb, early summer wildflower walks that lead north or south along that famous trail.

West of Ebbetts Pass, Hwy-4 winds through remote Hermit Valley, in the Mokelumne River drainage, where a handful of summer cabins stand on leased U.S. Forest Service land, surrounded by wilderness. From there, Hwy-4 humps over the next ridge, an 8,000-foot saddle known as Pacific Grade Summit, then drops down into the Stanislaus River watershed. Right at the summit lies a lovely reservoir with the unlovely name, Mosquito Lake, banked by rustic cabins amidst the forest.

Hwy-4 then descends to Lake Alpine, a rustic summer resort complete with bar, store and lodging. Though traditionally a fishing resort, **Lake Alpine Lodge** (209/753-6358) now caters to a more diverse clientele, providing boat and mountain bike rentals along with pleasant cabins and an excellent restaurant. Farther down the line, downhill and cross-country skiers from California's Central Valley flock in winter to the lodge and resort at **Bear Valley** (209/753-2327), which has also diversified its offerings with summer hiking and mountain biking, and two music festivals: the High Sierra Music Festival in June features rock and younger bands; in July and August, the Bear Valley Music Festival (800/458-1618) features classical music, jazz and pops.

Next stop along Hwy-4 is the **Calaveras Big Trees State Park,** where, a century ago, the giant sequoia trees were a must-see on any complete California tour. Today owned and managed by the state ($5 per car; 209/795-2334), the park every year welcomes thousands of visitors to hike through the roadside North Grove, where they can visit the Grizzly Giant, gawk at a great stump once used as a dance-hall floor, and enjoy the many other freakishly huge, but totally natural, specimens of nature. Accessible via a five-mile loop hike, the more remote South Grove receives far fewer visitors, though compared to North Grove it contains more sequoias and even larger specimens, including the Agassiz Tree, which is one of the top 10 largest trees in the world.

Though most people come in summer, winter snows make the trees stand out all the more, and if you approach from the west you can snowshoe or cross-country ski to your heart's content. The nice **campground** in the park is open all year; reservations are required in the summer ($16), but in fall and winter the sites are first-come, first-served ($12).

The nearest place to eat is a few miles farther back up Hwy-4 in "Beautiful Downtown Dorrington," where the historic **Dorrington Hotel** (closed Tues. and Wed.; 209/795-5800) serves Italian food in a frilly but friendly dining room; they also have a few B&B rooms available.

Dropping down into the Central Valley from Calaveras Big Trees State Park, Hwy-4 passes the historic Gold Country hamlet of Murphys near the ever-popular Columbia State Historic Park.

Walker River: Topaz, Coleville and Walker

South of the Topaz Lake, US-395 delves along the Walker River, through a land choked with sagebrush, aspens, and pinyon pine, through the ranches of Antelope Valley, and the humble settlements of Topaz and Coleville, both of which have populations in the high dozens (100 and 48, respectively) if the city limits signs are to be believed. A third community, Walker, has three cafes, and stands at the confluence of the Walker River and Lost Cannon Creek. **Lost Cannon Creek** takes its name from an interesting story. In 1844, after dragging a heavy brass howitzer for too many miles from the Missouri River, Capt. John C. Frémont finally decided that it was holding his expedition back in the deep Sierra snows, and decided to abandon it. Despite the place name, however, it's doubtful that Frémont left the cannon in Lost Cannon Canyon, for he entered the Sierra much further north. In any event, the cannon's recovery was never recorded, and its fate remains one of the enduring mysteries of the Sierra Nevada.

Hwy-108: Sonora Pass

The ruggedest paved route across the Sierra Nevada, this highway—the second-highest highway west of Colorado—is so steep, winding, and exposed in places that it almost doesn't seem to have made sense for anyone to build it. More's the reason to enjoy it, however, for it encounters the most striking mountain scenery of any trans-Sierra road, with the possible exception of the Tioga Pass Road (Hwy-120) through Yosemite National Park.

As is often the case with highway construction, the 82-mile-long Sonora Pass route was more the work of boosterism than of logic. Sonora business leaders in

1852, craving some of the lucrative trans-Sierra traffic that was then passing through Placerville, virtually built it with their tongues by sending promoters to the east side of the pass to advertise the advantages of the new Sonora Pass Route. A group of pioneers known as the Duckwall Party decided to give it a try, but after exhausting efforts to pick their route through canyon and cliff, they finally bogged down and had to be rescued by the good citizens of Sonora. The place where the rescue party met up with the pioneers is still called Relief Valley—and is still remote from any paved road. A hiker's paradise, the encompassing Hoover and Emigrant Wilderness Areas run clear to the borders of Yosemite National Park, all three together forming the second largest roadless area in the Sierra Nevada.

The present Sonora Pass route, completed as a toll road in 1864, crosses the crest about eight miles north of the original route. After turning west onto Hwy-108 from US-395, we soon come to the U.S. Marine Corps Mountain Warfare Training Center, a cold-weather military camp. Drive with care, as Marines often train along the road. (They also train in the surrounding wilderness, so don't be too unnerved if your peaceful hike up Silver Creek is interrupted by a platoon in camouflage armed to the teeth.)

The most resplendent scene along the highway might well be the view of 11,755-foot **Tower Peak** over the bosky, green pastures of Leavitt Meadow, seven miles west of US-395 and about nine miles east of Sonora Pass. A trailhead at the Leavitt Meadows campground off Hwy-108 leads to a fairly flat, 3.5 mile leg-stretcher hike across and along the Walker River, offering sublime views south to the Yosemite high-country.

Back on the road, while grinding relentlessly upward on switchbacks, look for pretty Sardine Falls on the south side before topping out at Sonora Pass at 9,625 feet. Sonora Pass marks the northern end of what is commonly called the High Sierra, the largely granitic crest that dramatically crescendos in elevation as it wends southward more than 250 trail miles, at or above the timber line almost all the way, to a final climax at the Mt. Whitney. The Pacific Crest Trail, chugging down from the Carson-Iceberg Wilderness on the north side of the road, cuts across the highway here in a haste to duck back into the Emigrant Wilderness, on the south. Great hiking in either direction.

West from Sonora Pass, the highway begins its relentless fall through mountains that overwrought Victorian guidebook writers might have described as "frowning," though the hearts of true wilderness lovers will smile to behold them. A great base of operations for exploring them afoot or on horseback is **Kennedy Meadows Resort** (209/532-9663), on a short spur road south of Hwy-108. With cabins, campground, pack station, and store, Kennedy Meadows makes a civilized HQ for trips south to Relief Valley and other remote points in the Emigrant Wilderness.

Eleven miles west of Sonora Pass, a prominent sign marks the trailhead for the short walk to the **Columns of the Giants**, a great leg-stretching jaunt right along the road. Like Devils Postpile National Monument, the Columns are a curious geological formation of basalt pickets exposed when glaciers sideswiped a fast-cooled lava flow. An easy, 0.7-mile trail loops from the parking lot to the base of the bluffs. Remnants of the Ice Age glacier are still present, hidden by talus, but felt in the cold breezes that blow through the rocks beneath the Columns. Near the trailhead, the Pigeon Flat campground spreads along the banks of the Stanislaus River.

Continuing its long haul west, Hwy-108 passes several resort communities, before reaching the foothills and the historic Gold Country town of Sonora.

Bridgeport

The classic cowboy town of Bridgeport (pop. 500; elev. 6,645 feet) sits smack in the midst of a huge basin of well-watered meadows, surrounded by silvery, snow-capped mountains. With Bridgeport Lake plainly visible to the north of town, and the jagged Sawtooth Ridge looming above the southwest horizon, Bridgeport is the seat of Mono County (with a delicate Victorian-era courthouse, built in 1880, along US-395 to prove it), and also serves as a supply center for people heading off to enjoy themselves fishing, backpacking, hiking, boating, and hunting.

The tiny town of Bridgeport plays a starring role in one of my all-time favorite movies, *Out of the Past*, a film noir classic starring Robert Mitchum as a former hood trying to start a new life in a new town—running a gas station here in Bridgeport, and falling in love with a nice local girl.

About the only reliable radio signal in the Bridgeport area belongs to **KIBS 97.7FM,** broadcasting modern country.

The historic Victorian **Bridgeport Inn** at 205 Main Street (760/932-7380) has been in operation since 1887. The restaurant offers a nice prime rib, and the bar still entertains its share of genuine cowboys; the Inn also offers a number of charming rooms, which can be quite expensive during peak holidays. A number of nifty old neon-signed motels line US-395 through Bridgeport—all advertising "fish-cleaning facilities"—but these tend to close in winter, and summer rates are higher than you might expect, hovering in the $75-to-$100-a-night range. Try the **Silver Maple Inn**, 310 Main Street (760/932-7383), next to the historic courthouse. Also good for food is the **Hays Street Cafe**, on US-395 at the south end of town.

For food, lodging, and fun, head five miles south of Bridgeport along US-395 to **Virginia Creek Settlement** (760/932-7780), which has a restaurant serving pizzas, steaks, trout and more, plus a variety of cabins and some creekside campsites, all on the site of a former Wild West mining camp known as Dogtown.

Twin Lakes
Of the many excellent trips from Bridgeport into the mountains, none is easier nor more beautiful than the well-signed road to Twin Lakes, which departs from downtown Bridgeport, zigzagging at right angles south and west through the fenced pastures of the Bridgeport Valley, 14 miles to the end of the road. Along the way the road passes several resorts of interest primarily to anglers, but everyone else comes for the hiking and the views of the spectacular Sawtooth Ridge, Yosemite's northern boundary. The best time to come is autumn, when the canyon is inflamed with color—yellowing leaves and the crimson Kokanee salmon which spawn from Upper Twin Lakes into Robinson Creek. Mono Village, at the head of the upper lake, is a major trailhead for backpackers bound for northeastern Yosemite National Park; the rustic **Annett's Mono Village** (closed in winter; 760/932-7071) has cabins ($50-125 a night) and camping (around $11 per night).

Hwy-270: Bodie
One of the largest genuine ghost towns in the West, Bodie was the site of a gold strike by Waterman S. Bodey in 1859. Despite the early boom, the town did not settle into its full stride until 1874, when corporate mining interests moved in, and the settlement turned into a bona fide city of 10,000 people—with a very nasty

reputation. Thanks to a high murder rate, the fruits of drunken gunplay, the "Bad Man from Bodie" achieved widespread notoriety throughout the old West. A story current during the town's heyday claimed that a young girl of a neighboring district, upon learning that her family was moving to Bodie, kneeled down to pray, "Goodbye, God, I'm going to Bodie." (A local booster apparently tried and failed to put a positive spin on the tale, by claiming that what she *really* said was "Good, by God! I'm going to Bodie!")

The big bonanza ended by 1884, but townsfolk continued to work the mines for many years after. Bodie became one of the first fully electrified cities in the world in 1893, when power lines were extended 13 miles from a small hydroelectric plant in Green Creek Canyon. After a 1932 fire burned all but 150 of the town's original 2,000 buildings, Bodie was quickly abandoned. The state of California bought the town in 1962, establishing a Bodie State Historical Park with a mandate for "arrested decay"—which means that natural deterioration of the buildings is repaired, but no improvements or restorations are allowed.

Thanks in part to its back-of-beyond location, and near-total lack of signs of the modern world, Bodie is a haunting place, dramatically ensconced in windswept, sagebrush-covered hills. A thousand stories peer back from the windows of homes and businesses abandoned in a rush, and left as they were. Old calendars and newspapers still decorate walls. An unfinished card game lies on a table. The coffin shop still has coffins. The doors of the old Methodist church stand ajar. Some of the houses are occupied by park rangers, and the Miners Union Hall on Main Street has been opened as a park **museum** (late May-mid-Oct. only, 9:30 AM-5 PM; $2; 760/647-6445), but otherwise, the place is truly a ghost town.

Leaving US-395 about seven miles south of Bridgeport, or 20 miles north of Lee Vining, the Bodie Road (Hwy-270) cuts east on two-lanes of pavement for 10 miles, whereupon it abruptly turns to gravel and dirt. The next three, jouncing miles of washboard road serve to provide a 19th-century cushion around Bodie. All roads in and out of Bodie are closed by winter snows, though the park stays open to welcome what few hearty skiers or snowshoers make the trip.

Between the Bodie turnoff and Lundy Canyon, **Conway Summit** is the highest point along US-395—a whopping 8,138 feet above sea level. Heading south from Conway Summit, the road gives a breathtaking panorama of the Mono Lake basin.

Lundy Canyon

Like many other eastern Sierra canyons, Lundy Canyon is amazing for how quickly it takes you from the sagebrush flats of the Great Basin desert into lush woodland clumps of aspen and pine. Located west of US-395 from the Hwy-167 junction, the place was settled in a flurry in 1879, after William Wasson discovered gold in Lake Canyon, which feeds from the south into Lundy Canyon. Boomtowns sprang up in both canyons—the higher one, called Wasson, to mine the ore, and the lower one, called Lundy, to mill it. Both were remote, hardscrabble places, especially through the long winter months, which did not put a halt to mining operations.

CADILLAC DESERT

From the 1849 Gold Rush to today's IPO millionaires of Silicon Valley, California has long been associated with great fortunes and instant riches, but the source of the state's greatest wealth is not gold or software code but a much more common commodity—water, the control of which has fueled some of the state's bitterest battles. The same story is true throughout the Southwest: however much money changes hands around the gaming tables of Las Vegas, most of the region is utterly bankrupt when it comes to that one essential ingredient—water—without which the entire western Sunbelt would dry up and blow away, leaving behind a ruined civilization fit for Ozymandias.

All of this is a complicated way of saying that most of the major cities of the western U.S.—Phoenix, Tucson, Las Vegas, Los Angeles, San Diego, even San Francisco—are living on borrowed water, if not borrowed time. The natural water supply in these places could not support even a tenth of the current populations, so each of these cities has constructed an elaborate system to bring in water from elsewhere.

As you might expect, the first, the biggest, and the brashest of these water projects ended up in Los Angeles, which blossomed from a dusty town into a maddening metropolis thanks to copious water taken from the Owens Valley, a mere 250 miles away. If you ever saw the movie *Chinatown,* you may be surprised to find out it's as close to a documentary as Hollywood ever gets: in 1913, after years of political machinations and dubious land deals funded by some of the richest and most powerful men in Southern California, the city of Los Angeles, under the direction of **William Mulholland** (for whom Mulholland Drive is named) completed construction of one of the largest and most controversial water projects in American history, the Los Angeles Aqueduct. The aqueduct is an undeniably impressive engineering feat—for example, it delivers over 400 million gallons of water daily, using gravity flow and siphons instead of pumps—but its qualities have been more than overshadowed by its flaws.

Originally conceived as a private enterprise by former L.A. Mayor Fred Eaton, who bought up Owens Valley water rights under the guise of being a cattle rancher, the stealth of its conception exploded into open warfare in the 1920s, when drought struck the Owens Valley and locals dynamited sections of the aqueduct to try to keep the remaining water for themselves. However, by that time Los Angeles had bought up over 90% of the Owens Valley land and almost all of its water, so their battle was lost and Owens Valley was doomed to a life as LA's most distant suburb. For all its significance, the Los Angeles Aqueduct is not much to look at—there's no Hoover Dam or other visibly impressive sign of its power—but it can be seen along US-395, running parallel to the highway from Mono Lake to near Mojave.

One of the few remaining structures at Lundy is the store of the **Lundy Lake Resort** (760/309-0415), whose portals are covered in vines, and whose walls are covered with old photographs. Hikers can climb to the site of Wasson on the remarkable old mining road built in 1881, and which can be seen cutting a sharp diagonal up the south wall, above Lake Lundy reservoir. The 3.4-mile hike gains 1,800 feet, passing ruined mining buildings and equipment above the shore of Crystal Lake and eventually reaching the gated entrance to the May Lundy Mine.

Mono Lake

Filling a huge basin in between towering peaks, Mono Lake has no outlet and is consequently three times saltier than the ocean. (Delightfully buoyant, the waters of Mono Lake will also sting the bejeezus out of your eyes or any cuts exposed to it!) Like Utah's Great Salt Lake, it is the remnant of a much larger prehistoric lake that once covered a vast area of the Great Basin.

Mark Twain was so impressed with Mono Lake, which he called "California's Dead Sea," that he devoted a chapter to it in *Roughing It*. By the mid-20th century, however, Mono Lake was in danger. In its insatiable search for drinking water, the city of Los Angeles tapped Mono Lake's sparkling inlet streams in the early 20th century. Deprived of inflow from four out of five feeder streams, the lake receded and doubled in salinity. Local people and conservationists from near and far feared that Mono Lake would soon become another Owens Lake, which had been siphoned off by Los Angeles, leaving nothing but a huge alkali flat whipped by incessant winds into stinging, blinding dust storms. The campaign to save Mono Lake garnered national attention, and a series of environmental lawsuits eventually pushed Los Angeles to partially relinquish its grip on the inlet streams. Since 1994, the shoreline recession has reversed direction and is once again rising.

The sights of Mono Lake are unique and remarkable. Start at the **Mono Basin Scenic Area Visitors Center** ($2; 760/647-3044), a half-mile north of Lee Vining on US-395. Aside from displays on the lake's geologic history and the life of the

native Kuzedika people, this outstanding U.S. Forest Service facility has an excellent bookstore covering every facet of the entire region. Rangers on duty can recommend many fine places that you will want to visit.

The most popular of natural sights on Mono Lake are the tufa (pronounced "TOO-fa") towers, grotesque, whitish, limestone pinnacles that formed where freshwater springs flowed into the alkaline waters. Exposed by the long-receding shoreline, the best place to see them is the at the **South Tufa** portion of the Mono Lake Tufa State Reserve ($2); to get there, drive six miles south from Lee Vining on US-395 and take the eastbound exit for Hwy-120; drive east on Hwy-120 for about five miles to the South Tufa parking area, on the left side of the road. Aside from a bizarre array of twisted hoodoos, the reserve is famous among birdwatchers for its thousands of California gulls, phalaropes, eared grebes, and other avian travelers along the Pacific Flyway who stop here to rest and pig out on the clouds of brine flies, their pupae, and the trillions of brine shrimp that breed in the lake.

Adjacent Navy Beach is Mono Lake's most popular swimming spot for the human species. This is also the launching spot for self-guided kayak tours of the lake, such as those offered by **Caldera Kayaks** (760/935-4942).

Lee Vining

The friendly crossroads town of Lee Vining—situated along US-395 above Mono Lake, next to the Hwy-120 turnoff to Yosemite —offers lodging, groceries, restaurants, gas, and other amenities. A humble but mighty fine spot to revive the spirits on a warm summer afternoon is **Mono Cones** on the east side of US-395 at the north end of town. Aside from better than usual burgers and shakes, the big draw here are the shaded backyard lawn and tables, a refreshing retreat not only out of the hot sun, but into the 1950s. Another throwback to kinder, gentler times is **Nicely's**, a family-run coffee shop along US-395 at 4th Street (760/647-6477), open for early breakfast (from 6 AM), plus lunch and dinner. For more upscale fare, check out the restored **Mono Inn**, overlooking Mono Lake at 55620 US-395 (760/647-6581), four miles north of Lee Vining. The Inn is owned and managed by Sarah Adams, a granddaughter of Ansel Adams, and many of the great photographer's works are displayed (and for sale) in the adjacent gallery.

To stay the night, try **El Mono Motel** (760/647-6310), which shares premises with the only espresso machine in town, at the Latte Da Cafe.

Hwy-120: Tioga Pass and Tuolumne Meadows

The most continuously hair-raising highway over the Sierra Nevada is Hwy-120 over Tioga Pass, and specifically the 13-mile stretch up Lee Vining Canyon between the junction of US-395 and the 9,945-foot crest. People who drive this official **Lee Vining Canyon National Scenic Byway** uphill from Mono Lake hug the inside wall, and miss the excitement; to fully appreciate it, you have to drive *down* it, steering gingerly twixt center line and the yawning chasm, with a drop as deep as 1,500 feet just below your right front fender.

Scary as it is in places, the Tioga Road is not the test that it was before realignment widened the old one-lane, cliff-hanging road in the early 1960s. Nosiree, compared to that, the present highway, two lanes wide and fenced with a guardrail, is a piece of cake.

The native **Kuzedika** people were a sub-tribe of the wide-ranging Paiute. The Kuzedika dwelled along Mono Lake's shores and were known to white settlers as the Mono Indians. "Mono" is a corruption of *Monache*, the name that the Yokut people, trading partners from the west slope of the Sierra Nevada, used to refer to the Kuzedika. *Monache* means "fly-eaters," and refers to the culinary delicacy and highly valued article of trade that the Kuzedika harvested in Mono Lake: the pupae of the alkali fly. Shelled and dried, they were a surprisingly nutritious (and reputedly tasty) food, as early pioneer travelers themselves attested.

Along US-395, some three miles north of Lee Vining, the **High Sierra Shrimp Plant** packages the other life form that thrives in the Mono Lake's salty waters—brine shrimp—for use as fish food.

South of Mono Lake, near South Tufa State Reserve, a fascinating trail climbs to the pumice rim of **Panum Crater** and circumnavigates it in full view of the towering Sierra Crest, which marches north and south like a snow-capped wall. This northern bulwark of the Mono Craters, America's youngest mountain range, last erupted about 600 years ago, plugging up the center of the crater with an obsidian dome.

Ten miles east of US-395, near the top of Tioga Pass, a 2.5-mile gravel road departs north to **Saddlebag Lake**, an angler's resort. This friendly place serves up simple meals and fine conversation at a snug dining counter that doubles as the resort store and office. Come here also to arrange a boat shuttle across the reservoir to the Twenty Lakes Basin, prime day-hiking, fishing, or backpacking country above 10,000 feet.

Every September since 1980, local running maniacs get together for an early Sunday run—not just any weekend jog, but a lung-straining, truly breath-taking run *up* Hwy-120, from Lee Vining to Tioga Pass.

Tioga Pass, at 9,945 feet, is the highest point on any main highway west of Colorado.

The heavily mineralized rocks near Tioga Pass sparked several short-lived mining booms in the 19th century. From the north side of Hwy-120, one mile east of Tioga Pass (which is marked by the ranger kiosk at the Yosemite National Park boundary), a 1.4-mile trail leads to a mine and two clapboard buildings, remnants of the 1874 rush to Bennettville. Another more rugged trail leaves directly from the parking lot at Tioga Pass, climbing in two miles to the godforsaken silver mining settlement of Dana (elev. 10,800 feet), with its stupendous views over the Gaylor Lakes and Gaylor Peak.

Crossing into Yosemite National Park at Tioga Pass ($20 per car, unless you promise not to stop anywhere in the park; 209/372-0265; for more see Yosemite National Park on page 132), Hwy-120 abandons its hard-edged character in favor of a gentle run through some of the prettiest meadows, forests, and mountains accessible by road in the Sierra Nevada. The most salubrious tract is **Tuolumne Meadows**, the heart of Yosemite's high country. Spread at the foot of the sharp-peaked Cathedral Range, at 8,600 feet in elevation, Tuolumne Meadows offers a simple mix of facilities, including a visitors center, store, campground, wilderness office for backpackers' permits, stables, rustic lodging, dining, and access to miles of spectacular backcountry trails, including such noteworthy stalwarts as the Pacific Crest, Tahoe-Yosemite, John Muir, and Yosemite High Sierra Camp Trails, all of which pass through here. **Tuolumne Meadows Lodge** (May-Sept. only; 559/252-4848) is a charmingly rustic affair, with a canvas dining hall serving excellent meals to lodge guests and walk-in diners alike, though dinner reservations should be made early in the day. The most spectacular short trail climbs one mile to the 9,450-foot summit of glaciated Lembert Dome, where the views stretch for miles over the meadows and peaks of Yosemite's high country. Other day-hikes lead to sub-alpine Elizabeth Lake and Cathedral Lakes, though unstructured hikes through the vast meadowlands are often the best. Bears are common visitors to the campgrounds, and if you stay overnight there is a good chance that you will see some.

From the Tuolumne Meadows area, the Tioga Road (Hwy-120) continues west toward Yosemite Valley, passing Tenaya Lake (Yosemite's largest) and striking views from Olmsted Point of Tenaya Canyon down to Clouds Rest and Half Dome.

June Lake Loop

South of Mono Lake, Hwy-120 continues east toward the Nevada border, crossing through the heart of the volcanic Mono Craters; from the junction, if you turn west instead, you'll be on scenic Hwy-158, the June Lake Loop. This 16-mile detour from US-395 loops past several large lakes and summer communities popular with the fishing crowds, though **June Mountain Ski Area** (760/648-7733) caters to a winter clientele. Sagebrush flats, forests, and the looming Sierra Crest combine to make this a very scenic drive, but as to hiking, the choices don't favor casual strollers. Just about all the trailheads along the loop road set off on rather brutal uphill tangents.

Obsidian Dome

Also known as Glass Mountain, this shiny black obsidian dome is reached by way of a signed dirt road (Glass Flow Road) that forks west from US-395, south of the southern June Lake Loop turnoff, right where US-395 becomes a divided freeway at 8,041-foot Deadman Summit. The black volcanic glass, used for making first-class blades, arrowheads, and weapon points, was one of the major trading items of the local Paiute tribes. Bring good shoes if you aim to climb the 600-foot-high peak, and try not to slip: the rock edges are razor sharp.

Mammoth Lakes

Bigger and better heeled than Bishop, the mountain town of Mammoth Lakes (pop. 4,785) carries itself like the most sophisticated place on the eastern Sierra. Catering to ski and snowboard crowds in winter, and hikers, campers, anglers, and mountain bikers in the snow-free months, Mammoth is a year-round resort. Among its offerings are a host of seasonal festivals, as well as nightlife, movies, a large variety of restaurants, coffeehouses galore, and all manner of lodging and other amenities. Lording over the entire region is 11,053-foot **Mammoth Mountain**, a very healthy volcano looming on the western end of town. Town boosters may not like the negative publicity, but geologists consider Mammoth Mountain to be one of the most seismologically active areas in California, and say that Mammoth is more likely to blow than any other volcano in California. (Not to put too much emphasis on the fleeting nature of things round here, but you might want to check out the so-called "Earthquake Fault," a 50-foot-deep fissure on the north side of Minaret Road, near the Mammoth Mountain ski lifts.)

The big draw, of course, remains the great outdoors. Four miles up the Lake Mary Road from the center of town lie the lovely Mammoth Lakes, all fully developed with cabins, campgrounds, and stores catering to anglers and campers. Trails from here lead to wilder Crystal, Barrett, and TJ Lakes, while more ambitious backpackers can hike to Duck Lake and link up with the John Muir Trail.

Most of Mammoth's many restaurants are located in the center of town, around the junction of Main Street (Hwy-203) and Minaret Road. **Whiskey Creek** (760/934-2555) is perenially popular and has the bonus of regular live music. Mountain bikers and downhill skiers will want to avail themselves of the large **Mammoth Mountain Inn**, (760/934-2581 or 800/224-2744), handily located right at the foot of the slopes, while cross-country skiers (and those in search of summer tranquility) may prefer the **Tamarack Lodge**, on Lake Mary Road (760/934-2442 or 800/237-6879), which has a two dozen cabins and a few rooms in the rustic log-cabin lodge.

For details on hiking, camping, or anything else to do with the outdoors in and around Mammoth, stop by the Inyo National Forest **visitors center** (760/924-5500), on Hwy-203 at the east end of town, three miles west of US-395. For more general information, contact the Mammoth Lakes **visitors bureau** (760/934-2712 or 888/466-2666).

Don't expect much scenic pleasure from the so-called Mammoth Scenic Loop, which runs northeast from the center of Mammoth, doubling back to US-395. It's not very scenic at all; locals claim the name is an upbeat euphemism for what is essentially an escape route, should the volcanic mountain make any sudden alterations to the main highway in and out of town.

Mammoth Mountain Ski Center (lift tickets around $50; 760/934-2571) has staked out the mountain with a maze of ski runs (3,100 vertical feet) that double as mountain-bike runs after the snow has melted. In summer, a gondola ($10) transports bikers and sightseers to the 11,053-foot summit, the highest point that you can reach in the Sierra Nevada without breaking a sweat (unless you're really scared of heights, that is).

Minaret Summit and Devils Postpile National Monument

In summer, one of the requisite activities for any visitor to the Mammoth area is to take in the view from Minaret Summit, five miles west of Mammoth Mountain on Minaret Road (Hwy-203). At 9,265 feet, Minaret Summit offers astonishing views of jagged Minaret Range, Mount Ritter, and Banner Peak; there are many who aver that the Sierra Nevada holds no finer view from any road. During summer months, Minaret Road is closed to vehicular traffic beyond this point, except to people with campground reservations and guests of the **Reds Meadow Resort** (760/934-2345), hidden away deep in the forest. The rest of us can ride the Devils Postpile **shuttle bus** (every half-hour; $9) from the Mammoth Mountain Inn, which lets you enjoy the fantastic views without worrying about the steep, one-lane stretches of highway. Some of the Sierra's most popular trails delve from trailheads along the Minaret Road into the Ansel Adams Wilderness, or the backcountry of Yosemite National Park, which is just a day's hike away. If there's room, hikers are allowed to hop on and off the shuttle, so you can explore different trailheads without needing a car shuttle.

With the possible exception of Giants Causeway in Northern Ireland, Devils Postpile National Monument (free; 760/934-2289), 14 miles west of Mammoth, is the most striking example of a columnar basaltic lava flow in the world. When the flow cooled, it cracked into rows of mostly six- to eight-sided columns, which were later exposed by glaciers. Fortunately, the sight itself is not as dry as its geological description; it looks like a natural quarry, and is surrounded by dense forest. An easy half-mile trail leads to the 60-foot-high face of these glassy stone pillars; be sure to take the spur trail to the top, where the polished tops of the columns resemble an exceptionally handsome tiled floor. A longer hike takes you another 1.5 miles each way to **Rainbow Falls**, where the Middle Fork of San Joaquin River dives 101 feet down a narrow gorge. In the middle of the day, when the sun hits the spray from the powerful falls, this is one of the prettiest sights of the eastern Sierra.

Hot Creek Geothermal Area

One of the largest geothermal springs outside of Yellowstone proves that volcanism, specifically the Long Valley Caldera, is alive and well in the Mammoth area. Hot Creek flows cold from the Sierra until it hits this pocket of boiling springs. The sulfurous air pops and bubbles with the sound of boiling water, steam rises from vents, and signs warn that many people have been flash-boiled to death by swimming too close to scalding vents hidden under the flowing creek. The U.S. Forest Service strongly exhorts people not to swim here at all, and closes the area completely after dark, but many people do brave the warm waters, hoping to find a soothing medium between the freezing cold river and the boiling volcanic vents that the rangers mark with signs and yellow caution tape. (Anglers take note: upstream from the hot springs area, fishing in Hot Creek is among the best in the West, strictly catch-and-release with barbless hooks.)

South of Hot Creek, US-395 runs past **Lake Crowley**, a huge flat expanse that is actually the most visible sign of the Los Angeles Aqueduct, which siphons water from here and delivers it to thirsty Southern California. The lake is named for the popular priest Father Crowley, who was known as the "Desert Padre" before his death in a car wreck on US-395 near Red Rock Canyon in 1940.

To get to the steaming springs of Hot Creek, take the Hot Creek Fish Hatchery Road exit from US-395, about 2.5 miles south of the Hwy-203 Mammoth turnoff; if you reach the airport, you're just south of Hot Creek. From US-395, head east and follow the signs for about three miles to the Hot Creek parking lot, where there are bathrooms (but no camping).

Tom's Place and Rock Creek

Three miles south of Lake Crowley, this tiny crossroads stop at 7,072 feet elevation is named for Tom Yerby, who set up shop here in 1919. The town comprises a store, some cabins, a cafe and gas pumps, and little else (760/935-4239); but 'tis enough to serve explorers of Rock Creek. The highest paved road in the Sierra, Upper Rock Creek climbs past campground after campground (all part of the Inyo National Forest, and costing around $12 a night), then ends at 10,250-foot Mosquito Flat, just below exquisite Little Lakes Valley, another of the many breathtaking alpine basins in the range. Because the trailhead is so high, the walk into the valley (along the remains of an old mining road) requires only small effort, which has made it one of the more popular day-hikes in the eastern Sierra. Though it's a fairly easy walk, the rewards are huge: wonderful alpine wildflowers and great views of Long Lake, Bear Creek Spire, and 13,715-foot Mt. Abbott.

Lower Rock Creek Canyon

South of Tom's Place, the 1990s realignment of US-395 cuts east, leaving a fine two-lane section of the old highway (now called Lower Rock Creek Road, west of US-395) to follow Rock Creek as it snakes through lava flows of the volcanic tableland down to the Owens Valley, an elevation drop of more than 3,000 feet in less than 10 miles. This lower canyon of Rock Creek makes for one of the prettiest early and late-season hikes in the region, and one of the most popular winter snowshoe routes. The trail splits conveniently into two parts. One begins near the Tuff Campground near Tom's Place, and runs about four miles south to where Lower Rock Creek Road crosses the creek. The second half starts at that same bridge and runs 4.6 miles down to where

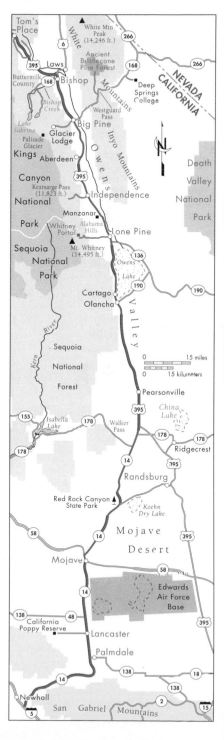

US-6, which comes across Nevada to join up with US-395 at Bishop, used to be the longest cross-country U.S. highway running between the tip of Cape Cod and Long Beach, California; it still runs east to Provincetown, Massachusetts, but Bishop is now the west end of the line.

Bishop's annual **Mule Days** celebrations, draws some 40,000 people to Bishop every Memorial Day weekend. The festival features the usual county fair fun plus a virtual mule rodeo—mule auctions, mule-powered chariot races, mule penning, and mule packing competitions—and a Saturday parade down Main Street, featuring so many mules it's counted as "the longest non-motorized parade in the USA." For information, call 760/872-4263.

it hits the historic **Paradise Resort** (760/387-2370), where rustic fisherman's cottages line the creek behind a cozy restaurant. Despite desert-like conditions in the lava flows, the creek supports a continuous oasis of Jeffrey pines and aspens that turn brilliant yellow and red in autumn.

Bishop

Bishop (pop. 3,680) sits at an elevation of 4,140 feet, in between the Owens Valley and the volcanic tablelands that characterize the Mono Lake and Mammoth Mountain region. Though Bishop itself is well shaded by trees that turn bright colors in fall, the town is completely surrounded by desert landscapes. That has not always been the case. In 1904, when Muholland began building the Los Angeles Aqueduct to siphon off the Owens River for the Los Angeles water supply, the Owens Valley was full of orchards and farms. Of course, the orchards and farms likewise were not "natural," either; before late 19th-century irrigation projects made orchard farming possible, the Owens Valley was a desert, and some naturalists and others credit Los Angeles with inadvertently *protecting* the valley from modern development. No water may mean no growth, but it has also meant no sprawl; how long the current staus quo will continue, no one can say.

Two excellent museums recount the region's history from prehistoric times to the present day. The first, chronologically, is the **Owens Valley Paiute Shoshone Cultural Center** (Mon.-Fri. 9 AM-5 PM, Saturday and Sunday 10 AM-4 PM; donation requested; 760/873-4478) which is located a mile west of US-395 at 2300 West Line Street (Hwy-168). The Cultural Center exhibits artifacts recounting Native American life and culture in the western Great Basin. It also has a nice gift shop, with some high-quality woven basketry. About five miles northeast of Bishop on US-6, the **Laws Railroad Museum and Historical Site** (daily 10 AM-4 PM; donation requested; 760/873-5950), marks the site of the old Laws train depot, where the *Slim Princess*—the narrow-gauge Carson & Colorado Railway—chugged and huffed and puffed between 1883 and 1960. Historic buildings from around the Owens Valley have been moved here and furnished with period furniture, creating a kind of faux ghost town of real buildings, and real pioneer history.

Bishop Practicalities

The biggest town of the Owens Valley, Bishop has everything you need for a vacation in the big outdoors, or indeed, a civilized respite from the same. Bishop's main street (US-395) hosts the town cinema and most of the restaurants, motels, and businesses. It also serves as the parade route for the annual Mule Days Celebration, held every Memorial Day weekend at the Inyo County Fairgrounds at the junction of US-395 and US-6. The Bishop Indian Reservation occupies the western half of the town, a mostly residential district recently brought into commercial prominence by the **Paiute Palace Casino** (760/873-4150), along US-395 on the north side of town.

Sunk between California's two tallest mountain ranges—the Sierra Nevada on the west and the White and Inyo Mountains on the east—the long **Owens Valley** is up to two miles deep in places, giving US-395 a near-continuous spectacle of sheer mountain escarpments as it runs its nearly 100-mile length. Though Bishop is the biggest town hereabouts, the best Owens Valley museum is in Independence, 60 miles farther south.

Because of the considerable passing trade, Bishop has more good places to eat than you might expect. There are greasy spoon diner-type breakfast places aplenty, or you can start the day with pastries and other goodies (like a loaf of their beloved sheepherder bread) from **Erick Schatts Bakery**, open from 7 AM at 608 Main Street. Schatts also does hefty deli sandwiches, but for a real carnivore fest, head to **Bar-B-Q Bill's**, 187 S. Main Street. For more substantial fare, try the homey **Petite Pantry**, with fresh pies and a nice outdoor deck, open all day along US-395 on the north side of town at 2278 N. Sierra Highway (760/873-3789). A local fine dining option is **Whiskey Creek**, 524 N. Main Street (760/873-7174), which offers steaks, fish, and seafood dishes in a cozy setting. If you're cruising through in the middle of the night, head to **Jack's Waffle Shop**, open 24 hours at 437 N. Main Street (760/872-7971); for healthier fare, head to the 24-hour **Von's supermarket**.

With so many wonderful campgrounds up Bishop Creek above the town, campers have a huge advantage over everyone else. However, for a place to stay in town, try the quiet and inexpensive **El Rancho**, west of US-395 at 274 Lagoon Street (760/872-9251), or choose from the chains that line Main Street (US-395), including Motel 6, Super 8, and Days Inn.

For details on hiking, camping, and outdoor recreation, stop by the Inyo National Forest **ranger station**, 798 N. Main Street (760/873-2500). For gear, maps, or more tips on where to go, check in with **Wilson's Eastside Sports**, 224 N. Main Street (760/873-7520). For general visitor information, contact the Bishop Area **visitors center**, 690 N. Main Street (760/873-8405).

Hwy-168: Bishop Creek and Lake Sabrina

Bishop's crown jewels stand to the west, in the Sierra Nevada. West Line Street (Hwy-168) splits off from the center of town and climbs steeply up along Bishop Creek. Hwy-168 ends at North Lake and Lake Sabrina (elev. 10,000 feet), where

some onerously steep but extraordinarily scenic trails fan out to a myriad of great fishing lakes, into the high country of Kings Canyon National Park and beyond.

Before the end of Hwy-168, another road cuts off

The Owens Valley was named in 1845 by explorer John C. Frémont, who named it after one of his officers, Richard Owens.

A curious feature of the foothills west of Bishop is **Buttermilk Country** (a.k.a. "The Buttermilks") reached via unpaved Buttermilk Road, which turns north off Hwy-168 about four miles west of Bishop. The Buttermilks are huge, rounded boulders that are popular with climbers and photographers.

south toward South Lake. At the junction is the large Four Jeffrey Campground, one of nine U.S. Forest Service campgrounds along Bishop Creek; all are $12-a-night sites (760/873-2400). From the end of the road at South Lake, a great trail climbs up over glaciated Bishop Pass into lovely Dusy Basin, full of wildflowers and granite glacial erratics.

Big Pine

A crossroads town with the slogan "Small Town, Big Back Yard," Big Pine (pop. 1,500) is best regarded for its proximity to two outdoor wonders, the Palisades Glacier and the ancient bristlecone pines. The "big pines" for which the town is named were all logged off in the late 1860s, milled into timbers for the many mines in the surrounding region.

West from town, Glacier Lodge Road follows Big Pine Creek to **Glacier Lodge**, an old resort that burned down in 1988, but which should rise again (maybe next year); in the meantime, you can stay at the rustic cabins ($70 a night; 760/938-2837). Glacier Lodge takes its name from, and offers stupendous views of, the Middle Palisade Glacier, one of three local icefields that rank as the largest remaining glaciers in the Sierra Nevada. (They're also the southernmost glaciers in northern hemisphere, if you keep track of such things.) The main Palisade Glacier, largest of the three, requires a strenuous hike of 4.5 miles to Big Pine Lakes Basin, a popular backpacking destination. After the Whitney Crest to the south, the Palisades are the second highest crest in the Sierra Nevada, and its peaks and sheer faces are a challenge to climbers.

GLACIER LODGE

OPEN YEAR ROUND BY PERMIT
On U.S.D.A. Forest Service Land

At the junction of US-395 and Hwy-168, the road east to the White Mountains and the Ancient Bristlecone Pine Forest, a giant sequoia, planted in 1913 and known as the **Roosevelt Tree**, stands alongside the Glacier View campground, run by Inyo County and costing just $5 a night.

Back in Big Pine proper, a good place to renew the spirits is at **Rossi's Steak and Spaghetti**, a classic family-friendly Italian restaurant on US-395 at 100 N. Main Street (760/938-2254). Stay the night at the **Big Pine Motel**, a well-maintained 1950s classic at 370 S. Main Street (760/938-2282), which has clean, $40-a-night rooms, picnic tables, BBQ grills, and lawn chairs arrayed in a tidy garden; who could ask for more?

For information on the nearby outdoors, especially if you're planning to head up to the White Mountains to see the bristlecone pines, stop by the **visitors center** at 126 S. Main Street (760/938-1136), north of town at the Hwy-168 turnoff east to the White Mountains. This office shares space with the local **chamber of commerce** (760/938-2114), so you can find out all you need to know about Big Pine.

Hwy-168: Ancient Bristlecone Pine Forest

Due east of Big Pine, Hwy-168 climbs up the narrow cleft of Westgard Pass, the parched 7,313 foot-high divide between the Inyo Mountains on the south, and on the north, the White Mountains, the second-highest chain of peaks in the Golden State. The White Mountains rise to over 14,000 feet and continue north to the

Nevada border (Nevada's Boundary Peak, at 13,140 feet, is the highest point in the Silver State). They are also home to the famous forests of bristlecone pine, believed to be the oldest living trees on earth. The sparse forests grow at high altitude in rocky soils, conditions which strangely stunt growth but stimulate longevity; though they live for thousands of years, the average height of these trees is a mere 25 feet. The oldest known living specimen, the Methuselah Tree, is 4,600 years old, which means it predates the Great Pyramid at Giza, and was already ancient when Socrates, Confucius, and Buddha were busy ruminating.

A spur road off Hwy-168, a mile east of US-395, leads south toward the amazing **Eureka Sand Dunes,** which tower up to 700 feet high. The dunes are within the recently expanded northern boundaries of Death Valley National Park.

To get to the bristlecone pines, which are 25 miles from Big Pine, fill up on gas and water (both of which are unavailable east of US-395), then drive 13 miles east on Hwy-168, and turn left (north) on White Mountain Road, at the sign that reads Ancient Bristlecone Pine Forest. Continue past aptly named Grandview Campground, which has two dozen primitive (there's no water, but no fee) campsites and a panorama view of the Owens Valley and across to the Sierra crest, and make your way 10 miles farther to Schulman Grove (elev. 10,050 feet). After visiting the Schulman Grove **visitors center** (daily June-October; $5 per car; 760/873-2500), consider taking one of two loops, the 1-mile Discovery Trail, or the 4-mile Methuselah Walk, which visits the grove where the world's oldest living thing (unmarked to discourage vandalism) resides. If you enjoy these, you can continue driving 11 miles deeper (and 1,000 feet higher) into the mountains along a rough, unpaved road to the **Patriarch Grove**, where you really get a feel for the desolate environment that creates these grotesquely stunted, though ancient survivors.

Independence

This handsome little town is less tourist-oriented than some other US-395 towns, but it still has everything you could need, plus some added attractions. The best of these is the small but wonderful **Eastern California Museum,** west of US-395 at 155 N. Grant Street (closed on Tuesday, 10 AM-4

LAND OF LITTLE RAIN

Fans of regional American literature will want to pay a visit to the Owens Valley home of prose poet Mary Austin (1862-1934), whose book *Land of Little Rain* captures the essence of life here in the shadow of the Sierra Nevada. Published in 1903, this slim volume was a clear precursor to the works of Edward Abbey, Wallace Stegner, and other writers on the true wild West. (Among Austin's many evocative details is her observation that the native Shoshone Indians lived like their trees—with plenty of land around.)

Mary Austin lived and worked in Independence, in a modest home at Market and Webster Streets, two blocks west of US-395. Although the house is marked with a bronze plaque, it is privately owned and not open to the public.

South of Westgard Pass, way back in the Inyo Mountains, lies one of America's most unusual centers of learning: **Deep Springs College,** founded in 1917 and run as a college and working cattle ranch. The two dozen or so students (all male) work instead of paying tuition, and study here for two years before going on to Ivy League and other top universities.

Midway between Big Pine and Independence, a dirt road heading east from the hamlet of Aberdeen marks the actual start of the Los Angeles Aqueduct. Water is diverted here from the Owens River into massive pipes, which form a siphon for the next 300 miles south. For more, see the special topic Cadillac Desert.

If you're looking for a classic small-town setting for your next 4th of July, Independence is hard to beat: there's a parade, a crafts bazaar, a BBQ, and after dark, fireworks aplenty. Festivities focus on Dehy Park, along Independence Creek on the north side of town.

West of Independence, the Onion Valley Road zigzags up the mountains along Independence Creek to the trailhead for the most popular east-side access into Kings Canyon National Park. **Kearsarge Pass** (elev. 11,823 feet), gets so much traffic that the local bears have started to rely on backpackers to bring them dinner. As a result, backpackers are required by law to carry their food in bear-proof canisters if leaving from the Onion Valley trailhead.

PM; contributions accepted; 760/878-0364), an excellent introduction to the history of the Owens Valley and surrounding region. The best displays are those on Paiute basketry, local writer Mary Austin (who lived just a block away), and the WWII Japanese-American internment camp at nearby Manzanar (see below); there's also a whole yard full of rusty farm equipment, untouched since Los Angeles took away the valley's water a century ago.

About three miles north of Independence, a historical marker is about the only remaining sign of **Camp Independence**, a Civil War-era U.S. Army fort that aimed to protect settlers from local Paiute Indians; the first soldiers arrived here on July 4, 1862, hence the name. Looming over the west side of US-395, the steeply roofed, half-timbered complex is one of the oldest and most exotic-looking fish hatcheries in the West, the Mt. Whitney Fish Hatchery. Built in 1915, the hatchery produces some 15 million trout eggs every year; most of these the fish are reared at other facilities up and down the eastern Sierra, and some three million fish are stocked in the region's lakes and streams to keep anglers happy.

Back in town, choose between a pair of diner-type places along US-395: the neon-fronted **Pines Cafe**, 104 S. Edwards (760/878-9907) or **Bill and Linda's Family Restaurant**, 306 S. Edwards (760/878-2377).

For a place to stay, consider the historic **Winnedumah Hotel**, 211 N. Edwards Street (760/878-2040), a Spanish Revival landmark that dates from the 1920s. Besides nice B&B rooms, the hotel also has HI-approved hostel dorms ($18 per person), and often hosts Elderhostel and other guided programs that take guests into surrounding mountains on photographic workshops, ghost town tours, and trail rides.

Lone Pine

The town of Lone Pine (pop. 2,060) lies at the deepest part of the Owens Valley, two vertical miles lower than the 14,495-foot summit of Mt. Whitney, highest point in the continental United States. The spectacular Sierra escarpment was thrust upward by a geologic process known as fault blocking. A horrendous example of this process destroyed the town in 1872, when an earthquake leveled nearly every building and killed 27 people in seconds; a small monument on US-395 north of town commemorates the calamity. As a result of the 1872 earthquake, the Sierra crest rose upward by 13 feet above the valley floor, and shifted horizontally by 20 feet; at such a rate, and taking into account the frequency of such massive quakes, geologists estimate that this part of the Sierra crest is rising at a rate of about a half-inch per year.

FAREWELL TO MANZANAR

Although the federal government plans to develop the site as a national historic monument, today almost nothing remains of the relocation camp at Manzanar that housed up to 10,000 people of Japanese ancestry, including many American citizens, during World War II. Located six miles south of Independence, nine miles north of Lone Pine, since 1992 the site has been preserved as the 814-acre **Manzanar National Historic Site** (daily dawn-dusk; free; 760/878-2932 or 213/662-5102). Manzanar is the most intact of the 10 main relocation camps constructed around the U.S., but almost nothing remains of the rows and rows of tar paper barracks, the well-tended gardens, or anything else, apart from the small cemetery (with its central "Soul Consoling Tower" monument) and the former school auditorium, which is now a garage and warehouse for the Inyo County Public Works Department. At the entrance, a pair of pagoda-roofed stone huts (which no doubt they were

During World War II, over 120,000 people of Japanese descent were forcibly removed from the western U.S. and imprisoned in camps like Manzanar for the duration of the conflict. Over half those imprisoned were American born; one-quarter were school-age children.

designed to make the inmates feel more at home, but can't help but make their incarceration here seem all the more cruel) are the most visible sign that anything unusual ever happened here. A nearby marker says it all: "May the injustices suffered here as a result of hysteria, racism and economic exploitation never emerge again." A self-guided tour booklet is available at the Inter-Agency Visitors Center in Lone Pine and at the Eastern California Museum in Independence. A Manzanar Pilgrimage takes place yearly on the last Saturday in April to remember and honor those who were interned in the camps.

Because of Hollywood's long-time love affair with the Alabama Hills (see below), Lone Pine is an old hand at entertaining celebrities. Many town restaurants and businesses display signed portraits of movie stars like John Wayne, Gene Autry, and Errol Flynn; check out the **Mount Whitney Restaurant**, 277 S. Main Street (760/876-5751) for a glimpse of Hollywood glossies, and maybe a plate of meat loaf, fried chicken, or chicken-fried steak. Another fine place to eat is just across the highway: the **Merry-Go-Round Restaurant**, 212 S. Main Street (760/876-4259), where you can dine on a similar range of all-American meals while sitting on a simulated carousel. (The room doesn't move, but is round and decorated with mirrors and other merry-go-round accoutrements.)

For fast food or a cool summer cone, choose between the **Frosty Chalet**, at the north end of town, and the **Frosty Stop**, at the south end of town. Choice accommodations include the friendly **Dow Villa Motel**, 310 S. Main Street (760/876-5521) with a 24-hour swimming pool and spa (ideal for moonlight admiration of Mt. Whitney).

You can get a good bearing on the region's recreational opportunities at the excellent **Inter-Agency Visitors Center** (760/876-6222), about one mile south of town at the junction of US-395 and Hwy-136, which heads east toward Death Valley.

It's an amazing fact that the **highest and lowest points in the continental USA** are on either side of Lone Pine. West of town, Mt. Whitney rises to 14,495 feet above sea level; 75 miles southeast of town, in Death Valley National Park, Badwater drops to 282 feet below sea level.

Alabama Hills

Few natural sights are more dramatic than the view of the Whitney Crest from the Alabama Hills, west of Lone Pine. These weather-worn hills are composed of orange-tinged granite boulders, piled in picturesque array. Their photogenic qualities were early recognized by Hollywood and Madison Avenue, which has shot hundreds of movies, TV shows, pilots, and Marlboro Man-type advertisements throughout the hills. Movie buffs will want to obtain a copy of the movie map published by the Lone Pine Chamber of Commerce, also available from the Inter-Agency Visitors Center in Lone Pine. Among the scattered locales, perhaps you'll find some favorite scenes from horse-operas by Tom Mix, Gene Autry, Hopalong Cassidy, and Roy Rogers (who in 1990 presided over the dedication of a historical plaque along Whitney Portal Road at the Movie Flat turnoff); movies that have used the Alabama Hills location include *The Lone Ranger, Gunga Din* (starring Cary Grant), *How the West Was Won* (see it in the original Cinerama, if you ever get the chance), Humphrey Bogart's classic *High Sierra,* and many more.

Many of the sites are located along unpaved Movie Road, north of Whitney Portal Road, and yet more are found along Horseshoe Meadows Road, south off of Whitney Portal Road. It's all BLM-administered public land, and you are basically free to explore, on or off the road. The BLM also manages the basic but free **Tuttle Creek Campground** (760/872-4881), off Horseshoe Meadows Road at the southwest edge of the Alabama Hills.

Every Columbus Day weekend, the **Lone Pine Film Festival** shows a selection of movies filmed in the Alabama Hills west of town. For details, phone 760/876-4444.

Whitney Portal

If you are not satisfied by distant views of Mt. Whitney from Lone Pine, drive 13 miles west up Whitney Portal Road for a closer look. The paved, double-lane road ends at 8,350 feet elevation in a narrow, glaciated canyon at the trailhead of the 10.5-mile Mt. Whitney Trail. As tempting as it might sound to hike to the top, the trail is so popular that it is strictly controlled by a quota system, and reservations (50 people per day are allowed up the trail) are snapped up months in advance. Even if you want to take a day-hike on part of the trail, you need to obtain a permit from the Mt. Whitney **ranger station** in Lone Pine (760/876-6200).

If you don't manage to snag a permit to hike up the peak, console yourself with the Mt. Whitney souvenirs at the small Whitney Portal store (open summer only); or better yet, take a hike downhill, on the Whitney Portal National Recreation Trail, which starts at the fishing pond and winds along Lone Pine Creek. A mile downhill from Whitney Portal, you can camp out and enjoy the Mt. Whitney view at the lovely U.S. Forest Service Whitney Portal campground ($12; 800/280-CAMP or 800/280-2267).

DEATH VALLEY NATIONAL PARK

Death Valley, at over 8,000 square miles (3.3 million acres), is by far the largest national park in the contiguous U.S. Its vast desert landscape is full of surprises: canyons so narrow and deep that you can stand on the bottom, with palms on both walls, and look up a thousand feet to a slit of sky; vista points that simultaneously gaze upon 14,000-foot Sierra peaks and valleys that plunge to well below sea level; and stretches of ground so level and wide that it distorts perspectives, making a distance of 14 miles look the length of a mere football field or two.

A true land of contrasts, Death Valley is a place where you can shiver on the slopes of Telescope Peak (elev. 11,049 feet) within sight of playas baking under the hottest temperatures ever recorded in the New World. The name Death Valley, first bestowed by gold seekers bound for California during the 1849 Gold Rush, is correctly applied only to the area at the center of the park that is below sea level; the park also contain numerous other valleys and mountain ranges, though all are equally inhospitable to casual visitors.

(continues)

At the west edge of Death Valley National Park, a last taste of moist verdure can be had at **Darwin Falls**, just west of Panamint Springs. The falls, which drop about 30 feet at the head of a creek, are less than a mile from the well-signed trailhead, two miles south of Hwy-190, the road from Lone Pine.

The heart of Death Valley is **Furnace Creek**, an oasis of date palms and tamarind trees on the floor of the valley itself. It was here that the second-hottest surface temperature on earth was recorded—134° F. Furnace Creek is also home to the park's widest range of gas, food, and lodging options (see below). A good first stop here is the **visitors center** (760/786-2331), on Hwy-190 next to the Furnace Creek Ranch motel and restaurant complex.

Among the natural sights that are easy to reach by paved road are the sand dunes and Mosaic Canyon, north of Furnace Creek near **Stovepipe Wells**. Both places are best explored on foot, but neither requires much exertion. *Beau Geste, Star Wars,* and other movies have been filmed on the Stovepipe Wells Sand Dunes, which are particularly fun for kids to explore. The namesake of Mosaic Canyon is the aggregate formation right near the entrance of the narrow slot gorge, which winds south from Stovepipe Wells for several miles.

From Furnace Creek, Hwy-190 leads southeast to **Zabriskie Point** and the much higher **Dante's View** (elev. 5,475 feet), both of which offer astounding views over the badlands of Death Valley, especially at sunrise and sunset. In between the two overlooks is a one-way road through Twenty Mule Team Canyon, which takes its name from the mule-pulled wagons that used to haul borax from Death Valley to the railhead at Mojave, 165 miles away.

Along the Badwater Road (Hwy-178) south of Furnace Creek, motorists can tour Artist Drive, a nine-mile scenic jaunt through intensely colorful badlands known as the **Artist's Palette**. **Badwater** itself is an alkali pond located 279.8 feet below sea level—the lowest point reached by road in the western hemisphere. If you want a more intense experience of Death Valley, a scenic alternative to the Badwater Road is the unpaved West Side Road, which runs along the west side of Death Valley for 30 desolate miles, from Artist's Palette to the foot of Jubilee Pass, where it rejoins the Badwater Road (Hwy-178). The actual lowest point—282 feet below sea level—lies in between the Badwater Road and the West Side Road, about three miles northwest of Badwater.

In the northern sections of the park, close to Scotty's Castle, volcanic **Ubehebe Crater** yawns 600 feet deep and 2,640 feet wide. Blown from the ground only a few thousand years ago by superheated steam, the hole was named by the native Shoshone; *ubehebe* apparently means "basket." From Ubehebe, two unpaved roads suitable only for high-clearance vehicles (though 4WD is usually not required) explore more distant corners of the park. One leads north and east to Eureka Dunes, among the highest sand dunes in the world, and continues on to Big Pine; another runs south to The Racetrack, a dry lake bed famed for its mysterious moving rocks.

If you have a high clearance vehicle and don't mind bumpy roads, be sure to take the one-way drive from Rhyolite through **Titus Canyon**. From a pass of 5,250 feet, the well-graded road visits the ghost town of Leadfield before squeezing into the narrows for a grand finale, twisting through the deep and narrow gorge. Titus Canyon is the easiest slot canyon in Death Valley to visit in a vehicle, though nearby Red Wall Canyon, two miles north, makes the more spectacular hike.

One more road should be on any Death Valley tour: the route to **Telescope Peak**. Though it's sometimes closed at higher elevations by snow in winter, the road gives a sense of the full spectrum of habitats and scenery comprised by the park; in summer, the drive offers respite from the unbearable heat of Death Valley, two miles below. Along the way you'll pass the ghostly remains of **Skidoo**, where some 700 gold miners and others lived between 1906 and 1917. From the end of the road, at Mahogany Flat campground, a five-mile trail leads to the summit of Telescope Peak, the highest point in the park, from where you can see both Badwater, the official lowest point in the USA, and Mount Whitney, the highest peak in the lower 48 states.

Along with Skidoo, and the amazing mansion known as Scotty's Castle (see special topic), the **Keane Wonder Mine** is probably the most extensive sign of human activity within the park. East of Stovepipe Wells along the Beatty Cut-Off (between Hwy-374 and Hwy-190), the remains of the Keane mine comprise an enormous stamp mill, a shattered cable car system, extensive mining pits (many gaping and extremely dangerous), and ruined buildings and piles of garbage galore. Few sights are more evocative of Death Valley's rich past and present enchantment than watching the sunset from the hillside amidst the ghosts of this vast industrial complex, now empty and forlorn.

Practicalities

While the most intense experience of Death Valley comes from getting out and roughing it in the less-than-hospitable desert, this vast park also offers days of fascinating exploration for travelers who put an emphasis on good roads and comfortable lodgings. Considering the extreme daytime temperatures (rarely below 100° F), by far the most sensible time to visit is from October through May. Furnace Creek offers a store, restaurants, a gas station, golf course, and motel-type lodging at the **Furnace Creek Ranch**. The nearby **Furnace Creek Inn**, a Moorish fantasy built exactly at sea level around an enchanting palm

(continues)

Death Valley does have vast areas of wilderness, where motorized traffic is blissfully restricted. These are open only to a special breed of hiker who knows how to cache water, find routes without trails, endure the incessant winds, and survive the harsh conditions of North America's hottest, driest landscape.

Innumerable **ghost towns** and **old mines** (as well as mines still being worked) dot the park. Take extreme care when poking around old ruins, because the abandoned ones are typically unstable, while the ones still worked do not welcome visitors. The ghost town of Rhyolite, outside the park's eastern entrance near Beatty, is the easiest to visit.

oasis, offers much more luxurious lodging and dining, at prices to match. Rooms at the Ranch cost around $100 a night; rooms at the Inn go for $250; reservations for either are handled by the same concessionaire, Amfac (760/786-2345).

Lodging and food are also available within the park at **Stovepipe Wells Village** (760/786-2387) and at the west edge of the park, halfway to Lone Pine along Hwy-190, at **Panamint Springs Resort** (760/482-7680). Some snacktype food, but no lodging, is available at Scotty's Castle. The relatively close towns of Beatty, Nevada, at the east edge of the park, and Shoshone, to the south, also offer amenities.

One of the largest campgrounds in the world has to be the **Sunset Campground**, along Hwy-190 just east of Furnace Creek Ranch—a massive desert parking lot with 1,000 first-come, first-served spaces, most of which are full throughout the peak winter season. The only campground that takes reservations (800/365-2267) is the **Furnace Creek Campground**, across the highway from (and much smaller than) sprawling Sunset. There are a half-dozen smaller campgrounds spread around the park, like the pleasant but primitive Wildrose Campground, on the slopes of Telescope Peak. All sites cost around $10 a night; for further information, call the visitors center (760/786-2331).

The only **gas stations** in and around the park are at Stovepipe Wells, Scotty's Castle, and Furnace Creek; expect to pay about 50 cents more per gallon than elsewhere. **Water**, Death Valley's other most precious commodity, is very hard to come by, so carry at least a gallon per person per day, plus another gallon just in case something goes wrong.

Into Nevada: Rhyolite and Beatty

South of Lone Pine, Hwy-136 meanders north along the foothills of the Inyo Mountains where it merges with Hwy-190 and continues east through the Panamint Valley and Death Valley National Park. At Stovepipe Wells, Hwy-190 veers southeast to Death Valley Junction, but our route along Hwy-374 continues northeast climbing very steeply up Daylight Pass (elev. 4,317 feet), which gives a wonderful panorama over the barren white plains of Death Valley. Continuing east, this road leads to Beatty, Nevada, the biggest town for miles, where Hwy-374 meets US-95. In between Beatty and the park boundary, you pass the big ponds of a gold-leaching operation, which marks the turnoff up the hill (north) to Rhyolite, one of the West's great ghost towns. Not so long ago, between 1905 and 1912 or so, Rhyolite was a booming gold mining town, the third largest settlement in Nevada, with some 53 saloons and as many as 10,000 residents. Now, vacant buildings—the schoolhouse, the grand First National Bank, some storefronts, and a Mission-style train depot—line Golden Street, the dusty main drag. Along with many photogenic ruins, Rhyolite is home to at least two real oddities: the **Bottle House**, built in 1906 out of some 50,000 multicolored glass bottles, and an extensive outdoor sculpture garden, created by Belgian artist Albert Szukalski. The whole town is protected by the Bureau of Land Management, which pays a resident "g/host" caretaker to look after things in the cooler months.

Continuing on Hwy-374, four miles east of Rhyolite, you reach Beatty, a friendly crossroads town that has gas stations, motels, cafes and, of course, casinos, like the funky **Exchange Club**, best known for its historic carved wooden bar, carted over from San Francisco in 1905. There are also at least two ice cream parlors, which are very welcome after any amount of time spent out in the surrounding desert in the summer. The big motel in town is the **Burro Inn**, on US-95 at 3rd Street (775/553-2225), with rooms from around $40.

The area around Beatty has been on the cusp of major changes since the U.S. government announced plans to store high-grade nuclear waste at a nearby site known as **Yucca Mountain.** Some 70,000 tons of radioactive materials, mostly from weapons programs, have to be kept safe for a minimum of 10,000 years—starting in 2003. Find out more from the U.S. Department of Energy's Yucca Mountain **visitors center,** between Rhyolite and Beatty on Hwy-374.

Death Valley Junction: The Amargosa Opera House

Leaving or approaching Death Valley from the southeast via Hwy-190, the first (or last) signs of civilization you'll see is also one of the most eccentric hotels in the West: the well preserved **Amargosa Hotel** (760/852-4441), a 1920s motor court at Death Valley Junction, a one-time borax mining company town 18 miles east of the boundary for Death Valley National Park, but still in California. Rooms here vary in size and comfort, but prices (around $50 a night) are uniformly low. The real at-

---

SCOTTY'S CASTLE

Though best known for its extreme temeratures and otherworldly landscapes, Death Valley has also attracted a fair number of strange humans, most notoriously the murderous Manson Family, who lived on the western edge of the park for many years in the late 1960s. Among the more hospitable local eccentrics was Walter Scott, a.k.a. "Death Valley Scotty," a self-promoting humbug who charmed investors into buying stakes in his secret gold mines, and who lived off the proceeds for years. Scotty's ingenious shenanigans paid off royally in the 1920s when he convinced a Chicago millionaire named Albert Johnson to spend his millions building a Moorish-style mansion in Death Valley. This enabled Scotty to retire from mining, and earn his room and board instead by spinning yarns and lending local color to Johnson family dinner parties.

Johnson's home, popularly known today as Scotty's Castle (daily 9 AM-5 PM; $8; 760/786-2392) is in Grapevine Canyon (Hwy-267), which feeds into the northern end of Death Valley. Often compared to the much grander Hearst Castle (see page 77), Scotty's Castle is indeed impressive, especially when you consider the location, miles from any materials or workers. The 25-room house has tons of well-crafted tile and woodwork, 15 fireplaces, a swimming pool (no swimming allowed, alas) and some very pleasant fountains, courtyards and gardens—not to mention the famous 1,121-pipe organ, which blasts out a tune at the end of every tour.

A variety of routes link Death Valley with Las Vegas. The quickest is from Beatty via US-95, which runs as a near freeway along the edge of the atomic-age Nevada Test Site, all the way to Las Vegas. An alternate route follows US-95 south to Hwy-160, which runs to Las Vegas by way of Pahrump and Red Rock State Park.

traction is next door, where the one and only Marta Beckett still dances at the Amargosa Opera House on winter weekend evenings. A refugee from the Broadway boards, Miss Beckett bought the whole town in the early 1960s, and proceeded to put on weekly ballet performances in the converted cinema— whether customers showed up or not. To keep herself company, she painted her own audience, a boisterous crowd of *trompe l'oeil* Renaissance figures arranged from ceiling to floor around the walls. Performances nowadays are usually sold out to live audiences (tickets cost $10; 760/852-4441).

South of Death Valley: Shoshone and Tecopa

Though they're too far away to be ideal bases for a Death Valley visit, a pair of California towns south of the park do offer some extra options for lodging, food and fun. The first of these, Shoshone, is located 28 miles south of Death Valley Junction, on Hwy-127 very near the junction with Hwy-178, which winds to the west along the bottom of Death Valley. Besides a gas station or two, you'll find the **Sho-**

shone Inn (760/852-4335). The next town south, Tecopa, is tucked away east of Hwy-127 on Tecopa Road. It is semi-famous for two things: the year-round Inyo County-run public hot springs (free) at the center of town, and the hundreds of snowbird RVers who flock here during the winter months. Tecopa also has the small but handy **HI Desertaire Hostel** (760/852-4580), on the Old Spanish Trail between the hot springs and Hwy-127.

From Tecopa, Hwy-127 runs due south to Baker, where it links up with the I-15 freeway, at the north edge of the vast Mojave National Preserve.

From the southern Owens Valley, scenic Hwy-178 is the first road to cross the Sierra Nevada Mountains since the Tioga Pass Road crossed Yosemite National Park. Starting from Hwy-14 at the northern fringe of the Mojave Desert, Hwy-178 climbs up through an intriguing forest of Joshua trees on the slopes of Walker Pass (elev. 5,245 feet), after which the road begins to drop down along the forested canyons of the Kern River before dropping into the vast Central Valley at Bakersfield.

China Lake and Randsburg

Compared with the wealth of adventure available in the upper Owens Valley along US-395, south of Lone Pine there is precious little to see or do. The Los Angeles Aqueduct has siphoned off the natural water supply, leaving once-huge Owens Lake high and dry. There are a few little communities along the highway where you can fill the tank or grab a soda, then get on the road again, but there's not a lot to grab you. Outposts like **Cartago,** which believe it or not was once on a thriving Owens Lake port; **Olancha,** a thriving little palace with two cafes and two gas stations; and **Pearsonville,** one-time "Hubcap Capital of the World," would all make great middle-of-nowhere settings for some low-budget B-movie, but not even the biggest booster could stake a claim to much more.

THE RIGHT STUFF

It may not look like much from the highway, but driving along Hwy-14 you pass through one of the more significant corners of contemporary California. The railroad town of Mojave is where aircraft designer Burt Rutan made and built the *Voyager*, the first plane to fly non-stop around the globe on a single tank of fuel (they landed with 18.7 gallons of fuel left in their tank). Piloted by Burt Rutan's brother, Dick Rutan, and co-piloted by Jeana Yeager, the *Voyager* took off from Edwards Air Force Base on December 14, 1987, and landed at Edwards again just over 9 days later. (The rear-engine *Voyager* was a innovative design, and commercial models based on its design have suffered from some terrible crashes. Pop singer John Denver was killed when he crashed his into California's Monterey Bay.)

Just north of Mojave, Hwy-14 is lined with dozens of retired military and passenger jets, parked in the middle of the desert; but the real nexus of all this aerospace is the cutting-edge testing ground at Edwards Air Force Base, which spreads over 65 square miles of dry lake beds, east of the towns of Mojave and Lancaster.

Along with the triumphant journey of *Voyager*, Edwards A.F.B. is probably best known as the site of most of the early landings of NASA space shuttles, which touched down here at the end of the first 45 trips. The Edwards test range also saw many other important aviation firsts, many of which never made the news because of national security concerns during the Cold War: this is the place where in 1947 Chuck Yeager (he of *The Right Stuff* fame) first broke the sound barrier in the X-1, and where the rocket-powered X-15 flew more than 4,500 mph and reached altitudes of more than 350,000 feet. These days military research still goes on, as does development and testing of unmanned and remote-controlled aircraft, solar-powered planes (like NASA's *Centurion*), and the next-generation space shuttle, the X-33.

Many parts of the base are strictly off-limits, but you can definitely learn a lot on one of the free, 90-minute tours (Mon.-Fri. at 10 AM and 1 PM; 661/258-3460), which take you through hangars to look at the experimental aircraft currently being tested here.

The aphorism known as **Murphy's Law** ("Anything that can go wrong, will go wrong.") has been around for ages, but the Murphy to whom it is popularly credited was an engineer (Capt. Edward A. Murphy) working at Edwards after WW II.

West of the highway, the southern end of the Sierra Nevada mountains start to blend into the Tehachapis, and to the east, the vast volcanic desert around China Lake is under the control of the U.S. Navy, which uses it to test weapons. Meanwhile US-395 drops down from the Owens Valley into the heart of the Mojave Desert. Near China Lake, some 65 miles south of Lone Pine, Hwy-14 splits off slightly to the west from US-395, following the route of old US-6 toward Los Angeles through Mojave, Lancaster, and Palmdale, while US-395 veers eastward, through the ghostly heart of the Rand Mountains mining district, which from the 1890s until the 1930s was a thriving producer of gold, silver, tungsten and other valuable metals. Located some 30 miles south of the US-395/Hwy-14 junction, the mining district centered upon the twin towns of Randsburg and Johannesburg, where the few cafes, saloons, markets, and antique stores that stand today are a far cry from the days when thousands of men, women and children lived here.

One of the world's largest stamp mills once pounded the ore at the massive Yellow Aster Mine in Randsburg; alas, the mine was destroyed by arsonists in 1969.

Red Rock Canyon State Park (661/942-0662), 20 miles northeast of Mojave along both sides of Hwy-14, protects a wall of bright red sandstone badlands that look like they belong in Utah. The park has been used as a backdrop for many movies, including *Jurassic Park*.

South of Randsburg, US-395 embarks on one of California's dullest drives, a beeline south across the desert finishing at the I-15 freeway, the modern replacement for old Route 66.

Hwy-14: Mojave, Palmdale, and Lancaster

Used by long-haul truckers and Los Angelenos bound for or returning from the wild High Sierra, Hwy-14 across the Mojave Desert is not exactly a scenic drive, but there are a few spots worth knowing about. The towns along here vary from burly railroad junctions and truck stops (like Mojave, at the Hwy-14/Hwy-58 junction), to booming Lancaster (pop.127,000!) and Palmdale (pop. 117,000!), which are low-budget satellite suburbs of Los Angeles.

Lancaster boasts a very nice stadium for the Class A California League **Lancaster Jethawks** (661/726-5400), and also marks the turnoff for one of the real treats of the region: the **California Poppy Reserve** (661/924-0662), 15 miles west of Hwy-14 along Lancaster Road, where in springtime, depending upon rainfall and other factors, the entire desert floor is covered in masses of brilliant golden orange flowers, California's state flower.

I-15 SURVIVAL GUIDE: CALIFORNIA

RUNNING DIAGONALLY ACROSS SOUTHERN CALIFORNIA, I-15 has replaced US-395 (and old Route 66) in places, and offers an alternative route between Los Angeles and Death Valley. For the most part, though, it's a busy freeway, carrying truckers and gamblers between San Diego, around the eastern fringes of Los Angeles, and Sin City (Las Vegas). Crossing the Mojave Desert, you might want to stop at:

MM 180: Main Street in the desert crossroads of **Barstow** is none other than historic Route 66.

MM 236: From the **Zzyzx Road** exit, go four miles south to a 60-room former hot springs resort that's now the California State University-run Desert Study Center (760/733-4266).

MM 239: The only real city between Barstow and Las Vegas, **Baker** is home to the World's Tallest Thermometer—134 feet tall, commemorating the all-time-high temperature, 134°, that was reached in Death Valley in 1913. The thermometer (call 800/204-TEMP for a current reading) stands over the visitors center for the expansive, 1.6 million-acre **Mojave National Preserve** (760/733-4040), which protects the vast desert area between I-15 and I-10.

MM 280: From the Nipton Road exit off I-10, head south and east for 10 miles and you'll come to the intriguing desert oasis of **Nipton**, which consists of twin sets of railroad tracks, a fully stocked grocery store, a campground with hookups, and the delightful Hotel Nipton (760/856-2335), a comfortable B&B with outdoor hot tubs for soaking while staring at the stars. East from Nipton, the Joshua Tree Parkway is lined with a wonderful dense forest of these weirdly anthropomorphic trees all the way to Searchlight, Nevada, near the west bank of the Colorado River.

MM 292: Looming up at the Nevada border, the casino-packed border town of **Primm** has one huge attraction: the 70 mph **Collossus** roller coaster.

From Lancaster, Hwy-14 climbs gently up 3,179-foot Soledad Pass, running along the back of the San Gabriel Mountains before linking up with I-5 at the north edge of the San Fernando Valley. For more on the route across Los Angeles, see pages 87-88; for more on Los Angeles itself, see the Survival Guide on pages 88-90.

GREAT BASIN AND SONORA DESERT: US-93

GREAT BASIN AND SONORA DESERT: US-93

The western half of North America is often described as a land of contrasts, and no route across it gives a sharper sense of the region's extremes than US-93. Besides traversing some of the most wild and rugged terrain imaginable— mighty mountains, endless valleys, raging rivers, and two very different deserts—and offering up-close looks at mile after mile of magnificent and almost completely untouched wilderness, US-93 also takes you right through the neon heart of what is surely the most extreme (and extremely visual) example of our contemporary "civilization": Las Vegas.

From the Idaho border, US-93 embarks on a journey that truly—if not officially —gives US-50 a run for the claim as the loneliest road in America, traveling top to bottom across the entire Great Basin desert. US-93 runs along the eastern edge of Nevada for 520 miles—500 of which take you through an exceptional degree of desolation: endless straight, narrow valleys, two-car traffic jams, and sparsely scattered towns. Crossroads like Wells, along I-80 in the northern half of the state, are big events; south of Wells, it's 130 miles to the next watering hole—Ely—beyond which the old mining camp of Pioche and the railroad town and desert hot springs of Caliente are the only wide spots in the road.Though not for the faint of heart (or anyone with an unreliable car), it's an unforgettably beautiful journey; after hours (or days, or weeks) of existential solitude, you drop down into the frenetic boomtown of Las Vegas.

North from Nevada, US-93 travels through some truly stupendous scenery— across the volcanic Snake River plain, through Sun Valley, the Sawtooth Mountains, and the Craters of the Moon National Park, then up into Montana and the Canadian Rockies. The entire route is described in my book *Road Trip USA: Cross-Country Adventures on America's Two-Lane Highways.*

Coming into Arizona across the top of Hoover Dam, US-93 cuts southeast the full length and half the breadth of the state. Starting at the Nevada border, US-93 makes a diagonal beeline toward the old Route 66 town of Kingman, one of the few watering holes in Arizona's northwest quarter. From the west end of the Grand Canyon, US-93 races southeast across the lush Sonora Desert—known as the "world's greenest desert," because of its abundant flora and fauna—through Phoenix and Tucson to the Mexican border. This last stretch is among the most fascinating 200 miles of highway in the country, taking you past such intriguingly diverse and unique sights as the controversial Biosphere II scientific research center, the country's only intact Cold War-era missile silo, and a pair of centuries-old churches, San Xavier and Tumacacori—two of the most captivating pieces of colonial-era architecture in the western U.S.

Jackpot

In every respect but one, Jackpot belongs more to Idaho than Nevada. Jackpot's visitors and workers mostly come from Idaho, as do its power and water; even its clocks are set to Idaho time. The one little exception, however, is pure Nevada: border-town gambling. Jackpot was founded in 1956, mere months after Idaho banned slot machines. The ban didn't, to be sure, reduce the demand, and Jackpot has thrived—as a pit stop in any of the town's casinos will attest.

Cactus Pete's (775/755-2321) is the 10-story tower you can see for miles; along with the big (30,000-square-foot) casino, it has a great snack bar, a buffet, gourmet restaurant, showroom, lounge, and 400 guest rooms ($50-150 a night). The rather pricey rooms—rated four diamonds by my AAA Tourbook, an honor usually reserved for big-city swank—are plush enough to be good value. Cactus Pete's also has a RV park, where the $12-a-night rate buys access to the hotel swimming pool and tennis courts. Under the same ownership, **The Horseshu** (775/755-7777), across the street, has cheaper rooms ($35-50 a night) and a good 24-hour coffee shop with typical Nevada meal deals. You can also stock up for the road at the supermarket next door.

Heading south from Jackpot, be sure to fill the tank before hitting the road; the next gas is more than an hour away.

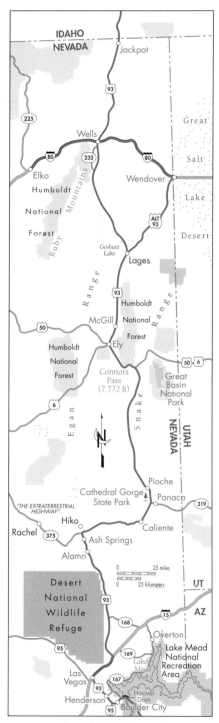

Two dozen miles north of the Idaho border, one place worth a stop is the summer-only **Nat-Soo-Pah** hot springs (208/655-4337), where you'll find a giant (125 by 50 feet) spring-fed swimming pool, a tree-shaded picnic area and snack bar, and a $10-a-night campground. Nat-Soo-Pah is about a mile south of Hollister, then three miles east on a well-signed road. There are a number of other natural springs in the area, so if you enjoy being in hot water, southern Idaho is a great place to explore.

Jackpot lies within the **Columbia Plateau** physiography of southern Idaho. This geographical anomaly is the only bit of land in Nevada that falls outside its two eminent deserts: the Great Basin, encompassing the top three-quarters of the state, and the Mojave, which covers the bottom quarter.

Every January, in the middle of winter, Wells holds **chariot races** on the west side of town. Some 50 teams (each consisting of a horse, a chariot and a driver) run around a track at the west end of town. For details, contact the visitors bureau (775/752-3355).

Wells

Some lone peaks, a stretch of badlands and buttes, and a couple of north-south-trending ranges usher US-93 down a long basin toward the little junction town of Wells (pop. 1,250). Just under 70 miles from Jackpot, at the interchange of US-93 and the I-80 freeway, Wells was named by the Central Pacific Railroad, which chose the site for a depot and town to make use of the plentiful springs in the hills a few miles northeast, a tributary of the Humboldt River. The old downtown—take a right on 6th Street and another right at the light—is the most intact abandoned "railroad row" on the entire mainline across northern Nevada. Wells provides an explicit illustration of the West's transition from rail to road to superhighway: the newest action in town is at the east and west exit ramps of I-80; between the exits, the business strip along 6th Street (old US-40), is pre-interstate vintage—1950s and even 1960s. The historic heart of town, on 7th Street along the railroad tracks, is pretty much out of business and derelict; commerce along the 125-year-old tracks is, of course, nearly extinct; food options are not especially exciting; and places to stay include a Motel 6.

Wells is situated at the northeastern base of the scenic **East Humboldt Range**. To get into the mountains, go under Wells's west exit ramp and follow the signs toward Angel Lake; the paved road (Hwy-231) climbs to 8,400 feet, passing one U.S. Forest Service campground and terminating at another. For details, contact the U.S. Forest Service **ranger station**, 140 Pacific Avenue (775/752-3342), at the west end of town, next to the very hospitable **Mountain Shadows RV Park** (775/752-3525).

Continuing down US-93 affords a different view of the East Humboldts. Ten miles south of Wells, you can take a right on Hwy-232, which makes a loop through luxuriant Clover Valley at the eastern base of the mountains, one of the most bucolic basins in Nevada. About six miles in from the highway is a right turn onto a rough dirt track. Look up to see **Hole-in-the-Mountain Peak**. Tallest peak in the East Humboldts (11,276 feet), it features a 30- by 25-foot natural window right through the top of the range in the thin rock 300 feet below its summit, presenting a spectacular little patch of blue (or silver, orange, or purple, depending on the time of day).

The Ruby Mountains

It's a long, solitary 140 miles between Wells and Ely. US-93 shoots down Clover Valley to the southern edge of the East Humboldts where Hwy-229, a maintained gravel road, cuts off southwest toward the Ruby Mountains, also known as the Nevada Alps. This is one of Nevada's most scenic ranges: 100 miles long, with more than a dozen peaks over 9,000 feet.

Though the drive down US-93 along their eastern flank gives you a good look at them, the best access to the 90,000-acre Ruby Mountains wilderness is from the west, where incredibly pretty ranch lands surround picturesque communities like **Lamoille**, gateway to gorgeous Lamoille Canyon and the heart of the Ruby Mountain Scenic Area.

For maps or more information on the Ruby Mountains, stop by the U.S. Forest Service **ranger station**, 976 Mountain City Highway (Hwy-225), at the west end of Elko (775/738-5171)

Detour: Elko
Gateway to the Ruby Mountains, and one of the most interesting places in Nevada, the engaging small city of Elko is 50 miles west of Wells via I-80. With only 15,000 residents, Elko is the fourth-largest city in the Silver State (behind Las Vegas, Reno, and Carson City), but away from the buzz of I-80 it still feels like a *very* small town. Best place to stop and get a feel for life here is the excellent **Northeastern Nevada Museum**, on the east side of downtown at 1515 Idaho Street (Mon.-Sat. 9 AM-5 PM, Sunday 1-5 PM; donations; 775/738-3418). Out front, a restored Pony Express cabin dates from the 1860s; inside are displays on railroads, pioneers, wildlife, and everything else to do with the middle of Nevada. Besides highlighting the

---

BONNEVILLE SPEEDWAY

Located in the middle of nowhere, west of the Great Salt Lake on the Utah/Nevada border, the vast salt flats of Bonneville cover some 150 square miles. Bonneville's broad, hard, flat, and unobstructed surface has made it a mecca for efforts to set ever faster land-speed records. The earliest speed records were set at Daytona Beach, Florida. But as top speeds increased, racers needed more room to maneuver safely. Bonneville's first world record (114 mph) was set in 1914. Ever since, racers—from Ab Jenkins in his bright red *Mormon Meteor,* to Gary Gabelich, who in 1970 set Bonneville's most recent record (622 mph) in his *Blue Flame*—have converged on Bonneville's 13-mile-long drag strip in pursuit of record-breaking speed. Craig Breedlove, in his car *Spirit of America,* was the first to exceed the 400, 500, and 600 mph marks here.

In recent years, problems with water dissolving the salt have made Bonneville less than ideal; racers like Richard Noble—whose team set the current record of 763 mph—have opted for the Black Rock Desert, 150 miles north of Reno, Nevada.

Still, every summer, hundreds of thrill-seekers descend on Bonneville, racing their hot rods in a series of time trials.

Mormon Meteor. The World's Greatest Unlimited Speed Record Maker, Bonneville Salt Flats, Utah. Holding All Speed Records from 10 Miles to 7,134 and from One Hour to 48 Hours

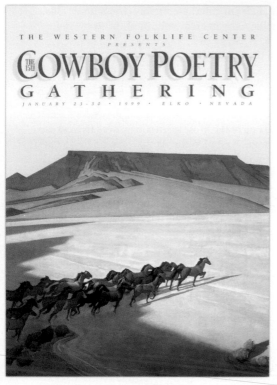

region's intermingled Basque and ranching cultures, the museum also provides a full introduction to the mining industry with a multimedia show telling you all you could ever want to know about gold and how it is got. (Did you know that it can take up to 100 tons of ore to recover a single ounce of pure gold?). Half-day tours of a real-life gold mine can be arranged through the museum.

The other place to stop in Elko is the **Western Folklife Center**, which hosts the very popular **Cowboy Poetry Gathering** (800/ 748-4466) every January. (The gathering takes place in January because that's the only time of year real cowboys—as opposed to the rhinestone type—get to take a break from their ropin' and throwin' and brandin'.) Readings and other cowboy poetry events take place elsewhere in Elko, but year-round the Folklore Center, housed in the old Pioneer Hotel at 5th and Railroad Streets, can supply you with all the books, tapes, and songbooks you could want. And if they don't have it, Nevada's largest cowboy outfitters, **J. M. Capriola's**, is just a block away, on Railroad Street.

'Elko also hosts a Cowboy Music Gathering the last weekend in June and a very big Basque-flavored 4th of July celebration. Take advantage of some of the fine restaurants such as the **Star Hotel** (775/738-9925), near the railroad tracks at 246 Silver Street, which is worth the drive for the delicious lamb chops and other dishes. Because of all the travelers passing through along I-80, rooms can be expensive and hard to find (impossible during the Cowboy Poetry Gathering, or any other big event).

If you're standing on Elko's Railroad Street wondering where the tracks have gone, they've been moved south, out from downtown to a strip along the Humboldt River.

For more information, or lists of lodging options, contact the **Elko Convention and Visitors Bureau** (800/248-ELKO or 800/248-3556).

Wendover

At the I-80 freeway, US-93 becomes the hypotenuse of an alternate route, which runs for 60 miles southeast to the Utah border at Wendover, then another 60 miles southwest to rejoin the mainline US-93 at Lages. Wendover, like Jackpot, is a thriving Nevada border town, with over 1,000 hotel rooms, five major casinos and as many new golf-course-view subdivisions. Wendover's claims to fame include

Wendover Will, the huge cowboy who welcomes you to Nevada along the Utah state line, outside the classy **Stateline** casino (775/664-2221 or 800/648-9668); the **Bonneville Salt Flats** and speedway, where most of the world's land-speed records have been set over the past 80 years (see the special topic); and **Wendover Air Force Base**, where in 1945 the crew of the *Enola Gay* trained to drop an atomic bomb on Japan.

Right at the border, the Stateline casino is linked by a pedestrian bridge with the equally classy **Silversmith** casino; the two are run jointly, and though either would be dwarfed by most anything on the Las Vegas Strip, here in Wendover they seem pretty darn flashy. Both these places have nice rooms for $45-145; rates are highest weekend nights, when you may prefer to opt for the cheaper motel-type places (Best Western, Days Inn, and more) across the Utah border. Food is pretty much limited to casino buffets and franchised fast food.

Between Wells and Ely, US-93 bends away from the heart of the Ruby Mountains, running southeast through Steptoe Valley on a marathon drive down an elongated basin, hemmed in by the Schell Creek Range on the east and the Egan Range on the west. The only signs of civilization on this stretch are two **road-houses**: one at **Lages** (78 miles south of Wells), the other at **Schellbourne** (40 miles north of Ely), where the rest area across US-93 has a historic plaque marking the route of the Pony Express.

McGill

Tiny McGill, 128 miles south of I-80 and 12 miles north of Ely, is a classic Nevada company town—its workaday life revolving for the first 50 years of the 20th century around a giant copper smelter. Mining company officials lived in the fancy houses

The McGill smelter's last skyscraping smokestack was felled in September 1993. At 750 feet, it was until then the tallest structure in Nevada.

around the "Circle" at the top of the hill just below the factory, while workers were housed according to their ethnic origins. The saloon and jail were conveniently right next door to each other (the jail is now in Ely), and steam from the copper furnaces was piped to heat the town's houses. The company's been gone for more than 15 years, but the layout remains, along with acres of fenced-off brick factory buildings painted with fading signs encouraging workers to behave safely.

A few of McGill's buildings have been converted to current uses, but most are closed. US-93, which runs along 4th Street at the foot of town, attracts most of the businesses, including **Marie's Cafe**, the town's main place to eat, a Frosty stand (for burgers and shakes), and the **McGill Club**, right on US-93 down the street in the old Cyprus Hall. Boasting "The Oldest Back Bar in the State," the latter is considered one of Nevada's finest by connoisseurs of Silver State licensed establishments.

The junction of US-93 and US-50, the legendary "Loneliest Road in America," is just east of Ely, which is described in the US-50 chapter on pages 250-251.

Connors Pass and Major's Place

Southeast of Ely, US-93—spliced together with US-50 and US-6 into a single two-lane highway—continues for 25 miles before crossing the narrow waist of the Schell Creek Range at Connors Pass (elev. 7,722 feet), one of only two fractions of US-93 in Nevada that climb above the tree line. (Unlike most of the rest of the country, tree line in Nevada has a lower, as well as an upper, limit: no trees grow below roughly 4,000 feet.) As you ascend toward the pass, the air cools and freshens, the single-leaf piñon and Utah juniper appear and thicken, and, cresting the summit, the mighty Snake Range—including 13,061-foot Wheeler Peak—comes into view.

At Major's Place, where there's cold beer and banks of slot machines waiting for you in a roadhouse called **Major's Station** (775/591-0430), US-93 splits off from US-50 and US-6, the latter two heading east toward Utah, while US-93 cuts south for 80 long, solitary miles to the next contact with humans, at Pioche. The highway rolls along Spring and Lake Valleys, ushered on its way by the Schell Creek, Fairview, Bristol, and Highland Ranges on the west and the Snake and Wilson Creek Ranges on the east.

> Nevada's one and only national park, **Great Basin National Park,** stands along the slopes of Wheeler Peak, off US-50 some 30 miles east of US-93. For details, see pages 251-253.

> Note that there are **no services**—no gas, no food, no lodging or organized camping, not even a video rental store—for the long haul between Major's Place and Pioche.

Pioche

The only places that are more than a ghostly outline of civilization in the nearly 300 miles of Great Basin desert that US-93 crosses between Ely and Las Vegas are the wildly different towns of Caliente, Panaca, and Pioche. The oldest and most northerly of the three, Pioche (pop. 800; pronounced "pee-OACH") is a one-time mining boomtown that had its heyday well over a century ago. Being so remote (exponentially more then than now), during the 1870s Pioche descended to a level of anarchy that rivaled that of Bodie and Tombstone, and more than 50 men were killed before anyone died of natural causes.

Corruption, too, was the order of the day, and you can tour Pioche's "Million Dollar" **Lincoln County Courthouse**, on Lacour Street, for a graphic demonstration. Designed in 1871 at an estimated cost of $26,000, the courthouse wasn't completed until 1876, to the tune of $88,000. Then, unable to pay off the principal, the county commissioners kept refinancing the debt while interest accrued year after year. By the time the debt was paid off, in 1937, the courthouse had cost a million bucks, been sold (for a whopping $150), and been replaced by a more modern structure. Now restored, the old courthouse is open for self-guided **tours** (daily 10 AM-4 PM; donations; 775/962-5182) of the offices, the courtroom, and the old jail.

The eclectic **Lincoln County Museum** (Tues.-Sun. 10 AM-4 PM; free), on Main Street (Business 93) at the center of town, is another good stop, as are nearby historic buildings such as the **Thompson Opera House**, the **Commercial Club**, and the **Gem**, an intact, still-in-use 1920s movie theater. The rusting remains of an **aerial tramway** that ran through Pioche in the 1920s, carrying ore to the stamp mills, can be explored—cables, cars, and all—from various points in town. Two state parks along Hwy-322 to the east (Echo Canyon and Spring Valley, 12 and 20 miles from town, respectively) round out your

Pioche-area sightseeing and offer the best **camping**.

On the practical side, Pioche also has the **Motel Pioche** (775/962-5551), on Lecour Street near the Million Dollar Courthouse, as well as the **Silver Cafe**, open daily for Mexican and American breakfasts, lunches, and dinners right on Main

Street (775/962-5124), a Chevron station, and a used-book store housed in the old mining company headquarters, the Book Mine.

Panaca Spring, a fine local **swimming hole** with warm, sweet water, is found just outside town. Take 5th Street north past the baseball diamond and a rusty old steam engine, toward a big cottonwood tree about a half-mile beyond where the pavement ends.

Panaca and Cathedral Gorge

Panaca, 11 miles south of Pioche (165 miles north of Las Vegas), and a mile east of US-93 on Hwy-319, was founded in 1864 by Mormon farmers attracted to the valley by the plentiful water of Panaca Spring, in what was then a part of Utah. The mining strikes at nearby Bullionville and Pioche disturbed their peace briefly, but Panaca—which has a single gas station/minimart, the **Skittles and Vittles** cafe, a school, and lots of houses—has a strong sense of tranquillity and timelessness rarely felt in the rest of Nevada.

Just west of US-93, a mile north of Panaca, **Cathedral Gorge State Park** is a mini-Grand Canyon of eroded mud. A lake once covered this deep gully, and silt and clay were washed to the bottom by streams and creeks. The lake dried up, exposing the sediments, and erosion (which never sleeps) sculpted them into the fantastic procession of formations that you see today. The **campground** ($7 per site; 775/728-4467) here has shade trees, flush toilets, even showers.

Caliente

To Pioche's mining and Panaca's farming, Caliente (pop. 1,100), 15 miles south, adds railroading. This small town was built around the San Pedro, Los Angeles, and Salt Lake Railroad tracks in the early 1900s, a short while before Las Vegas itself was founded. Built in 1923, the **Union Pacific Depot** (which still receives Amtrak service on the Las Vegas-Salt Lake City line) is the nerve center of Caliente. It's being restored to house government offices and an art and local-history gallery.

Caliente supports two gas stations and three motels, the best of which is the **Hot Springs** (775/726-3777), off US-93 on the north side of town. Here your room comes with use of big Roman-inspired tubs, whose fire-hydrant faucets fill the five-foot-square, four-foot-deep tubs in three minutes flat with clean, soft, 105° water. Roadfood is limited to three choices: the **Knotty Pine** coffee shop and pool hall; the **Branding Iron** cafe, across from the depot; and **Carl's Sandwich and Burger Shop**, next to the post office on US-93, which does a fine green chili cheeseburger and great shakes—well worth a stop on a hot summer afternoon.

Rainbow Canyon

From the south end of Caliente, where US-93 bends to the west, Hwy-317 heads straight south on one of Nevada's most scenic and least-known drives. Pass under a railroad trestle, and a few idyllic farms and ranches lining Meadow Wash, then suddenly the road is bounded by the colorful volcanic-tuff cliffs of Rainbow Canyon. After two miles or so you pass the small gem of **Kershaw-Ryan State Park** (day-use only), with hiking trails winding through 240 acres of oak and cottonwood trees that thrive along nearly permanent springs. Beyond here, some five miles south of Caliente, numerous pictographs, petroglyphs and other signs of Native American presence can be seen around Etna Cave.

The Hwy-317 pavement ends after 21 total miles of Rainbow Canyon ranches and railroad trestles, but in dry weather you can continue 38 miles through Kane Springs Valley to connect back up with US-93, 31 miles north of the I-15 freeway. If your car is up to the drive, and the weather's fine, the Rainbow Canyon route makes a shorter (in miles) and much more interesting alternative to the long, lonely, extraterrestrial tour along US-93.

Hiko and the Extraterrestrial Highway

South from Caliente, US-93 bends due west for 43 miles. Newman Canyon, just outside of town, has tall, sheer, smooth volcanic-tuff walls similar to Rainbow Canyon's. You twist and climb out of the canyon to cross the Delmar Range at **Oak Springs Summit** (elev. 6,237 feet), where the juniper trees are a welcome change from the low desert scrub. Beyond is an even rarer sight—not only for this highway but for any highway: a little interface zone in which the junipers grow right next to Joshua trees. This is the first indication of the change from Great Basin desert, which lies to the north, to the front edge of the Mojave Desert, which spreads south and west. Pahroc Summit is next (just under 5,000 feet), then Six Mile Flat, and then Hiko, where Hwy-375—the heart of the "Extraterrestrial Highway"— heads northwest through Rachel to US-6, Tonopah, and the back door to Bishop, California. (See the special topic The Extraterrestrial Highway for more.)

Ash Springs and Alamo

From the Hwy-375 junction, US-93 turns due south again and enters some unexpectedly lush country, in the midst of which three large and faithful springs provide plentiful water for alfalfa farms and cattle ranches—as well as for the only bona fide lakes that US-93 encounters in more than 400 miles of its Nevada leg. Ash Springs—consisting of a single combination gas station/restaurant/bar called R Place—is named after the nearby water source, which is believed to be part of a vast aquifer underlying much of eastern Nevada; earthquakes have thrust this particular water to the surface.

Twelve miles south of Ash Springs is Alamo, whose two motels, two truck stop gas stations, and 24-hour "Del Pueblo" Mexican restaurant are the only real services between Caliente and Las Vegas. Four miles south of town is Upper Pahranagat Lake; an old road runs along the eastern shore, with camping and picnic sites and big cottonwoods —one of the most idyllic spots on the whole Nevada portion of US-93. The water is close enough to the source at Ash Springs that it's relatively warm year-round. Lower Pahranagat Lake, a bit farther south, freezes in the winter.

THE EXTRATERRESTRIAL HIGHWAY: THE TRUTH IS OUT THERE

West of US-93, the U.S. government has turned the 3.5-million-acre expanse of Nellis Air Force Range, stretching nearly to Death Valley and the California border, into its most top-secret laboratory and testing ground. H-bombs, U-2 spy planes, Stealth bombers, you name it—this is where projects no one is supposed to know about exist.

The fallout—literal and figurative—from the nuclear bomb tests at the Nevada Test Site (which fills the southwestern third of the range) has abated in the post-Cold War era, so it's not totally surprising that something else has emerged to fill that void. What is surprising is that, like Roswell, New Mexico, this lonely corner of the world has become the focus of an ongoing controversy pitting government secrecy against allegations that the Air Force has been using a corner of the base known as "Area 51" to study UFOs and extraterrestrials. (Much of the controversy surrounding Area 51 is pretty silly, but for a serious study of the phenomenon read *Dreamland: Travels inside the Secret World of Roswell and Area 51*, by Phil Patton.)

Fueled in part by tabloid stories claiming an extraterrestrial creature is being kept alive at Area 51 in a high-security compound underneath Groom Lake—and also by local businesspeople's realization that UFO tourism can't hurt their economy—the hoopla has focused on the tiny village of **Rachel**, which has become to UFO-spotters what Dallas' grassy knoll is to JFK conspiracy theorists. Rachel (pop. 99), the only visible community along the 92-mile stretch of Hwy-375, is a block-long strip that holds the **Area 51 Research Center**, a mobile home that doubles as a command post for UFO-spotters. The more lighthearted **Little A-Le-Inn** is a typical bar and grill where you can munch on Alien Burgers, down drinks with names such as the "Beam Me Up, Scotty" (Jim Beam, 7UP, and Scotch), and peruse UFO-related key chains, fridge magnets, and T-shirts. The A-Le-Inn (775/729-2515) also has rooms for around $30 a night.

Since 1997, Hwy-375, the main road through Rachel and past Groom Lake and Area 51, has been officially known as the Extraterrestrial Highway, promoted by the state along the lines of their "Loneliest Road" campaign. So far, the promotion has consisted of a few brochures and four roadside signs. Apart from the signs (which are alien green, of course), the other main "sight" out here (as opposed to "sightings," which still occur fairly frequently) is the mysterious "black mailbox," a supposed beacon for UFOs, 29 miles southeast of Rachel along Hwy-375.

Upper Lake is also home to the administration and maintenance facilities for the **Desert National Wildlife Refuge**, at 1.5 million acres the largest refuge in the Lower 48. Elusive desert bighorn sheep enjoy protection within this huge habitat, alongside which US-93 travels the length of the aptly named Sheep Range. The road descends gradually into rocky and barren desert until finally, 70 miles from Alamo and 125 miles from Caliente, it merges with the I-15 freeway for the high-speed haul into the Big Glow, Las Vegas.

If you want to avoid Las Vegas entirely, you can do so by following a very scenic route along the shores of Lake Mead. The route, which leaves US-93 30 miles north of the junction with I-15 and loops east of Las Vegas along Hwy-168 and Hwy-169, rejoining US-93 at Hoover Dam, is described below on pages 212-213.

Radio station **KBAD 920 AM** broadcasts all the hits of the 1940s and early 1950s, plus play-by-play of Las Vegas Stars baseball games.

Driving Las Vegas

If you time the drive into Las Vegas so you arrive around dusk, the western sky sports a purple sunset while the horizon shines brightly from a billion amber street lights stretching from one end of the valley to the other. But wait: you're still more than 30 miles out! The downtown and Strip skylines are clearly discernible for a full half hour before you get to Ground Zero, but even though the roadway widens to four-lane freeway, the halcyon trip down Nevada's nothingness lingers till the last possible moment. And then the transition is insanely abrupt: the deep desert, then wham!—Sin City.

Almost everybody who drives into Las Vegas comes by way of the I-15 freeway, which runs between Los Angeles and Salt Lake City and which connects with US-93 some 20 miles northwest of the Strip. From the south and Hoover Dam, use the new I-515 freeway, which carries US-93 and US-95 on a snaking figure-S between Henderson and Fremont Street in downtown Las Vegas.

Las Vegas has to be the easiest city in the world to drive: everything lines up along, or in relation to, one big road—**The Strip**, the 10-mile barrage of bright lights and architectural extravagance that stretches along Las Vegas Boulevard, running parallel to I-15 southwest from the compact downtown area. US-93 actually bypasses The Strip, veering southeast along Fremont Street and the Boulder Highway—or along the I-515 freeway. (Other roads in Las Vegas are named after the big hotels near their intersections with the Strip; hence you find Sahara Avenue, Desert Inn Road, Flamingo Road, and Tropicana Avenue, one after another from downtown.)

If you visit Las Vegas, it's all but required that you drive at least a little of the Strip (which *is* an official scenic route)—preferably around 2 AM, when the usually busy traffic has subsided a little. Starting near downtown at the Strosphere Tower, things start to pick up at the Venetian, its impressive replica of St. Mark's Square standing across from the pirate ships of Treasure Island and the erupting volcano of The Mirage. Then comes Caesar's Palace, the dancing fountains of Bellagio, and the erstaz Eiffel Tower of Paris, then my personal favorite: New York, New York, with its mini-Coney Island roller coaster rumbling through the scaled-down trademark Manhattan skyline, anchored by the Statue of Liberty. Across the street, in fluorescent hues, is the comic Camelot of Excalibur, then the glass pyramid of Luxor, then, surprisingly suddenly, the desert.

LAS VEGAS SURVIVAL GUIDE

LAS VEGAS IS THE BIGGEST, BRIGHTEST, AND BRAZENEST boomtown in the world, and this is its biggest boom. In the past decade, multiple mega resorts and another dozen major hotels, dressed up as mock everything—from Venice to Paris to New York City—have opened here. The city can now claim nine of the 10 largest hotels in the world and more than 100,000 rooms—more than New York and Chicago *combined*. Twenty-five million visitors lose five billion dollars in the casinos here every year, and as more and more resorts begin catering to general "vacation fun," rather than just gambling, there's no end in sight—so long as the water supply holds out.

If Frank Sinatra and the "Rat Pack" personified the swaggering spirit of Las Vegas, there's one person who embodied its over-the-top glitz: pianist Liberace, whose collection of candelabras, cars, and flamboyant costumes is on display at the **Liberace Museum**, 1775 E. Tropicana (daily 10 AM-5 PM; $7; 702/798-5595).

Still, gambling is the biggest game in town, and here are a few of the many places you can "play" (and one place you can watch professional baseball being played).

Binion's Horseshoe, 1238 Fremont Street (702/382-1600 or 800/237-6537). The quintessential old-time gambling joint, which hasn't changed much from the good old gangster days. Home of the World Series of Poker, with its $1,000,000 prize.

Caesar's Palace, 3570 Las Vegas Boulevard South (702/731-7110 or 800/634-6661). The most famous of them all—from the day it opened in 1966 until 1991, when the Mirage was completed, Caesar's was the classiest, the most expensive, and the first truly "themed" hotel in Las Vegas.

El Cortez, 600 Fremont Street (702/385-5200 or 800/634-6703). The oldest (1941) casino still in operation, once owned by Bugsy Siegel.

Hard Rock Hotel/Casino, 4555 Paradise Road (702/693-5000 or 800/473-7625). For anyone under 50, this is the coolest place in town. It's off the Strip and small by Vegas standards, but where else can you play Jimi Hendrix slot machines (a line of "Purple Haze" pays $200) while listening to nonstop classic rock 'n' roll?

Luxor, 3900 Las Vegas Boulevard South (702/262-4444 or 800/288-1000). The most distinctive casino here—housed inside a mammoth (29-million-cubic-foot) glass pyramid at the southern end of the Strip. Above the casino, stage sets of city streets hold high-tech attractions: motion simulators, 3-D and IMAX movies, and "virtual reality" arcade games.

MGM Grand, 3799 Las Vegas Boulevard South (702/891-7777 or 800/929-1111). The biggest, with the world's largest gaming hall—at 171,000 square feet, it could encompass 85 four-bedroom houses. The rest of the place is huge, too: 5,000-plus rooms, 23 eateries, an arena and showroom, a monorail, and an amusement park.

The Mirage, 3400 Las Vegas Boulevard South (702/791-7111 or 800/627-6667). The most opulent, with a rainforest, a 50,000-gallon aquarium, white tigers on display (this is the home of Siegfried and Roy), and the most "Beautiful People."   *(continues)*

New York, New York, 3790 Las Vegas Boulevard South (702/740-6969 or 800/693-6763). "The Greatest City in Las Vegas" is a convincing re-creation of the Big Apple, complete with replicas of the Statue of Liberty, the Chrysler Building, and a Coney Island roller coaster that races around the roof. The casino area feels like tidy versions of real NYC streets, right down to steaming sidewalk grates.

Treasure Island, 3300 Las Vegas Boulevard South (702/894-7111 or 800/944-7444). The free pirate show—right on the Strip in front of the casino—plays every 90 minutes starting at 1:30 PM. Not to be missed.

Las Vegas Stars, 850 N. Las Vegas Boulevard (702/386-7200). The Class AAA farm club of the San Diego Padres play their home games at Cashman Field. Games are broadcast on KBAD 920 AM.

Practicalities

McCarran International Airport (LAS), one of the 10 busiest in the country, is only a couple of miles east of the Tropicana/Strip intersection. The local bus fare is $1, low in cost but high in adventure. Limos and shuttles will take you to your hotel or motel for less than $5. Taxis from the airport are about $10 for Strip destinations, $15 for downtown. There are also all the usual rental car companies. (If you'd like to pretend that the whole thing is a hallucination, a mere mirage in the Mojave Desert, you can barrel straight through Las Vegas on the I-15 freeway. But don't turn your head! It's an illusion only if you see it with one eye.)

If you're going to brave a tour through the belly of the beast, your exits are all off I-15: Main Street for downtown; Sahara, Spring Mountain, Flamingo, and Tropicana (these are names of streets as well as casinos) for the Strip.

If you're staying overnight, you'll enter the wacky and somewhat wicked world of Las Vegas lodging. Rates, depending on the time of year, time of the week, and sometimes even the time of day, can be as low as $19 for a decent hotel room, or as high as $229 for a dive. If you want to stay in a hotel, you should try to make reservations at least a week in advance.

If you're blowing in without a reservation, it's wisest to stop at a pay phone, look under "Hotels" in the Yellow Pages, and call around. You'll quickly find out whether the town is sold out, has a few rooms at top dollar, or can put you up reasonably. Don't even bother with this on a Friday or Saturday, or during a big convention (like Comdex, when every room within 100 miles is booked up) or a boxing match, when the town is *always* sold out. A final note: If you'll be schlepping a lot of luggage, Las Vegas hotel rooms are a *long* way from parking spaces in the high-rise garages and huge lots, though the parking is free.

One of the most comfortable, reasonably priced places to stay is **Circus Circus**, 2880 Las Vegas Boulevard South (702/734-0410 or 800/634-3450), which has cheap rooms (doubles from $25 a night) at the center of the Strip, with a carnival midway, circus acts, and low-stakes table games. **Excalibur**, 3850 Las Vegas Boulevard South (702/597-7777 or 800/937-7777), is 100% over-the-top Vegas kitsch, in the form of a turreted castle dwarfed by one of the world's largest hotels—4,032 rooms, usually around $50 a night. Across the Strip, the **Tropicana**, 3801 Las Vegas Boulevard South (702/739-2222 or 800/468-9494), is a real desert oasis, with lots of swimming pools (including one 300 feet long) and spacious, 1950s-style rooms and public areas. The **Desert Inn**, 3145 Las Vegas Boulevard South (702/733-4444 or 800/634-6906), where Howard Hughes lived during his reclusive years, is now owned (along with half of Vegas, it seems) by the ITT-Sheraton conglomerate, but the "DI" is still the same as it always has been: a sedate, high-roller haven amidst the glitzy bustle of the Strip.

Finally there's **Motel 6**, 195 E. Tropicana Avenue (702/798-0728), "The World's Largest Motel 6" (880 rooms) and also the most expensive, starting at $45 a night.

For great cheap food, try the snack bars downtown, especially at the Horseshoe, Golden Gate, and El Cortez; on the Strip, at the Boardwalk, Westward Ho, and Slots A Fun. Fast-food courts are found at the Riviera, Caesar's, and MGM, and there's a neon McDonald's on the Strip. The best all-you-can-eat buffet is at the **Rio Suites Casino**, away from the Strip at 3700 W. Flamingo Road, west of I-15; Main Street Station, Texas Station, and Fiesta (in that order) also have good buffets. Every major hotel has a 24-hour coffee shop; the Desert Inn, the Mirage, Binion's Horseshoe, Caesar's, and Gold Coast have good ones.

For more information, the main Las Vegas visitors center is next to the Convention Center at 3150 Paradise Road (702/892-0711). The *Las Vegas Review-Journal* is the big morning daily, the *Las Vegas Sun* the smaller afternoon paper.

Escape from Las Vegas

The most popular day-trip out from Las Vegas is south to Hoover Dam, but there are many other ways to escape the onslaught of neon and slot machines. If you have a whole day or more, you can drive two hours north to the pristine deserts of Death Valley or two hours east to the red rock wonderlanda of Zion and Bryce National Parks. In a long afternoon, you can get away to other natural beauty spots. The most remarkable of these is only a half-hour from the bustle of the Strip: high on the slopes of 11,919-foot Mount Charleston, hiking just over a mile brings you to **Mary Jane Falls**, cascading through conifer forest. The trail starts at a well-signed parking area, north of Las Vegas via US-95, then 17 miles west along Hwy-157 to Echo Road; call the Toiyabe National Forest (702/873-8800) for details.

If you'd rather do a drive-through tour, a better option may be the sandstone gorges of the **Red Rock Canyon National Conservation Area**, a half-hour west of Las Vegas via Charleston Boulevard (Hwy-159). Popular with cyclists, a 13-mile loop winds up through the canyon, with numerous short trails leading into rugged side canyons. There's a $5 entry fee per vehicle; call the BLM-run **visitors center** (702/363-1921) for further information.

Henderson

Southeast of Las Vegas, US-93 joins US-95 along Nevada's newest freeway, I-515, which connects Las Vegas with the rapidly growing industrial city of Henderson. Henderson itself is relatively young, even by Nevada standards. In 1941, the War Department selected this site, due to its proximity to unlimited electricity generated by then-six-year-old Hoover Dam, for a giant factory to process magnesium, which was needed for bombs and airplane components. Ten thousand workers arrived and within six months had built the plant and a town for 5,000 people. After the war ended, the factory was subdivided for private industry. Since then, Henderson has grown to be the third-largest city in Nevada, behind Las Vegas and Reno—the only three population centers in Nevada with more than 100,000 residents.

Though it doesn't even try to compete with the attractions of Las Vegas, Henderson does have two large and three small casinos (including the world's largest bingo parlor), and the very good **Clark County Heritage Museum** (daily 9 AM-4:30 PM; $1.50), located two miles south of town at 1830 S. Boulder Highway. A great place to take the kids is a tour of **Kidd's marshmallow factory** (call for directions; 702/564-5400).

South of Henderson, US-93/95 climbs up and over 2,367-foot Railroad Pass, and just beyond is the junction where US-95 cuts south, heading along the Colorado River to Laughlin, Nevada; Needles, California; and Yuma, Arizona. US-93 continues east, and a little north, to Boulder City.

Boulder City

Like Henderson, Boulder City (pop. 12,600) was founded and built by the federal government to house workers at Hoover Dam—then the largest construction project ever undertaken. Though the dam was completed in 1935, Boulder City continued under federal ownership and management for another 25 years; in 1960, an Act of Congress conferred independent municipal status on the town.

Long-time residents purchased their houses, and alcohol consumption was permitted for the first time in the town's history—though gambling remained forbidden. To this day, almost a half-century after "independence," Boulder City remains the only town in Nevada that expressly prohibits gambling, which may explain why it feels more like the Midwest than a suburb of Sin City.

If you're interested in the men and machines involved in building the dam (which was completed two years *ahead* of schedule), the small but interesting **Boulder City/Hoover Dam Museum** has walls full of old photos and other exhibits inside the historic (and newly restored) **Boulder Dam Hotel**, 1305 Arizona Street (702/293-3510). The hotel also has a good dining room and is home to the local chamber of commerce office, too. A handful of old motels and some nifty old-fashioned diners, such as the **Coffee Cup** and the **1950s Cafe**, line up along the Nevada Highway (a.k.a. the US-93 "Business Route"), the main street through Boulder City, but the real draws are just below Boulder City—at the dam, of course, and the lake behind it.

Hoover Dam

Approaching Hoover Dam from the Nevada side, in the eight miles from Boulder City you pass a Nevada Welcome Center, a National Park Service visitors center for Lake Mead National Recreation Area, and a peculiar parade of electrical generators, transformers, and capacitors all secured by cyclone fencing topped by razor wire and barbs to keep out intruders.

If you like what you see and hear on the main Hoover Dam tour, ask about the much longer "hardhat" tour (every half-hour; $25; 702/293-8321), which takes you behind the scenes and shows off the project's inner workings and impressive engineering.

US-93 slows to a crawl approaching the bronzed glass of the **visitors center** (daily 8:30 AM–5:30 PM; $4, plus $2 parking; 702/294-3523), which opened in 1995, 10 years behind schedule and $100 million over budget. Inside, movies and displays are designed to keep visitors occupied before they join one of the very popular 45-minute **tours** of the dam (daily 8 AM–6 PM in summer, 9 AM–3 PM rest of year; $8). These descend 53 stories to the humming turbine room, then step outside for a look *up* at the massive monolith, which is nearly a quarter-mile across, 726 feet tall, 660 feet thick at the base, and made of a mere seven million tons (that's only 14 billion pounds) of concrete.

Crowds often throng the visitors center, and you may have to wait all day for a tour, but don't go

I-15 SURVIVAL GUIDE: NEVADA

RUNNING DIAGONALLY ACROSS SOUTHERN NEVADA, I-15 links San Diego with Salt Lake City by way of Las Vegas. The much prettier section of I-15 across Utah is covered in the Canyonlands Loop chapter, but in Nevada you might want to stop at some of the following interesting sights:

MM 0: Looming up along the California/Nevada border, the casino-packed town of **Primm** has one huge attraction: the 70-mph **Collossus** roller coaster.

MM 34-40: Running just north of the famous Strip, I-15 gives an unforgettable look at **Las Vegas.**

MM 63: Junction with US-93, which runs north to Caliente, Pioche, and Ely.

MM 93: Head south to **Overton** for the unique Lost City Museum and access to Lake Mead National Recreation Area.

MM 123: Just before the Arizona state line, which also marks the boundary between Pacific and mountain time zones, obscenely green golf courses in the middle of the barren desert have made **Mesquite** Nevada's fastest-growing city. The trip along I-15 across northwestern Arizona lasts for a mere 30 miles, but it's a beautiful drive, as the freeway passes through the scenic Virgin River Gorge.

Hoover Dam marks the border between Nevada and Arizona, and between the Pacific and Mountain **time zones,** so set your clocks and watches accordingly (and remember, Arizona does not use daylight saving time). Heading south, you'll pass no towns or services for some 75 miles, until you reach Kingman on old Route 66, so stock up and fill up in Boulder City before proceeding.

away without visiting the *old* visitors center, which is across the highway from the new one (and free). Here, in a 1940s-era theater, the story of the Colorado River basin and how it was saved from floods by reclamation projects, irrigation, and electrification is told by a big map, which is lit up by spotlights at appropriate historical and geographical points. It's high in kitsch value, and not a bad education, either. Fast food (with lake views) is available next door, at the irresistible **Hoover Dam Snacketeria.**

Continuing along, US-93 rolls right over the top of the gargantuan wedge of Hoover Dam; parking is free on the Arizona side of the dam.

Hwy-167: Lake Mead, the Lost City Museum, and Valley of Fire State Park

Lake Mead, the largest man-made lake in the Western Hemisphere, contains roughly 30 million acre-feet, or just over nine *trillion* gallons. It irrigates some 2.5 million acres of land in the U.S. and Mexico and supplies electricity—from 17 electrical turbines inside the dam's base—to millions and millions of people. The lake is also a very popular recreation site, with thousands of water skiers and fisherfolk flocking to its 500 miles of shoreline year-round.

Along the western shores of Lake Mead, one of the most interesting drives in southern Nevada doubles as a detour around Las Vegas: Hwy-167 runs the entire length of the lake, between I-15 near Mesquite, where the Virgin River ebbs into the lake, and Hoover Dam, which holds back the waters of the Virgin and Colorado Rivers.

At the north end of Lake Mead, the quiet farming town of **Overton** is home to the excellent **Lost City Museum** (daily 8:30 AM-4:30 PM; $2; 702/397-2193), which docu-ments the remnants of the ancient Anasazi or "Basketmaker" community, which emerged here around A.D. 800, then vanished mysteriously centuries later. The ruins were subsequently partially inun-dated by the rising waters of Lake Mead. The museum, housed in New Deal-era gallery that replicates Anasazi architec-

ture, displays hundreds of arti-facts related to the Anasazi and later Paiute and Pueblo cultures.

South from Overton, if the hills above Lake Mead seem to be burning, don't worry. Turn west on Hwy-169 to see why: the brilliant red, orange, and gold sand-stone spires of Valley of Fire State Park stretch for miles along the hilltops. At one of the most spectacular settings in this spec-tacular park, along Hwy-169 15 miles from the lakeshore (about 75 miles from Las Vegas), the main **visitors center** (daily 8:30 AM-4:30 PM; $4 per car; 702/397-2088) has exhibits explaining the more than 500 million years of sedimentation and erosion that went into the creation of the Valley of Fire's amazing landmarks. The visitors center is also the place to find out about the park's many pictographs, hiking trails, and camp-ing opportunities.

Between Valley of Fire and Las Vegas, scenic Hwy-167 fol-lows along Lake Mead all the way to the outskirts of Hender-son, but if you want to save time (and save your shocks from the fairly bumpy road surface), it's quicker to take I-15 to exit 75 and enter Valley of Fire from the western side.

Lake Mead Recreation Area: Eastern Shore

Most people visit Lake Mead, which covers some 160,000 acres and includes over 500 miles of shoreline, from the extensively developed Nevada side. The only access on the eastern (Arizona) side is from **Temple Bar**, 19 miles south of Hoover Dam, then another 27 miles northeast on a good paved road; a small marina has boat rentals and a motel (520/767-3211 or 800/752-9669).

The best access points to the western shore of Lake Mead are, from north to south, at **Overton Beach** (702/394-4040), where there's a marina, good fishing, a beach and an RV park; **Echo Bay**, where there's a nicer beach (no shade or lifeguard), another RV park, and a resort with rooms and a restaurant (702/394-4000); **Las Vegas Bay**, where you get a great lake view (but no good beach); and **Boulder Beach**, where there's a large shady campground and the appropriately named rocky beach.

South of Hoover Dam, US-93 runs parallel to the older version of the highway, with numerous old bridges and sections of gravel roadway standing along the modern four-lane freeway.

Along with low-price, low-key riverside gambling, Laughlin is also home to the massive **Mohave Generating Station**, which burns millions of tons of high-sulfur coal annually, producing enough power for over a million homes across California and Arizona—and enough pollution to stain the air with a dull brown haze for hundreds of miles. There are plans to install pollution control equipment, but we'll have to wait and, if possible, see.

Laughlin is one of the hottest inhabited places in the country—an all-time high temperature of 125° F was registered here in 1994.

Stretching to both sides of the border, downstream from Hoover Dam, the Lake Mead Recreation Area also incorporates the smaller Lake Mojave, clearly visible from US-93 and most easily accessible at **Willow Beach**, 14 miles south of Hoover Dam and four miles west of US-93.

Detour: Laughlin, Nevada

From Hoover Dam via US-95, and via Hwy-68 from US-93 just north of Kingman, a detour heads west to the Nevada side of the Colorado River. There, Laughlin, Nevada, a booming gambling resort, seems even more mirage-like than Las Vegas. Lacking the glitz and pizzazz of Vegas but offering cheaper rooms (under $20 is not uncommon) and the almost unheard-of attraction of river views from the casino floors, Laughlin epitomizes the anything-goes character of Nevada gaming.

The history of Laughlin—or rather, the lack of it—is impressive even by Nevada standards. Starting with a run-down bait shop he bought in the mid-1960s, Michigan-born entrepreneur Don Laughlin envisioned the fantasyland you see today, opening his **Riverside Hotel** (800/227-3849)—still a local favorite—in the late 1970s and drawing visitors from all over Arizona and Southern California. Laughlin's independent mini-empire was eclipsed in the 1980s by the big shots: Harrah's built the luxurious **Del Rio** (800/447-8700), Circus Circus opened the steamboat-shaped **Colorado Belle** (800/47-RIVER), and the **Flamingo**

Hilton (800/352-6464) added another 2,000-room palace in 1990. Fortunes have ebbed and flowed ever since, but Laughlin is still well worth a look or an overnight stay.

For further information, contact the Laughlin Chamber of Commerce (702/298-2214 or 800/227-5245).

Chloride

Back on US-93, marked by a big "C" inscribed in the hillside above it, the near-ghost town of Chloride (pop. 352), 53 miles south of Hoover Dam and 15 miles north of Kingman, then four miles east of the highway on a paved, well-marked road, is the oldest and among the most evocative former mining camps in Arizona. Following the discovery of silver here in the 1860s, mining activities continued through the 1940s; the town is now preserved by its dedicated residents.

A couple of stores and cafes still cling to life, and occasional festivals and flea markets draw sizeable crowds of visitors. Mostly what there is to see are the odd bits of "folk art" so often found in the American desert: strange sculptures made of rusting metal and odd bits of junk, plus comical tributes to the mythology of the Wild West, such as a fake "Boot Hill" cemetery with laconic epitaphs and hand-painted signs playing up the apocryphal legacy of the local "Hangin' Judge" Jim Beam.

From Chloride, it's another 15 miles along arrow-straight US-93 to Kingman, which is covered in the Route 66 chapter.

Kingman marks the intersection of US-93 and I-40. Before the I-40 interstate by-passed it in the 1970s, Kingman was a vital desert oasis on the famous Route 66. For more on the "Mother Road" and Kingman, see the Route 66 chapter, beginning on page 276.

Hualapai Mountain Park

East from Kingman, US-93 follows I-40 for over 20 miles before turning south again, but parallel to the freeway a well-marked 14-mile road leads up from the desert to Hualapai Mountain Park, where pines and firs cover the slopes of the 8,417-foot peak. Hiking trails wind through the wilderness, and there's a **campground** ($6) and a few rustic **cabins** ($25) built by the CCC during the New Deal 1930s.

For detailed information or to make reservations, contact the **ranger station** (520/757-3859), near the park entrance.

Wickieup and Nothing

The long stretch of US-93 between Kingman and Phoenix is very busy, and sections have been upgraded to four-lane freeway to handle the many heavy trucks that rumble up and down it. There's not a lot to stop for, though the ranch town of Wickieup, 32 miles south of I-40, has **Luchia's Restaurant and Trading Post** (great pies!), and scenic Burro Canyon has a BLM campground set amidst impressive lava flows. The town of Nothing, midway between I-40 and Wickenburg, has a sevice station—nothing more.

Wickenburg

In the middle of the Arizona desert, 60 miles northwest of Phoenix and 130 miles from Kingman, **Wickenburg** (pop. 4,500) grew up as a gold-mining camp in the 1860s and has survived as a low-key resort community. A few

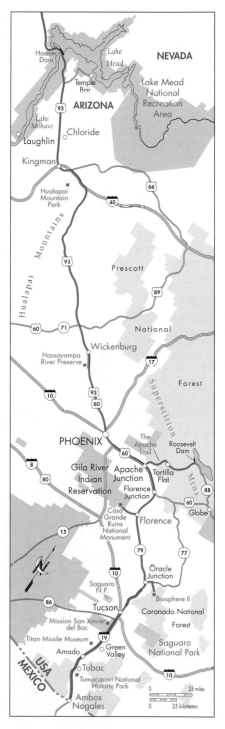

PHOENIX SURVIVAL GUIDE

THE MILLION-PLUS PEOPLE WHO HAVE SETTLED IN THE "VALLEY OF THE SUN" in and around the Arizona capital of Phoenix have nearly succeeded in obliterating any sense that the land here ever was—and in fact still is—a desert. Golf courses, swimming pools, lakes, and waterfalls are everywhere, with only a few carefully coiffed cacti remaining to testify to the natural state of things.

Phoenix really is a sprawling mess, expanding by acres every day, with no end (or beginning or middle, for that matter) in sight. But there is something oddly charming about the place—an anything-goes, Wild West spirit, manifest in the city's ongoing ability to grow and thrive despite the almost total lack of natural advantages.

The best thing about visiting Phoenix is the chance to explore the marvelous **Heard Museum**, 2301 N. Central Avenue (Mon.-Sat. 9:30 AM-5 PM, Wednesday till 9 PM, Sunday noon-5 PM; $7; 602/252-8840), among the best museums anywhere devoted to the native cultures of the Southwestern U.S. The recently expanded permanent galleries trace the history and diversity of prehistoric peoples and contemporary tribes, while changing exhibits focus on specific themes. Don't miss the amazing collection of Hopi kachina dolls, collected by hotelier Fred Harvey and the late U.S. Senator Barry Goldwater.

Another treat: **Taliesin West**, 108th Street at the east end of Cactus Road (daily 9 AM-4 PM; $10; 480/860-2700), where every winter from 1937 until his death, in 1959, Frank Lloyd Wright lived, worked, and taught, hand-crafting the complex of studios, theaters, and living quarters that survives as an architecture school. This monument to Wright's social and aesthetic ideals is located on a beautiful foothill site, once all alone but now at the edge of Phoenix's ever-encroaching suburban sprawl.

It's altogether appropriate that a city named for the mythological symbol of rebirth from ashes should be home to the **Hall of Flame**, 6101 E. Van Buren Street (Mon.-Sat. 9 AM-5 PM, Sunday noon-4 PM; $4), which displays one of the world's largest collections of fire fighting equipment in a series of air-conditioned industrial sheds in Papago Park. Across the street, the headquarters of the **Salt River Project** holds a lobby full of displays tracing the 2,500-year story of Phoenix's water supply, from prehistoric Hohokam canals to Mormon times and on up through today.

Last but not least, there's the "BOB," the Banc One Ballpark, downtown home of the **Arizona Diamondbacks** (602/514-8400). It's the only major league ballpark with its own outfield swimming pool.

Practicalities

Phoenix, sixth-largest city in the U.S., sits at the junction of the east-west I-10 freeway and north-south I-17 freeway from Flagstaff. Completing the high-speed overlay are other state-of-the-art local freeways, including the Hwy-202 Loop, Hwy-51, and the US-60 "Superstition Freeway." Note that Phoenix proper is surrounded by a half-dozen legally independent communities—upscale Scottsdale, Mormon Mesa, studenty Tempe—differentiated only by the design of their streets signs. Phoenix's busy Sky Harbor International Airport is just over a mile southeast of downtown and has all the shuttle services and car rental companies you could need.

Though there is skeletal bus service, trying to get around town without a car is hazardous to your health. In a word, *drive*.

There are tons of highway motels in and around the Valley of the Sun, and a number of gorgeous winter resort hotels. A prime example of the latter, the **Biltmore Hotel**, 24th and Missouri Streets (602/955-6600 or 800/950-0086), is an absolutely beautiful, Frank Lloyd Wright-style resort complex tucked away on spacious grounds on the far north side of Phoenix. Even if you can't manage the $250-a-night (and up) rates, stop by for a look, maybe even a meal or a drink. More reasonably priced places to sleep include **Holiday Inn-Old Town Scottsdale**, 7353 E. Indian School Road (602/994-9203 or 800/695-6995), near Scottsdale's Center for the Arts, with rooms from $50-150, depending upon season. Downtown, the **San Carlos Hotel**, 202 N. Central Avenue (602/253-4121 or 800/528-5446) is a well-maintained older hotel whose rooms cost $50-100 a night. The **HI Phoenix Hostel**, 1026 9th Street (602/254-9803) has dorm beds for around $15 a night.

The classic roadfood stop in Phoenix is the **Tee Pee**, 4144 E. Indian School Road, a characterful and always crowded place serving huge and very cheap plates of old-style Ameri-Mexican food. Other Mexican places range from **Such Is Life**, 3602 N. 24th Street, which specializes in southern Mexican cuisine—with especially delicious *mole* sauces. For something a bit hotter, brave the salsa at **Los Dos Molinos**, 8646 S. Central Avenue (closed Mon.), in the old Tom Mix house at the foot of South Mountain.

The Phoenix area **visitors bureau** puts out the usual hotel and restaurant listings and other practical information for travelers; contact them downtown at 400 E Van Buren Street (602/254-6500). The main newspaper is the Arizona *Republic*.

South of Wickieup, a section of US-93 is known as the **"Joshua Tree Parkway"** because it passes through some 15 miles of these oddly contorted cacti, which cover the rolling hills between 20 and 35 miles north of Wickenburg. The most intense concentration is 30 miles from town, around mile marker 170.

From Wickenburg, Hwy-89 runs north and east into the mountains, passing through historic gold mining towns of Prescott and Jerome on its way through scenic Sedona to Flagstaff.

At Wickenburg, US-93 officially comes to an end, replaced from here south to Phoenix by joint US-60/89.

crusty prospectors still search for a strike, and cowboys are often seen riding through town, which makes Wickenburg a pleasant place to get a feel for the Old West, especially during the winter months when temperatures are mild and the sun shines nearly every day.

Wickenburg's reliably good winter weather accounts for the number of **dude ranches** dotting the surrounding desert, most of which are intended for long stays (at least a week) rather than passing travelers; for a complete list of properties (which includes one owned by Merv Griffin), or any other information, contact the **visitors center** (520/684-5479) in the old railroad depot on Frontier Street, a block west of US-93.

Two blocks south along Frontier Street and the railroad tracks, at the US-60/US-93 junction and Wickenburg's only stoplight, the **Desert Caballeros Western Museum** (Mon.-Sat. 10 AM-5 PM, Sunday 1-4 PM; $5) gives a broad overview of regional history, and contains a good (if slightly snooty) collection of Western art and sculpture (including works by Frederic Remington, Charley Russell, George Catlin, and Thomas Moran) along with the usual desert rat displays of odd rocks and barbed wire.

Though Wickenburg tends to showcase its cowboy history, it's also home to one of the best-preserved gold mines in the state. The **Vulture Mine** (daily 8 AM-4 PM; $5; 520/377-0803), about 15 miles southwest of town, was open from the 1860s until 1942 and has never been dismantled or restored.

Most of the places to eat in Wickenburg are lined up along east-west US-60 (Wickenburg Way); try the **Gold Nugget** coffee shop at 222 E. Wickenburg Way, across from the **Best Western Rancho Grande** (520/684-5445 or 800/528-1234). For some fun after dark, check out the **Saguaro Theater**, marked by a concrete cactus at 176 E. Wickenburg Way (520/684-7189); this 1930s theater shows films and sometimes hosts performances by the local amateur dramatic society the Desert Stagers.

Hassayampa River Preserve

One of Arizona's very few stretches of riverside ecology preserved in its natural state, the Hassayampa River Preserve, three miles southeast of Wickenburg on US-60/89, is a great place to break a journey. For most of its way, the Hassayampa River runs underground, but here it rises to irrigate a dense forest of willows and cottonwood trees, which in turn shelter animals like bobcats and javelinas and an amazing variety of birds—over 200 species, from songbirds to raptors, are listed in the preserve's birders' guide.

South of Wickenburg and the Hassayampa River Preserve, the highway crosses over the canal of the **Central Arizona Project,** which provides Colorado River water to Phoenix and Tucson.

The Nature Conservancy, which owns and operates the preserve, runs a small **visitors center** (Wed.-Sun. 8 AM-5 PM in winter, 6 AM-noon in summer; $5 donation; 520/684-2772), where you can pick up trail guides and maybe join a guided walk.

Across the Valley of the Sun

From the northwest, this route arrives in ever-growing metropolitan Phoenix, also called the Valley of the Sun, by way of US-60/89. The highway passes through the retirement communities of Sun City and Sun City West. From the western out-skirts of Phoenix, the most direct route follows Grand Avenue all the way to the downtown area, where you can follow the old main road, Van Buren Street, or hop onto the freeway system and hope you don't get too lost—it's a crazy and confusing city, so spread out it can seem to take forever to get anywhere.

The "old road" route picks up again at Apache Junction, on the far eastern edge of metropolitan Phoenix.

The Apache Trail
and the Superstition Mountains

East of Phoenix, US-60 runs as a four-lane free-way through the shopping-mall suburbs of Tempe and Mesa, but the sprawl ends suddenly around Apache Junction, which marks the beginning of the scenic Apache Trail. Winding along the Salt River and named for the tribe that dominated the area a century ago, the Apache Trail was created in the early 1900s as a supply road during the construc-

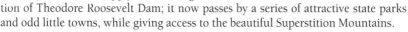

tion of Theodore Roosevelt Dam; it now passes by a series of attractive state parks and odd little towns, while giving access to the beautiful Superstition Mountains.

SPRING TRAINING: CACTUS LEAGUE BASEBALL

The arrival of the Arizona Diamondbacks in 1998 culminated a long but limited history of baseball in the Grand Canyon State. Though it had never before had a major-league team of its own, Arizona has long welcomed out-of-state teams for pre-season spring training—since 1947, when the Cleveland Indians and New York Giants first played at Tucson's HI Corbett Field (now the training home of the Colorado Rockies). Every February and March, hun-dreds of ball players at all levels of the game come here to earn or keep places on professional teams, and the daily workouts and 20-odd exhibition games of what's known as "Cactus League" baseball attract thousands of hard-core fans as well.

Tucson still gets a fair share of the action, though the metropolitan Phoenix area hosts the bulk of the teams and the tourists. Though they're not necessari-ly played to win, Cactus League games are held in modern 10,000-seat stadia that approach the major leagues in quality, and the smaller sizes give you an up-close feel you'd have to pay much more for during the regular season. (Your chances of snagging balls during batting practice are infinitely better here, too.)

Tickets for games cost $5-15, and are available through Ticketmaster (480/784-4444) and at the stadium box offices.

From the US-60 freeway, take Idaho Road (exit 11) north onto the well-signed Hwy-88. After five miles, the suburbs give way to the wild desert of **Lost Dutchman State Park** ($3 day-use fee), named for a legendary gold mine located nearby. Two miles farther is the overlook for the 4,535-foot phallus of Weaver's Needle, beyond

which the road passes several reservoirs before reaching the entertaining tourist-trap hamlet of **Tortilla Flat** (pop. 6), 18 miles from US-60, named after the Steinbeck novella (which has nothing to do with Arizona, but who cares?), and home to a good cafe, a saloon with frequent live music, and a small motel.

Beyond Tortilla Flat, the road turns to dirt, twisting and turning through spectacular desert country for the next 27 miles to Roosevelt Dam, then heading southeast to join US-60 near Globe, at the western edge of the San Carlos Apache Indian Reservation, 50 miles east of Phoenix.

For information on the Apache Trail or on hiking and camping in the Superstition Mountains—contact the U.S. Forest Service **ranger station** in Mesa (602/ 835-1161).

Hwy-79: Florence and Casa Grande Ruins National Monument

From Apache Junction, US-60 runs southeast for 15 miles to Florence Junction, where Hwy-79 (old US-89) cuts off to the south at **Florence**. One of Arizona's oldest towns, but now best known as the site of the state's largest prison, Florence has a pleasant, non-touristy Main Street of bars, general stores, and junk shops, parallel to and a half-mile west of the highway. The penal history is documented in gruesome detail at the **Pinal County Historical Museum** (Wed.-Sun. noon-4 PM; donations), 715 S. Main Street, where an actual hangman's noose and chairs from the retired gas chamber are displayed along with photos of people put to death. **McFarland State Historic Park**, filling the circa-1878 courthouse, documents another aspect: Florence's role as the site of a large World War II POW camp that was home to more than 5,000 Axis prisoners.

The most popular destination around Florence is the **Casa Grande Ruins National Monument** (daily 8 AM-5 PM; $4 per car), eight miles west of town off Hwy-287, which preserves some of the state's largest and most perplexing prehistoric remains. A small **visitors center** at the entrance gives some

While the route along Hwy-79 is far more scenic, the I-10 freeway between Phoenix and Tucson is considerably faster.

Cowboy actor **Tom Mix** died on October 12, 1940, when he crashed his 1937 Cord Phantom into a ditch along Hwy-79 and was decapitated by his suitcase. The site is marked, by a riderless horse, in a rest area 19 miles south of Florence.

background on the Hohokam people who, approximately six centuries ago, built the four-story "big house" and the surrounding village. But no one knows what the building was used for, or why it was abandoned.

South of Florence, Hwy-79 follows the **Pinal Pioneer Parkway,** the old main road between Phoenix and Tucson. The route is now lined with a series of interpretive signs pointing out palo verde trees, saguaros, and other desert flora.

Biosphere II

One of the most ambitious, controversial, and just plain bizarre schemes to have been hatched in recent years, Biosphere II stands in the Arizona desert at the northern foot of Mount Lemmon. Developed by a New Age group called Synergia Ranch and funded by Texas billionaire Ed Bass, Biosphere II was originally intended to simulate the earth's entire ecosystem in order to test the

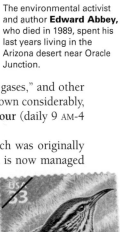

possibility of building self-sustaining colonies on other planets. A crew of four "biospherians" spent two not-entirely-self-sustained years sealed inside, emerging in 1993, when another crew took their place.

Amidst allegations of corruption and deceit, the founders of Biosphere II were unceremoniously fired by Mr. Bass in 1994, and the project has since been redirected to focus on pure research. Though the Biosphere II is still treated as a sealed system, there are no longer any people locked inside, and scien-

The environmental activist and author **Edward Abbey,** who died in 1989, spent his last years living in the Arizona desert near Oracle Junction.

tists study the causes and effects of global warming, "greenhouse gases," and other ecosystem changes. Media attention and tourist traffic have died down considerably, but you can still visit the very pretty site and take a self-guided **tour** (daily 9 AM-4 PM; $12.95, kids under 5 free; 520/896-6200 or 800/828-2462).

Located in a lovely desert canyon, the Biosphere facility (which was originally constructed in the 1970s as a corporate retreat for Motorola and is now managed by Columbia University) also offers good meals in a small cafe and comfortable and inexpensive accommodations—rooms cost $60-100 a night depending upon the time of year, and there are tennis courts and a swimming pool. To reach Biosphere II, follow Hwy-79 to Oracle Junction, 25 miles north of Tucson, then turn east onto Hwy-77 for six miles; at the Biosphere II signs, turn south and follow the driveway for just over two more miles to the parking area, ticket booth, and gift shop.

Catalina State Park

Just south of Biosphere II along Hwy 77, 15 miles north of downtown Tucson, the western foothills of the lovely Santa Catalina Mountains hold one of the many oases that are tucked away across the Sonora Desert. The 5,500-acre Catalina State Park preserves the remnants of a prehistoric Hohokam village, a more recent cattle ranch, endless hillsides of saguaro and spring wildflowers, and seasonal creeks that (when full) have swimming holes and waterfalls. Trails lead through the park and up into the wilder reaches of the Coronado National Forest

all the way to the 9,157-foot summit of Mount Lemmon. One of the most popular trails follows a creek up Romero Canyon, past sycamores and cottonwood trees to the Romero Pools, a popular three-mile day-hike. If you want to stay overnight, there's a first-come, first-served campground with showers ($10 for tents, $15 for RV hookups; 520/628-5798); day use parking is $5.

Tucson marks the junction of this US-93 route with our Southern Pacific: US-80 route, which begins on page 322.

Across Tucson

From Oracle Junction, Hwy-77/Oracle Road winds around the western Catalina Mountains, following a series of one-way surface streets into compact downtown Tucson, which fills the area between the I-10 freeway and 6th Avenue, the main highway before the interstate was built. South of town, 6th Avenue becomes the Old Nogales Highway, the old road south to Mexico. Running past the small Tucson airport, the Old Nogales Highway holds a few funky old motels, the Indian-run Desert Diamond Casino, and **Jimmy's Diner**, an old railroad dining car serving up cheap breakfasts and BBQ beef sandwiches to an eclectic clientele.

Continuing south, the Old Nogales Highway veers among extensive pecan groves in various alignments along the Santa Cruz River. Repeatedly crisscrossing the I-19 freeway, it offers a slower (and frequently—though not frustratingly— dead-end) alternative to the fast lane.

Mission San Xavier del Bac

Among the most strikingly memorable of all the Spanish colonial missions in the Southwest, Mission San Xavier del Bac was built more than 200 years ago and still

TUCSON SURVIVAL GUIDE

THOUGH IT'S LESS THAN HALF THE SIZE OF PHOENIX, Tucson is at least twice as nice a place to visit. With a lively university community, some of the most beautiful desert landscapes anywhere on earth, and more palpable history than anywhere in the Southwest outside New Mexico, Tucson is well worth taking the time to get to know. It also makes an excellent jumping-off point for visiting the Wild West towns of Tombstone and Bisbee to the east along old US-80 in the state's southeast corner.

However, with daytime temperatures averaging more than 100° F, Tucson is hotter than heck from early May to late September, so try to visit during the rest of the year. Spring is especially nice, with wildflowers blooming and spring training baseball bashing away, but it's also the most expensive time to be here—room rates in March are easily double those the rest of the year.

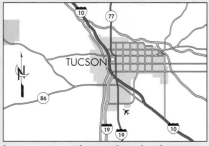

Many of Tucson's biggest attractions (Biosphere II, Mission San Xavier del Bac, the Arizona Sonora Desert Museum, and Saguaro National Park) are outside the city limits and covered under various road trips, but the downtown area is worth a wander, especially for the many historic buildings that have been spared from the redeveloper's wrecking ball. Most prominent of these old adobes is the **Fremont House**, 151 S. Granada Avenue, next to the Convention Center, built in 1858 and later rented out to frontiersman John Frémont during his term as Governor of the Arizona Territory in 1878.

East of downtown, the nicely landscaped 350-acre University of Arizona campus, which spreads between Speedway Boulevard and 6th Street, holds the engaging historical exhibits of the **Arizona State Museum** (Mon.-Sat. 10 AM-5 PM; Sun. noon-5 PM; donations; 520/621-6302) and one of the country's preeminent photography collections in the **Center for Creative Photography.**

In the foothills of the Santa Catalina Mountains, which rise north of Tucson, **Sabino Canyon** (daily 8:30 AM-dusk; 520/749-2861), with its seasonal waterfalls and a (nearly) year-round creek, is a great place to stretch your legs while getting a sense of how pretty and vibrant the desert can be. Sabino Canyon is 17 miles east of downtown, well signed off Tanque Verde Road.

Southeast of Tucson, off I-10 at the Kolb Road exit, **Davis-Monthan Air Force Base** holds one of the very strangest sights in the entire Southwest desert: rows and rows and rows of surplus military aircraft, lined up for what seems like miles. You can glimpse them from the highway, but for the full experience you have to sign up for one of the very popular tours (9 AM on Monday and Wednesday only; free; 520/228-3358).

(continues)

Also on the southeast side of town, the **Tucson Sidewinders** (520/325-2621), the Class AAA farm club of the Arizona Diamondbacks, play at Tucson Electric Park, off I-10 at Ajo Way.

Practicalities
The main I-10 freeway runs diagonally from northwest to southeast along usually dry Santa Rita River at the western edge of town. Tucson stretches east from here for over 10 miles and north toward the foothills of the Santa Catalinas. The main east-west route across town is Speedway Boulevard, but there are numerous parallel roads as well.

Tucson's very small **airport** is south of I-10, eight miles from downtown, with all the usual shuttle and car rental companies.

In addition to the usual highway motels, Tucson has some characterful places to stay, from restored downtown hotels to luxurious vacation resorts. One of the latter is the **Hacienda del Sol**, 5601 N. Hacienda del Sol Road (520/299-1501), a historic guest ranch, built as a posh girl's school in the 1920s and now a quiet, intimate getaway, with a pool, tennis courts, great sunset views, and one of Tucson's best restaurants (The Grill). Another historic property, the **Arizona Inn**, 2200 E. Elm Street (520/325-1541 or 800/933-1093), is perhaps *the* classic Arizona resort, little changed since the 1920s, when it was a favorite winter haunt of the Rockefellers and other elites. The Arizona Inn offers very comfortable accommodations on lovingly landscaped grounds, near the University campus; room rates are reasonable—especially off-peak, when they drop to under $100 a night.

Downtown holds many more accommodation options, starting with the lively **Hotel Congress**, at 311 E. Congress Street (520/622-8848 or 800/722-8848). This youth-oriented

Life has its ups and down, but nowhere is this truer than at Tucson's **Yoseum**, 2947 E. Grant Road (Mon.-Sat. 9 AM-6 PM; free; 520/322-0100), a yo-yo museum opened by the son of yo-yo pioneer Donald Duncan. The museum showcases more than 1,000 yo-yos and offers free yo-yo lessons.

serves the native Tohono O'odham (a.k.a. "Papago") people. Known as the "White Dove of the Desert" because of the gleaming white plaster that covers its adobe walls, balustrades, and twin bell towers (one of which is domed), this landmark edifice was designed and built by Franciscan missionaries beginning in 1778; outbuildings date to the mid-1750s, and the mission was originally founded in 1700 by the Jesuit priest Eusebio Kino, who also established another mission farther south, at Tumacacori.

South of San Xavier along the Old Nogales Highway, or east from I-19 exit 80, the **Asarco Mineral Discovery Center** (Tues.-Sat. 9 AM-5 PM; free; 520/625-7513), in the town of Sahuarita, offers you a chance to learn all you ever wanted to know about mining, smelting, and processing raw copper. You can also take a guided tour ($6) of a working copper mine.

Rising from the flat desert plain, San Xavier presents an impressive silhouette, but what's most unforgettable is the Mexican folk-baroque interior, covered in intensely wrought sculptures and paintings of saints and religious imagery. Currently under restoration by a team brought in from Italy, these paintings and figurines are among the country's finest example of folk art, using painted mud to simulate marble, tiles, and crystal chandeliers.

hotel and hostel doubles as a cafe and nightclub, right at the heart of downtown; dorm beds run $15, rooms $50. Many steps up on both the price and the comfort scale is **El Presidio Inn**, 297 N. Main Street (520/623-6151), an intimate bed-and-breakfast in lovely old adobe home at the center of town.

One of the most enjoyable places to eat in all Arizona is the quirky **Cafe Poca Cosa**, right downtown at 88 E. Broadway (in the lobby of the Clarion Hotel). Adventurously creative Mexican food, served up in large portions at low prices, is the specialty here—try anything in a *mole* sauce and you won't be disappointed. Across the street at 20 S. Scott Avenue, the restaurant's original location is now **Little Cafe Poca Cosa**, open for breakfast and lunch versions of the same delicious food. On the west side of downtown is **El Charro**, 311 N. Court Avenue, "the oldest family-operated Mexican restaurant in the USA," so they say, serving up inexpensive food (and margaritas) since 1922 in a turn-of-the-century downtown house. The same neighborhood also holds **Janos**, 150 N. Main Avenue (520/884-9426), possibly the best restaurant in the state, serving delicious (and very expensive) nouvelle cuisine in a landmark adobe home. Reservations strongly recommended.

For more all-American food, you may have to head east of downtown, perhaps to the **Big A Restaurant**, 2033 E. Speedway Boulevard (next to the university), *the* place to eat burgers, drink beer, and watch sports on TV. Also great—for food, if not for ambience—is **Jack's Original BBQ**, 5250 E. 22nd Street, a bare-bones barbecue place with succulent meats, tasty sweet-potato pies, and the best beans west of Texas.

The **Metropolitan Tucson Visitors Bureau**, 130 S. Scott Avenue (520/624-1817 or 800/638-8350), has tons of information on Tucson and the surrounding regions. There are two daily newspapers (the morning *Daily Star* and the afternoon *Tucson Citizen*), while the free *Tucson Weekly* has the best listings of nightlife and current events.

The mission (daily 8 AM-6 PM; donations; 520/294-2624) is well signed and easy to reach, just 10 miles south of downtown Tucson off I-19 exit 92, then a half-mile west. Across the plaza from the church is a small Tohono-owned and -operated complex of craft galleries, plus a very good taco stand.

Titan Missile Museum

In just the 15 miles south of San Xavier Mission, you can travel from the colonial 1700s to the Cold War 1960s by stopping at the Titan Missile Museum, the only Inter-Continental Ballistic Missile (ICBM) silo anywhere in the world preserved intact and open to the public. On the north side of the sprawling stucco retirement community of Green Valley (pop. 13,231), just west from I-19 off exit 69 on Duval Mine Road, the silo was in active use from 1963 until 1982. It was declared a National Historic Landmark in 1994 and is now open for **tours** (daily 9 AM-5 PM; $7.50; 520/625-7736).

The tours, which take around an hour, involve donning a hard hat and descending downstairs into the control room of the hardened silo, which still contains a 110-foot-tall Titan missile (de-activated, of course). Also on display are a partly dismantled rocket engine and a "re-entry vehicle," which would have held the nuclear-tipped warhead.

In Amado, just west of I-19 at the Arivaca Road exit, a huge concrete cow's skull marks the entrance to a small cantina, one of a long series of businesses that have tried to make a go of this unique location. Across the highway is the popular **Cow Palace** restaurant, which is open daily 8 AM-9 PM. The road west to Arivaca is a motorcyclist's dream of a highway, roller-coastering over the mountains for more than 40 miles, ending up eventually at the Mexican border village of Sasabe.

Between Tubac and Tumacacori, the Anza Trail follows a brief portion of the route taken in 1775 by explorer **Juan de Anza**, who led a group of colonists across the deserts to establish the city of San Francisco in 1776.

South of Tucson, signs on the I-19 freeway to the Mexican border gives all distances in metric measurements. The speed limit, however, is still the same old 65 mph.

Tubac

Another good place to stop between Tucson and the Mexican border is Tubac, 45 miles from Tucson, just east of I-19 at exit 34. One of the first European outposts in what's now Arizona, Tubac was established as a Spanish presidio in 1751; a century later, it boomed with the opening of gold mines nearby. The town's lively history is recounted at the **Tubac Presidio State Historic Park** (daily 8 AM-5 PM; $1) on the east side of town, from where you can walk a short (4.5-mile) portion of the **Anza Trail** south to Tumacacori and get a real sense of what it was like on the Spanish colonial frontier.

Scattered around a dusty central plaza, just west of the presidio park, Tubac has developed into a small but diverting arts-and-crafts colony, with local artists frequently showcased in the **Tubac Center for the Arts** (Tues.-Sat. 10:30 AM-4:30 PM, Sunday 1-4:30 PM; free), on the north side of the plaza. A short walk south of the plaza, an excellent book shop, **Tortuga Books**, and the popular **Cafe Fiesta**, which has very good salads and sandwiches, share space in the Mercado del Baca shopping complex at 19 Tubac Road.

Tumacacori National Historic Park

The preserved ruins of an impressive Spanish colonial mission stand at the center of Tumacacori National Historic Park (daily 8 AM-5 PM; $2), 19 miles north of Nogales and just three miles south of Tubac, off I-19 exit 29. The site was used by missionaries as early as 1691, but it wasn't until 1800 that they set to work building the massive adobe church. Though never finished, thanks to Apache raids and the Mexican Revolution, Tumacacori stands as an impressive reminder of the religious passion of the friars and their efforts to convert local tribes.

Directly across from Tumacacori is a rare sight—a Greek cafe. A half-mile north is **Wisdom's**, which serves reliable Mexican and American food.

Ambos Nogales

Arizona's busiest border crossing, Nogales is also perhaps the most pleasant of all the "international" cities along the U.S./Mexico border. Despite being divided by an ugly corrugated steel fence, it gets promoted as *Ambos Nogales* ("Both Nogales"). The twin cities are economically dependent on one another—especially post-NAFTA—but the influx of illegal immigrants caused a crackdown (sometimes referred to as "Operation Gatekeeper") by the federal border patrol, resulting in as many as 500 arrests and deportations every day. The devalued peso has meant that fewer Mexicans can afford to come across and shop at Safeway, but Americans still while away evenings drinking cut-price beer in cantinas south of the border. Apart from the intriguing little **Pimeria Alta Historical Society Museum** (daily 9 AM-5 PM; donations), which documents cross-border history in the storefront-sized Old City Hall on Grand Avenue, 400 yards north of the border crossing, there are few real sights to see. But if you just want to spend an hour or two shopping for souvenirs and practicing your Spanish, Nogales Mexico is a painless place in which to do it. (Ironically, however, you'll find that shopkeepers south of the border speak better English than do those on the U.S. side.) Avenida Obregon, two blocks west of the railroad and main highway from the border crossing, is the main drag, lined by a lively range of bars, restaurants, and hotels.

To save hassle (and time) crossing the border, drivers should park their cars on the U.S. side—on the streets or in the $4-a-day lots—and walk across. Border formalities are minimal, and U.S. dollars are accepted on both sides. Though prices for most things on the Mexican side aren't dirt cheap, they are usually around 20% lower than in the U.S.

From Nogales, Mexican Highway 15, the primary route along the Gulf of California and the Pacific coast, heads south through Hermosillo and Guaymas to Mazatlán, Guadalajara, and beyond. There's also good bus service to and from Nogales from the rest of Mexico, but the stations are a half-mile south of "The Line."

Jazz bassist and composer **Charles Mingus** was born in Nogales on April 22, 1922, but soon after moved to L.A. with his father, a railroad worker.

For more information on travel in Mexico, see "Crossing the Border" in the US-80 chapter on page 325.

THE LONELIEST ROAD: US-50

THE LONELIEST ROAD: US-50

Running across the magnificent landscapes of the Rocky Mountains and Sierra Nevada and the desiccated basin-and-range deserts of Utah and Nevada, US-50 is one of the country's sublime long-distance drives. Still mostly two-lane highway from California to the eastern edge of Colorado, a road trip along US-50 can also be a journey along the timeline of national development. Heading west to east, you can travel back in history from the cutting-edge, high-tech contemporary Silicon Valley, through the Gold Rush country of the California foothills, and follow the footsteps of pioneers along the routes of the Pony Express and the Santa Fe Trail, across what still feels like the old Western frontier.

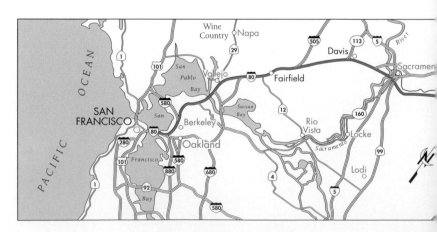

Heading east from San Francisco across the heavy-duty, heavy-traffic Oakland Bay Bridge, the route across California starts off along the busy I-80 freeway through the urbanized San Francisco Bay area. Passing diverse bayfront towns, including blue-collar Oakland and collegiate Berkeley, the busy and often congested eight-lane I-80 can easily be avoided if you take a short but memorable detour across the watery flatlands of the Sacramento Delta. Beyond Sacramento, the state capital of California, US-50 finally emerges, first as a freeway but later as a two-lane mountain road climbing through the heart of the Sierra Nevada foothills, where many small towns slumber in a Gold Rush dream of the 1850s. Continuing east, US-50 winds through endless tracts of pine forest before cresting the Sierra to reach alpine Lake Tahoe, a year-round resort lying astride the California-Nevada border.

The Nevada portion of the route, dubbed "The Loneliest Road in America" by travel writers and tourist boards, is one of the most compelling long-distance drives in the country—provided you find miles and miles of little more than mountains, sagebrush, and blue sky compelling. Between Lake Tahoe in the west and Great Basin National Park on the Utah border, US-50 traverses more than 400 miles of corrugated country, climbing up and over a dozen distinct mountain ranges while passing through four classic mining towns and the state capital, Carson City. Early explorers mapped this region, Pony Express riders raced across it, and the long-distance Lincoln Highway finally tamed it, but the US-50 byway has always played second fiddle to I-80, the more popular route across the state.

For most of the way across Utah, US-50's role has been usurped by the high-speed I-70 freeway, but if you have time to take a couple of detours you'll be rewarded with incredible scenery. Most of this is concentrated in the southeastern corner of the state, where a number of parks, including Canyonlands and Arches National Parks, preserve the sandstone canyon country of the Colorado Plateau. In the west a few old mining towns stand amidst the arid desert of the Great Basin. Distances are huge and services few and far between, but if you have the time and plan ahead, this is one of the most satisfying and memorable corners of the country.

Driving across southern Colorado on US-50 takes you through almost every landscape landlocked North America has to offer. From the geological wonderland

of the Colorado River plateau, the route climbs up and over the 13,000-foot Rocky Mountains, which form a formidable wall down the center of the state. Continuing east, the alpine meadows, deeply etched river canyons, and snow-covered peaks of the southern Rockies slowly fade away into the flat, agricultural prairies that stretch east across the middle of the country—best seen from atop Pike's Peak, which provides a grand panorama and a fitting end to this journey.

Oakland's native son Jack London worked in factories and along the waterfront near present-day Jack London Square before becoming the first writer to earn $1 million with his pen.

In the past decade Oakland has suffered one disaster after another. The 1989 earthquake did far more damage (and killed twice as many people) in Oakland than it did across the bay in San Francisco, and in 1991 a terrible fire destroyed 3,000 hillside homes, killing 27 people.

San Francisco is easily accessible from both Berkeley and Oakland via the high-speed, trans-bay **BART** trains, which run under the bay between a half-dozen East Bay stations and downtown San Francisco.

Oakland

Though many dismiss it as the West Coast equivalent of Newark, New Jersey, the hardworking and long-suffering city of Oakland (pop. 365,000) is actually a lively and intriguing place. The main attraction for visitors is its waterfront **Jack London Square** honoring the city's favorite prodigal son. Covering a few blocks at the foot of Broadway, this modern outdoor shopping complex contains a large bookstore, a couple of restaurants, an ancient log cabin supposedly lived in by Jack London in the Yukon Territory, and last but not least, the truly funky **Heinold's First and Last Chance,** a rickety old saloon that's the only survivor from the waterfront's wild past, right on the water at 56 Jack London Square. Nearby, at the foot of Clay Street, is the landing for the **ferry boat** ($4.25 each way, under-5 free; 510/522-3300) that cruises across to the Embarcadero in San Francisco, and to Angel Island State Park in the middle of the bay.

Oakland's other main draw is the excellent **Oakland Museum** (Wed.-Sat. 10 AM-5 PM, Sunday noon-5 PM; $6; 510/238-2200), housed in a landmark modernist ziggurat on the east edge of downtown at 1000 Oak Street. Inside, exhibits cover everything from California's natural history to the photography of Dorothea Lange. An in-depth look at the state's popular culture is highlighted by a lively display of Hollywood movie posters, neon signs, jukeboxes, and classic cars and motorcycles.

From Oakland, you have a choice of two routes out of town: east along the old Lincoln Highway, by way of today's I-580 freeway, or northeast along I-80, which links up with the official start of US-50 at the state capital in Sacramento. Both routes are described below.

Berkeley

The intellectual, literary, and political nexus of the San Francisco Bay Area, left-leaning Berkeley (pop. 120,000) enjoys an international reputation that overshadows its suburban character. The town grew up around the attractively landscaped University of California campus, which during the 1960s and early 1970s was the scene of ongoing battles between "The Establishment" and unwashed hordes of sex-and-drugs-and-rock-and-roll-crazed youth protesting against the war in Vietnam. Today Berkeley quietly maintains a typical college town feel, and its setting is superb, looking out across the bay to the Golden Gate and San Francisco.

The square-mile **University of California** campus sits at the foot of eucalyptus-covered hills a mile east of the University Avenue exit off the I-80 freeway. Wander along Strawberry Creek, admiring the mix of neoclassical and postmodern buildings. Berkeley's cacophonous main drag, Telegraph Avenue, runs south from the heart of campus in a crazy array of tie-dye and tarot, lined by a half-dozen good cafes and some of the country's best bookstores.

There are dozens of good-value places to eat and drink in Berkeley, including one of the best breakfast joints on the planet, **Bette's Ocean View Diner**, 1807 4th Street (510/644-3230), two blocks from the I-80 University Avenue exit, at the center of a boutique shopping district. Berkeley also has many top-rated restaurants, including world-renowned **Chez Panisse**, birthplace of California cuisine, located in the heart of Berkeley's gourmet ghetto at 1517 Shattuck Avenue (reservations essential; 510/548-5525).

Old US-50: Altamont Pass

If you're interested in following the real route of old US-50, which was part of the historic Lincoln Highway in the days before highways were numbered, be prepared to take what seems like the long way around. From downtown Oakland, the old road wound southeast along MacArthur and Foothill Boulevards, the approximate route of today's I-580 through Castro Valley and Dublin—once separate communities but now immersed in the general East Bay sprawl.

Some 30 miles east of the bay, the old Lincoln Highway passed through the heart of **Livermore**, where a nifty old garage has been preserved as the **Lincoln Highway Museum**, on Portola Avenue near L Street. Dating from 1915, the same year the Lincoln Highway was opened from coast to coast, the tin-paneled garage is full of old fire trucks, farm equipment, and other items of historical interest. It's an all-volunteer effort, so unfortunately it's open only by appointment (925/449-9927). In contrast, Livermore is also home to the ultra high-tech **Lawrence Livermore National Laboratory**, where scientists are turning away from weapons research and development toward more peaceful endeavors; there's a visitors center and special tours (reservations required; Thurs. 1:30 PM; free; 925/422-6408).

East of Livermore, up until 1938 or so, the old Lincoln Highway/US-50 route followed Altamont Pass Road up and over 741-foot **Altamont Pass**, now home to the ghostly Summit Garage and a huge wind farm full of modern windmills. From Altamont Pass, the old Lincoln Highway/US-50 route ran east along 11th Street through the center of **Tracy**, which is now a booming suburban community. The route then bent north along old Hwy-99 to Sacramento, where the original old road rejoins the current US-50.

The big "C" above the University of California campus is over 100 years old. It was the first of these giant letters, which have since been mimicked on hillsides all over the country.

While Berkeley students were rioting in the streets in 1968, a Berkeley plumber was putting the finishing touches on the air-bubbling bath device that bears his name—**Jacuzzi**.

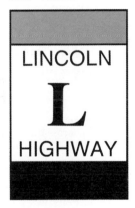

Altamont is probably best known as the site of the Rolling Stones' notorious 1969 "Gimme Shelter" concert, which was held at the **Altamont Speedway**, southeast of the pass off the I-580 connection to southbound I-5. There's no plaque about the concert, but races and classic car shows are still held here on summer weekends.

The town of Vallejo served as state capital of California on two different occasions in the Gold Rush years of the early 1850s.

I-80: Vallejo

Vallejo is west of the I-80 freeway on the north side of the Carquinez Straits, through which the Sacramento and San Joaquin Rivers flow into San Pablo Bay, the northern portion of San Francisco Bay. It's a blue-collar maritime town still reeling from the closure of its huge and historic Mare Island naval shipyard, which from 1854 to 1994 built and maintained many of the country's fighting ships and submarines. An early state capital of California, Vallejo's bona fide attraction these days is **Six Flags Marine World** (Wed.-Sun. 9:30 AM-5:30 PM, daily till 6:30 PM in summer; $34; 707/643-6722), on the north side of town just west of I-80, with 160 acres of elephants, tigers, sea lions, and killer whales, some of which perform tricks on cue. There's also an adjacent theme park with the usual array of thrill rides—one admission gets you into all three parks—the oceanarium, wild animal park, and theme park.

Vallejo effectively marks the edge of the Bay Area. Once you cross over the hills east of here, the landscape turns suddenly flat and agricultural, with a few pockets of suburbia, and the roadside alternates between farmland and mini-mall sprawl.

Detour: Napa Valley
Vallejo also marks the turnoff from I-80 onto Hwy-29, which links up with Hwy-12 and runs west through the celebrated Wine Country of the Napa and Sonoma Valleys. The Sonoma Valley is most easily reached from the west, via US-101 (see

---

I-80 SURVIVAL GUIDE: CALIFORNIA

HEADING NORTHEAST FROM SAN FRANCISCO, the I-80 freeway is the fastest route across the Sierra Nevada mountains, and unlike some freeways it actually has some spots to look for, such as:

MM 26: Sitting on the south side of the Carquinez Straits, the company town of **Crockett** rises above the big C&H sugar mill, whose flashing neon sign lights up the night sky.

MM 64: A not-quite historic landmark of roadside Californiana, the Giant Orange in **Dixon** is still in business, now selling tacos instead of the fresh orange juice, for which it was designed.

MM 79: West of **Sacramento**, a big sign marks the start of US-50, which runs all the way across the country to Ocean City, MD—3,073 miles away.

MM 117: Turn off onto Lincolnway in **Auburn** and you'll be on the Lincoln Highway, the nation's first cross-country road, opened in 1915.

MM 174: Named for the unfortunate group of travelers who got caught unprepared for winter in 1846, 7,227-foot **Donner Summit** is the high point of I-80's run across the Golden State.

MM 208: California/Nevada border.

pages 50-51); the Napa Valley is 10 miles northwest of I-80, and stretches north from the top of San Pablo Bay along the banks of the Napa River for over 30 miles.

There are two main routes through the Napa Valley, and the quality of your experience will vary depending upon which road you're on. Hwy-29 is the main route, running as a fast, four-lane freeway in the southern half of the valley, then dropping down to a busy Main Street in the north. Parallel to Hwy-29, about a mile to the east, is the **Silverado Trail**, a winding, two-lane road that takes twice as long but is at least twice as pretty. The main advantage of Hwy-29 is that it takes you to the heart of the Napa Valley's most popular towns and wineries; this is also its main disadvantage, since weekend traffic can cause major delays. The most satisfying Napa tours take advantage of both roads: cruising up Hwy-29 and down the Silverado Trail, for instance, with many detours along the country lanes that wind between them.

Whole guidebooks have been written describing the wonderful restaurants, resorts, and wineries of the Napa Valley; here are a few highlights that should help you spend a pleasant day or two here, or longer, without spending the megabucks you can easily dish out on a Wine Country tour.

At the south end of the valley, the workaday town of Napa usually doesn't feature on most visitors' itineraries, but the next town to the north, **Yountville**, definitely does. Its main drag, Washington Street, a block east of Hwy-29, is home to one of the very finest restaurants in the world—chef Thomas Keller's **French Laundry**, at 6640 Washington Street (707/944-2380), where multi-course prix fixe dinners of inventive haute cuisine cost around $100 a head. For those of more modest means, Yountville also boasts the eminently affordable **The Diner**, 6476 Washington Street (707/944-2626), an excellent Mexican-American breakfast, lunch, and dinner place, with comfy booths and a long counter.

Midway up the valley, the hamlet of **Oakville** has two great draws: the excellent, informative (and free!) tours at the famous **Robert Mondavi Winery** (800/666-3284), and the selection of picnic goodies at the equally famous Oakville Grocery, right across Hwy-29. Oakville is also the starting point for one of the only drives across the mountains to the Sonoma Valley, by way of the Oakville Grade, which drops down to Glen Ellen and Jack London State Historic Park.

Set into lovely gardens alongside a creek and a mature grove of redwood trees, the **Napa Valley Museum** (Wed.-Mon. 10 AM-5 PM; $5; 707/944-0500), west of Yountville on the grounds of the landmark California Veterans Home, is a great place to stop and get a feel for the history of local culture and viticulture.

North of Oakville, winery after prestigous winery (Beaulieu, Grgich Hills, Franciscan, Heitz, and many more) line the highway before it turns into the Main Street of super-quaint St. Helena, one of the few really wanderable Napa Valley towns. Immediately north of St. Helena, a very French allée of mature trees shades the road past yet more wineries, including stately Beringer, one of Napa's most historic, and the former Christian Brothers estate, now home to the Culinary Institute of America (C.I.A) and its fine-dining restaurant, **Greystone** (707/965-1010).

At the north end of the Napa Valley, the historic hot springs resort of **Calistoga** (home of the famous bottled water) is the most humble and easy-going of the Wine Country towns. Founded in 1860 by Gold Rush entrepreneur Sam Brannan, Calistoga has the usual array of great restaurants—try Cajun-spiced **Catahoula**, 1457

Lincoln Avenue (707/942-2275), or the outdoor terrace at the **Calistoga Inn**, 1250 Lincoln Avenue (707/942-4101). Additionally, there are many relaxing spas that take advantage of the naturally heated spring water. Take the waters (and maybe a massage or a mudbath) at **Indian Springs**, 1712 Lincoln Avenue (707/942-4913) or a half-dozen others. In between meals and spa visits take time to explore the **Sharpsteen Museum**, 1311 Washington Street, a block north of Lincoln (daily 10 AM-4 PM; free).

The modern I-80 route overlays the old US-40 route, which was part of the Victory Highway and an alternate route on the Lincoln Highway back in 1927 when the Carquinez Straits were first bridged. Many portions of the old transcontinental highway are still there, often as frontage roads along the freeway. An untouched section east of Davis, on the north side of I-80, is now a billboard-lined bike path.

About three-quarters of all the precipitation that falls on California makes its way back to the ocean by way of the broad watery delta formed by the Sacramento and San Joaquin Rivers. Unless, of course, this water is diverted for use in agriculture or as drinking water—as most of it is, ending up as far away as Los Angeles.

I-80 Towns

Between Vallejo and Sacramento, I-80 passes through an ever more suburbanized corridor of towns such as **Fairfield** (pop. 78,000), home of Travis Air Force Base, the Herman Goelitz **Jelly Belly** jelly bean factory (tours and tastings daily 9 AM-3 PM; free; 800/522-3627), and a huge Anheuser-Busch beer refinery that's also open for free tours (Tues.-Sat. 9 AM-4 PM). The other biggish city on the route is **Vacaville** (pop. 71,500), home to the state's largest psychiatric prison, a ton of factory outlet stores, and the biggest steak sandwiches in creation, served up for lunch and dinner daily at the **Merchant and Main Bar & Grill**, 349 Merchant Street (707/446-0368).

Approaching Sacramento, I-80 races past **Dixon**, where one of California's few surviving "giant orange" roadside stands is now a great Mexican restaurant, just south of the freeway, and **Davis**, home to a University of California campus that's renowned around the world for its wine-making school. A quiet former farm town where bikes tend to outnumber cars, Davis has a couple of places that merit a turn off the freeway, including a stretch of the historic Lincoln Highway, on Olive Drive along the north side of I-80. Two miles north of I-80, right off Hwy-113 on Covell Boulevard, **Dos Coyotes** (530/753-0922) serves outstanding burritos in a busy restaurant hidden away in the Davis Commons shopping mall.

Detour: The Delta

When most Americans think of the "Delta," they probably think of the Mississippi Delta, with its rich history of cotton and the blues. But in Northern California, the Delta is the Sacramento Delta, the 1,000 square mile area of marshlands, farms, and ghost towns that fills the space between San Francisco Bay and the foothills of the Sierra Nevada mountains. Bypassed by all the big roads, and with a population that's smaller now than it was a century ago, the Delta is also a wonderful place for doing some serendipitous traveling, turning off onto levee roads to follow the dozens of different river channels, canals, and inlets that checkerboard this vast watery plain.

The main north-south route through the Delta is sinuous Hwy-160, which winds along the banks of the Sacramento River between the heart of Sacramento and the eastern edge of the Bay Area, running into Hwy-4 at unlovely Antioch. The main east-west road, Hwy-12, takes a more angular route, running between Fairfield along I-80 and the farm town of Lodi, along I-5. The two routes cross at the heart of the Delta in the town of **Rio Vista**, a very popular riverside spot for windsurfing, and perhaps best known as the home base of land speed racer Craig Breedlove and his "Spirit of America" team.

In terms of destinations, the two best Delta places are just upstream from Rio Vista, along Hwy-160. The first place you reach, **Isleton**, is full of tin-roofed shacks and fishing tackle shops (including one knowingly called the Master Baiter); in the 1990s, Isleton gained some notoriety when its sheriff decided to pay his salary by selling concealed weapons permits to anyone who asked.

The next stop, **Locke**, is among the more evocative historical places in the state—its single, narrow street is crowded by ancient wooden buildings, many of which seem on the verge of collapse. Locke dates back a century or more, to a time when its predominantly Chinese residents, having completed the transcontinental railroad across the Sierra Nevada mountains, were toiling to build the many levees that made the Delta lands farmable. Though the town has a couple of art galleries (including one called Locke Ness), a grocery store, and the rarely open historical Dai Loy Historical Musuem, Locke is best known as the home of **Al the Wop's** (916/776-1800), a popular bar and Italian-American cafe dating back to 1934. A prototypically funky saloon where the walls and ceiling are covered with business

From I-80 south of Vacaville, the quickest and most interesting way to get out of the fast lane is to follow Hwy-12 east, past the Budweiser and Jelly Belly factories. Quickly leaving the contemporary suburban world behind, you find yourself in what feels like a time warp, as the road roller-coasters across a dozen miles of grassy hills to the wonderful **Western Railway Museum** (Wed.-Sun. 11 AM-5 PM; $6; 707/374-2978), which runs historic trains and streetcars on a variety of scenic trips around the still-rural countryside nearby.

Lording over the Delta, at the east edge of the East Bay, **Mt. Diablo** rises high above the generally flat landscape, and its summit (which you can drive to) offers one of the broadest panoramas anywhere—200-odd miles in every direction, from the Sierra crest west to the Farallon Islands, and north and south over the entire Central Valley.

Between Folsom and the Sierra Nevada foothills, US-50 is an eight-lane freeway—and one of the California Highway Patrol's more lucrative **speed traps**, especially costly for westbound (downhill) travelers.

At Placerville, US-50 crosses scenic Hwy-49, which runs along the Sierra Nevada foothills through the heart of the Gold Country. Starting in the north beyond beautiful Nevada City (see page 122), Hwy-49 winds down through one historic town after another, all the way to the gates of Yosemite National Park, 150 miles to the south (see page 132).

cards, dollar bills, and road signs, Al's serves burgers and steak or chicken with a side of spaghetti for dinner.

Sacramento, which marks the junction of US-50 with old Hwy-99, is covered in our Central Valley and National Parks: Hwy-99 chapter, see pages 125-127.

Folsom

Though it can seem like just another Sacramento suburb, surrounded by mini-malls and housing tracts along the north side of the US-50 freeway, Folsom is actually among the more historic communities in California. A gold-mining supply center that served as western terminus of the short-lived but legendary Pony Express, Folsom retains its historic core of 1860s buildings along Sutter Street. One of these, said to be the oldest Wells Fargo office still standing, is now a local history **museum**, at 823 Sutter Street (Wed.-Sun. 11 AM-4 PM; free). North of town, the American River—lined by a very attractive cycling and hiking path that runs all the way downstream to Old Sacramento—has been impounded behind the state's oldest hydroelectric dam to form Folsom Lake. Two miles east of Folsom's city hall, north off Natoma Street, the bleak granite walls of **Folsom State Prison** hold some of California's most violent offenders; outside the wall are a pair of museums, one showing (and selling) artwork by prisoners, the other documenting the story of the oldest prison in California and the many outlaws imprisoned and executed there over the years. Alas, neither makes any mention of Folsom's most famous, fictional inmate, Johnny Cash. Though Cash sang of being "Stuck in Folsom Prison," he was never in prison here (or anywhere else, for that matter).

If you want to follow the old road between Sacramento and Folsom, take Folsom Boulevard, though it has very few surviving signs of its heritage. One of these, fortunately, is the **Sheepherder Inn** restaurant at 11275 Folsom Boulevard (916/635-6886), just as popular today as it was when it opened back in 1912. Now surrounded by anonymous hotels in the town of Rancho Cordova (which is the western base of the IRS), the Sheepherder is not Basque, as its name suggests, but instead offers a meaty range of traditional American meals—prime rib, steaks, chops, and smoky BBQ—in a lively, vaguely English, half-timbered dining room.

Placerville

The main US-50 stop in the Sierra Nevada foothills, Placerville (pop. 8,400; elev. 1,860 feet) takes its name from the placer gold deposits recovered from the South Fork of the American River, which flows just north of town. The historic core of Placerville is well preserved, with a few cafes and bars paying homage to its rough-and-tumble past. The main reminder of the town's Gold Rush heritage is the **Gold Bug Mine** (daily 10 AM-4 PM in summer, weekends only rest of the year; $1), a mile north of US-50 off the Bedford Avenue exit. A stamp mill and other mining equipment stand outside the entrance to the mine tunnel, which you can explore on a self-guided tour.

If you want to investigate the region's many evocative Gold Rush-era remnants, Placerville makes a good base, with its handful of motels (including a Best Western and a Days Inn) on the old highway frontage along Broadway, on the south side of the modern freeway. Broadway also holds one of Placerville's few holdouts against fast food or over-the-top tearoom Victoriana: the **Shoestring**, a roadside shack on Broadway a mile up from downtown, serving hot dogs, pastrami sandwiches, and shoestring french fries since 1959.

Another great old Gold Country haunt can be reached by a short drive south of US-50. The ancient-feeling and very popular **Poor Red's Barbecue** (530/622-2901) is housed in a Gold Rush-era stagecoach station in the hamlet of El Dorado, five miles south of Placerville on Hwy-49. Here you'll find full lunches and dinners (BBQ ribs, chicken, and great margaritas!) for very little money.

Detour: Coloma and the Gold Discovery State Historic Park

The actual site where the 1849 California Gold Rush began, Sutter's Mill has been reconstructed as part of **Gold Discovery State Historic Park** (daily 8 AM-dusk; $5 per car; 530/622-3470) in Coloma. Now a fairly idyllic place along the banks of the American River, Coloma is nine miles north of Placerville on Hwy-49. Back in the winter of 1848, a team of Mormon laborers hired by John Sutter to build a sawmill discovered traces of gold in the tailrace of the mill they were constructing. The news got out and within a year thousands of would-be gold miners were flocking here and elsewhere in the Sierra foothills, hoping to make their fortune. Few did, but California was never the same. Ironically, Coloma itself hasn't changed all that much since before the discovery of gold—the really big deposits of gold were found elsewhere. The popular, 275-acre state park holds a replica of Sutter's Mill (rangers hold demonstrations throughout the day), some historic stores, and a cemetery, above which a monument stands over the grave of James Marshall, the mill's foreman who spotted the first nugget of gold and who never profited from his discovery.

The park is also a prime spot for whitewater rafting and kayaking, especially on weekends in spring and summer, so don't be surprised to find the place thronged with wet-suited and Teva-shod hordes.

Throughout the Gold Rush era, Placerville was known as Hangtown, with a reputation for stringing up petty thieves and other lawbreakers. An effigy still hangs at the center of town, in front of a bar on Main Street.

A historical plaque at 543 Main Street in Placerville marks the site of wheelwright **John Studebaker's** Gold Rush-era workshop. You might recognize the name: after he moved back to South Bend, Indiana, his wheelbarrow business expanded into carts, then ammunition wagons for the Civil War, and later yet into some of America's classiest-looking cars and pickup trucks.

American River and Lover's Leap

Some 20 miles east of Placerville, US-50 changes suddenly from a four-lane freeway into a twisting, narrow, mostly two-lane road over the crest of the Sierra Nevada mountains. The usually busy highway, which every year is battered and frequently closed by winter storms, runs right alongside the steep banks of the American River, passing luxuriant groves of pine, fir, and cedar, with numerous old resorts and vacation cabins lining the highway. Many of the resorts, however, seem to have fallen on hard times, and many cabins have actually fallen into the river, which has suffered from serious flooding in recent years. One place along the highway that has stayed in fine shape is the **Strawberry Lodge**, 43 miles east of Placerville at 17510 US-50 (530/659-7200). This rustic, hiker- and mountain-bike-friendly haunt has a nice restaurant and around 50 moderately priced rooms, many overlooking the river.

If you turn off US-50 south from the Strawberry Lodge, a half-mile dirt road brings you across the American River to the fairly basic, U.S. Forest Service-run Lover's Leap campground. Very popular with the rock-climbers who test themselves on the range of beginning to ultra-expert routes etched into the cracked face of Lover's Leap, the campground is rich in history as well: from 1914 until the 1930s, what's now the main road through here used to be part of the legendary Lincoln Highway. You can still see advertising signs painted onto rocks along the well-signed, mile-long route: the first state highway in California. Before the auto age the route served as the main wagon road across the mountains to the gold and silver mines of the Comstock Lode, and before that it was used by the riders of the Pony Express.

Continuing uphill from Strawberry, about six miles west of the summit, the towering granite cliff of Lover's Leap stands out to the south of the highway; to the north, from the Twin Bridges parking area, a rough two-mile scramble along Pyramid Creek leads to the delicate cascade of **Horsetail Falls**, a serene destination. The falls, which can be seen from the highway, are inside the boundary of the Desolation Wilderness, so you need a permit to hike or stay overnight. For details, contact the U.S. Forest Service **ranger station**, five miles east of Placerville (530/644-6048), on the south side of US-50.

After climbing east up US-50's steepest set of hairpin turns, you'll pass the Sierra-at-Tahoe ski area and a couple of vacation camps before reaching 7,365-foot Echo Summit and some great views of the Lake Tahoe basin. The shining blue waters beckon you along another steep stretch of US-50, downhill this time, if you're heading east, to the lakeshore itself. (Unfortunately, the vista is marred by the grey concrete scar of the Lake Tahoe airport, which sits smack dab between you and the lake.)

South Lake Tahoe

One of the biggest and deepest lakes in the country, straddling the Nevada/California border at 6,220 feet above sea level, Lake Tahoe is a beautiful sight from any angle—from the crest of the alpine peaks surrounding it, from a car or bicycle as you cruise along the shoreline roads, or from a boat out on the lake itself.

Sitting, as the name suggests, at the southern end of Lake Tahoe, the ungainly resort community of South Lake Tahoe is a place of multiple personalities. On the

California side, low-rise motels line the US-50 frontage, and the atmosphere is that of a family-oriented summer resort, with bike-rental stands and T-shirt shops clogging the roadside. Across the Nevada border in the town of Stateline, glitzy 20-story casinos rise up in a sudden wall of concrete and glass, ignoring the surrounding beauty in favor of round-the-clock "adult fun"—gambling, racy nightclub revues, and more gambling. A few strategically placed pine trees work hard to retain a semblance of the natural splendor, but in peak summer season it's basically a *very* busy stretch of road on both sides of the state line.

Despite the lake's great popularity, year-round prices for Tahoe accommodations are surprisingly low; with three **Travelodges**, a **Motel 6**, and dozens of others to choose from, you shouldn't have trouble finding something suitable for around $50 a night. The most charac-

terful place to stay is the rustic, family-friendly **Camp Richardson Resort** (530/541-1801 or 800/544-1801), with cabins and a historic hotel right on the lake off Hwy-89 at Jamison Beach, two miles northwest of the US-50/Hwy-89 junction; they also have boat, bike, and kayak rentals, and a trio of campgrounds with showers (two are on the inland side of Hwy-89).

Though the Stateline casinos all have fine dining restaurants galore, food, alas, is not really a strength. For a carbo-loading breakfast head to the **Red Hut Waffle Shop** at 2749 Lake Tahoe Boulevard (US-50), or for burgers and shakes, stop by the **50's Drive-In**, farther east on Lake Tahoe Boulevard. Away from the roadside, right on the lake at Camp Richardson, you can enjoy good food (burgers, grilled fish, and great steaks) and frequent live music at the beachfront **Beacon** (530/541-1801).

For a truly unforgettable meal, you may have to cruise around to Crystal Bay on Lake Tahoe's north shore, where the

Midway between Echo Summit and South Lake Tahoe, Hwy-89 turns off along the crest heading south toward **Hope Valley**, a mostly undeveloped and wonderfully scenic region known for its wealth of fishing and hiking opportunities. See the High Sierra and Death Valley: US-395 chapter on page 164 for more.

In winter, the Tahoe area is an extremely popular ski resort—**Heavenly** (775/586-7000) on the south shore and **Squaw Valley** (530/583-6985) in the north are among the largest and busiest ski areas in the U.S.; both have sightseeing chairlifts in summer.

Lake Tahoe is 12 miles wide, 22 miles long, and has 72 miles of coastline and is over 1,000 feet deep in places.

LAKE TAHOE LOOP

Lake Tahoe is spectacular from pretty much any point along its shore, but to really get a feel for all its facets nothing beats a leisurely drive (or long days' bike ride) all the way around it, 72 miles if you don't backtrack or take any detours. It doesn't really matter where you start or finish—just be sure you stop, early and often, and get out of the car (or off your bike).

Starting in the south at South Lake Tahoe, you'll find some of Lake Tahoe's most enjoyable places are only a few minutes away, off Emerald Bay Road (Hwy-89). In summer, get a taste of Lake Tahoe in the early days by visiting the **Tallac Historic Site**, four miles west of the US-50/Hwy-89 junction, where some seriously-monied mansions have been preserved as a state park—complete with a nice little beach. For details on the many hikes up into the mountains above this part of Lake Tahoe, stop by the U.S. Forest Service **ranger station** at 870 Emerald Bay Road (530/573-2674), which marks the turnoff to the Tallac Historic Site. North of here you'll find one of the pair of parks that wrap around the gorgeous fjord-like inlet of Emerald Bay is **D.L. Bliss State Park** (daily 8 AM-dusk; $5; 530/525-7277) with miles of trails, two campgrounds, and a sandy beach in the far north end, at Rubicon Point.

The west and north shores of Lake Tahoe look and feel more commercial and developed, dotted with vacation homes, resort hotels, and lake-view restaurants—but precious few parks and picnic areas. Crossing east on Hwy-28 into Nevada, you'll start on the 30-mile Nevada portion of the lakeshore's 72 miles, passing the border-straddling **Cal-Neva** lodge-casino, a truly rustic spot (with a real log exterior and huge boulders in the lobby) that opened in the 1920s and was owned in the 1960s by Frank Sinatra. East of the Cal-Neva, through the privately-owned, ultra-exclusive enclave of Incline Village and past the ersatz **Ponderosa Ranch**, a theme park inspired by the TV show *Bonanza*, the scenery picks up again as Hwy-28 runs right along the lakeshore for another 15 miles before edging away from the lake toward the US-50 junction. The section south of the Hwy-28/US-50 junction is another stunner, as the road is carved into the granite walls, most clearly at the landmark Cave Rock Tunnel, a dozen miles north of the Stateline casinos.

Around Lake Tahoe, be aware that most of the actual lakeshore is private property, so access can be difficult and frustratingly rare. Also, traveling in a clockwise direction keeps you on the lake side of the road, and so has the least obstructed views—and the easiest access to lakeside turnouts.

From the north shore of Lake Tahoe, a pair of highways—Hwy-89 from Tahoe City via Squaw Valley, and Hwy-267 from Kings Beach—link the lake with the I-80 freeway at Truckee.

wonderful **Soule Domain** serves roast meats, pastas, and other deliciously inventive dinners in a cozy log cabin that stands across from Cal-Neva lodge, right on the California side of the Nevada border. Reservations strongly recommended; call 530/546-7529.

Stateline

Right where US-50 crosses from California into Nevada, the casino complex at Stateline forms: for a few short blocks, it's a mini-Las Vegas, with four 20-story resort hotels towering over the lakeshore. **Harvey's** (800/648-3361) started it all in the 1940s, with six nickel slot machines, still in use in a corner of the casino; it's now the largest, with over 650 lakeside rooms. **Harrah's** (800/648-3773), across US-50, is the most opulent—

For a thrill-seeking alternative east from Stateline and Lake Tahoe, take the very steep **Kingsbury Grade** (Hwy-207) down to historic Genoa and the Nevada state capital, Carson City. See the High Sierra and Death Valley: US-395 chapter on pages 161-162 for more.

its luxurious 500-square-foot suites are yours to enjoy for a mere $200 a night. Altogether, over 2,000 rooms are available, combined with at least that many more across the California border. The multitudes of game-hungry visitors that converge here create a definite charge in the rarefied atmosphere when the casino tables are turning at full speed, and it's also a great place to catch your favorite performers, or a Vegas-style floor show.

Nevada Beach and Zephyr Cove

From the casino district at Stateline, US-50 winds along Lake Tahoe's southeastern shore for over 20 miles, passing by a pair of waterfront parks at Nevada Beach and Zephyr Cove (where you can ride the faux paddlewheeler MS *Dixie* on a two-hour cruise across the lake). Otherwise, lakeshore access is severely limited, since most of the waterfront is privately owned, though numerous roadside turnouts (most easily accessible to westbound, lakeside travelers) offer ample opportunities to take in unforgettable views.

Midway along the lake's eastern shore, US-50 turns sharply and begins climbing up and over the 7,140-foot crest of Spooner Summit, all the way giving great views of the tantalizing blue gleam below. At the summit, stretch your legs by taking a quick hike on the Tahoe Ridge Trail, a work-in-progress which will eventually circumnavigate the entire Lake Tahoe basin. Dropping down swiftly from Spooner Summit into the Great Basin desert, US-50 links up with US-395 for the final few miles into Carson City.

I-80: Donner Pass

Though US-50 has the great advantage of actually winding along Lake Tahoe, the quickest and most popular way to get to, or across, the Sierra Nevada mountains is the I-80 freeway over Donner Pass. Splitting off from US-50 at Sacramento, I-80 veers further north, along a route blazed by early pioneer wagon trains and later followed by major transcontinental routes: the Central Pacific Railroad in 1867 and the Lincoln Highway in 1914. The scenery here is as compelling as the history, and apart from the lack of a lake view it's an enjoyable drive—especially if you take the time to turn off the freeway.

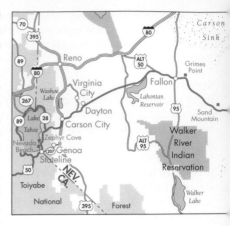

About a half-hour east of Sacramento, I-80 cruises through the historic Gold Rush town of **Auburn**, which still retains a small town feel, and a nice stretch of the old Lincoln Highway, still signed as Lincoln Way, goes through downtown Auburn. East of here the road climbs steeply, passing by the historic Gold Rush camp at Dutch Flat—where a great old log cabin roadhouse, the **Monte Vista Inn** (530/389-2333) has been serving travelers wonderful dinners and fresh pies since the 1930s—before shifting from the American River to the Yuba River watershed at the edge of the expansive Tahoe National Forest.

Continuing up, the real highlights are around 7,239-foot-high Donner Pass, which is impressive from the freeway but a million times more so from old US-40, aka the **Donner Pass Road**, which turns off I-80 at Soda Springs and runs along the south side of the freeway. It's only about 10 miles, or three freeway exits, but what a road: carved out of granite cliffs that provide some of the Tahoe area's most challenging rock climbing, the usually traffic-free road twists along at the edge of the world, high above the emerald waters of Donner Lake, with numerous pullouts for you to enjoy the High Sierra views.

At the bottom of the pass, the east end of Donner Lake has been set aside as **Donner Memorial State Park** (daily 8 AM-dusk in summer only; $5; 530/582-7892) where a statue of heroic pioneers stands near the site where 42 of 89 travelers in the legendary Donner party starved to death during the winter of 1846-47; the survivors resorted to cannibalism. Two miles further east, the town of **Truckee** (pop. 2,400; elev. 5,280 feet) marks the turnoff south to Lake Tahoe and is a great stop in its own right. A variety of cafes, diners, bars, and bike-and-ski shops line Commercial Street, the main drag along the busy railroad tracks.

At the end of summer, Donner Pass Road is closed for a few days so that **motorcycle riders** can race along its twisty curves. For dates and further details, contact the visitors bureau in Truckee (530/587-2757). All summer long, hikers can enjoy a quieter experience by heading off along the Pacific Crest Scenic Trail, which runs through the wilderness north and south from Donner Pass, near the Boreal ski area; for details, contact the Tahoe National Forest (530/587-3558).

At Carson City, the Nevada state capital, US-50 crosses US-395, a wonderful old highway that runs along the east side of the High Sierra crest, from Reno south through the Owens Valley past Death Valley—all the way to Los Angeles. Carson City, along with Reno and the nearby mining camp of Virginia City, are all covered beginning on page 156.

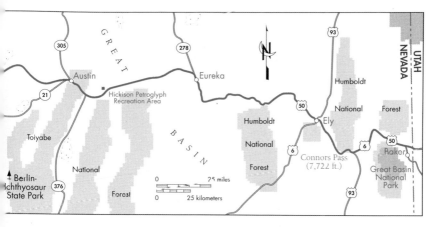

Dayton

On the north side of US-50, just east of the turnoff for Virginia City, Dayton is one of the oldest settlements in Nevada. Gold was first discovered here in 1849, and later the town's massive stamp mills pounded the ore carried through the massive Sutro Tunnel from the fabulous Comstock Lode in the mountains above. The historic town center is little more than two blocks of Main Street north from the traffic light on US-50. Here you can choose from a couple of combination cafes-and-saloons, including the **Old Corner Bar** at 30 Pike Street, a favorite hangout of John Huston, Arthur Miller, Marilyn Monroe, and company, when they were in Dayton in 1960 to film *The Misfits*.

East of Dayton, around Lahontan Dam, irrigated fields of alfalfa quickly give way to 50 miles of sandy desert, tumbleweed, and scruffy grasses.

Fallon

Coming into Fallon, especially if you've crossed the Great Basin deserts of Utah and Nevada that stretch to the east, can be a

About the only radio station along this stretch of US-50 is Fallon's **KBLB 980 AM,** which plays a fairly standard array of country hits.

shock to the system. First, relative to Nevada's other US-50 towns, Fallon is big: straddling the US 50/US-95 junction, with about 7,000 residents and all the attendant shopping malls, traffic lights, and fast-food franchises. Second, but perhaps more striking, Fallon is green: alfalfa, onions, garlic, and cantaloupes as far as the eye can see. Otherwise, Fallon offers the ATMs, gas stations, and motels lining US-50, as well as the usual Pizza Huts and Subways, and a handy 24-hour grocery store. My favorite road food stop is **Bob's Root Beer**, a burger stand at the west edge of town; for a quaint place to stay, try the **Lariat Motel**, 850 W. US-50 (775/423-3181), with a dozen $35-a-night rooms and a great neon sign. It offers a central location, too—across the road from Fallon's casinos.

Though it had long existed as a crossroads for the surrounding mining camps and was first laid out as a town around the turn of the century, Fallon didn't really begin to grow until the completion of Lahontan Dam west of town in 1915 brought irrigation water from the Carson River. Besides agriculture, Fallon's other main employer is the U.S. Navy, whose air base and target range is now an important training center for carrier-based fighters and bombers—the "Top Guns" of Tom Cruise fame.

While it's not an overwhelmingly attractive place, Fallon does have what they accurately call "The Best Little Museum on the Loneliest Road in America," the eclectic and engaging **Churchill County Museum** (Mon.-Sat. 10 AM-5 PM, Sunday noon-5 PM; free) at 1050 S. Maine Street, less than a mile south of US-50. Filling an old Safeway supermarket, the exhibits contain native Paiute basketry, clothing, and hunting gear, the usual pioneer quilts and clothing plus a player piano; the gift shop sells a wide range of books and historical postcards.

Grimes Point and Sand Mountain

The 110 miles of US-50 between Fallon and Austin, the next town to the east, look pretty empty on most maps, but there's more to see than you might think. In the midst of a U.S. Navy target range, where supersonic fighters play electronic war games across the alkali flats, there are historical plaques marking Pony Express and

Butterfield Stage way stations, a solitary brothel, and two unique attractions—a singing sand dune and an extensive petroglyph site.

Ten miles east of Fallon, the extraordinary grouping of petroglyphs at Grimes Point is not to be missed. Just 100 yards north of US-50, a self-guided trail leads past hundreds of images etched into the lichen-covered, espresso-brown basalt boulders. Some 8,000 years ago, when the carvings were made,

---

I-80 SURVIVAL GUIDE: NEVADA

RUNNING EAST FROM RENO ALONG THE ROUTE OF OLD US-40, the "Victory Highway," I-80 is the most traveled route to Utah and beyond, and has a few places along its 400-odd miles that merit a quick stop or more. If you're racing through, be sure to check out:

MM 12: The casinos of **Reno**, the "Biggest Little City in the World," mark the start of our road trip south along US-395.

MM 83: US-95 runs south to **Fallon**, western end of the Loneliest Road in America, US-50.

MM 178: At **Winnemucca**, a slice of a giant redwood tree in the middle of the desert marks the eastern end of the "Winnemucca to the Redwoods" highway; the town also boasts one of the better Basque restaurants in a state famous for them: **San Fermin**, 485 W. Winnemucca Boulevard (775/625-2555).

MM 301: Elko (see pages 199-299)

MM 352: Wells (see page 198)

MM 411: The Nevada/Utah state line also marks the boundary between Pacific and mountain time zones.

Grimes Point was on the shores of now-vanished Lake Lahontan, a prime hunting and fishing ground for prehistoric Great Basin peoples. These days fast and fierce lizards, and the occasional antelope, share the arid setting with a huge array of abstract and figurative images that have been pecked and chiseled into the rock faces. If you're intrigued and want to know more, stop by the excellent Churchill County Museum in Fallon (see above) or join a BLM-run guided tour (775/885-6000) of nearby **Hidden Cave** where significant archaeological remains have been uncovered.

Sand Mountain, 15 miles east of Grimes Point, 84 miles west of Austin, and just a quarter-mile north of US-50, is a giant sword-edged sand dune that makes a deep booming sound when cascading crystals oscillate at the proper frequency—somewhere between 50 and 100 hertz. On weekends you're more likely to hear the sound of unmuffled dirt bikes and dune buggies, but at other times the half-hour trudge to the top is well worth making, to watch the swirls of sand dance along the ridges.

At the turnoff to Sand Mountain, a battered sign marks the official (solar-powered!) **"Loneliest Phone on the Loneliest Road in America."**

Near Sand Mountain, surrounded by salt-encrusted mud flats about 150 yards north of US-50, a squat wooden cross and a short picket fence set in a rocky base mark the burial site of three French-Canadian sisters, Jennie, Emma, and Louise LeBeau. The girls, aged nine, six, and three, respectively, died of diphtheria here in 1865. Local good samaritans, including longtime Fallon residents John Johnson and his late father Johnnie, have tended the graves in the years since, and a small plaque remembers the hundreds of other people, and thousands of animals, who perished on the long journey west.

Austin

Some 110 miles east of Fallon and 70 miles west of Eureka, tiny Austin (pop. 300) huddles well above 6,000 feet on the north slope of the mighty Toiyabe Mountains. The steep incline of Main Street (US-50) as it passes through town is symbolic of the precariousness with which Austin has clung to life since its 10-year mining boom ended—in 1873. Unlike Fallon or Eureka, which wear their prosperity on their sleeves, Austin hangs on to the rustic, steadfastly un-whitewashed nature that was once—and in some places, remains—central to Nevada's character.

According to local legend, a Pony Express rider accidentally discovered silver ore here in 1862, and the rush was on. Prospectors fanned out from Austin (which was named after the Texas hometown of one of its founders) to establish Belmont, Berlin, Grantsville, Ione, and dozens of other boom-towns-now-turned-ghost towns; roughly $50 million in gold and silver was shipped out over the next 10 years. Since then Austin has experienced a long, melancholy decline, though recent efforts to mine the abundant turquoise and barium in the region have met with some success.

A two-minute drive (at 10 mph) along Main Street takes you past all there is to see in Austin today. The impressive steeples of the Catholic, Methodist, and Baptist churches dominate the townscape, while at the west (downhill) end of town you can glimpse **Stoke's Castle**, a three-story stone sentinel built in 1897 and lived in for all of a month. It looks best from a distance, looming over the cemeteries at the west end of town,

Forty-five miles east of Fallon at the town of Middlegate, Hwy-361 heads south to the magnesium-mining company town of Gabbs. About 20 miles east of Gabbs lies fascinating **Berlin-Ichthyosaur State Park** (775/867-3001), which holds an only-in-Nevada combination: the 100-year-old ghost town of Berlin and a 225-million-year-old marine fossil quarry. Camping is available year-round, and guided tours of the town and the fossil beds are given weekends in summer.

but if you want to get closer, follow Castle Road for about a half-mile south from US-50.

For its 300 residents, Austin has three gas stations (it's a long way to the next town, so fill up here), three bare-bones motels, and a pair of cafes: the ancient **International**, moved here board by board from Virginia City in 1863, and the **Toiyabe Cafe**. Both are right on Main Street, and open early (around 6 AM), and close early (around 9 PM).

Hickison Petroglyph Recreation Area

Bookended by 7,000-foot mountain ranges at either end, the route between Austin and Eureka is perhaps the longest, flat-test, straightest stretch of the entire trans-Nevada length of US-50, over 70 miles of Great Basin nothingness. Cattle ranches fill the plains, which were crisscrossed by early explorers like John C. Frémont, who passed through in 1845, as well as by the Pony Express. Such recent history, however, pales in comparison to the relics from the region's prehistoric past, particularly the fine petroglyphs carved into the rocks on the eastern side of 6,594-foot Hickison Summit, 28 miles east of Austin and 46 miles west of Eureka.

Now protected as part of the BLM-operated Hickison Petroglyph Recreation Area, the petroglyphs stand in a shallow sandstone draw on the north side of the highway. A half-mile trail loops through sagebrush, junipers, and piñon pines from the parking area-*cum*-campground past dozens of these enigmatic figures, some of which are thought to date back as far as 10,000 B.C. Somewhat surprisingly, so far they are mostly graffiti-free.

Across Nevada, US-50 follows the path of the Lincoln Highway, the nation's first transcontinental route.

Eureka, Nevada

Right in the middle of a 100-mile stretch of spectacular Great Basin scenery, Eureka is one of the most engaging and enjoyable stops in the state. Unlike a lot of places along the Loneliest Road, Eureka is fairly thriving, thanks to numerous gold mines still in operation in Eureka County, including one of the largest and most productive in the United States, the Newmont Mine near Carlin.

The four blocks of 100-year-old buildings lining the steeply sloping, franchise-free Main Street (US-50) are a mix of well-restored brick and wood storefronts alongside less fortunate ruins, some merely sets of cast-iron pilasters holding up false fronts. The focal point is the grand 1879 **Eureka County Courthouse**, still in use. Behind it stands the **Eureka Sentinel Museum** (Mon.-Fri. 11 AM-5 PM, shorter hours weekends), with displays explaining the lively local history as well as type-setting equipment and printing presses of the newspaper published here from 1870 to 1960.

Besides being an intriguing place to stroll around (walking-tour booklets are available from the Sentinel Museum and many local shops), Eureka is also a good place to break a journey. The historic but recently restored **Jackson House** hotel (775/237-5577) on Main Street is a fine choice and it also has a bar and a good restaurant. Main Street also boasts a new Best Western. The best place to eat, drink, and be merry is the lively **Owl Club** cafe and casino, also on Main Street; good

THE PONY EXPRESS

Of all the larger-than-life legends that animate the annals of the Wild West, none looms larger than that of the Pony Express. As is typical of frontier adventures, accounts of the Pony Express are often laced with considerable exaggeration, but in this case the facts are unusually impressive. Beginning in April 1860, running twice a week between St. Joseph, Missouri, and Sacramento, California (where it was linked with San Francisco by steamship), the Pony Express halved the time it took to carry news to and from the West Coast, making the 1,966-mile trek in just 10 days. Eighty riders (including 14-year-old William "Buffalo Bill" Cody, who made the record single run of 322 miles) were employed to race between some 190 stations en route, switching horses every 10-15 miles and averaging 75 miles per run—day or night, in all kinds of weather, across 120° F deserts or snowbound Sierra passes.

Covering nearly 2,000 miles of the wildest and ruggedest land on the frontier, the Pony Express established the first high-speed link between the two coasts. At a time when the nation was divided against itself, with the Civil War looming on the horizon, the Pony Express connection played a key role in keeping the valuable mines of California and Nevada in Union hands. A private enterprise that lasted just 18 months, and which lost considerable amounts of money before being put of out business for good, the Pony Express proved that overground connections across the still-wild western U.S. were both necessary and possible.

The completion of the transcontinental telegraph on October 28, 1861 made the Pony Express obsolete overnight, and not so much as a saddle survives from this legendary endeavor. Apart from a few postmarked letters, and various statues and plaques marking the Pony Express route, there are very few tangible signs of it today. The most evocative sites stand all alone in the dry Nevada desert, within easy access of the US-50 highway. East of Fallon, Nevada, for example, the highway runs right on top of the old Pony Express route, and the remains of two relay stations can still be seen. One is at **Sand Springs**, at the foot of Sand Mountain. More substantial remains survive at **Cold Springs**, 32 miles east, where plaques recount the history and a short trail brings you to what was once among the most isolated and dangerous of the Pony Express stations.

steaks, a 150-year-old bar, and some chatty card sharks will all help you while away a few hours.

Ely marks the junction of US-50 and our US-93 route, which is covered beginning on page 196.

Ely

Ely (pop. 4,756; pronounced "E-lee," as in Robert) is a sprawling crossroads community where US-6, US-50, and US-93 all intersect. For nearly 100 years Ely was a boomtown flush with the wealth from the massive Kennecott-owned Liberty Pit copper mines, Nevada's largest and longest-lived mining venture, which produced over a billion dollars' worth of ore while employing nearly 10,000 people at its peak during the 1950s.

The state-run Nevada Commission on Tourism sponsors a tongue-in-cheek promotion in which travelers along US-50 can earn themselves a certificate saying **"I Survived the Loneliest Road in America"** by getting their official US-50 travel passports stamped at locations along the highway. For details, contact the commission at Capitol Complex, Carson City, NV 89710 or call 800/237-0774.

Mountains of mine tailings tower over US-50 west of Ely, and five miles west of town, near **Ruth**, there's a turn marked Historic Mining Viewpoint that leads south along a part-paved, part-dirt road for just over a mile to a viewpoint high above the huge crater where hundreds of tons of ore were dug. The Magma mining company is currently leaching the metal out of the previously discarded ore and has encircled the viewing area with historical photographs of the old mining operations, alongside chunks of rock—all of which are labeled to explain their history and geologic makeup.

After the mines closed down in 1982, the railway that had shuttled pay dirt from the mines to the smelter was abandoned. The entire operation was turned into **Nevada Northern Railway Museum** (Wed.-Sun. 9 AM-4 PM; $3; 775/289-2085) in 1985, and now you can take a 90-minute, 14-mile loop tour of the rail yards aboard the Ghost Train, a 1910 Baldwin Steamer. The train leaves from the depot at the north end of East 11th Street and uses a ton of coal and 1,000 gallons of water; trips are offered weekends only, and tickets cost around $15.

Ely's other main stop is the **White Pine Public Museum**, 2000 Aultman Street (US-50), which has a wide-ranging collection of minerals, mining implements, and Pony Express memorabilia on display.

Apart from mining history (and motels, 24-hour gas stations, and the only supermarket for many miles) there's not a whole lot to Ely. The heart of town is a neon-rich few blocks of Aultman Street (US-50) west of the US-93 junction, centering upon the landmark **Hotel Nevada** (775/289-6665), with its giant cowboy and a neon-lit slot machine on its marquee. Inside there are real (as opposed to video) slot machines, pool tables, a cafe, and a bar with nightly live music. Rooms upstairs start at a bargain $25. Another place worth stopping at is the **Copper Queen Casino** (775/289-4883), on the south side of Ely, where pricey motel rooms open directly onto a lobby shared by banks of slot machines and a small swimming pool. Also nice is the quiet **Four Sevens Motel**, a block north of Aultman at 500 High Street (775/289-4747); chains have arrived more recently, in the form of a Holiday Inn and a Motel 6.

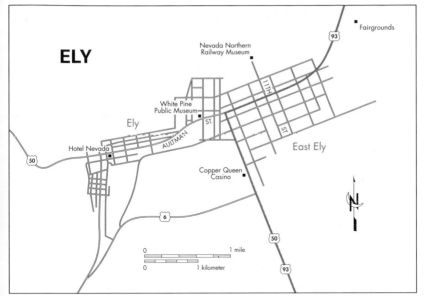

The nicest and most memorable place to stay in Ely has to be the **Steptoe Valley Inn**, a Victorian B&B with all the trimmings, located north of US-50 on 11th Street, near the Northern Nevada Railroad depot (open seasonally; 775/289-8687).

For food, Ely has three coffee shop-style restaurants, plus franchised fast food, including a newish McDonald's. A better bet: down a milk shake at the soda fountain inside **Economy Drug** at Aultman and 7th Streets.

The route east toward Great Basin National Park is an official "scenic route," rolling across sagebrush plains and climbing over the Schell Creek and Snake mountain ranges through dense groves of pine and juniper.

Connors Pass and Majors Place

East of Ely, US-50, spliced together with US-6 and US-93 into a single two-lane highway, continues for 25 miles before crossing the narrow waist of the Schell Creek Range at 7,722-foot Connors Pass. As you ascend toward the pass, the air cools and freshens, the single-leaf piñon and Utah juniper appear and increase and, cresting the summit, the mighty Snake Range, including 13,063-foot Wheeler Peak, comes into view.

East of the pass, at Majors Place (where there's a roadhouse, but no reliable gas), US-93 cuts due south, heading 80 long, solitary miles to the next contact with humans at Pioche, while US-50 heads east toward Great Basin National Park.

Great Basin National Park

Approaching Nevada from the east, travelers are greeted by the towering silhouette of **Wheeler Peak**, at 13,063 feet the second highest mountain in the state; from the west, similarly sheer escarpments tower over lush green open range for miles and

The world's oldest known bristlecone pine, dubbed **Prometheus,** was cut down on Wheeler Peak by the U.S. Forest Service in 1964, which discovered too late that, at 4,900 years old, the tree had been the oldest living thing on earth. A cross section of the trunk is displayed at the Bristlecone Convention Center, 150 6th Street in Ely (775/289-3720 or 800/496-3350).

Ely's lively **KELY 1230 AM** plays "the best of everything": oldies from the 1950s and 1960s, plus Rush Limbaugh all morning long.

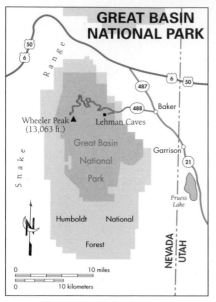

miles along US-50. On October 27, 1986 some 77,000 acres around Wheeler Peak were designated as Great Basin National Park, but its remote location has kept it one of the least-visited national parks in the United States. Hikers and campers will have no trouble finding solitude amidst the alpine forests, ancient bristlecone pines, glacial lakes, and small ice field.

Despite all this beautiful alpine scenery so close at hand, many visitors go no farther than the park's centerpiece, **Lehman Caves**. Geological forces have been sculpting Lehman Caves for roughly 70 million years, but they weren't noticed until homesteader Absalom Lehman stumbled upon the small entrance to the caves in 1885. They were declared a national monument in 1922, and since then only minor improvements have been made, leaving the mind-bending limestone formations alone—no flashy light-and-sound show, just hundreds of delicate stalagmites, stalactites, helictites, aragonites, and the like. A variety of guided tours ($2-4), ranging from short ones to mile-long, 90-minute rambles are conducted at intervals throughout the day; on some summer evenings at 6 PM there's a memorable candlelight tour. Tours leave from the small **visitors center** (daily 8 AM-5 PM, longer in summer; 775/234-7331), which has details of hiking and camping in the park, as well as exhibits on Great Basin wildlife—from birds and bats to mountain lions. There's even a small and surprisingly good summer-only **cafe**.

Thanks to the well-maintained **Wheeler Peak Scenic Drive**, which starts near the vistor center and passes through all the major Great Basin climate zones while climbing from 6,500 feet to over 10,000 feet in a dozen steep miles, the wilderness areas of the park are easily accessible to people willing to take a short hike. At the

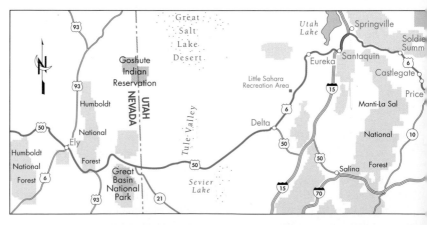

end of the road, camp at the breathtaking Wheeler Peak Campground ($5), and take an easy walk to Theresa Lake, headwaters of Wheeler Creek. From here, you can climb the steep (3,000 uphill feet in 4 miles) trail to the summit, or wind around its base to the park's tiny ice field (Nevada's only glacier) and the immortal grove of bristlecone pines, the oldest living things on the planet, a full 2,000 years older than the second oldest species, the giant sequoias. This is one of very few places where these tenacious trees grow—the other main grove is in the White Mountains, over the California border east of Big Pine—and you can't help but walk softly in their twisted, tormented presence—a full-size bonsai. Alas, not everyone feels so humble: in 1964, a U.S. Forest Service scientist attempting to date the trees here without doing an expensive core sample chose one at random and cut it down, only to discover later that it had been the oldest living thing on the face of the earth—4,900 years old. Not a good career move for *him.*

If you're not camping and being self-reliant, or if you are and want a break, the nearest food and drink to Great Basin National Park can be found at the foot of the park in tiny **Baker** (pop. 55), which boasts one gas station, a post office, the seven-room **Silverjack Motel** (775/234-7323), and the friendly, homey **Outlaw Cafe and Bar**, which serves breakfast, hefty burritos, and beer from early till late.

The state border marks the line between time zones: Nevada is on Pacific standard time, while Utah is on mountain standard time. Adjust your clocks and watches accordingly.

Back on US-50, straddling the Utah/Nevada border is the **Border Inn** cafe/gas station/motel, and the **Hitchin' Post** bar, all open 24 hours a day (775/234-7300). (The gas pumps are technically across the border in Utah, where taxes are lower, so the gas is cheaper than it might be.) Apart from this and Baker, the only other reliable services are in Ely, 70 miles west, or in Delta, 88 miles to the east, so pass by at your peril.

From Delta, US-50 officially cuts southeast via I-15, linking up with I-70 at Salina for the trip east to Grand Junction. Our route, however, follows US-6 (old US-50) toward the Great Salt Lake area, then east over the Wasatch Front, rejoining official US-50 (now I-70) at Green River.

Delta, Utah

About 85 miles east of the Nevada border, the landscape changes suddenly from barren desert to lush pastures around the town of Delta, which is irrigated by the Sevier River. Delta bills itself as the "Gateway to Great Basin National Park," offer-

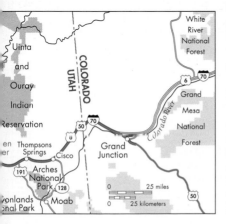

ing a **Best Western** and other motels, gas stations, and a large supermarket—but it has very little else to attract visitors. One place worth a stop is the small **Great Basin Museum** (Tues.-Sat. 10 AM-4 PM; free), a block north of Main Street at 328 W. 100 North Street. The museum features exhibits of minerals, arrowheads, and local history, including a small display of artifacts relating to **Topaz Camp**, an internment camp set up in the Utah desert west of Delta by the U.S. government to imprison persons of Japanese descent during WW II.

Little Sahara Recreation Area

From Delta, the route follows the Sevier River northwest, racing across the feature-less desert for 32 miles before reaching the well-posted turnoff north to the Little Sahara Recreation Area. Visible from the highway four miles north of US-6, the park holds 60,000 acres of sand dunes and sagebrush flats; but the prettiest parts are preserved for hikers and campers, though the hordes of motorcyclists and ATVers hurtling around can overwhelm any sense of peace and tranquillity, turning it into a campground from hell.

SALT LAKE CITY SURVIVAL GUIDE

WITH NO OTHER BIG CITY FOR AT LEAST 500 MILES in any direction, for weary travelers Salt Lake City (pop. 160,000) can still sometimes seem like the oasis that it is, naturally. Taking its name from the undrinkably alkaline Great Salt Lake, the city is actually blessed with abundant fresh water, thanks to the rain- and snow-making properties of the Wasatch Range, which rises knife-like to the east. Founded by Mormons in 1847, and effectively controlled by Mormon elders ever since, Salt Lake City is not exactly a thrilling place, but it's clean and pleasant enough to merit a detour. Most of what there is to see has to do with the Mormon church, officially known as the Church of Latter-day Saints, which has its worldwide headquarters at **Temple Square** downtown. (Street numbers and addresses are measured from here, not the nearby state capitol, which goes to show just how predominant the church is in local life.) On the west side of Temple Square are the amazing genealogical libraries the Mormons maintain; a block east of Temple Square is the **Beehive House**, preserved as it was in the 1850s, when Brigham Young lived here. In the basement of the capitol, a history museum displays the amazing **Mormon Meteor**, the 18-cylinder, 750-horsepower machine in which Ab Jenkins set the land speed record at Bonneville Salt Flats in 1931.

If you want to see (or swim in, or taste) the Great Salt Lake, head west on I-80 to exit 104, where a free state park (with a beach) spreads west from the site of **Saltaire,** a wonderfully eclectic bathing resort that burned down in 1970.

Though Salt Lake is a pretty, clean, and tidy city, it's not exactly *fun*. For that you have to head up into the many lovely canyons (Big Cottonwood or Little Cottonwood, to name just two) that climb east into the looming Wasatch Mountains; both offer heavenly hiking, and some of the world's finest skiing. Or, you can take a trip farther east to historic **Park City**, a quick half-hour drive via the I-80 freeway. Now famous for its skiing (and as the home of the Sundance Film Festival), Park

City (pop. 6,800; elev. 7,000 feet) started in the 1860s as a silver mining camp, and still retains dozens of turn-of-the-century buildings along its photogenic Main Street. Park City has a full range of accommodations, and some of Utah's best restaurants; for details, contact the **visitors bureau** inside the Park City Museum, 528 Main Street in the old Ciy Hall (801/649-6100).

The mountains above Salt Lake City hold some of the country's best ski resorts (Park City, Alta, and Snowbird), which will host the **Winter Olympics** in 2002.

Practicalities

Salt Lake City has a great, don't miss road food stop: **Bill and Nada's Cafe**, 479 S. 600 Street East (801/359-6984), an all-night diner with a truly great jukebox and greasy-spoon food that ranges from incredible to indigestible. For reliably great food in a beautiful setting, head two miles east of town (past the massive "This is the Place" monument) to **Ruth's Diner**, 2100 Emigration Canyon (801/582-5807), featuring great breakfasts and a lively bustling crowd. For dinner, the nearby **Santa Fe Restaurant** (801/582-5888) has great views and a full range of authentic, spicy Southwestern food.

Along with all the usual motels and hotels, Salt Lake City has some very nice B&Bs, many in historic homes on or around the landmark-loaded South Temple Street. One of these is the **Brigham Street Inn**, 1135 E. South Temple Street (801/364-4461), which has nine rooms in a lushly restored 1890s Queen Anne mansion; rates run $125-195 a night.

For more information on Salt Lake City and the surrounding region contact the **visitors bureau**, in the Salt Palace Convention Center at 90 S. West Temple Street (801/521-2822).

564—Bathing Scene, Great Salt Lake, Utah.

Eureka, Utah

Fifty miles east of Delta, 20 miles west of the I-15 freeway, the weather-beaten town of Eureka (pop. 750) climbs steeply up surrounding mountainsides at the heart of the once-thriving Tintic Mining District, where as recently as the 1930s thousands of miners dug millions of dollars' worth of gold, silver, copper, and lead out of the ground every year. Now the massive wooden head frames of long-closed mine shafts stand high above the houses and prefab trailers that cling to the slopes, while fading signs advertise abandoned businesses along Main Street.

Though diehard residents still speak of plans to reopen one or more of the mines, prosperity seems a distant dream in Eureka, and while it's not quite a ghost town, it is well on its way there. The glory days are recounted in the small **Tintic Mining Museum**, next to city hall on Main Street, and at the west edge of town a historical plaque stands alongside the heavy timber head frame of the Bullion-Beck Mine, once one of the area's most productive.

Santaquin and Springville

Heading east from Eureka, our route bends across rock-strewn sagebrush hills around the southern shore of Utah Lake toward the I-15 freeway. Utah Lake, which is freshwater in contrast to the briny expanse of the Great Salt Lake to the north, used to be much larger than it is now, before so much of it was diverted to water the apple, peach, and cherry orchards that line US-6 around Santaquin—whose three gas stations are the last reliable source of fuel for westbound travelers until Delta, 70 miles to the southwest.

From Santaquin, follow the I-15 freeway north to Springville, where you'll find a truck stop that's as clean and comfortable as any in the U.S.: the **Mountain Springs Travel Center** (801/489-3641), which, besides good food, cheap gas, and $40-a-night rooms, offers free showers with every fill-up.

From Springville, the Salt Lake City megalopolis stretches north along I-15 for nearly 100 miles, from Provo to Ogden.

Detour: Dinosaur National Monument and Vernal

If you're traveling between Salt Lake City and the Denver area, but don't have time to follow our road trip route along old US-50 through Utah's national parks and around Pike's Peak, a good alternative to tedious I-80 is to follow old US-40. Splitting off from I-80 at Park City, US-40 bends south and then east around the wild

Uinta Mountains (one of the few east-west ranges in the United States) and then continues through stupendous alpine scenery and abundant outdoor recreation, as well one of the world's greatest concentrations of fossillized **dinosaurs**. Located just before the Colorado border, and just north of US-40, 80-acre **Dinosaur Quarry** (8 AM-7 PM in summer, till 4:30 PM rest of year; $10 per car; 435/789-2115) is a unit of the larger Dinosaur National Monument, a 325-square mile park straddling the Utah-Colorado border. Over the years Dinosaur Quarry has provided enough brontosaurus bones to fill Carnegie Hall. (Well, to be exact, the bones ended up at the Carnegie Museum of Natural History in Pittsburgh, Pennsylvania.)

Between 1909 and 1924, some 350 tons of bones, belonging to a dozen different dinosaur species, were dug up here; nowadays excavations are continuing, but the fossils are left in place. Despite the *Jurassic Park* connotations of the name, Dinosaur National Monument has very few fossils outside of the quarry—what it does have is 325 square miles of limestone canyons carved by the Green and Yampa Rivers.

The region's largest town, Vernal (pop. 8,000), has more fun with the dinosaur connection than the National Park Service does. The town's mascot is a 40-foot-tall pink fiberglass dinosaur (nicknamed "Dinah"), which stood for 41 years (1958-1999) stood outside the Dine-A-Ville Motel, on the Main Street stretch of old US-40. When the motel was demolished to make way for a credit union, Dinah made her way to a new home in a park at 1500 E. Main Street. (Her mate, a pint-sized *T. rex*, wasn't so lucky; he now stands alone in the median strip.) Near downtown Vernal, the **Dinosaur Gardens** at the Utah Field House of Natural History, 235 E. Main Street (8 AM-9 PM in summer, till 5 PM the rest of year; $5 per car or $2 per person; 435/789-3799), have 17 different full-size dinosaur statues set in realistic environments, while displays inside identify fossils and trace the region's significant human history, too.

Next door to the Dinosaur Gardens, the helpful folks at the **Vernal Welcome Center** (daily 8 AM-5 PM; 435/789-7894) can help with tips on places to stay and eat around town.

Soldier Summit

Heading southeast from the greater Salt Lake City area, the drive along US-6 (old US-50) up and over 7,477-foot Soldier Summit is truly beautiful, as the two-lane highway passes through bright red sandstone canyons along the stark eastern side of the towering Wasatch Front, then twists alongside pines and cottonwoods to the crest. The summit itself, where there's a handy gas station-cum-general store (their motto: "Radiators Filled, Bladders Emptied"), marks the boundary between the Colorado River drainage and the Great Basin.

About 10 miles northwest of Vernal, the **Dry Fork Petroglyphs** are considered to be some of the country's finest rock art, consisting of a series of life-sized human figures, many adorned with headdresses and other ornaments. The art is on private property, at the end of the Red Cloud Scenic Drive, well-signed and open to well-behaved visitors.

Castlegate and Helper

Dropping down from Soldier Summit, US-6 joins up with US-191 to become US-6/191, winding along the Price River through Castlegate, a steeply walled sandstone canyon lined with working coal mines, many of which you see from the highway. While most mining companies now rely on heavy machinery to do the dirty work of digging out the coal, the Castlegate area was the site of the two worst mining disasters in Utah history: 200 men and boys killed at nearby Scofield on May 1, 1900 and another 173 killed in a 1924 explosion in Castlegate.

Helper (pop. 2,148), at the downstream edge of Castlegate, six miles northwest of Price, is a classic railroad town preserved almost unchanged for nearly a century. The six-block downtown area, fronting onto the tracks, includes so many turn-of-the-century brick- and stone-fronted buildings that it's been declared a National Historic District—though the sad truth is that most of these have stood abandoned since the railroad switched to diesel power in the 1950s. Before that, Helper was a

BUTCH CASSIDY AND THE HOLE-IN-THE-WALL GANG

Long before Paul Newman played him alongside Robert Redford's Sundance Kid, Butch Cassidy was one of the great outlaw legends of the Wild West. Thanks to his habit of sharing the proceeds from his crimes with the widows and children of men killed or ruined by bankers and cattle barons, Butch Cassidy earned a reputation as the "Robin Hood of the Wild West." That, plus the fact he never killed anyone while committing his crimes, gained him popular admiration from the cowboys, miners, and homesteading pioneers among whom he worked his trade.

Born Robert Leroy Parker to a family of Mormon farmers in Beaver, Utah, on Friday the 13th of April, 1866, the man who came to be known as Butch Cassidy spent his youth as a ranch hand in Utah, Colorado, and southern Wyoming. The first major crime attributed to Butch Cassidy is the robbery of a bank in Telluride in 1889, which netted him and his three accomplices some $20,000. From 1894 to 1896 he was imprisoned in Wyoming for cattle theft, and following this he joined up with Harry Longabaugh (a.k.a "The Sundance Kid") and the rest of the Hole-in-the-Wall gang. Together they robbed over a dozen banks, trains, and stagecoaches throughout the West, netting an estimated $350,000 in five years. One of their many daring heists was the daylight robbery of a coal-mining company in Castlegate, Utah, in April 1897; while the payroll was being taken from a train, Butch simply grabbed the satchel and rode off in a cloud of dust, $9,000 richer.

According to the movie and many others, Butch and Sundance died in 1909, in a shoot-out in South America. But some people (including his sister, who lived until the 1970s) say that Butch survived to a ripe old age, living in Spokane, Washington under the name William T. Phillips until his death in 1937.

buzzing boomtown; it earned its name in 1892 when the Denver and Rio Grande Railroad built a depot and roundhouse here to hold the "helper" engines that were added to trains to help push them over Soldier Summit, 25 miles to the west. Though the line of boarded-up hotels, bars, and pool halls along Main Street may not encourage you to linger, the excellent **Western Mining and Railroad Museum** (Mon.-Sat. 9 AM-5 PM in summer; donations; 435/472-3009) at 296 S. Main Street contains enough exhibits on railroading and coal mining, not to mention the region's diverse immigrant cultures, to keep you occupied for an hour or more. There's also a fine assembly of WPA-era artwork, and a brief display recounting the exploits of Butch Cassidy and his gang, who raided banks and rustled cattle throughout the region in the late 1890s, hiding out in surrounding hills. Behind the museum, an outdoor lot displays some of the giant machines used in the coal mines, which unlike the railroad still employ a large number of local people.

The one Main Street business showing any sign of life last time I passed through was the **Sunshine Video and Tanning Salon**, at the middle of town. Along with the double-barreled services suggested by its name, it also has a soda fountain serving up milk shakes ($1.50) and a pool table. Other Helper storefronts seem to serve as "phantom galleries," displaying some surprisingly lively artwork in the windows of otherwise dead spaces.

Price

The largest city in eastern Utah, Price (pop. 8,712) is located roughly midway between the I-15 and I-70 freeways, 65 miles northwest of the town of Green River. Coal is so prevalent in the area that roadcuts reveal solid black seams, but the town itself is lush and green, thanks to irrigation provided by the Price River, which flows south from town into the Green River.

You won't miss much by following the bypass around the town center, though the small **Prehistoric Museum** at 155 E. Main Street (daily 9 AM-6 PM in summer; donations) is worth a look for its extensive displays on the Native American cultures of the region, and for its range of full-sized dinosaur skeletons, including a stegosaurus and a mammoth. Many of these were reassembled from fossils collected from the **Cleveland-Lloyd Dinosaur Quarry**, 30 miles south of town on Hwy-10 near Cleveland (daily 10 AM-5 PM in summer; $2; 435/637-5060). Price also has all the highway services travelers might need: numerous gas stations, places to eat, and six motels, including a Days Inn.

Southwest from Price, bound for Green River and the I-70 freeway, US-6/191 runs alongside the busy Denver and Rio Grande mainline railroad through a region of arid plateaus highlighted every few miles by brilliantly colorful, weirdly sculpted sandstone mesas. Though barren and empty at first glance, the region is particularly rich in two things: coal mines and, more unusually, dinosaur bones (Why do you think they call them fossil fuels?)

Green River marks the junction of US-50 with our Canyonlands Loop, a road trip through Arches, Canyonlands, Bryce, and Zion National Parks as well as other national and many state parks in southern Utah. The Canyonlands Loop begins on page 354.

The 250-mile long Book Cliffs north of Green River, forming the south edge of the Tavaputs Plateau, are the longest continuous escarpment in the world.

An unsuccessful oil test well drilled in the 1930s resulted in **Crystal Geyser,** an unusual cold-water gusher that shoots mineral water 100 feet in the air two or three times a day. To find it, head east two miles from downtown Green River on Frontage Road, then cross under the interstate and continue along about 10 miles of graded dirt to the east bank of the river.

Green River is also semi-famous for its delicious melons, grown with water from the river and celebrated during the **Melon Days** festival in September.

Green River

Straddling the eponymous river on the north side of the I-70 freeway, Green River (pop. 744) makes a handy base for exploring southeastern Utah, but it offers very little in itself. The town holds numerous 24-hour gas stations and a handful of motels, including a nice **Best Western**, a **Motel 6**, and the small **Mancos Rose Motel** at 20 W. Main Street (435/564-9660), which has the cheapest rooms.

A fine place to eat is the **Tamarisk**, overlooking the Green River at 870 E. Main Street (435/564-8109), and open all day. Another good choice is **Ben's Cafe**, 115 W. Main Street (435/564-3352), serving modestly-priced Mexican and American food in a diner atmosphere of orange vinyl and countertop jukeboxes, open daily for lunch and dinner. The most unusual place is **Ray's Tavern**, 25 S. Broadway (435/564-3511), a classic roadhouse with dining tables made out of tree trunks, plus pool tables, an excellent selection of beer, and a short but effective menu of steaks, chops, and burgers.

Even if you don't need fuel, food, or a place to sleep, Green River offers one very compelling reason to stop: the spacious modern **John Wesley Powell River History Museum** (daily 8 AM-8 PM in summer; 8 AM-5 PM the rest of the year; $2; 435/564-3427). In 1869 Powell and his crew were the first to travel the length of the Colorado River through the Grand Canyon (though the legendary explorers started their epic adventure in Green River, Wyoming, not here in Utah), and this spacious modern museum, on old US-50 along the east bank of the Green River, is the best single repository of artifacts relating to their feat. The collection concentrates on Powell in particular (he's depicted by a scarecrow-like dummy, strapped into a wooden dory) and on water transportation in general, but there are also displays chronicling the adventures of other early explorers (including Juan de Oñate in 1605 and the Dominguez and Escalante expedition in 1776), and of fur-trappers, miners, and Mormons—all of whom contributed to the exploration and mapping of the American West.

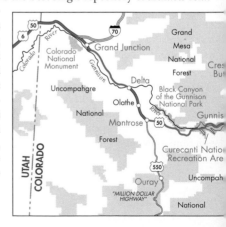

Grand Junction

In Colorado some 30 miles east of the Utah border, US-50 finally diverges from the high-speed I-70 freeway at the city of Grand Junction (pop. 29,034) on the Colorado River. After all the empty desert that surrounds it, Grand Junction feels much bigger than you'd expect, with its thriving old downtown, complete with cobblestoned streets, odd bits of outdoor sculpture, great antique shops—and tons of free parking.

Like the rest of western Colorado and eastern Utah, the Grand Junction area is especially rich in two things: the scenic splendor of rivers and red-rock canyons, and fossilized dinosaurs. A fine array of fossils are on display in the **Museum of Western Colorado** (Tues.-Sat. 10 AM-5 PM; $2; 970/242-0971), downtown at 248 S. 4th Street and in the museum's Dinosaur Valley faux fossil beds, two blocks away at 362 Main Street.

Catering to passing traffic, Grand Junction's I-70 frontage has all the motels and places to eat you could want, but downtown holds one really nice older place, the **Hotel Melrose** at 337 Colorado Avenue (970/242-9636), which has clean and comfortable rooms from $20, $25 with private bathroom—just look for the red neon sign.

More complete listings are available from the **visitors center** off I-70 at exit 31 (970/244-1480).

Colorado National Monument

Rising nearly 2,000 feet above the Colorado River, southwest of Grand Junction, the brilliantly colored cliffs of Colorado National Monument are simply impossible to miss. You get panoramic views over miles and miles of the Colorado Plateau

Green River also makes a good base for exploring the remote wilderness of the **San Rafael Swell,** a massive fold and uplift of the earth's crust that spreads west of town to both sides of the I-70 freeway.

For westbound travelers, there's a helpful Utah state **welcome center** on I-70 at Thompsons Springs, 39 miles west of the Colorado border.

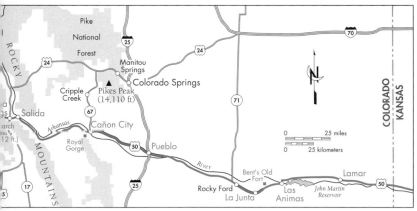

from the tops of deep canyons that are alive with piñon pines and cottonwood trees nestling at the foot of sheer rock walls. The 23-mile-long **Rim Rock Drive** winds along the tops of the cliffs, giving quick access to numerous trails for up-close looks at the various layers and hues of sandstone and shale that have eroded over the eons into masses of sculpted stone.

To reach the monument from US-50 in downtown Grand Junction, follow Grand Avenue west to Broadway (Hwy-340) across the river; the monument's main entrance is four miles southeast of town, and there's another, off I-70 exit 19, at the northern end of the park. Both are well signed, and an entry fee of $5 per car is charged, though cyclists brave enough to tackle the steep climb are usually waved through for free.

There's a large **visitors center** (daily 9 AM-5 PM; 970/858-3617) at the main entrance, and a basic **campground** four miles from the northern entrance to the monument, near the top of the Book Cliffs.

Delta, Colorado

From Grand Junction, US-50 briefly becomes a four-lane freeway, then reverts to two lanes and follows the Gunnison River as far as Delta (pop. 3,789). The half-dozen murals of elk and local agricultural products support Delta's claim that it is "The City of Murals," but the biggest attraction to travelers is the reconstructed **Fort Uncompaghre** (Wed.-Sun. 10 AM-4 PM; $3.50; 970/874-8349), at the confluence of the Gunnison and Uncompaghre Rivers on the northwest side of town. One of the best and most authentic "living history" museums in the country, the city-sponsored fort re-creates the lifestyles of trappers and traders who first settled in the western Rocky Mountains in the early 1820s. Ed Maddox, the fort's well-versed live-in guide, takes you around the small palisaded compound, discussing the historical context of the fur trade while demonstrating (and encouraging visitors to take part in) the arts and crafts necessary for frontier life: metalworking, tanning, and tomahawk-throwing, not to mention hunting, shooting, and fishing.

If you're inspired by the fort to go out and play mountain man (or woman), Delta is the location of the main **ranger station**, 2250 US-50 (970/874-6600), for the trio of national forests that cover a combined three million acres of the surrounding mountains. Uncompahgre National Forest, southwest of Delta, has over 100 peaks topping 13,000 feet (Uncompahgre Peak reaches to 14,309 feet); to the north, Grand Mesa National Forest has many quickly accessible alpine meadows, lakes, and campgrounds; and to the east Gunnison National Forest stretches along the Continental Divide, north from the Black Canyon.

Delta makes a good base for exploring the area, with its fair share of motels (including a **Best Western**) and (mostly fast-food) restaurants. It's also home to a classic piece of roadside Americana: the log-and-stone cabins of the **Westways Court Motel**, 1030 Main Street (970/874-4415) on US-50 in the center of town.

Southeast of Delta, US-50 runs along the banks of the Uncompaghre River, passing lots of farms and one very large Louisiana-Pacific lumber mill at Olathe, midway to Montrose.

Montrose

With the San Juan Mountains standing out to the south, and Black Canyon just up the road, Montrose, a small farming community that spreads from the heart of the fertile Uncompaghre (pronounced "un-com-PA-gray") Valley, makes a good base for exploring the region. Though the town itself is less charming than many others in the region (with a population of 9,000 souls it's roughly twice as big but only half as interesting as nearby Delta, for example), it does have plenty of motels and places to eat, especially along US-50 east of downtown.

In the middle of Montrose, US-550 splits off south from US-50 toward Ouray and the Million Dollar Highway. Eight miles east of Montrose, Hwy-347 turns off north from US-50 toward the Black Canyon of the Gunnison.

US-550: Ouray

Rising up from the ranchlands of Montrose and Ridgway, where the John Wayne movie *True Grit* was filmed, US-550 climbs up past dense groves of quaking aspens along the bottom of a deep, red-walled canyon. Soon after it enters the Uncompahgre National Forest, the road runs through the center of historic Ouray (pop. 644; elev. 7,706 feet), a historic Rocky Mountain mining camp and vacation spot that fully retains its late Victorian character. Colorful blocks of turreteted towers and daintily filligreed cottages line Main Street, which includes many welcoming respites from the road, such as the 1890s St. Elmo Hotel, 426 Main Street (970/325-4951), where you can enjoy comfortable B&B rooms from well under $100 a night. Even if you're just passing through, be sure to stop at the Outlaw, 610 Main Street, a rustic steakhouse that's rich with Wild West ambience.

The spectacular setting has earned Ouray the right to call itself the "Switzerland of America," and there's no better way to savor the scenery than to do so while soaking in the natural hot springs at Ouray Hot Springs Pool (winter noon-9 PM, summer 10 AM to 10 PM; $7; 970/325-4638) that bubble up along US-550 at the north end of town, filling what must be one of the world's largest swimming pools. At the south end of town, another must-see sight is Box Canyon Falls, where the waters of Clear Creek crash 300 feet through a narrow gorge.

For more information on Ouray, or details on the many great jeep trails that climb up old mining roads all over the area, contact the visitors bureau (970/325-4746 or 800/228-1876).

Black Canyon of the Gunnison National Park

Some of the hardest and oldest rocks on earth form the sheer walls of 2,000-foot-deep Black Canyon of the Gunnison, the deepest and most impressive gorge in the state. The river cutting through the canyon falls faster than any other in North America—dropping 2,150 feet in under 50 miles, averaging

A Montrose ranch was the childhood stomping ground for **Roy Stryker,** who directed the New Deal-era photography project that hired Walker Evans, Dorothea Lange, and other sensitive and powerful photographers who went on to fame and fortune. The project was undertaken under the auspices of the Farm Security Administration with the mission to document and witness the events of the Great Depression for posterity.

Along US-550 about five miles south of Montrose, the **Ute Indian Museum** (daily 9 AM-5 PM; $2.50; 970/249-3098) has exhibits on the life and culture of the native Ute Indians, with a special focus on the exploration and mapping of the Colorado plateau region, which the Utes made possible through their assistance of Europeans and Americans, starting with the Dominguez and Escalante expedition of 1776.

If the drive along US-550 whets your appetite for Rocky Mountain scenery, you're in luck: the Million Dollar Highway also serves as the centerpiece of an ambitious 235-mile scenic loop tour, dubbed the **"San Juan Skyway,"** which runs south and west from Silverton to Durango and Mesa Verde National Park, north to the resort town of Telluride then back to Ouray to rejoin the Million Dollar Highway and start all over again. The Silverton-Durango Mesa Verde stretch is covered in our Four Corners Loop.

THE MILLION DOLLAR HIGHWAY

No matter what you want from a scenic drive, Colorado's famous Million Dollar Highway has it in spades. Loaded with sublime natural scenery, historically fascinating and visually appealing small towns, and, most of all, sheer driving pleasure, the Million Dollar Highway more than lives up to its name. One of the best-loved roads in the country, this classic stretch of two-lane blacktop forms a swirling ribbon through the San Juan Mountains, the wildest and ruggedest peaks in the Colorado Rockies. Marked on maps and by road signs as US-550, which runs north to south between Gunnison River ranchlands and the Southern Ute Indian Reservation, the "Million Dollar" tag is generally applied to the 25 steep and twisting miles that link Ouray and Silverton, a pair of remote gold and silver mining communities, but it's also an appropriate nickname for the entire 110 miles of US-550 that link Montrose with Ouray and Durango.

As you might expect of a road born in a Wild West mining country animated by tales of million-dollar fortunes earned, lost, and hoped-for, the history of the Million Dollar Highway is rife with legend. The route was first blazed by the so-called "Pathfinder of the San Juans," a five-foot-tall Russian immigrant named Otto Mears who was working as a U.S. mail carrier between Silverton and Telluride. By 1882 Mears had created a lucrative toll road which he parlayed into a sizeable empire of roads and railroads, but his original hand-carved route through the mountains formed the basis of today's Million Dollar Highway.

Even the origin of the "Million Dollar" name is clouded in myth. Some say it was first used after an early traveler, complaining of the vertigo-inducing steepness of the route, said "I wouldn't go that way again if you paid me a million dollars," while others claim that it derives simply from the actual cost of paving the route in the 1930s. But the favorite explanation is also the most likely: when the highway was first constructed, the builders used gravel discarded by nearby gold and silver mines, only to find out later that this dirt was actually rich in ore and worth an estimated "million dollars."

The Million Dollar Highway starts in the north at the old mining town of Ouray (rhymes with "hooray"), which sits in a granite amphitheater surrounded by so many towering peaks that it's often called the "Switzerland of America." Grand hotels and ornate cottages, many of which date from the gold and silver mining heyday of 100 years ago, still line the dense jumble of streets, and Ouray is also home to one of the world's largest natural hot springs, whose waters fill the open-air "Million Gallon Hot Springs."

South from Ouray, the Million Dollar Highway twists as it climbs over 3,000 vertical feet on sweeping hairpin turns. The literal high point of the route comes just 14 miles south of Ouray at 11,018-foot Red Mountain Pass, one of the highest points in the whole U.S. highway system. From the pass you get up-close views of a trio of rusty red volcanic peaks, and a more distant panorama of pyramidal Mt. Abrams, Engineer Mountain, and the white limestone bulk of White House Mountain. To give a sense of the ruggedness of this mountain landscape, the resort town of Telluride is just 3 miles west of Red Mountain Pass as the crow flies, but driving there is a 40-mile trip.

Back on the Million Dollar Highway, head frames, shanty-like cabins, and other remains of mining operations (some bearing evocative names like "Yankee Girl" and "North Star Sultan") can still be seen on the heavily forested hillsides that turn brilliant with color in fall. After another 10 incredibly scenic miles, you reach the fabled mining camp of Silverton, with its immaculately preserved Grand Imperial Hotel and gold-domed courthouse marking the southern end of the Million Dollar Highway.

nearly 100 feet per mile within the main canyon—and the canyon bottom is so rugged that there are no trails along it. Unless you're a serious mountaineer, you'll have to content yourself with looking down into the canyon from the rim, which is accessible on the north side from a dirt road off Hwy-92 from Delta, and more easily on the south, from US-50 via Hwy-347.

The **visitors center** (daily 9 AM-6 PM in summer; 970/249-7036) on the south rim provides details on hiking trails and camping and can tell you more than you ever wanted to know about the canyon's unique geology: for instance, unlike the Grand Canyon with its layers of exposed rock, the Black Canyon is basically one solid hunk of stone.

Late in 1999, the Black Canyon of the Gunnison was expanded by some 7,500 acres and upgraded from National Monument to National Park status.

Midway between Ouray and Red Mountain Pass, a stone monument honors the brave efforts of the snowplow drivers who've lost their lives fighting to keep the road open during winter storms.

Curecanti National Recreation Area

Upstream from the Black Canyon turnoff (that is, east), US-50 parallels the Gunnison River, renowned for its excellent trout and landlocked salmon fishing, though sadly the once-raging waters have been backed up behind dams to form a series of reservoirs, jointly managed as the Curecanti National Recreation Area (970/ 641-3128). Midway between Montrose and the town of Gunnison, the highway crosses Blue Mesa Dam, where Hwy-92 cuts off north for a scenic detour around the Black Canyon of the Gunnison, rejoining US-50 at Delta.

Gunnison

A crossroads cattle town with rapidly growing recreational opportunities and the only airport for miles, Gunnison (pop. 4,636) is livelier than many Colorado towns thanks to Western State College, whose students were responsi-

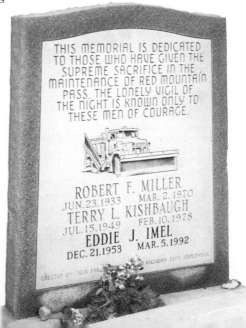

THIS MEMORIAL IS DEDICATED TO THOSE WHO HAVE GIVEN THE SUPREME SACRIFICE IN THE MAINTENANCE OF RED MOUNTAIN PASS. THE LONELY VIGIL OF THE NIGHT IS KNOWN ONLY TO THESE MEN OF COURAGE.

ROBERT F. MILLER
JUN.23.1933   MAR. 2.1970
TERRY L. KISHBAUGH
JUL.15.1949   FEB.10.1978
EDDIE J. IMEL
DEC. 21.1953   MAR. 5.1992

ERECTED BY THEIR FAM...   HIGHWAY DEPT. EMPLOYEES

ble for the huge W that covers a mountainside north of town. To get a feel for Gunnison, stop by the lively **Steaming Bean** coffeehouse, downtown off US-50 at the Hwy-135 junction. Motels, including a **Days Inn**, **Super 8**, and **Econo Lodge**, line up along US-50, making Gunnison a handy base for exploring the region.

The rocks exposed deep in the Black Canyon of Gunnison are primarily dark Precambrian granitic schist, formed in one solid piece an estimated 1.7 billion years ago. The rim rocks include streaks of pinkish pegmatite, which are a mere billion years old.

Crested Butte

If you're taken with the scenery around Gunnison and want to see more, head north along Hwy-135 and the Gunnison River to the area's skiing, fishing, and mountain-biking center, Crested Butte (pop. 898), 25 miles away. As in Telluride and Aspen, this 100-year-old gold-mining camp has won a second lease on life thanks to tourism, though Crested Butte is comparatively low-key and somewhat off the beaten path. Skiers in search of solitude flock here in winter to cruise the 1,100-plus acres of Mount Crested Butte (970/349-2222 or 800/544-8448), while in summer Crested Butte is a mountain biking mecca, with miles and miles of mining roads and single-track trails winding through the mountains. The town also has some of the best restaurants in the state, according to the Denver *Post* and others. Start the day at the **Bakery Cafe**, open daily at 7 AM at 3rd and Elk downtown, and later recharge your batteries with a burger, steak, lamb chop, or other hunk of meat (and a beer or two) at the **Wooden Nickel**, nearby at 222 Elk Street (970/349-6350); the very popular and fairly pricey **Soupçon**, on Elk and 2nd (970/349-5448) offers some of the nicest meals for miles. To while away an evening, a couple of other places can be found within stumbling distance, including the **Idlespur Brewpub**, 226 Elk Avenue, and the **Powerhouse**, 130 Elk Avenue, a lively Mexican cantina.

The most interesting and enoyable place to stay in Crested Butte has to be the **Claim Jumper**, 704 Whiterock Avenue (970/349-6471), where the six B&B rooms are all packed full of jumbled Americana—Ethyl's Room, for example, has everything from an old gas pump to a working jukebox. Three blocks north of Elk Avenue, the **HI Crested Butte International Hostel**, 615 Teocalli Avenue (970/349-0588), has dorm beds for $15 in summer, $23 in winter.

For further information, contact the **chamber of commerce** (970/349-6438 or 800/545-4505), on the south side of Crested Butte. For details on the plentiful **camping**, riding, and hiking in the surrounding Gunnison National Forest, check in at the U.S. Forest Service **ranger station** in Gunnison (970/641-0471).

One of the many great hiking and mountain-biking routes in the Crested Butte area climbs through the Gunnison National Forest, over Pearl Pass to the elite environs of Aspen. It's 20-odd miles by foot or bike, but nearly 200 miles by road.

The first European explorers to pass through this part of the Rockies were the Spanish missionaries **Dominguez and Escalante**, in 1776.

Monarch Pass and Poncha Springs

East of Gunnison, the landscape changes swiftly as US-50 (and a few masochistic bicyclists) climb steeply through a gorgeous alpine landscape of meadows and cattle ranches toward 11,312-foot Monarch Pass. The pass marks the highest point on US-50 and straddles the Continental Divide: the 30 feet of annual snowfall on the east side of the pass end up in the Atlantic, while (in theory, at least) moisture falling farther west makes its way to the Pacific. There's a ski and snowboarding area here in winter, and in summer you can ride a **tram** (daily 8 AM-6 PM; $5) or hike to a nearby summit for a 360-degree view over the Rocky and Sangre de Cristo Mountains.

At the eastern foot of Monarch Pass, the tiny town of Poncha Springs has a pair of places perfect for weary travelers: a truck stop featuring great Mexican food and the historic **Jackson Hotel**, 6340 US-285 (719/539-4861). The Jackson is a former-1870s stage stop that has hosted (or at least claims to have hosted) every Wild West figure from Billy the Kid to Teddy Roosevelt. Rooms are a bargain at around $40 a night.

Detour: Great Sand Dunes National Monument

Cruising across Colorado along US-50, the splendid alpine scenery makes it hard to believe that sand dunes to match the Sahara can be viewed if you take a fairly quick detour south to the little-visited Great Sand Dunes National Monument. Here towering dunes, some reaching 700 feet high, cover nearly 40 square miles of the San Luis Valley. The sand dunes form a starkly contrasting foreground to the Sangre de Cristo Mountains that rise behind them; nature trails, a campground ($10, with flush toilets but no showers), and a **visitors center** (daily 8:30 AM-4:30 PM; $3; 719/378-2312) are the only facilities available. The dunes are some 75 miles south of US-50 via Hwy-17, 14 miles north of Alamosa, then 16 miles east via a good but partly gravel road.

The nearest towns to the Great Sand Dunes National Moument are the sleepy potato-farming burgs of Alamosa and Monte Vista. To tempt road-tripping visitors, Alamosa has an alligator farm, while Monte Vista is home to a unique example of roadside Americana: the **Movie Manor**, a combination drive-in movie theater, restaurant, and Best Western motel at 2860 W. US-160 (719/852-5921 or 800/771-9468). You can watch movies (for free!) from the comfort of your motel room, though the screen is so far away it's about the same size as watching movies on TV. Fun, though, and unique, for sure; where else can you snuggle down beneath the covers, gazing out the window as the sun sets and the lights come up on the full-screen figures swaggering through their latest Hollywood hits against a backdrop of snow-capped 14,000-foot peaks?

The Movie Manor has been in action since 1955, when George and Edna Kelloff bought the site of an abandoned airport and built the Star Drive-In Theater, which was an immediate success. As the Kelloff family grew, they had the bright idea of developing the drive-in into a complete resort, and in 1964 the first motel units were constructed, with large picture windows and piped-in sound bringing the big screen into each of the 14 bedrooms. There are now 28 rooms altogether, all of them with full modern conveniences; rates run about $50 a night.

Before the nightly movie screening, the adjacent Academy Award Restaurant and Lounge serves a full menu of New Mexican and American food in a dramatically (pun intended) decorated dining room, with forged handprints and signatures of Hollywood stars (and Kelloff family members) set into concrete.

If you think of alligators, chances are you picture them basking in the Florida sun, but the Rocky Mountain town of Alamosa —an hour south of Poncha Springs, and 7,500 feet above sea level—has over 100 of these tropical creatures, forcibly transplanted to the geothermal hot springs of the **San Luis Valley Alligator Farm** (daily 7 AM-7 PM; $4; 719/378-2612), 17 miles north of Alamosa on Hwy-17, near the turnoff east to the Great Sand Dunes.

Every December, Salida lights up a tree on Christmas Mountain with 10,000 bulbs.

Salida Hot Springs, next to the visitors bureau on US-50 at Rainbow Avenue, is the largest in the state; the water is piped in from Poncha Springs, up the road. The WPA-built indoor pool and baths are open year-round; call 719/539-6738 for times and prices.

Salida

Sitting alongside the Arkansas River east of Monarch Pass, Salida (pop. 4,737; elev. 7,038 feet) is a riverfront railroad town gradually switching over to the tourist trade. Close your eyes to the sprawl of Wal-Mart, McDonald's, and other chains along US-50 and head a few blocks north to the historic downtown. Here, a half-dozen brick buildings along 1st Street house some slightly hippyish cafes—the **Laughing Ladies** and the **First Street Cafe** are both good bets—and outdoor supply shops, including **Headwaters**, 228 N. F Street (719/539-4506) right along the river, which rents and sells mountain bikes and kayaks and is the best source of information on the area's wealth of recreational opportunities.

East of Salida, rafters can be seen riding the rapids of the Arkansas River for most of the next 45 miles. Steeply walled sandstone gorges alternate with broad meadows and sagebrush plains all the way to Royal Gorge and Cañon City.

Royal Gorge

It would be easy to object to the rampant commercialism of Royal Gorge (daily 7 AM-6 PM; $12; 719/275-7507), but if you don't mind seeing impressive works of humankind amidst a stupendous show of nature's prowess, it's worth a visit. The gorge itself is unforgettable—its sheer red granite cliffs drop over a thousand feet straight down to the Arkansas River. The experience is enhanced by a number of civil engineering feats, including aerial trams, incline railways, and an impossibly delicate suspension bridge, all enabling visitors to experience the area in diverse ways. You can look down from the rim, dangle from a gondola across to the other side, and from there follow a short nature trail that offers good views of Pike's Peak. Later, you can walk back across the wooden planks of the 1929 bridge—which claims to be the highest in the world and feels like a rickety old seaside pier—then drop down on a funicular to the gorge's bottom. At the bottom, you can stand alongside the raging river listening to its roar and admire the famous Denver and Rio Grande Railroad line that passes through the gorge, in places suspended out over the river from the solid rock walls.

The main problem with Royal Gorge, apart from the steep admission fee, is that to get there you have to run a gauntlet of some of the tackiest tourist traps in creation, the worst of which is the self-proclaimed "Real Historic Buckskin Joe—Gunfights and Hangings Daily." Similarly hyped outfits line the well-marked, two mile-long road to Royal Gorge, which cuts south from US-50 eight miles west of Cañon City.

Cañon City

One of the last remaining Wild West towns in the lower 48 states, Cañon City (pop. 12,687) is carved out of the eastern flank of the Rocky Mountains. Over a mile high and surrounded by a ring of 14,000-foot peaks, Cañon City's short Main Street, a block north of US-50, is lined by workaday saddle shops, gun shops, book shops, and many saloons (eight in four blocks!). But the local economy prospers not so much from tourism as from prisons: 14 in all, including Colorado's newest, the maximum-security penitentiary nicknamed "Supermax," and its oldest, the **Territorial Prison** (daily 9 AM–5 PM; $3) at the west end of Main Street, in which 32 cells have been preserved as a somewhat gruesome but compelling museum. The $60 million Supermax prison holds the nation's most notorious inmates, including Oklahoma City bomber Timothy McVeigh, Ramzi Yousef (mastermind of the World Trade Center bombing), Unabomber Ted Kaczynski, and actor Woody Harrelson's alleged hit-man dad Charles. The historic Territorial Prison's most famous guest was Alferd Packer, a miner and Wild West gunslinger convicted of cannibalism and other crimes.

Despite the notoriety of its prisons, Cañon City's main attraction is the surrounding scenery, particularly the views along **Skyline Drive**, accessible from just west of town. It's a three-mile, one-way drive across the top of an 800-foot hill, as close to riding a roller coaster as you're likely to get while inside a passenger car. Royal Gorge to the west (which Cañon City owns and operates) is another major draw, so Cañon City makes a good base for explorations, with a few moderately priced motels like the **Pioneer**, 201 Main Street (719/269-1745) next to the old prison, plus a **Days Inn**, and a **Best Western**. Best place for cheap food and drink is **The Owl**, 626 Main Street, a combo cigar store, soda fountain, diner, and pool hall at the heart of the lively Main Street business district north of US-50.

For further information, contact the **chamber of commerce** (719/275-2331 or 800/876-7922), at 403 Royal Gorge Boulevard, on US-50 at the center of town.

Detour: Pike's Peak and Manitou Springs

The highest point you can drive to in the continental United States, Pike's Peak has been a road trip destination since 1901 when the first car (a two-cylinder Locomobile Steamer) made its way to the 14,110-foot summit. Opened as a toll road in 1915, the Pike's Peak Highway now winds its way to the top—climbing nearly 7,000 vertical feet in under 20 miles, with no guardrails to comfort you or block the amazing 360-degree Rocky Mountain panorama. The road is now owned and operated by the city of

In spring and summer, all along US-50 west of Cañon City, you can see rafters racing along the wild Arkansas River. Many companies offer guided trips, including Arkansas River Tours (800/321-4352) and River Runners (800/525-2081).

convicted cannibal Alferd Packer

According to the WPA *Guide to Colorado*, the poet **Joaquin Miller**, who served as mayor, judge, and minister in Cañon City's early days, wanted to change its name to Oreodelphia, to highlight the region's many gold mines. Local miners, however, protested, insisting that "the place is a canyon, and it's goin' to be called Cañon City."

Phantom Canyon Road is one of the West's most scenic drives, a six-mile-drive on an unpaved but easily passable route that winds north to the town of **Cripple Creek**. The town started out as a mining camp but is now a prosperous gambling town. Phantom Canyon Road is located off US-50 about 25 miles west of Pueblo and seven miles east of Cañon City.

After a visit to the top of Pike's Peak in 1893, Katharine Lee Bates wrote the words to "America the Beautiful."

The Pike's Peak Hill Climb has been held around the 4th of July almost every year since 1916. Top Indy Car, NASCAR, and Formula One racers like Bobby Unser sometimes compete, hitting speeds of up to 100 mph on the twisting mountain road. The rest of the year, cars and racing memorabilia are displayed in a mouthful of a museum, the **Pikes Peak International Auto Hill Climb Educational Museum** at 135 Manitou Avenue (daily 9 AM-5 PM; $5; 719/685-1400).

Colorado Springs, which charges a $5 per person toll (daily 7 AM-6 PM, summer only); go early, before the clouds and haze build up, for the best long-distance views.

And if the views aren't enough, another good reason to climb Pike's Peak is that to get there you pass through the delightful old resort town of **Manitou Springs.** A National Historic District, Manitou Springs has all the grand hotels, hot springs, tourist traps, and cave tours you could want, plus my very favorite pinball arcade in the entire world—dozens of ancient machines in perfect working order, and still charging the same nickel or dime that they did in the 1920s, '30s, and '40s.

Besides places to play, Manitou Springs also has some classic places to stay, like the historic cabins of the **El Colorado Lodge,** 23 Manitou Avenue (719/ 685-5467), arrayed around four acres of pine trees, with fireplaces, a pool (and a horseshoe pit!), all for a bargain $40-55 a night.

North of Manitou Springs, the 1,350-acre **Garden of the Gods** (daily 5 AM-11 PM; free) is a photogenic geological outcropping of red sandstone spires, some rising to heights of 300 feet.

Pike's Peak and Manitou Springs are along US-24, just west of Colorado Springs. From US-50, Hwy-115 runs north from just outside Cañon City to Colorado Springs, where you can take I-25 north to reach US-24. For more information, contact the **visitors bureau,** 354 Manitou Avenue (719/685-5089 or 800/642-2567).

Pueblo

At the foot of the mountains, along US-50 38 miles east of Cañon City and 150 miles west of the Kansas border, the heavily industrialized city of Pueblo (pop. 98,640) spreads to both sides of the Arkansas River. Colorado's third-largest city, Pueblo was founded by legendary African-American fur-trapper **Jim Beckwourth** in 1842, but the town really grew in the 1870s following the arrival of the railroad and the discovery nearby of vast amounts of coal. Steel mills, including some of the largest west of the Mississippi, still stand around the fringes of the pleasant, tree-lined downtown area, but Pueblo is increasingly more bucolic than brawny, and the historic areas are slowly filling up with artsy cafes, book shops, and antique stores, especially along Union Avenue on the south side.

US-50 bypasses the center of town, crossing I-25 with its usual phalanx of motels, including a Motel 6, a Holiday Inn and a Super 8, and fast-food franchises. Don't be too put off by all this—stop at the **visitors bureau** (719/543-1742) on US-50 just west of I-25 and pick up listings and walking-tour maps of Pueblo's many engaging historic districts.

US-50 and its sibling, US-56, follow the route of the historic Santa Fe Trail east across the rest of Colorado and all of Kansas to its end in Independence, Missouri.

La Junta

For eastbound travelers La Junta (pop. 7,637), a busy railroad town on the banks of the Arkansas River, is where we begin tracing the historic Santa Fe Trail. In Spanish *la junta* means the junction—an apt name since the town has long been a key crossroads, first on the Santa Fe Trail and now as the division between the main line and the Denver branch of the Santa Fe Railroad, and as the junction of US-50 and US-350. Besides gas stations and a good range of places to eat (Mexican restaurants are a particular strength, and **Christina's** on Colorado Avenue, a half-block south of US-50, is very popular), a two-screen movie theater, and an ancient-looking barber shop, La Junta also offers the excellent **Koshare Indian Museum** (Tues.-Sun. 9 AM-5 PM; $2), on the campus of Otero Junior College on the south side of town. Sleep cheap at the **Mid-Town Motel**, 215 E. 3rd Street (719/384-7741).

A dozen miles west of La Junta, **Rocky Ford** is a small and quiet farming community that comes alive every August during a celebration of its nationally known cash crop, cantaloupes.

Unfortunately for westbound US-50 travelers, La Junta also marks the spot where the "Mountain Branch" of the Santa Fe Trail finally cuts away to the south, following what's now US-350 through the Comanche National Grassland and continuing over Raton Pass into New Mexico and Santa Fe.

Bent's Old Fort

From La Junta, a worthwhile detour along the north bank of the Arkansas River takes you to one of Colorado's most evocative historic sites, Bent's Old Fort (daily 8 AM-6 PM in summer, 9 AM-4 PM in winter; $2). It lies eight miles east of La Junta, or 15 miles west of Las Animas off US-50 onto Hwy-194. Built in 1833 by the fur traders William and Charles Bent, Bent's Fort was the Southwest's most important outpost of white civilization until 1848, when war with Mexico and increasing unrest among the local Arapahoe, Apache, and Cheyenne tribes put an end to their business. The fort was known as a stopping place for travelers, trappers, and explorers, including John C. Frémont, Francis Parkman, and just about every other Wild West luminary.

William Bent ran Bent's Fort on the Arkansas River from 1833 to 1848. Besides minding the store Bent served as an unofficial ambassador to area tribes.

Though it was abandoned and left to decay for over 100 years, the large adobe fort has been authentically rebuilt by the National Park Service, and now stands as a palpable reminder of the early years of the frontier era. Thick adobe walls, 15 feet tall with circular bastions at the corners, protect a roughly 100-square-foot compound. Rangers dressed in period clothing work as wheelwrights, coopers, and carpenters, or process the many buffalo hides and beaver pelts piled up in storerooms.

SANTA FE TRAIL

For over half a century, beginning in the 1820s and lasting until the railroads were completed in the 1880s, the Santa Fe Trail was the primary link between the midwestern heart of the U.S. and the distant Southwest. Starting in the east around present-day Kansas City, and in use under Spanish, Mexican, and American flags, the Santa Fe Trail angled west along the banks of the Arkansas River, splitting near what's now Dodge City into two routes: the Mountain Branch, which US-50 follows across southern Colorado, and the quicker but more dangerous Cimarron Cut-off, across Comanche homeland that is today's Oklahoma Panhandle. The two routes rejoined near Las Vegas (Las Vegas, New Mexico, that is), before climbing the Sangre de Cristo Mountains and edging north into what was then, as it is now, the capital of the Southwest, Santa Fe.

Unlike many of the routes across the Wild West frontier, the Santa Fe Trail was established by commercial traders rather than emigrant pioneers, and travel along it was active in both directions: merchants from the U.S. brought manufactured goods by the wagonload, which they exchanged mainly for Mexican silver. First blazed by trader William Becknell in 1821, the year the newly independent government of Mexico opened the border (which had been kept closed under Spanish rule), the 750-mile-long trail was surveyed by the U.S. government in 1826. Traffic increased slowly until the end of the Mexican-American War brought Santa Fe, and all the land in between it and the border, under U.S. control in 1848. Military forts were established to protect traders from the marauding Comanche and other native tribes; by the start of the Civil War commerce along the trail reached a peak, with over 5,000 wagons making the trek to Santa Fe, carrying over $5 million worth of trade goods every year. The extension of the railroads across the Great Plains in the 1870s diminished the importance of the trail, and by 1880, when the Santa Fe Railroad reached Santa Fe itself, the trail became a part of history.

Across southern Colorado, today's US-50 follows the Santa Fe Trail almost exactly, through preserved and restored outposts like the historic trading post known as Bent's Old Fort. Southwest from La Junta, the old trail ran roughly underneath today's US-350 as far as Trinidad, Colorado. But New Mexico has the most numerous historic sites, and even though many are within sight of the I-25 freeway it's still possible to get a powerful sense of what the trail might have been like—provided you take the time to park the car and walk even a few hundred yards in the footsteps that crossed here a century ago.

The following are some of the most evocative sites along the Santa Fe Trail, west to east.

Santa Fe, NM: The oldest city in North America, preserving a vivid taste of its overlapping Native American, Spanish, Mexican, and American past. See pages 412-417 for more.

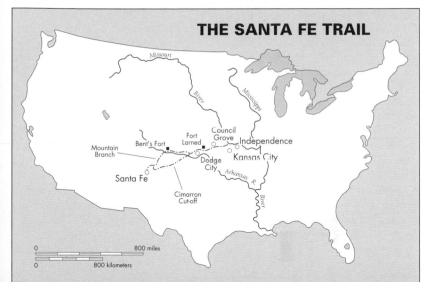

THE SANTA FE TRAIL

Las Vegas, NM: Once a truly wild Wild West town, named like its Nevada sibling for the lush meadows that surround it, Las Vegas has a nice old plaza along the Gallinas River and a wonderful array of late-Victorian buildings. Along with the Santa Fe Trail heritage, this is also the place where President Teddy Roosevelt recruited the bulk of his "Rough Riders" to do dubious battle in the Spanish-American War. The town is located just west of the I-25 freeway, about an hour northeast of Santa Fe.

Fort Union National Monument: Located a half-hour north of Las Vegas, just west of I-25, Fort Union was once the largest US Army outpost in the Southwest. It was crucial to American settlement of New Mexico from the 1850s until the 1890s, by which time the West had been won. All that remain today are the crumbling walls and some artifacts in a visitors center, but the surrounding grasslands give a good sense of what frontier life was really like.

Cimarron, NM: Located about an hour's drive east of Taos via US-64, Cimarron is a quiet little place set in gorgeous mountains—the world's largest Boy Scout camp, the 220-square-mile **Philmont Ranch**, is just south of town. The mountain branch of the Santa Fe Trail ran right through, along what's Hwy-21; the faster but more dangerous Cimarron Cutoff cut off south of town on a beeline across the desolate Jornada del Muerto, rejoining the main route near Dodge City, Kansas.

Bent's Old Fort, CO: A reconstructed adobe trading post along the banks of the Arkansas River in the Rocky Mountain foothills. See page 271 for more.

Las Animas

The farming community of Las Animas (pop. 2,481) takes its name from the Arkansas River tributary originally known as **Rio de las Animas Perdidas en Purgatorio**—the River of Lost Souls. Las Animas is also the place where, on November 15, 1806, Lt. Zebulon Pike first laid eyes on the Rocky Mountains peak that now bears his name—Pike's Peak, 120 miles to the northwest.

Beyond Las Animas, US-50 continues its gradual descent across the Rocky Mountain foothills. The area was first known as Big Timbers for the tall cottonwoods that grew here along the Arkansas River, though most of these trees were cut down soon after the arrival of white settlers. In the 1840s and 1850s, local Cheyenne, Arapaho, Kiowa, and Apache tribes bartered bison hides at William and Charles Bent's trading post, and Wild West explorer **Kit Carson** died here on May 23, 1868, in his family home at what was then the U.S. Army's Fort Lyon, south of present-day US-50. Carson's remains were later moved to Taos, New Mexico, and his lands were flooded after the Arkansas River was dammed to form the large John Martin Reservoir, which stretches most of the way downstream to Lamar.

THE MOTHER ROAD: ROUTE 66

THE MOTHER ROAD: ROUTE 66

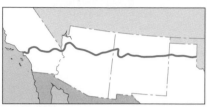

The mystique of Route 66 continues to captivate people around the world. Running between Chicago and Los Angeles, "over two thousand miles all the way," in the words of the popular R&B anthem, this legendary old road passes through the heart of California and the Southwest on a diagonal trip that takes in some of the regions's most archetypal roadside scenes. If you're looking for great displays of neon signs, rusty middle-of-nowhere truck stops, or kitschy Americana, you're likely to do as the song says and "get your kicks on Route 66."

The pleasures of driving through some of prettiest parts of California and the Southwest—from the Santa Monica beaches, past the Grand Canyon, to the Native American pueblos of New Mexico—are almost nonstop. But another compelling reason to follow Route 66 is to experience the road's ingrained timeline of contemporary America. Before it was called Route 66—and long before it was even paved,

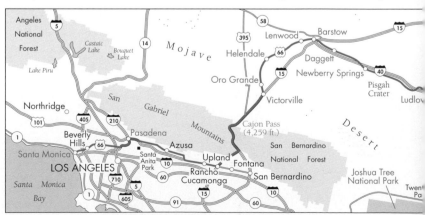

in 1926—this corridor was traversed by the National Old Trails Highway, one of the country's first transcontinental roads. Because it wound through small towns across the Southwest, for three decades before and after WW II it earned the title "Main Street of America," lined by hundreds of cafes, motels, gas stations, and tourist attractions. During the Great Depression, hundreds of thousands of farm families, displaced from the Dust Bowl, made their way west along Route 66 to California, following what John Steinbeck called "The Mother Road" in his vivid portrait, *The Grapes of Wrath*. After WW II, thousands more people expressed their upward mobility by heading west for good jobs in the suburban idyll of Southern California. They, too, followed Route 66, and the road came to embody the demographic shift from the Rust Belt to the Sun Belt.

Beginning in the late 1950s and continuing gradually over the next 25 years, old Route 66 was bypassed section by section as the high-speed interstate highways were completed. As recently as 1984, when the last stretch of freeway (at Williams, Arizona, near the South Rim of the Grand Canyon) was finished, Route 66 was finally officially decommissioned. But the old route is still alive and well, designated "Historic Route 66," and serving as a scenic alternative to I-40 all the way from California to Texas.

Though it is no longer a main route across the country, Route 66 has retained its mystique—in part due to the very same effective combination of hype, hucksterism, and boosterism that animated it through its half-century heyday. It was here that the American concept of driving tour as vacation first flourished. Billboards and giant statues along the highway still hawk a baffling array of roadside attractions, tempting passing travelers to "Sleep in a TeePee" (like the one at Holbrook, Arizona), to see live rattlesnakes and other creatures on display in roadside menageries, or to stay in "Tucumcari Tonight1,500 Motel Rooms."

The same commercial know-how and shameless self-promotion has helped the towns along the old route stay alive. Diners and motels play up their Route 66 connections, however tenuous. And, thanks to the numerous guidebooks and magazine articles that proclaim the charms of the old road, many bona fide Route 66 landmarks are kept in business by nostalgic travelers intent on experiencing a taste of this endangered American experience. That said, along many stretches of Route 66, the contrast characterful old-road landscape and contemporary franchised freeway culture is painfully sharp. Many quirky old motels and cafes hang on by a thread of hope, sit vacant, or survive in memory onlyall for want of an interstate exitand for many stretches you'll be forced to leave the old two-lane and follow super slabs that have been built right on top of the old road.

Route 66 covered in this book passes through a marvelous cross-section of American scenes, from the golden sands and sunshine of Los Angeles, across the arid Mojave Desert, past the canyons and mesas of the desert Southwest, finally winding up near that classic symbol of America's obsession with the automobile, Cadillac Ranch. Route 66 offers an unforgettable journey into America—then and now—whether you are motivated by an interest in its history, feel a nostalgic yearning for the good old days the route has come to represent, or simply want to experience firsthand the amazing diversity of people and landscapes that line its path.

From the beautiful beaches of Santa Monica, through the citrus-rich inland valleys, over mountains and across the demanding Mojave Desert, Route 66 passes through every type of Southern California landscape. The road survives intact almost all the way across the state, marked for most of its 315 miles with "Historic Route 66" signs. In the Mojave desert, the route is also marked as the "National Old Trails Highway," which was its title before the national numbering system went into effect in the late 1920s.

Santa Monica

Old Route 66 had its western terminus at the edge of the Pacific Ocean in Santa Monica, on a palm-lined bluff a few blocks north of the city's landmark pier. In Palisades Park, where Santa Monica Boulevard dead-ends at Ocean Boulevard, a brass plaque marks the official end of Route 66, the "Main Street of America" but also remembered as the "Will Rogers Highway," one of many names the old road earned in its half-century of existence. (The small plaque remembers Rogers as a "Humorist, World Traveler, Good Neighbor"—not bad for an Okie from the middle of nowhere.)

From Santa Monica Pier, where **Pacific Park** amusement park has bumper-car rides (great for working out your road rage), a small roller coaster, a five-story solar-powered Ferris wheel, and one of the country's nicest old carousels (this 1922 Looff is the one seen in the movie *The Sting*), a broad pedestrian walkway leads a mile south to Venice Beach, heart of bohemian L.A.

Back on Route 66, two blocks east of the ocean, stretch your legs at **Santa Monica Place**, an indoor/outdoor shopping mall and icon of contemporary Southern California urban culture; north from the mall, the three pedestrianized blocks of Third Street Promenade are among the liveliest in Southern California—people actually walk, enjoying street performers, dozens of trendy cafes, many good book shops, and multiplex movie theaters.

Will Rogers

In between the mall and the beach, the **Santa Monica HI Hostel**, 1436 2nd Street (310/393-9913), has 200 dorm beds all for under $20 a night—an ideal budget base for seeing Los Angeles. If you're willing to spend 10 times more money, you can enjoy a night at the lovely Art Deco **Shangri-La Hotel**, 1301 Ocean Avenue (310/394-2791), or the only hotel actually on the beach, swanky **Shutters-on-the-Beach**, south of the pier at 1 Pico Boulevard (310/458-0030 or 800/334-9000).

Pick up full details on things to do and places to eat and sleep in and around Santa Monica at the **visitor information booth**, right at the end of old Route 66 at 1400 Ocean Avenue (310/393-7593).

Just south of the Will Rogers plaque marking the west end of Route 66, an unlikely building (the Senior Recreation Center) holds an unusual attraction: the **Camera Obscura** (daily 9 AM-5 PM; free). A camera obscura (another of Leonardo da Vinci's inventions) is a device that uses a mirror and prism to reflect images of the outside world onto, in this case, a circular screen at the center of a pitch-dark room. Turn a crank and the mirror rotates, showing a 360-degree panorama of the Santa Monica coast.

Route 66 across Los Angeles

Diehard old-roads fans will be pleasantly surprised to know that Route 66 across Los Angeles still exists, almost completely intact. Heading east from Santa Monica—and now marked by prominent beige road signs as "Historic Route 66 1935-1964"—old Route 66 follows Santa Monica Boulevard through the hearts of Beverly Hills (where Will Rogers once was mayor) and West Hollywood (where the old railroad tracks have been converted into a linear sculpture park in the middle of the road). Continuing east, through Hollywood itself, Santa Monica Boulevard runs past **Hollywood Memorial Cemetery** (daily 9 AM-5 PM; free; 323/469-1181), where such luminaries as Rudolf Valentino and Mel Blanc are entombed, overlooked by the water tower of legendary Paramount Studios. Route 66 then merges into Sunset Boulevard for the long winding drive to downtown L.A., ending at the historic core of the city: Olvera Street and the Plaza de Los Angeles State Historic Park.

East of downtown L.A., you have your choice of Route 66 routings. You can hop onto the Pasadena Freeway for a trip back to freeways past—opened in 1939, when it was called the Arroyo Seco Parkway, this was California's first freeway and featured such novel (and never repeated) concepts as 15-mph exit ramps and stop signs at the entrances. Or you can follow Figueroa Street—which in L.A. is known as a "surface street." Signed as "Historic Route 66," it runs parallel to the freeway past some fascinating pieces of Los Angeles, new and old, including the concrete-lined Los Angeles River, hilltop Dodger Stadium, and the nifty **Southwest Museum** (Tues.- Sun. 10 AM- 5 PM; $5; 323/221-2164), an extensive and unusual collection of Native American art and artifacts from all over western North America, Arizona to Alaska. Though the museum itself, standing on Mount Washington, is very small, the collection is enormous; there have been plans to open a second display space in a more central location on Wilshire Boulevard, so phone and ask.

The sights and sounds of Los Angeles, along with select places to eat and sleep, are covered in a Survival Guide on pages 88-90.

Pasadena

The historic Pasadena Freeway unceremoniously drops you short of Pasadena, but following Figueroa Street (or getting off the Ventura Freeway at the Colorado

Colorado Boulevard Bridge

Colorado Boulevard in Pasadena holds the annual Tournament of Roses Parade, every New Year's Day before the famous Rose Bowl football game.

The San Gabriel Valley takes its name from old **Mission San Gabriel Arcangel**, which still stands at 537 W. Mission Drive (daily 9 AM-4 PM; $1; 626/457-3035). Despite suffering extensive earthquake damage, the mission is an interesting spot, though not as evoacative as others in the chain.

Boulevard exit) brings you into town with a bang, on the **Colorado Boulevard Bridge**, an elegant concrete arch that soars over Arroya Seco at the western edge of Pasadena. The arch long marked the symbolic entrance to Los Angeles from the east. Just east of the bridge, on old Route 66 at 411 W. Colorado Boulevard, the **Norton Simon Museum** (Thurs.-Sun. noon-6 PM; $4; 626/449-6840), has a medium-sized but impeccably chosen collection of western and southeast Asian art, ranging from Hindu sculpture to one the world's foremost collections of Degas paintings, drawings, and sculptures.

Though it doesn't have anything like the Hollywood cachet of Malibu or Beverly Hills, the Pasadena area has always been the home of L.A.'s elite—in spirit if not always in fact. In the early years of the 20th century, when L.A. was first booming, Arroyo Seco was among the most desirable places to live, and that era left behind some of the most important architecture in Southern California. The greatest landmark is the distinctive **Gamble House** (Thurs.-Sun. noon-3PM; $5; 626/793-3334), located at 4 Westmoreland Place, off the 300 block of N. Orange Grove Boulevard, an 8,800-square-foot arts-and-crafts masterpiece built in 1908 by architects Charles and Henry Greene as a winter home for the heirs to the Proctor and Gamble fortune. Nearby are many other "Greene and Greene" houses, as well as works by Frank Lloyd Wright—not to mention college football's Rose Bowl, which hosts one of the country's oldest and proudest sporting events every New Year's Day.

Back on old Route 66, the blocks of downtown Pasadena east of the Norton Simon Museum have been undergoing a real renaissance in the recent years. Renamed Old Pasadena, the district is increasingly filled with upscale boutiques and trendy cafes taking over and restoring blocks of historic 1920s buildings.

For more information on Pasadena, contact the **visitors bureau**, 171 S. Los Robles Avenue (626/795-9311).

San Marino: The Huntington Library, Museum, and Gardens
If you want to experience a little more than Route 66 and its roadside Americana, head southeast from Pasadena to exclusive San Marino, where one of the world's great museum collections is on display in the 600-acre former estate of one of Southern California's true magnates, streetcar millionaire Henry Huntington. The library contains all sorts of unique books and documents and preserves thousands more (over 3 million documents in all) for the benefit of scholars, but the real draw is

the art gallery, which displays an excellent collection of British and European painting and sculpture, with major works by Reynolds, Gainsborough, and others.

The Huntington, which is to genteel Pasadena what the flashy Getty Center is to West L.A., is not particularly high-profile or cutting-edge, but it's one of the world's top museums nonetheless. There are also fine assemblages of American art (including Gilbert Stuart's familiar portrait of George Washington) and architecture, but for my money (despite what the people at the admission desks may lead you to believe, the Huntington *is* free) the best part of the Huntington is its splendid **gardens**, which cover 120 acres in a series of mini-ecosystems, distilling the essence of Australia, Japan, South America, and, in the country's largest cactus garden, the American Southwest.

The bookshop is first-rate as well, with numerous scholarly journals as well as art books, postcards, greeting cards, and prints. The Huntington (Tues.-Fri. noon-4:30 PM, Saturday and Sunday 11 AM-4:30 PM; donations; 626/405-2141) is located at 1151 Oxford Road, a mile east from the end of the Pasadena Freeway.

Henry Huntington (1850-1927) was the nephew of Southern Pacific Railroad baron Collis P. Huntington. Henry made his own fortune building the Pacific Electric streetcar system which once crisscrossed Los Angeles. The books and art on display were collected by him and his aunt Arabella, both of whom are buried in a mausoleum surrounded by orange groves on the north side of the Huntington Library.

The San Gabriel Valley

East of Pasadena—though effectively swallowed up in Southern California's neverending sprawl—the San Gabriel Valley used to be the westbound traveler's first taste of Southern California. After crossing the Mojave Desert and the high mountains, Route 66 dropped down into what might have seemed like paradise: orange groves as far as the eye could see, a few tidy towns linked by streetcars, and houses draped in climbing roses and bougainvillea. The San Gabriel Valley embodied this suburban ideal until the mid-1950s, when Route 66 gave way to high-speed freeways and the orange groves were replaced by endless grids of tract houses.

In the 1950s, San Bernardino was where **Maurice and Richard McDonald** perfected the burger-making restaurant chain that bears their name. In 1961, the McDonald brothers sold their company to Ray Kroc, and the rest is fast-food history.

If you're willing to search and to close your eyes to mini-mall sprawl, Route 66 still offers a window onto this golden age. Winding between Pasadena and San Bernardino, along the foothills of the sometimes snowcapped San Gabriel Mountains, the old road links a number of once-distinct communities.

East of Pasadena, old Route 66 runs alongside the I-210 freeway (which ends at La Verne, one-time base of David Koresh and his ill-fated Branch Davidian followers). The old road followed Colorado Boulevard, turning into Foothill Boulevard around the landmark **Santa Anita** racetrack. (The Marx Brothers filmed *A Day at the Races* here.) Foothill Boulevard, which is signed as "Historic Route 66," jogs east along the foothills through **Azusa**, home of the classic Foothill Drive-In theater; collegiate **Claremont**; and **Upland**, where the grass median strip holds a statue of the pioneer "Madonna of the Trail," which officially marked the western end of the National Old Trails Highway, the immediate precursor to Route 66.

At **Rancho Cucamonga**, Foothill Boulevard crosses the I-15 freeway, which is the quickest route over Cajon Pass. Rancho Cucamonga, once famed for its vineyards—a few of which survive amidst the suburban sprawl—is now best known as the home of the Epicenter, where the very popular **Cucamonga Quakes** (909/481-5000) play Class A baseball and a statue of Jack Benny welcomes you through the turnstiles. (If you ever heard his radio show, which featured the catchphrase "Anahein, Azusa, and Cucamonga," you'll know why he's here.)

East of the Giant Orange, at the western edge of San Bernardino, another remnant of old Route 66 road culture is closed but still standing: the 19 concrete tepees that form the **Wigwam Motel**, at 2728 W. Foothill Boulevard.

Hula Ville, formerly California State Landmark No. 939, bordered old Route 66 on the west side of Victorville. It's gone through hard times since the 100-year-old creator and caretaker, "Fry Pan" Miles Mahan, passed away in 1996, but the hundreds of beer bottles and hand-lettered memorials to sundry bums, hobos, and other travelers he called his friends have been preserved in the California Route 66 museum in town.

East of the I-15 freeway, one of the San Gabriel Valley's few still-healthy roadside sights sits on the south side of old Route 66, next to the classic **Bono's Old Route 66 Cafe**, 15395 Foothill Boulevard. The cafe, run by same family since 1936 (yes, they're related to the late Sonny of Cher fame) still churns out big portions of family-friendly breakfasts and lunches. But the real attraction is **Bono's Giant Orange**, an orange-shaped stand which during the 1920s offered thirsty Route 66 travelers "All The Orange Juice You Can Drink—10¢." In good shape—and slated for eventual reopening as a juice stand—the Giant Orange is one of the last of the dozens of giant roadside fruits all over California which used to tempt passersby to stop and sample their wares. Others survive in the Central Valley (near Chowchilla along Hwy-99, and in Dixon off I-80), but this is the best-preserved of them all.

The old Route 66 alignment continued east for another 15 miles, passing through the former steel mill town of Fontana, birthplace of the Hell's Angels' Motorcycle Club (and L.A. culture critic Mike Davis), before bending north at San Bernardino to join I-15 at the summit.

Cajon Pass

A few picturesque stretches of the old road go up and over Cajon Pass, though old Route 66 is no longer a through route; the main road is now I-15. On the desert side of the summit, turn off the freeway at the "Oak Hills" exit and stop for a burger and fries at the **Summit Inn**, one of the few survivors of the old road businesses along this stretch of highway.

Victorville: Roy Rogers

It takes about two hours to get here from the west end of Route 66, but it's not until you reach Victorville—the distant extent of Los Angeles' sprawl—that old Route 66 begins to seem real. As real

as Hollywood cowboys, anyway. Victorville, a rapidly growing desert community of over 50,000 residents, is home to the **Roy Rogers and Dale Evans Museum** (daily 9 AM-5 PM; $6; 760/243-4547), west of I-15 at the Roy Rogers Drive exit, a living memorial to America's favorite cowboy and cowgirl. Along with an encyclopedic collection of old movie stills and posters stand the taxidermied remains of Roy and Dale's favorite animals—Roy's horse Trigger (a larger-than-life concrete copy of Trigger stands in front of the museum as well), Dale's horse Buttermilk, and their dog Bullet—plus hundreds of trophy heads of other less-loved creatures. Nearly up until the day he died in 1998, Roy himself was on hand to welcome visitors, and the homespun charm of the museum he and Dale created here perfectly suits the characters they created, onscreen and off. However much the name "Roy Rogers" makes you think of anodyne suburban restaurants, the real Roy Rogers was a comic-book hero come to life, and he really did embody all those Boy Scout virtues that are so easy and fun to sneer at.

That said, the Roy Rogers Museum really does reveal a lot about a certain generation—the rural-born, survivors of the Depression and World War II who came of age in and set the tone for the all-American 1950s and are now our "seasoned citizens." In their museum, Roy and Dale really opened their hearts, displaying so many family photo albums and worldly knickknacks that you feel you're nosing around their living room. Whatever you may think about the politics—or about killing wild animals, which Roy did with glee—you simply have to admire his taste in cars: check out the 1960s Pontiac Bonneville, with a Texas Longhorn hood ornament, saddle leather upholstery, and—best of all—a gear shift lever in the shape of a six-shooter.

Victorville is also home to a small new **California Route 66 Museum**, on the old road at 16849 D Street (Thurs.-Sun. 10 AM-4 PM; donations; 760/261-US66), with a small but growing collection of road signs, photographs, and reminiscences, plus the remnants of Hula Ville.

Old Route 66 follows 7th Street through town, past a few neon-signed old motels including the **New Corral**, 14643 7th Street (760/245-9378), with its animated bucking bronco, and the large **Best Western Green Tree Inn**, with its 24-hour restaurant, just off the freeway at 14173 Green Tree Boulevard.

For more information, contact the **Victorville Chamber of Commerce** (760/245-6506).

With an area of more than 20,000 square miles (some 90% of it desert), San Bernardino County is the largest county in the United States.

The **Mojave Desert** is one of the driest places on the planet; parts of it receive less than three inches of rainfall in an average year, sometimes going for more than two years without getting a single drop.

Trigger

Old Route 66 Loop: Oro Grande, Helendale, and Lenwood

Between Victorville and Barstow, old Route 66 survives as an "old roads" trek across the Mojave Desert. The 36-mile route, called the Old National Trail Highway, parallels the railroad tracks and the usually parched Mojave River, passing through odd little towns like Oro Grande, which is still home to a huge cement plant and lots of roadside junk shops. Outside Barstow at the west end of Main Street, keep an eye out for the Christian Motorcycle club sign welcoming you to Lenwood, a crossroads near where the old road reconnects with I-15.

Midway between Victorville and Barstow is Helendale, where you can find the nearly famous stripper's museum, Exotic World, a mile west of old Route 66—call 760/243-5261 for directions, because it's hard to find.

EXOTIC WORLD

Victorville is about as far as you can get from the bright lights and bump-and-grind of a big city, but the sprawling desert east of the city is the unlikely home of the world's only museum dedicated to the art and craft of striptease dancing —Exotic World. Exotic World fills many rooms in the ranch house of Dixie Lee Evans, a former burlesque dancer who, during the early 1960s, was semi-famous for her striptease impersonations of Marilyn Monroe. Dixie personally guides visitors through the extensive collection, which includes dozens of elaborate costumes as well as posters, photos, props (including one of fan-dancer Sally Rand's famous fans), and rare movies. Most of the items on display were assembled by another burlesque dancer, Jennie Lee, who ran a strip club in San Pedro, California, and who started the collection in order to document the forbidden story of striptease. Jennie Lee's effort to preserve the history of burlesque and the dancers who made the "hubba-hubba" happen, is carried on by Exotic World's Burlesque Hall of Fame, a wall of 8-by-10 glossies remembering the shimmying efforts of such striptease luminaries as Lily St. Cyr, Tempest Storm, Blaze Starr, Sally Rand, and Gypsy Rose Lee.

Despite the X-rated connotations of striptease, Exotic World is not at all seedy or licentious, and Dixie's energetic and illuminating presentation makes it well worth the detour. Located on a former goat ranch, behind a set of elaborate wrought iron gates at 29053 Wild Road, just north of old Route 66 in Helendale, Exotic World (Tues.-Sun. 10 AM-4 PM; donations; 760/243-5261) is about 17 miles east of D Street from Victorville—call Dixie for directions and reservations.

Barstow

Though by population it's less than half the size of Victorville, the burly railroad and transportation center of Barstow (pop. 21,495) seems a much bigger place. Located midway between Los Angeles and Las Vegas, at the point where I-15 veers north and I-40 takes the place of old east-west Route 66, Barstow was the first large watering hole west of the Arizona border. Judging by the numerous truck depots arrayed around town, that's a role it still plays. It's scruffy and a little scary in the way railroad towns can be, and along Main Street—the old Route 66 corridor—many of the old cafes and motels are now closed and boarded up, including the landmark **El Rancho Motel** at 112 E. Main Street—the one whose 100-foot neon sign is supported by a pair of massive pylons visible from all over town.

At the center of town, just north of old Route 66, the faded old Harvey House Casa del Desierto hotel, next to the train station, looks like the Doge's Palace in Venice, its gothic-style arcades a substantial reminder of a time when travel meant more than just getting somewhere.

Northeast of Barstow, **Calico Ghost Town** (daily 9 AM-5 PM; $6; 800/TO-CALICO or 800/862-2542) is an enjoyably silly resurrection of the silver mining camp that boomed here during the 1890s.

Daggett and Newberry Springs: *Bagdad Cafe*

East of Barstow all the way to the Arizona border, old Route 66 survives in a series of different stretches alongside the I-40 freeway. The first place of interest, Daggett, is a rusty old mining and railroad town six miles east of Barstow along the north side of the freeway. A couple of abandoned hotels keep company with the still-functioning **Daggett Restaurant**, which serves bowls of chili and ice-cold beers along the south side of the tracks. Old Route 66 runs due east from Daggett, past the region's current claim to fame, the acres of shiny mirrors of the **Solar One power plant**, an experimental electricity generating station three miles from Daggett and north of the old road.

Fifteen miles east of Daggett come the next I-40 junction and the next small town, Newberry Springs, where the popular Percy Adlon movie *Bagdad Cafe* was shot at the town's one and only cafe. The newly renamed **Bagdad Cafe**, is open daily 6 AM-8 PM and offers the best food on this stretch of old Route 66. The old road continues along the south side of I-40 for another 25 miles, passing the lava flows of Pisgah Crater before crossing over to the north of the freeway for the final 10 miles into Ludlow, where old Route 66 rejoins the freeway.

Amboy Crater has been the focus of a contentious plan which would turn the entire area into a massive trash dump, eventually forming a mountain 400 feet tall, a mile wide, and three miles long, growing by up to 21,000 tons a day.

Old Route 66 Loop: Ludlow, Amboy, and Chambless

If you want a quick and convincing taste of what traveling across the Mojave Desert was like in the days before air conditioning and cellular phones, turn south off I-40 at Ludlow, 50 miles east of Barstow, and follow the well-signed "National Old Trails Highway," one of the many monikers Route 66 has carried over the years, on a 75-mile loop along the old road. At Ludlow, two gas stations, a coffee shop, and a motel represent civilization between Barstow and Needles. The old road bends slightly southeast here, passing first through Bagdad, a now-defunct turn-of-the-century gold mining town. Continuing east, old Route 66 cuts across another lava flow—this one part

According to Route 66 historian Tom Teague, author of *Searching for 66*, Santa Fe Railroad supply points across the Mojave Desert were named in alphabetical order: Amboy, Bristol, Cadiz, Danby, Essex, Fenner, Goffs, Home, Ibex, Java, and Klinefelter.

Almost 1.5 million acres between I-40 and I-15 have been set aside as the **Mojave National Preserve,** which includes some huge sand dunes and a historic railroad depot at Kelso, 33 miles north of Amboy. Another of the many places here worth visiting is **Mitchell Caverns** (760/928-2586), at the center of Providence Mountains State Recreation Area, 25 miles north of I-40 at the end of Essex Road.

Huge chunks of the Mojave Desert have been used as military training grounds since WW II, when **Gen. George Patton** used this area to prepare his tank battalions for battle in the North African desert. As many as 90,000 soldiers were based here during the war years; the remains of the camp can still be seen in the desert along Crucero Road, just north of the I-40 Ludlow exit.

of the Amboy Crater—beyond which another road heads 50 miles south to Twentynine Palms and Joshua Tree National Park.

Midway along the old road loop, Amboy (pop. 2) is a museum-worthy assembly of roadside architecture that has survived solely due to the willpower of its longtime lord, master, and owner since 1938, Buster Burris. Once traffic dropped off with the construction of I-40, the whole town—complete with a classic late-1940s roadside cafe called Roy's, a disused motel, and a set of gas pumps—went up for sale. It remained for sale for decades, until Buster finally found a buyer in 1996. Still photogenic, Amboy is well worth a stop, but the new owners haven't made many friends with their high prices and lack of hospitality—charging $1 for a glass of water, for example.

From Amboy, it's another 48 miles back to I-40 at the town of Fenner. If you're keen on traveling as much of the old road as possible, another stretch of Route 66 runs east from Fenner on a roller coaster of undulating two-lane blacktop, parallel to the railroad track through the desert hamlet of **Goffs.** Fifteen miles east of Goffs, old Route 66 joins up with US-95, which continues north to Las Vegas, 90-odd miles away. US-95 also runs south, linking up with the I-40 freeway 10 miles west of Needles.

Needles

Founded soon after the Santa Fe Railroad came through in 1883 and named for the group of sharp stone spires that stand near where I-40 crosses the Colorado River from Arizona, Needles (pop. 5,191) is one of the hottest places in the country, with summertime highs hovering between 100° and 120° F for months on end. Though unbearable in summer, Needles is a popular place with winter snowbirds escaping colder climes. It also has a very rich Route 66 heritage. The stretch of old Route 66 through Needles—along Broadway, alternating along both sides of the freeway—holds a slew of old-road treasures. The

The Amtrak station in Needles stands next to what was formerly El Garces Hotel, one of many palatial railroad hotels run by **Fred Harvey.**

Needles was the boyhood home of late *Peanuts* cartoonist **Charles Schulz** and was featured in the comic strip as the desert home of Snoopy's raffish sibling, Spike.

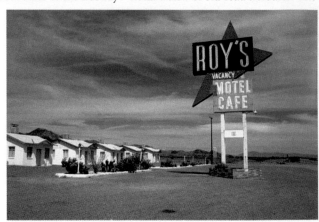

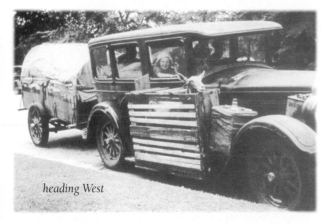

heading West

magnificent El Garces Hotel, which is undergoing long-term renovation and transformation into a historical museum. The Route 66 Motel, with its great arrow-shaped sign. Across the street from the "Welcome to Needles" wagon, the motor court at 304 Broadway was known as the Palm Motel during its heyday and later briefly brought back to life by Hank Wilde as a nostalgic B&B in the early 1990s. It's since closed again, but stop by and see if its fortunes have improved—and hope for a sense of the *real* old Route 66.

Despite the unforgiving summer weather, Needles is a friendly town well worth getting to know. Drive around awhile to get your bearings, and stop by the **chamber of commerce** office (760/326-2050), at Front and G Streets, across from the El Garces, for a free map or other useful information.

Lake Havasu City and London Bridge

The first stop east of the Colorado River, nine miles from the border and 23 miles south of I-40, Lake Havasu City is a thoroughly modern vacation town built around a thoroughly odd centerpiece: London Bridge, brought here stone by stone between 1967 and 1971. Terribly tacky souvenir shops and faux London pubs congregate around the foot of the bridge, which spans a man-made channel, but the bridge itself is an impressive sight.

Unless you plan to retire here—or simply relax on a boat on the river—there's not a lot to do at Lake Havasu. Have an English muffin and a cup of tea, pay your respects, and take a photograph or two, then hit the road again. That said, Lake Havasu has managed to turn itself into one of the country's most popular destinations for college kids on Spring Break, when thousands of late adolescents head to the beaches of **Lake Havasu State Park**, off Hwy-95 at 699 London Bridge Road (520/855-2784).

From Needles, it's a quick 25-mile drive north along the Colorado River into Nevada to visit the gambling center of **Laughlin.** Since the mid-1980s, Laughlin has boomed into a sparkling city with huge casinos and more than 10,000 cheap rooms.

Crossing the Colorado River between Arizona and California, look downstream from the I-40 freeway to see the arching silver steel bridge that carried Route 66 up until, somewhat ironically, 1966. It's still in use, supporting a natural gas pipeline. Beyond it, the red-rock spires for which Needles is named rise sharply out of the desert plains. The border here was the site of illegal but effective roadblocks during the Dust Bowl, when California vigilantes turned back migrant Okies if they didn't have much money.

If you're not a die-hard Route 66 fan when you get there, traveling even short stretches of the old route across Arizona is bound to convert you. The high-speed I-40 freeway gives quick access to some of the best surviving stretches of the old road, and these are some of the most captivating parts of Route 66 anywhere. Starting at the Colorado River, the route runs from the arid Mojave Desert up into the mountains around Oatman, then rejoins I-40 at Kingman. East of Kingman, the old road diverges again, running past dozens of remarkable old highway towns along some of the oldest and longest still-driveable stretches of the Mother Road, before climbing up toward the dense pine forests that surround the Grand Canyon.

LAKE HAVASU'S LONDON BRIDGE

It may not have stood out as an exemplar of the finest engineering when it spanned the River Thames, but London Bridge is a marvelous sight in the middle of the Arizona desert. A replacement for a series of bridges that date back to medieval times (inspiring the children's rhyme "London Bridge is Falling Down"), this iteration was constructed (in London) in the 1830s. In 1967, it was determined that the bridge was no longer able to handle the demands of London traffic. It was replaced by a modern concrete span, and the stones of the old one were put up for sale.

Bought by property developer Robert McCulloch for $2.4 million, the 10,246 blocks of stone were shipped here and reassembled (at a cost of another $3 million), and a channel was cut under it to bring water from the Colorado River. The Lord Mayor of London flew in to attend rededication ceremonies in October 1971. The bridge now stands as the centerpiece of a retirement and resort community that's home to some 25,000 residents. There's no admission charge to see this oddly compelling sight, its finely carved stonework standing aloof from the tacky stucco, mock-Tudor souvenir shops lining the base of the bridge.

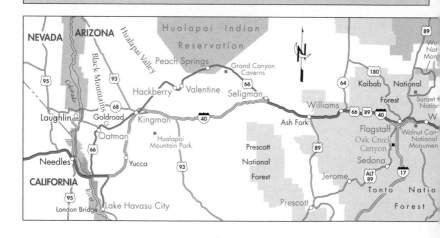

Old Route 66: Oatman

One of the most demanding, desolate, and awesomely satisfying stretches of the old road climbs from I-40 along the Colorado River, beginning just east of the California border and rejoining the freeway at Kingman. Following at first along the wildlife refuge that lines the Colorado River, the old road then cuts across a stretch of desert that brings new meaning to the word "harsh." The narrow, roughly surfaced roadway passes few signs of life on this 50-mile loop, so be sure you and your car are prepared for the rigors of desert driving.

From I-40 and the California border, take the Park Moabi exit and follow Hwy-95, then Hwy-66, due north; you can also reach Hwy-95 directly from Needles or from Laughlin, Nevada. (Westbound drivers have it the easiest—simply follow the well-signed "Historic Route 66" west from Kingman, exit 44 off I-40.) Whichever way you go, you can't avoid the steep hills that bring you to Oatman (elev. 2,700 feet), an odd combination of ghost town and tourist draw that's one of the top stops along Route 66. A gold mining town whose glory days had long faded by the time I-40 passed it by way back in 1952, Oatman looks like a Wild West stage set. But it's the real thing—awnings over the plank sidewalks, bearded roughnecks (and a few burros) wandering the streets, lots of rust, slumping old buildings. The gold mines here produced some two million ounces from their start in 1904 until they panned out in the mid-1930s. At its peak, Oatman had a population of over 10,000, with 20 saloons and a half-dozen hotels lining three-block Main Street. The old **Oatman Hotel** (520/768-4408), was where Clark Gable and Carole Lombard spent their first night after getting married in Kingman in 1939 (the room is preserved behind a Plexiglas door today). You can sample Oatman's highly recommended Navajo tacos, have a beer in the hotel's downstairs bar, or spend the night for $35-50 in a room hardly changed in the last half-century.

Saloons and rock shops line the rest of Main Street, where on weekends and holidays Wild West enthusiasts enact the shootouts that took place here only in the movies. Oatman does get a considerable tourist trade, but after dark or in winter the town reverts to its rough-and-tumble ways, and the conservative, libertarian bent of most of the local population ensures that nothing is likely to change Oatman's crusty charms.

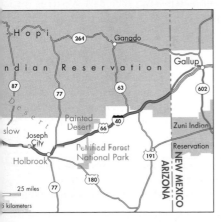

For more information, contact the small but helpful **chamber of commerce** (520/768-8070).

East from Oatman, the road passes the recently reactivated gold workings at **Goldroad** before climbing up and over the angular Black Mountains. Steep switchbacks and 15-mph hairpin turns make the 2,100-foot change in elevation over a very short eight miles of blacktop. The route then continues for another 20 miles into Kingman, which seems like a bustling metropolis after this hour-plus roller coaster of a drive.

At **Yucca,** Arizona, just south of I-40 exit 26, and 18 miles west of Kingman, the Ford Motor Company maintains an automobile "proving ground," where cars are run for countless miles around an oval track in the hottest summer heat.

For the hits of the 1960s, tune to Kingman's "Radio Crazy," **KRCY 105.9 FM.**

Andy Devine

The stretch of Route 66 through Kingman has been renamed in memory of favorite son **Andy Devine,** who was born in Flagstaff in 1905 but grew up here, where his parents ran the Beale Hotel. One of the best-known character actors of Hollywood's classic era, the raspy-voiced Devine usually played devoted sidekicks, the sort of roles also taken by Gabby Hayes—whom Devine, in fact, replaced in the later Roy Rogers movies. Devine's most famous role was as the wagon driver in the classic 1939 John Ford Western, *Stagecoach.* He remained active in films and TV until his death in 1977.

Kingman

The only town for miles in any direction since its founding as a railroad center in 1880, Kingman (pop. 12,750) has always depended upon passing travelers for its livelihood. Long a main stopping place on Route 66, it still provides the only all-night services on US-93 between Las Vegas and Phoenix and along I-40 between Flagstaff and Needles. The town remains more a way station than a destination despite the increasing number of people who have relocated here in recent years, attracted by the open space, high desert air, and low cost of living.

Everything that's ever happened in and around Kingman is documented to some degree at the **Mojave Museum,** 400 W. Beale Street (Mon.-Fri. 10 AM-5 PM, Saturday and Sunday 1-5 PM; $1), right on US-93 a block south of I-40. Besides the usual dioramas and displays on regional history, there's an extensive section devoted to local Hualapai culture and crafts, as well as samples of turquoise mined nearby. There's also a display on the life of local boy Andy Devine and a photograph of Clark Gable and Carole Lombard, who fled Hollywood to get married in Kingman's Methodist church.

Quite a few of the old Route 66 cafes and motels still flourish alongside the old road, now called Andy Devine Avenue through town. Modern development borders the I-40 freeway. Among many places to eat are the very good **Mr. D's Route 66 Diner,** right downtown and—thanks to its bank of neon—impossible to miss, and the **House of Chan,** 960 W. Beale Street, on US-93 a block north of I-40, which serves a full menu of American food as well as Cantonese specialties. Besides the usual chain motels—two nice Best Westerns, two Days Inns, a Holiday Inn, and a Travelodge—accommodation options include the pleasant **Hill Top Motel,** 1901 E. Andy Devine Avenue (520/753-2198). The Hill Top may be due for everlasting infamy as the place Timothy McVeigh stayed for a week before blowing up the Murrah federal building in Oklahoma City.

For more information, or to pick up a copy of the town's very good Route 66 brochure, stop by the Kingman **visitors center,** housed in a recently converted old powerhouse along Route 66 at 120 W. Andy Devine Avenue (520/753-6106).

Kingman sits at the junction of I-40, old Route 66, and US-93, which runs north to Las Vegas and south to Phoenix, Tucson and Mexico. US-93 is covered beginning on page 196.

BOOKS ON ROUTE 66

Considering the old road's great fame, it's hardly surprising that more than a dozen books still in print deal with the Route 66 experience. Some are travel guides, some folk histories, others nostalgic rambles down what was and what's left of the Mother Road. Photographic essays document the rapidly disappearing architecture and signage, and at least one cookbook collects recipes of dishes served in cafes along the route. The following is a sampling of favorite titles—most of which can be found in stores along the route if not in your local bookstore.

• *The Grapes of Wrath,* John Steinbeck (Viking, 1937). The first and foremost Route 66–related story, this compelling tale traces the traumatic travels of the Joad family from Dust Bowl Oklahoma to the illusive Promised Land of California. Brutally vivid, *The Grapes of Wrath* was an instant bestseller at the tail end of the Depression and was the source of Route 66's "Mother Road" appellation.

• *A Guide Book to Highway 66,* Jack Rittenhouse (University of New Mexico, 1989). A facsimile reprinting of the self-published 1946 book that the late author sold door-to-door at truck stops, motor courts, and cafes along the route.

• *Route 66: A Guidebook to the Mother Road,* Bob Moore and Patrick Grauwels. The most detailed driving guide to old Route 66, packed with mile-by-mile instructions and information as well as photographs and illustrations. Spiral bound for on-the-road ease of use.

• *Route 66: The Mother Road,* Michael Wallis (St. Martin's Press, 1987). A richly illustrated and thoroughly researched guide to the old road. This is more armchair companion than practical aid, but the book captures the spirit of Route 66, and the writer has been a key promotional force behind the route's preservation and rediscovery.

• *Route 66 Traveler's Guide,* Tom Snyder (St. Martin's Press, 1990). State-by-state description of Route 66, with an emphasis on the stories behind the sights you see. Illustrated with 1930s-era auto club maps adapted to show the path of modern freeways but still evoking the spirit of the old road.

• *Searching for 66,* Tom Teague (Samizdat House, 1996). More personal than other titles on Route 66, this book of vignettes describes the author's interactions with many people along Route 66 who have made it what it is. As a bonus, Teague's book is illustrated with fine pen-and-ink drawings by Route 66 artist Bob Waldmire.

Hualapai Mountain Park

To escape the summer heat, Kingmanites head south along a well-marked 14-mile road to Hualapai Mountain Park, where pines and firs cover the slopes of the 8,417-foot peak. Hiking trails wind through the wilderness, where there's a campground ($6) and a few rustic cabins ($25) built by the Civilian Conservation Corps during the New Deal 1930s. Contact the ranger station (520/757-3859) near the park entrance for detailed information or to make reservations.

Old Route 66 Loop: Hackberry and the Hualapai Reservation

Probably the most evocative stretch of old Route 66 runs northeast from Kingman through the high desert Hualapai Valley, along the Santa Fe Railroad tracks through all-but-abandoned towns bypassed by the interstate. Leaving Kingman on a 20-mile-long straightaway, the road (now named Hwy-66) bends back south around the Peacock Mountains through the old railroad town of Hackberry, home to the ever-evolving **International Bioregional Old Route 66 Visitors Center and Preservation Foundation.** A marvelous establishment, created by renowned Route 66 artist Bob Waldmire, the center serves multiple purposes: the 22-acre site includes everything from cactus gardens to a solar oven, and the main building, built in 1934 as the Hackberry General Store, now houses a museum and gift shop. The center's library—with its books on Route 66 and complete works of Thomas Paine, Thomas Jefferson, and other free thinkers—disappeared when Bob moved back to Springfield, Illinois, to write a biography of his father, the inventor of the Corn Dog. For more information on Hackberry or the center, call or write: P.O. Box 46, Hackberry, AZ 86411 (520/769-2605).

Downhill from the Route 66 center, the town of Hackberry itself grew up along the original alignment of Route 66, which continues east across a small section of the Hualapai Indian Reservation, at whose center lies the village of Valentine. Another 10 miles east brings you to the town of Truxton, where the **Frontier Cafe,** on the south side of the highway, is the one reliable place to eat in this sparsely populated region—good pie and great chat, open weekdays 7 AM-7 PM, weekends 9 AM-5 PM. **Grandma's Bar,** across the highway, gives you another chance to sample local lore and lifeways.

Another mile east is the boundary of the main Hualapai (pronounced "WALL-ah-pie") reservation lands. The 1,500-strong tribe has its community center at the town of **Peach Springs,** which marks the halfway point of this 90-mile, old-roads loop and offers at least one reason to stop: the comfortable and well-placed new **Hualapai Lodge** (520/769-2230 or 888/255-9550), which has spacious $75-a-night hotel rooms, and the River Runners restaurant, right on Route 66. Apart from this, Peach Springs is mostly a prefab Bureau of Indian Affairs housing project with few services, though a photogenic old Route 66 filling station sits in the center of town.

Peach Springs is also the starting point for the 22-mile trip along Diamond Creek Road, which, weather willing, allows people in normal passenger cars the chance to drive down to the Colorado River—and the chance to say you drove to the bottom of the Grand Canyon. Get a permit ($4) and up-to-date information at the Hualapai Lodge.

Havasupai Indian Reservation: Supai

Midway between Peach Springs and the Grand Canyon Caverns, Hwy-18 cuts off to the northeast toward the Havasupai Indian Reservation, which includes one of the most beautiful and untrammelled (as well as wettest and greenest) corners of the Grand Canyon, **Havasu Canyon**. The 62-mile road north from Route 66 ends in a parking lot at mile-high Hualapai Hilltop, from where a somewhat arduous (especially in summer) eight-mile trail drops down to the village of Supai (pop. 550; elev. 3,200 feet), at the edge of Havasu Canyon. In Supai, the tribally owned and operated **Havasupai Lodge** (520/448-2111) has rooms with air-conditioning and private baths for around $80, less in off-season; there's also a cafe serving breakfast, lunch, and early dinner (try the Indian Taco—kidney bean chili piled on fry bread).

Besides the amazing scenery, Supai offers visitors the chance to send a postcard home via pack train—the only postal service in the country still using animals, with a postmark to prove it.

At the heart of Havasu Canyon, stretching along Havasu Creek from about 1.5 to 5 miles down from Supai, a series of waterfalls cascade down sandstone cliffs, forming clear turquoise pools of cool water—ideal for a summertime swim. The tallest of these, Mooney Falls, drops nearly 200 feet and takes its name from a hapless prospector who fell to his death here in 1880, dangling for hours before his climbing rope broke. If you're feeling brave, you can follow in his footsteps along a rough trail that descends (with the help of iron bars and a few carved footholds) to the bottom of the falls.

To get the complete Havasu Canyon experience, come prepared to camp out at the very basic but beautifully situated Havasu Campground, located between Havasu and Mooney Falls; tent sites cost around $10 a night per person, and there is no camping allowed anywhere else. Campfires and mountain bikes are also banned.

To visit Havasu Canyon, whether you're camping or planning to stay at the lodge, you must make reservations in advance; it is not a feasible day trip, since the hike in and out again is a 20-mile roundtrip. Contact the lodge if you want to stay there; call Havasupai Tourist Enterprise (520/448-2141) to arrange payment of the entrance fee ($15 per person) and any camping fees.

Grand Canyon Caverns

A dozen miles east of Peach Springs, 26 miles from I-40, a large green sign along old Route 66 marks the entrance to Grand Canyon Caverns (daily 10 AM-5 PM, 8 AM-6 PM in summer; $8.50; 520/422-3223), which has somehow managed to survive despite being bypassed by the I-40 superslab. Once one of the prime tourist draws on the Arizona stretch of Route 66, the Grand Canyon Caverns were discovered and developed in the late 1920s and still have the feel of an old-time roadside attraction. Start your tour at the gift shop, buy a ticket, and hop on the elevator, which drops you 300 feet to underground chambers, including the 18,000-square-foot Chapel of the Ages. Tours last about 45 minutes. There's also a motel (doubles run $25 in winter, $50 in summer) and a restaurant on the site.

Seligman

At the east end of the long loop of old Route 66, the sleepy little town of Seligman (pop. 510; pronounced "SLIG-man") is a perfect place to take a break before or after rejoining the interstate hordes. The town retains a lot of its historic character—old sidewalk awnings and even a few hitching rails —and offers lots of reasons to stop. Two of the biggest are brothers Angel and Juan Delgadillo, ringleaders of local Route 66 preservation efforts. Angel is the town barber, and his shop is a pilgrimage point for old roads fans; Juan, a practical joker, runs the wacky **Snow Cap Drive-In** a block to the east. The burgers, fries, and milk shakes there are plenty good, but Juan's sense of humor is more than a little strange: he has handles on doors that don't open, a sign that says "Sorry, We're Open," and a menu advertising "Hamburgers without Ham." Behind the restaurant —in snow, rain, or shine—sits a roofless old Chevy decorated with fake flowers and an artificial Christmas tree. Ask Juan why.

Between Seligman and Ash Fork, a nice section of the old two-lane Route 66 runs just north of and parallel to the I-40 freeway.

Apart from the Delgadillo brothers, Seligman also has a very good cafe, the **Copper Cart**, at the center of town; a neat old mock-Tudor railroad station that once doubled as a Harvey House hotel and restaurant; a half-dozen motels including the **Historic Route 66 Motel**, 500 W. Route 66 (520/422-3204), and the sign for the Unique Motel. After dark, head to the **Black Cat** saloon, where actor Nicolas Cage has been known to stop in for a drink or two.

Detour: US-89 to Prescott and Jerome

Between Ash Fork and Flagstaff, a 100-mile scenic loop winds south from I-40 along Hwy-89 and Hwy-89A, passing through Prescott, Jerome, Sedona, and Oak Creek Canyon. Some of the best parts are toward the Flagstaff end of the loop. But the western half, around Arizona's original capital, Prescott (pop. 26,592; elev. 5,346 feet) has plenty to offer. Founded as a gold mining town in 1864, Prescott has evolved into a popular vacation and retirement town, but the historic core retains its feel, with old saloons lining "Whiskey Row," on the west side of the central courthouse square.

East from Prescott, Hwy-89A makes a wonderfully scenic drive past 7,743-foot Mingus Mountain before dropping down into photogenic Jerome (pop. 403; elev. 5,400 feet), the liveliest and most interesting "ghost town" in Arizona. Set on steep streets that switchback up the mountainside, Jerome is an old copper mining camp that has turned itself into a thriving artists community, with many nice shops, galleries and cafes, and almost no touristy schlock.

> The copper mines at Jerome were originally worked by Native Americans as far back as the 1580s, when Spanish missionaries first described them. Three hundred years later, American entrepreneurs expanded the mines, which were operated by the Phelps Dodge Corporation until 1953.

Park wherever you can and walk around, enjoying the incredible views out over the Verde Valley to the San Francisco peaks and beyond. And be sure to stop at one or both of the Victoriana-packed saloons (the **Spirit Room** and **Paul and Jerry's**), and the local history **museum**, 200 N. Main Street (daily 9 AM-4:30 PM; $1) above the Public Library.

At the north (uphill) edge of town, a mile off Hwy-89 at the end of Perkinsville Road, the **Gold King Mine** (daily 9 AM-5 PM; $3) captures the feel of old Jerome through acres of ancient-looking machinery (sawmills, pumps, hoists, and ore cars—most of which is kept in working order), plus ramshackle cabins, a blacksmith shop, an assay office, even an intact old gas station dating from Jerome's 1920s heyday. The many antique cars and trucks (including a pristine 1923 Buffalo Springfield road roller) are as much a draw as the mining equipment, most of which survives from the small Gold King gold mine that opened here in 1890.

For food or a fine shot of espresso, try the **Flatiron Cafe**, 416 Main Street, at the downhill edge of town, or neighboring **Pizza Heaven**. Across the street, in an impossibly tiny Victorian cottage (a former bordello), the **House of Joy** (open for dinner only, Saturday and Sunday only, cash only) serves some of the state's best European-style meals; if you want to try it, reserve a table as soon as you can (520/634-5339).

Being here early in the morning or at sunset really brings out the beauty of Jerome. Fortunately for overnight visitors, a number of Jerome's old homes have been turned into quaint B&Bs, all with panoramic views. Try the **Ghost City Inn**, 541 N. Main Street (520/634-4678), or the more upscale **Surgeon's House** 101 Hill Street (520/639-1452), both of which have rates in the $80-a-night range.

For further information on Jerome and the surrounding area, contact the **visitors bureau**, 317 Main Street (520/634-2900). East of Jerome, Hwy-89A drops down into the Verde Valley, then winds northeast toward Flagstaff by way of scenic Sedona, which is covered below.

Williams

The last Route 66 town to be bypassed by the I-40 freeway, Williams (pop. 2,532; elev. 6,780 feet) held out until the bitter end, waging court battle after court battle before finally surrendering on October 13, 1984. Despite the town's long opposition, in the end Williams gave in gracefully, going so far as to hold a celebration-cum-wake for the old road, highlighted by a performance atop the new freeway overpass by none other than Mr. Route 66 himself, the late great Bobby Troup.

Williams today is primarily a gateway to the Grand Canyon, but it also takes full tourist advantage of its Route 66 heritage. The downtown streets sport old-fashioned street lamps, and every other store—including the friendly and well-stocked world headquarters of **Route 66 Magazine**, at 326 W. Route 66 (520/635-4322)—sells a variety of Route 66 souvenirs, but the town is still a charming place, much more than a bedroom community for Grand Canyon-bound travelers.

Apart from the Route 66 connections, Williams' pride and joy is the vintage **Grand Canyon Railway**, which whistles and steams its way north to the canyon every morning March-Dec., taking roughly two hours each way and allowing a three-hour layover—or longer, if you go up one day and come back another. Call for current schedules and fares (roundtrip tickets cost around $50; 800/THE-TRAIN or 800/843-8724), or stop by the historic depot, a former Harvey House hotel restored in 1990.

As any good road trip destination must, Williams has at least one decent place to eat breakfast, **Old Smokey's Pancake House**, 624 W. Bill Williams Avenue, at the west end of town. The town is also home to a landmark old Route 66 restaurant, **Rod's Steak House**, 301 E. Bill Williams Avenue, in business since 1946.

For a place to stay, try any of the town's many motels, such as the **Westerner Motel**, 530 W. Bill Williams Avenue (520/635-4312 or 800/385-9313), or the British-run **Norris Motel** (520/635-2202), at the far west end of town; rates vary with the seasons, starting at less than $30 a night but rising to twice that in summer.

For more information, contact the **chamber of commerce**, 200 W. Railroad Avenue (520/635-4061).

Flagstaff

Flagstaff (pop. 54,280; elev. 7,000 feet) is an enjoyable, energetic city high up on the Coconino Plateau. The old railroad and lumber-mill town was given a new lease on life by an influx of students at Northern Arizona University and by the array of ski-bums and mountain bikers attracted by the surrounding high mountain wilderness. It's a major gateway to the Grand Canyon and the Native American lands of the Four Corners region, and it richly enjoys the natural beauty of its forested location. So in many ways it has hardly blinked since the demise of old Route 66 (now Santa Fe Avenue), which still winds along the railroad tracks through the center of town. That said, Flagstaff still takes pride in the past, notably in the form of the **Museum Club**, 3404 E. Route 66 (520/526-9434), an old roadhouse brought back to life as a country-western nightclub and ad-hoc nostalgia museum. There are also dozens of vintage neon signs along the old Route 66 alignment: check out the Western Hills Motel and the Grand Canyon Cafe downtown and the Flamingo Motel five blocks west.

In his 1945 *Guide Book to Highway 66,* Jack Rittenhouse wrote, "Cowboys and Indians can be seen in their picturesque dress on Flagstaff streets year 'round."

Flagstaff also has a pair of non-Route 66-related attractions. First and foremost of these stands on a hill at the west end of town, reachable from the west end of Santa Fe Avenue: the **Lowell Observatory**, established in 1894 by Percival Lowell and best known as the place where, in 1930, the planet Pluto was *(continues on page 301)*

GRAND CANYON NATIONAL PARK

Driving an hour north from Williams or Flagstaff will bring you to one of the wonders of the natural world, the Grand Canyon of the Colorado River. Two hundred miles long, a mile deep, and anywhere from five to 15 miles across, the Grand Canyon defies description, and if you're anywhere nearby you really owe it to yourself to stop for a look. The most amazing thing about the Grand Canyon, apart from its sheer size and incredible variety of shapes and colors, is how different it looks when viewed from different places (artist David Hockney has said that the Grand Canyon is the only place on Earth that makes you want to look in all directions—up, down and side to side—at the same time), so be sure to check it out from as many angles, and at as many different times of day, as you can. A book like this one can do little more than hint at all there is to see and do, but if you have time for nothing else, take a quick hike down into the canyon to get a real sense of its truly awesome scale.

The great majority of the more than five million people who visit the Grand Canyon each year arrive at the South Rim and gaze down into the Grand Canyon from Mather Point, where the entrance road hits the edge of the gorge. The park visitors center and most of the food and lodging is located a mile west at Grand Canyon Village. Beyond Grand Canyon Village, West Rim Drive winds west, leading past the J.W. Powell Memorial at Hopi Point (from where you get great views of the Colorado River, which otherwise can be surprisingly hard to see) and a series of other viewpoints before ending up at Hermit's Rest, eight miles from Grand Canyon Village—where there are yet more stupendous views as well as restrooms, drinking fountains, and a gift shop.

The **West Rim Drive**, which was built for tourists by the Santa Fe Railroad in 1912, is closed to cars throughout summer, but frequent shuttle buses stop at all the viewpoints. A seven-mile hiking trail runs west from the Powell Memorial to Hermit's Rest, and a three-mile paved nature trail links the Powell Memorial with Grand Canyon Village. *(continues)*

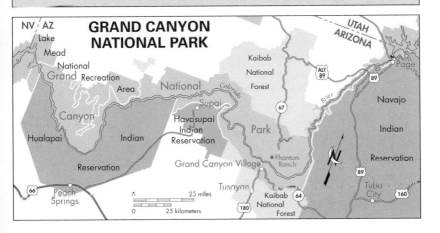

East from Mather Point, **East Rim Drive** runs for 25 miles, stopping first at aptly named Grandview Point, 12 miles from Grand Canyon Village and a half-mile north of the East Rim Drive. This is, literally and figuratively, a high point of any Grand Canyon tour, giving a 270-degree panorama over the entire gorge. Continuing east, the road passes a small Anasazi pueblo at Tusayan Ruins before ending with a bang at **Desert View Watchtower**, an Anasazi-style tower set right at the edge of the canyon. Though it looks ancient, the tower was created for tourists in 1932, designed by Mary Colter, also the architect of the Bright Angel Lodge and most of the wonderful old "Harvey House" hotels that lined Route 66 across the Southwest.

A FREE GOVERNMENT SERVICE
GRAND CANYON
NATIONAL   **PARK**
U.S. DEPARTMENT   NATIONAL PARK
OF THE INTERIOR   SERVICE

From the watchtower, the road continues along the rim through the east entrance, then drops down to the crossroads town of Cameron and the Little Colorado River (see below for more).

Grand Canyon Hikes

To get a real feel for the Grand Canyon, you have to get out of the car, get beyond the often overcrowded viewpoints that line the South Rim, and take a walk down into the depths of the canyon itself. The most popular and best-maintained path, the **Bright Angel Trail**, descends from the west end of Grand Canyon Village, following a route blazed by prospectors in the 1890s. It's an all-day, 17-mile hike down to the Colorado River and back, but there are rest stops (with water) along the way. A shorter day-hike cuts off to **Plateau Point**, 1,300 feet above the river and a 12-mile round trip from the South Rim. If you can finagle a reservation, you can extend the stay (and delay the climb back up) by staying overnight at Phantom Ranch (see below), another three miles from Plateau Point on the north side of the Colorado River, which is traversed by a pair of suspension bridges. Nearby **Bright Angel Campground** has space for more than 100 people, but reservations and a backcountry camping permit are required; call the main visitors center for details.

Another interesting old trail drops down from Grandview Point to Horseshoe Mesa, where you can still see the remnants of an old copper mine that closed in 1907. This a six-mile roundtrip and gives an unforgettable introduction to the Grand Canyon.

Many avid Grand Canyon hikers prefer to start at the comparatively untraveled North Rim. But no matter where you go, when hiking down into the canyon remember that it will take you twice as long to hike back up again, and *always carry water*—especially in summer—at least a quart for every hour you're on the trail.

It may give a sense of the immensity of the Grand Canyon to know that, while the North Rim is a mere 6-10 miles from the South Rim as the crow flies, to get there by road requires a drive of at least 215 miles. See page 380 for detailed coverage of the North Rim, which is much higher (and less visited) than the South Rim, as part of our Canyonlands Loop road trip.

Practicalities

Most of what you'll need to know to enjoy your Grand Canyon visit is contained in the brochure you're given at the entrance, where you pay the $20-per-car fee (Golden Eagle and other passes are accepted). Once in the park, the very good **visitors center** (daily 8 AM-5 PM; 520/638-7888) in Grand Canyon Village has information about the park's many hiking trails, the canyon's geology, the burro rides that take you down and back up again, and anything else to do with the Grand Canyon.

Yaki Point in winter

To make advance reservations for accommodations—a good idea at any time of year but essential in the peak summer months—phone the park concessionaire, **Amfac** (303/297-2757 in advance, 520/638-2631 same-day), which handles reservations for the six very different lodges in Grand Canyon Village. The most characterful and best-value place to stay is the **Bright Angel Lodge**, which overlooks the canyon; the cheapest rooms (around $65) share bathrooms, while others have canyon views and fireplaces (for around $150-200). In between, there are some rustic cabins (around $100). The coffee shop here is open all day, and the lobby fireplace shows off the rock strata, in proper chronological order, that form the walls of the Grand Canyon. The other historic lodge is the **El Tovar Hotel**, built in 1905 but recently renovated; rooms here start around $150 and top out at more than $300 a night. The El Tovar also has the park's best restaurant—and a comfy piano bar to help while away the night.

For a basic motel bed, there are four other lodges in Grand Canyon Village, offering more than 750 rooms altogether, costing $75-125 a night. There's also a very nice lodge at the North Rim, open in summer only.   *(continues)*

It's more of an effort to reach, but the best place to get a feel for the Grand Canyon is splendid **Phantom Ranch**, a rustic complex of cabins and dormitories way down in the canyon, on the north side of the Colorado River. Space here is usually taken up by people on overnight burro-ride packages (which cost around $300), but in off-season particularly you may be able to get a bed without the standard six months (or more) advance reservation. Ask at the desk in the Bright Angel Lodge, or call 520/638-3283.

Tusayan, near the south entrance to the Grand Canyon, is where the park service plans to concentrate all future development, like the massive National Geographic IMAX Theater that gives a 35-minute, $8 taste of the canyon's beauty and immensity—if and when cars and tour buses are finally banned from the South Rim and replaced by the proposed light rail train.

Reservations for camping (800/365-CAMP) at the South Rim are also essential in summer. The largest facility, **Mather Campground,** is across from the visitors center and is open year-round; the more than 300 sites (no hookups) cost $15 a night; coin-operated showers are available. Sites with RV hookups are available at nearby **Trailer Village** (303/297-2757 in advance, 520/638-2631 same-day) for around $20 a night. There's another campground at Desert View, near the east entrance, and backcountry camping (overnight permits required) is available at established sites deep in the canyon.

If all the in-park accommodations are full, hundreds of rooms are available in Williams and Flagstaff, and right outside the park's southern boundary at **Tusayan,** where you can choose from a Best Western, a Holiday Inn Express, and a Quality Inn.

Tusayan (which has the third-busiest airport in Arizona) is also headquarters for a half-dozen companies offering airplane and helicopter tours of the canyon; you can't miss their billboards, but details of prices (think $200 a hour) and trips can be got from operators such as **Papillon** (520/638-2419) or **Grand Canyon Airlines** (520/638-2407).

"VIEW FROM EL TOVAR HOTEL"—GRAND CANYON NATIONAL PARK, ARIZONA.   FROM PAINTING BY GUNNAR WIDFORSS.

discovered. A visitors center (daily 9 AM-5 PM in summer, shorter hours rest of the year; $3) has descriptions of the science behind what goes on here—spectroscopy, red shifts, and expanding universes, for example—and the old telescope, a 24-inch refractor, is open for viewings 8-10 PM most nights in summer. For more detailed information, call the observatory at 520/774-2096.

Flagstaff's other main draw, the **Museum of Northern Arizona** (daily 9 AM-5 PM; $5; 520/774-5213), perches at the edge of a pine-forested canyon three miles northwest of downtown via US-180—the main road to the Grand Canyon. Besides providing background on the geology and natural history of the 130,000-square-mile Colorado Plateau region (highlights include a cross-section of the Grand Canyon and a full-size reconstruction of a fossilized Dilophosaurus), extensive exhibits detail the vibrant human cultures of northern Arizona, from prehistoric Anasazi to contemporary Hopi, Navajo, and Zuni. Founded in 1928 by scientist and artist Harold and Mary Colton, whose pottery, textiles, katsina dolls, and baskets form the core of the 5-million-artifact collection, the museum also has an excellent gift shop featuring fine Native American jewelry.

Flagstaff's San Francisco Street was named not for the California city but for the nearby volcanic peaks, so called by early Spanish missionaries and still held sacred by the native Hopi Indians.

Flagstaff very nearly became an early movie center, when young **Cecil B. DeMille** stopped here briefly while scouting locations to shoot the world's first feature-length film, a Western called *The Squaw Man*. It was snowing in Flagstaff that day, so he moved on to L.A.

Downtown Flagstaff has more than enough espresso bars (probably a dozen within a two-block radius of the train station) to satisfy its many multiply pierced, twentysomething residents. There are also ethnic restaurants specializing in Greek, Thai, German, or Indian, so finding suitable places to eat and drink is not a problem. For breakfast and lunch, it's hard to beat **Kathie's**, a cozy cafe at 7 N. San Francisco Street.

Accommodations, too, are plentiful. You can pick either the motel with the most appealing sign or step back into an earlier time and stay at the classy old **Hotel Monte Vista**, right on old Route 66 at 100 N. San Francisco Street (520/779-6971 or 800/545-3068). It was good enough for Gary Cooper and has been restored to Roaring Twenties splendor.

For more complete listings or other information, contact the **visitors center**, right downtown at 101 W. Route 66 (520/774-9541 or 800/842-7293).

Detour: Sedona and Oak Creek Canyon

Most visitors head for the Grand Canyon, but smaller and still scenic Oak Creek Canyon, just south of Flagstaff, has one great advantage over its world-famous neighbor: you can drive through it, on scenic Hwy-89A. Starting right at the edge of Flagstaff (contained within the Kaibab National Forest, the entire canyon is protected from commercial development), this red sandstone gorge has been cut into the surrounding pine and juniper forests by eons of erosion. The most popular place to enjoy Oak Creek Canyon, **Slide Rock State Park** (daily 8 AM-5 PM, till 6 PM in summer; $5 per car; 520/282-3034), 18 miles south of Flagstaff and seven miles north of Sedona, is a 55-acre day-use-only area focused on the long, natural rock chute for which the park is named. Nearby **Slide Rock Lodge** (520/282-3531) has motel rooms starting around $70 in summer, plus BBQ grills for the do-it-yourself cook; this is about the cheapest indoor accommodation in the area. For camping, try the U.S. Forest Service-operated **Manzanita Campground** (520/282-4119; $10), a mile south of Slide Rock on Hwy-89A.

At the south end of Oak Creek Canyon, 25 miles from Flagstaff, the otherworldy landscape surrounding Sedona (pop. 16,000) has made it one of the nation's most popular haunts—particularly for New Age visitors, who in the past 20 years have made Sedona into a world-famous center for shamanism, psychic chaneling, and aromatherapy. First settled as a farming community around the turn of the 20th century, in the 1950s the red rock spires that dominate the local landscape began to attract the attention of Hollywood movie makers. But Sedona was still a fairly sleepy farm community until as recently as the early 1980s. Since then, it has quadrupled in population, accompanied by mini-malls, franchised fast-food and pink stucco resorts sporting New Ages themes.

Despite the rampant sprawl—and the high hotel rates, which average $140 a night—Sedona is still well worth a look, especially if you can get away from the town and explore some of the surrounding wilderness. Topo maps and information on day-hikes and longer treks are available from the U.S. Forest Service **ranger station**, 250 Brewer Road (520/282-4119). West of Sedona, Hwy-89 runs along the Verde Valley before climbing up into the mountains to the old mining town of Jerome.

Walnut Canyon National Monument

The most easily accessible of the hundreds of different prehistoric settlements all over the southwestern U.S., Walnut Canyon National Monument (daily 8 AM-4 PM, 7 AM-5 PM in summer; $4; 520/526-3367), which contains some 300 identified archaeological sites, is also one of the prettiest places imaginable. Piñon pines and junipers cling to the canyon walls, and walnut trees fill the canyon floor. On the edge of the canyon, a small visitors center gives historical background, but the real interest lies below, on a short—though very steep—path that winds through cliff dwellings tucked into overhangs and ledges 400 feet above the canyon floor.

The entrance to the monument lies seven miles east of Flagstaff, accessible from I-40 exit 204.

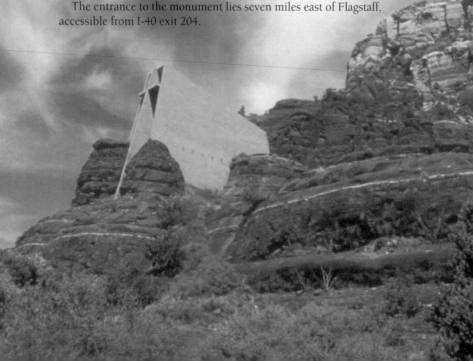

Detour: Sunset Crater and Wupatki National Monument
Running north from Flagstaff toward the Navajo Nation and the east entrance to Grand Canyon National Park, US-89 is a fast, divided four-lane freeway, which makes the change from Flagstaff's green forest to red rock desert plateau all the more swift. Though there isn't much to see right along the highway, the views are amazing in any direction—north across the desiccated Colorado Plateau, east across the colorful Painted Desert, west to the forests of the Kaibab Plateau, or south to the angular San Francisco

Peaks, including 12,663-foot Mount Humphreys, the highest point in Arizona.

This route is somewhat longer than the US-180 route to the Grand Canyon, but in other ways it's far superior—not least because it gives access to a huge variety of scenery and historic sites. The first of these, 12 miles north of Flagstaff and three miles east of US-89, is **Sunset Crater Volcano National Monument** (daily 8 AM-5 PM; $4; 520/526-0502). The 1,000-foot-tall black basalt cone is tinged with streaks of oranges and reds and capped by a sulfur-yellow rim—hence the name, which was bestowed by explorer John Wesley Powell in 1892. You can hike through the lava field that surrounds the cone, but the cone itself is off limits (as is the crater). The visitors center and a basic **campground** (with water, but no showers or hookups; $10) are at the entrance, three miles east of US-89.

Sunset Crater marks the start of a scenic loop that winds around for some 30 miles through neighboring Wupatki National Monument (daily 8 AM-5 PM; $3; 520/ 679-2365). The monument protects the remains of a prehistoric Native American community. The residents are thought to have been ancestors of the Hopi, who lived here between 1100 and 1225 A.D. Hundreds of ruins—most in very fine condition—are spread over the 35,000-acre monument. Coming from Sunset Crater, the first ruin you reach, **Big House**, stands among cinder ones and gives a grand prospect over the Painted Desert stretching to the east. Next comes the small visitors center, then the largest ruin, 100-room **Tall House**, which stands near a ceremonial amphitheater and a very rare ball court, which may indicate a link with the Mayan cultures of Central America.

Cameron is named in memory of a cantankerous prospector-turned-early-promoter of the Grand Canyon. Ralph Cameron blazed the Bright Angel Trail (then charged tourists $1 to use it) and did everything he could to obstruct the government from taking over "his" canyon—even going so far as to get elected U.S. Senator (in 1920) so he could try to eliminate the newly established National Park.

Back on US-89, 20 miles north of the north entrance to Wupatki, the crossroads settlement of Cameron stands at the junction with Hwy-64, which heads up (and up) to the east entrance of Grand Canyon National Park. A mile north of the Hwy-64 junction, along the south bank of the Little Colorado River, historic **Cameron Trading Post** (which also has an $80- a-night motel and an RV park; 520/679-2231) stands next to an equally historic one-lane suspension bridge, built in 1911 (and now carrying an oil pipeline). Cameron makes a good alternative to Tusayan, should all in-park accommodations be full.

From Cameron, Hwy-64 runs west along the Little Colorado River Gorge, which Hopi cosmology considers to be the place where man emerged into the present world. This deep canyon leads into the much larger Grand Canyon, while Hwy-64 climbs for 30 miles up to the east entrance of Grand Canyon National Park, which is described in detail above.

Cameron, at the east end of the Grand Canyon, is near two other road trip routes described in this book. The Canyonlands Loop, which runs north through Monument Valley and west to the North Rim of the Grand Canyon, is described beginning on page 354, while the Four Corners Loop, which tours Santa Fe, Mesa Verde, the Hopi mesas, and the other Native American lands, is described beginning on page 398.

Midway across Arizona, old Route 66 climbs onto the forested (and often snowy) Kaibab Plateau for a look at the mighty Grand Canyon. East of Flagstaff, the old road is effectively submerged beneath the freeway, which drops down to cross desolate desert, passing through desiccated towns and the Petrified Forest National Park. Remnants of numerous old roadside attractions—Indian trading posts, wild animal menageries, and Holbrook's famous "Sleep in a Teepee" Wigwam Village—all survive in varying degrees of preservation along this eastern section of Route 66.

Don't Forget: Winona

East of Flagstaff, following old Route 66 can be a frustrating task, since much of the roadway is blocked off, torn up, or both. Unlike the long stretches found in the western half of Arizona, here the old road exists only in short segments running through towns. Most of the way you're forced to follow the I-40 freeway, turning off at exit after exit. One such short segment runs through the only place mentioned out of sequence in the song "Route 66" ("Flagstaff, Arizona, don't forget Winona"). Alas, today it's little more than a name on the sign at I-40 exit 211.

East of Winona, the route drops swiftly from the cool pines onto the hot red desert, but old-road fanatics will want to take the time to explore what remains of two old-time tourist traps along the next 20 miles of highway. First of these is **Twin Arrows**. If you're lucky, a pair of red arrows will point you toward a small but thriving cafe, right off the freeway at exit 219. Continuing east, approaching exit 230, the freeway crosses deep Diablo Canyon, where an old Route 66 bridge still spans the dry wash, and the walls of a half-dozen bleached buildings are all that's left of the **Two Guns Trading Post** (just south of exit 230). A roadside attraction par excellence, Two Guns had a zoo full of roadrunners, gila monsters, and coyotes—one building still has a sign saying Mountain Lions. According to various reports down the Route 66 grapevine, Two Guns has been on the verge of reopening in recent years, but most of the time the old road is blocked by a sign reading No Trespassing by Order of Two Guns Sheriff Department. That's probably a good thing, since the old buildings are all dangerously close to collapse. It's an evocative site, nonetheless, and photogenic in the right light.

Meteor Crater

Three miles east of Two Guns and six miles south of I-40 exit 233 sits Meteor Crater (daily 8 AM-5 PM, longer hours in summer; $8). This is Arizona's second-most-distinctive hole in the ground, formed by a meteorite some 50,000 years ago and measuring 570 feet deep and nearly a mile across. The crater is a privately owned tourist attraction, offering an Astronauts Hall of Fame as well as a chance to look down into the huge hole (you can't climb down into it, however).

SONGS OF ROUTE 66

"Route 66"

If you ever plan to motor west,
Travel my way, that's the highway that's the best,
Get your kicks on Route 66.

It winds from Chicago to L.A.,
More than 2,000 miles all the way,
Get your kicks on Route 66.

Now you go through St. Looey, Joplin, Missouri
And Oklahoma City is mighty pretty.
You'll see Amarillo, Gallup, New Mexico,
Flagstaff, Arizona, don't forget Winona,
Kingman, Barstow, San Bernardino.

Won't you get hip to this timely tip:
When you make that California trip,
Get your kicks on Route 66.
Get your kicks on Route 66.

One of the most popular road songs ever written, and a prime force behind the international popularity of Route 66, "Route 66" was penned by the late jazz musician and TV actor Bobby Troup in 1946, while he was driving west to seek fame and fortune in Los Angeles. Troup consistently credited his former wife Cynthia, with whom he was traveling, for the half-dozen words of the refrain. The rest of the song simply rattled off the rhyming place-names along the way. Despite its apparent simplicity, it caught the ear of Nat King Cole, who made it into a hit record (Cole also established the definitive pronunciation as "root," rather than "rout," as repeated in later renditions by everyone from Bob Wills to the Rolling Stones).

If you haven't heard the song for a while, the compilation tape and CD *The Songs of the Route 66—Music from the All American Highway* features a jazzy version by Troup himself along with some lively Route 66–related songs, including a world-weary "What's Left of 66" by traveling troubadour Jason Ecklund. The tape or CD is available at souvenir stores en route and from Lazy SOB Records, P.O. Box 49884, Austin, TX 78765.

Winslow

Winslow, Arizona, didn't make it into Bobby Troup's original Route 66 hit list. But the town more than made up for it a generation later with the Eagles tune "Take It Easy," which begins, "Standin' on a corner in Winslow, Arizona," a line that has caused more people to turn off in search of the place than anything else ever has. What you may actually *find* in Winslow is not a lot, actually. Chain motels and fast-food franchises stand at either end of town around the I-40 exits. In between, a

Winslow and Holbrook are the nearest towns to the Navajo Nation Indian Reservation, home of radio station **KTNN 660 AM,** which broadcasts a fascinating mélange of Navajo chants and Jimi Hendrix riffs. It's also the only station in the U.S. that broadcasts Dallas Cowboys football games in Navajo.

couple of cafes and cheap motels are the only signs of life along the old Route 66 frontage, which followed 2nd Street eastbound and 3rd Street westbound.

In between the I-40 and Route 66 is the funky **Old Trails Museum,** 212 Kinsley Street (Tues.-Sat. 1-5 PM; 520/289-5861), which sells a range of "Standin' on the Corner" T-shirts and displays a few reminders of Winslow in its heyday. Down the block, on 2nd and Kinsley, a little sign stakes a claim to being the corner the Eagles sang about. In 1994, Eagles songwriter Don Henley donated $2,500 to help beautify the spot with an appropriate monument.

At the west end of Joseph City, right off I-40 exit 274, stop at the **Jackrabbit Trading Post**—the one whose signs you will probably have noticed over the past hundred miles— and take a picture or buy a postcard of the giant jackrabbit, one of a long line of creatures who have stood here since 1949.

Holbrook

Holding a concentrated dose of old Route 66 character, Holbrook (pop. 4,686) is definitely worth a quick detour off the I-40 freeway. More than the other Route 66 towns in the eastern half of Arizona, it still feels like a real place, with lively cafes and some endearing roadside attractions. Be sure to stop at **Joe and Aggie's Cafe,** at the center of town, or **Romo's,** across the street. And be sure to check out the dinosaur collection outside the **Rainbow Rock Shop,** a block south on Navajo Boulevard near the railroad tracks. Best of all, stop for the night at the marvelous **Wigwam Village,** 811 W. Hopi Drive (520/524-3048), at the western edge of town, and sleep in a concrete tepee. One of about a dozen such accommodations across the country, this one opened in 1950 but was fully modernized in 1988. Rooms cost around $35 a night, so you really should stay here at least once in your life.

Another worthwhile place to stop is the **Navajo County Museum** (Mon.-Fri. 8 AM-5 PM, plus Saturday in summer; free), in the old Navajo County Courthouse, four blocks south of I-40 at the corner of Navajo Boulevard (old Route 66) and Arizona Street. The collections are wide-ranging, and you can walk downstairs to the old county jail, which was in use from 1899 until 1976. The museum is next door to the **Holbrook Chamber of Commerce** (520/524-6558), which has walking- and driving-tour maps and general information on the town.

Painted Desert and
Petrified Forest National Park

The easternmost 60 miles of I-40 across Arizona are little more than a long speedway, since any sign of the old road has been lost beneath the four-lane interstate. One place that's worth a stop here is Petrified Forest National Park (daily dawn-dusk; $10 per car). The polished petrified wood on display in the visitors center is gorgeous to look at, but seeing the stuff in its raw natural state

is not particularly thrilling. The story of how the wood got petrified is interesting, though: about 225 million years ago, a forest was buried in volcanic ash, then slowly embalmed with silica and effectively turned to stone. You can take a look at 93,000 acres of the stuff outside the visitors center.

While the park contains a vast array of prehistoric fossils and pictographs as well as the petrified wood, one of the more interesting sights is the old **Painted Desert Inn**, a Route 66 landmark during the 1920s and 1930s that was converted into a museum and bookstore after the park service took it over in the 1960s. There are no services here, but there's a handy Fred Harvey restaurant and gas station at the visitors center. And the desert views, especially at sunrise or sunset, are worth waiting around to see.

East of the park, along the New Mexico border, Arizona welcomes westbound travelers with an overwhelming display of trading-post tackiness—huge concrete tepees stand at the foot of brilliant red-rock mesas, while gift shops with themes ranging from TV's *F Troop* to *Dances With Wolves* hawk their souvenirs to passing travelers.

Thirty-eight miles north of I-40 from exit 333, a mile west of the town of Ganado, the **Hubbell Trading Post National Historic Site** is a frontier store preserved as it was in the 1870s, when trader John Hubbell began buying the beautiful rugs made by local Navajo weavers.

Stretching for more than a dozen miles across the border between the two states, Hwy-118 runs north of the I-40 freeway, following old Route 66 between exit 357 in Arizona and exit 8 in New Mexico.

Gallup, New Mexico

Despite the obvious poverty and other signs of genuine despair, Gallup (pop. 21,000) is a fascinating town, founded in 1881, when the Santa Fe Railroad first rumbled through. Calling itself The Gateway to Indian Country, because it's the largest town near the huge Navajo and

other Native American reservations, Gallup has some of the Southwest's largest trading posts offering great deals—and one of the best strips of neon signs you'll see anywhere on old 66.

For travelers intent on experiencing a little of the charms of old Route 66, Gallup is home to **El Rancho**, 1000 E. Route 66 (505/863-9311), a delightful old

hotel lovingly restored to its 1930s glory. Built by a man who claimed to be a brother of movie director D.W. Griffiths (his last name was Griffiths, but that was the only actual connection), the El Rancho feels like a national park lodge, with a large but welcoming two-story lobby dominated a huge stone fireplace. All the rooms in the old wing are named for the movie stars who stayed here over the years—W.C. Fields, John Wayne, the Marx Brothers (a room that sleeps six), even Ronald Reagan. Signed glossies of these and many other actors and actresses adorn the halls. Rooms cost $40-75 a night for two people, depending upon the individual room and the time of year. El Rancho also has a good restaurant, serving regional food daily 6 AM-10 PM, and a gift shop selling souvenirs and fine jewelry, pottery, and rugs made by Native American craftspeople. The shop's owner, Armand Ortega, is one of Gallup's most respected crafts dealers.

Gallup also hosts the annual **Inter Tribal Ceremonial**, perhaps the largest Native American gathering in the country. Held every August in Red Rock State Park, eight miles east of Gallup, the event culminates in a Sunday parade that brings 30,000 people out to line old Route 66 through town. For details on the ceremonial, which lasts five or six days and includes a rodeo, traditional dances, powwows, and a beauty show, call 505/863-3896.

For further listings or more information, contact the Gallup **visitors bureau**, on the north side of I-40 exit 22, at 701 Montoya Boulevard (505/863-3841 or 800/242-4282). The staff will no doubt try to direct you away from the many classic motels lining Route 66, such as the **Log Cabin Lodge**, in the middle of town, offering rooms for as little as $15-20 a night, $85 a week. And many of these are indeed sufficiently scary-looking to give your mother sleepless nights. For peace of mind, though (if the El Rancho is fully booked), you'll also find all the usual chains here: three Best Westerns, two Holiday Inns, nearly 2,000 rooms in all.

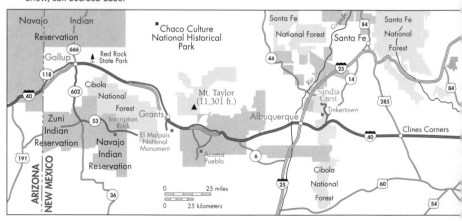

Detour: Inscription Rock and El Malpais

Western New Mexico is among the most beautiful places on the planet. One of the best drives through it, Hwy-53, loops south of I-40 between Gallup and Grants across the Zuni and Ramah Navajo Indian Reservations. Skirting the southern foothills of the 9,000-foot Zuni Mountains, the route follows ancient Indian trails that Coronado used on his ill-fated 16th-century explorations, winding past piñon-covered hills, open grasslands, and the fascinating graffiti collection of El Morro National Monument. Better known as Inscription Rock, El Morro's 200-foot-tall sandstone cliffs have been inscribed by travelers for centuries, including Juan de Oñate, who wrote his name with a flourish in 1605, after he discovered the Gulf of California.

Atop the cliffs are the partially excavated remains of a small Anasazi pueblo dating from around A.D. 1200. A two-mile loop trail to the inscriptions and the ruins starts from a small **visitors center** (daily 8 AM-5 PM; till 7 PM in summer; $4 per car; 505/783-4226), where exhibits outline the history of the site. The trails are closed an hour before sunset, so get here early enough in the day to enjoy the beautiful scenery. There is also a small campground (pit toilets, no showers) amidst the junipers.

East of Inscription Rock, Hwy-53 crosses the Continental Divide (where there's a roadside rest stop), then winds along the edge of the massive El Malpais lava flow—thousands of acres of pitch-black, concrete-hard, glassy sharp rock, capped by volcanic cones and underlain by miles of pitch-black, bat-filled lava tubes. For information, and tips on traveling in the desolate but eerily beautiful area, stop by the small **Malpais Information Center**, on Hwy-53 (505/783-4774) south of I-40 and old Route 66 at Grants.

Of all the stretches of old Route 66 in the Southwest, western New Mexico has the most to see and the most interesting topography, with sandstone mesas looming in the foreground and high, pine-forested peaks rising in the distance. Paralleling the Santa Fe Railroad, the route passes through the heart of this region, and numerous detours—to Inscription Rock and Chaco Canyon, among others—make unforgettable stops along the way.

Every bit as magical and memorable as the cliff dwellings of Mesa Verde National Park, the extensive archaeological remains protected within **Chaco Culture National Historical Park** are well worth your time. Though it's an hour's drive from I-40, mostly via unpaved roads, the park is one of the wonders of the Southwest desert; for details, see the Four Corners Loop on page 408.

Grants

Along with the usual Route 66 range of funky motels and rusty neon signs, the former mining boomtown of Grants is home to the unique attraction of the **New Mexico Museum of Mining** (Mon.-Sat. 9 AM-6 PM, Sunday noon-6 PM; $3), right downtown on old Route 66 (Santa Fe Avenue), at the corner of Iron Avenue. Most of the exhibits trace the short history of local uranium mining, which began in 1950 when a local Navajo rancher, Paddy Martinez, discovered an odd yellow rock that turned out to be high-grade uranium ore. Mines here once produced half the ore mined in the U.S., but production ceased in the early

1980s. From the main gallery, ride the elevator down to the highlight of the museum: a credible re-creation of a uranium mine, complete with an underground lunch room emblazoned with all manner of warning signs.

Across the street from the Mining Museum, the **Uranium Cafe** is still in business (we hope), serving up breakfast and lunch every day and dinner on Friday and Saturday. Just look for the neon atomic-cloud sign, a Route 66 landmark. Motels line the old Route 66 frontage, most with rates in $30-a-night range.

Midway between Grants and Gallup, I-40 crosses the 7,250-foot Continental Divide, where the Top O' the World dance hall used to tempt travelers off old Route 66. From here (exit 47), it's possible to follow the old road for 30 miles, running east along I-40 as far as Grants.

Broadcasting on **530 AM** around the Acoma area, actor Ricardo Montalban narrates the story of the pueblo's conquest by the Spanish, and the story of the building of San Esteban church high atop the mesa.

Acoma Pueblo: Sky City and Enchanted Mesa

A dozen miles east of Grants and 50 miles west of Albuquerque, one of the Southwest's most intriguing sites, Acoma Pueblo, stands atop a 357-foot-tall sandstone mesa. Long known as Sky City, Acoma is one of the very oldest communities in North America, inhabited since A.D. 1150. The views out across the plains are unforgettable—especially the Enchanted Mesa on the horizon to the northeast.

Few people live on the mesa today, though the many adobe houses are used by Pueblo craftspeople, who live down below but come up to the mesa-top to sell their pottery to tourists. To visit, stop at the visitors center at the base of the mesa and join a guided tour (daily 8 AM-4 PM, till 7 PM in summer; $8; 505/470-4966 or 800/747-0181). You're taken by bus to the mesa-top; the tour either begins or ends with a visit to **San Esteban del Rey Mission**, the largest Spanish colonial church in the state. Built in 1629, the church features a roof constructed of huge timbers that were carried from the top of Mount Taylor on the backs of neophyte Indians —a distance of more than 30 miles.

Acoma Pueblo is 15 miles south of I-40, from exit 96 (eastbound) or exit 108 (westbound). Between these two exits, another stretch of old Route 66 survives, passing crumbling tourist courts and service stations and flashy new gambling casinos, across the Laguna and Acoma Indian Reservations.

Albuquerque

Located roughly at the center of New Mexico, the sprawling city of Albuquerque (pop. 463,300) spreads north and south along the banks of the

Rio Grande and east to the foothills of 10,000-foot Sandia Crest. By far the state's biggest city, Albuquerque is a young, energetic, and vibrantly multicultural community. Among many features, it boasts a great stretch of old Route 66 along Central Avenue right through the heart of the city—18 miles of diners, motels, and sparkling neon signs.

Apart from the Route 66 legacy, one of the best parts of the city is **Old Town**, the historic heart of Albuquerque. Located a block north of Central Avenue, at the west end of the route's cruise through the city, Old Town offers a quick taste of New Mexico's Spanish colonial past—with a lovely old church, the circa-1706 San Felipe de Neri—as well as shops and restaurants set around a leafy green plaza. An information booth in the plaza has walking-tour maps of Old Town and other information about the city. Another Old Town attraction—one that carries on the Route 66 tradition of reptile farms and private zoos—is the **Rattlesnake Museum** (daily 10 AM-6 PM; $2), 202 San Felipe Street, where you can see a range of rattlers from tiny babies to full-sized diamondbacks, about 50 altogether.

A very different look into New Mexico's varied cultural makeup is available at the **Indian Pueblo Cultural Center** (daily 9 AM-5:30 PM; $3; 505/843-7270 or 800/766-4405), a block north of I-40, exit 158, at 2401 12th Street. The center is owned and operated by the state's 19 pueblo communities; its highlight is a fine museum tracing the history of the region's Native American cultures, from Anasazi times up to the Pueblo Revolt of 1680. The contemporary era is represented by video presentations and a mock-up of a typical tourist—camera, shorts, and all. There's also a small cafeteria where you can sample food such as fry bread and Navajo tacos. On most weekends, ceremonial dances are held in the central courtyard, free, and open to the general public.

The best range of places to eat lies within walking distance of Old Town. It includes the very good Mexican food at **La Hacienda**, 302 San Felipe Street, with a front porch overlooking the plaza; and the mix of Mexican and American diner food at **Garcia's**, 1736 W. Central Avenue beneath a glorious neon sign. The excellent **Route 66 Diner** was housed in an old Phillips 66 station at 1405 E. Central Avenue, near the University of New Mexico campus, until it burned down in 1995. It reopened in February 1996 and serves top-quality burgers, malts and shakes, and regional specialties such as blue corn pancakes, 8 AM-midnight, Sunday till 10 PM. Another old Route 66 landmark, **Mac's La Sierra**, serves up "Steak in the Rough" and other beefy specialties in a cozy, dark wood dining room west of town at 6217 W. Central Avenue.

As is true throughout most of New Mexico, Albuquerque has a ton of inexpensive accommodations, with all the usual chain motels represented along the interstate frontage roads. For the total Route 66 experience, stay the night at the **El Vado**, 2500 W. Central Avenue (505/243-4594), a well-maintained 1930s motel

Just north of I-40 via Unser Boulevard in Albuquerque, the **Petroglyph National Monument** (505/899-0205) protects some 20,000 ancient rock art pictures, drawn on the volcanic escarpment between 1300 and 1650 A.D.

If you're here in summer, check out a home game of the L.A. Dodgers Class AAA farm club, the **Albuquerque Dukes**. For schedules and prices, call 505/243 1791.

Albuquerque was also the home of the great travel writer and war correspondent **Ernie Pyle**. His old house, at 900 Girard Avenue, a half-mile south of Central Avenue, later became the city's first public library, which includes his collected works and a few personal items on display.

Though most people associate computer giant Microsoft with Seattle, the company actually began here in Albuquerque in 1975, in a series of dingy Route 66 motels.

Albuquerque's "Coyote Radio," **KIOT 102.5 FM,** plays a lively range of alternative popular music, from Hank Williams and John Lee Hooker to Talking Heads and the Grateful Dead.

True completists of the Route 66 tour—and anyone interested in the art and architecture (not to mention food) of the American Southwest—will want to make a detour to the state capital, Santa Fe, which is covered in our Four Corners Loop on pages 412-417. The original Route 66 alignment ran north from Albuquerque along the I-25 corridor, then curved back south from Santa Fe along what's now US-84 to rejoin I-40 west of Santa Rosa. The most interesting driving route between Albuquerque and Santa Fe these days is the Turquoise Trail along Hwy-14, which runs behind Sandia Crest and continues north through Madrid, joining I-25 at La Cienega.

between Old Town and the Rio Grande; it may not be as clean and comfortable as a modern Super 8, but the price is right and the neon sign is fantastic. The nicest old hotel has got to be the grand **La Posada**, a block off old Route 66 at 125 2nd Street (505/242-9090 or 800/777-5732), one of the first inns built by New Mexico-born hotel magnate Conrad Hilton; doubles here start at $85 a night.

For more information, contact the Albuquerque **visitors center**, 121 Tijeras Road (505/842-9918 or 800/733-9918).

Tinkertown and Sandia Crest

Not that there's any shortage of wacky roadside Americana along what's left of Route 66, but one of the most endearing of them all, Tinkertown (daily 9 AM-6 PM April-Oct.; $3; 505/281-5233), is a quick 10-minute drive north of the old road. Like an old-fashioned penny arcade run riot, Tinkertown is a marvelous assemblage of more than a thousand delicately carved miniature wooden figures, arranged in tiny stage sets to act out animated scenes—a circus Big Top complete with side show, a Wild West town with dance hall girls and a squawking vulture—all housed in a ramshackle building made in part out of glass bottles and bicycle wheels, created over the past 45 years by Ross and Carla Ward and family. It's impossible to describe the many odds and ends on show here—one display case holds more than 100 plastic figures taken from the tops of wedding cakes, for example—especially since the whole thing is always being improved and, as it were, tinkered with—but the spirit of the place is aptly summed up in its motto: "We Did All This While You Were Watching TV." The Dalai Lama loved it, and so will you.

To get to Tinkertown, turn off I-40 at exit 175, six miles east of Albuquerque, and follow Hwy-14 for six miles, toward Sandia Crest. Tinkertown is on Hwy-536, 1.5 miles west of the Hwy-14 junction, hidden off the highway among the juniper trees.

Sandia Crest itself is another 12 miles uphill at the end of Hwy-536, a National Scenic Byway; the ridge offers a phenomenal panorama from an elevation of 10,678 feet. Some 80 miles of hiking trails wind through the surrounding Cibola National Forest. Back on Hwy-14, four miles north of I-40, the **Sandia Mountain Hostel** (12234 N. Hwy-14 in Tijeras; 505/281-4117) offers clean bunks in a bike-friendly environment.

Hwy-14: The Turquoise Trail

The most interesting route between Albuquerque and Santa Fe, Hwy-14, continues north behind Sandia Crest along what's now touted as the Turquoise Trail, passing through series of photogenic ghost towns dating from New Mexico's 19th-century mining booms. Much of the gold that was mined in **Golden**, 20 miles north of Albuquerque, played out nearly as quickly as it began. A dozen miles farther along, the much longer-lived town of **Madrid** (usually pronounced MAD-rid), was a booming coal-mining company town in the 1880s. At that point, its population was greater than that of Albuquerque. Madrid was later famed for its annual

*on the
Turquoise
Trail*

displays of Christmas lights (one guidebook says that the airline TWA used to re-route its flights so passengers could see the show). It now boasts dozens of old workers' cottages, many of which have been restored by New Age-minded settlers who have brought Madrid back to life as an arts-and-crafts center.

At the north end of the Turquoise Trail, 20 miles south of Santa Fe, is **Cerrillos**, the town that inspired the name of the route. Responsible for something like 90% of the turquoise mined in ancient North America—stones mined here in pre-colonial times made it as far south as Aztec Mexico—the turqoise mines around Cerrillos were later joined by gold and silver mines, many of which are still being worked. Cerillos still looks the part of a Wild West boomtown, and many movie and TV shows have taken advantage of its dusty streets and 1890s false-front buildings.

Following old Route 66 across New Mexico gives you a great taste of the Land of Enchantment, as the state calls itself on its license plates. There is less of the actual "old road" here than in other places, but the many towns and ghost towns along I-40—built more or less on top of Route 66—still stand.

Santa Rosa

The I-40 freeway has bisected the town of Santa Rosa (pop. 2,263) and cut its old Route 66 frontage in two. But for over 65 years, travelers crossing New Mexico along Route 66 and I-40 made a point of stopping here for a meal at the **Club Cafe**, "The Original Route 66 Restaurant Since 1935." Thanks to signs lining the road for miles in both directions, emblazoned with the smiling face of the "Fat Man," the Club Cafe became nationally famous for its always-fresh food. Despite its "EZ-OFF, EZ-ON" location right along the interstate, the restaurant closed in 1992 but has been on the verge of reopening many times since. If you're lucky, it will be open when you pass through. If not, try Joseph's, on old Route 66 a half-mile southwest of I-40 exit 275, which has very good food at reasonable prices.

Clines Corners, midway between Albuquerque and Santa Rosa, off I-40 exit 218, is a truck-stop cafe that dates back to 1934 and is, as the signs say, Worth Waiting For—for the huge gift shop if not for the unexciting food.

East of Santa Rosa, along the south side of I-40 as far as Cuervo, you can trace one of the older stretches of Route 66—only partly paved, and best traveled in a 4WD or on a mountain bike. Here, you get an indelible sense of what travel was like in the very early days, when less than half of the route's 2,400-odd miles were paved. Another stretch of old Route 66 now serves as the runway for Santa Rosa's small airport.

Along I-40 near Cuervo, Ricardo Montalban broadcasts a brief, State of New Mexico-sponsored history of Route 66 on **530 AM.**

Along the Pecos River via US-84, some 50 miles southwest of Santa Rosa, the gravesite of Wild West legend **Billy the Kid** lies outside the town of Fort Sumner. The grave, two miles east of town, then three miles south, at the end of Billy the Kid Road, is part of a private museum (daily 9 AM-5 PM; $3; 505/355-2942) adjacent to the historic fort—where 7,000 Navajo people were imprisoned from 1864 to 1869.

The line between Texas and New Mexico marks the boundary between central and mountain time zones. Set your clocks and watches accordingly.

In Glenrio, just over the border from New Mexico, a rapidly decaying sign advertises the "First/Last Motel in Texas."

Most of the Texas Panhandle's 20 inches of annual rain falls during summer thunderstorms that sweep across the plains between May and August.

Santa Rosa's other main attraction is the unique **Blue Hole,** an 80-foot wide, 80-foot-deep artesian well filled with crystal clear water. Blue Hole draws scuba divers from throughout the western states to practice their underwater techniques. At around 61°, the water is too cold for casual swimming, but in the summer heat it's a great place to cool your heels. Blue Hole is well signed at the end of Blue Hole Road, a half-mile south of old Route 66.

Tucumcari

Subject of one of the most successful advertising campaigns in Route 66's long history of roadside hype, Tucumcari (pop. 6,831), also known as "the town that's two blocks wide and two miles long," looks and sounds like a much bigger place than it is. In fact, Tucumcari Boulevard, which follows the route blazed by old Route 66 through town, stretches closer to *seven* miles between interstate exits. And the city does have a little of everything, including a great range of neon. But it can be hard to explain the attraction of the town once trumpeted in hundreds of signs reading, "Tucumcari Tonight—2,000 Motel Rooms." (A new ad campaign plays on this legacy, though the signs now read, "Tucumcari Tonight—1,500 Motel Rooms.")

Hype or no hype, Tucumcari is a handy place to break a journey. Even if you think you can make it to the next town east or west, you won't regret stopping here for a night. The famous **Blue Swallow Motel,** 815 E. Tucumcari Boulevard (505/461-9849), which no less an authority than *Smithsonian* magazine called "the last, best, and friendliest of the old-time motels," is under new ownership. But thanks to the warm hospitality of its late owner, Lillian Redman, few who stayed there during her long reign would disagree.

Across Route 66 from the Blue Swallow stands another survivor, the old **Tee Pee Trading Post,** worth a look to add to your collection of Southwest or Route 66 souvenirs. For a place to eat, try the Mexican food at **La Cita,** under the turquoise and pink sombrero at 812 S. 1st Street, on the corner of old Route 66.

Vega and Old Tascosa

Between Amarillo and the New Mexico border, the landscape is identical to what lies east of the city: endless flat plains dotted with occasional oil derricks and Aermotor windmills. Vega, midway between the border and Amarillo, is a sprawling cow town that marks the turnoff onto US-385, which heads north to the remains of Old Tascosa. During the 1870s, the town was one of the wildest on the Texas frontier. Twenty-two miles north of I-40, just east of US-385 on the north bank of the Canadian River, a few buildings, a barbed-wire museum, and an old Boot

CLOVIS' CLAIMS TO FAME: BONES AND ROCK

South of Tucumcari, at the edge of the desolate Llano Estacado that stretches south and east across the Texas Panhandle, the city of Clovis is a large railroad and ranching town that has two unique claims to fame. One is that it was the site of the oldest archaeological remains ever found in North America. In the 1930s, archaeologists dug up bones and arrowheads that proved human habitation dating back as early as 9000 B.C.; some of these artifacts are on display at the **Blackwater Draw Museum** (daily 10 AM-5 PM; $2; 505/562-2202), on US-70 about 10 miles south of Clovis.

Clovis is also semi-famous for having played a part in early rock 'n'roll: Buddy Holly came here from Lubbock, across the Texas border in the late 1950s to record "Peggy Sue," "That'll Be The Day," and other early classics. (Other Lubbockites did the same.) You can tour the restored studios, which are located at 1313 W. 7th Street but open only by appointment (505/356-6422).

For more information, contact the Clovis **chamber of commerce**, 215 N. Main Street (505/763-3435).

Hill cemetery have been preserved; the entire townsite is part of **Cal Farley's Boys Ranch** (daily 8 AM-5 PM; free; 806/372-2341), a working 10,000-acre cattle ranch that doubles as a foster home for some 400 troubled teenagers.

Amarillo

The Texas Panhandle was the southern extent of the buffalo-rich grasslands of the Great Plains, populated by roving bands of Kiowa and Comanche Indians as recently as 100 years ago. At the heart of the Llano Estacado, midway across the Texas Panhandle, Amarillo (pop. 157,615—and do pronounce the "l"s) is a busy big city that retains its cowboy roots as center of the local ranching industry, which

Known as the Panhandle because of the way it juts north from the rest of Texas, this part of the route traverses a nearly-200-mile stretch of pancake-flat plains. Almost devoid of trees or other features, the western half, stretching into New Mexico, is also known as the Llano Estacado (Staked Plains), possibly because early travelers marked their route by driving stakes into the earth.

In Amarillo, radio station **KIXE 940 AM** ("Kicks," as in "get your") plays a lively variety of 1940s swing and earlier jazz, as well as crooners such as Bing and Perry, to help get you in the Route 66 mood. The best alternative is on the other dial, where the local Amarillo College station, 89.9 FM, boasts of playing "less music from dead guys."

raises some two million head of cattle each year. Today, oil and gas production, as well as trucking and Route 66 tourism, have joined ranching as the region's economic basis.

Old Route 66 may have been obliterated by I-40 most of the way across Texas, but in Amarillo it survives as a main business strip, lined with the remains of roadside businesses, a select few of which are still open for a cup of coffee and a sharp taste of the living past. Route 66 followed 6th Street through Amarillo, past the brick-paved blocks of the Old San Jacinto district around Western Avenue—where you can wander amongst ancient-looking gun and saddle shops and numerous Wild West-themed clothing shops. East of downtown, follow East Amarillo Boulevard past a line of authentic honky-tonks around the 20-acre **Western Stockyards**, at Grand Avenue and 3rd Street. Livestock auctions are held here most weekday mornings; Tuesday is the biggest day. Visitors are welcome and there's no entry fee. Phone for details (806/373-7464).

You'll find one health-food place, the **OHMS Cafe**, downtown at 619 S. Tyler Street, but Amarillo is known for its many good steakhouses. These include the **Iron Horse Cafe**, 401 S. Grant Street, housed in the old train depot near the stockyards, and probably the most famous, **Big Texan Steak Ranch**, which started along Route 66 and now stands on the east side of Amarillo off I-40 exit 74, marked by a false-front Wild West town and a giant cowboy atop a billboard. This is the place where your 72-ounce steak is free if you can eat the whole thing—plus a table full of salad, baked potato, and dessert—in under an hour. If you don't make it, the cost is around $50; regular meals and very good non-contest steaks are available as well.

There's a $35-a-night motel featuring a Texas-shaped swimming pool at the **Big Texan** (806/372-5000), and dozens of inexpensive chain motels (two Travelodges, two Comfort Inns) stand along the I-40 and I-27 frontages, so rooms shouldn't be hard to find. For more complete listings or other information, contact the **visitors center** (806/373-7800 or 800/692-1330).

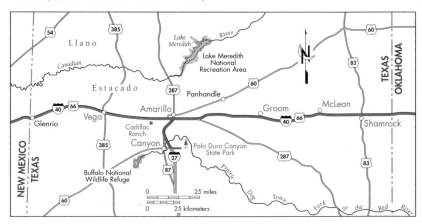

CADILLAC RANCH

No, you're not seeing things—there really *are* nearly a dozen Cadillacs upended in the Texas plain west of Amarillo, roughly midway between Chicago and L.A. Two hundred yards south of I-40 between the Hope Road and Arnot Road exits (62 and 60, respectively), some six miles west of Amarillo, where old US-66 rejoins the interstate, the rusting hulks of 10 classic Caddies are buried nose-down in the dirt, their upended tail fins tracing design changes from 1949 to 1964.

A popular shrine to America's love of the open road, Cadillac Ranch was created by the San Francisco–based Ant Farm artists' and architects' collective in May 1974, under the patronage of eccentric Amarillo helium millionaire Stanley Marsh 3 (not III, please). The cars were all bought—some running, some not—from local junkyards and used-car lots at an average cost of $200 each. Before the Cadillacs were planted, all the hubcaps and wheels were weld-

ed on—a good idea, since most of the time the cars are in a badly vandalized state. Every once in a while, an advertising agency or a rock band will tidy them up for use as backdrops in photo shoots. In August 1997, the Cadillacs got another 15 minutes of fame when Marsh decided to dig them up and move them a mile west from where they'd been—to escape the ever-expanding Amarillo sprawl and preserve the natural horizon.

Visitors are allowed any time, day or night, and there's a well-worn path from the frontage road if you want a closer look.

Palo Duro Canyon State Park

Lovely Palo Duro Canyon, one of the most beautiful places in all of Texas, is just 25 miles southeast of Amarillo, east of the town of Canyon via the I-27 freeway. Cut into the Texas plain by the Prairie Dog Fork of the Red River, Palo Duro stretches for more than 100 miles, with canyon walls climbing to over 1,200 feet. Coronado and company were the first Europeans to lay eyes on the area, and numerous Plains tribes, including Apache, Kiowa, and Comanche, later took refuge here.

From the end of Hwy-217, a well-paved road winds past the park visitors center, from where a short trail leads to a canyon overlook. Beyond here, the road drops down into the canyon and follows the river on a 15-mile loop trip through the canyon's heart. It's prettiest in spring and fall and fairly popular year-round; for more information, or for camping reservations, contact the **visitors center** (daily 8 AM-5 PM; 806/488-2227).

Canyon: Tex the Giant Cowboy

On your way to or from Palo Duro Canyon, be sure to stop by the Cowboy Cafe, on US-60 west of Canyon, marked by the towering statue of Tex, the giant cowboy (47 feet tall and weighing seven tons). Not that you need one, but another great reason to visit Canyon is the excellent **Panhandle-Plains Historical Museum** (Mon.-Sat. 9 AM-5 PM, Sunday 1-5 PM; donations), one of the state's great museums, with extensive exhibits on the cultural and economic life of the Panhandle region and its relations with Mexico, the Texas Republic, and the United States. The museum, which is housed in a WPA-era building on the campus of West Texas A&M University, has a special section on rancher Charles Goodnight, who once owned a half-million acres here and was also an early advocate of saving the bison from extinction. His cabin is preserved in the Pioneer Town behind the museum.

Groom

The town of Groom, 40 miles east of Amarillo on the north side of I-40 at exit 113, holds two of the more eye-catching sights along old Route 66. One of these is a water tower that leans like the Tower of Pisa, causing drivers to stop and rub their eyes, then pull out the camera to take some snapshots to show the folks back home. The other landmark is even harder to miss: a gigantic stainless steel cross, erected by a religious group in 1995 and easily 150 feet tall.

Both of these sights are along the I-40 freeway, but if you head south into town, another photo opportunity awaits: the ruins of the 66 Courts motel court, highlighted by a rusty old Edsel in the driveway.

McLean

Founded around the turn of 20th century by an English rancher, Alfred Rowe (who later lost his life on the *Titanic* in 1912), McLean is now perhaps the most evocative town along on old Route 66. Bypassed only in the early 1980s, the old main drag is eerily silent, with a few businesses—a barber shop, a boot shop, and some motels, including one with a fine Texas-shaped neon sign—holding on despite the drop in passing trade.

McLean is now headquarters of the state's **Historic Route 66 Association**, and efforts are being made to preserve the town in prime condition. This explains the lovingly restored Phillips 66 station at 1st and Gray Streets, and the many other odds and ends on display around town. The center of activity here is the wonderful **Devil's Rope Museum** (Tues.-Sat. 10 AM-4 PM, Sunday 1-4 PM—or "as long as people keep coming"; free; 806/779-2225), 100 S. Kingsley Street, at the east end of downtown. The museum has a huge room full of barbed wire ("devil's rope") and some of the most entertaining and educational collections of Route 66 memorabilia you'll find anywhere. No hype, just lots of good stuff and friendly people telling you all about it.

East of McLean along the old Route 66 frontage, north of the freeway near exit 148, a skeletal sign commands: Rattlesnakes Exit Here. McLean marks the end of our Route 66 tour across the Southwest; sights peter out east of here, though a few remnants still stand, awaiting nostalgic photographers. A nice stretch of late-model Route 66 continues through the little town of Erick, Oklahoma, where the old highway has been renamed Roger Miller Boulevard in memory of the late "King of the Road," who grew up there. To follow Route 66 east to Chicago, pick up a copy of *Road Trip USA: Cross-Country Adventures on America's Two-Lane Highways.*

SOUTHERN PACIFIC: US-80

SOUTHERN PACIFIC: US-80

Following old US-80 and its contemporary equivalents along the US-Mexico border takes you through more varied cultural and physical landscapes than you'd probably expect. Throughout this journey you can shift from one world to another and another—from bustling city to endless desert to pine forested mountains—in the time it takes to eat a taco or two.

From the Pacific bays and golden beaches of San Diego, you can choose between two routes as you head east across Southern California: the high-speed I-8 freeway, or a more winding drive along the Mexican border. We've focused on the slower, more southerly route that follows the remnants of old US-80 through sleepy border towns and past a pair of unique roadside attractions—the funky old Desert View Tower, and the oddly endearing "Official Center of the World" at tiny Felicity. Also included is a quick side trip south of the border to beer-making Tecate. But no matter which way you choose, eventually you'll have to cross many monotonous miles of barren, dry, and inhospitable desert.

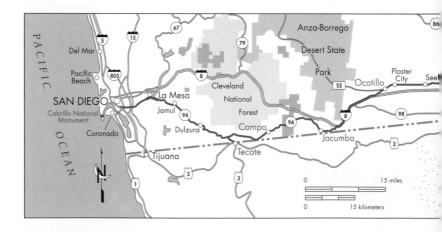

Between the Colorado River, which divides Arizona from California, and the Phoenix-Tucson megalopolis in the middle of the state, there is not very much to attract the traveler off the freeway. However, a couple of detours can take you to the unique Organ Pipe Cactus National Monument, or even further south, down into Mexico to Puerto Penasco, a quaintly low-key fishing port on the Sea of Cortez. The semi-shortage of interesting places in the western half of Arizona is more than made up for by the wealth of fascinating things to see in the state's southeast corner. Here you'll find such legendary sites as Tombstone—home of Boot Hill and the OK Corral—and other finely presented reminders of the state's Wild West heritage, along with some of Arizona's most beautiful natural scenery.

Between Arizona and Texas, the I-10 freeway has replaced the more congenial two-lane US-80 across the part of New Mexico known as the Bootheel, for the way it steps down toward Old Mexico. Until the Gadsden Purchase of 1853, all this was part of Mexico, and the Hispanic influence definitely still dominates the Anglo-American. The few towns here, like Lordsburg and Deming, were founded and remain primarily based on the railroad, and offer little for the passing traveler, though a long but worthwhile detour takes you from the desert up into the forested mountains, historic homeland of the Apache Indians, to see one of the best-preserved remnants of the prehistoric Anasazi, protected as the Gila Cliff Dwellings National Monument. Continuing east, at least one more place is definitely worth a stop: the historic village of Mesilla, looking like a Western movie set, with adobe cantinas surrounding around a dusty plaza. Mesilla is just south of the region's one big city, Las Cruces, which serves as a gateway to another unique sight: the magical white gypsum dunes of the White Sands National Monument.

South of here along the Rio Grande, after passing through fields of chili peppers and the industrial, international twin cities of El Paso and Juarez, to maximize scenic interest our route bypasses the oil rigs that line old US-80 to follow the significantly more attractive route along US-180 through the beautiful Guadalupe Mountains National Park, a little-visited but absolutely unforgettable wilderness that stands adjacent to the totally different but equally remarkable Carlsbad Caverns National Park. These neighboring parks let you go from some of the world's deepest, largest and most beautiful underground caves to the highest point in Texas; if that's not enough, from here you can take a detour north to visit supposed extraterrestrials in New Mexico's unremarkable UFO capital, Roswell.

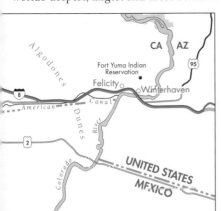

Point Loma: Cabrillo National Monument

The sturdy headland that protects San Diego's extensive harbor from the open Pacific Ocean, Point Loma has long been occupied by the military, whose many fences, radio towers, and gun emplacements all seem to disappear at the very tip, where the Cabrillo

National Monument (daily 9 AM-5 PM; $5 per car; 619/557-5450) protects a breath-taking 150 acres of cliffs and tidepools. Set aside in 1913 to remember the efforts of Portuguese sailor Juan Cabrillo, who explored the California coast in 1542, there's also an old lighthouse, some nice trails, and a visitors center describing the whole shebang.

San Diego marks the southern end of our Pacific Coast Highway road trip, which is described on pages 30-101. For details on visiting San Diego, see the San Diego Survival Guide on pages 99-101.

Across San Diego: Old US-80

From Point Loma and the Pacific Ocean, old US-80 bends south past the airport (named for Charles Lindbergh, and featuring one of the most hair-raising landing patterns of any big American airport) and through downtown along 12th Avenue and Market Street, then veers north again along the Cabrillo Freeway (one of the oldest in the country) through historic Balboa Park, home to the San Diego Zoo, a replica of London's old Globe Theater, and many grand Spanish Colonial-style buildings that have been standing here since the 1915 Panama International Exposition.

East of San Diego, old US-80 follows El Cajon Boulevard, past San Diego State University and a dozen miles of unsightly but surviving motels, cafes, and gas stations, before it reaches the foothill town of La Mesa, where you can leave old US-80 (which runs alongside the high-speed I-8 freeway), and turn onto the two-lane blacktop of Hwy-94. Twisting to the southeast around the 4,000-foot peaks of the Cleveland National Forest, Hwy-94 traverses classic Southern California landscape: rolling, chaparral-covered hillsides rising above grassy ranch lands and stately valley oaks.

Detour: Tecate

After passing through **Jamul** and **Dulzura,** two quiet ranching towns that appear on the verge of extinction as San Diego rapidly approaches, some 40 miles east of downtown along Hwy-94 you'll spot a sign marking the turnoff south to the Mexican border town of Tecate (pop. 45,000). Known around the world as the source of tangy Tecate beer—by most accounts, the brew that started people drinking beer with a squeeze of fresh lime—Tecate is in the top tier of enjoyable border towns, if only by virtue of being cleaner, quieter and much less "touristy" than Tijuana. Potential stops include the usual restaurants, cantinas, and souvenir shops; but the main stop is the **Tecate Brewery** itself, the biggest building in town, located on Avenida Hidalgo a half-dozen blocks from the border. Free **tours** (Saturday 10 AM-4 PM) include samples.

Because of insurance concerns, it's a good idea to leave your car on the U.S. side of the border and cross into Mexico on foot; if you want to make an extended visit into Mexico, consider the drive east along Hwy-2, which winds east through Mexicali and the vast desert of the Pinacate National Park before touching the U.S. border again in southern Arizona, near the Sea of Cortez resort of Puerto Penasco. East of Tecate, Hwy-94 runs along the U.S. side of the border for 41 miles before joining the I-8 freeway.

CROSSING THE BORDER

At dozens of sleepy little towns across Southern California, Arizona, New Mexico, and Texas, the temptation to nip across the border and see something of our southern neighbor can be strong. It's only a hop and a skip away, and the crossing is usually simple and hassle free, but before you go it's good to know a few things about international customs—both in the official and unofficial sense of the word, as the U.S. Customs Service is not something to take lightly.

All that a U.S. citizen needs to cross the border for 72 hours or less (and to be readmitted to the U.S.) is proof of citizenship—a passport, basically—and the burden of proof is on the traveler. Often, you can get by with just a driver's license, or simply an American-looking face, but this is risky business and you could well be turned back. To stay longer or to travel beyond the border areas, you need a *tarjeta de turistica* (tourist card), which is available free of charge from Mexican tourist offices, consulates, or government offices at the ports of entry.

If you're thinking of heading south to stock up on Mexican beers or a rug or other handicraft, note the following rules: all merchandise is subject to a $400 duty-free limit, above which U.S. customs will charge a 10% duty based on fair retail value. Alcohol imports by individuals are limited to a whopping liter every 30 days—about two cans of beer—and it is illegal to import Mexican versions of trademarked items (perfumes, watches, even cans of Coke) that are also sold in the United States. So don't risk having to leave something behind at the border—ask before you buy.

The most important advice I can offer is that, because of insurance and other legal concerns, you should leave your car on the U.S. side of the border and cross into Mexico on foot. If you do want to drive across, be sure you have a policy that specifically covers travel in Mexico—the travel club AAA is a good source, since these policies must be written by Mexican companies, and they have reciprocal contacts. Insurance, which costs around $3 a day plus a small one-time administration fee, is essential—if you are involved in any kind of collision in Mexico, even a tiny fender bender, the police are required to impound the cars and hold the drivers in jail until the responsibilities are decided—not how you want to spend your time. If you're tempted to cross the border simply to fill up on cheap Mexican gas, be aware that prices are often much higher in Mexico than in the U.S. Also, because of a different rating method, the 92 octane unleaded ("Magna Sin" in Mexico) is the same as 87 octane gas in the U.S.

For more detailed information on traveling across the border, pick up a copy of Joe Cummings's excellent *Northern Mexico Handbook* (800/345-5473).

Campo

Campo marks the southern end of the **Pacific Crest Trail**, which winds for 2,638 miles between Canada and Mexico.

Set in a broad valley midway between Tecate and the I-8 freeway, tiny Campo (pop. 1,102) has one main attraction, the **San Diego Railroad Museum** (Saturday, Sunday, and holidays 9 AM-5 PM; free; 619/595-3030), easy to find at the west end of town on Forest Gate Road. Along with an extensive outdoor collection of old locomotives and carriages, the museum offers rides (11 AM and 2:30 PM; $10) on restored steam- and diesel-powered trains, including a 16-mile round trip through the surrounding countryside. Occasionally, the museum also offers all-day trips ($35) south to Tecate, Mexico.

Jacumba

South of the I-8 freeway on a surviving stretch of the old US-80 highway, Jacumba is a former spa and resort town where Clark Gable, Marlene Dietrich, and countless others soaked themselves silly in the free-flowing natural hot springs. Established in 1852 as a station on the stagecoach mail route across the desert, Jacumba had its heyday during the 1920s, and while little remains apart from the water, it makes a great offbeat place to stop. The mineral-rich hot springs still flow into outdoor pools and private Jacuzzis at **Jacumba Hot Springs Spa**, 44500 Old US-80 (760/766-4333), which includes motel rooms for around $40, and has a good on-site restaurant and bar.

Ocotillo: The Desert View Tower

For more information on visiting **Anza-Borrego State Park,** see our Central Valley and National Parks: Hwy-99 chapter on pages 152-153, or contact the ranger station in Borrego Springs (760/767-4205).

Southern gateway to the splendid, 600,000-acre Anza-Borrego State Park, the largest and wildest desert park in the country, Ocotillo lies north of the I-8 freeway on the old US-80 highway (designated S2 on maps). Ocotillo itself is little more than a gas station-cum-grocery store, bar, and volunteer fire station, but five miles west of town the Desert View Tower (daily 9 AM-5 PM; $3; 760/766-4612) is well worth searching out. The four-story, cut-stone structure was built in 1922 by Burt Vaughn (who owned much of neighboring Jacumba) to commemorate the pioneers who struggled across the arid desert. Inside the tower, a small but interesting museum displays a haphazard collection of desert Americana such as Navajo blankets and Native American artifacts, with similar items on sale in the gift shop. At the top of the tower, an observation platform offers views across 100 miles of desert landscape, sliced by the I-8 freeway.

Across the parking lot from the tower, a hillside of quartz granite boulders has been carved with dozens of three-dimensional figures. Most of the figures are of skulls, snakes, and lizards—with real lizards sometimes racing each other across the rocks—and the whole ensemble was created during the Depression by an out-of-work engineer named W.T. Ratliffe.

The Desert View Tower stands at a cool 3,000 feet above sea level, six miles east of the Jacumba turnoff from I-8, at the In-Ko-Pah Road exit; billboards point the way. East of the tower, old US-80 is designated as S80 and runs parallel to I-8 all the way east to El Centro, passing through ghostly old industrial towns like Seeley and Plaster City, where a section of original US-80 roadbed survives along the south side of the current highway.

El Centro

Located some 50 feet below sea level, midway across California at the heart of the agricultural Imperial Valley, El Centro (pop. 31, 384) was founded in 1905 and has since bloomed into a bustling small city, thanks to irrigation water diverted from the Colorado River. Melons, grapefruit, and dates are the region's prime agricultural products, along with alfalfa grown to feed the many dairy cows. There's not a lot here that doesn't depend upon farming.

El Centro is the best place to break a journey between San Diego and the Arizona border; fill your gas tank if nothing else. Places to eat include **Millie's Restaurant**, a popular truck-stop cafe on 4th Street south of I-8, and the usual franchise fast-food places. All the national motel chains are here as well, along with neon-signed local ones along the I-8 Business Loop, advertising rooms for as little as $18 a night.

The Algodones Dunes

In the middle of the southern Mojave Desert, 42 miles east of El Centro, a rest area south of the I-8 freeway at the Grays Well Road exit gives access to the enticing sands of the Algodones Dunes, which stretch to both sides of the freeway for over 50 miles. (The much-wilder northern end of the Algodones Dunes is covered on page 153.) The slender dunes, which measure over 10 miles across and reach heights of 200 feet, sometimes cover the highway in blowing sandstorms. Though you can amble around on foot, be aware that the dunes themselves are under constant abuse from hordes of motorcycles and dune buggies.

If you're really really interested in old highways, you won't want to miss the reconstructed remnants of a **wooden plank road**, built across the sands in 1914 and later used as part of the original US-80 highway. Preserved by the dry desert air, and arranged to form a 100-foot section across the dunes, this fenced-off museum

From atop the Desert View Tower, you can see places where the excavations for I-8 have left sections of the old US-80 roadway stranded on man-made mesas, 50 feet or more higher than the modern freeway

From 1858 to 1861 the original **Butterfield Stage**, which carried mail and passengers from St. Louis to San Francisco, followed the approximate route of I-8 across Southern California. The route across the desert was originally blazed by Spanish explorer Juan de Anza, on his way from Mexico to found San Francisco in 1775.

El Centro is the winter home of the aerial acrobats of the U.S. Navy's **Blue Angels,** who can sometimes be spotted practicing their loops and rolls in the skies above the city. El Centro is also the birthplace of **Cher.**

From El Centro, it's a quick 10 miles south across the Mexican border to **Mexicali,** capital of Baja California and a busy big city focused more on commerce than on catering to tourists.

When driving in the desert, always keep the gas tank as full as possible, and always carry at least one gallon of drinking water per person. In case of trouble, stay with your car. Don't walk off in search of help; let it find you.

piece is along the south side of the I-8 freeway, two miles west of the Grey's Well Road exit. The All-American Canal, which waters the Coachella Valley, runs along the north side of the I-8 freeway.

FELICITY, CALIFORNIA USA

Felicity: "The Center of the World Pyramid"

One of the odder sites in the desert Southwest—and competition for this title is pretty fierce—sits just north of the I-8 freeway in the tiny but happily named town of Felicity (pop. four). Local resident Jacques-Andres Istel—author of a children's fairy tale concerning a scholarly, firebreathing dragon named Coe who lives at the center of the world reading fireproof books and eating the nearby Chocolate Mountains—convinced France, China, and Imperial County that Felicity is, legally and officially, the center of the world.

A 25-foot-high pink terrazzo pyramid stands above the exact spot, which you can visit on regular guided **tours** (daily 10 AM-5 PM, late November to mid-April only; $1; 760/572-0100); the fee also buys a certificate saying you've stood at "The Official Center of the World." You can climb a set of stairs that used to belong to the Eiffel Tower and sift through sundry souvenirs in the gift shop.

Winterhaven

The last California town before the Colorado River, Winterhaven is the modest center of the Quechan community on 44,000-acre Fort Yuma Indian Reservation. A few reminders of its pre- and post-colonial past are displayed inside the small **Fort Yuma Indian Museum** (daily 8 AM-noon, 1-4 PM; $1; 760/572-0661) alongside the white-walled St. Thomas missionary church. Both structures overlook the Colorado River from atop Indian Hill off the end of 1st Street.

The **Colorado River** forms the border between California and Arizona, (and Arizona and Mexico), and marks the line between the Pacific and mountain time zones.

Yuma

Among the hottest and driest towns in the country, Yuma (pop. 57,000) was first settled in 1779 at the site of one of the few good crossings along the Colorado River. Dozens of decaying old adobe buildings around town testify to Yuma's lengthy history, and a select few places are preserved as historic parks.

The **Yuma Crossing** (daily 10 AM-5 PM; $3; 520/329-0471), along the river and I-8 at 206 N. 4th Avenue, has been restored to its appearance prior to the arrival of the railroad in 1876, when supplies for U.S. troops throughout the Southwest arrived here by steamboat from the Gulf of California.

407 OCEAN TO OCEAN HIGHWAY AND SOUTHERN PACIFIC BRIDGES.

ACROSS THE COLORADO RIVER, YUMA, ARIZONA

At the time the railroad arrived, a full century after its founding by Spanish missionaries, Yuma became the site of Arizona Territory's main prison. Built in 1876 out of stone and adobe by convicts struggling in the 120° heat, over the next 33 years until it was closed in 1909, the prison earned a reputation as the "Hellhole of Arizona," due in large part to the summer heat and the brutality of its regime, though park rangers emphasize the fact that the 3,000 prisoners had access to a library and other facilities unusual at the time. Now preserved as the state-run **Yuma Territorial Prison** (daily 8 AM-5 PM; $3), well-posted along the north side of I-8 at the 4th Avenue exit, the site consists of a few of the cells and the main gate, as well as a small museum.

From the prison, a rickety pedestrians-only steel bridge leads across the Colorado River to California and the **St. Thomas mission church** on the Quechan Indian Fort Yuma Reservation. The entire riverfront area, much of it under the I-8 bridge, is being restored as the Yuma Crossing State Historical Park.

Along with the usual national franchises, Yuma has a number of decent places to eat, ranging from the big breakfasts and afternoon BBQ at **Brownie's Cafe**, open daily 6 AM-9 PM at 1145 S. 4th Avenue (old US-80), to the pool tables, burgers, and sandwiches at ancient **Lutes Casino** 221 S. Main Street (520/782-2192) in the historic old downtown area. Voted the "Best Place to Stop in Yuma" by the *Arizona Republic* newspaper, Lutes is the oldest pool hall in the state (open since 1901) and its friendly barn-like hall full of old photos, political posters, street signs, and all manner of junk, is well worth a look—at least for its passionately played domino games. Children are welcome, and souvenir T-shirts are available.

Along with the national chains (two Motel 6s and a Travelodge), places to sleep in Yuma include the pleasant **Yuma Cabana**, 2151 S. 4th Avenue (520/783-8311 or 800/874-0811), with palm trees, a nice pool and a complimentary breakfast, all for rates in the $40-50 range.

Yuma to Gila Bend: I-8

Spanning 110 miles of barren desert east of Yuma, between the U.S. Air Force's 14 million-acre Barry M. Goldwater Bombing Range and a U.S. Army Proving Ground, the I-8 freeway follows

Along with dozens of Spanish-language stations north and south of the Mexican border, Yuma's **KBLU 560 AM** plays oldies and local news.

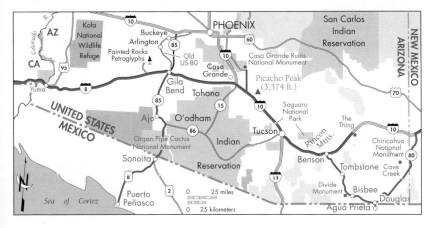

the route of early Spanish explorers and settlers on the flat but forbidding Camino del Diablo, along the banks of the usually dry Gila River.

East of 767-foot-high Telegraph Pass, 20 miles outside Yuma, the old US-80 highway reappears along the north side of the freeway, running through old-time desert outposts. If you're hungry, the flyspeck ranching community of **Tacna** has a great place to eat: **Basque Etchea**. Take I-8 exit 42, then head north across the rail-road tracks. It's open every day but Monday 11 AM-10 PM for burgers and lamb chops and a full menu of other Mexican, American and Basque dishes. **Dateland**, 25 miles farther east along I-8, has a convenience store, a cafe and gift shop selling dates in all possible forms, including milk shakes.

Gila Bend

The only place approaching a town between Yuma and Phoenix or Tucson, Gila Bend (pop. 1,747) is regularly the "Hottest Spot in the Country"—a title of which it is so proud that, more than once, it's been caught inflating the numbers. First settled as a main stop on the Butter-field Stage route, Gila Bend has some photogenic old motels and all the gas stations, rest rooms and restaurants you could reasonably expect to find in the middle of the Arizona desert.

Twenty-two miles west of Gila Bend, off I-8 at exit 102, Painted Rocks Road leads 11 miles north to a BLM-managed site where an array of **petroglyphs**, carved into the boulders by the Hohokam people around A.D. 1400, cover the rocks.

One unique place to eat is the **Outer Limits Coffee Shop**, open 24 hours at 401 E. Pima Avenue, downtown off exit 115. Marked by a flying-saucer-shaped sign, it's part of the **Best Western Space Age Lodge** motel (520/683-2273 or 800/528-1234). Both are essential stops for any Jetsons-aged traveler, though recent refubishment (after a 1998 fire) has diminished some of the Space Age charms.

Old US-80 to Phoenix

I-8 is by far the fastest way east from Gila Bend to Tucson and beyond, but if you have the time and inclination to follow the old road, it took the long way around: from Gila Bend US-80 veered north across the usually dry Gila River along what's now an unmarked county road, looping east through the towns of Arlington, Palo Verde, and **Buckeye**, where a 40-odd-foot statue of "Hobo Joe" stands along Baldy Street, a block south of Monroe Street. East of Buckeye, US-80 ran through downtown Phoenix on Van Buren Street (which was also US-60 and US-70), before heading south to Tucson.

Between Phoenix and Tucson, the I-10 freeway parallels our US-93 road trip route, which runs about 20 miles to the east, along Hwy-79. From Phoenix, the route passes such enticing desert oddities as the famous Biosphere II earthbound space station, and a memorial to cowboy actor Tom Mix. Phoenix and Tucson, and the alternate route between them, are covered on pages 216-225.

If you're interested in following the route of old US-80 across California and western Arizona, pick up a copy of the entertaining and informative *Old US-80 Highway Traveler's Guide,* by Eric J. Finley. Nicely illustrated, with many helpful maps, the 144-page book is available for $13.95 postpaid from Narrow Road Communications, PO Box 42852, Phoenix AZ 85080 (602/996-4595).

Detour on Hwy-85 South: Organ Pipe and Into Mexico

From Gila Bend, Hwy-85 runs south from I-8 toward the beautiful and totally deserted Organ Pipe Cactus National Monument, which lies astride the Mexican border. The first 40 miles runs across the gigantic Luke Air Force Bombing and Gunnery Range that stretches west nearly to California, then passes through the lovely little copper-mining town of **Ajo** (pop. 5,264)—pronounced "AH-ho." Ajo looks like an ancient colonial community, with a pair of churches and an arcade of small shops surrounding a central plaza, right along Hwy-85, but the whole place is actually a modern industrial complex, founded and constructed starting in 1917 by the New Cornelia Mining Company to exploit massive deposits of low-grade copper ore. Despite being the third most productive mine in the U.S., mining ceased in 1986 after a drop in copper prices. Though the town is still tidy and proud, you can't help but notice people here would be a lot happier if the mine—a huge pit cut into the hill, at the top of La Mina Avenue—were still being worked. The Ajo **chamber of commerce,** on Hwy-85 near the plaza (520/387-7742), can help with maps and suggestions of places to eat or sleep.

A dozen miles from Ajo, south of the "Y" in the road that gave a name to the crossroads community of **Why,** the sprawling **Organ Pipe Cactus National**

Monument was named for the candelabra-shaped cactus that grows here and nowhere else in the country. A fine example of Sonoran desert landscape, the park protects all manner of flora and fauna—lizards, birds, foxes, bobcats, and bighorn sheep—as well as its namesake cactus, which is similar to a saguaro but grows many slender arms from a single, central base. Springtime, when wildflowers can turn the desert into a glowing palette of blues, yellows, reds and purples, is definitely the time to be here; in summer, daytime temperatures rarely drop into the double digits.

The main park visitors center (daily 8 AM-5 PM; $4 per car; 520/387-6849), at the south end of the monument, 22 miles south of Why and just five miles from the Mexican border, has the usual interpretive displays to introduce you to this vibrant if dessicated ecosystem. There's a large, first-come first-served campground (water but no RV hookups; $8) across the road, and two scenic drives into the Organ Pipe backcountry start here, too. One heads west into the Puerto Blanco Mountains on a one-way, 53-mile-long dirt road; the other is half as long, and heads east up Ajo Mountain past some of the park's most impressive groupings of Organ Pipe and other cacti.

Before driving into Mexico, be sure you have valid car insurance, since American policies are not valid there; fortunately, Mexican insurance can be purchased from a number of places along the road, and the cost is minimal ($3-5 a day, plus a $10, one-time "policy fee").

Between the border and Puerto Peñasco, to the west of Hwy-8 you can clearly see the gnarled volcanic cerros and pyramid-shaped cones of the **Gran Pinacate**, the otherworldly desert that stretches west to the mouth of the Colorado River.

Rocky Point: Puerto Peñasco, Mexico

When you're stuck in the middle of the Arizona desert, the only ocean you'll see always turns out to be a mirage, but if you head south, over the border into Mexico, the sea is closer than you might think. Just 65 miles from the border, 210 miles from Tucson or Phoenix, the surprisingly quaint shrimp-fishing port of Puerto Peñasco offers respite from the endless desert, and a definite change of pace from the go-getting rat race of contemporary America.

The one and only road to Puerto Peñasco, which many Americans call "Rocky Point," passes through the Organ Pipe Cactus National Monument, hitting the border at **Lukeville**, where in addition to the customs and immigration facilities (which are closed from midnight to 6 AM), there's a gas station, a convenience store (Mexican car insurance sold here; 520/387-3546), and a post office officially named "Gringo Pass, Arizona 85341."

Once in Mexico, pass through the dusty border town streets of Sonoita and follow the well-signed main road (Hwy-8) south for about 60 miles.

Once in Puerto Peñasco, stay on the main road and make your way to the waterfront (called *malecon* in Spanish), where a handful of touristy restaurants overlook the broad open blue waters of the Sea of Cortez. At the whitewashed seafood market, hawkers will insist on selling you bags full of fresh jumbo shrimp (*camarones*), but unless you want to clean and cook your own, eat at **Mary's**, a low-key cafe right on the water, in the middle of the market, selling wonderful fresh tacos made from shrimp or whatever fish was caught that day (usually flounder or mahi-mahi).

Picacho Peak

Looming like a giant battleship alongside the I-10 freeway, 75 miles southeast of Phoenix and 40-odd miles northwest of Tucson, 3,374-foot Picacho Peak has served as a Sonora Desert landmark for as long as there have been people here to see it. Native Americans, Spanish explorers, American pioneers, you name it, they've used the volcanic peak to keep them on track. Now a state park, Picacho Peak also played a role in the Civil War, as the official westernmost battlefield of the war was fought here on April 15, 1862, when a dozen Union soldiers skirmished with 17 Confederate cavalrymen. These days people come here to enjoy the saguaro cactus and the desert wildflowers (in spring mainly, when they're at their most colorful), or to hike to the summit (two miles each way, with roughly 1,500-feet elevation gain) for a desert panorama. The park is open for day use ($4 per car; 520/466-3183) and camping (tents $10, RVs $21).

Saguaro National Park: Tucson Mountain

Northwest of Tucson, the more popular (and free!) half of Saguaro National Park protects extensive stands of saguaro cactus as well as ancient petroglyphs, spring wildflowers, and generally gorgeous desert scenery. From I-10 at Cortaro (exit 246), a loop road runs southwest, then back east through rugged, mountainous terrain; though popular, this road is a great place to get a feel for the Sonora Desert landscape. A newish **visitors center** (daily 8 AM-5 PM; free; 520/733-5158) has details of the many hikes here, the longest of which winds its way to the 4,687-foot summit of Wasson Peak.

There's more hiking, and camping, in the adjacent **Tucson Mountain Park** (520/883-4200), where **Old Tucson Studios** (daily 9 AM-7 PM; $14.95) has the old movie sets used to film more than 300 movies and TV shows; these days, the "action" is mostly staged gunfights and dance hall revues.

Located on a 6,875-foot mountain, 12 (very steep!) miles off Hwy-86 (the road to and from the Organ Pipe Cactus National Monument) and some 56 miles southwest of Tucson, **Kitt Peak National Observatory** controls over 20 different telescopes that run the gamut of traditional and modern technology; the largest are some 500 feet long, and up to 20 stories tall. Learn all about them at the visitors center (daily 10 AM-3:30 PM; $2 donation; 520/318-8726), or take a free tour which, alas, doesn't allow you to look through any of the telescopes.

Halfway across Arizona, and midway between Phoenix and Tucson, near Casa Grande the I-8 freeway merges into the I-10 freeway, the "Christopher Columbus Transcontinental Highway," which runs cross-country between Los Angeles and Jacksonville, FL.

Along the freeway at the foot of Picacho Peak, a sprawling **ostrich farm** lets you feed the ungainly beasts or purchase a variety of ostrich-made products.

The saguaro cactus, whose creamy white blossoms are the Arizona state flower, blooms in April and May.

Tucson Mountain Park is also home to the excellent **Arizona Sonora Desert Museum** (daily 8:30 AM-5 PM, longer hours in summer; $8.95 Dec.-April, $9.95 May-Nov.; 520/883-2702). Apart from spending a lifetime in the desert itself, there's really no better place to get a sense of the abundant flora and fauna of the Sonora Desert than this creatively presented zoological park.

From Tucson Mountain Park, Gates Pass Road drops down into Tucson's main east-west road, Speedway Boulevard.

Across Tucson: Old US-80

From the north and west, the best old road introduction to Tucson is the so-called **Miracle Mile**, a wonderful few blocks of slightly seedy neon-signed old motels, right off the I-10 freeway, exit 255. From here, old US-80 follows a series of one-way surface streets into compact downtown Tucson, first following 5th Avenue, then 6th Avenue, the pre-interstate main highway. South of town, 6th Avenue becomes the Old Nogales Highway, the old road south to Mexico, which crosses the freeway and hits **Benson Highway** (I-10 Business), another old road now serving as a freeway frontage. This is another pretty scruffy part of town, with old motels renting rooms by the month (or by the hour), and you don't miss much by jumping on the I-10 freeway for the ride east.

Tucson, which marks the junction with our road trip along US-93, is covered in the Tucson Survival Guide on pages 223-225.

Saguaro National Park: Rincon Mountains

A dozen miles east of Tucson, on the slopes of the Tanque Verde and Rincon Mountains, the eastern half of the fabulous Saguaro National Park covers 57,000

acres of rolling desert landscape, which climbs through oak woodland up to conifer forest at the park's highest elevations. Named in honor of the anthropomorphic saguaro (SWA-row) cactus, which here reach heights upwards of 40 feet and live as long as 200 years, the monument is best seen by following one-way, eight-mile Cactus Forest Drive, along which numerous trails give close-up looks at the multi-limbed succulents. For more information, and details of hiking and overnight backpacking opportunities, stop at the **visitors center** (daily 8 AM-5 PM; 520/733-5153), where the $5-per-car entry fee is collected.

South and east from the Rincon Mountains on the historic "Old Spanish Trail" highway, or seven miles north from I-10 exit 279, **Colossal Cave** (daily 9 AM-5 PM, longer hours in summer; $7.50; 520/647-7275) is a huge old limestone cavern (said by some to be the largest of its type in the world) which offers, if nothing else, a cool escape from the sweltering summer heat. One of the state's most enduring tourist attractions, Colossal Cave was used in Wild West times by a group of train robbers who escaped here with $62,000; the money bags were recovered, but not the money.

Benson and Kartchner Caverns State Park

On the banks of the San Pedro River, Benson (pop. approx. 4,000), already home to a large and stable population, was founded as a Santa Fe railroad connection to booming Tombstone and the Mexican harbor town of Guaymas. Trains still rumble through town, but there's not much to see apart from fading roadside signs. The **Horse Shoe Cafe**, 154 E. 4th Street across from the railroad tracks, is where locals have been going to eat since 1937. Four chain motels (a Super 8, a Best Western, a Day's Inn and a Holiday Inn Express) stand along I-10 at exit 304.

> Benson's radio station **KAVV 97.7 FM** plays lots of good Waylon-and-Willie-type country hits, plus captivating accounts of local news and activities.

Though Amtrak trains now stop here only by advance request, Benson's railroad heritage is kept alive by the entertaining **San Pedro and Southwestern Railroad** (schedule varies; trips cost $26; 520/586-2266), which winds far from any road along the San Pedro River, ending up at the ghost town of Charleston, 26 miles away.

Near Benson, one of Arizona's most long-awaited "openings" has been that of **Kartchner Caverns State Park**, a massive limestone cavern—over two miles long —that is rated by experts as one of the 10 most beautiful in the world. Discovered by a pair of avid cavers back in 1974, it took 25 years of negotiation and $27 million worth of careful construction of tunnels and facilities before the cave was opened to the general public in November 1999. Since people have been waiting so long for the caverns to be open, for now advance reservations are all but required if you want to take a tour ($14) of the 150-foot-square Throne Room, with its 60-foot ceiling, or the larger but less lofty Rotunda. The caverns, which are kept at near 100% humidity by a set of air-locks at the entrance, are remarkable for their diverse and delicate formations, including over 30 different types of stalactites, stalagmites, columns, draperies, shields and helictities, not to mention the longest "soda straw" in the U.S.—a thin tube of limestone over 21 feet long but only a quarter-inch in diameter.

Kartchner Caverns State Park is south of I-10 exit 302, nine miles from Benson via Hwy-90; if you don't manage to join a tour, it's still worth stopping at the 23,000-square-foot **visitors center** (daily 7:30 AM-6 PM; $10 per vehicle; 520/586-4100), which includes videos of the cave and full-scale replicas of its features (including the famous "soda straw"). There's also an above-ground hiking trail through native hummingbird habitat, and a 63-site campground ($15) with full hookups.

> The **Willcox Commercial Store** on Railroad Avenue downtown is the oldest commercial building in Arizona—Geronimo used to shop here. On the same block is the **Rex Allen Arizona Cowboy Museum**, which explores the life, times and sequined wardrobe of the Willcox-born movie and TV star.

I-10: Amerind Foundation and The Thing!

From Benson, our main route cuts south on old US-80 (now Hwy 80) toward Tombstone and Bisbee, while I-10 races east over mountains that 100-plus years ago were a stronghold of Apache warriors under Geronimo and Cochise. If you're following the interstate, a couple of sights are worth looking for. The more satisfying of these, the Amerind Foundation Museum (daily 10 AM-4 PM; closed Monday and Tuesday in summer; $3; 520/586-3666), lies 12 miles east of Benson, off Dragoon Road a mile southeast of I-10 exit 318. Started in 1937, the private, nonprofit museum is devoted to the study of local Native American cultures, with everything from ancient arrowheads to contemporary Pueblo pottery on display in the spacious mission-style buildings. Not surprisingly, the best collections are of Hopi, Navajo, and Apache artifacts, with well-presented exhibits of ceremonial and domestic objects—kachina dolls, rugs, and ritual costumes.

Advertised by signs all along the freeway, one of the country's odder roadside attractions stands atop 4,975-foot Texas Summit, between Benson and Willcox along I-10 at exit 322: **The Thing** (hours vary; 75 cents admission). A gas station, a gift shop, and a Dairy Queen stand in front of a prefab shed full of stuff ranging from a Rolls Royce once used by Adolf Hitler to The Thing itself, a mummified corpse whose "secret identity" has yet to be revealed. "What is it?" the signs ask . . . .

In the mountains north of Willcox, 30 miles from I-10 exit 340 along a bumpy dirt road, the Nature Conservancy operates the remote **Muleshoe Ranch Preserve** (520/586-7072), offering overnight lodgings in adobe casitas or a two-room stone cabin ($75-100 a night for two people), plus a small campground (water, but no RV hookups; $6). Especially in spring, birdwatchers flock to the preserve, which sits along a year-round stream at the foot of the Galiuro Mountains.

East of The Thing, the town of Willcox is another old railroad town, which during the winter is famous for its migratory **sandhill cranes**, some 10,000 of whom linger south of town at the seasonal lake known as Willcox Playa, which is visible from I-10. In early fall, don't be surprised to see apple orchards being harvested: Willcox is at the heart of Arizona's prime apple growing region, and while it's not on the scale of Washington state, there are seasonal fruit stands along most local country roads. Willcox is also the best turnoff from I-10 for visitors heading to the lovely Chiricahua National Monument, described below.

Tombstone

While I-10 races east over the mountains between Tucson and New Mexico, a more scenic route, promoted by tourism authorities as the Cochise Trail, winds south on old US-80 through the Wild West town of Tombstone, "The Town too Tough to Die." The route loops along the Mexican border before rejoining I-10 across the New Mexico border.

Though it's just 22 miles south of the freeway, and regularly inundated by bikers, RVers and busloads of tourists, the rough-and-ready mining town of Tombstone (pop. 1,220) has kept itself looking pretty much as it did back in the 1880s, when 10,000 miners called it home and one of the more mythic events of the Wild West took place here: the shoot-out at the OK Corral.

Historians, and everyone in Tombstone, still debate the chain of events of October 26, 1881. Was Wyatt Earp a sharp-shooting savior, out to make Tombstone safe for decent society? Or was he really a grandstanding cowboy whom history has romanticized? Decide for yourself after hearing all sides of the story. The **OK Corral** (daily 8 AM-5 PM; $2.50) is still there, a block south of Fremont Street (old US-80), on Allen Street between 3rd and 4th Streets, with life-sized, black-leather-clad figures taking the places of Virgil and Wyatt Earp facing down the Clanton brothers. Next door to the OK Corral, the entertaining **Historama** (daily 9 AM-4 PM; $2.50) re-creates the events at the OK Corral through animatronic figures and a movie narrated by none other than Vincent Price.

The dead men, and many hundreds of others, ended up at **Boot Hill Cemetery** (daily 8 AM-6 PM; free), along the highway at the northern edge of town, where you can wander among the wooden grave markers inscribed with all manner of rhyming epitaphs. (An example: "Here lies Lester Moore, Four slugs from a .44, No Les, No More.") The Boot Hill Cemetery is the real thing, and the souvenirs in the large gift shop at the entrance are as wonderfully tacky as they come.

Though the OK Corral and Boot Hill are both fun, the best place to learn about Tombstone's real, as opposed to mythic, history is at the **Tombstone Courthouse State Historic Park**, at 3rd and Toughnut Streets (daily 8 AM-4 PM; $2.50). Built in 1882, and in use until the 1930s, this old courthouse building holds 12,000 square feet of artifacts (including an authentic gallows from the 1880s) documenting and describing the *real* Wild West.

Considering the huge numbers of people who descend upon Tombstone every day, and the gauntlet of T-shirt shops catering to them, the town is still a very appealing place to visit. Eat breakfast, lunch, or dinner at family-friendly **Nellie Cashman's**, 5th and Toughnut Streets, Tombstone's oldest eatery, founded in 1882 by the eponymous Irishwoman. Enjoy a cold beer or a "shot of whisky in a dirty glass," at the **Crystal Palace Saloon**, 420 E. Allen Street, or at the local biker hangout **Legends of the West**, two doors down at 414 E. Allen Street. Places to stay are not extensive, nor very expensive: try the centrally located, $50-a-night **Tombstone Motel**, on the main road at 502 E. Fremont Street (520/457-3478), or the slightly plusher Best Western, a mile north.

Every summer, every day—sometimes every hour on the hour—theatrical **gunfights** are reenacted all around Tombstone, at places like "Six Gun City" just south of the historic area, and in mid-October, the whole town comes alive with a weekend of shoot-outs and parades during Helldorado Days. Tough-looking "outlaws" hand out flyers to drum up business all over town, but for details and schedules in advance, contact the Tombstone **visitors center,** 4th and Allen Streets (520/457-2211).

FLY'S PHOTOS

Wild West photographer Camilius S. Fly, whose work forms one of the primary records of life in frontier Arizona, had his main studio in Tombstone, now restored as part of the OK Corral. What Matthew Brady was to the Civil War, Fly was to Tombstone in its 1880s heyday. His images, displayed in the small gallery, include some of the earliest photos taken of Chiricahua Apache warrior Geronimo, as well as shots of Wyatt Earp, "Doc" Holliday, and many others.

Divide Monument

About 20 miles southeast of Tombstone, three miles west of Bisbee at the 6,030-foot Mule Pass summit of old US-80, the much-abused stone obelisk of the Divide Monument commemorates the convict-laborers who first constructed the road in 1913. The monument stands in a somewhat scruffy parking area directly above the modern tunnel, and from it you get a great panorama view of the surrounding Mule Mountains.

Bisbee

Bisbee offers what has to be the most unusual accommodations in Arizona: the **Shady Dell RV Park,** on US-80 a mile east of Bisbee at 1 Douglas Road (520/432-3567), where you can stay the night—or longer—in one of seven well-restored 1940s Airstream, Silver Streak, and Spartanette trailers, all filled with period furnishings. Rates are a bargain $30-45 per night, and include use of a VCR stocked with classic B-movies. You can also pitch a tent or pull up your own RV, too. And don't miss the Shady Dell's vintage Valentine diner, named **Dot's,** serving breakfast and lunch Tues.-Saturday.

A classic boom-and-bust mining town, Bisbee (pop. 6,288) is one of the most satisfying off-beat destinations in Arizona, combining scenic beauty, palpable history and a good range of places to eat, drink, and enjoy yourself. Climbing up winding streets lined by 100-year-old structures—Victorian cottages, board shacks, and stately brick churches—Bisbee has attracted a diverse population of desert rats, bikers, working artists, and New Age apostles, all of whom mix amiably in the town's cafes and bars.

The heart of Bisbee—which around the turn of the 20th century was the largest city between El Paso and the West Coast—lies north of old US-80 along Main Street, stretching west from the **Bisbee Mining and Historical Museum** (daily 10 AM-4 PM; $3), which displays dioramas, old photos, and sundry artifacts inside the old Phelps Dodge company headquarters. Main Street has many cafes, antique shops, art galleries, and restaurants.

The main event in Bisbee is the **Queen Mine**, which was in operation until WW II. Put on a hard hat and a miner's lamp, and take a train ride down into the mine shafts and tunnels (where the temperature averages 47° F), where retired miners will give you an unforgettable feel for what used to be Arizona's main industry. Hour-long **tours** (daily 9 AM-3:30 PM; $10; 520/432-2071) leave every 90 minutes from the Queen Mine building, just south of downtown along old US-80.

One of Arizona's most unforgettable sights, the massive **Lavender Open Pit** forms a gigantic polychrome crater along Hwy-80, just south of the Queen Mine. Named not for its color—which is more rusty red than purple—but for a mine superintendent, Harry Lavender, this was a true glory hole with ore deposits that provided the bulk of Bisbee's eight billion pounds of copper before they were shut down in 1974. The Queen Mine also offers hour-long tours ($7) of this mile-wide, 1,000-foot-deep pit.

At the center of Bisbee, the **Copper Queen Hotel**, looming over downtown at 11 Howell Street (520/432-2216), has been the best place to stay since it opened in 1902. Most of the rooms have been upgraded to include modern conveniences without losing their old-fashioned charm, and rates start at around $75. Another nice place to stay is the **Bisbee Inn**, 450 K Street (520/432-5131), at the far eastern edge of downtown, overlooking Brewery Gulch and offering 20 antique-furnished B&B rooms (some with shared bathrooms) from about $50-80 for two.

The Copper Queen Hotel has a good restaurant and popular bar; other good bets include the cafes on the plaza next door. For a much-better-than-average dinner (Wed.-Sat. only), try the gourmet **Cafe Roka**, in the center of town at 35 Main Street (520/432-5153). Brewery Gulch, which runs north from Main Street at the east side of downtown Bisbee, once held over 50 different saloons and gambling parlors; it's considerably quieter now, but still home to such fun haunts as the **Stock Exchange** bar, inside the old Bisbee Stock Exchange, and **St. Elmo's**, which has live music most nights.

For further information, walking tour maps, or details of special events, contact the Bisbee **visitors center**, 7 Main Street (520/432-5421).

The Border: Douglas and Agua Prieta

Like Bisbee, the border town of Douglas (pop. 12,822) grew up on copper mining, which here lasted until fairly recently: the huge smokestack of the Phelps-Dodge smelter a mile west of town was in operation until 1987, processing ores from mines in Mexico. Now most of the economy revolves around cross-border trade with *maquiladora* plants in its much larger Mexican neighbor, Agua Prieta (pop. 80,000), which in the past decades has quadrupled in size.

Douglas boasts a fabulous attraction: the landmark **Gadsden Hotel**, 1046 G Avenue (520/364-4481). Rebuilt in 1928 after a fire destroyed the 1907 original, the spacious gold-leafed lobby—one of the grandest public spaces in the state—has a pretty Tiffany-style stained-glass mural decorating its mezzanine. The small and basic rooms start at a bargain $35, and there's also a good Mexican-American restaurant and a very popular bar, the Saddle and Spur, its walls decorated with over 200 cattle brands from area ranches.

La Vuelta de Bisbee, a highly competitive professional cycling race held every April, sees hundreds of world-class riders racing up and down Bisbee's steep streets. There's also a 4th of July Soap Box Derby.

One of the more infamous events in Bisbee's busy history occurred in July 1917, when over 1,000 miners on strike for better pay and conditions were forcibly deported—literally railroaded out of town and dumped in the desert outside Columbus, New Mexico.

Travel along the Mexican border is enlivened immeasurably by the many radio stations, varying from the country twang of Douglas's **KDAP 96.5 FM** to the many south-of-the-border stations, like Radio Sonora **101.3 FM,** that play a part-English, part-Spanish Tejano mélange typified by songs such as "Mama, No Deje Que Sus Hijos Grow Up To Be Vaqueros."

Agua Prieta was the site of skirmishes between revolutionary **Pancho Villa** and the Mexican army.

Across the street from the Gadsden Hotel, a few doors down from the ornate facade of the Grand Theater, the **Grand Cafe**, 1119 G Street, is another great place to sample some very good and very cheap border town Mexican food.

East of Douglas along the border, a gravel road runs for 16 miles to the historic **John Slaughter Ranch**, one of the largest in the Southwest, now restored and preserved in its original 1880s condition (Wed.-Sun. 10 AM-3 PM; $3; 520/558-2474). The extensive acreage has been protected as the San Bernardino National Wildlife Refuge.

*A stone monument along Hwy-80, a half-mile east of the tiny town of Apache, points out the nearby site of Skeleton Canyon, where Apache warrior **Geronimo** finally surrendered to the U.S. Army in 1886, effectively ending the "Indian Wars."*

Cave Creek, Portal and Paradise

For the 50-odd miles between Douglas and the New Mexico state line, old US-80 cuts diagonally across the southeast corner of Arizona, a rugged country of mountains, canyons, and volcanic outcrops rising above sagebrush plains. There's not much to see along the highway, but to the northwest rise the enticing Pendregosa Mountains, whose forested peaks, now protected as part of the Coronado National Forest, long served as sanctuary to Chiricahua Apaches and sundry outlaws and wanted men.

Birdwatchers know Cave Creek as the only U.S. home of W.C. Fields' favorite bird, "my little chickadee"; so many other rare species can be seen that the Museum of Natural History has established a field station here, with rooms ($65; 520/558-2396) occasionally available to visitors.

While you can also reach them from the north via Willcox off I-10, the best access to the mountains from the south is via the aptly named hamlet of **Portal**, west of old US-80 from the New Mexico border, where the **Portal Peak Lodge, Store and Cafe** (520/558-2223) is a welcoming oasis, offering fresh food and comfortable rooms (around $65 for two, including breakfast).

Above Portal rise the sheer cliffs of Cave Creek Canyon, which writer William Least Heat Moon described in *Blue Highways* as "one of the strangest pieces of topography I've ever seen," its pale sandstone walls looking like a sun-bleached twin of Utah's Zion National Park. A narrow but passable (except in winter) 20-mile dirt road from Cave Creek climbs west, past the ghost town of **Paradise** then over the mountains' pine-covered, 7,600-foot-high crest.

Much of southeastern Arizona is still open range, so keep an eye out for livestock on the highway.

Chiricahua National Monument

The dirt road from Paradise, or the more prosaic approach from I-10 via Hwy-186 from Willcox, 36 miles to the northwest, brings you to the foot of the intriguing Chiricahua National Monument, a veritable "Wonderland of Rocks" whose contorted shapes were formed out of soft volcanic stone by eons of erosion. One of the most remote areas of the Southwest, the Chiricahuas are home to mountain lions, bobcats, bears and even javelinas, but the main attraction is the odd geology, which differs from anywhere else in the state. A good overview of the pinnacles and encompassing wilderness can be had from 6,870-foot-high **Massai Point**, at the end of the paved park road. There's a small **campground** (water, but no RV hookups; $8) a half-

mile from the visitors center, and in summer a shuttle bus ($2) runs to Massai Point, allowing hikers to make the trek through the park—downhill, without needing a car shuttle. One of the most intense concentrations of odd geology (Big Balanced Rock, Duck on a Rock, Kissing Rocks, and others) is along the Heart of Rocks trail, which also starts at Massai Point.

The **visitors center** (daily 8 AM-5 PM; $6 per car; 520/824-3560) near the monument entrance has more information on hiking, camping, and wildlife-watching opportunities in the Chiricahuas. Be aware that there are only very limited services —gas, food, or lodging—anywhere near the park.

Across New Mexico, towns along the interstate post road signs that total up their tourist services. At last count Deming, for example, had 27 gas stations, 21 restaurants, and 13 motels.

Lordsburg and Shakespeare

Coming in from southeastern Arizona, old US-80 rejoins the I-10 freeway at a crossroads community aptly called Road Forks, and 15 miles farther east the freeway swerves south to bypass the town of Lordsburg (pop. 2,951). Named not from any religious conviction but in honor of the Southern Pacific railroad engineer who plotted it in 1880, Lordsburg has little to offer other than its 17 gas stations, 11 cafes (try **El Charro** along the train tracks at the center of town), and 10 motels, which line "Motel Drive," the three-mile-long I-10 Business Route (old US-80).

Like something out of *The Andromeda Strain*, Lordsburg (which was John Wayne's supposed destination in the movie *Stagecoach*) feels oddly abandoned, as if everyone has just packed up and left town. In fact, one of the best reasons to stop is that New Mexico's best preserved ghost town, Shakespeare, sits three miles south of Lordsburg on a well-marked dirt road. Briefly home to some 3,000 silver miners during the early 1870s, Shakespeare was abandoned when the mines dried up, only

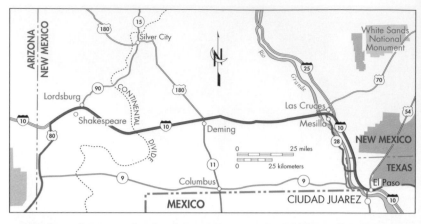

to be reborn during another brief mining boom in the 1880s. By the 1930s it was turned into a ranch by the Hill family, whose descendants still live here, care for the buildings, and conduct irregularly scheduled guided **tours** (weekends 10 AM and 2 PM; $3; 505/542-9034) of the Grant House saloon, the general store (where you can buy books and postcards), and the Stratford Hotel, where Billy the Kid washed dishes as a young boy.

Detour: Gila Cliff Dwellings National Monument

Silver City, an evocative old mining town high in the mountains roughly 45 miles from Lordsburg or Deming, was another early stomping ground of Wild West outlaw **Billy the Kid** and makes an excellent sidetrip off I-10. The name comes from silver mines worked here after the Civil War, but the biggest industry hereabouts are the open-cast copper mines at nearby Santa Rita, and the oldest industry was turquoise, mined in ancient times by the Mogollon Anasazi. The Mogollon also built the region's biggest draw: the Gila Cliff Dwellings National Monument (daily 8 AM-5 PM; free; 505/536-9461), located a steep 50 miles north of Silver City, at the end of scenic Hwy-15.

The area around the Gila Cliff Dwellings, at the headwaters of the Gila River, is reputed to have been the birthplace of Apache chief **Geronimo**.

Tucked into deep caves above a year-round stream, the cliff dwellings here were inhabited between A.D. 100 and 1100—a very long time, compared to other Anasazi sites. The Gila dwellings are not as immediately impressive as those at Mesa Verde or elsewhere, but they seem more human-scale and liveable—and since you're allowed to wander through them unescorted, it isn't hard to sit still and imagine what it might have been like to live here, high up in the forested mountains.

Midway between Lordsburg and Deming, where I-10 imperceptibly crosses the 4,585-foot Continental Divide, **Bowlin's Trading Post** sells fireworks, rattlesnake eggs, and sundry other road trip essentials, as advertised by dozens of billboards along the highway.

Deming's own **KNFT 102.9 FM** plays Top 40 country hits of the past 25 years.

Deming

Some 60 miles east of Lordsburg, halfway to Las Cruces, the dusty ranching and farming community of Deming (pop. 10,970) advertises itself as "Deming—Home of Pure Water and Fast Ducks." This motto, which is repeated on billboard after billboard along I-10, makes more sense than it may seem to at first:

Deming's water comes from the underground Mimbres River, and every year at the end of August the town hosts duck races (for living ones, not the rubber kind) with prizes of some $10,000 going to the winners. And if you didn't happen to pack your own duck, you can rent one for a $10 entry fee on the spot.

All this is little more than a clever ploy to get travelers to turn off tedious I-10 and visit their city. Fortunately, Deming's not a bad place, boasting the excellent **Deming-Luna-Mimbres Museum**, 301 S. Silver Street (Mon.-Sat. 9 AM-4 PM, Sunday 1-4 PM; donations), three blocks south of Pine Street (old US-80), Deming's main drag. Besides the usual range of old pottery, sparkling rocks, and pioneer artifacts, the museum displays an endearing collection of old toys, dolls, quilts, and dental equipment, even a braille edition of Playboy—well worth a quick look at the very least.

Rooms range from local places like the neon-signed **Butterfield Stage Motel**, at 309 W. Pine Street (505/544-0011) to a Best Western, a Holiday Inn, and a big Motel 6 (off I-10 at exit 85). Best place to camp is southeast of town in **Rockhound State Park** ($8; 505/546-1212), where besides finding nice sites with hot showers you can collect up to 15 pounds of geodes, agates, opals or quartz crystals—something the rangers urge you to do.

Las Cruces

Spreading along the eastern banks of the Rio Grande, at the foot of the angular Organ Mountains, Las Cruces (pop. 62,126) is the commercial center of a prosperous agricultural and recreational region. Named for a concentration of pioneer grave markers, Las Cruces was first settled by Spanish missionaries but is now a thoroughly modern, American-looking place, with all the motels you could want (from Motel 6 to an upscale Hilton), but only a couple of places really worth searching out, such as **Nellie's**, a Mexican restaurant famed for spicy salsas and delicious chile cheeseburgers, housed in a little brown box at 1226 W. Hadley Street, off Valley Boulevard on the northwest edge of downtown.

Thirty-two miles south of Deming, hugging the Mexican border, **Pancho Villa State Park** (dally 8 AM- 5 PM; $3; 505/531-2711) preserves the site where, on March 9, 1916, around 1,000 guerillas under the charge of revolutionary Pancho Villa attacked a small U.S. Army outpost, Camp Furlong, and the neighboring town of Columbus, killing 18 people. In response, U.S. forces under the command of Gen. John "Blackjack" Pershing chased Villa back into Mexico, using aircraft and mechanized ground forces together for the first time in military history.

In southwestern New Mexico, the I-10 freeway roughly parallels the route followed in the 1850s by the **Butterfield Stage**, the 2,800-mile-long main overland link between St. Louis and San Francisco.

Along US-70 some 50 miles northeast of Las Cruces, **White Sands National Monument** protects over 60,000 acres of gleaming white gypsum dunes, the tallest of which rise over 60 feet in height. A scenic 16-mile loop drive ($3 per car) is open during daylight hours, and during summer (June-Aug.), park rangers offer nighttime walks guided by the light of the moon. For dates and other details, call the visitors center (505/479-6124).

Mesilla

The best thing about Las Cruces is its nearness to a truly neat little place, the historic village of Mesilla, three miles southwest of Las Cruces via Hwy-28. Low-slung adobe buildings set around a shady central plaza hold a couple of historic sites—including an old jail from which Billy the Kid escaped in 1880—and a pair of excellent cantina-type restaurants, including very popular **La Posta** and less pricey but equally good **El Patio.**

Mesilla was founded across the Rio Grande on the Mexican side of the border in 1848, after the treaty that ended the Mexican-American War gave everything to the north of the river to the Americans. Six years later, Mesilla became (legally at least) American again, after the Gadsden Purchase bought the entire, 30,000-square-mile "Bootheel" region for $10 million.

Another place to eat is on the main road south of the historic center: the **Old Mesilla Pastry Cafe,** which has great pastries all day (Wed.-Sun.) and a full range of Mexican-American breakfasts; it's not historic, but it is delicious.

Also in Mesilla, on Barker Road across Hwy-28 from the plaza, the **Gadsden Museum** (daily 9-11 AM and 1-5 PM; $2) traces local history from pre-conquest to current times.

Hwy-28: Juan de Onate Trail

Southeast from Las Cruces and Mesilla, our route dips south across the Texas border to El Paso, then continues on US-180 for some 60 miles east before re-entering New Mexico at Carlsbad Caverns National Park. For the run to El Paso you have your choice between I-10 or the slower and much more scenic Hwy-28, the Juan de Onate Trail, which avoids the freeway and runs through the pecan groves, pepper fields, and dusty small towns that spread along the west bank of the Rio Grande.

This part of New Mexico is chile country, and there's no better place to sample the great variety of spicy peppers than at **Chope's** (505/233-9976), an unpretentious cinderblock cafe along Hwy-28 in La Mesa, roughly midway between Mesilla and El Paso. House specialty here is *chiles rellenos*—whole chiles stuffed with cheese and deep-fried.

One of my all-time favorite roadside finds is right behind Chope's, in the front yard of an unforgettable old man named Francisco Alaniz. A former boxer who fought under the name "Kid Chimuri," the 90-year-old Alaniz has created a remarakble sculpture garden using cast-off industrial and consumer goods, aka "junk." Old trophies, advertising signs, mass-produced statues—they're all combined into visually delightful little scenes, featuring everything from Don Quixote to a replica of the "Little Boy" A-Bomb ("Built by Lazy Ignorant People—Tested in Japan"). Stop by for a guided tour.

A TORTILLA BY ANY OTHER NAME

Carne adovada, calabacitas, posole, sopaipillas . . . . Menu items like these put you squarely in the lower left-hand quadrant of any U.S. map. But how do you know whether you're eating traditional New Mexican cooking, Southwestern cuisine, or the popular hybrid known as Tex-Mex? Truth is, they're all hybrids, launched nearly five centuries ago when the Spanish brought European spices and domestic animals to combine with indigenous ingredients. As Spanish and Mexican settlers followed El Camino Real north from Chihuahua to Santa Fe, culinary distinctions grew out of regional variations in locally grown products along the way.

What's new is the categories: a generation ago, folks just helped themselves to "Mexican food." Still, certain characteristics distinguish each cuisine. In New Mexico, the chiles set the dishes apart—and set your taste buds afire. New Mexico's Mesilla Valley is to chiles what California's Napa Valley is to wine production. When you order a local specialty, the server may ask, "Red or green?"—referring to red or green chiles. You can ask which is hotter and order accordingly, or try a little of each one.

A tip for tender palates: if the chile's heat has you reaching for your Dos Equis, don't. Like water on gasoline, beer, soda pop, and even ice water only spread the fire. Try milk or, failing that, chew on a tortilla.

Tex-Mex, as its name implies, draws from both sides of the international border, from grazing lands where *vaqueros* roast meat over mesquite fires. Hearty foods like *carne asada* (grilled meat) are accompanied by refried beans, guacamole, flour tortillas, and *pico de gallo*—an essential tomato and chile salsa. Fajitas, too, once signaled Tex-Mex territory, but that was before the rest of the country discovered the tasty strips of skirt steak.

When the food fusion goes farther afield than Mexico and the American Southwest, as in, say, Southwestern roasted chile bruschetta or spring rolls with green chile, you know you've entered the nebulous realm of contemporary Southwestern cuisine, and all bets are off. The world-class chefs of Santa Fe recognize no limits, creative or otherwise. The world is their blue-corn fried oyster.

(And speaking of oysters—just because you're in the desert doesn't mean you have to do without seafood. The Sea of Cortez is a quick hop over the border, and supplies the region's restaurants with oxymoronic jumbo shrimp, delicious sea bass, and many other fresh-from-the-sea treats.)

El Paso

Part of the largest international community in North America, El Paso (pop. 515,342) was originally settled because of its location at one of the safest crossings of the Rio Grande. It later grew into a vital way-station on the transcontinental Butterfield Stage and Southern Pacific Railroad. As its name suggests, for most people El Paso is a place to pass through, but there are many things here for visitors to enjoy.

Q. Why do they call it Texas?
A. Because it "Texas" so long to drive across.

One of the most interesting aspects of El Paso is the border itself, which for years followed the Rio Grande (known as the

El Paso has at least three unique claims to fame: it's the home of **Tony Lama** boots, which are available at significant discounts at four showrooms around town; the "World's Largest Harley Davidson Dealership," **Barnett's,** is along I-10 at Lee Trevino Drive; and the **University of Texas-El Paso** (UTEP) campus, along I-10 west of town, which has the only buildings in North America designed to look like Tibetan monasteries. UTEP is also significant for sports fans: way back in 1966, UTEP (which was then called Texas Western) became the first college in history to win the NCAA basketball championship with all African-American starters.

Río Bravo in Mexico), whose frequent changes in course caused innumerable problems for the two governments. Finally, in 1963, the river was run through a concrete channel so it could not change course. The border is now the location of the **Chamizal National Memorial**, on San Marical Street off Paisano Drive, where a small museum (daily 8 AM-5 PM; free) tells the border story and is surrounded by a pleasant green park. The Bridge of the Americas leads across to Ciudad Juárez on the Mexican side.

Another unique attraction hidden away amidst El Paso's horizontal sprawl is the Spanish colonial missions that still stand southeast of downtown. The oldest missions in what is now the United States, this trio of churches—Ysleta, Socorro, and San Elizario—stand along the well-signed "Mission Trail," between the Rio Grande and I-10, roughly 15 miles from the center of town.

Along with the missions, all of which are still in use, El Paso holds a number of small special-interest **museums**, including ones dedicated to such diverse subjects as the U.S. Border Patrol, Napoléon Bonaparte, and frontier medicine. Four more—the U.S. Army Air Defense Artillery Museum, the Third Cavalry Museum, the Museum of the Non-Commissioned Officer, and the Fort Bliss Museum —are located at Fort Bliss, tracing El Paso's significant military history. All four are free and open daily 9 AM-4:30 PM.

Places to eat in and around El Paso tend, not surprisingly, to specialize in Tex-Mex food. Peruse the menus at **JJ's Drive-In**, 5320 Doniphan Avenue, off I-10 exit 11; at classic old **Forti's Mexican Elder**, 321 Chelsea Street east of downtown near the Paisano Avenue exit off I-10; and at

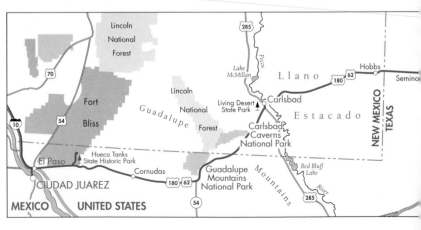

El Paso's hard-to-find Concordia Cemetery (it's just northwest of the I-10/US-54 junction) is the final resting place of **John Wesley Hardin,** the "Fastest Gun in the West" before he got killed in 1895. There are efforts to have him dug up and moved elsewhere; phone the El Paso visitors bureau for the latest details.

For the first 35 miles east of El Paso, US-180 runs along the southern edge of gigantic **Fort Bliss,** which stretches north for 50 miles into New Mexico and is home to about 20,000 U.S. troops.

Grigg's, east of town near Fort Bliss at 9007 Montana Avenue (US-180), which has been serving classic New Mexican food since 1939. One unique option: breakfast (and a car wash!) at the **H&H Coffee Shop,** 701 E. Yandell Avenue.

El Paso's finest place to stay is the grand old **Camino Real Paso Del Norte Hotel,** 101 S. El Paso Street (915/534-3000), one of the classiest hotels anywhere, with a beautiful bar off the lobby and rates (starting around $100) lower than you might think. All the usual mid-range chains are here too, plus a handy HI-approved youth hostel at the historic **Gardner Hotel,** 311 E. Franklin Street (915/532-3661).

For maps or more information on El Paso or neighboring Juárez, contact the **visitors bureau** downtown at 1 Civic Center Plaza (915/534-0696 or 800/351-6024).

Detour: Ciudad Juárez

Largest by far of the Mexican border cities, Ciudad Juárez (pop.

While in Texas, why not catch a Texas League baseball game? The **El Paso Diablos** (915/755-2000) play April-Aug. at Cohen Stadium, north of I-10 via the "North-South Freeway." Games are broadcast on **KROD 600 AM.**

1.2 million, and growing fast) is a compelling, disturbing, exciting and very worthwhile place to visit. Though the city sprawls through miles and miles of some of the worst pollution and direst poverty in Mexico—thanks in part to abuses of the *maquiladora* system—the downtown areas offer a quick taste of the country, and a half-hour walk can take you very far away from the USA. From the El Paso side, don't drive, park and walk down Santa Fe Street from downtown and cross the bridge on foot.

This crossing drops you at the head of Avenida Juárez, the main drag, lined by cantinas and nightclubs and stalls and stores selling everything from mass-produced "crafts" to knock-off designer goods and Cuban cigars. (The latter items will be confiscated if you try to bring them back into the U.S.)

About a half-mile south of the border, at the junction with Avenida 16 de Septiembre, Avenida Juárez brings you to the heart of Ciudad Juárez, where the very good historical museum (Tues.-Sun. 10 AM-6 PM; free), housed in the old customs building, and a large, often packed cathedral give glimpses into the city's history and culture. Among the many restaurants and bars along Avenida Juárez, a couple to check out are the **Kentucky Club**, 629 Avenida Juárez, a 1930s-looking bar that could be used as a set for some Raymond Chandler underworld adventure. Legend has it that Marilyn Monroe got drunk here, celebrating her Juárez divorce from playwright Arthur Miller. Next door, **Martino's** is a very popular Mexican restaurant. Be warned, however, that many Juárez bars double as brothels—these tend to have giveaway names like The Pink Lady.

The 70-mph section of US-180 east of El Paso is also signed as **Camino Buena Suerte**, the "Good Luck Highway."

Food and drink aside, the best thing about a trip south is the chance to enjoy some **Lucha Libre**, professional wrestling, Mexican style. Dramatic and impassioned bouts (US$5 for a ringside seat) are held Sunday nights in the large municipal auditorium near the cathedral.

Hueco Tanks State Historic Park

In the 100 miles of arid West Texas desert between El Paso and the Guadalupe Mountains, look forward to precious little but the tiny Hueco Tanks State Historic Park (daily 8 AM-dusk; $2; 915/857-1135) on the fringes of Fort Bliss, some 30 miles east of El Paso, then eight miles north on Hwy-2775. Established to preserve the approximately 3,000 pictographs painted on the syenite basalt boulders, the 850-acre park also protects the remains of a stagecoach station and an old ranch house. The "tanks" of the title are naturally formed rock basins, which collect rainwater and have made the site a natural stop for passing travelers, from prehistoric natives to the Butterfield stagecoach. Unfortunately sometimes the "historic" graffiti is overwhelmed by more contemporary spray-paint versions, but the site is pleasant enough, with a popular campground and good opportunities for birdwatching and rock-climbing.

Some 35 miles east of the Hueco Tanks turnoff, the tiny highway town of **Cornudas** has a nice cafe—"Home of the World Famous Cornudas Burger"—and a row of false-fronted Wild West buildings.

Guadalupe Mountains National Park

One of the few un-hyped wonders of Texas, Guadalupe Mountains National Park covers the rugged peaks that rise along the New Mexico border, 110 miles east of

Climb **Guadalupe Peak,** the highest point in Texas at 8,749 feet, via a very steep three-mile-long trail from the main visitors center along US-180. The change in elevation from the surrounding plains makes the Guadalupe Mountains a great place for watching thunderstorms.

Along with New Mexico, El Paso and the Guadalupe Mountains area follow mountain standard time zone. The rest of Texas is on central standard time.

El Paso. Formed as part of the same Capitan Reef of 250 million-year-old limestone as the great caverns of Carlsbad, the Guadalupe Mountains, a cool contrast to the surrounding desert, rise in sheer faces about 2,000 feet above the desert floor and offer the chance to experience many different and contrasting ecosystems side by side, within easy reach of the highway.

Even if you're not prepared to do any serious hiking—which is really the best way to experience the grandeur of the park or to see signs of the abundant wildlife (including mountain lions) —the quickest way to get a feel for the Guadalupes is to walk the half-mile **nature trail** that runs between the main **visitors center** (daily 8 AM-4:30 PM; free; 915/828-3251) and the remains of a Butterfield stagecoach station, passing well-signed specimens of all the major desert flora. If you have more time, head to **McKittrick Canyon**, off US-62/180 in the northeast corner of the park. From the small **visitors center** (daily 8 AM-4:30 PM; free; 915/828-3251) at the end of the road, a well-marked, well-maintained, and generally flat 3.5-mile trail winds along a stream, through a green landscape that changes gradually from the cactus of the Chihuahuan Desert to the oaks, walnuts, and maples of the inner canyon. It's best in spring, when the desert wildflowers bloom, or in autumn, when the hardwoods turn color.

Camping is available on a first-come, first-served basis at Pine Springs Campground near the main visitors center, and at numerous sites in the backcountry.

Carlsbad Caverns National Park

Carved out of the solid limestone of Capitan Reef by eons of dripping water, the Carlsbad Caverns contain over 30 miles of underground caves, some over 1,000 feet across. A two-mile trail (daily 8 AM-3:30 PM in summer, last entry at 2 PM rest of year) drops steeply from the large visitors center; or you can board an elevator (daily 8 AM-3 PM; $6 adults, $3 children; 505/785-2232) and ride 750 feet straight down to the "Big Room," where after wandering among the countless stalactites, stalagmites, and other formations, you can chow down on cheeseburgers at a classic 1950s-style cafeteria. Everyone has to ride the elevator back to the surface.

The trail down to the caverns closes early in the afternoon so that visitors don't interrupt the increasingly popular spectacle of the **Bat Flight,** in which hundreds of

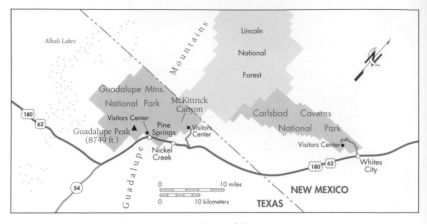

thousands of Mexican freetail bats swirl out of the caverns at sunset. Every evening (usually around 7 PM, except in winter when the bats have migrated to Mexico), rangers give a brief free talk about bats—proselytizing about how really great and harmless they are—waiting for them to set off into the night.

The nearest places to stay and eat are in **Whites City**, a giant complex of motels, restaurants, pinball arcades and souvenir shops along Hwy-180 at the turnoff to the park. Rooms at the two **Best Westerns** (505/785-2291, 800/CAVERNS or 800/228-3767) there cost about $60 a night.

The one highlight of Whites City's tourist clutter is the bizarre but captivating **Million Dollar Museum** ($3), which displays 10 rooms full of rifles, dollhouses, antique furniture and Native American artifacts.

Carlsbad

Twenty miles northeast of the Carlsbad Caverns, the town of Carlsbad (pop. 25,000) makes its living from the 750,000 tourists who visit the caves every year and it has the motels to prove it: lining Canal Street (aka US-180, the "National Parks Highway"), the main road through town, you'll find national chains like Best Western, Holiday Inn, Motel 6, and Travelodge, and funkier local counterparts like the **Stagecoach Inn**, 1819 S. Canal Street (505/887-1148). There's also one very good Mexican restaurant, the **Casa de Cortez** at 506 S. Canal Street, a plain brown-brick building where locals come for heaping helpings of *frijoles refritos* and *chiles rellenos;* no booze and no credit cards, but great fresh *sopaipillas.*

North of Carlsbad Caverns, state-run radio station 530 AM broadcasts Ricardo Montalban continuously recounting the story of the famous **Goodnight-Loving cattle trail,** which ran along the nearby Pecos River.

Apart from the caverns, the Carlsbad area boasts the **Living Desert State Park** (8 AM-sunset; $3), four miles northwest off US-285, which shows off the plant and animal life of the arid Chihuahuan Desert region.

US-180: The Llano Estacado

From Carlsbad, US-180 crosses the Pecos River, then snakes across the barren Llano Estacado, the "Staked Plain," which covers most of eastern New Mexico and the Texas Panhandle. Supposedly named by early explorers who drove wooden stakes into the ground to mark their way, the Llano Estacado area is pretty much the same on both sides of the border—flat, dry, and mostly devoid of settlement.

For eastbound travelers, this is the place where oil first becomes noticeably important—pumpjacks can be seen pumping away from here all the way to Alabama.

As part of a federal program known as WIPP—the Waste Isolation Pilot Plant—the underground potash mines east of Carlsbad are in the process of being adapted into a contentious disposal site for the nation's **nuclear waste.**

This is also cowboy country, thanks to the extensive pastures irrigated by water pumped up from aquifers deep underground. For travelers, however, the dominant image is of land stretching out far and wide: mile after mile after mile of endless flat cotton fields, interrupted every now and then by brilliant green alfalfa fields and a few surprisingly large towns like **Hobbs,** New Mexico (pop. 29,115), right on the border, its main street lined by various "Drilling Supply" companies and huge piles of old pipe. The Texas side is dotted with towns like **Seminole** (pop. 6,342), **Lamesa** (pop. 10,809, pronounced "la-MEE-sa"), which has an intact old Dairy Queen Drive-in along US-180, and **Gail**, which has the friendly Caprock Cafe and hosts an annual Fiddler's Festival. These towns seem like bustling hives of activity after the open, red-earth prairie in between them.

ROSWELL: UFO CENTRAL

If you can remember anything about the summer of 1997, this word will probably ring a few bells: Roswell. Seventy-five miles north of Carlsbad, Roswell (pop. 44,650) has become a catch-word for flying saucers, UFOs, extraterrestrials, and a complicated U.S. government cover-up of all the above. The cover-up is the one thing that's pretty much a given, since the Air Force has gone so far as to deny officially that anything ever happened in Roswell—which is equivalent to a confession, in the minds of UFO believers. Everything else about Roswell is, so to speak, up in the air.

The Roswell story goes something like this: in July of 1947, at the start of Cold War hysteria, something strange and metallic crashed into a field outside town, and the Army Air Corps (teams of tight-lipped operatives wearing special suits and dark glasses, no doubt) came and recovered it. Reports to the effect that a flying saucer had landed in Roswell appeared in the local paper, and quickly spread around the globe, only to be denied by the government, which claimed the "flying saucers" were actually weather balloons. Thirty-one years later, a retired military intelligence officer from the Roswell base sold a story to the *National Enquirer,* repeating details of the 1947 "flying saucer" crash, and telling of his subsequent capture of extraterrestrial beings. This in turn spawned countless other stories, books and videos, and spurred the growth of a battery of tourist attractions and events in and around Roswell, including at least two "museums": the **UFO Enigma Museum** at 6108 S. Main Street (Mon.-Sat. 9:30 AM-5:30 PM, Sunday noon-5 PM; $1; 505/825-2389), four miles south of Roswell near the Roswell Air Force Base, and the **International UFO Museum and Research Center**, in downtown Roswell at 114 N. Main Street (daily 11 AM-5 PM; free; 505/625-9495).

CANYONLANDS LOOP:
THE GRAND CIRCLE

CANYONLANDS LOOP: THE GRAND CIRCLE

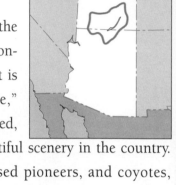

O n its way around the heart of the Colorado Plateau, this Canyonlands Loop trip, within what is sometimes called the "Grand Circle," passes through some of the most rugged, forbidding, and jaw-droppingly beautiful scenery in the country. Once the domain of Indians, callused pioneers, and coyotes, southern Utah and northern Arizona have gradually come to the attention of the world—first and foremost for the variegated landscape, which is like nowhere else on earth. Barren deserts, snow-capped mountains, and sheer-walled river canyons thousands of feet deep make this region truly, in the words of author Wallace Stegner, "a country that calls for wings." Such wonders of the natural world, including the Grand Canyon and five other national parks, are mostly accessible by road, but their farther reaches still beg to be explored on foot, mountain bike, raft, or jeep.

> This was the country the Mormons settled. . . . Its destiny was plain on its face, its contempt of man and his history and his theological immortality, his Millennium, his Heaven on Earth, was monumentally obvious. Its distances were terrifying, its cloudbursts catastrophic, its beauty flamboyant and bizarre and allied with death. —Wallace Stegner, *Mormon Country*

This region, the last in the lower 48 states to be explored and mapped, is full of the signs and presence of distinctly foreign cultures, from the ruins of the long-gone Anasazi to the more modern but still solidly traditional Navajo and Mormons. It's a rough-edged and unforgiving country, where most of the roads weren't even paved until the 1960s (and where many still aren't). But if you use common sense (carry water, and keep an eye on the gas gauge!), the region offers you a chance to browse the wares at Indian trading posts, swim under desert waterfalls, and wander through ghost towns dried like skeletons in the ceaseless sun.

Starting in central Utah (see our US-50 route), at the interstate fuel stop of Green River, this loop heads south along US-191 to the adventure hub of Moab, gateway to the sandstone wonders of Arches and Canyonlands National Parks. Continuing south, you can take a detour to the natural bridges and ancient ruins of Cedar Mesa or keep going to the wide open reaches of the Navajo Indian Reservation. Largest in the country, with as many parks and monuments per square mile as its neighboring states, the semi-autonomous Navajo Nation is guarded in the north by the famous sandstone towers of Monument Valley and bounded on the west by the Grand Canyon, on the south by historic Route 66, and on the east by Anasazi-rich canyons described in our Four Corners Loop route (see pages 398-443).

The best map by far of the Canyonlands area is the Automobile Club of Southern California's *Indian Country,* available from most AAA offices and just about everywhere on the Colorado Plateau.

Heading back north from the edge of the Grand Canyon, the route crosses the Colorado River at houseboat-dotted Lake Powell, which backs up behind the smooth face of Glen Canyon Dam for hundreds of miles across the desert, providing some surreal images of man's odd place in the natural order of things here in this arid, barren desert. Bending west, after climbing onto the cool, high Kaibab Plateau, you can follow a spectacular spur to the North Rim of the Grand Canyon, that eroded abyss far beyond the reach of verbal superlatives and panoramic photos. Next stop is the gorgeous gorge of Zion Canyon National Park, beyond

THE CATHEDRAL BRYCE CANYON NATIONAL PARK, UTAH

Over the desert and the canyons, down there in the rocks, a huge vibration of light and stillness and solitude shapes itself in the form of hovering wings spread out across the sky from the world's rim to the world's end. —Edward Abbey, *Desert Solitaire*

which our route rolls north between two pine-covered plateaus with tongue-twisting names: the Markagunt, capped by Cedar Breaks National Monument, and the Paunsaugunt, whose eastern edge falls off into the rosy spires of Bryce Canyon National Park.

East of Bryce Canyon, scenic Hwy-12 winds it patient way across the northern border of the huge new Grand Staircase-Escalante National Monument, with enough diversity of landscape to make two or three national parks. The area is dotted with many tiny Mormon settlements, most of which were almost completely cut off from the outside world until the middle of the 20th century. After climbing up to the 9,400-foot summit of the route over Boulder Mountain, Hwy-12 joins Hwy-24, which slices through the massive ridge of the Waterpocket Fold and Capitol Reef National Park before cutting across the Martian landscape of the San Rafael Desert, just west of Green River.

One $10 **entrance fee** will get you in to all three Canyonlands districts for one week (The Maze is free). **Vehicle campgrounds** in the Island in the Sky and Needles Districts offer sites on a first-come, first served basis and fill quickly from spring to fall. **Backcountry camping** reservations ($10 per trip) can be made through the main Canyonlands reservation number (435/259-4531) up to two weeks ahead of time—after that, whatever sites are left are available on a walk-in basis only. There are also overflow campgrounds for self-contained RVers—basically, parking lots.

Canyonlands National Park: Island in the Sky

There's not a lot to see along the stretches of I-70 and US-191 that link Green River and Moab, but some of the Southwest's most unforgettable places are only a turn or two away. Twenty-one miles south of I-70, nine miles north of Moab, Hwy-313 heads west from US-191 and climbs onto the Island in the Sky, a wedge-shaped mesa high above the sheer canyons of the Green and Colorado Rivers. The closest to Moab of the park's three districts, the Island in the Sky section is also the easiest to experience in a short time, with paved roads leading right to **Grand View Point**, overlooking hundreds of square miles of canyon country.

For hiking advice, natural history, and weather reports (lightning is a real danger out here in the open at 6,000 feet), start at the main **visitors center** (daily 8 AM-6 PM in summer; 435/259-4712), 22 miles west of US-191. Short trails lead from the pavement to **Aztec Butte**, **Neck Spring**, **Whale Rock**, and an overlook above **Upheaval Dome**, a huge crater-like formation whose origins are still hotly debated among geologists. You've probably already seen pictures of the view through **Mesa Arch**, perched on the very edge of the precipice, on posters or calendars somewhere in southeastern Utah. Longer trails lead down a thousand feet to the **White Rim**, from which it's another long descent to either river. The multi-day trip around the entire rim is popular with mountain bikers and off-road drivers.

The **Willow Flat campground** has 12 sites ($5) and a great view but no water. In fact, bring all the water you'll need for your entire visit—there's none available besides a drinking fountain at the visitors center.

Dead Horse Point State Park

On the way in to or out from the Island in the Sky along Hwy-313, seven miles east of the visitors center, you'll pass the turnoff for Dead Horse Point State Park, which

I-15 SURVIVAL GUIDE: UTAH

QUICKER BUT FAR LESS SCENIC than our loop tour through the Canyonlands region, I-15 provides the fastest access between Zion and Bryce National Parks and the rest of the world. From the small town of Hurricane—the gateway to the national parks—you can zoom 130 miles southwest to Las Vegas, or north to Salt Lake City. The choice is yours, but along the way you might enjoy:

MM 0: Crossing a short 30-mile stretch of Arizona, I-15 runs through the scenic (and almost totally undeveloped) **Virgin River Gorge**. Just over the Nevada state line, which also marks the boundary between the Pacific and mountain time zones, the scene changes suddenly: obscenely green golf courses in the middle of the barren desert have made **Mesquite** Nevada's fastest growing city. Las Vegas is another 90 miles—about an hour away, at typical highway speeds.

MM 10: An impressive Mormon Temple, and many other significant Church of Latter Day Saints sites, make the town of **St. George** worth visiting, though the roadside is packed with all the usual franchised sprawl.

MM 40: Head a few miles east from here to explore the amazing Kolob Canyons section of Zion National Park.

MM 132: Junction with I-70, running east to Green River and Moab through the scenic gorge of the Sevier River.

MM 178: Junction with westbound US-50, the self-proclaimed Loneliest Road in America.

MM 260: Junction with eastbound US-6, which runs to Moab.

---

enjoys much the same views as Island in the Sky but smaller crowds. The name supposedly came from a herd of horses left to graze at the end of the point, who became confused about the way out and died of thirst within sight of the river below. A visitors center, a mile or so from the end of the road, has information on hiking, history, and geology; ask here for directions to **Thelma and Louise Point**, where the heroines (actually stunt dummies) hurtled off into what was supposed to be the Grand Canyon at the end of the movie. Near the visitors center is a nice campground, with water and power but no showers.

Canyonlands—already Utah's largest national park—may soon become even bigger. The **Canyonlands Completion Proposal** would more than triple the park's area by expanding its boundaries beyond the current straight, arbitrary lines to the more natural contours of the watersheds of the Colorado and Green Rivers.

Arches National Park

The reason most people come to this desolate-looking part of Utah is to take a spin through this, the southwest's most famous park. Arches National Park is packed with thousands of brilliantly colored sandstone arches, spires, fins, walls,

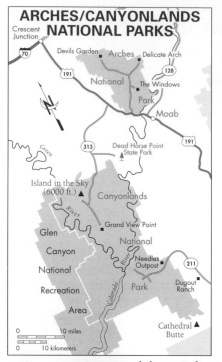

and pinnacles. Add in easy accessibility and a great view of the La Sal Mountains and it's easy to see why millions of visitors a year brave the crowds to soak up the scenery. Families and RVers love Arches, since it's easy to see almost everything in a day and all the scenic highlights are within a mile or two (and often much less) of the roadside.

At the entrance gate, five miles north of Moab on the east side of US-191, pay your admission ($10 per vehicle) and stop by the **visitors center** (daily 7:30 AM-6:30 PM from spring to fall; 435/259-8161) for books, maps, advice, and information on the park's geology and natural history. From here, the 20-mile paved loop road climbs swiftly up the sandstone cliffs before passing the **Courthouse Towers** and the famous, 3,600-ton **Balanced Rock**. Turn right here to reach **The Windows**, a pair of large arches only a short walk from the parking area, or continue farther in for the turnoff to **Wolfe Ranch**, a turn-of-the-century settlement near a panel of Ute Indian petroglyphs. This is one end of the 1.5-mile hike to **Delicate Arch**, which has effectively become Utah's state symbol, emblazoned on everything from license plates to shot glasses.

Toward the end of the scenic drive, longer trails lead into the **Devil's Garden**, a seven-mile loop to impossibly thin **Landscape Arch**, a 306-foot span that dropped a large chunk in 1991. Guided ranger hikes (sign up at the visitors center in the morning) are the only way to see the **Fiery Furnace**, a maze of stone fins that are actually cooler in summer than the surrounding desert. Get an even earlier start to snag a spot in the **Devils Garden Campground** ($10), which fills up by 8 AM daily in the summer and usually spring and fall, too.

Early settlers had more descriptive names for what's now called Delicate Arch. These included "Old Lady's Bloomers" and "Cowboy Chaps."

Moab

The undisputed tourist epicenter of Utah's canyon country, Moab (pop. 5,500) has survived as complete a transformation—actually, two—as any town in the West. First came Charlie Steen's discovery of uranium in 1952, which transformed a sleepy ranching community into a mining boom town almost overnight as fortune-seekers combed the hills with Jeeps and Geiger counters. Left high and dry toward the end of the Cold War, Moab was reborn once again when mountain bikers discovered the unequaled riding on the surrounding mining roads and slickrock. It didn't take long for word to get out as well about the two national

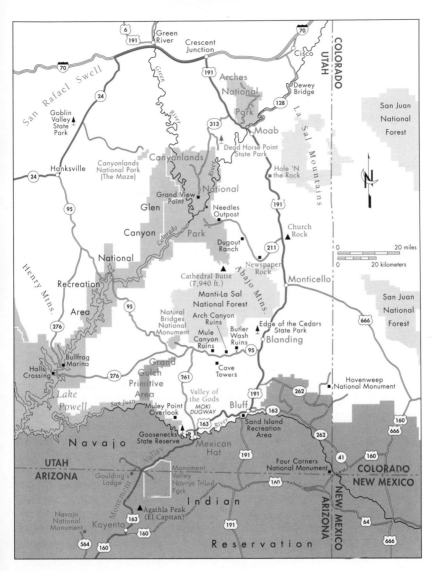

parks (Arches and Canyonlands) and assorted other outdoor attractions within easy distance, and Moab's reputation as an international fun spot was soon set in sandstone.

Fast-food franchises and T-shirt stores now line Main Street, but Moab hasn't given up its quirky but solid sense of community. Grizzled ranchers rub elbows with Lycra-clad mountain bikers, European tourists, and college students from Colorado in bars and at the City Market, yet everyone coexists surprisingly well. On the whole, the town tends toward the liberal end of things; the spirit of Edward

(continues on page 362)

ADVENTURES IN AND AROUND MOAB

The options for fun in the sun in Moab and vicinity are almost unlimited. Just about the only thing the town doesn't have is a ski mountain (though a chairlift *was* installed recently up one side of the valley). Dozens of outfitters are available to sell you gear and point you in the right direction, whether you want to explore on your own or have someone guide you down the river, along a trail, up or down a cliff, or through a canyon.

Mountain Biking

Moab's modern era all started with a bike trail—namely, the **Slickrock Trail**, originally a motorcycle path over the petrified sand dunes northeast of town. Mountain bikers soon found that their tires stuck just as tightly as motorcyclists' did to the sandstone swells, and a legend was born. One of the most famous bike trails in the world, Slickrock is no cake walk—over 10 miles of up and down, no coasting, with 100-foot dropoffs and nothing to cushion a fall. Over 100,000 riders attempt it each year—most choosing wisely to start on the 2.5-mile practice loop. To reach the trailhead, take 100 South toward the mountains from Main St., then follow the signs to Tusher St. and Sand Flats Rd., where you'll have to pay a $4 entrance fee per car ($2 per bike). (The Moab landfill, along the way, is considered "America's most scenic dump" for its view over the La Sals.)

Easier trails around Moab include **Gemini Bridges** and **Monitor and Merrimac**, both north of town. **Hurrah Pass** and **Amasa Back** explore the mesas along the Colorado to the south, and **Porcupine Rim** heads past the entrance to Slickrock up into the foothills of the La Sals before skirting Castle Valley for a hair-raising descent to UT-128. **Poison Spider Mesa** and the **Moab Rim** are both so difficult that they can be deadly for the incautious. Most of the half dozen or so bike shops in town rent bikes, and you can book tours with **Kaibab Mountain Bike Tours**, 391 S. Main (435/259-7423) and **Western Spirit Cycling**, 478 Mill Creek Dr. (435/259-8732).

Four-Wheeling

Many of the back roads beloved by mountain bikers were blazed by ranchers and uranium prospectors and are still popular with 4WD enthusiasts, who gather by the hundreds for the **Easter Jeep Safari**. Pick up a map and route info at **Farabee Adventures** 83 S. Main (435/259-7494), or **Slickrock 4X4**, 284 N. Main (435/259-5678), both of whom rent Jeeps by the day. **Tag-A-Long Expeditions**, 452 N. Main (435/259-8946), organizes 4WD trips around Moab and in the Needles district of Canyonlands and also runs raft and jetboat trips on the Colorado.

Hiking

Countless trails snake through the desert and hills around Moab. Hikers can reach the **Portal Overlook** and **Corona Arch** from UT-279, which runs along the Colorado toward the Island in the Sky district of Canyonlands National Park. In the same neighborhood, the **Hidden Valley** trail leads into the Behind the Rocks area, a maze of sandstone fins similar to the Fiery Furnace at Arches. **Hunters Canyon**, off Kane Creek Blvd., passes Hunter Arch and a deep pool of water perfect for a dip on a hot day. **Coyote Shuttle** (435/259-8656) and **Roadrunner Shuttle** (435/259-9402) both offer trailhead shuttle services (for mountain bikers, too).

Rafting

Moab's second-biggest outdoor draw takes advantage of both of the rivers that join in Canyonlands National Park to the south. Needless to say, all raft trips should include life jackets, and those on overnight trips need to carry firepans and portable toilets. Permits are necessary to float through Canyonlands National Park.

The **Green River** runs smooth through Labyrinth and Stillwater Canyons over the 124 miles from Green River State Park to the confluence with the Colorado. You can take out at Mineral Bottom below Island in the Sky, shortening the trip to 64 miles. It's possible to run the minor rapids of "The Daily," the section of the Colorado River above Moab, on your own in a single day (hence the name); start at Hittle Bottom off UT-128 and take out near town. South of Moab, the Colorado is placid all the way to where it joins the Green, called the confluence—a three- to five-day float.

You'll definitely want an experienced guide through Cataract Canyon below the confluence, where 26 rapids with names like Hell-to-Pay and the Big Drops give some of the wildest rides in the country. To take you the 112 miles to Hite Marina, contact **Sheri Griffith Expeditions, Inc.,** 2231 S. Hwy. 191 (435/259-8229) or **Western River Expeditions,** 1371 N. Hwy. 191 (435/259-7019). **Tex's Riverways,** 691 N. 500 West (435/259-5101) runs motorboats up and down the Colorado, and can pick up rafters who'd rather not paddle back upstream.

Other Pursuits

Stop by the **Moab Rock Shop**, 600 N. Main (435/259-7312), for gear and information on great nearby **rock climbing**. There are many moderate routes up the Wingate sandstone cliffs along the Colorado off UT-279, and the cracks at Indian Creek on the way to the Needles District are world famous. **Desert Highlights**, 208 E. 200 South (435/259-4433), offers **canyoneering** trips throughout the area. This exciting, relatively new sport involves minor rock scrambling and ropework to get into canyons that would otherwise be too difficult or dangerous.

After becoming an instant multimillionaire from his La Vida uranium mine, Charlie Steen built himself a huge house overlooking town (now the **Sunset Grill**, 435/259-7146) and stayed around to become a pillar of the community.

A brochure available from the Information Center lists all the movies that have taken advantage of Moab's amazing scenery, including *City Slickers II, Indiana Jones and the Last Crusade, Geronimo, Rio Grande,* and *Cheyenne Autumn.*

Abbey, author of the environmental classic *Desert Solitaire* (about his stint as an Arches ranger decades ago) is invoked so often it can seem like he's just in the next room.

Start at the **Moab Information Center,** at Main and Center (435/259-1370), for information on just about anything in the area and a large selection of books, maps, and posters. Here they can tell you about Moab's long list of annual events, including September's **Moab Music Festival** and October's **Fat Tire Festival.**

Moab Practicalities

John Wayne stayed at the **Apache Motel,** 166 S. 400 East (435/259-5727; $65 d), while filming *Rio Bravo* nearby in 1950. And the **Gonzo Inn,** 100 W. 200 South (435/259-2515; $109 d), offers an offbeat take on luxury lodgings. Chain motels, camp-

grounds, and B&Bs, such as the gorgeous **Castle Valley Inn,** up in the La Sals (435/259-6012; $155 d), fill to capacity in the summer months—contact **Moab/ Canyonlands Central Reservations** (800/748-4386) for advance bookings. At the cheapest end of Moab's long list of accommodations is the **Lazy Lizard International Hostel,** 1213 S. US-191 (435/259-6057), with dorm beds for $8 and private rooms for $22.

The choice of restaurants is almost as wide, starting with the Grand Marnier French toast at the **Jailhouse Cafe,** 101 N. Main (435/259-3900), open for breakfast daily in the historic courthouse, which boasts two-foot-thick adobe walls. **Honest Ozzie's Cafe and Bakery,** 60 N. 100 West (435/259-8422), also does a good breakfast, but it's hard to beat their lunch of pecan-crusted salmon fish-and-chips on the shady outdoor patio, served daily. Locals flock to the **Fat City Smoke House,** 36 S. 100 West (435/259-4302), for spicy BBQ, and **Poplar Place Pub and Eatery,** 11 E. 100 North (435/259-6018), for microbrews and gourmet pizzas. An evening out usually starts at one of Moab's two brewpubs: **Moab Brewery,** 686 S. Main (435/259-6333), and **Eddie McStiff's,** 57 S. Main (435/259-2337), which also has a dance floor.

If you need a respite from the desert and you're not up for climbing into the La Sal Mountains, stop by the **Scott M. Matheson Wetlands Preserve** (435/259-4629), a lush 875-acre marsh between Moab and the Colorado River. Over 180 species of birds have been spotted among the cottonwood and Russian olive trees. Turn onto Kane Creek Boulevard (from the McDonald's on Main Street), and head southwest three quarters of a mile to the marked parking area.

Hwy-128: Along the Colorado River

If you need to get back to I-70 but aren't in a hurry, take a spin up Hwy-128. It runs along the eastern bank of the Colorado River, offering plenty of spots to float, camp, and hike. **Negro Bill Canyon,** a deep, green cleft starting three miles up from US-191, leads to Morning Glory Natural Bridge, the sixth-longest in the country at 243 feet. Farther up the 23-mile road you'll pass

Castleton Valley, whose flat bottom is filled with farms beneath the rust-colored sandstone spires of the **Fisher Towers**. Castleton Tower, one of the tallest, is considered one of the classic desert tower climbs in the country. (You can access one end of the **La Sal Mountain Loop Road** from the upper end of the valley.) Keep going to **Dewey Bridge**, a one-lane suspension bridge used until 1986, and the eerie ghost town of **Cisco**, abandoned after construction of the interstate. Hwy-128 links up with I-70 at exit 202, 40 miles east of Green River, roughly 30 miles west of the Colorado border.

For more on Grand Junction and the trip across Colorado, see pages 260-270.

Hole 'N the Rock

Heading south from Moab on US-191, don't miss the unique Hole 'N the Rock, a 14-room home that took Albert Christensen a dozen years to carve out of a sandstone cliff. The 5,000-square-foot residence—whose front room did double duty for years as a roadside cafe—includes bedrooms furnished with the original 1950s furniture, a fireplace with a 65-foot chimney drilled through the rock, the inevitable taxidermy collection, a roomful of religious portraits Christensen painted, and a sculpted bust of F.D.R. Christensen carved into the outside wall.

The Hole 'N the Rock is about 15 miles south of Moab and can be seen on short guided tours (daily 9 AM-6 PM; $2.50; 435/686-2250). There's also the requisite very large gift shop.

Canyonlands National Park: The Needles

Some 40 miles south of Moab, or 15 north of Monticello, bulbous Church Rock marks the turnoff from US-191 into the heart of Canyonlands National Park. From here, US-211 snakes westward before dropping into the valley cut by Indian Creek, a truly spectacular 30-mile drive around the feet of looming mesas.

Ten miles west of US-191 is **Newspaper Rock**, where ancient passersby carved everything from bear tracks to mounted warriors into the dark desert varnish as many as 4,000 years ago. There's a BLM-managed campsite under the cottonwoods by the water, and plenty of other petroglyphs in nearby canyons.

A few miles farther, at the mouth of Cottonwood Creek, sits the **Dugout Ranch**, a private spread that was once part of the largest cattle operation in Utah. Recently purchased by The Nature Conservancy on the condition that it continue as a working, conservation-minded ranch, the Dugout still holds cows and the occasional Marlboro photo shoot. From here you can see the unmistakable Six-Shooter Peaks, which mark the entrance to this district of the park.

Newspaper Rock

The **Needles District** of Canyonlands National Park (435/259-4711) takes its name from distinctive red and white spires of Cedar Mesa sandstone jumbled like an alien city skyline just east of the confluence of the Green and Colorado Rivers. Stop at the new **visitors center** (daily 8 AM-6 PM, spring through fall) for a quick video introduction to the funky local geology and to check what's in bloom. The Squaw Flat vehicle campground has 16 sites ($10).

If you make it the five-and-a-half miles out to the **Confluence Overlook,** you'll notice that the Green River is actually brown and that the Colorado flows green.

Just outside the park boundary, the **Needles Outpost** (435/979-4007) offers a campground, showers, a small food and souvenir store, and expensive gasoline. They're open more or less regularly from spring to fall.

Most visitors come this far to explore the backcountry, either on foot or in a vehicle. Four short self-guided trails leave the paved main road (Cave Springs shelters an old cowboy camp), and miles of longer paths snake over the slickrock and down into canyon bottoms. Druid Arch and Chessler Park are both popular day-hikes; the latter loop includes the famous Joint Trail section, through deep, narrow cracks in the stone. Other loops of 10 miles or less connect Squaw, Big Spring, and Lost Canyons. And the rugged Peekaboo Trail crawls across two miles of slickrock after three miles in the canyons. Backcountry camping permits are $10, regardless of how long you're out.

The Needles abound in archaeology, with canyons chock-full of Anasazi ruins and rock art. Upper Salt Creek Canyon harbors the most; take at least three days to explore this section, starting at Cathedral Butte just outside the southern park boundary. If you're not a hiker, don't despair; rough 4WD roads wind up Lavender, Horse, and Salt Creek canyons and to an overlook above the Colorado river gorge. Tower Ruin, Paul Bunyan's Potty (a horizontal arch), and pictographs at Peekaboo Spring in lower Salt Creek can be seen on one day-use permit ($5). If you're up for a challenge—and are paid up on your insurance—take a scouting walk before tackling short but brutal Elephant Hill, which claims new victims every year. The back side, which is even worse than the front, includes one section with such tight corners that vehicles have to shift into reverse and back down part of the way.

Monticello

Nestled at the eastern foot of the **Abajo Mountains** this sleepy burg serves as a quieter alternative to Moab as a base for explorations of the Canyonlands area. Founded in 1888, Monticello (pop. 1,800; elev. 7,050 feet) was named after Thomas Jefferson's country retreat in Virginia. If you're planning to spend the night, the **Grist Mill Inn**, 64 S. 300 East (435/587-2597; $92 d), offers accommodations in a turn-of-the-century flour mill, and the **MD Ranch Cookhouse**, 380 S. Main Street (435/587-3299), has good steaks and sandwiches and a Western-themed gift shop.

The friendly folks at the **information center**, 435 N. Main Street (800/574-4386), can provide information on the parks and other public lands in the area. For guided "ed-ventures" into the nearby wilds, contact the **Four Corners School of Outdoor Education** (435/587-2859), which runs rafting, hiking, and backpacking trips with a conservation bent.

The **Abajos**—also called the Blue Mountains—take their name (meaning "lower" or "below" in Spanish) from early explorers who looked down on the mountains from the higher (and more northerly) La Sals. Look toward the northern (right-hand) end of the Abajos for a patch of trees resembling a horse's head with a blaze on its muzzle.

Blanding

This biggest town in Utah's largest county (San Juan) sits smack in the middle of the numinously haunting grounds of the Four Corners region's most famous long-lost culture, the Anasazi. Displays on the lifestyle and artifacts of these enigmatic ancient people fill the museum at the **Edge of the Cedars State Park**, 660 W. 400 North (daily 9 AM-6 PM; $2 per person or $5 per car; 435/678-2238). Many of the artifacts, including much of the extensive pottery collection, were found by locals on souvenir-hunting excursions (long before such an expedition became something that could land you in jail) in the countless canyons nearby. A partially excavated Anasazi pueblo stands behind the museum, backed by a view of the Abajo Mountains.

Delve even deeper into the past at the **Dinosaur Museum**, 754 S. 200 West (Mon.-Sat. 9 AM-5 PM; $2; 435/678-3454), a cavernous building filled with bones and fossilized tracks of creatures including the Allosaurus, Utah's state fossil. The museum also houses a great collection of posters from old dinosaur movies including *The Beast of Hollow Mountain* and *The Valley of Gwangi*. At the edge of town, the **Nations of the Four Corners Cultural Center**, 500 S. 700 West, has a free network of self-guided trails leading past recon- structed Mormon pioneer cabins, rusting farm machinery, Navajo hogans, and an observation tower.

Blanding has a deeply conservative Mormon streak, which helps explain why it's totally alcohol-free.

Just south of town on US-191 sits **Huck's Museum and Trading Post** ($3; 435/678-2329), a log building filled with local memorabilia, sundry knickknacks, and a gigantic private collection of Anasazi artifacts in the back room. Across the road, the **Blue Mountain Trading Post** (435/678-2218) has an attractive collection of Navajo and Hopi crafts. Don't miss the large private collection of woven baskets in *their* back room.

If you come across an Anasazi artifact in your explorations of the backcountry, keep in mind that it's a felony to disturb anything on federal land. Leave it in place, note the location, and tell a ranger what you found—you just might get your name on a display in a visitors center.

Detour: Hwy-95

Built only in 1946 and unpaved until 1976, the **Bicentennial Highway** climbs across Cedar Mesa, an area so rich in archaeology the route has been nicknamed the "Trail of the Ancients." Although not everyone liked the idea of opening the remote plateau to tourism (this road was one target of Edward Abbey's band of environmental saboteurs in his novel *The Monkey Wrench Gang*), Hwy-95 is one of the easiest means of access to canyons filled with ruins, arches, and bridges that were once almost completely beyond reach.

From Blanding, Hwy-95 slices through the jagged teeth of the Comb Ridge monocline before reaching the turnoff for **Butler Wash ruins**, where a mile-long trail leads to an overlook above an Anasazi cliff dwelling occupied around A.D. 1200. Look for the treacherous hand-and-foot trail chipped into the rock to the left of the alcove. A few miles farther (between mileposts 107 and 108) is the turnoff

Chances are that those tiny, clawed prints you see in sandy canyon bottoms belong to a **ringtail cat**— which isn't a cat at all, but rather a member of the raccoon family.

On **August 25,** admission is free to all National Parks and monuments in the country, to celebrate the date the National Park System was established in 1916.

Archaeologists can determine with amazing accuracy when ancient structures were built, thanks to a procedure called **tree-ring dating.** Core samples from wooden beams in ruins are compared to a master tree-ring "map" created from hundreds of samples. Large rings indicate wet years, narrow rings drought. When the patterns match, scientists can tell the exact year the tree was cut.

From Hwy-95 near Natural Bridges, you can tour the surreal landscapes around Lake Powell by following Hwy-276 on a loop west through Halls Crossing; the entire route is described below (and in the reverse direction).

It's hard to imagine a more remote hotel than the **Fry Canyon Lodge** (435/259-5334), on Hwy-95 20 miles west of Natural Bridges National Monument. Established in 1955 as a mining supply center, the building served as a post office and school before being transformed into a cozy getaway (rooms cost $60-75) with attached restaurant and gas station.

for **Arch Canyon,** where anything from a day-hike to an overnight trip leads to more Anasazi ruins and artifacts. Six miles west, you'll hit **Mule Canyon,** where a circular tower and stone kiva have been excavated and stabilized by the BLM. Head two miles southeast to reach **Cave Towers,** with half a dozen towers and several cliff dwellings.

West of here, Hwy-95 provides access to ancient Grand Gulch and the remote Natural Bridges National Monument. Then it bends north across the upper reaches of Lake Powell.

Grand Gulch Primitive Area

The Kane Gulch Ranger Station, five miles south of Hwy-95 on Hwy-261, is the starting point for the 23-mile loop through Bullet Canyon and Kane Gulch into the 37,000-acre Grand Gulch Primitive Area. This beautiful canyon, chock-full of Anasazi pictographs and ruins of cliff dwellings and other buildings, is getting so popular that the BLM has set up a permit system ($8 per person overnight, $2 for day use; 435/587-1532). Across Hwy-261 from Grand Gulch, the loop connecting **Owl and Fish Creek Canyons** is another popular backpacking route. Head clockwise, descending into Owl Creek first, and leave two to three days for the 15-mile journey—more if you plan on exploring any side canyons.

Natural Bridges National Monument

Three natural sandstone bridges spanning White Canyon were set aside by Theodore Roosevelt in 1908 as Natural Bridges National Monument. The overlook drive permits even non-hikers a chance to enjoy the views of Sipapu, Kachina, and Owachomo —formed when the desert river changed course and cut through gigantic fins of rock. Short, steep trails lead to the bases of the bridges—as well as to numerous Anasazi ruins scattered about. Stop first at the **visitors center** ($6 per vehicle; 435/692-1234), next to which is a wonderfully quiet and very cheap campground ($5). All power used in the park comes from the sun, by way of the **solar array** across the road from the visitors center. The largest such array in the world when it was built, in 1980, the solar array contains a quarter of a million solar cells that produce up to 100 kilowatts. Push a button, and the (solar-powered) tape player blasts out an informative recording telling you all about it.

Upper Lake Powell

From Natural Bridges, Hwy-95 winds northwest along White Canyon to the upper end of Lake Powell, enclosed by the **Glen Canyon National Recreational Area** ($5 per vehicle) and administered by the National Park Service. The artificial lake formed by Glen Canyon Dam reaches as far up the Colorado River as its junction with the Dirty Devil, the last river in the continental U.S. to be discovered and named (by John Wesley Powell's expedition).

Where Hwy-95 crosses the Colorado River at the top of Lake Powell, **Hite Marina** (435/684-2457) caters to boaters and anglers by offering boat rentals, a launching ramp, a store, and a campground. From here you have the option of continuing north on Hwy-95 to Hanksville and Capitol Reef National Park or you can follow a wonderfully scenic route back to Natural Bridges by taking Hwy-276 south through the foothills of the Henry Mountains—the last range to be named and mapped in the U.S. and now home to the only free-ranging herd of buffalo in the country. At **Bullfrog Marina** (435/684-2243)—home to the luxury **Defiance House** hotel—the ferry *John Atlantic Burr* crosses Lake Powell (up to six times daily,

$9 per car) to the smaller **Hall's Crossing Marina** (435/684-2261). Both marinas offer boat rentals, lake tours, campgrounds, stores, and ranger stations. From Hall's Crossing, Hwy 276 heads east off the edge of the Clay Hills and Red House Cliffs to rejoin US-95 at Natural Bridges.

Bluff

After chipping and dragging their way across half of southeast Utah, the bone weary Hole-in-the-Rock expedition (see special topic) decided that this was far enough and settled in 1880 along the banks of the San Juan River. A few hundred people still live in the hard-won town, which has evolved into a bit of an anomaly in this conservative corner of the state—a liberal, artistic enclave with relatively few Mormon residents.

Recapture Lodge
TOURS OF THE BIG COUNTRY

With a comfy feel, the family-run **Recapture Lodge** (435/672-2281) offers modestly priced motel rooms ($38-48 d), a pool, on-site hike down to the San Juan River, and free nightly slide shows on the surrounding area. Also in Bluff, the **Desert Rose Inn** (435/672-2303) dates to the turn of the century. At one end of Bluff's historic loop, lined with 19th-century Mormon stone houses, sits the timeworn **Cow Canyon Trading Post and Restaurant** (dinner Thurs.-Mon.; 435/672-7208), whose gourmet Southwest cooking with fresh local produce is so popular that reservations are usually necessary. They also stock an eclectic collection of souvenirs, art objects, and books. Look for the upscale **Twin Rocks Trading Post and Cafe**, 913 E. Navajo Twins Drive (435/672-2341) at the foot of the

THE AMAZING STORY OF HOLE-IN-THE-ROCK

In 1879, Mormon Church President John Taylor called on a group of believers to colonize Montezuma Creek in southeastern Utah to secure a remote corner of the rapidly expanding Mormon empire and "breed goodwill among the Indians." And so they went, 236 people—many of them recent arrivals to the western desert—in 82 wagons surrounded by hundreds of horses and cattle, on one of the most arduous journeys in the history of the American West.

From the start, they knew the trip would not be easy. Leader Silas Smith had chosen to cut straight across the barren Escalante Desert to save 250 miles over alternate routes to the north and south. Cattle could find hardly any forage in the wasteland, and Mormon wives, lacking wood, had to burn weeds and sagebrush to cook their food.

In December, with snow blocking any hope of retreat through the mountains behind them, the ragged party reached the edge of Glen Canyon, took one look over the 1,800-foot drop, and immediately sent Smith and two boys back to Salt Lake for blasting powder, mining equipment, and food. When the three men returned, the pioneers sat down to figure out how to get everything down to the river in one piece.

Plagued by bitter cold and dwindling food, 60 men set about building a road where, as author Wallace Stegner writes, "God certainly never intended a road to be." While one team hung from the cliff edge in barrels, chiseling blasting holes to widen and level an existing crack, another group essentially began tacking a road onto the sheer rock face below it. They drove two-foot cottonwood stakes into holes gouged every 18 inches into the sandstone. On the stakes they piled rocks, dirt, and vegetation. And, gradually, a makeshift road began to take shape. Far below, a third team was busy building a ferry on which to cross the river.

On January 25, after six weeks of backbreaking labor, the Hole-in-the-Rock road was finished. By February 10, everyone was down with all their possessions. Amazingly, no lives had been lost—human or otherwise—though many had been injured and all were exhausted. In their descent, the settlers had worn the road down to almost nothing, so there would be no going back. It took a week to get across the river and up the steep wall on the other side. (A Ute Indian to whom the settlers told the story of their amazing feat called them liars and rode away insulted.)

But things quickly got even worse. Scouts trying to find a route ahead almost died of thirst and starvation and only found the way by following a herd of mountain sheep. It took almost four months for the settlers to travel another 150 miles—an average of two miles a day—as they pulled, pushed, and dragged the wagons over slickrock and through sandy wash bottoms. By the time they reached the banks of the San Juan River, everyone had had enough. The planned six-week trip had taken six months, and nobody had the strength or will to push on another mile. Instead, they established the town of Bluff, which faltered over the years but always managed to pull through, perhaps drawing strength from the spirit of its founders.

unmistakable Navajo Twins rock formation towering over the town. Inside, the Simpson family has amassed a wide selection of high-quality rugs, jewelry, and baskets. Great homemade pies help keep the **Turquoise Restaurant** (435/672-2433) in business.

Bluff is the starting point for a popular, modestly challenging **raft trip** down the San Juan River. Most groups put in at the Sand Island Recreation Area three miles west of town on US-191, which has primitive camping and an impressive panel of pictographs. From here it's a three-day float to Mexican Hat through class III rapids and the famous Goosenecks (see below), then another three to six days to Clay Hills Crossing just above Lake Powell. Contact the BLM office in Monticello (435/587-2144) for permits and information. **Wild River Expeditions** (435/672-2244) have been doing this and other nearby river runs since 1947. **Far Out Expeditions**, 7th and Mulberry (435/672-2294), and **Bluff Expeditions**, 189 N. 3rd Street East (435/672-2446), both offer guided tours of the local area by foot and vehicle.

Mexican Hat and the Goosenecks of the San Juan River

Named after a rock formation a mile to the north that looks like an upside-down sombrero, this tiny town, like many in the Southwest, is more notable for what it's near than for what it contains. Mexican Hat itself is little more than a few gas stations and hotels, such as the Western-themed **Mexican Hat Lodge**, on Main Street (435/683-2222), where you can have an expensive steak cooked in the outside restaurant by a cowboy over a swinging grill. Off the highway, the very nice **San Juan Inn and Trading Post** (435/683-2220) has motel-type rooms seemingly carved into the sandstone cliffs; and the on-site **Old Bridge Bar and Grill** is a great place to unwind and rinse the dust out of your mouth after a day in the desert.

Head any direction outside of town, though, and things get very interesting quickly, starting with the vivid grays and oranges staining the cliffs overhead. Head north on Hwy-261, then sharply west on Hwy-316 to reach the **Goosenecks State Reserve**, where the San Juan river has carved a series of tortuous curves 1,000 feet deep in the flat desert. The Goosenecks of the San Juan River are textbook examples of **entrenched meanders**, which begin when a waterway winds across a relatively flat surface. If the landscape is lifted upwards, as it has been in the Colorado Plateau, the river cuts deeper and deeper into the ground, eventually becoming trapped in the wide curves it's cut.

Hwy-261: Valley of the Gods

From Mexican Hat and the Goosenecks of the San Juan River, Hwy-261 makes an amazing run north past Grand Gulch to Hwy-95 and Natural Bridges National Monument. Just over 10 miles north of Mexican Hat, a dirt road (good enough for cars, but impassable when wet) leads east on a 17-mile loop through the Valley of the Gods, a sort of Monument Valley in miniature—and without the crowds. The road passes the remote **Valley of the Gods Bed & Breakfast** ($95; 970/749-1164), with four rooms in a snug stone ranch house—and the best porch for at least 50 miles. In the east, the Valley of the Gods road reconnects with US-163 north of Mexican Hat, 18 miles southwest of Bluff.

Early in the last century, the names "Moki," "Moqui," and "Mokee"—as used in designating the Moki Dugway—were applied to the ancient culture we now call the Anasazi.

In more ways than one, it's easy to lose track of time at the intersection of Utah, Arizona, and the Navajo Reservation. All three are on mountain time, but only Utah and "The Res" participate in daylight savings time. (Arizona has enough sun already.) So, from April to October, make sure to set your watch *forward* one hour if you enter Utah, New Mexico, or the reservation from Arizona, and *back* an hour when crossing into Arizona.

Heading north from the Valley of the Gods turnoff, Hwy-261 heads straight up the sheer edge of Cedar Mesa in a series of white-knuckle gravel curves known as the **Moki Dugway.** You'll probably be ready for a breather after climbing 1,100 feet in three miles, so take the dirt road west at the very top to stunning **Muley Point Overlook**, with the San Juan goosenecks in front and Monument Valley on the southern horizon.

Monument Valley

Heading south on US-163 toward the Arizona border, it's easy to believe you've suddenly driven into a car commercial, or off into a Western-movie sunset. Visual cliche or not, the stone monoliths of Monument Valley Navajo Tribal Park are among the classic sights of the American road, etched into the world-wide imagination by countless frames of celluloid and souvenir postcards.

At an intersection on the state line, a four-mile road leads east to a **visitors center** (daily 7 AM-7 PM in summer; $2.50; 435/727-3287), which perches on the edge of the valley where mesas of Cedar Mesa sandstone—including the Totem Pole and the distinctive Mittens—loom like a celestial rock garden. The Navajo-run visitors center includes a restaurant, snack bar, and gift shop, and dozens of tour companies have set up booths in the parking lot offering trail rides, hikes, and vehicle tours through the monument. Some of the spots in the campground (first-come, first-served; $10) have great views of the valley.

From the visitors center parking lot, a 17-mile dirt loop road passes through the heart of Monument Valley. It also passes many Navajo homes, since the valley is still inhabited, so you're not supposed to walk far from the road (though you can

stop and take pictures of the many redrock formations). The main stop on this self-guided route is John Ford Point, in memory of the Hollywood director whose movies —including *Stagecoach* (1937) and *The Searchers* (1956), both starring John Wayne—indelibly established Monument Valley as an archetypal Western American scene.

Goulding's Lodge and Oljato Trading Post

If you turn west off US-163, away from the visitors center, you'll end up at Goulding's Lodge and Trading Post, which Harry Goulding and his wife, "Mike," started in the 1920s in a 10-man tent. After per-

suading director John Ford that the local scenery made an ideal movie backdrop, the Gouldings opened a lodge that became a second home to stars such as John Wayne, whose name is inscribed in the guest register of the trading post (now a free museum). Set at the foot of a wall of red sandstone, the Goulding's complex includes an immaculate modern lodge ($98-145; 435/727-3231) as well as John Wayne's cabin, a stagecoach, and the Stagecoach Dining Room. Navajo-led 4WD tours of Monument Valley leave daily. Nearby are a grocery store and campground (March-Oct. only, $14 tent, $22 RV) with full hookups and an indoor pool.

A little over seven miles east of Goulding's Lodge sits the Oljato Trading Post (435/727-3210), built in 1921 and one of the oldest still in operation. Step past the rusting gas pumps into the U-shaped "bullpen" for everything from hose clamps to ice-cream sandwiches. In back, the original structure still has a few things for sale, along with museum pieces and old photo albums. They don't sell gas any longer, however, and the airstrip is growing weeds, but this gem hasn't closed yet. The current owners also offer trail rides in the area.

The Navajo consider all of Monument Valley to be one huge hogan (ceremonial lodge), with the traditional eastern-facing door situated near the visitors center.

The buttes of Monument Valley are formed of Cedar Mesa sandstone on top of sloping bases of Halgaito shale. Over millennia, the softer shale has eroded more quickly, causing the sandstone to fracture vertically into the towering formations. Many are capped by red ledges of Organ Rock shale.

Students of Monument Valley High School run the **Changing Winds Inn** (520/697-3948), which has a two-bedroom apartment and rooms in a mobile home for $59-79 d including breakfast.

Between Kayenta and Tuba City, this Canyonlands Loop trip runs in tandem with our Four Corners Loop, which loops around the Four Corners region through the anceint remains of Mesa Verde National Park, Canyon de Chelley, and Chaco Canyon, before winding east to the modern hot spots of Santa Fe and Taos. Full coverage begins on page 398.

Just north of Kayenta along US-163 juts the jagged volcanic thumb of **Agathla Peak,** renamed El Capitan by Kit Carson. This is believed to be the center of the Navajo world, set in place by the Holy People to prop up the sky.

Even if you're not in the mood for a Double Whopper, stop at the Burger King in Kayenta to see the displays on the "**Navajo Code Talkers,**" brave Native American U.S. Marines who, during WWII battles at Guadacanal, Iwo Jima, and elsewhere in the South Pacific spoke Navajo as a code to baffle the enemy and keep their messages secret. Around 100 Navajo Marines, including the father of the Burger King owner, acted as "code talkers," calling for artillery strikes and conveying other essential military secrets—including details of the A-bomb deployment.

Kayenta

The main commercial center of the northern Navajo Nation, Kayenta (pop. 4,400, elev. 5,641 feet) grew out of a trading post established back in 1910. It is now primarily dependent upon two things: tourism, especially in nearby Monument Valley, and the massive strip mines on Black Mesa, which the Navajo Nation leases—controversially—to Peabody Coal. Kayenta has a big supermarket called **Basha's,** a half-dozen restaurants, and two hotels: a $100-a-night **Holiday Inn** (520/697-3221) at the US-160/US-163 junction, and the less expensive **Best Western Wetherill Inn** (520/697-3231), on US-163 a mile north of US-160.

There's a **flea market** held near the community center on US-163 every Wednesday.

Navajo National Monument

Twenty miles south of Kayenta, Hwy-564 leads north to this tiny reserve, which protects two of the largest, most impressive Anasazi ruins in the Southwest. To help preserve the 700-year-old ruins intact, ranger-led tours are the only way to go. You have a choice of a five miles roundtrip to **Betatakin** or 17 miles roundtrip to **Keet Seel.** If you're up for the hike, both are worth the effort. Betatakin can be seen on a six-hour roundtrip day-hike, which departs twice daily (at 9 AM and noon, at last report). Keet Seel, accessible only on an overnight trip, is the

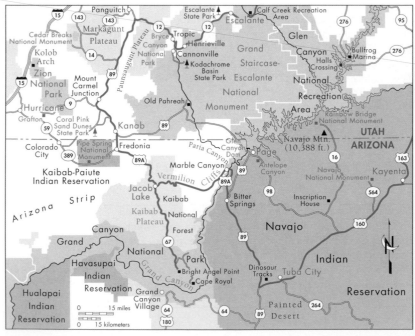

Inhabitants of Keet Seel and Betatakin kept their stored food safe from rodents by designing ingenious sealed storage chambers. Small raised openings were built with recessed edges into which stone slabs fit perfectly, held in place by poles slid through wooden loops set into the masonry on either side.

largest Anasazi ruin in Arizona—an entire town of over 100 rooms tucked under a cliff overhang. Entrance, permits, and camping are free, but group size is limited, so reservations at least the day before are a good idea (summer only; 520/ 672-2366).

For the less ambitious or more time-constrained, a very pleasant one-mile trail leads from the main visitors center to overlooks above Betatakin—which looks tiny from this distance, despite being set in an alcove that's over 450 feet high. There's a nice, small **campground** (first-come, first-served; free) next to the visitors center, the best place to sleep if you're planning to visit the ruins up close.

Tuba City

The urban center of the western Navajo reservation, Tuba City (pop. 7,750) sits just off US-89 between Flagstaff and Page. Most travelers zip past on their way to the North Rim of the Grand Canyon without a second glance. But those who turn off onto US-160 enter the surrealist landscape of the **Painted Desert**, where pastel pinks, rust, tan, lime, and grays stain the barren hillsides. The soils around here, laid down as silt and volcanic ash during the age of the dinosaurs, are mostly bentonite, a clay that shrinks and swells so much as it gets wet and dries that hardly anything can grow in it. The Navajo call this area *halchíltah*, meaning "among the colors."

Traveling along US-160 southwest of the Navajo National Monument, keep your eyes peeled for a sighting of the electric train that carries coal between the Black Mesa mines and the power plant at Page. It makes three trips each day, and about one-third of its 88-mile journey is right along the north side of the highway. If you're an Earth First fan, this was the train that George Hayduke and Company wanted to blow up in Edward Abbey's marvelously mischievous novel *The Monkey Wrench Gang.*

Twenty miles northeast of Tuba City on US-160, the **Old Red Lake Trading Post** (520/283-5194) is steeped in history. Started in 1891 by the Babbitt Brothers Trading Company, the post was acquired as payment of a debt for an early settler who was shot in a card game.

Three miles west of Tuba City along the north side of US-160, eight miles east of the US-89 junction, **Vans Trading Company** (520/283-5343) has a huge selection of Navajo rugs in one corner of a large supermarket. They auction off dead pawn items on the 15th of every month—a good time to find inexpensive jewelry. From the center of Tuba City, head north on Main Street to find the **Tuba Trading Post** (520/283-5441), established in 1870, with its two-story octagonal showroom and a wide selection of quality crafts and souvenirs.

At the intersection of US-160 and AZ-264, the **Tuba City Truck Stop Cafe** (520/283-4975) serves their "world famous" Navajo tacos—a heaping helping of beans, lettuce, tomatoes, and cheese on top of fry bread—beneath signed photos of various celebrities who have stopped in for a bite.

If you're staying in the area and want to have a close encounter with some earnest Navajo youth, students at the Greyhills High School run the **Greyhills Inn** (520/283-6271) as part of a training program in hotel management. Hostel beds are $17, and rooms with shared baths run $50 per person. Ari-

Dead pawn, a term you'll often hear in trading posts, refers to items that were pawned (left as collateral for a short-term loan), never reclaimed by their owners, and subsequently put up for sale.

zona's only high school-run radio station, KGHR (91.5 FM), is also based here, broadcasting an interesting mix of country, classical, rock, and Native American music, plus National Public Radio programs.

The **Tuba City Flea Market** is held behind the community center every Friday. A little bit of everything is for sale—car parts, used clothing, medicinal herbs, turquoise jewelry. And when you need a breather, you can listen to the sounds of Navajo over a bowl of mutton stew and fry bread. The **Western Navajo Fair** is held in the Rodeo and Fair Grounds every October on the first weekend after Columbus Day.

A hand-lettered sign about five miles southwest of Tuba City on US-160 marks the turnoff for a set of **dinosaur tracks,** where for a small fee Navajo children will show you three-toed footprints, petrified eggs, and even an embedded claw from an ancient Dilophosaurus. Like those portrayed in *Jurassic Park,* the "running dinosaurs" evident here lived some 65 million years ago.

From Tuba City, this Canyonlands Loop diverges north toward Page and Lake Powell, away from our Four Corners Loop, which circles east across the Hopi mesas to New Mexico. The Four Corners route along Hwy-264 through the Hopi lands is described beginning on page 401.

Originally built around 1880, **The Gap Trading Post** (520/283-5635), 17 miles north of the Tuba City turnoff on US-89, has been rebuilt twice—most recently in solid stone—after repeated fires. It's now a Thriftway gas station, with a decent selection of jewelry, rugs, and other crafts.

Page

The tidy little town of Page (pop. 8,500) was built from scratch in 1957 to house workers building the Glen Canyon Dam—at the time one of the largest construction projects in the world. Since then, Page has become the tourist center of far northern Arizona, retaining most of its pre-fab, company-town feel.

The **John Wesley Powell Memorial Museum,** 6 N. Lake Powell Boulevard (daily in summer 8 AM-6 PM; 520/645-9496), houses an excellent collection covering early cultures, river runners, and natural history; it's also a local information center.

Budget travelers will be happy to hear that Page has plenty of inexpensive accommodations on 8th Avenue, starting with the **Lake Powell International Hostel,** 141 8th Avenue (520/645-3898), with beds for $12-15 and rooms with shared bath for $35-45. **Bashful Bob's Motel**, on 8th Avenue at 750 S. Navajo Drive (520/645-3919), and **Le Lu's Sleep Ezzze Motel**, 105 8th Avenue (520/608-0273), both have clean, comfortable rooms for under $50. Chain hotels galore are sprinkled throughout the town, led by the **Courtyard by Marriott** (520/645-5000) at US-89 and N. Lake Powell Boulevard, whose **Pepper's** restaurant, voted one of Arizona's 100 best in 1995, commands an expansive view of the dam, lake, and desert. Other eating options tend toward the generic; **Bella Napoli**, 810 N. Navajo Drive (520/645-2706), and **Dos Amigos**, 608 Elm Street (520/645-3036), are two local favorites for Italian and Mexican, respectively.

Heading between the north and south rims of the Grand Canyon, you have two options for crossing the Colorado River: US-89A across Navajo Bridge at Lees Ferry, and US-89 farther north at Page. After leaving US-89A at Bitter Springs, US-89 heads north to Page through **Antelope Pass**, a 300-foot gash in the Echo Cliffs at 6,533 feet.

JOHN WESLEY POWELL AND THE CANYONS OF THE COLORADO RIVER

Of the many chronicles of the exploration of America's western frontier, few have stood the test of time better than those written by John Wesley Powell, the one-armed engineer who led the first expedition down the Colorado River through the canyons of Utah and Arizona. Until Powell's journey, the entire Colorado Plateau region, roughly 200 miles wide and some 500 miles long, was a large blank space on the map, simply labeled "unexplored."

Powell's life story reads like something out of Horatio Alger. Born in upstate New York in 1834, "Wes" Powell grew up in the Midwest and attended various frontier colleges—where he taught himself the fundamentals of geography, geology, and other natural sciences. Volunteering for service in the Civil War, he rose to the rank of major despite losing the lower part of his right arm at the Battle of Shilo. After the war, he took up a position as professor of geology in Illinois and led summer research trips to the Rocky Mountains in search of fossils.

In 1869, thanks to his wartime friendship with then-President Grant, he secured a small measure of federal funding for an ambitious survey of the Colorado River and its as-yet-unexplored canyons. Powell organized a party of 10 men, who set off in four boats from the newly completed Union Pacific Railroad at Green River, Wyoming, on May 24, 1869. Three months, 900 miles, one mutiny, and many near-disasters later, Powell and party emerged at the mouth of the Grand Canyon, the first people to pass through the canyon by river.

Two years later, Powell repeated the journey with a different crew, taking more time to do scientific studies and to compile an accurate map. In subsequent years, he recounted his adventures in government reports as well as newspaper and magazine articles and eventually published a detailed journal, *The Exploration of the Colorado River and its Canyons*, complete with dozens of dramatic illustrations. Powell's enthusiastic accounts of magnificent red-rock canyons are the most readable and evocative descriptions of the region to this day—required reading for any interested traveler.

In Page, **Blair's Dinnebito Trading Post,** 626 N. Navajo Drive (520/645-3008), was the birthplace of the black-background Dinnebito style of Navajo weaving. Along with a large selection of rugs, kachinas, pottery, baskets, and paintings, they also stock raw wool, saddle leather, and pawned jewelry.

From Page, you can hop aboard float trips run by **Wilderness River Adventures** (50 S. Lake Powell Boulevard; 520/645-3279) down the placid, winding stretch of the Colorado through Marble Canyon to Lees Ferry. If you'd like to stretch your legs, head up to the **Rimview Trail,** an eight-mile bike and foot path around the edge of Manson Mesa, with great views of the lake and desert. Start from the nature trail at the north end of town near the Lake View school.

Antelope Canyon

In spite—or perhaps because—of recent publicity, **Antelope Canyon Navajo Tribal Park,** 2.5 miles east on Hwy-98 ($5 per person; 520/698-3347), is another popular outing from Page. Discovered in 1931 by a 13-year-old girl, the slot canyon is 120 feet deep and only a few yards wide in spots. The rosily lit sandstone curves are a photographer's dream (bring a tripod and cable release, and try to shoot near noon). Dozens of companies in town, such as **Antelope Canyon Tours,** 18 N. Lake Powell Boulevard (520/645-9102), offer guided excursions for $10 and up. **Water Holes Canyon,** six miles south of Page on US-89, is another great slot hike.

Like any narrow slot canyon, Antelope Canyon is prone to flash flooding from storms upstream, even if the sky is blue overhead. If your Navajo guide tells you to get out, *get out.* This is something 11 European tourists failed to do in 1997, and it took months to recover their bodies from the mud and debris.

The best **view of Glen Canyon Dam** can be found across US-89 from Page, behind the Denny's coffee shop.

Glen Canyon Dam and Lower Lake Powell

Page's raison d'être is Glen Canyon Dam. Plugging Marble Canyon a few miles west of town, the dam consists of nearly five million cubic yards of concrete—poured around the clock for three years. Free tours of the dam's cave-cool innards—from the gigantic turbines and transformers to an incongruous patch of green grass at the base—are given at the National Park Service's **Carl Hayden visitors center** (daily 7 AM-7 PM in summer; free; 520/608-6404) on the west side of the US-89 bridge.

Lake Powell itself seems like a startling turquoise mirage wavering between the red rock and blue sky. It's real enough, though, with more miles of shoreline than the entire American West Coast and enough water when full to cover 27 million acres a foot deep. Just about anything you could want to do on, under, or near its surface is available at **Wahweap Marina** (520/645-2433), just west of the dam. Wahweap is the largest marina in the Glen Canyon National Recreation Area ($5 per car). A veritable desert navy of boats bobs at anchor in front of the luxury **Wahweap Lodge** (520/645-2433), whose Rainbow Room Restaurant offers a panoramic

DAM DEBATE

When Interior Secretary Bruce Babbit brought a sledgehammer down on McPherrin Dam near Chico, California in 1998, the symbolic blow—ostensibly for the good of spawning salmon—struck more than the dam itself. In recent years, cracks have appeared in an entire ideology begun more than a century ago, when settlers first began using dams and irrigation to feed crops and cities in the deserts of the American West. And nothing has aroused controversy more heated than the 710-foot face of Glen Canyon Dam.

Water has always been the limiting factor in the settlement of the West. And it's a problem whose solutions are, at best, temporary. Dam supporters include ranchers, farmers, developers, and anyone else who benefits from having large quantities of water where it doesn't occur naturally (i.e., most of the U.S. between Colorado and California). Also benefiting, though, are government agencies such as the Bureau of Reclamation and the U.S. Army Corps of Engineers, which threw dams up by the hundreds in the early and middle 20th century. These groups espouse such benefits as pollution-free power, irrigation, flood control, and smooth waterways to transport goods.

On the other hand are scientists, conservation groups, and fish and river lovers, who cite growing evidence of the catastrophic effects dams have on river ecosystems—fish runs devastated, fertile banks turned barren—as well as practical considerations (surpluses of crops and power) and even aesthetics, such as golf courses in Phoenix and the fact that the Colorado River no longer even reaches the Gulf of California, instead trickling to nothing in the sands of Mexico.

Many dam opponents, or "breachers," see Glen Canyon Dam as environmental author Edward Abbey did: as the ultimate symbol of the bulldozing of the West by overeager engineers and shortsighted developers. From the moment the last spillway closed, on March 13, 1963, the dam's opponents have mourned the loss of one of the West's most beautiful canyons, pointing

(continues)

out how the river ecosystem is so altered that trout—cold, clear-water fish, mountain fish—now thrive in the once warm and muddy river; how sediment has filled one seventh of the lake; and how pollutants have become so concentrated that pregnant women are warned to stay out of the water. They're in for a fight from the three million tourists who enjoy Lake Powell every year, as well as anyone who pulls in a share of the $400 million those tourists spend, or who still draws water from the lake or power from the dam.

Abbey advocated the dam's destruction for decades in his novels and essays, but only recently has the idea begun to seem possible. The environmental group Earth First! kicked off its career in 1981 by unfurling a gigantic plastic "crack" down the face of the dam. In 1994, the Glen Canyon Institute was formed to lobby for the resurrection of Glen Canyon. Two years later the Sierra Club—which had not opposed the dam in the first place in a Faustian bargain to keep two more out of Dinosaur National Monument—called for the draining of Lake Powell. The proposal was heard before a subcommittee of the House Committee on Resources in September 1997, but no action has been taken yet.

Over all this hangs the subtle irony of naming the dam after the canyon it covered, and the artificial lake after the explorer and scientist who spent much of his life campaigning against the unwise use of the West's most precious resource.

view of the lake. Rooms range $159-239, depending on the season. Ask at the front desk about boat rentals and tours, including trips across the lake to Rainbow Bridge National Monument and shorter tours aboard the *Canyon King* paddlewheeler. There's also a gas station, an RV park ($23), a campground ($13), and a picnic area within a mile of the lodge.

Detour: Hwy-98 and Rainbow Bridge National Monument

Heading east from Page, Hwy-98 passes Antelope Canyon and the gigantic, coal-fired **Navajo Generating Station**, which squats like a smoking spaceport in the flat desert. Providing electricity to Phoenix and other Arizona cities, the plant burns coal dug from the controversial strip mines farther south on the Navajo Reservation.

Toward the eastern end of the 67-mile Hwy-98 is the turnoff for *Inscription House* and the beginning of the route around 10,388-foot Navajo Mountain to Rainbow Bridge National Monument. It once took weeks by mule from anywhere to arrive at this largest natural bridge in the world (275 feet across and 290 feet high), which is now lapped by the sluggish waters of Lake Powell. If you don't have access to a boat and don't want to join a mass tour from Wahweap Marina, the only other way to see the multihued sandstone span is to hike (13-14 miles each way) from the end of the Navajo Mountain Road (Hwy-16). Since the route crosses Navajo Nation lands, you'll have to get a $10 permit from tribal offices in Window Rock (520/871-6647), Cameron (520/679-2303), or LeChee (520/698-3347) ahead of time.

Rainbow Bridge is considered a sacred religious site by local tribes, so please respect their beliefs by not walking under it or approaching it too closely.

US-89A: Along the Vermilion Cliffs

After splitting off its parent road, US-89A crosses the Colorado at **Marble Canyon**, an area of spectacular scenery with the smooth-topped Vermilion Cliffs on one side and the rough-edged Echo Cliffs on the other. When it was opened in 1929, the original **Navajo Bridge** was the highest cantilevered steel arch in the world—467 feet above the river—and the only place to cross in the 600 miles between Moab and the Hoover Dam. The road itself wasn't even paved until 1937. Today, the bridge has been replaced by a stronger, wider twin, and the old bridge is open only to pedestrians, with a picnic center and interpretive center at the western end.

Before the bridge went up, **Lees Ferry**, six miles upstream, was the only way across. Mormon scapegoat John D. Lee hid out here in 1871 after being accused of masterminding the massacre of a party of settlers up north in 1857. Before he was caught and executed, Lee built the **Lonely Dell Ranch** with the help of Emma, the 17th of his 19 wives. The ranch is now open to the public, along with a group of crumbling stone buildings by the riverbank. Today, Lees Ferry is the traditional put-in for whitewater raft trips through the Grand Canyon.

West of the bridge along US-89A, a few rustic places along the foot of the Vermilion Cliffs offer lodging and local guiding services for rafting, fishing, and hiking. Rooms at the **Marble Canyon Lodge** (520/355-2225) go for $65 d in summer. The **Vermilion Cliffs Bar & Grill** (520/355-2230) has a fly shop on the premises, and the modern, moderately priced **Cliff Dwellers Lodge**, eight miles west of Marble Canyon (rooms $70; 520/355-2228), has a gas station, a small store, and a restaurant.

Jacob Lake and the Kaibab Plateau

From both east and west, US-89A climbs steeply into the evergreen forests of the Kaibab Plateau, surprisingly cool after the heat of the desert below. At Jacob Lake, a tiny pond at an elevation of almost 8,000 feet, US-89A joins with Hwy-67, which heads south toward the edge of the abyss. The **Jacob Lake Inn** ($75-90; 520/643-7232) has fresh-baked bread and milk shakes at the lunch counter and year-round rooms and cabins. **Allen's Trail Rides** (435/644-8150), across the road, organizes horseback trips lasting an hour to several days into the Kaibab National Forest. The U.S. Forest Service **Jacob Lake Campground** has primitive sites for $10.

From Jacob Lake, Hwy-67 reaches almost 9,000 feet as it winds toward the North Rim of the Grand Canyon through the parklike meadows and pine-clad hills of the **Kaibab National Forest**, one of the prettiest in the lower 48 states. Buried by

As it crosses the southern boundary of the new Grand Staircase-Escalante National Monument, US-89 passes the upper end of **Paria Canyon,** which you can explore on a beautiful three- to four-day hike to Lees Ferry with deep narrows, arches, Anasazi ruins, and rock art. Contact the BLM Paria Canyon Ranger Station, 30 miles west of Page and 45 miles east of Kanab, for details and permits (435/644-2672).

Ten miles west of the BLM Paria Canyon Ranger Station, US-89 passes a sandstone obelisk marking the turnoff for **Old Pahreah,** a weathered wooden movie set where parts of The Outlaw Josey Wales and episodes of Gunsmoke were filmed. The six-mile dirt drive is worth it simply for the kaleidoscopic colors banding the cliffs. A bit farther on, the actual **Pahreah townsite,** deserted in the 1930s due to flooding and the exhausting of nearby gold mines, sits on the banks of the Paria River.

During construction of the original Navajo Bridge, parts had to be shipped from one side to the other all the way though Needles, California—an 800-mile trip just to travel 800 feet across the river!

If you see a huge silhouette gliding across the sun near the Vermilion Cliffs, it might be one of six **California condors** released near here in 1996. The gigantic birds, which can reach 10 feet from wing to wing, haven't been seen in this area in 70 years. By 1987, there were only 27 left in the world—all in captivity.

snow in winter, the road is open mid-May to mid-October, weather permitting—for updates, call 520/638-7888 or the U.S. Forest Service visitors center at Jacob Lake (520/643-7298). About halfway to the canyon you'll come upon the homey 1927 **Kaibab Lodge** (rooms and cabins $70-80; 520/638-2389), with Adirondack chairs in front of the fireplace.

North Rim of the Grand Canyon

Though only about 10 miles from the South Rim as the raven flies, the less-developed North Rim of Grand Canyon National Park is more than 200 miles away by road. Consequently, it sees far fewer visitors. However, you can still depend on the same stupendous views of this wonder of the natural world—and the same precipitous trails down to the Colorado River 5,000 feet below—you'll just encounter a few thousand fewer people than you would on the South Rim. At more than 1,000 feet higher, the North Rim is also significantly cooler in the summer—daily highs reach the mid 70s, rather than the 80s or 90s seen on the other side.

At the gate, pay your $20 entrance fee (or flash your Golden Eagle pass) and grab a copy of the park newsletter for details on where to go and what to see. Built in 1928, the log-beam **Grand Canyon Lodge** (520/638-2631, reservations 303/297-3175) boasts two porches and an octagonal Sun Room with huge windows to take advantage of the view from the edge of the canyon. Rooms and cabins range $65-105 per night, and it's a good idea to make reservations as far ahead as possible.

COLORADO RIVER TRIP OPERATORS

Dozens of concessionaires offer trips through the rapids of the Grand Canyon, one of the most famous stretches of whitewater in the world—even after the completion of Glen Canyon Dam. Various options include motorized boats, oar-powered rafts, and supported kayak trips, taking anywhere from three to 16 days to get from Lees Ferry to Lake Mead. It's also possible to join or leave a trip at Phantom Ranch. Here are a few local operators:

Diamond River Adventures, Inc.	**Hatch River Expeditions, Inc.**
P.O. Box 1316	P.O. Box 1200
Page, AZ 86040	Vernal, UT 84078
800/343-3121, 520/645-8866	800/433-8966, 435/789-3813
Grand Canyon Expeditions Company	**Tour West**
P.O. Box 0	P.O. Box 333
Kanab, UT 84741	Orem, UT 84059
800/544-2691, 435/644-2691	800/453-9107, 801/225-0755

Wilderness River Adventures
P.O. Box 717
Page, AZ 86040
800/992-8022, 520/645-3296

The same goes for the restaurant, which serves all three meals. Reservations are wise, too, at **North Rim Campground** (800/365-2267), with sites ($15-20), showers, laundry facilities, and a grocery and camping store.

A 23-mile scenic drive leads east to the overlook at **Cape Royal**, passing half a dozen more view points along the way, many with picnic areas and short trails. Those who venture into the canyon—the only way to gain a true appreciation of the sheer size of the thing—can take the **North Kaibab Trail** all 15 miles from Bright Angel Point to the bottom, where the nine cabins at **Phantom Ranch** (520/638-2631, reservations 303/297-3175) were built from river stones in the 1920s and 1930s. The steeper, unmaintained **North Bass** and **Thunder River** trails also go all the way to the bottom; the latter passes a river that gushes out of a sheer limestone cliff and flows directly into the Colorado, making it the shortest in the world. Wherever you go, it's going to cost $20 for a hiking permit plus a $4 per person per day impact fee, making long trips with a group the most economical way to go. Call the **Backcountry Information Line** (Mon.-Fri. 1-5 PM; 520/638-7875) for details and helpful advice.

Grand Canyon hikers should keep in mind that temperatures can rise to well over 100° F in the inner gorge in the summer—even when it's balmy on the rims—and that it typically takes twice as much time, energy, and water to climb up out of the canyon as it does to descend into it. Carry *at least* one gallon of water per person per day from spring to fall.

Trans-Canyon Shuttle (520/638-2820) sends vans from the North Rim to the South Rim and back daily from May to October.

Kanab

Established as a fort in 1864, until well into the 20th century Kanab was farther from a railhead than any other settlement in the U.S., making it by some estimates the country's most inaccessible town. Hollywood was here even before paved roads, taking advantage of the area's gorgeous scenery at the foot of the pine-dotted Vermilion Cliffs to film more than 50 movies and TV series, including *Drums Along*

By the early 1900s, cattlemen had exterminated all the mountain lions on the Kaibab Plateau. This led to a large population of mule deer. When the hapless animals began to starve, someone had the bright idea of moving all 75,000 deer into and across the Grand Canyon in a grand "deer drive." Cowboys beat pots and pans and shot pistols to frighten the animals into moving, but not a single one stepped down the trail. Eventually the government reintroduced the cougar onto the plateau.

the Mohawk, Have Gun Will Travel, and Planet of the Apes. Even though nothing's been filmed here since 1978, Kanab's still proud of its "Greatest Earth on Show" and has retained a retro air—part Route 66, part Western kitsch, part genuine article—of neon signs and false storefronts, making it the kind of place where you're not surprised to see a real cowboy (a real one) riding a horse down Main Street.

Start at the town **information center**, 78 S. 100 East (Mon.-Fri. 8 AM-9 PM, Saturday 8 AM-5 PM, Sunday 10 AM-2 PM; 435/644-5033) for directions to the many turn-of-the-century pioneer homes open to the public, including the 1885 **Kanab Heritage House**, at Main and 100 South. Next for most visitors —especially those on tour buses—is **Denny's Wigwam**, 78 E. Center (435/644-2452), an unmistakable stone gift shop in the center of town with a huge selection of Western crafts, clothing, souvenirs, and even fudge and ice cream. If you continue ambling down Center, you'll reach **Frontier Movie Town**, 297 W. Center (435/644-5337), a gloriously unabashed tourist trap that hasn't actually been in any movies yet but does boast a barn and stable used in The Outlaw Josey Wales. Knock back a frosty one in the saloon, have your picture taken in the Olde Tyme Photo Parlour, and hang around for a gunfight and comedy show over dinner, served daily.

A little more than five miles north of Kanab on US-89 is another of those only-in-America places, this one a natural sandstone cave that was used in the early

1950s as a dance hall and bar. Since then, the **Moqui Cave** (Mon.-Sat. 9 AM-7 PM; $4; 435/644-2987) has added a set of faux-Anasazi ruins out front and an impromptu museum inside, showing native artifacts, dinosaur tracks, fossils, foreign money, and one of the largest collections of fluorescent minerals in the country. (The radioactive slag of West Virginia glows ominously brightly.)

The **Canyonlands International Hostel**, 1433 E. 100 South (435/644-5554), has seen better days, but at $10 a bed it's the cheapest in town. A handful of inexpensive motels line 100 East on its way out of town toward Fredonia. The surest relic of Kanab's movie past is the **Parry Lodge**, 89 E. Center (435/644-2601), a quaint, pastel motel opened in 1931. Along with autographed photos outside the "Dining Room of the Stars," the lodge has labeled rooms where celebrities such as Ronald Reagan stayed over the years. The motel has an outdoor pool and rooms for around $50. Another holdover, the **Frostop Drive-in**, 210 S. 100 East (435/644-2274), has been turning out Mexican food, burgers, and shakes since 1964. **Wildflower Health Food**, 18 E. Center (435/644-3200), provides a healthy, inexpensive alternative with soup and salad deals for lunch, and the florid **Wok Inn**, 86 S. 200 East (435/644-5400), offers Chinese food that's surprisingly good for being this deep in the desert heart of Utah.

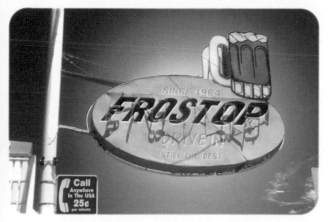

If you're lucky enough to be around Kanab in mid-July, don't miss the music at the **Southern Utah Fiddle Championships & Bluegrass Music Festival** (435/644-5330). Two months later, in mid-September, Kanab hosts the **Western Legends Round-up,** with cowboy poets, square dancing, and more music (call Denny's Wigwam for information).

Set as it is at a crossroads just over the border from Arizona, Kanab has many options for coming and going. US-89 heads north through the Vermilion Cliffs toward Panguitch, passing Mount Carmel Junction (the turnoff for the east entrance to Zion National Park) after 17 miles. To the east, the same road cuts across the southern boundary of the Grand Staircase-Escalante National Monument before reaching Page and the Glen Canyon Dam. US-89A zips south to Fredonia just across the state line, from where AZ-389 leaves to the west across the Kaibab-Pauite Indian Reservation, passing Pipe Spring National Monument and Colorado City before turning into Hwy-59 on its way to St. George and I-15. The other branch of US-89A continues south into the Kaibab National Forest and Jacob Lake, gateway to the North Rim of the Grand Canyon (see above).

Almost the entire 12,000-square-mile, million-plus-acre chunk of Arizona north of the Grand Canyon and west to the Nevada border was recently set aside as the **Grand Canyon-Parshant National Monument.** The two main access roads into this remote region head south from Hwy-389 toward 8,028-foot Mount Trumbull, but there are no real facilities and the Bureau of Land Management, which oversees the monument, plans to keep things that way.

Coral Pink Sand Dunes State Park
Northwest of Kanab, huge dunes of salmon-colored sand—erosional remnants of the Navajo sandstone you see in every direction—have accumulated in a small basin 10 miles west of US-89. Although a majority of the park's acres are given over to the ravages of off-road vehicles, 265 acres have been set aside for those who prefer to kick off their shoes and play Lawrence of Arabia for an afternoon. The state park itself ($4 per car; 435/648-2800) has a campground and not much else.

Colorado City and Fredonia, Arizona, both just across the border from Utah, began life as refuges for renegade Mormon polygamists in the 1880s and are still home to many extended multi-wife families.

Pipe Spring National Monument
Four springs in the middle of the desert gave rise to an oasis of rich grasslands that attracted native tribes and settlers for centuries. Today the grounds of Pipe Spring National Monument (daily 8 AM-4:30 PM; $2; 520/643-7105) encompass a 19th-century Mormon cattle ranch complete with longhorns and Winsor Castle, a stone fort that received the first telegram in Arizona, way back in 1871. (The eponymous "Winsor" was not

The **Short Stop Market** in Fredonia serves coffee by the hour: as many cups as you can drink in however long you pay for.

a member of the English royal family, but an imperious foreman on the cattle ranch by the name of Anson P. Winsor.) Park rangers help organize a variety of "living history" actvities to evoke pioneer life. Adding a touch of modernity, the local Paiute tribe runs a small casino just north of the monument boundary.

Zion National Park

Second only to Grand Canyon—maybe —in sheer jaw-dropping grandeur, the chasm carved by the Virgin River through southwest Utah combines deep slot canyons, waterfalls, a fiery geological palette, and some of the largest chunks of rock you may ever see, anywhere. With elevations ranging from 3,700 to more than 9,000 feet, Zion shelters everything from sandstone desert to mossy gardens, all of it connected by paved and unpaved roads and a network of backcountry trails.

Only a short hop east of the I-15 freeway less than three hours by car from Las Vegas, Zion sees more than its fair share of visitors—close to three million annually. If you can plan your trip outside of the peak months of June through August, all the better. Traffic in the main canyon road has gotten so bad that the park plans to open a park-and-ride **shuttle service.** As in most popular parks, the secret to shedding the crowds at Zion—even in the summer—can be summed up in three rules: go early, go far, and return late. A few hundred yards from almost any trailhead, you can have the place almost to yourself.

Hwy-9 leads through Virgin, Rockville, and Springdale to the park's south entrance, where the **visitors center** (daily 8 AM-7 PM spring through fall; 435/772-3256) has a museum, shows an introductory video, and boasts a great view of the **Towers of the Virgin,** formed—like most of Zion's peaks—from thousands of feet of brilliant red Navajo sandstone.

Beyond the visitors center, a seven-mile paved road leads through the heart of the park, winding up leafy Zion Canyon past the feet of other heavenly rock formations such as the **Sentinel,** the **Great White Throne,** and the **Three Patriarchs,** continuing north past the **Zion Lodge** (435/772-3213), where $100-a-night cabins, complete with fireplace and front porch, sit among the trees. The lodge also has a restaurant, open daily for all meals.

A good alternative to Zion's chronic traffic problems (at least until the shuttle service gets rolling) is a guided **tram tour** from the Zion Lodge, which lets you concentrate on the scenery instead of the road. A bike is even better—rentals are available in Springdale.

The **Temple of Sinawava** marks the end of the park road and the beginning of the **Zion Narrows,** one of the most popular hikes in the park, right up the slippery bed of the Virgin River.

Likened to walking on greased bowling balls, this route heads upstream (or down, if you're through-hiking) to a deep, shadowy slot section hundreds of feet deep. At 16 miles each way, the narrows make for a long day-hike or more reasonable over-nighter—either way, plan on wading (up to waist deep) through the Virgin River almost the entire way.

Many shorter, less imposing trails lead from the scenic drive, taking visitors to such magnificent spots as the **Emerald Pools** and **Weeping Rock**, where Zion's constant supply of water has created startling hanging gardens of moss, ferns, and flowers. If you're not afraid of heights, head up the **Angels Landing Trail**, a five-mile roundtrip that climbs 1,488 feet up a sheer-edged summit to a dizzying view of the canyons. This one's not for the fainthearted—it's so steep by the end that chains have been installed for safety, and it's one of the few trails in the country where you can look down and see rock climbers on multi-day pitches coming up *below* you.

Nicknamed "Yosemite in Sandstone," Zion boasts a huge variety of big-wall **climbing routes** up its sheer rock faces. Pick up a guidebook or give Zion Adventures (listed below) a call for route information and advice.

Zion National Park Practicalities

Springdale, the park's gateway town, offers plenty of places to stay, ranging from the **Zion Campground Motel**, 479 Zion Park Blvd. (435/772-3237), with rooms for $45, to the luxury **Best Western Zion Park Inn**, 1215 Zion Park Blvd. (435/772-3200), where doubles are $99. The **Desert Pearl Inn**, 707 Zion Park Blvd. (435/772-3234), has an attractive outdoor spa and rooms from $74 off-season to nearly twice that in the summer.

The Zion Adventure Company (435/772-1001) has an **adventure day camp** for kids that includes climbing, swimming, and hiking at $50 per day.

For a garlic burger or burrito, try offbeat **Oscar's Cafe**, 948 Zion Park Boulevard (435/772-3232), open for breakfast from 7 a.m. Long waits for fresh gourmet pizza are the norm (and worth it) at the **Zion Pizza & Noodle Company**, 868 Zion Park Boulevard (435/772-3815), open daily for dinner and for lunch as well on weekends. Also good (and popular) is the **Bit and Spur Saloon**, a Mexican place with a lively bar at 1212 Zion Park Boulevard (435/772-3498).

During the day, look for the orchards a few miles west of town to find the **Spingdale Fruit Company**, 2491 Zion Park Boulevard (435/772-3822), an organic market with a shady picnic area.

Bike Zion (800/4SLICKROK or 800/475-4576) offers mountain-bike rentals and guide services, and the **Zion Adventure Company** (435/772-1001) offers plenty of gear and advice for climbing, hiking, and canyoneering and also runs a trailhead shuttle service.

Set on an old ranch in the rolling countryside four miles outside of Zion's east entrance, the **Buffalo Bistro** (435/648-2778) serves fresh game hen, rabbit, wild boar, rattlesnake, and buffalo in the form of sausages, burgers, and steaks for lunch and dinner Tues.-Sunday.

The trail to **Kolob Arch,** one of the largest in the world at 310 feet, is but one of the highlights of the Zion National Park's Kolob Canyon section. Northwest of Zion Canyon, and most easily accessible from an entrance off I-15 exit 40, the Kolob Canyons are much less visited but every bit as memorable as the main park sights.

East from Springdale across the southernmost corner of Zion National Park, the **Zion-Mt. Carmel Highway** heads on an impressive 11-mile route winding through a set of rock tunnels. Large vehicles (wider than 7 feet 10 inches, or over 11 feet tall) may require an escort; call the Zion visitors center (433/772-3256) for details.

Hurricane: Pah Tempe Hot Springs

A half-hour west of Springdale, almost back to the I-15 freeway in the town of **Hurricane** (HUR-i-kun), you'll find the **Dixie Hostel**, at 73 S. Main Street (435/635-8202), with dorm rooms for $15. A better reason to come here is **Pah Tempe Hot Springs**, 825 N. 800 East (435/635-2879), where natural mineral-water springs flow directly into the Virgin River. A small, quaint resort offers B&B accommodations ($66-77) and massage available by appointment. To soak in the hot springs for the day (and at night, when the cave-like pools are especially magical) will cost you $10.

Grafton

The ghost town of Grafton, between Springdale and Hurricane, was settled in 1859 and abandoned by the 1930s. Crumbling buildings in the town are undergoing renovations and may not be all that photogenic, but don't miss the wooden headstones in the cemetery—and the headstone that reads simply, "Killed by Indians." Grafton's most recent claim to fame is that the "Raindrops Are Falling on My Head" bicycle scene from *Butch Cassidy and the Sundance Kid* was filmed here in 1969.

To get to Grafton, turn south from placid Rockville onto Bridge Road (a.k.a. 200 East) and cross the Virgin River on a historic steel truss bridge—built by the National Park Service in 1924 as part of the original road route between Zion and the North Rim of the Grand Canyon. Beyond the bridge, there's a "Y" in the road; to reach Grafton follow the "No Outlet" branch, or take the left side and amble along a truly scenic, eight-mile backroad route that links up with Hwy-59 through Pipe Spring National Monument and the Arizona Strip.

Detour: Cedar Breaks National Monument

Whichever way you ascend onto the Markagunt Plateau from US-89—via Hwy-14 or Hwy-143—be ready for a spectacular drive that climbs and climbs through lumpy, volcanic hills clad with forests of pine, fir, and aspen—more like Colorado than Utah. Volcanic activity as recent as 1,000 years ago has left cinder cones, sink-holes, lava tubes, vents, and jumbles of igneous boulders among dozens of lakes. Both routes, lined by primary-color patches of alpine wildflowers in the summer, are frequently closed by snow from late fall to early spring.

The air is getting thin by the time you reach Cedar Breaks National Monument, where the **visitors center** ($4 per car; 435/586-9451) is set on the western edge of the plateau at 10,350 feet. A five-mile scenic drive parallels the edge of a three-mile-wide bowl of eroded rocks stained brilliant colors by minerals including iron oxide (red), limonite (yellow), and manganese (blue). Cedar Breaks looks a lot like Bryce Canyon in miniature but has the advantages of being more remote—meaning less crowded—and facing west, making sunset, rather than sunrise, the best time for viewing. Five overlooks share the hundred-mile view all the way to the Escalante Desert, and there are a campground and a few short trails along the edge.

Bryce Canyon National Park

Probably the most painfully photogenic of southern Utah's five national parks, Bryce Canyon isn't actually a canyon at all. Instead, it's a gigantic amphitheater filled with a psychedelic assortment of limestone hoodoos, spires, and precariously balanced rocks colored every imaginable shade of cream, lemon, peach, and rust.

Most of this scenic section of the Pink Cliffs, eroded out of the eastern edge of the Paunsaugunt Plateau, is visible from a dozen or so viewpoints along a 17-mile scenic drive, making it popular with the drive-though crowd. Since it's facing east, you'll have to get up for sunrise to see the formations lit up to full effect. Hikers can choose from 61 miles of trails leading along the edge and down into the fantasyland of rocks; the park ranges from 9,100 feet elevation at the rim to 6,500 in the valley. The **Under-the-Rim Trail**, the longest in the park, winds 22.5 miles from one end of the road to the other, but you can reach shorter portions of it from the numerous trailheads along the rim. The eight-mile **Fairyland Loop Trail**, descending from the viewpoint of the same name, is a ranger favorite.

As usual, start at the **visitors center** (daily 8 AM-4:30 PM; 435/834-5322), at the north end of the scenic drive, where you can see a slide show on the park's geology, find out the subject of that night's campfire talk, or, in winter, borrow snowshoes for a tour of the redrock spires dusted with snow.

Along US-89 between Zion and Bryce National Parks, the roadside holds some unusually wacky (for Utah) attractions: rock shops (and a rock church) in Mount Carmel, and, in Orderville, a Wild West souvenir shop decorated as Fort Apache.

Bryce Canyon was named for Mormon pioneer **Ebenezer Bryce**, who lived here in the late 19th century with his wife Mary. Leaving for Arizona after only a few years, all Bryce had to say of the beautiful amphitheater was that it was "a helluva place to lose a cow."

Bryce Canyon National Park Practicalities

In the middle of the park, **Bryce Canyon Lodge** (April-Nov. only; 435/834-5361 or 303/292-2757) is the only remaining lodge of the handful built by the Union Pacific Railroad in the Southwest in the 1920s. The lodge is set back from the edge

The Paiute Indians, Bryce Canyon's original inhabitants, told of the **"Legend People,"** who once lived in a beautiful city built for them here by Coyote. When the legend people misbehaved, they were turned to stone, and remain standing in the valley to this day.

The drive approaching Bryce Canyon along Hwy-12 is a thrill in itself. From the east, you get a great view of the "canyon" from below, gazing up from the town of Tropic. If you're driving toward Bryce from the west, the vivid vermilion hoodoos of **Red Canyon,** just off US-89, offer a preview of the colors to come. There's a Forest Service **visitors center** (daily 8 AM-6 PM in season; 435/676-8815) among the evergreen Ponderosa pines in Red Canyon, where you can pick up information on nearby trails.

Canyon Trail Rides (435/679-8665) offers guided horseback trips through Bryce Canyon, Zion, and the North Rim of the Grand Canyon, ranging from two hours to a full day.

In 1949, photographers from *National Geographic* used a new type of film to shoot the multi-hued sandstone arches and spires just south of Cannonville on Hwy-12. Since then, the area has been set aside as **Koda-chrome Basin State Park** ($4 per car; 435/679-8562), which offers a year-round campground ($12), short hiking trails, and horseback and stagecoach rides.

(the story has it that this one was supposed to be temporary until another larger lodge could be built right on the canyon rim), so don't expect great views, but it does have a restaurant, gift shop, and rooms and cabins for around $100. Nearby are two **campgrounds** ($7) and a grocery store.

The **Bryce Canyon Information Line** (800/444-6689) can help with reservations outside the park, at places such as the **Best Western Ruby's Inn** (435/834-5341), a monstrous resort-style spread just north of the park boundary, complete with pools, spa, gas stations, and rodeo arena. It's open year-round, with rooms starting at $90 in season. For cheaper accommodations, head west on Hwy-12 to the city of **Panguitch** (pop. 1,400), where a host of inexpensive motels, including the **Blue Pine Motel**, 130 N. Main Street (435/676-8197), have rooms in the $40-50 range. Historic brick and stone buildings line the town's classic western Main Street. You'll find red checkered tablecloths and deer heads on the wall at **Cowboy's Smoke-house**, 95 N. Main Street (435/676-8030), with great mesquite BBQ. **Foy's Country Corner Restaurant**, just across the street (435/676-8851), has offered American standards at low prices since 1935. Look for the forest-green 1941 Cadillac in front of **Thunder Horses Mercantile**, 47 N. Main Street (435/676-8900), which features an eclectic collection of western books and knickknacks and is home to the Buffalo Java gourmet coffee shop.

East of the park on Hwy-12, the town of **Tropic** has more mid-priced accommodation choices, such as the **World Host Bryce Valley Inn**, 200 N. Main Street (435/679-8811), and **Doug's Country Inn Motel**, 141 N. Main Street (435/679-8600), both with rooms for around $60.

Hwy-12: Grand Staircase-Escalante National Monument

One of the west's most beautiful drives, Hwy-12 winds between Bryce Canyon and Capitol Reef National Parks across the northern edge of the huge—and hugely controversial—new Grand Staircase-Escalante National Monument. Passing from green livestock-grazing fields near Henrieville, across slickrock desert and up to almost 10,000 feet at the top of the Aquarius Plateau, Hwy-12 showcases the amazing diversity of this rugged landscape—which was one of the last blank spots on the map of the United States.

Set aside by President Clinton in a surprise presidential declaration in 1996 (signed into law at the North Rim of the Grand Canyon, in *Arizona*, no less), the Grand Staircase-Escalante National Monument was founded in controversy. Utah politicians were enraged that they hadn't been consulted in the planning, and tensions have arisen among local ranchers, miners, and farmers, who feel that their land and way of life is being legislated out of existence. Meanwhile, newly arrived environmentalists and government workers are scrambling to protect the huge area.

The fate of the 60 billion tons of coal—the largest deposit in the U.S.—underneath the Grand Staircase-Escalante National Monument is still undecided.

At 1.7 million acres, the Grand Staircase-Escalante National Monument dwarfs the surrounding national parks (it's bigger than all of Utah's other national parklands combined), yet it's so new that it's not even on most maps. In spite of the fact that parts of Hwy-12 weren't even paved until the last few decades, thousands of visitors are already pouring in to this previously little-known wonderland of cliffs, canyons, and desert plateaus.

Three roughly defined areas make up the monument. The **Grand Staircase** itself takes it name from a series of gaudily colored cliffs stepping downward to the Colorado River to the west. The ancient Fremont and Anasazi cultures once overlapped on the rugged **Kaiparowits Plateau** down the middle, which shelters bighorn sheep and significant coal deposits. To the east, the **Escalante Canyons** contain dinosaur tracks and historic pioneer routes along the eponymous river and its tributaries.

For information on the monument and its almost limitless possibilities for exploration on foot or mountain bike or in a vehicle, contact the **Escalante Interagency visitors center** (daily 7:30 AM-5:30 PM; 435/ 826-5499), at 775 W. Main Street in Escalante. You can also try the BLM's **Kanab Resource Area Office**, 318 N. 100 East (435/644-2672), or the **Paria Canyon Ranger Station**, on US-89 west of Kanab (435/644-2672).

Trails and 4WD roads such as the **Hole-in-the-Rock Route**, the **Burr Trail**, and the **Boulder Mail Trail** lead to natural bridges, slot canyons, river gorges, and places with names like Spooky Gulch and the Cockscomb. Overnight backcountry permits are free.

Escalante

Founded by Mormons in 1875, this tiny town (pop. 800) sits at an elevation of 6,000 feet between the Kaiparowits and Aquarius Plateaus. As the main crossroads for the new national monument, it's also at the center of a controversy—among the pioneer homes and barns, you'll see signs demanding that the government give locals back their "back yard," and for every "Wild Utah" bumper sticker, you'll see one proclaiming "Wilderness: Land of No Use."

Just west of town, **Escalante State Park** ($4 per vehicle; 435/826-4466) has self-guided nature trails past rainbow chunks of petrified wood, plus a reservoir for fishing and swimming and a campground. The nicest place to spend the night outside of the backcountry is the modern **Rainbow Country Bed & Breakfast Inn**, 586 E. 300 South (435/826-4567), with a large sun deck and rooms for $65. Another option is the **Prospector Inn**, 380 W. Main (435/826-4653), near the solidly American **Golden Loop Cafe**, 39 W. Main Street (435/826-4433). Stock up on camping gear at **Escalante Outfitters**, 310 W. Main Street (435/826-4266), or just stop by for a slice of pizza and an espresso.

A good introduction to hiking the Escalante deserts starts at the **Calf Creek Recreation Area,** 16 miles east of Escalante on Hwy-12 ($2 day use, $7 to camp). There, a 5.5-mile hike leads up a sandstone canyon to Lower Calf Creek Falls, which plunges 126 feet into a sandy pool.

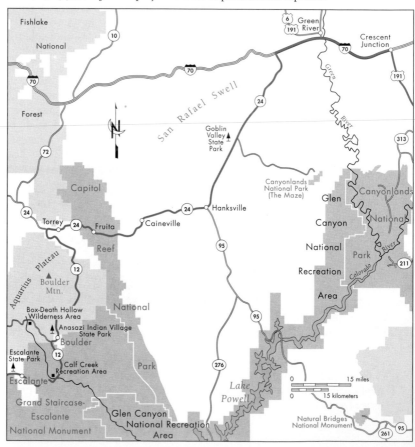

Boulder

The drive along Hwy-12 between Escalante and Boulder (pop. 100; elev. 6,640 feet) is one of the most breathtaking in the Southwest, following the slender neck of a plateau, then dropping into and climbing out of the deep canyon of the Escalante River; the drive from the north, up and over Boulder Mountain, is equally stunning. Apart from the drives in and out of Boulder, the main reason to take a spin through this tiny, pretty town is the **Boulder Mountain Lodge** (435/335-7480), a gorgeous wooden hotel set around an 11-acre pond and waterfowl sanctuary, along Hwy-12 at the Burr Trail junction. Very tastefully decorated with quilts, wood furniture, and flowers, the lodge has rooms for $75-100 a night, as well as the **Hell's Backbone Grill**, cooking up some of the best fare in southern Utah.

Just up Hwy-12 is the **Anasazi Indian Village State Park** (daily 8 AM-6 PM; $5 per car; 435/335-7308), set near the site of an 87-room Anasazi village that has been excavated and partially reconstructed. **Pole's Place** (435/335-7422), across the street, has good burgers and shakes at their walk-up window, and **Hall's Store** has been selling gas, fishing licenses, and sundries since 1961.

To get out into the backcountry, try **Red Rock 'n' Llamas** (435/559-7325), which runs three- to four-day pack trips to Glen Canyon, Rainbow Bridge, and the Escalante and Colorado Rivers; or **Escalante Canyon Outfitters** (435/335-7311), which uses horses.

> Boulder was the last town in the U.S. to receive its mail by mule, which it did until 1935.

> East from Boulder, the 37-mile **Burr Trail** is paved as far as the Capitol Reef National Park boundary. Beyond that, it turns into a wild but usually passable five-mile dirt drive, switchbacking (over 800 feet in a half-mile) over the Waterpocket Fold. It rejoins pavement again on the east side of the park, and rejoins "civilization" at the Bullfrog Marina on Lake Powell.

Detour: Hell's Backbone Road

Even if it didn't have such a great name, the **Box-Death Hollow Wilderness Area**, in the hills west of Boulder, is worth a visit just for the drive there, along humbling Hell's Backbone Road. Starting from Hwy-12, three miles southwest of town, the 40-mile dirt road winds along sheer ridgetops and over gorges, with views all the way east to the Henry Mountains. Along the way, seven miles west of Boulder, you'll pass the **Boulder Mountain Ranch** (435/335-7480), a sort of dude ranch with lodge rooms, cabins, and horseback rides—for an afternoon, or a longer trek along the Great Western Trail.

Boulder Mountain

Northeast from Boulder, Hwy-12 winds up and over the flank of Boulder Mountain, past overlooks so panoramic that they take in more area than some entire eastern states. Topping out at an elevation of 9,400 feet among the meadows, pines, and aspens of the **Dixie National Forest**, this stretch of road wasn't paved until 1985. If you can time it to catch the best of the fall color, you'll be blown away, but it's an unforgettable tour *any* time of year, with views across the red rocks of Capitol Reef and the Waterpocket Fold to the Henry Mountains and distant La Sals, high above Moab on the Colorado border. There are many nice U.S. Forest Service campgrounds along Hwy-12, all first-come first-served, all with water but little else; contact the ranger station in Torrey (435/425-3702) for details.

Approaching Torrey and the west entrance to Capitol Reef, the tall pines give way to sagebrush plains as Hwy-12 drops down from the mountains into the Fremont River valley.

Capitol Reef National Park

This undiscovered jewel is the second-largest national park in Utah, but it receives only a fraction of the crowds of its more famous neighbors. Visitors who don't just zip through the northern tip on Hwy-24 are often amazed at the diversity of the terrain around the Waterpocket Fold, a gigantic wrinkle in the earth's crust running more than 1,000 miles in all from north to south. It almost boggles the mind to imagine the forces it must have taken to fold the surface of the planet like carpet over a stair-step, but it's hard not to be equally amazed by the colors, surreal rock formations, and even oasis of green in this relatively unknown park.

There's no fee to drive through on Hwy-24, but if you turn south on the scenic drive you'll eventually have to pay $4 per car (or flash your Golden Eagle Pass). First you'll pass the park **visitors center** (daily 8 AM-7 PM in summer; 435/425-3791), right in the middle of the **Fruita historic district**, where Mormon settlers

The "Capitol" part of the name of Capitol Reef came from the fact that the huge, round white domes of sandstone reminded early settlers of the capitol building in Washington. The other half of the park's name stems from the fact that many Western pioneers had spent time on the high seas, so anything that blocked travel—such as a huge ridge of rock—they called a "reef."

planted orchards on the green banks of the Fremont River. Fruita is home to a number of weathered old buildings dating to the early part of the century, and the one-time "Eden of Wayne County" is still also startlingly lush, with fruit trees producing apples, cherries, peaches, and pears in summer and fall (visitors are encouraged to pick their own). There's a pleasant shady picnic area among the cottonwood and willows, and a campground ($8) farther down the road.

Head down the 12.5-mile **scenic drive** to reach the turnoff for **Grand Wash Road** past **Cassidy Arch**, where Butch Cassidy is said to have hidden out. Keep going south past the **Egyptian Temple** and the **Golden Throne** —two of the park's more unusual rock landmarks—to reach the beginning of the dirt road down **Capitol Gorge**. The gorge is basically a slot canyon you can drive part of the way through. (Before the current Hwy-24 was built in the 1960s, this used to be the only way vehicles could cross the Waterpocket Fold.) At the end of the road, a short trail heads onward to Fremont **petroglyphs** and the **Pioneer Register**, where passing settlers carved their names in the canyon wall near the turn of the century.

Back up on Hwy-24 is historic **Fruita Schoolhouse** and more petroglyphs high on the rocks. If you have 4WD, take a spin down the **Notom-Bullfrog Road**—which parallels the Waterpocket Fold all the way to Bullfrog Marina on Lake Powell—or the rougher track into **Cathedral Valley**, north of Hwy-24. Hikers can take longer trails through slot canyons and to overlooks on top of the Fold. Backcountry permits are free.

Capitol Reef
National Park

Capitol Reef National Park Practicalities

A cottonwood-lined mile or so of Hwy-24 west of the park makes up the center of **Torrey**, with a few noteworthy places to stay and eat. The **Cafe Diablo**, 599 W. Main Street (open daily for dinner; 435/425-3070), may not look like much from the outside, but the nouveau Southwestern dishes, such as macadamian sea bass, are outstanding. Another surprisingly good restaurant can be found at the **Capitol Reef Inn & Cafe**, 360 W. Main Street (435/425-3271), where fresh local ingredients are combined daily for all meals. Southwestern-style rooms with handmade furniture are $42 d. Perched on a hill over the Hwy-12 junction, the **Sky Ridge B&B** (435/425-3222) has great views, antiques, and delicious morning fare for $93-138 per night.

The **Alpine Anglers Flyshop**, 310 W. Main Street (435/425-3660), houses **Boulder Mountain Adventures** and is the place to go to arrange fly-fishing and other backcountry trips. Educational expeditions are the specialty of **Wild Hare Expeditions**, 116 W. Main Street (435/425-3999), ranging from two hours to multi-day trips. They also run a trailhead shuttle for nearby hikes.

Hwy-24: Capitol Reef to Goblin Valley

After Hwy-24 cuts east through the Waterpocket Fold, the surrounding landscape becomes positively lunar, a barren badlands of pale tans, purples, grays, and yellows. The struggling town of **Caineville** sits smack in the midst of this otherworldly scenery, where Cathedral Valley eases into the San Rafael Desert. Businesses here have closed, and local kids have to ride a bus 60 miles each way to and from school every day. But you still might find the offbeat **Luna Mesa Cafe** open (435/456-9122), serving Mexican and American food daily behind a rose-covered porch. A mile farther on is the **Mesa Farm Market** (435/979-8467), a small organic farm and produce stand with fresh salads and the self-proclaimed "best coffee in the state." (It *is* pretty good.)

Continuing east, following the sluggish, meandering Fremont River downstream, the next crossroads is **Hanksville**; as you pass through, look for the **scrap-metal dinosaur skeletons**

Hanksville marks the junction of Hwy-24 with scenic Hwy-95, which roughly bisects this Canyonlands Loop, running south across the top of Lake Powell toward Natural Bridges National Monuments and the sandstone landmarks of Monument Valley.

—especially the one with the hood and trunk lid of a Volkswagen Beetle for a skull—in front of the Desert Inn Motel. The **Hollow Mountain Gas & Grocery**, in Hanksville, at the junction of Hwy-24 and Hwy-95, was actually hollowed out of a sandstone hillside.

Twenty miles north of Hanksville, Hwy-24 passes the turnoff for **Goblin Valley State Park** (435/564-8110), which is another 12 miles down paved and gravel roads. Imagine Bryce Canyon sculpted in chocolate and left out in the sun too long, or a valley full of drooping sandstone mushrooms stranger than anything in Alice's Wonderland, and you'll have an idea of what to expect here. And the best part is that you can hike among and even climb the formations. Admission is $4 per vehicle, and campsites (available by advance reservation at 800/322-3770) are $10 per night.

Detour: Canyonlands National Park (The Maze) For the determined and well-prepared, the rugged area of this park known as "The Maze," east of Hwy-24 and west of the Green and Colorado Rivers, rewards the time and effort it takes to reach it. Totally inaccessible until the uranium rush in the 1950s put through some (very rough) roads, it still receives fewer than 1,000 visitors a year despite its status as part of Canyonlands National Park. The Maze is remote even by the standards of the Southwest. But if you have the time, it's one of the most beautiful and unspoiled parts of this beautiful region.

Look for the turnoff from Hwy-24, just south of and across from the turnoff for Goblin Valley State Park. From the highway, 46 miles of graded dirt road lead to the **Hans Flat Ranger Station** (435/259-2562), at the border of the Glen Canyon Recreation Area. From there, it's another 14 miles to the top of the **Flint Trail**—where the roads start to get *really* bad. If you have a high-clearance 4WD you can make it to the **Maze Overlook** or the **Golden Stairs**, then descend by foot or vehicle into the **Land of Standing Rocks** and, finally, the **Dollhouse** at the edge of the Colorado River canyon. Wherever you go and however you get there, you're more or less on your own, so you should be as self-sufficient as possible and carry plenty of water (sources are few and far between) and maps—it's not called "The Maze" for nothing.

Closer to Hwy-24, **Horseshoe Canyon** is a detached portion of the park protecting some of the canyon country's most outstanding pictographs. Follow the signs along 24 miles of graded dirt road to the parking and camping area at the canyon's rim, then hike another four miles down in to get to the famous **Great Gallery**, where more than 50 figures were painted on a long wall thousands of years before Christ. Towering up to 10 feet tall, the limbless figures sweep upwards like flames from a bonfire, presided over by the haunting, hollow-eyed "Holy Ghost."

San Rafael Swell

West of Hwy-24, the San Rafael Swell is a huge, kidney-shaped anticline (a bulge in the earth's surface) that stretches 80 miles from north to south on both sides of I-70. The southern section is marked by the **San Rafael Reef**, a jagged line of hills over 2,000 feet tall marking the Swell's eastern boundary. Numerous **slot canyons** slice through this forbidding topography, often joined in pairs with names like Ding and Dang, Chute and Crack, and Little Wild Horse and Bell. Check in with the BLM office in Price (435/637-4584) for information, and pick up maps and guidebooks (Steve Allen's *Canyoneering: The San Rafael Swell* is the best; it's available from the University of Utah Press) in Moab.

From the Hwy-24/I-70 junction, it's a quick 11 miles east to Green River and US-50, the beginning and end of this Canyonlands Loop.

FOUR CORNERS LOOP: NATIVE AMERICA

FOUR CORNERS LOOP: NATIVE AMERICA

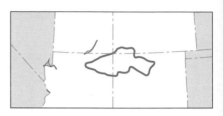

U ntil you've been there and seen it with your own eyes, it's nearly impossible to imagine the overwhelming beauty of the region known as the Four Corners. Named because it's the only place in the U.S. where four states—Arizona, Colorado, New Mexico, and Utah—come together, the Four Corners region is characterized by high plateaus, towering mesas, angular mountains, and an ever-present Native American history and cultural vitality.

The unique geographical conjunction that gives this region its name is probably the least interesting thing about it. Traveling here, you have the chance to sample an incredible variety of landscape and diversity of human cultures. Starting at the exact Four Corners, our route heads counterclockwise through the heart of the Navajo Nation, a semi-autonomous entity within the boundaries of the United States. With nearly 250,000 members—about half of whom live here on the reser-

vation—the Navajo are by far the largest Native American tribe, though their presence here dates only to around 1500. Most Navajo live spread out on small ranches dotted around the 25,000-square-mile nation, which stretches over the borders of Utah and New Mexico. Driving around, you're likely to spy modern pickup trucks parked in front of traditional Navajo dwellings, known as hogans. You're also likely to see signs of the controversial coal and uranium mines and the massive pair of coal-fired power plants which are all part of the unique Navajo-American melange.

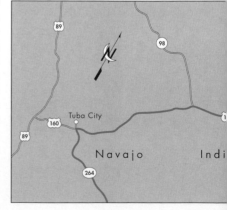

Perhaps the most compelling thing about traveling around the Navajo lands is the landscape itself. Besides world-famous Monument Valley, the northern gateway of the Navajo Nation (covered in the adjacent Canyonlands Loop, the Navajo lands also contain some of the finest remnants of the prehistoric Anasazi peoples, who built the fabulous cliff dwellings preserved in the Navajo National Monument and the Navajo-run Canyon de Chelly National Monument.

Stranded on a series of island-like mesas at the center of the Navajo Nation, the Hopi—predecessors and longtime rivals of the Navajo—are perhaps the clearest relatives of the vanished Anasazi. Once famous for religious snake dances (which in the early 20th century attracted tourists in droves) performed at the clifftop village of Walpi, the Hopi have become more guarded, still making fine jewelry, katsina dolls and other crafts for public consumption, but keeping their ceremonial life private.

Heading east into New Mexico from the Hopi and Navajo lands, before you reach Santa Fe and Taos, set aside some time to explore an earlier capital of the Southwest: the Anasazi pueblo preserved as Chaco Culture National Historic Park. Located high up on the Continental Divide, the intricately constructed city here was thought to have been the ceremonial center of the Anasazi empire. Nowadays, it's about as far off the beaten track—20 miles of dusty dirt road from the nearest paved highway—as you can get. Another Anasazi remnant, the cliff houses of Bandelier National Monument, sit just west of Santa Fe. In a clear case of cosmic irony, these ancient dwellings are right next door to the U.S. government laboratories at Los Alamos, where the atomic bombs that destroyed Hiroshima and Nagasaki were developed.

The historic, artistic, cultural, and culinary capital of the Southwest, Santa Fe is a lively small city. Along with everything else, it makes a refreshing change from the dusty wilderness of the rest of the Four Corners region. North from Santa Fe, a twisting scenic route aptly known as the High Road climbs up the Sangre de Cristo Mountains to the arts colony of Taos, a historic small town that has a little of everything that makes New Mexico so intoxicating—Native American culture, Wild West history, beautiful scenery, fine art, and fine food.

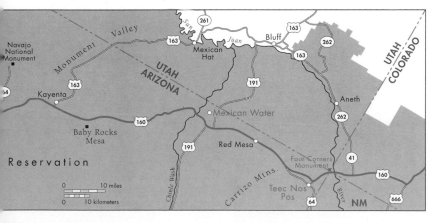

From Taos, our route heads into the mountains of Colorado, passing through the mining-camp-turned-mountain-bike-mecca of Durango on the way to Mesa Verde National Park, where the most stunningly sited Anasazi ruins anywhere are tucked into sheer cliffs at what feels like the top of the world. No matter how many—or how few—other Anasazi remnants you see here in the Southwest, Mesa Verde is a place you'll never forget.

By far the best map of the Four Corners area is the Automobile Club of Southern California's ***Indian Country,*** available from most AAA offices and just about everywhere on the route.

The term **Anasazi,** which means "ancient enemies" or "enemies of my ancestors" in Navajo, is coming under fire for its negative connotations by contemporary tribes who claim them as ancestors. Today, you'll often hear the term "ancestral Puebloans" used instead.

The Four Corners Monument

One of the better examples of Tourist Man's neverending search for novelty, the Four Corners Monument (daily 8 AM-5 PM, 7 AM-7 PM in summer; $1.50 per person) marks the only spot where four U.S. states meet. The borders of Colorado, New Mexico, Utah, and Arizona—and hundreds of eager visitors every day—all come together at this otherwise unremarkable spot, which is located at the north end of a short driveway, off US-160 from the New Mexico "corner." The actual convergence is surrounded by a circle of flagpoles and marked by a concrete slab in which are embedded the four state seals and the motto "Here Meet, Under God, Four States." Visitors take turns climbing up to a short platform to take pictures of their fellow travelers standing in four states at once, while dozens of Navajo souvenir, crafts, and fry bread stands form an outer wall around the monument.

The actual spot was established and mapped as the mutual border way back in 1875, but Four Corners only became the tourist attraction it is today after the US-160 highway was opened in 1962. The Four Corners Monument is operated as a Navajo tribal park; Golden Eagle and other park passes are not accepted, and there's no camping (or water) available. (There are some portable toilets, though, if you're desperate.)

Teec Nos Pos and Mexican Water

South and west of the Four Corners Monument, US-160 runs across the Navajo Nation along the south side of the Utah-Arizona border. At Teec Nos Pos, where US-160 is joined by US-64 from Farmington, a pair of trading posts and gas stations stand astride the crossroads, while the impressive (and uranium-rich) Carrizo Mountains rise up to the south. Similarly small communities line the route west, past the bright red sandstone of Red Mesa to Mexican Water ("Home of the Red Mesa Redskins"), where another trading post and gas station combo is joined by the **Mexican Water Restaurant**, known for its very good Navajo Tacos.

South from Mexican Water, US-191 runs along Chinle Wash to the west end of Canyon de Chelly National Monument. Seven miles west of Mexican Water along US-160, the **Navajo Trails Motel** (520/674-3618) offers the only rooms for many miles; doubles cost around $60 a night.

Kayenta marks the junction with our Canyonlands Loop, which heads 24 miles north to Monument Valley (and beyond) and west to Lake Powell, the North Rim of the Grand Canyon, and Zion and Bryce National Parks in southern Utah. The two routes run together between Kayenta and Tuba City; those two towns, and the stretch of US-160 between them, are covered on pages 372-374.

Somewhat ironically, the Four Corners Monument is actually on Navajo Nation land, legally distinct from any of the four states that supposedly meet here. Adding to the nominal confusion, the Arizona corner is officially part of Apache County, though that tribe's reservation is hundreds of miles to the south.

From just north of the Four Corners Monument, you can turn west off US-160 onto Hwy-41, which leads across the northern Navajo Nation through the oil-drilling center of Aneth, then, via Hwy-262 and Hwy-163, to the Mormon town of Bluff and on to Monument Valley.

Former Navajo Nation chairman **Peter MacDonald**, who was sentenced to 14 years in prison for corruption in the early 1990s, grew up in the Teec Nos Pos community.

Third Mesa: Old Oraibi

Heading east from the mainly Navajo community of Tuba City, this is the first substantial Hopi community you encounter. It's also the oldest. In fact, Old Oraibi is considered to be one of the oldest inhabited places in North America, with signs of occupation dating to well before A.D. 1300. Located on top of what's known as Third Mesa, around 40 miles east of Tuba City, Old Oraibi

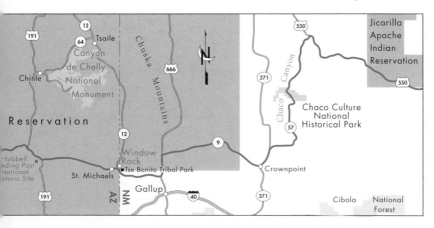

About 10 miles east of Kayenta, right along the south side of US-160, **Baby Rocks Mesa** is a miniature Bryce Canyon of eroded sandstone spires. It's also a popular spot for Navajo Nation police to catch speeders. Consider yourself warned.

One might prefer some great hierarchical significance to the names First, Second, and Third mesa, but the real reason behind the order is simple: the names were given by Spanish explorers coming from Santa Fe in the east; they were named simply in the order in which they were encountered.

Though many Hopi religious ceremonies are strictly for Hopi only, some dances and other ceremonies may be open to the visiting public. The Hopi Cultural Center will usually have details, but exact dates and times are set by the individual villages and are rarely announced until the morning of such events. This can make planning a visit to the mesas more than little frustrating, but, as the T-shirts say, Don't Worry, Be Hopi.

The two villages at the base of First Mesa—Polacca and Hano—are inhabited not by Hopi but by **Tewa Indians**, who settled here in the 1680s after the Pueblo Revolt in New Mexico.

(o-RY-bee) doesn't cater to visitors to any great degree, but there is a crafts shop and, unless the village is closed for a religious ceremony, you're free to wander the dusty old streets.

Old Oraibi is not called "old" simply for its long history—the adjective is used mainly to distinguish it from *New* Oraibi, a neighboring community—also known as **Kykotsmovi**—two miles east along Hwy-264. Kykotsmovi is the nominal center of tribal government, though since the Hopi tribe is organizd primarily on a village-by-village basis, the "central" tribal government is a fiction created to deal with the U.S. government.

In between the two Oraibis along Hwy-264, Pumpkin Seed Point is a great stop, offering grand views of the Hopi Buttes, 40 miles to the southeast.

Second Mesa: the Hopi Cultural Center

By and lage, the Hopi people do not seem very interested in popularizing their beliefs or using their lifestyles to entertain tourists, but there is one place you can go for an introduction: the Hopi Cultural Center (Mon.-Fri. 8 AM-5 PM; $3; 520/734-6650), which sits at the center of the Hopi reservation, more than a mile high atop Second Mesa. Housed in a modern Pueblo-style building comprising a museum, a crafts shop, a restaurant, and a motel, this is *the* place to get a feel for the Hopi way of life. The musem has exhibits explaining Hopi history and cosmology, with special focus on kachinas, the colorful dolls that represent ancestral spirits and are such a vivid key to the Hopi imagination. The crafts shop showcases the intricate silver inlay jewelry for which Hopi artists are famous, and the restaurant has reliably good food, including many dishes that use sacred Hopi blue corn (you can even get blue corn Corn Flakes). The motel (520/734-6651) has over 30 clean and pleasant rooms, costing around $85 a night; these are very popular during the peak summer months, so reserve ahead as early as you can—especially for weekends, when most dances and other ceremonial events are held on the mesas.

First Mesa: Walpi

No matter how much you read and learn about Hopi history and culture, nothing can prepare you for the spectacular, magical sight of the most traditional Hopi village, Walpi. It will take your breath away. Sitting, or perhaps floating, on a narrow, knife-edged island at the far west end of First Mesa, Walpi is a tiny village (pop. 30), with a small central plaza surrounded by ancient houses built of the same stone as the mesa itself. At Walpi, the mesa top is barely 150 feet across at its widest point (15 feet at its narrowest, near the entrance), and the cliffs drop off swiftly, tumbling down hundreds of feet to dry-farmed fields of corn. The village seems to hover in midair, barely connected to the distant horizon.

HOPI KACHINAS

More than mere playthings or tourist souvenirs, Hopi kachinas are an integral part of Hopi life. Representing a variety of 300 different deities—from gods of sun and rain to evil ogres—each kachina plays a particular role in the religious and social life of the Hopi community. The kachina doll is but one form these spirits can take; the kachina spirits also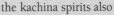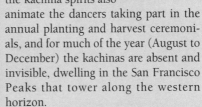

The traditional spelling of "kachina" is being replaced by the linguistically more correct "katsina."

animate the dancers taking part in the annual planting and harvest ceremonials, and for much of the year (August to December) the kachinas are absent and invisible, dwelling in the San Francisco Peaks that tower along the western horizon.

But it's the dolls that most people identify with the kachinas. That's understandable, since the dolls are among the most intricate and beautiful works of Native American art. Their primary purpose is to introduce children to the rich mythology underlying Hopi life, but they have also become a lucrative source of income for their carvers. Besides representing the kachina sprits, these dolls can also represent other Hopi cultural characters, especially the playful clown figures like the black-and-white "koshares" and the popular "koyemsi," or mudheads. Most of the kachinas you'll see offered for sale are not proper Hopi kachinas at all but rather mass-produced by non-Hopi. Because each one can take a week or more to make, real Hopi kachinas cost $300 and up. Some of the best collections of kachina dolls are in the Heard Museum in Phoenix, the Northern Arizona Museum in Flagstaff, and the Southwest Museum in Los Angeles. In Hopi country, you can usually see some fine examples in the Hopi Cultural Center.

Walpi still looks exactly as it did when the first photographers came through, in the 1880s. Residents live without water or electricty; it's a bit like a museum and can be visited only if you are accompanied by a Hopi guide. Guided tours (daily 9:30 AM-4 PM; donations of $5 or more per person recommended; 520/737-2262) take about 45 minutes, can have from one to a half-dozen guests, and start at Ponsi Hall in the neighboring village of Sichomovi. Ponsi Hall lies at the end of the only paved road (very steep—no RVs) up to First Mesa from Hwy-264. Try to come on a weekday, since summer weekends are the busiest times of the Hopi calendar and Walpi is closed to outsiders during religious ceremonies.

A word about time zones: the Navajo Nation and the Hopi Nation are both on mountain time, but the Navajo Nation observes daylight savings time while the Hopi (and the rest of Arizona) do not. So from April through October, Navajo Nation time is one hour ahead of the Hopi Nation and all of Arizona.

Keams Canyon

A U.S. government Bureau of Indian Affairs (BIA) town just east of the Hopi reservation boundary, Keams Canyon is an unlovely place with an unlovely past: historically used as a coal mine, in 1863 this was where Kit Carson assembled the military forces he used to remove the entire Navajo tribe east on the notorious "Long Walk" to Fort Sumner in eastern New Mexico. Nowadays there's a gas station, a small cafe, a hospital, and the very basic **Keams Canyon Motel** (520/738-2297).

Canyon de Chelly National Monument

The shared history of the Southwest is nowhere more vivid than at beautiful Canyon de Chelly National Monument, the only national monument legally owned and operated by someone other than the U.S. government—the Navajo Nation. The towering sandstone walls of Canyon de Chelly (pronounced "de-SHAY") still hold remnants of Anasazi cliff palaces as impressive as those at Mesa Verde, but history here doesn't end 600 years ago. After the Anasazi vanished, the Navajo moved in, planting the peach trees that Kit Carson and the U.S. Cavalry later chopped down as part of the cruel but effective efforts to drive the Navajo from the region.

Canyon de Chelly sits at the heart of the Navajo Nation, stretching east from **Chinle**, a mid-sized Navajo town on US-191, roughly 30 miles north of Hwy-264 and 50 miles south from US-160, all the way to the New Mexico border. A pair of highways run from the monument entrance in Chinle east along the north and south rims of Canyon de Chelly, offering amazing scenic overlooks over 1,000 feet straight down into the broad sandstone gorge.

About six miles east of the vistor center is the parking area for **White House Ruin**, the only place visitors are allowed into the canyon to visit without a guide. The hike is about 2.5 miles roundtrip, down to the ruin (and up again) on a steep but very pretty trail. The **South Rim Drive** winds for about 22 miles east from the visitors center, ending up at the 800-foot tower of **Spider Rock**, the spiritual home of the legendary Spider Woman—who taught the Navajo to weave.

The **North Rim Drive** winds from the visitors center along the mesa top, after eight miles passing the viewpoint for the circa-A.D. 700 A.D. Anasazi cliff palace called **Antelope House**. Another eight miles along is the even more spectacular Anasazi ruin known as **Mummy Cave**, which features a prominent central tower and was inhabited for more than 1,000 years—until approximately A.D. 1300. Another eight miles along, outside the monument boundary, the North Rim Drive reaches the Navajo village of **Tsaile**. Here the Navajo Community College campus runs the small but intriguing **Ned Hatathli Museum** (Mon.-Fri. 8 AM-5 PM; free), displaying local arts and crafts. If you're lucky, in summer you may be able to get a room in a dorm here; call for reservations (520/724-6782).

Almost all of Canyon de Chelly itself (everything except the trail to White House Ruin) is closed to unescorted visitors, but it's still home to Navajo farmers, many of whom double as tour guides, taking visitors (on horses, on foot, or in open-topped old surplus troop transport half-tracks) through the canyon and explaining its geological makeup and historical significance. Tours can be arranged through the Thunderbird Lodge or through the main Canyon de Chelly visitors center; see below for details.

In recent years, there have been problems with **theft** from cars along the rim drives at Canyon de Chelly, so be sure to hide any valuables and lock your car doors.

Canyon de Chelly Practicalities

Canyon de Chelly, unlike most national parks and monuments, is kept in its natural, undeveloped state. There are no real visitor facilities—not even a campground—within the canyon itself; all the nearest food and lodging is found between the canyon and the nondescript town of **Chinle**, on the western boundary. The limited facilties means that you may have to base yourself in Window Rock, Kayenta, Gallup, or Holbrook—all of which are at least an hour away—so reserve a room as early as you can.

The closest and most atmospheric place to stay, **Thunderbird Lodge** (520/674-5841 or 800/679-2473) is a former trading post and dude ranch located right at the mouth of the canyon. The lodge, which also has a good, cafeteria-style restaurant in the old historic trading post, is now the best place to connect with a **guided tour** of the canyon. The Jeep tours offered, which rattle along the sandy canyon floor and splash across streams, are either half-day (departing 9 AM and 2 PM; about $35) or full day (9 AM; $60, including lunch).

Other lodging options include an ersatz adobe **Holiday Inn** (520/674-5000 or 1-800/HOLIDAY), which has a swimming pool and is net door to reliably good **Garcia's Restaurant**, and the **Best Western Canyon de Chelly** (800/528-1234). Both are on the road between Chinle and Canyon de Chelly. Chinle itself has a supermarket, a bank with an ATM, and some fast-food restaurants, but little else.

The one and only Canyon de Chelly campground, **Cottonwood**, is next to the Thunderbird Lodge. It's free, but it's first-come first-served and very basic—there are no showers and sometimes no water at all.

For more complete information on visiting Canyon de Chelly, contact the **visitors center** (daily 8 AM-5 PM, until 6 PM in summer; free; 520/674-5500), which has introductory exhibits on the geology and cultural history of the canyon. This is also the place to get in touch with local Navajo guides offering hiking or horseback tours into the canyon.

Hubbell Trading Post
National Historic Site
Just south of Hwy-264, midway between the Hopi mesas and the city of Gallup, New Mexico, you'll find a rare survivor: a real-life Wild West trading post. Now managed by the National Park Service but otherwise unchanged since its turn-of-the-century heyday, the Hubbell Trading Post (daily 8 AM-5 PM, till 6 PM in summer; free; 520/755-3475) was built in 1871. It remained in business until the 1960s, providing supplies to the Navajo in exchange for wool and crafts. Navajo weavers are often on-site, demonstrating the art and craft of rug-making. You can also tour Hubbell's home, which is decorated with some fine (and very valuable) examples of Native American art.

Window Rock: Capital of the Navajo Nation
Established in 1934 and much more the adminstrative than the spiritual capital of the Navajo Nation, the sprawling town of Window Rock (pop. 8,000; elev. 6,750 feet) sits astride the Arizona-New Mexico border about 24 miles northwest of Gallup. The rock itself for which the town is named (known as *Teghahodzani* in Navajo) is about a half-mile north of Hwy-264, east of Hwy-12. With a 50-foot

"window," the rock is set in a lovely, shady park; nearby stands the hogan-like octagonal Council Chamber where the Navajo Nation Council meets to set tribal policy.

The main tourist attractions, such as they are, in Window Rock line Hwy-264. The **Tse Bonito Tribal Park,** a quarter-mile east of Hwy-12 at the foot of Haystacks Rocks, has a small zoo (free) with many native mammals (cougars, bobcats, goats, sheep), birds of prey, and reptiles. There's also basic camping available here. Nearby, the **Navajo Nation Museum** (Mon.-Fri. 8 AM-5 PM; donations; 520/871-7371) has items tracing Navajo history and culture, and next door, the modern **Navajo Nation Inn,** 48 W. Hwy-264 (520/871-4108), has 56 motel rooms (doubles cost around $75) and a very popular coffee shop (great for eavesdropping on Navajo shop talk). There's also a Day's Inn along Hwy-264 on the west side of town.

On the west edge of Window Rock, the historic community of St. Michaels was founded in 1896 as a Franciscan mission, and many of its monks made valuable contributions to the Navajo people—creating the written Navajo alphabet, for example.

Window Rock is the broadcasting base of radio station **KTNN 680 AM,** the "Voice of the Navajo Nation." KTNN fills the airwaves with classic country-western tunes, occasional Navajo chants, and Dallas Cowboys football games—with play-by-play in Navajo.

Detour: US-666 to Shiprock

Between Window Rock and Gallup, Hwy-264 is a fast, four-lane freeway, pausing only at the intersection with US-666. Running north, to Cortez, Colorado, and beyond, US-666 takes a very scenic route along the eastern foot of the Chuska Mountains, and the 90-mile drive is highlighted by one of the great landmarks of the desert Southwest: Shiprock (known in Navajo as *Tse Bidahi* or "winged rock") is a 1,700-foot-tall

The annual **Navajo Nation Fair** takes place in Window Rock the week after Labor Day and features powwow dance competitions, rodeos, fry bread contests, even a Miss Navajo beauty pageant.

volcanic plug with long thin igneous fins that resemble sails. These fins (or dikes, as they're also called) are more than a mile long but only 10 feet wide in places. You can see Shiprock very well from US-666. Red Rock Road (Hwy-33), which runs south and west from US-666, can take you closer—to within a mile—but there's no direct access, since the rock is considered sacred by the Navajo.

The sprawling mining town also known as Shiprock (pop. 7,200; elev. 7,192 feet) is seven miles north and east of the Shiprock pinnacle and offers basic gas-food-lodging services, but few reasons to linger.

The quickest route east from Window Rock to Albuquerque and beyond is I-40, which runs a little farther south and is covered in our Route 66 chapter, on pages 276-319.

Chaco Canyon

To reach Chaco Canyon from I-40 and old Route 66, it's a 60-mile drive, north along Hwy-371 from Thoreau (pronounced "threw") via Crown Point, then east along Hwy-9, the final 21 miles along a bumpy dirt road, Hwy-57. From Window Rock and US-666, take Hwy-9 all the way, avoiding the detour south through Gallup along I-40. Coming from the north and east, it's about the same distance and difficulty to get here from Cuba, a crossroads town northeast of the park on Hwy-44.

The routes passing into and out of ancient Chaco Canyon are generally awful—rutted at the best of times and virtually impassable during inclement weather. But persevere and you'll eventually come to the wonderful **Chaco Culture National Historic Park** (daily 8 AM-5 PM; 505/786-7014), which preserves the remnants of what was once among the largest civilizations in North America. The rough going in and out of Chaco Canyon—and the fact that there are no gas services, food concessions, or hotels anywhere nearby—keeps this archaeological treasure free from the overcrowding that can ruin other national park visits: only about 85,000 people visit during an entire year, which is as about many as visit the Grand Canyon on a single long weekend. Though for scenic beauty the setting here may not compete with other Anasazi ruins, in terms of fascinating history and the amazing degree to which it's been preserved, Chaco is without peer. Make every possible attempt to see it.

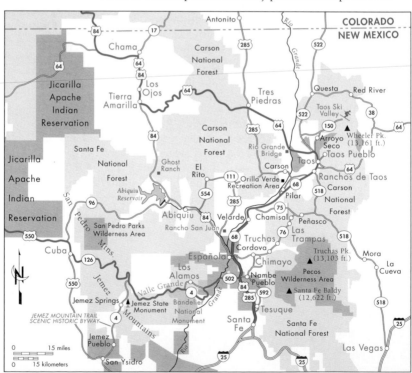

The highlight of Chaco Canyon is **Pueblo Bonito**, perhaps the most brilliant ruin in the Southwest, a massive semicircular "great house" that once stood four stories tall in places and encompasses many kivas (underground worship chambers) and interconnected cells. Pueblo Bonito—the ritualistic and cultural center of a Chacoan culture that may once have comprised some 150 settlements throughout the Four Corners region—is the most substantial and architecturally refined structure surviving from ancient Anasazi culture. Many other ruins are spread around the park, including an amazingly accurate astronomical observatory (closed to the public) atop Fajada Butte, many other smaller pueblos, and some 450 miles of ancient paved roads—some of them 30 feet wide and running arrow-straight for miles across the desert—which linked Chaco with other ancient Anasazi communities throughout the Southwest.

It's believed that many of the people who lived in Chaco Canyon and Mesa Verde a millenium ago eventually settled in the Rio Chama and Rio Grande valleys. Today's Pueblo people, their direct descendants, reject the popular term Anazasi, which, in the language of their Navajo rivals, means "ancient enemies."

Pueblo Bonito and other archaeological features are accessible only during daylight hours, via an eight-mile, one-way **loop road** that starts next to the park **visitors center**, where you should check in, pay the entry fee ($8 per car; Golden Eagle passes accepted), and meander through a small museum on Chaco Culture. Near the visitors center is a basic, first-come first-served **campground** ($10) with tables, fireplaces, and pit toilets; camping is limited to seven days. The bare-bones quality of these campsites and the rest of the facilities at Chaco is in some ways their greatest asset: the nights come alive with bursts of shooting stars and there's no traffic to muffle the sounds of nature.

Cuba

From Chaco Canyon, it's a 20-mile drive north to reach US-550/Hwy-44, and the first 16 miles are along a dirt road. On the main highway, there's a gas station and mini-mart where you can restock on fuel, water, and snacks. From there, head south along US-550/Hwy-44 for roughly another 60 miles to Cuba (pop. 760), a town of few people and fewer attractions but a good base for exploring Chaco Canyon, the San Pedro Parks Wilderness Area, and the Jemez Mountains.

If you're simply passing through, pop inside **Frostee Freez**, 6453 Hwy-44 (505/289-3341), an ice cream stand festooned with dwarf statuary and other kitschy figurines and where cool drinks, banana splits, and malts come in huge portions. More substantial—and reasonably tasty—diner fare is dished up at the **Cuban Cafe**, 6333 Hwy-44 (505/289-0275), a locals' joint on the south side of town. If you're here for the evening, on the other hand, by all means spend the dinner hour at the best restaurant between Farmington and Bernalillo, **El Bruno's**, 6448 Hwy-44 (505/289-9429), a sprawling Mission-inspired spread filled with chile ristras, decorative masks, and colorful Southwestern art. Margarita-marinated chicken and tender ribeye steaks are among the offerings.

There are a few zero-frills but clean motels in Cuba, including the **Cuban Lodge**, 6332 Hwy-44 (505/289-3475), and the dated but dirt-cheap **Frontier Motel** (505/289-3474). To find out more, contact or visit the Cuba **Regional Visitors Centers**, at the junction of US-550/Hwy-44 and Hwy-126 (505/289-3808).

Hwy-126: Cuba to Valle Grande

In summer (and only when it's fairly dry), adventurers should consider bypassing US-550/Hwy-44 south of Cuba and cutting over the San Pedro and Jemez Mountains to Hwy-4 via Hwy-126, a minimally maintained dirt road that passes through startlingly lush and magnificent scenery (and cuts many miles off the trip). Drivers regularly see coyotes, elk, foxes, beavers, and turkeys along this drive, which takes you past meadows of wildflowers and tall grass, moist coniferous forests, translucent creek beds, and a few secluded camping areas—you'll hardly believe that the arid and monochromatic high-desert landscape northwest of Cuba is just 20 miles behind you.

At its east end, Hwy-126 drops down into the volcanic caldera of Valle Grande, linking up with Hwy-4 between Jemez and Los Alamos.

A mile north of Jemez Springs on Hwy-4 is **Jemez State Monument** (505/829-3530), which preserves the ruins of the Church of San Jose, a 1600s edifice whose foundation and some six- to eight-foot walls have been excavated in recent years.

Hwy-4: Jemez Mountain Trail Scenic Historic Byway

From Cuba, unless you opt for the Hwy-126 shortcut over the mountains, continue southeast along US-550/Hwy-44 for another 40 miles to San Ysidro, the southern end of Hwy-4 and the Jemez Mountain Trail Scenic Historic Byway. Following this road north and east, you'll climb rapidly and tortuously toward Los Alamos, winding high alongside the Jemez River and the Jemez Mountains, passing Jemez Pueblo and then the town of Jemez Springs. The road gradually winds through beautiful red rock formations; occasionally you'll pass roadside stands hawking foods and crafts from Jemez Pueblo, which is not open to the public.

Tiny **Jemez Springs** has a few galleries and restaurants but is most famous for its sulfur-rich geothermal waters—whose curative powers may be experienced at the **Jemez Springs Bath House**, 62 Hwy-4 (505/829-3303), renowned for its mineral baths, herbal wraps, therapeutic massage, and facials. Grab a bite to eat at the **Laughing Lizard Inn & Cafe**, (505/829-3108), which serves healthful food and also has some overnight rooms. Or nosh on baked goods and sip lattes at **San Diego Canyon Bakery & Coffee Shop**, 17502 Hwy-4 (505/829-3956).

Valle Grande

After driving for several more miles through the steep, rocky, densely wooded terrain, east of the junction with Hwy-126 from Cuba, the view from Hwy-4 suddenly opens onto one of the most memorable sights in New Mexico: Valle Grande, a 14-mile-wide, 3,000-foot-deep caldera—-the largest in the world—-that formed when a massive volcano erupted and subsequently imploded 1.2 million years ago. From the scenic roadside overlook, 8,500 feet above sea level, you'll often see elk running from the nearby woods down the slope, and you'll also no doubt eye the infinitesimal brown-and-white flecks way, way down in the base of the valley. (Those flecks are cows.) Valle Grande is but one component of 94,000-acre Baca Ranch, a private holding that has been off-limits to the public for many years. The present owners have been trying to get the Nature Conservancy and the U.S. government to raise funds to purchase the property and open it to public use—-it's speculated this handsome little patch of paradise will fetch from $100 to $150 million.

MANHATTAN ON THE MESA

Look at maps and books on New Mexico from the 1930s and you'll find nary a mention of Los Alamos, about 35 miles northwest of Santa Fe and now a compact, bustling town of 18,300 registering the highest per capita income in the state. Like many communities in the Southwest, Los Alamos was created expressly as a company town. But the workers here weren't mining iron, tending freight trains, or hauling lumber. At Los Alamos, for at least the first 20 years of its existence, virtually everybody there worked for America's foremost nuclear research facility, Los Alamos National Laboratory (LANL). The lab still employs some 10,000 area workers.

That's right, just a few miles from the ancient Anazasi cave dwellings of Bandelier National Monument, a team of many of the best scientists in the world, led by a brilliant and morally conflicted J. Robert Oppenheimer, built Fat Man and Little Boy, the atomic bombs that in August 1945 devastated Hiroshima and Nagasaki. LANL was created in 1943 under the auspices of the intensely covert Manhattan Project, whose express purpose it was to expedite an Allied victory in World War II. Indeed, Japan did, of course, surrender— but the weapons fostered a full-blown Cold War between the United States and its Soviet *ally* that lasted for another four-and-a-half decades.

The laboratory works hard today to promote its broader platforms, including "enhancing global nuclear security" but also finding new ways to detect radiation, fight pollution, and reduce environmental risks associated with nuclear energy, as well as to further studies of the solar system, biology, and computer sciences. For a sense of what goes on there, be sure to visit LANL's highly engaging **Bradbury Science Museum**, 15th Street and Central Avenue (Sat.-Mon. 1-5 PM, Tues.-Fri. 9 AM-5 PM; free; 505/667-4444), whose exhibits offer a surprisingly frank and provocative examination of such thorny topics as atomic weapons and nuclear power.

Bandelier National Monument

An hour's drive west from Santa Fe, the amazing Anasazi cliff dwellings preserved at Bandelier National Monument (daily 8 AM-4:30 PM, longer hours in summer; $10; 505/672-0343) are a great introduction to the enigmatic ancient people of the Southwest. The prehistoric Pueblo Indians who lived at Bandelier occupied these dwellings from about A.D. 1200 to A.D. 1500, in between the abandonment of Chaco Canyon and the formation of the various Pueblo communities.

From the visitors center and museum near the entrance, a short and rather easy paved path leads along the bottom of Frijoles Canyon, alongside the base of a sheer cliff containing a number of ancient pictographs and dwellings carved into recesses. Several of these can be accessed via a system of paths and ladders. There are also longer trails here, such as the five-mile roundtrip trek past a springtime waterfall into the Rio Grande gorge.

SANTA FE SURVIVAL GUIDE

Once you penetrate Santa Fe's Paseo de Peralta—the historic ring road encircling the 17th-century city center —leave your car at one of the many parking lots or garages and see Santa Fe on foot.

NEW MEXICO'S STATE CAPITAL, and one of the prime vacation destinations in the country, Santa Fe has been at the center of Southwest life and culture for centuries, but its swirling hordes of vacationers, and its vast infrastructure of hotels, restaurants, art galleries and souvenir shops, haven't (yet) ruined what has long been one of the most enjoyably un-American cities. The historic Plaza and its surrounding blocks may occasionally draw comparisons to Walt Disney World's Epcot Center, but make no mistake: Santa Fe is the real McCoy, and it takes relatively little effort to look past the city's contemporary commercial veneer to examine and appreciate the oldest real city in the United States, the cultural crossroads of a region that has supported human life for thousands of years.

It makes the most sense to begin your tour of Santa Fe at its center, the **Plaza**. This will help you get not only your geographical bearings but also a historical context with which to appreciate the rest of Santa Fe. On the north side of the Plaza, the **Palace of the Governors** (Tues.-Sun. 10 AM-5 PM; $5), is the oldest public building in America. Dating from 1610, the

SANTA FE CHAMBER MUSIC FESTIVAL

THE EIGHTEENTH SEASON   July 8–August 20, 1990

SANTA FE CHAMBER MUSIC FESTIVAL

THE NINETEENTH SEASON July 7 - August 19, 1991

Georgia O'Keefe was such a fan of the Santa Fe Chamber Music Festival that she donated rights to many of her paintings for use as posters—which the festival sells to raise money.

palace served as residence for Spanish, Mexican, and, later, American territorial governors until 1909, when the New Mexico legislature voted to turn the building into the Museum of New Mexico. The museum contains an excellent overview of the building's and the city's tumultuous history, numerous artifacts and documents, and an exhaustive collection of regional photographs. The Museum of New Mexico comprises three additional attractions as well—the Museum of Fine Arts, the Museum of Indian Arts and Culture, and the Museum of International Folk Art—and functions in cooperation with the privately run Georgia O'Keeffe Museum. All five facilities are open Tuesday through Sunday 10 AM-5 PM; admission is $5 to each, but for just $10 you can buy a pass that allows admission to all five museums over a five-day period. Call 505/825-6471 for more information.

To get a sense of the life and work of the woman who did as much as anyone to fix Santa Fe in the American mind, walk two blocks west from the Plaza to the **Georgia O'Keeffe Museum**, 217 Johnson Street (Tues.-Sun. 10 AM-5 PM; $5; 505/827-6451), which displays more than 120 pieces of the late artist's works. Many of the paintings here depict the landscape in and around her home at Abiquiu, where she lived for 40 years.

Shops, shops, and more shops (plus a few cafes and restaurants) line the streets emanating from the Plaza. Many of these have a decidedly upscale bent;

Just north of town on US-285/84, you'll pass the almost open-air state-of-the-art **Santa Fe Opera** facility (July and August; $20-120; 505/986-5900 or 800/280-4654). If you want to take in one of the world-class productions here, book as early as possible (weeks ahead if you can).

If you're interested in classical music, the Santa Fe Opera isn't the only game in town. Tickets for **Santa Fe Chamber Music Festival** events are less expensive, and the concerts are held in a variety of atmospheric old Santa Fe buildings. Perfomances are mid-July to late August; for details, call 505/983-2075.

(continues)

there are about 250 art galleries alone in Santa Fe, for instance (though the most engaging and scenic stretch of them is found along narrow and tree-lined Canyon Road, which runs east from Paseo de Peralta up into the foothills above town). Some of the Plaza-area shops offer ragged if amusing selections of cheap curios and souvenirs, and still others are packed to the rafters with genuinely intriguing artifacts, rugs, old books, and other great stuff.

If you want to keep focused on Santa Fe's ancient (by North American standards) history, saunter about the blocks fringing the Plaza's eastern edge, and check out the grand and oft-photographed **St. Francis Cathedral**, 213 Cathedral Place (505/982-5619). In 1927, Santa Fe habitué Willa Cather published one of her most famous novels, *Death Comes for the Archbishop,* a thoughtful and quite moving thinly fictionalized account of French archbishop Jean Baptiste Lamy's near-obsessive ambition to build this cathedral. In fact, it's still unfinished—the odd flat tops of the bell towers were designed to support twin steeples, which they never received. Today, local statutes bar any building from standing taller than those bell towers.

Across the street from the cathedral, you can see exhibits of contemporary Indian art at the **Institute of American Indian Arts Museum** (daily 9 AM-5 PM; $5; 505/988-6211), at the corner of Palace Avenue and Cathedral Avenue.

Once you've done the downtown tour, hop in the car and cruise south along the Old Santa Fe Trail (past the Zia Indian-inspired state **capitol building**) and up a hill to what is known as Museum Plaza, a compound comprising two more of the Museum of New Mexico sites plus the free **Wheelwright Museum of the American Indian**, which presents traditional Indian arts and crafts. The excellent **Museum of Indian Arts and Culture** offers a survey of indigenous life in northern New Mexico over the past several centuries, with especially notable exhibits of both traditional and contemporary pottery, rugs, and other art.

If you have time for only one attraction in this area, though, make it the **Museum of International Folk Art**, a truly innovative collection of some 125,000 provocative artworks, some fashioned out of fairly mundane recycled household goods, and others illuminating the toys and crafts common to different cultures around the world. There are areas where kids can play and create art, and several displays focusing on Hispanic arts and culture.

For a short but rewarding excursion, head north out of town on Washington Avenue. This becomes scenic Bishop's Lodge Road, climbing over the hills and then down alongside a stream toward the village of Tesuque. Along the way, you'll pass the exclusive **Bishop's Lodge** resort ($125-600 a night; 505/983-6377), which has been fashioned out of Archbishop Lamy's former estate —drop by the lobby and ask for the key to see Lamy's small private chapel.

As you enter the artsy little village of Tesuque (te-SOO-key) itself, note the entrance to the **Shidoni Foundry and Gardens** (Mon.-Fri. noon-1 PM, Sat. 9 AM-5 PM; free; 505/988-8001) on your left. In the early 1970s, Shidoni founder

Santa Fe's **New Mexico Public Lands Information Center,** 1474 Rodeo Road (505/438-7542), is stocked with brochures, maps, and guidebooks on national parks and forests, Bureau of Land Management holdings, and lakes and rivers. It's a one-stop clearinghouse for recreation and outdoors permits and licenses, too.

Tommy Hicks bought what had been a small apple orchard and developed it into a one of the nation's preeminent fine arts foundries, where dozens of artists pour some 10,000 pounds of bronze each month to create stunning, sometimes life-size scultpures.

From Shidoni, continue into the village of Tesuque proper, stopping at the wonderfully inviting **Tesuque Village Market**, on Hwy-591 (505/988-8848). This little country store of yore is a scene—locals and others flock here en masse for green chile tuna melts, fresh-baked pies and cookies, tasty burritos, Frito pie, and a fine array of gourmet groceries, microbrews, and other delicacies.

Practicalities

It's a pleasant surprise that only moderately deep pockets are needed to find memorable accommodations in Santa Fe. Just off the plaza and close to the Georgia O'Keeffe museum are a pair of small gems: **Adobe Abode**, 202 Chapelle Street (505/986-0972), and the **Grant Corner Inn**, Grant Avenue (505/983-1526). The former, as the name suggests, consists of several large adobe-style rooms, each with modern baths, upscale amenities, and eclectic antiques and folk furnishings. The creaky Victorian Grant Corner Inn represents a departure from the typical Southwestern-style accommodations around town. This wood-frame beauty exudes charm and gentility, as rooms have period antiques, Waverly-print fabrics and wallpapers, eyelet curtains, four-poster beds, and other similarly quaint touches. One of the better values in Santa Fe is another rambling Victorian, the 1886 Queen Anne **Preston House**, 106 Faithway Street (505/982-3465), which also has rooms in two neighboring late-19th-century cottages, and a few more in a traditional adobe dwelling across the way. Brass beds, ceiling fans, and stained-glass windows fill the rooms. All of these properties include a full breakfast in their rates, which start between $70 and $100.

> **Frito pie** is quite the local delicacy (although the recipe allegedly originated in Texas in the 1930s, when Daisy Doolin, the mother of the Dallas-based founder of Frito-Lay, poured chili over her Fritos and found that she liked it). Santa Fe's now-defunct Plaza Woolworth's served one of the more memorable versions for many years, and its replacement, the Five and Dime Store, carries on the tradition. Other good bets for this dish are the Tesuque Village Market and the Plaza Restaurant.

If money isn't an issue, consider the wonderfully handcrafted **La Fonda de Santa Fe**, on the plaza at 100 E. San Francisco Street (505/982-5511 or 800/523-5002), which dates to the earliest days of America's occupation of the city—an oasis in the eyes of weary trappers and traders having trod into town via the Santa Fe Trail. A hidden secret here is the distinctive cocktail bar in the Bell Tower of the hotel, vantage for some of Santa Fe's best sunset views.

If all the desirable places are full, or if you're tight on funds, cruise along busy, overbuilt Cerrillos Road, where you'll find all the chain hotels and motels—Comfort Inn, Fairfield Inn, Hampton Inn, Holiday Inn Express, La Quinta, a particularly cheap Motel 6, and a nice Doubletree Inn. However, be warned that atmosphere along here is nonexistent; cars parked overnight have been broken into on numerous occasions in the past, so bring your valuables inside with you.

(continues)

For complete listings of accommodation options, and for information on anything else to do with Santa Fe, contact the **Santa Fe Convention and Visitors Bureau,** north of the Plaza at 201 W. Marcy Street (505/984-6760 or 800/777-2489).

With recipes that show the influence of more than 2,000 years of Native American culture (which contributed three major staples: beans, corn, and squash), some 400 years of catholic inclusion (chiles, cilantro, cumin, onions, garlic, wheat, rice, and both beef and pork), and a liberal dash of American inventiveness, Santa Fe restaurants serve the world's oldest, newest, and, some say, tastiest cuisines—often all side-by-side on the very same plates. Menu offerings include dishes like a buttermilk corn cake with smoky chipotle-chile shrimp (and a side of red chile onion rings), chile rellenos stuffed with roast duck and black bean mole sauce, or blue corn turkey enchiladas. Prices vary from dirt cheap (rare) to outrageous ($35 for designer tacos!), and attitude is everything, but if you like to eat, Santa Fe's fine food is at least as much a draw as its rich history and magical mountain light.

In a city where green chile stew is a fixture on dozens of menus, **Tia Sophia's,** 210 West San Francisco Street (505/983-9880), stands head and shoulders above the rest, especially in the morning when folks pack this place for an early fix of this spicy New Mexican dish. Breakfast burritos are similarly adored here (open only from morning to mid-afternoon). Another outstanding source of filling New Mexican breakfast fare is **Tecolote Cafe,** 1203 Cerrillos Road (505/988-1362), convenient to the motel row along Cerrillos. An addictive variation on the breakfast burrito is the famed breakfast quesadilla (with scrambled eggs, applewood-smoked bacon, Jack cheese, and guacamole), served at **Cafe Pasqual's,** 121 Don Gaspar Avenue (505/983-9340).

Hyped to the utmost degree, the most famous place in Santa Fe has to be Mark Miller's **Coyote Cafe,** a block south of the Plaza at 132 W. Water Street (505/983-1615). Coyote serves terrific contemporary Southwestern fare on a $40 three-course prix fixe menu, but the tone here can be a tad pretentious. For high-quality cooking that's half the price but still delicious, grab a seat at the Coyote's bustling, open-air rooftop cantina. If you're seeking the ultimate high-end Santa Fe dining experience, however, book a table at **Geronimo,** 724 Canyon Road (505/092-1500), where the historic adobe dining rooms make a perfect setting for entrees such as oven-roasted halibut, wrapped in banana leaf and served with a Meso-American plantain-and-black bean habañero sauce.

If you'd rather avoid these flashy newcomers, a source of delicious, all-American comfort food is the ersatz coffee-shop-style **Plaza Restaurant,** on the Plaza at 54 Lincoln Avenue (505/982-1664), which has been serving no-nonsense meals since it opened in 1918. Part of the fun here is the constant clatter of dishes and silverware, the old-fashioned tile floor, and a rear wall with a giant mural map of the Southwest. If you don't have time for a full meal (the New Mexico meatloaf is a specialty), pop in for a helping of Frito pie. In the evening, join Santa Fe's old guard at the **Pink Adobe** (also called simply "The

Pink"), 406 Old Santa Fe Trail (505/983-7712), a vaunted supper club once frequented by the likes of Willa Cather and Igor Stravinsky. The hearty Continental cooking here is about as retro as a 1962 Cadillac, but that's half of the fun; the other half comes from the kitschy **Dragon Room Bar**, a popular late-night hangout.

And if you want to avoid "Santa Fe" food entirely, you'll find a globally influenced menu at **Prana**, 320 S. Guadalupe Street (505/983-7705), a chic spot where pan-Asian fare like pad Thai noodles or Korean beef beggars' purses served with a piquant apricot-chile dipping sauce offer a bracing alternative to New Mexican cooking. Located along funky Guadalupe Street, **Whistling Moon**, 402 N. Guadalupe St. (505/983-3093), draws a quirky, untouristy crowd by serving fantastic Middle Eastern and Mediterranean fare.

Got a case of the late-night munchies and seeking a huge, juicy burger? Head to the **San Francisco Street Bar and Grill**, 114 W. San Francisco Street (505/982-2044). For plates piled high with authentic Spanish tapas and paellas (and glasses brimming with fine Spanish riojas), saunter over to **El Farol**, 808 Canyon Road (505/983-9912), a rollicking decades-old bar-cum-eatery with rough-hewn plank floors and cozy low ceilings.

Los Alamos

From Bandelier National Monument, head slightly west and turn north onto Hwy-501 to reach downtown Los Alamos, the wealthiest town in New Mexico—thanks to the presence of so many well-paid engineers and scientists working at Los Alamos National Laboratory (LANL). Check out the Bradbury Museum downtown, then visit the small but interesting **Los Alamos Historical Museum**, housed on the original site of LANL, at 1921 Juniper Street (Mon.-Sat. 10 AM-4 PM, Sunday 1-4 PM; free; 505/662-6272). Exhibits detail the once-volatile geological history of the volcanic Jemez mountains, the 700-year history of human life in this area, and more on the Manhattan Project. It's rather jarring to observe ancient Anazasi potsherds and arrowheads in one display and photos of a bombed-out Nagasaki in the next.

With several restaurants and some nice motels and hotels, Los Alamos is a good place to stay the night. For proximity to Bandelier and Los Alamos, consider the pleasant **Bandelier Inn**, 10 miles south of Los Alamos at 132 Hwy-4 (505/672-3838 or 800/321-3923), a motor lodge with several kinds of suites, plus RV hookups. Some suites have kitchenettes, and all rooms have microwave ovens and refrigerators. In Los Alamos, you can grab lunch or dinner at the very hip **Central Avenue Grille**, 1789 Central Avenue (505/662-2005), which specializes in stone-fired pizzas and microbrews. At press time, Los Alamos had experienced a devastating fire. Call ahead to confirm openings.

Espanola

From Los Alamos, head back down off the mesa via Hwy-30 to reach the biggest town between Santa Fe and Taos—Espanola. Founded in the 1880s as a stop on the Denver and Rio Grande Railroad, Espanola lacks the colonial charm of either of

Espanola is famous for its burger joints, all strung along Hwy-68, from the local **Dandy Burger** (505/753-4234)—a drive-in that's been around for more than 30 years—to **Blakes Lotaburger** (505/753-3611), a New Mexico institution, and several fast-food chain representatives.

Among Espanola's modern wonders are the many low-riders you'll see cruising the streets. Mostly classic 1960s cars that have been retrofitted with lowered chassis and hydraulics that allow the cars to jump, bump, and grind, they're often painted with spectacular murals—from religious art to scenes of the region's landscape.

its famous neighbors, but it's a rather busy little place with many great cheap restaurants but few accommodations and even fewer reasons to stick around for more than a meal.

Two especially noteworthy dining options in town include **El Paragua**, on Hwy-75 at 603 Santa Cruz Road (505/753-8852), which began as a lemonade-cum-taco stand in the late 1950s and has grown into a massive compound over the years, with viga ceilings and ornately decorated dining rooms. You'll be hard-pressed to find a better margarita in New Mexico, the chile rellenos are truly fresh (not the freezer-paroled versions you'll find in most places), and the *caldo talpeno*—a stew of chicken, avocado, garbanzo beans, chipotles, and spices—will forever redefine your sense of chicken soup.

Less renowned and lower on ambience, **Jo Ann's Ranch O Casados**, in the Walgreens Shopping Center on Hwy-68 at 418 N. Riverside Drive (505/753-2837), might just serve the best food between Santa Fe and Taos. You'll probably recognize the faded red-and-white-striped roof (yes, the building used to house a Kentucky Fried Chicken), but inside you'll find a cozy spot with eager servers and serape-draped windows. Jo Ann's makes its own blue-corn tortillas and raises its own chiles on a farm several miles north of Espanola, where all the produce and ingredients used in their food is grown. Chicken-fried steak is great here, but the specialties are sopaipillas stuffed with beans and cheese, *carne adovada* (beef with red sauce), and *menudo con posole* (tripe with hominy). Breakfast is also served all day.

Detour: Rancho San Juan

Just a couple miles north of US-84 on US-285 is one of the most wonderful and secluded getaways in New Mexico, maybe even the Southwest: **Rancho de San Juan** (505/753-6818 or 800/726-7121; $175-350 a night), a 225-acre adobe compound nestled below the high cliffs of Black Mesa. Most of the 17 rooms at this understatedly luxurious and very romantic getaway are suites, set around a central courtyard, though there are cottages farther out amid the wilderness. All rooms have museum-quality southwestern furnishings, stereos with CD players, and local artworks; some rooms have fireplaces, Jacuzzi tubs, and full kitchens. A spa is slated to open soon, and a lavish four-course prix-fixe dinner is available (by reservation only) in the intimate restaurant Wed.-Sun.—it's the only Mobil four-star dining experience in the state.

Even if you're unable to stay at Rancho de San Juan, consider dropping by for a hike up to a fascinating sandstone shrine that has been carved out of a ledge overlooking the inn. The shrine's smooth curvaceous walls reveal the expert craftsmanship of artist Ra Paulette, and great views of Georgia O'Keeffe country can be had farther up the trail, beyond the shrine. The grounds are free to guests of the inn, $5 for non-guests (the public is welcome daily 9 AM-2 PM; you must register at the front desk). You won't see anything like this place anywhere else in region.

A PUEBLO PRIMER

Driving around northern New Mexico, you'll encounter one Native American pueblo after another, but the main signs you'll see of Pueblo Indian culture are likely to be large, flashing neon ones— advertising flashy new casinos and low prices on cigarettes. These excessively commercial teasers may lead you to think northern New Mexico's Pueblo tribal heritage has dissipated over the years, but in fact many of these pueblos offer visitors a remarkable variety of cultural and historic diversions, plus great hiking and outdoors opportunities.

The 19 distinct pueblos in northern New Mexico have been occupied continuously for anywhere from several hundred to more than a thousand years. They are sovereign nations that have been recognized as such by the United States and "old" Mexico; the current boundaries reflect land grants established by the Spanish crown during colonial times. Policies about admission fees and hours vary considerably among the pueblos, and many of them are closed to nonmembers at various times during the year (mainly during religious observations and ceremonials). It's always a good idea to phone ahead before visiting any pueblo; once you arrive, pay close attention to the local rules and customs, and above all, conduct yourself with respect toward your hosts. Always check with tribal officials about each pueblo's policy on photography. In most cases, you have to pay something like $5 for a permit before taking pictures on pueblo grounds. Permit or no permit, you should always ask permission before photographing anyone.

It may seem as if visiting a pueblo involves an awful lot of regulations, but remember that these are sacred, centuries-old working communities operated as sovereign nations. For general information on the New Mexico pueblos, contact the **Indian Pueblo Cultural Center**, 2401 12th Street NW in Albuquerque (505/843-7270 or 800/766-4405).

The following list details some of the most capitivating pueblos for visitors:

Acoma Pueblo (505/470-4966): Perhaps the oldest continuously occupied city in North America, Acoma ("Sky City") sits atop a magical mesa. See page 310 for more.

Nambe Pueblo (505/455-2036): Just south of Chimayó, this pueblo contains several adobe buildings dating to the time of earliest habitation, in 1300. Probably the greatest draw here are the myriad recreational opportunities: visitors can hike to Nambe Falls, camp or picnic, and ride horseback on the many trails that climb into the Sangre de Cristo Mountains. *(continues)*

Picuris Pueblo (505/587-2919): On the High Road south of Taos, this is one of the oldest pueblos. It was visited by Spaniards as early as 1591. It has only recently began to develop an approach toward tourism and currently contains a small museum and a beautiful chapel dating to the late 1700s.

San Ildefonso Pueblo (505/455-3549): Famed for the black-on-black pottery technique of the tribe's most famous member, the late Maria Martinez, this pueblo overlooks a pretty plaza shaded by cottonwood trees, near Bandelier National Monument and the banks of the Rio Grande. Fine pottery is sold here, and a museum houses many early works of art and religious treasures; to see many more Martinez originals, visit the Millicent Rogers Museum in Taos.

San Juan Pueblo (505/852-4400): An interesting pueblo because of the way it has mixed tradition with modern entrepreneurial skills—in the summer of 1999 they opened the massive Okhay Casino Resort, complete with a hotel and golf course, on Hwy-68 north of Espanola.

Santa Clara Pueblo (505/753-7326): This pueblo west of Espanola is famous for two things: red-and-black pottery and the ancient Puye cliff dwellings in the foothills of the Jemez Mountains. The remains of the 1,000-year-old 750-room dwelling are concentrated atop a tall mesa; wooden ladders lead up the trails, just as at Bandelier National Monument. From the top of the mesa you'll see the entire Rio Grande Valley laid out below, with the Jemez and Sangre de Cristo ranges on either side.

Taos Pueblo (505/758-9593): The most famous of all the pueblos, this stands just north of the town of Taos. See page 431 for more.

Zuni Pueblo (505/782-4481): Stretching west to the Arizona border, this sprawling pueblo, famed for its intricately carved animal fetishes, is thought to have been one of the golden "Seven Cities of Cibola," for which the Spanish conquistador Coronado came searching in 1540.

US-84: Abiquiu

There's only one reason that people who don't live there have heard of the tiny village of Abiquiu, on US-84 some 30 miles northwest of Espanola: Georgia O'Keeffe. In 1945, the artist bought a large but forlorn late-18th-century Spanish colonial adobe compound just off Abiquiu Plaza. She had the place renovated and its three-acre grounds spruced up. Following the 1946 death of her husband, photographer Alfred Stieglitz, she left her home in New York City and began dividing her time permanently between homes here and at Ghost Ranch (see below). The Abiquiu home, which became a studio and has figured prominently in some of her works, may be visited, but only via an hour-long guided tour (groups limited to 12 persons) every Tuesday, Thursday, and Friday April through November. A minimum $20 (tax-deductible) donation is required, as are reservations—the tour is sometimes booked as far as three or four months in advance (505/685-4539).

Apart from the Georgia O'Keeffe home, there's almost nothing to see in this small, insular community, and locals understandably discourage tourists from parading about the small plaza. Picture-taking is strictly forbidden anywhere in town, and unless you're visiting on the aforementioned tour, you'll probably find it best to avoid Abiquiu's village altogether. That said, the **Cafe Abiquiu** and the **Abiquiu Inn**, just south of Abiquiu village on US-84 (505/685-4378 or 800/447-5621), can be found in a gracious adobe compound consisting of hotel rooms, a restaurant, beautiful gardens, an enormous gift shop (selling exceptionally fine Hispanic, Native American, and Middle Eastern rugs and handicrafts), an art gallery, and the offices of the Georgia O'Keeffe home and studio (tours depart from here). Accommodations are an excellent and reasonably priced alternative to those in Santa Fe and Taos. Especially appealing are the lavishly decorated four-person casitas, with woodstoves or fireplaces and tiled baths. The restaurant has a long eclectic menu, from yellowfin tuna sandwiches to steaks and gyro platters—good food and a warm, appealing ambience.

At the southern tip of Abiquiu Reservoir, Hwy-96 turns off to the west around the San Pedro mountains, offering some stunning views before intersecting with Hwy-44 just north of Cuba. From either Taos or Santa Fe, Hwy-96 is an enjoyable and reasonably direct way to reach Chaco Canyon, and a beautiful road through peaceful farming communities, over hills, and around bends.

Ghost Ranch: Georgia O'Keeffe

If you've even a remote interest in the life and work of famed Southwestern painter Georgia O'Keeffe, or if you're simply seeking a rewarding day trip from Taos or Santa Fe, consider a trip to Ghost Ranch, on the northern outskirts of Abiquiu. O'Keeffe spent many years in this part of New Mexico, and quite a few of her most famous works depict this desiccated but enchanting region. Driving along US-84 north from Abiquiu, subjects of O'Keeffe works dot the entire area, from the tall vermilion and ocher cliffs surrounding deep blue Abiquiu Reservoir to many old adobe homes and churches.

Ghost Ranch proper encompasses some 20,000 acres. In the 1930s, the property was bought and operated as a dude and cattle ranch by conservationist and publisher of *Nature Magazine*, Arthur Pack. In 1934, Pack invited O'Keeffe here to visit; six years later, he sold the artist a seven-acre parcel with an adobe house, in which she lived summer and fall for most of the rest of her life. In 1955, he donated the remainder of the property to the Presbyterian Church. The church continues to use the original structures and about 55 acres of the land as the **Ghost Ranch Conference Center** (505/685-4333), now the site of retreats and workshops open to the public (on everything from arts and crafts to archaeology).

The public is encouraged to drop by the conference center and hike the many trails traversing the property (just register first at the conference center). The old O'Keeffe property is off-limits, though as you walk the trails you'll experience the region in the way O'Keeffe often depicted it.

A final and quite engaging element of Ghost Ranch is the **Ghost Ranch Living Museum** (Tues.-Sat. 9 AM-4 PM; $3; 505/685-4312), just north of the conference center on US-84. Donated by the church (at Pack's behest) to the National Park Service in 1970, the museum is now administered by the Carson National Forest. A nature trail threads among native trees and wildlife enclosures (containing beavers, prairie dogs, brilliant red-and-blue-headed wild turkeys, and formidable elk); newer exhibits trace mankind's inhabitance and utilization of the land around Ghost Ranch for more than 1,000 years.

Hwy-68: Along the Rio Grande

From Ghost Ranch, backtracking to Espanola will bring you to a choice of routes to Taos. With all the hype about the High Road, it's sometimes easy to forget that the Low Road—i.e., Hwy-68, the main road between Santa Fe and Tao—is a devastatingly beautiful way to go. If you're in the area for more than a few days, make a point of trying both routes. On Hwy-68, be sure to keep an eye out for the Rio Grande Gorge, which reveals itself dramatically as you climb the steep hillside north of Pilar.

Much of Hwy-68 traces the route of the narrow-gauge Chili Line railway, defunct for decades now. Note the many produce stands, especially around Velarde, where you'll find seasonal fruits, juices, vegetables, and ristras (strands of chile peppers); Hunt's, the Fruit Basket, and Salazar's are all reliable options. The Chili Line's former terminus, **Embudo Station** (505/852-4707 or 800/852-4707), 25 miles south

of Taos, now houses a popular restaurant with one of the only riverside patios in all of New Mexico. Outstanding locally produced beer and wine are the drink specialties, while the menu focuses on a mix of American and New Mexican dishes (baby back ribs, chicken stuffed with artichokes and polenta, black-bean-and-feta burritos). The village of Embudo Station (pop. 21) also has a gift shop, smokehouse store, and rafting outfitter.

Farther north along Hwy-68, 10 miles south of Ranchos de Taos, the **Rio Grande Visitors Center** (505/751-4899), at Pilar, is a great place to pick up information on rafting, fishing, and hiking the Rio Grande. River-rafting is a major activity in northern central New Mexico; the center provides a list of approved outfitters but also gives advice and guidelines on tackling some sections on your own. Two popular stretches are the 17-mile Taos Box, which runs from Arroyo Hondo (just north of Taos) beneath the Rio Grande Bridge and through a spectacular section of the gorge, ending at the Orilla Verde Recreation Area near Pilar; and the Lower Gorge, a 12-mile stretch that begins where Taos Box ends.

Across from the Rio Grande Visitors Center, you'll find the tongue-in-cheek named **Pilar Yacht Club** (505/758-9072), a small cafe where you can pick up burritos, burgers, baked goods, and various sundries (including fishing tackle, sunglasses, newspapers, and river-rafting equipment). Next door is the **Rio Grande Gorge Hostel**, Hwy-68 (505/758-0090), a charming adobe building with purple doors and a garden of campy lawn ornaments. There's a small dorm room, an efficiency with two beds, and two curious dome-shaped units behind the adobe (these make for a romantic and highly affordable getaway).

At the Pilar Yacht Club, turn right onto Hwy-567 and follow the road down into the **Orilla Verde Recreation Area**, where there's a small ranger station (505/758-4060) and several good campgrounds strung along or just across from the Rio Grande River. Arroyo Hondo is one of the prettiest of the sites, as it's right by the water and quite secluded; Petaca has attractive stone-and-adobe lean-tos; and Taos Junction Campground is the most spectacular, offering fine views through the river gorge. There's no swimming allowed in the river here, but fishing (brown and rainbow trout and northern pike) is common (pick up a license first at the Rio Grande Visitors Center). If you'll be spending any time or camping in this area, register at the ranger station ($3 day-use, $7 overnight, per vehicle).

Hwy-567 crosses the small bridge over the Rio Grande, passes Taos Junction Campground, then switchbacks up the steep dirt (but maintained) road that hugs the western wall of this dramatic canyon. At the top of the ascent, Hwy-567 is paved again; continue west through the tiny village of Carson, and make a left (heading south) once you reach US-285.

After about 10 miles south on US-285, you'll come to the turnoff on the right for Hwy-111. This road climbs through a pass between the Ortega mountains (to the north) and Cerro Colorado (to the south) before intersecting with Hwy-554, which leads into El Rito. El Rito is an alluring artists' community and farming town with a little-known New Mexican restaurant, El Farolito, 1212 Main Street (505/581-9509), right on the town's tree-shaded main drag.

> Hikers may wish to stop at the trailhead for the **La Vista Verde Trail**, about a half-mile of switchbacking up Hwy-567 from Taos Junction Campground. It's an easy 2.5-mile loop, offering amazing views down into the gorge, plus archaeological sites along the trail.

The High Road: Chimayó

Though the route along Hwy-68 between Santa Fe and Taos is plenty pretty, if you really want to get a feel for northern New Mexico, take the "High Road," which winds east of Hwy-68 through a series of remote mountain communities before dropping down into Taos. Starting in Santa Fe, work your way past Tesuque and continue a half-dozen miles north along US-285/84, past the turnoff west to Los Alamos and Bandelier National Monument, to Hwy-503, where the High Road to Taos begins in earnest. This twisting roads slopes up into the foothills of the Pecos Wilderness Area, where the 12,000-foot Santa Fe Baldy and Sierra Mosca mountain peaks loom high above you.

Almost immediately after you pass Nambe Pueblo, you'll enter **Chimayó** (often mispronounced—the emphasis is on the final syllable), a center of Spanish weaving tradition for more than 250 years. Note the brilliant red sandstone hills that rise above this area as far as the eye can see—Chimayó takes it name from the Tewa Indian term for this colorful geology. A few notable attractions have earned Chimayó the greatest following among the towns on the High Road to Taos. Much of the activity revolves around **Rancho de Chimayó**, a gallery and restaurant (505/351-4444) on Hwy-98 run by the Jamarillo family, residents of this community since the late 17th century. The restaurant opened in 1965 inside a simple 19th-century adobe house that has been added onto over the years and now consists of landscaped patios and several warm and inviting dining warrens. Local New Mexican fare is served, but the ambience accounts more for the success of this place than the actual cooking, which is good but not extraordinary. Still, it's a mob scene on weekends. Just down and across the road, the Jamarillos also operate **Hacienda Rancho de Chimayó** (505/351-2222), the fanciest of the few accommodations you'll encounter along the High Road. The hacienda is set amid cacti gardens, an enchanting courtyard, and the town's trademark red cliffs. Eight rooms, with antique or wooden beds, fireplaces, and private baths, open onto the courtyard. And with rates ranging from $69 to $105, this place is a bargain compared to Santa Fe's hotels.

Several weaving shops line the area's roads. Start at the most famous of them, **Ortega's de Chimayó** (505/351-4215), where the eighth generation of this artisan family shows fine weavings in the form of blankets, place mats, shawls, vests, purses, and pillows. They also operate an adjoining gallery that sells art, gifts, books, music, and more.

It's quite possible to become overwhelmed by the number of quaint, historic cathedrals and chapels dotting northern New Mexico. Many of these lie on Indian pueblos, others anchor busy plazas. Some draw a steady stream of both tourists and pilgrims, while others serenely stand guard over the community, appreciated by few outsiders. Among both devoted worshipers and curious onlookers, one church in this region evokes a more fervent and dedicated following than any other: the **Santuario de Chimayó**, on Hwy-98 just south of Rancho de Chimayó. Built in 1816, Santuario de Chimayó, often called the "Lourdes of New Mexico," carries on a Lourdes-like tradition of healing the sick and the infirm. This belief is rooted in the legend of the sickly Abeyta, who was directed in a vision to build the chapel on this site, whereupon he was miraculously healed. In a room off the sanctuary, discarded crutches and braces hang from the walls, and small photos, rosary beads, and burning candles line several tables.

A gaudy carnival of shops and gift stands leads up to the sanctuary—images of Christ and the Dr. Pepper logo hang side by side over one doorway; through others you'll find stalls hawking everything from crèche statuary to tattoos of Our Lady of Guadalupe, not to mention more than a few "you break it, you buy it" signs.

Head northeast on Hwy-76 from Chimayó toward Truchas, and after climbing through the high desert for about four miles you'll come to signs for **Cordova,** a very small village that is highly acclaimed for woodworking. There are no formal shops with regular hours, but signs at the end of many driveways off the highway indicate small galleries. Assuming it's sometime between late morning and early afternoon, you'll typically find artisans displaying or making their wares.

Truchas

You may recognize the high (elev. 8,400 feet) and breathtakingly beautiful village of Truchas as the shooting location for the film *The Milagro Beanfield War,* directed by Robert Redford. This small, close-knit community of perhaps 1,000 residents hugs a sheer cliffside, offering views back toward Chimayó, with the Sangre de Cristo Mountains to the east and the Jemez Mountains to the west. Due east, you can't miss the often snow-capped tip of Truchas Peak, which at 13,103 feet is the second-tallest mountain in New Mexico.

Truchas is a mostly Hispanic community that has grown from a Spanish land grant established in 1754. Early settlers built irrigation ditches that extended from the neighboring mountains, and some of these 250-year-old acequias still serve the community today. (Battles over the precious resources of lumber and water would figure prominently in the villages along the High Road for many years; one such altercation sets the stage for *The Milagro Beanfield War.*) Electricity and running water weren't introduced in Truchas until 1950. At that point, the military projects in Los Alamos, about 40 miles away, sparked a limited degree of job growth. Nevertheless, Truchas today seems to have relatively little contact with (or interest in) the outside world, which makes a refreshing change from the hyper-tourism of areas around Santa Fe.

As you first enter town, consider stopping by **Los Siete Gallery**, which has very nice tinware and weavings. Farther along, Hwy-76 turns left toward Ojo Sarco and

Las Trampas. On your right at this intersection stands the cheerful **Truchas Mountain Coffeehouse Gallery.** Owner Sharon Adee can provide a wealth of information not only on Truchas but also on the extensive collection of photos, paintings, and jewelry sold inside. You can also pick up baked goods, espresso, sodas, and juice, and admire the glorious views from the southwest-facing windows of the gallery.

Before continuing along Hwy-76, make a brief detour by driving straight through the village of Truchas; just past the coffeehouse gallery, you'll notice **Tafoya's Truchas General Store,** which has a pay phone, snacks, and a few antiques. Farther along are more art galleries, and well beyond them lies **Rancho Arriba** (505/689-2374; $70), one of the most dramatically situated accommodations in New Mexico. Curtiss Frank bought this site in 1961 and over many years with great effort and ingenuity built this remarkable adobe and most of the furnishings within it. Several nearby trails lead into the Sangre de Cristo Mountains, and the star-gazing here at night is awe inspiring.

Las Trampas

Between Truchas and the Picuris Pueblo, the hamlet of Las Trampas is best known for its remarkably well-preserved church, the eye-catching **San Jose de Gracia.** In 1966, with a rather perplexing disregard for local culture and history, the highway department slated the 1760 structure for demolition; local preservationists rallied and successfully fought to save it. Walk inside to appreciate the flat mud-plastered roof, the intricate religious carvings, paintings around the altar dating to 1800, and the hand-hewn floorboards—it is said that local villagers were buried under these floorboards (this practice continued through the 18th and 19th centuries but has ceased in the last 100 years or so). It's hard to see them without somebody pointing them out to you, but you may also find faded blood stains on these wooden planks—reminders of the Penitentes, who faithfully reenacted the crucifixion of Christ inside the church.

Near the church, poke your head inside **La Tiendita and Taste of Trampas,** a rambling gallery of jewelry, crafts, and weavings, plus a small takeout food counter. It's not a reason in itself to visit Trampas, but it bears a quick visit if you've got some free time. A couple more miles up Hwy-76, many of the dirt roads and modest adobe houses in the sleepy village of **Chamisal** date to the community's origin in the mid-1850s. A little more than two miles north of here, Hwy-76 meets with Hwy-75 at a T intersection, which marks the western reaches of Peñasco.

Truchas and the several communities farther north on the High Road to Taos are characterized by an insularity that may surprise you if you've spent most of your time in Santa Fe. The lack of a commercialized and heavily developed tourist infrastructure makes this part of the state all the more special, and its residents considerably less jaded by the sight of visitors. By the same token, be careful not to tread on private property or snap pictures of residents without first asking permission—a little courtesy and discretion go a long way here.

The **Penitentes** are an order of devout Roman Catholics living mostly in small villages throughout northern New Mexico, including many of the small towns on the High Road to Taos. The Penitentes are famous—or infamous—for their 18th- and 19th century practice of especially faithful passion plays. In these, a procession of members flogged themselves with heavy whips and one member (chosen by drawing lots) was nailed to a real cross—a ritual that often ended in death. Archbishop Lamy sought to end what he considered to be the barbaric rites of the Penitentes, and eventually the church banned these orders in 1899. The Catholic Church lifted the ban in 1947 on the condition that the Penitentes cease any rituals that might result in injury. But the orders are highly secretive, and rumors persist that at least some of the severe practices are still carried out today.

From Peñasco, it's a short drive east to the final turn on the High Road, north onto Hwy-518. On the way, note Hwy-73, a dead-end road that leads five miles up into the Carson National Forest and one of the region's most popular (and secluded) campgrounds, **Santa Barbara** (505/587-2255), which lies directly in the shadows of 12,175-foot Trampas Peak. North of here, Hwy-518 soars high over the Picuris Mountains and through Kit Carson National Forest before descending into Ranchos de Taos, the southern section of Taos proper—the views toward town and beyond that across the broad mesa to the west merits a good, long stare (there's a scenic pull-out along the route).

Detour: Hwy-518 to Las Vegas

From where Hwy-75 meets with Hwy-518 for the final run into Taos, you can take a stunning detour off the High Road by heading east on Hwy-518 over the Sangre de Cristo Mountains to Las Vegas, New Mexico, about 60 miles away. Along this drive you'll pass the funky, family-oriented ski village of Sipapu (505/587-2240 or 800/587-2240), the farming town of Mora, and a restored mill at La Cueva, before finishing at historic Las Vegas, whose plaza is surrounded by stately Victorian buildings and towering shade trees. Las Vegas was an important stopping point on the historic Santa Fe Trail; now it's on I-25, so it's possible to make this trip as a loop from Santa Fe, an hour's drive away via the interstate.

Ranchos de Taos

Reaching Taos from the south, you first enter Ranchos de Taos, centered at the intersection of Hwy-68 (Paseo del Pueblo Sur) and Hwy-518. The original Hispanic settlement contains two sites worthy of exploration, but note that Hwy-68 in this part of town has become increasingly littered with fast-food restaurants, chain motels, and irritating shopping centers.

With this in mind, turn west from Hwy-68 onto Hwy-240 to better appreciate this southern end of the greater Taos Valley. At the junction stands the **San Francisco de Asis Church**, (daily 9 AM-noon and 1 PM-4 PM; $2; 505/758-2754), which was built over many decades and completed in 1816. Georgia O'Keeffe (and literally countless subsequent imitators) immortalized

There are good and bad aspects of experiencing northern New Mexico during one of its ferocious monsoon **rainstorms** (most common July-Aug.). High winds, lightning, and creeks and arroyos that swell with little or no warning (never attempt to cross a flooded road if you can't clearly see the highway surface through the water). On the other hand, the brilliant contrast of adobe against a forbidding charcoal sky makes for incredible photographs—especially late in the day, when the sun often produces breathtaking rainbows.

this church by unconventionally (and brilliantly) painting it from the back, where it is a squat assemblage of adobe walls and buttresses. From the front, it is crowned with three white crosses and a pair of belfries; the sanctuary is treasured for its striking reredos and one painting that allegedly gives off a mystical glow in the evening.

Looping north and west, follow Hwy-240 past cattle farms and old adobe homesteads, crossing the Rio Pueblo, and then winding north until you reach **La Hacienda de los Martinez** (daily 10 AM-4 PM, longer hours in summer; $5; 505/758-0505). This Spanish colonial fortress, rambling and filled with period furnishings, provides as intimate a look at Spanish colonial living as you'll find anywhere in New Mexico. Artisans here offer arts and crafts demonstrations on a regular basis. In the early 1800s, the Martinez spread stood as the northern terminus of El Camino Real (the Royal Road), the main trade route from clear down in Mexico City.

At La Hacienda, Hwy-240 becomes Ranchitos Road. Continue on this road and make a right onto Ledoux Street, which leads to a pair of longstanding arts attractions. The **E.L. Blumenschein Home and Museum**, 222 Ledoux Street (daily 11 AM-4 PM, longer hours in summer; $5; 505/758-0505), boasts a fine collection of early Taos art and many fine European and Spanish colonial antiques as well as a painstakingly preserved example of an early (circa 1790) pueblo home. A few doors away is the state's second-oldest art collection, the **Harwood Museum**, 238 Ledoux Street (Wed.-Sat. 10 AM-5 PM, Sunday noon-5 PM; $4; 505/758-9826), which has a very good permanent exhibit of 19th-century retablos (devotional paintings on wood), plus an eclectic mix of Taos Society works, contemporary pieces in all media, and many rotating exhibits.

From here, continue north along Ledoux Street to reach the Taos Plaza, where you can park to explore the remaining area museums on foot.

Taos

Even longtime locals admit to feeling a lump in their throats as they approach Taos, either in a descent on Hwy-518 from the High Road, an ascent on Hwy-68 from the Low Road, or on an even plane from the west on US-64. No matter the vantage point, the high desert's brilliant collision with the precipitous Sangre de Cristo mountain range never fails to inspire wonder. Situated at 7,000 feet, Taos is quite a bit smaller than Santa Fe and has about one-tenth the population but holds a wide selection of diversions, including a plethora of respected art museums and perhaps the nation's most famous still-functioning Native American pueblo.

The Plaza, which anchors Taos proper, was laid out in 1796 and figured prominently in the history of New Mexico during the following century, as frontiersmen including Kit Carson used the town as a base for their western explorations. Early in the 20th century, Taos came of age as an artists' colony, and pretty soon dozens of luminaries had moved here. These included the eccentric socialite Mabel Dodge Luhan, who established something of an artists' coven here in 1917—guests to her home included Ansel Adams, Aldous Huxley, D. H. Lawrence, Georgia O'Keeffe, and Thomas Wolfe. Taos remains a remarkably eclectic community today, with a strong presence of Native American, Hispanic, and Anglo residents.

On the north side of the Plaza stands the 1933 **Taos County Courthouse**, now containing art galleries. Vibrant murals and frescoes painted by local artists decorate the former courtroom upstairs. A couple of doors down, visit the **Taos Trading Company**, an old-fashioned soda fountain with a tile floor and deco-style

stools, all surrounded by a showroom of Coca-Cola memorabilia and kitschy souvenirs (the Frito pies, vanilla Cokes, and ice cream cones served here are, in fact, quite tasty). Just north of the Plaza is a tree-shaded courtyard of small shops and galleries, plus a handful of eateries, which extends across Bent Street—this picturesque pedestrian way evokes the alluring charms of Taos better than the Plaza, which is somewhat more touristy and predictable.

Walk east of the Plaza, crossing Paseo del Pueblo Norte, and you'll find several more galleries and boutiques, plus the **Kit Carson Home and Museum**, 2 Ledoux Street (daily

The **Museum Association of Taos** offers a combination pass very like the one offered by the Museum of New Mexico in Santa Fe: pay $20 and receive admission to the town's seven major museums (Hacienda Martinez, Harwood, Blumenschein, Kit Carson, Fechin, Van Vechten-Lineberry, and Millicent Rogers). The pass is good for a full year and is fully transferable, so you can pass it along to a friend if you're unable to visit every place during your stay.

9 AM-5 PM with longer hours in summer; $5; 505/758-0505). The rugged frontiersman and his wife, Maria Josefa Jamarillo, lived here from the 1840s until their deaths in the late 1860s; it now contains relics of his life, guns, and Hispanic and Indian art pieces.

Paseo del Pueblo Norte holds two of the arts attractions in town. The **Fechin Institute**, 227 Paseo del Pueblo Norte (Wed.-Sun. 10 AM-2 PM with longer hours in summer; $4; 505/758-1710), celebrates the life and work of Russian émigré Nicolai Fechin (1881-1955). His woodcarvings, paintings, drawings, wrought-iron handmade furnishings, and decorative elements fill this magnificent adobe house, infusing it with a distinctive Russian flair. A bit farther up the road, at the turnoff for the Taos Pueblo, the **Van Vechten-Lineberry Taos Art Museum**, 501 Paseo del Pueblo Norte (Wed.-Fri. 11 AM-4 PM, weekends 1:30 AM-4 PM; $5 (505/758-2690), contains a remarkable collection of works created by early Taos artisans, including many by the late Duane Van Vechten-Lineberry, who lived and painted here for many years up until her death in 1977. In 1994, her husband Edwin C. Lineberry and his second wife, Novella, opened this expansive museum—built around the original studio and tree-shaded grounds—as a tribute to his first wife.

Back on Paseo del Pueblo Norte, continue north through the El Prado section of town and turn left to reach the **Millicent Rogers Museum**, Millicent Rogers Road (Tues.-Sun. 10 AM-5 PM, daily in summer; $6; 505/758-2462), arguably the most intriguing art collection in the state. Rogers (1902-53), a glamorous heiress of the Standard Oil Company and successful fashion designer, kept company with some pretty important artists during her years in Taos. Three years after her death, her estate and its estimable collection of southwestern fine arts opened to the public as a museum; it has been expanded dramatically in the years since through major donations and acquisitions.

Contrary to popular misconception, the museum is not Rogers' former home—she lived in town, in a fairly modest adobe. However, her fast-growing collection was moved in the late 1960s to this large homestead and was greatly expanded in the mid-1980s by architectural icon Nathaniel Owings (of Skidmore, Owings & Merrill). Contained within these walls is a very fine survey of Indian, Hispanic, and Southwestern art, jewelry, and weaving through the ages, including many pieces from the Maria Martinez pottery collection. It's not difficult to lose yourself for a few hours in this place.

Nearby, head to the intersection of US-64, Hwy-150, and Hwy-522—where you'll find what locals refer to as "the blinking light," even though a fully operational traffic signal was installed here in 1997. From here, Hwy-150 leads right up through Arroyo Seco and into the Taos Ski Valley. The village of Arroyo Seco is a perfect, unspoiled place to spend an afternoon, with a smattering of very nice galleries and some excellent spots for lunch, notably Casa Fresen and Momentitos de la Vida. Abe's Cocina (505/776-8516), a simple little tavern and grocery store, makes some of the best homemade tamales around. Pick up heavenly ice cream cones at Taos Cow (505/776-5640).

In a crowded office off the lobby of the historic La Fonda de Taos (505/758-2211), you can view nine salacious paintings by the English novelist **D. H. Lawrence,** who spent time in Taos in the 1920s. A single attempt at an exhibition of the paintings was mounted in London, but Scotland Yard banned them and closed the exhibit. For $3 you can check the collection out for yourself—and read the strange story of how they came to be owned by La Fonda's late owner and how he offered to trade them to the British government in exchange for the return of the Elgin Marbles to Greece.

Taos Practicalities

The long-favored accommodation in the Plaza is the Taos Inn, 125 Paseo del Pueblo Norte (505/758-2233 or 800/826-7466), a charming 39-room adobe structure part of which dates to the 1600s. Bright southwestern bedspreads and country antiques fill the rooms, some of which have fireplaces. The historic hotel is also home to two of Taos' favorite eating and drinking spots—Doc Martin's and the Adobe Bar.

If wide-open mesas and unbelievable views are a priority, consider one of the B&Bs north of town in Arroyo Seco. Salsa del Salto, Hwy-150 (505/776-2422 or 800/530-3097), has perhaps the best facilities of any in these parts, with a pool, tennis court, and hot tub. The 10 rooms at this adobe compound range from modest-sized to quite capacious, and all have contemporary handmade southwestern furnishings (a few also have fireplaces and whirlpools). With unobstructed mountain and mesa views for 100 miles from every window, the intimate Little Tree, Hondo-Seco Road (505/776-8467 or 800/334-8467), has one of the best settings of any accommodation in the Southwest. Rooms are tastefully furnished, with latilla ceilings, native furnishings, and colorful handmade quilts. A grove of cottonwood trees shelters the aptly named Cottonwood Inn (505/776-5826 or 800/324-7120), at the junction of Hwy-150 and 230, near Arroyo Seco. Built by an offbeat local artist named Wolfgang Pogzeba, the rambling adobe was converted into an inn some years back and now

After a fire raged through the north side of the Plaza in 1932, resulting in the loss of several historic structures, concerned residents formed the **Taos Volunteer Fire Department**. In appreciation of the department's efforts, Taos artists have made a point of donating works to the fire department —more than 100 impressive paintings to date. Drop by the station on Camino de la Placita, by the Taos Civic Plaza and Convention Center, for a free peek.

In and around Taos, tune in to **KTAO 101.9 FM,** the "World's Only Solar Powered Radio Station," playing a lively range of alternative-minded folk, rock, and world music. The station increased from 3,000 to 50,000 watts in 1991, using only solar panels and batteries. Each June, the station also throws a respected music festival. Call 505/758-0815 or 505/758-8609 for information or to make requests.

has several characterful rooms, many with kiva fireplaces, balconies, terraces, and hot tubs.

Set on a hill within walking distance of the plaza, the **Mabel Dodge Luhan House** (505/751-9686) is a fascinating place to stay. Once the center of the Taos art colony, it was later owned by actor Dennis Hopper, and now offers comfortable, characterful accommodations (and great breakfasts) at reasonable rates ($85-110 a night). Stay in Tony's Room, and your bathroom will have a window painted by D. H. Lawrence.

Good moderate-priced motels in Taos include the **El Monte Lodge**, 317 Kit Carson Road (505/758-3171 or 800/828-TAOS), with adobe casitas amid a grove of cottonwood trees, and the basic, cheap, but exceptionally clean and well-run **Sun God Lodge**, 919 Paseo del Pueblo Sur (505/758-3162 or 800/821-2437), a 45-room, two-story complex with rooms overlooking a shady courtyard. A longtime favorite of backpackers and budget travelers, the **Abominable Snowmansion** hostel, on Hwy-150 in Arroyo Seco (505/776-8298), has dorm rooms for $13 to $18, plus private rooms, cabins, teepees, campsites, and a fun common area with a fireplace, pool tables, and piano. There are several chain motels in Taos on Hwy-68 as you enter town. None of them are especially remarkable except for a very nice and quite new **Hampton Inn**, at 515 Paseo del Pueblo Sur (505/737-5700 or 800/HAMPTON), which has an indoor pool.

Taos dining offers everything from down-home luncheonettes to upscale chi-chi (but still rather unpretentious). Starting in the south, two nearly neighboring restaurants in Ranchos de Taos have developed such a wildly loyal following in recent years that it's nearly impossible to score a table at either one in high season without reservations several days in advance. The **Trading Post Cafe**, Hwy-68 at Hwy-518 (505/758-5089), serves stylish California-Italalian bistro-style fare; down Hwy-68 a short distance, the romantic **Joseph's Table**, 4167 Paseo del Pueblo Sur (505/751-4512), has a short but sweet menu specializing in delicious contemporary American fare such as baked salmon with a roasted-tomato vinaigrette and pizza with caramelized onions, bacon, and gruyère cheese.

Even as trendy new eateries continue to proliferate in and around town, the region's favorite upscale standby, **Doc Martin's**, in the historic Taos Inn at 125 Paseo del Pueblo Norte (505/758-1977), remains a huge hit, as much for its charming dining room as for the stellar fare. Entrees include apple-cider pork tenderloin, grilled sea bass with bouillabaisse, and lacquered duck. The expansive hotel and restaurant compound is named for the only doctor in all of Taos county from the 1890s until his death in 1935. Even if you don't eat here, be sure to poke your head inside, or maybe have a drink in the lobby's **Adobe Bar**, admiring the vaulted latilla ceiling and stained-glass cupola. **Stakeout** (505/758-2042), which is perched high on a hill above Hwy-68, is *the* place in town—maybe even in all of New Mexico—to go for fantastic sunsets that unfold across the Rio Grande gorge and the broad mesa extending for miles beyond it.

For some of the best New Mexican fare around the region, head to **Tim's Chile Connection,** Hwy-150 (505/776-8787), whose menu borrows also from Mexico and other regions of the Southwest. Several rustic dining rooms and a spacious open-air patio with outstanding views toward the Sangre de Cristos accommodate big crowds, who partake of such specialties as shrimp-chipotle enchiladas, black bean tostadas, and sweet-corn tamales.

Most of the great lunch spots in Taos, however, serve regionally focused fare, oftentimes amid bare-bones trappings. A longtime locals' joint, the **Northtown Restaurant,** 908 Paseo del Pueblo Norte (505/758-2374), is where you're apt to see local politicos, newspaper editors, business owners, and other prominent Taoseños. Northtown specializes in slow-smoked barbecue and weighty sandwiches (the "ultimate" grilled cheese is slathered in Swiss, cheddar, avocado, tomato, onion, and sprouts). The linoleum floors and paneled walls fit the no-nonsense image of this place perfectly, just as they do at nearby **El Pueblo Cafe,** 625 Paseo del Pueblo Norte (505/751-9817), a raggedy-looking greasy spoon diner that serves food into the late hours. El Pueblo specializes in wonderful tamale platters, waitresses who call you "hon," and stuffing sticking out of most of the vinyl booths. **Bent Street Deli,** 120 Bent Street (505/758-5787), on the edge of the pedestrian mall north of the Plaza, offers about two-dozen creative sandwiches served all day, plus a full slate of entrees varying wildly in their culinary origins, from Italian chicken parmigiana to shrimp and veggies in a Brazilian coconut-tomato-peanut sauce.

Despite the spartan surroundings, you owe it to yourself to sample the best tacos, burritos, and tostadas in town. Located behind the Central Taos Motorbank (if you need it, pick up some cash at the drive-through ATM; this place doesn't take plastic), **The Burrito Wagon,** Tiwa Lane and Paseo del Pueblo Sur (505/751-4091), is really an old tan camper surrounded by a few picnic tables. Inexpensive and thoroughly satisfying dining options abound in Taos: for breakfast, check out **Michael's Kitchen,** 304 Paseo del Pueblo Norte (505/758-4178), famous for its fresh-baked bread and pastries.

Taos Pueblo

Two miles northeast of the center of town, at the end of Taos Pueblo Road, Taos Pueblo (daily 8 AM-4:30 PM, closed Jan.-March and certain religious occasions; $10; 505/758-1028 or 505/758-9593) is one of New Mexico's real treasures, a walled village comprising two multi-story pueblos (the North and South houses), St. Jerome's Church, the ruins of Old San Gerónimo Church (and its adjacent burial ground), and the Pueblo Plaza, which has sustained life continuously for the past 1,000 years. This historic village is neither a museum nor a theme park but a real

As fascinating as the Taos Pueblo is, a visit here is not inexpensive. When planning, be sure to factor in admission, various permit fees for photography or even painting (still cameras $10; video cameras $25), and the requisite tips if you take one of the highly recommend guided tours offered throughout the day.

Taos Pueblo has joined other pueblos and reservations in the region by opening the **Taos Mountain Casino** (505/737-0777). It's fairly diminutive now, but the pueblo hopes to turn the current Best Western Kachina Lodge, near the turnoff for the pueblo, into a full-scale casino-resort hotel. Not everyone in Taos—or even in the pueblo—is completely behind this project, but it does appear to be moving steadily forward toward an opening around 2004.

functioning community, and visitors are expected to behave in a respectful manner toward their hosts. In return, you'll be able to explore those areas open to outsiders and glimpse a bit of a remarkably well-preserved culture. As you wander about the pueblo, you'll see quite a few shops, selling pottery flecked with bits of mica, turquoise jewelry, moccasins, fresh-baked bread, and a fair share of modern-day souvenirs (mugs, T-shirts, and more).

About 150 tribal members reside within the main buildings of the pueblo, and nearly 1,800 more Taos Indians live elsewhere on the adjoining reservation. At the pueblo itself, neither electricity nor modern plumbing are used; the tribe's sole source of water is the Rio Pueblo, which is fed from the sacred Blue Lake in the Sangre de Cristo Mountains, high above the reservation. In the plaza, wooden drying racks and ovens are used for food preparation. While everybody here speaks English, Tiwa is the pueblo's primary language, and generations continue to pass it on.

Many Native Americans in New Mexico practice Catholicism, as they have since the Spanish colonized this region. The historic St. Jerome Church stands as evidence to the pueblo's devout faith. The structure dates to 1850 and is named for the patron saint of the Taos Pueblo. It was built to replace the original Old San Geronimo Church, which the US cavalry sacked and burned in 1847 following the assassination of governor Charles Bent, who was murdered in his Taos home. During the altercation, the Taos Indians—including many women and children—barricaded themselves inside San Geronimo; about 150 of them died in the ensuing melee. The former courtyard of the demolished church was transformed—appropriately and sadly—into a graveyard (visitors are not permitted to enter these grounds).

If you can, come during one of the sacred religious ceremonies, held year-round at the pueblo. Some of these are open only to tribal members, but about a dozen welcome visitors, including a Christmas Eve procession; several corn dances held in May, June, and July; and a Turtle Dance that ushers in the New Year (photography is not allowed, even by permit, during these events). Whenever you arrive, be sure to take one of the tours of the Pueblo, which will undoubtedly help illuminate both the tensions and the mutual understandings that exist between tribal members and the outside world.

Taos Ski Valley

There are eight major ski valleys in northern New Mexico. But serious ski fanatics cite Taos Ski Valley, 20 miles northeast of town at the end of Hwy-150, as one of the most challenging and beautiful ski areas in the nation. The area is equally appealing in summer, though, since daily high temperatures rarely exceed 80° F (you should bring a light jacket even in July and August); there are several trails leading from the resort area, passing alpine lakes or through deserted copper mining camps; and you can even still ride the Lift No.1 chairlift (Thurs.-Sun. 10 AM-

4 PM; late June to Labor Day; $6), either hiking up or back and riding the other way, or riding both ways. The valley's elevation is 9,207 feet, and it receives more than 300 inches of snow in an average year. Ski season is late November to early April. There are several restaurants and hotels up here, but unless you're here to ski it's nicer and cheaper to stay elsewhere; for more details, call 505/776-8220 or 800/992-7669.

Forming a full-day's 85-mile circuit of the Carson National Forest around 13,161-foot Wheeler Peak, the **Enchanted Circle National Scenic Byway** follows US-64 east past the Angel Fire ski area, then heads north and west on Hwy-38 through the towns of Red River and Questa, returning to Taos on Hwy-522.

US-64: the Rio Grande Bridge

From Taos, toward Chama and the Four Corners region, if you drive west on US-64 for about eight miles, you'll cross one of the most-visited attractions in the area—the Rio Grande Gorge Bridge, the second-highest bridge in the U.S. highway system. The 650-foot-high bridge is a sight to see (it's appeared in several movies, including *Natural Born Killers* and *Easy Rider*). You can also walk across it and peer down into the gorge below—a view breathtaking for some, genuinely terrifying for anyone prone to vertigo.

As you drive west just beyond the bridge, keep an eye out on your right for the colony of futuristic-looking domiciles, called "earthships," clustered amid the sage bushes. The self-proclaimed **Earthship World Headquarters** comprises a number of these structures built of recycled tires and aluminum cans, mud, and straw bales. The self-sustaining community collects its water in rain cisterns and uses the sun and the wind to generate power.

Tres Piedras

After crossing the Rio Grande Bridge, continue on US-64 west to the small town of Tres Piedras. One building here is visible from at least a mile away: a large hot-pink adobe, one of the more curious structures in the state. Owned by a reticent but passionate collector of southwestern art named Ken Nelson, the **Old Pink Schoolhouse**, US-285 at US-64 (open by chance or appointment; 505/758-7826), is one of the most fascinating and provocative art galleries you'll ever find. About a dozen enthusiastic dogs greet guests, who enter through the rear courtyard and walk into this former schoolhouse, which is also Nelson's home. The entire place is open for viewing—religious iconography abounds, including many images of Our Lady of Guadalupe. Inside, amid the scent of burning incense, you'll find folk art, mixed media, collectibles, rags, and tapestries from both the local area and Mexico depicting beautiful and sometimes disturbing themes.

From Tres Piedras, US-64 continues over the dramatic San Juan Mountains toward Tierra Amarilla and Chama. In winter, this road is closed and you must reach Chama by turning north in Tres Piedras onto US-285 and proceeding just over the Colorado border to the village of Antonito. This detour really doesn't take all that much longer and passes over much of the same spectacular mountainside that's visible from the famous Cumbres & Toltec Scenic Railroad, which terminates at Antonito.

Tierra Amarilla and Los Ojos

At the junction of US-64 and US-84, a dozen miles south of Chama, the town of Tierra Amarilla is a worn-looking place whose one slice of grandeur is the

Italianate-inspired Rio Arriba Courthouse. Just north of the the center of town, a turn off US-64/84 leads a mile west into one of the loveliest villages in the Chama valley, Los Ojos. Here in this once-agrarian community you'll find a smattering of artists' studios, most of them in rustic buildings with corrugated metal roofs. A must-see is **Tierra Wools** (505/588-7231), where the Hispanic weaving tradition has been practiced since the 1600s; many families of northern New Mexico made their livings spinning, farming, and shepherding, and weaving continues to be a major cottage industry throughout the Rio Chama Valley. The large showroom here displays fine wool rugs, and a back room contains about a dozen looms, where you can see unfinished works, tapestries, and rugs in progress. On many days you can come and watch the weavers work, spinning and hand-dyeing the wool. In addition, the **Tierra Wools B&B** (505/588-7231) offers simple but elegant rooms with saltillo tiles, turquoise-painted trim, kitchenettes, and handsome Tierra Wools rugs hanging on the walls—this place is a real treasure that few visitors ever hear about.

Drop by the neighboring **Pastore's Feed and General Store** (505/588-7821), which is also a frame shop and art gallery. Here, under a pressed-tin ceiling, you can order lunch, a latte, soda, or sweets. In the same village, the **San Jose Church**, a lovely old building with a tall belfry, adobe walls, a metal roof, and stained-glass windows, contains a breathtakingly beautiful altar and statuary of saints along the sanctuary walls.

Parkview Fish Hatchery is just down the road from Los Ojos—it's one of four hatcheries in northern New Mexico, the spawning ground for many of the 1.5 million Rio Grande, lake, cutthroat, rainbow, and brook trout raised each year by New Mexico Department of Game and Fish. For 25 cents you can grab a handful of feed and toss it out into the pools of fish. A few fishing and hunting artifacts are displayed in a small exhibition room.

Chama

High up in the Tusas Mountains, a dozen miles south of the Colorado border, forests of aspen and pine and vast meadows of wildflowers surround the old railroad town of Chama (pop. 1,300; elev. 7,900 feet), whose booms and busts have largely coincided with the vicissitudes in the popularity of train transportation. The town was born around 1880, when gold and silver miners struck paydirt in the San Juan Mountains, and workers piled in to construct the Denver and Rio Grande Railroad. Gambling halls, moonshine stills, speakeasies, and brothels were a fixture along the main drag, Terrace Avenue.

The town still contains quite a few historic houses and buildings fashioned out of spare hand-hewn railroad ties. And, surrounded by national forests, it's a popular base for fishing, boating, camping trips, and for cross-country skiing and snowmobiling in winter. Otherwise, though, it's home to relatively few diversions. The reason most casual travelers venture here is to take a ride on the historic narrow-gauge **Cumbres & Toltec Scenic Railroad** (daily at 10:30 AM, mid-May to mid-October; $35-55; 505/756-2151 or 800/724-5428), a string of vintage open-air carriages pulled by a coal-fired steam engine along 64 miles of twisting railroad from Chama to Antonito, Colorado. You'll pass over ancient trestles, around breathtaking bends, over 10,000-foot passes, and high above the Los Pinos River. If the terrain looks at all familiar, it may be because you saw the train's guest appearance in the extended opening sequence of *Indiana Jones and the Last Crusade*. On the ride, you'll hear the echo of the whistle as you pass through narrow canyons, and you'll catch glimpses of the Los Pinos River.

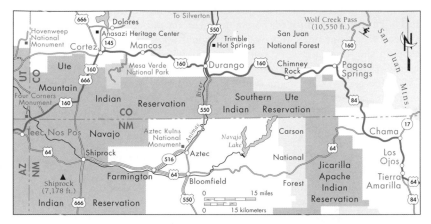

Trains leave from both ends of the line, meeting midway at Osier Station, where passengers disembark for lunch; after this, half-day riders return to their starting point by train, while full-day riders continue on to the other end, coming home by bus. It makes the most sense to choose this latter option, as making the full trip takes only an additional two hours (for a roundtrip total of eight hours) and assures you new and thrilling scenery the entire way—even on the bus ride back along scenic Hwy-17. To follow the railroad route by car, take Hwy-17 north and east from Chama, entering Colorado over 10,222-foot Chama Pass; US-64/84 winds in a westerly direction toward Farmington, New Mexico, with US-84 branching off long before then and curving up toward Pagosa Springs, Colorado.

Chama offers some affordable, serviceable eateries and pleasant motels. The two best accommodations are the **Chama Trails Inn Motel**, 2362 Hwy-17 at the US-64/84 junction (505/756-2156 or 800/289-1421), whose rooms have refrigerators, TVs, phones, and many whimsical touches (from chile ristras to kachina dolls); and the slightly more upscale **Vista del Rio Lodge**, 2595 US-64/84 (505/756-2138), a timber-faced motor lodge with bright, clean, newly furnished rooms and a hot tub on the premises.

For meals, check out the **Whistle Stop**, 423 S. Terrace Avenue (505/756-1833), a storefront cafe on the main road, directly across from the railroad station. Steaks, seafood, and a fair number of both American and Southwestern dishes are offered. The best steaks in town (plus some pretty good Mexican cooking) are served at **High Country**, on Hwy-17 just north of US-64/84 (505/756-2384), where a high-kitsch Old West theme puts patrons in a lively mood for drinking and socializing. Across the street, **Viva Vera's** (505/756-2557) has been Chama's favorite Mexican restaurant since the 1920s, but the blandly seasoned food and indifferent service may leave you wondering why.

Aztec Ruins National Monument
Two main routes branch out from Chama. One goes north into the heart of the San Juan Mountains along US-84, toward Pagosa Springs, Colorado; the other heads west, following US-64 for over 100 miles across the Jicarilla Apache Reservation toward Farmington and Aztec Ruins National Monument. Around A.D. 1100, this

was one of the largest of many pre-Columbian cities in today's Four Corners region, linking the Mesa Verde community with the one at Pueblo Bonito in Chaco Canyon. The name Aztec was mistakenly applied by early American settlers, who thought the three-story, 500-room structure was related to the great Mexican culture (it wasn't). Despite considerable "restoration" efforts undertaken in the 1920s and 1930s, Aztec Ruins is well worth visiting if you've enjoyed any of the other Anasazi sites. The fact that the ruins here—especially the Great Kiva that stands at the center of the complex—have been manhandled and reconstructed has at least one real upside: park service anthropologists are more willing than elsewhere to let visitors clamber in and around the place, squeezing through narrow doorways to get a palpable sense of what life might have been like for the people who built it—400 years before the "discovery" of the New World.

Before or after exploring the ruins, be sure to stop in the **visitors center** (daily 8 AM-5 PM, till 6 PM in summer; $4; 505/334-6174), which has a small museum displaying Anasazi pottery shards, jewelry, and textiles found here. Park rangers also give guided tours and interpretive talks inside the Great Kiva.

The ruins are located on Ruins Road, a half-mile north of US-550, just west of the sleepily pleasant small town of **Aztec,** which was founded in 1890 along the banks of the Animas River and proudly preserves its many historic buildings.

The best range of accommodations in the area is southwest of Aztec in the big, busy coal and oil city of **Farmington** (pop. 34,000), on the eastern edge of the Navajo Nation. Choose from two each of Motel 6, Super 8, and Holiday Inn as well as about a dozen others.

South of Farmington, a smaller Anasazi site is the centerpiece of **Salmon Ruins and Heritage Park,** right off US-64, two miles west of Bloomfield. There's a small museum (daily 9 AM-5 PM; $3) on site.

Farmington is home to one of the best radio stations in the Southwest: **KNDN 960 AM,** "The Indian Station," broadcasting the best classic country music (from Hank Williams to George Jones) with almost all patter and advertising in Navajo.

The prettiest route from the national monument is US-550, which runs north along the river, linking up with US-160 across the Colorado border in Durango.

Pagosa Springs

If you prefer mountain scenery to ancient history, head north into Colorado from Chama, along US-84 to Pagosa Springs (pop. 1,200; elev. 7,095 feet). This is a small but rapidly growing resort community tucked away at the heart of the San Juan Mountains, the youngest and among the most rugged of all in the Rocky Mountains chain. Taking its name from the natural 153° hot springs treasured by the native Ute and Navajo tribes (Pagosa is Ute for "healing waters"), Pagosa Springs was more a lumber town than a vacation spot until the recent development of golf courses and the small but popular Wolf Creek Ski Area (800/754-9653) began drawing more casual visitors.

Pagosa Springs is still not really a major destination, but it's well worth a stop. For hearty Mexican food, try the **Elkhorn Cafe,** downtown at 438 Main Street; east of town along US-160, choose from **Branding Iron BBQ** or the **Ole Miners Steakhouse.** You can stay the night at the **Spring Inn,** a block south of US-160 at 165 Hot Springs Boulevard (970/264-4168), where rooms start at $80. The room price includes a soak in the dozen different outdoor riverfront pools, all fed by natural hot springs. Use of the pools for non-guests costs $10.

East from Pagosa Springs, US-160 makes an incredibly scenic jaunt over the Continental Divide at 10,550-foot Wolf Creek Pass, then drops down along the headwaters of the Rio Grande into the agricultural San Luis Valley, home of the Great Sand Dunes National Monument.

Durango

Founded as a supply and smelting center for surrounding gold and silver mines, Durango (pop. 12,400; elev. 6,500 feet) is a picturesque and very popular base for visitors exploring the Four Corners and southern Rocky Mountain regions. The whitewater Animas River flows right alongside the downtown area, attracting river rafters in droves. Mountain bikers race through the nearby mountains along old mining trails, but the real activity is along Main Avenue, where a dozen blocks of historic, turn-of-the-century buildings, stretching north from the depot of the historic Durango-Silverton steam train, house an engaging variety of brewpubs, bike shops, art galleries, and cafes. One of the latter is the friendly **Durango Diner**, 957 Main Avenue (970/247-9889), where gigantic pancakes and delicious green chile burritos start the day off right. A block away, you can hang out with Durango's bike-and-board crowd at **Carver's**, 1022 Main Avenue (6 AM-10 PM; 970/259-2545), serving coffees, snacks, full meals, and fresh-brewed beer.

Well-maintained Victorian-era hotels located downtown include the **General Palmer**, 567 Main Avenue (970/247-4747), next to the Silverton steam train depot, and the stately **Strater**, 699 Main Avenue (970/247-4431 or 800/247-4431). Durango also has many nice old motels along the north end of Main Avenue, such as the **Silver Spur**, 3416 Main Avenue (970/247-5552 or 800/748-1715), where John Wayne once stayed. Apart from a new mattress and a few other essentials, his room (#104) is still decorated the same as it was when The Duke slept here. And at $50 a night, the price is right. For budget travelers, the **HI Durango**, 543 E. 2nd Street (970/247-9905), offers hostel beds for $12-15.

For details on rooms, river-rafting, rodeos, and anything else to do with Durango and the surrounding area, contact the **visitors bureau**, along the river at 111 S. Camino del Rio (970/247-0312 or 800/525-8855).

Midway between Pagosa Springs and Durango, on Hwy-151 three miles south of US-160, the fascinating but generally inaccessible Anasazi ruins at **Chimney Rock** comprise dozens of ruins covering six square miles. For information on the summer-only guided tours, contact the U.S. Forest Service **ranger station** in Pagosa Springs (970/264-2268).

Summer nights in Durango are best spent at the many **rodeos** held at the La Plata County Fairgrounds, just north of town. The 4th of July weekend sees the Cowgirl Classic, the state's only all-female rodeo; the Ghost Dancer All-Indian Rodeo is held on Labor Day; and the Durango Pro Rodeo can be enjoyed weeknights from June to August.

Detour: Silverton

One of the prettiest 50-mile drives imaginable starts north from Durango and follows US-550 high up into the Rocky Mountains to the old mining camp of Silverton. Though the drive is amazing enough, to really get a feel for the history (and to be free from having to keep your eyes on the road), take a ride on the unforgettable **Durango and Silverton Narrow Gauge Railroad** ($50; 970/247-7733 or 888/872-4607), which has been in active use since 1882. Still coal-fired and steam-powered, the locomotives huff and puff from the streets of downtown Durango, spewing soot and cinders and blocking traffic, then proceed north alongside US-550 all the way to Silverton, a mining town little changed since its 1880s heyday, with bars and hotels lining the dusty streets.

Silverton is also the southern end of the legendary Million Dollar Highway, which climbs north over the mountains to Ouray; this amazingly scenic drive is covered in the US-50 chapter on pages 264-265.

If you're staying in one of the older motels along Main Avenue on the north side of Durango, take advantage of the free trolley bus that rambles between there and downtown.

On the road to Silverton, north of Durango near the very popular but unpretentious Purgatory ski area (800/525-0892), the equally unpretentious **Trimble Hot Springs** (970/247-0111) has been soothing travelers for over a century.

Mancos

Midway between Durango and Mesa Verde National Park, US-160 passes through the small town of Mancos, which has a photogenic downtown area located just south of the highway. Mancos was the home of the Wetherill family, who "discovered" Mesa Verde while wandering through the canyons looking for lost cattle and subsequently balanced their efforts to preserve the sites and bring them to appropriate anthropological and scholarly attention by leading safaris into the region to hunt for pottery and other souvenirs. The historic **Old Mancos Inn**, 200 W. Grand Avenue (970/533-9019), is a very pleasant place to stay, with rooms running $30-50 a night, depending on whether you share a bathroom; the hot tub is open to all guests. The same building houses the excellent **Dusty Rose Cafe**, which serves above-average breakfasts and, for dinner, upscale Italian food. The town holds one of the better souvenir shops in the Four Corners region: **The Hogan Trading Post** (970/533-7117), marked by a miniature forest of giant red arrows on the north side of US-160, just west of downtown. (Each of the arrows is a telephone pole, painted red and adorned with feathery fronds.)

North of Mancos, one of the region's more unusual places to stay is the **Jersey Jim Lookout** ($45 per night; 970/533-7060), a former Forest Service fire lookout now open for up to four overnight guests—55 feet above the forest floor.

Mesa Verde National Park

The beautiful, top-of-the-world environs of Mesa Verde National Park form a perfect backdrop for this stupendous archaeological site. If you're not familiar with the amazing Anasazi cities whose remnants dot the Four Corners region, come here for an unforgettable introduction to this enigmatic ancient culture. If you have visited and been fascinated by other Anasazi ruins, you still haven't seen anything until you've experienced the stupendous cliff palaces at Mesa Verde.

The prisitine setting (at elevations ranging from 7,000 to 8,500 feet), the limits on the numbers of visitors (only approximately 50 people a day are permitted to visit the two most stunning and fragile sites, Cliff Palace and Balcony House), and most of the buildings themselves all conspire to make Mesa Verde one of the true must-sees of the Southwest. Mesa Verde gained national park status in 1906—it is the only national park dedicated to the preservation of man-made, as opposed to natural, creations.

The greatest concentration of sites is at Chapin Mesa, where a nice **museum** (daily 8 AM-5 PM, till 6:30 PM in summer; free; 970/529-4465) gives a great introduction to the Mesa Verde story—with New Deal dioramas aplenty. From the museum, a short but steep hike drops from the junipers and piñon pines atop the mesa down to **Spruce Tree House** (daily 9 AM-5 PM), where more than 100 rooms huddle in a 90-foot-deep alcove.

South of Chapin Mesa, one-way loop Ruins Road leads past the photogenic, four-story **Square Tower House** and continues on past **Sun Point**, which offers great afternoon views of **Cliff Palace** on the opposite side of the canyon. Sun Point is where, on a snowy December 18, 1888, ranchers Richard Wetherill and his brother-in-law Charlie Mason saw and named Cliff Palace, describing it as a "magnificent city."

To reach Cliff Palace or **Balcony House**, take the eastern half of the Ruins Road loop. To tour Cliff Palace—the largest Anasazi cliff dwelling, where some 250 people once lived in a magnificent, 200-room apartment building 100 feet below the mesa top—be prepared to clamber up and down five ladders. Touring Balcony House is much more strenuous (and potentially heart-stopping, for those with a fear of heights): visitors climb down a 32-foot ladder to enter a small alcove that hangs some 500 feet above the canyon floor. Tours of each begin every half-hour and take about an hour; get the mandatory advance **tickets** ($1.75) from the Far View Visitors Center.

Two miles east of the entrance to Mesa Verde National Park, the **Reptile Reserve** (daily 9 AM-5 PM; $4; 970/533-7532) is a throwback to old-fashioned roadside tourism, offering a chance to see hundreds of rattlesnakes up close and personal. For a small fee, you can have a photo taken of yourself and your favorite fanged friend, and the gift shop sells some unique souvenirs.

The oldest remnants at Mesa Verde are the many simple pithouses all over the mesa top. These date from around A.D. 700; the famous cliff palaces were inhabited for only a century or so, before the entire community disappeared around A.D. 1300. Most anthropologists figure that the displaced Mesa Verdeans evolved into today's Hopi and Pueblo Indians.

For a less crowded experience of Mesa Verde, during the peak summer season you can head west from the Far View Visitors Center to Wetherill Mesa, where Anasazi ruins include the Long House, the second-largest in Mesa Verde.

Because of the prevalence of archaeological features all over Mesa Verde National Park, there is very little public access to the backcountry; no hiking or camping is allowed outside established areas. If you do chance upon an artifact, leave it where it is and don't be tempted to take it home as a souvenir: disturbing or removing antiquities can win you a $100,000 fine or up to 20 years in federal prison.

Mesa Verde National Park Practicalities

Mesa Verde is located on a high tableland, 36 miles west of Durango and 10 miles east of Cortez. South from US-160, the park road climbs steeply for about four miles, passing the park's one and only campground—very large, rarely full **Morefield**. There are nearly 500 sites costing $10 (full hookups $17), and showers, a grocery store, and nightly campfire programs (at 9 PM) make this a very comfortable base for seeing the park.

Another 11 miles brings you to the **Far View Visitors Center** (May-Sept. only, 8 AM-5 PM; free; 970/529-4543), where most park visitors stop first. This is the place to pick up the mandatory tickets for tours of the Cliff Palace, Balcony House, and Long House ruins. The park's only hotel, the 150-room, $100-a-night **Far View Lodge** (970/529-4421), is right next door; there's also a gas station and a cafeteria here.

The main ruins are further south—six miles to Chapin Mesa, and another six beyond that to Balcony House—a good hour's drive south from US-160, if you obey speed limits or get stuck behind a lumbering RV or two. The distances involved, and the strict limits the park service puts on numbers of visitors, can make Mesa Verde difficult to enjoy in passing; set aside at least one full day if you want to get the whole Mesa Verde experience. Though summertime can be crowded, there isn't much of a shoulder season. From October until May, the lodge, the campground, and most of the cliff dwellings are closed; only Spruce Tree House ruin is kept open for visitors year-round.

Cortez

A ranching supply town at the foot of Mesa Verde, about 35 miles northeast of the Four Corners Monument, Cortez is a busy little town that stretches for miles along the main highways, east-west US-160 and north-south US-666.

For a taste of what visiting Mesa Verde was like at the dawn of the automobile age, take a hike along the **Knife Edge Trail,** which climbs up from the north end of Morefield campground along the original access road to the cliff palaces, offering great views (especially at sunset) over the vast valleys below.

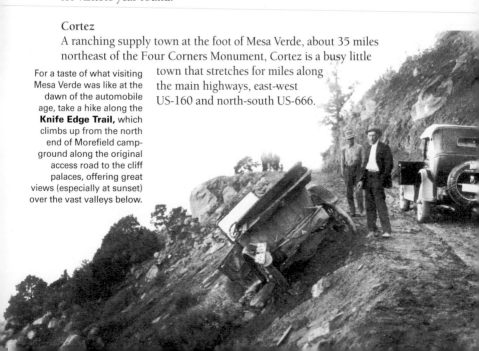

North and east from Cortez, Hwy-145 completes the top-of-the-world scenic drive known as the **San Juan Skyway**. The high point in this western section is the picturesque old mining camp and upscale resort town of **Telluride,** about 100 twisting miles away. Other sections of the San Juan Skyway are covered elsewhere in this book: south of Ouray on US-550, the Million Dollar Highway is described on page 264; the route to Silverton is described after the Durango entry, above.

Downtown Cortez is compact and very pleasant, with shops, an old movie theater, and a pair of reliably good restaurants lined up along Main Street (US-160). For breakfast, lunch or dinner, the family-friendly **Homesteaders**, 45 E. Main Street (970/565-6253), has everything from burgers to pasta dishes, and a few doors down, the **Main Street Brewery**, 21 E. Main Street (970/564-9112), has fresh beer, burgers, and fish 'n' chips.

Fans of roadside Americana who also treasure a good cup of coffee will want to visit one of my favorite finds in the whole Southwest: the **Silver Bean**, 410 W. Main Street (970/946-4404). Located on the west edge of Cortez, at the US-160/US-666 junction, and housed in a classic 1960s Airstream trailer, the Silver Bean serves up eye-opening java and simple breakfast fare (pastries, burritos, and more), with a counter inside and a small patio out front.

Nine miles north of Cortez and three miles west of Dolores at 27501 Hwy-184, the BLM-operated **Anasazi Heritage Center** (daily 9 AM-5 PM; $3; 970/882-4811) presents some of the millions of ancient artifacts unearthed prior to the filling of McPhee Reservoir, Colorado's second-largest "lake." Two Anasazi ruins—known as Dominguez and Escalante in memory of the early Spanish explorers—are just outside the museum.

South and west of Cortez, US-160 runs through a short stretch of verdant irrigated ranchlands, which last until you reach the Ute Mountain Indian Reservation. There, the land reverts to its natural sun-baked brown, and a small casino (and RV park) beckons travelers to stop.

Detour: Hovenweep National Monument

One of the most remote properties in the National Park system, Hovenweep National Monument lies astride the Utah/Colorado border—a long, slow 30-mile drive west of Cortez via McElmo Canyon Road. The name Hovenweep, which means "deserted valley" in Ute, is very appropriate; if you ever want to get away from it all, this is a good place to be. Though visitor numbers have doubled since the roads were paved, Hovenweep still only handles around 40,000 people a year. Facilities are being upgraded, with a new visitors center (daily 8 AM-5 PM; $6; 435/459-4344 or 970/749-0510) and some new trails, but there's no lodge and no

Visible from all over the Four Corners region, **Sleeping Ute Mountain** rises to 9,977 feet above the otherwise flat plain southwest of Cortez (from where it most resembles a sleeping man). The "head" is in the north, the "feet" in the south.

food available for miles, so come prepared. (It's primitive enough that the water taps at the small first-come first-served campground seem luxurious; in fact, the rates are cut in half during winter—from $10 to $5 a night—when the water is shut off.) If you're ready to rough it a little, Hovenweep may end up being a highlight of your Southwest trip: the night sky is unbelievably bright, the desert usually so still that you can hear coyotes wailing, and the many intriguing ruins will keep your imagination reeling for a long time to come.

The Anasazi ruins protected here, only a small portion of which have been excavated and restored, are noted for their stone towers. The most impressive group is known as the **Square Tower Ruins**, which include examples of all the main building types at Hovenweep: a square, a D-shaped, an oval, and a round tower. Square Tower Ruins has long been the main visitor focus at Hovenweep, and at press time the old ranger station near the campground was being replaced by the new visitors center, a half-mile away, where you should start your tour. From the new center, a

short half-mile jaunt leads to an overlook down into the shallow canyon, while a longer two-mile loop actually drops down into the canyon, passing a number of outlying ruins, including the impressive Hovenweep Castle, before approaching the medieval-looking sandstone Square Tower itself.

There are many other Anasazi remains all over the monument, but these are not even signposted. If you want to explore, get details and directions from the main visitors center, but don't disturb anything, and keep an eye out for rattlesnakes.

From Hovenweep, you can head east and return to Cortez; head west along well-paved Hwy-262 and join our Canyonlands Loop road trip between Blanding and Bluff (see pages 365-367); or head south along Hwy-262 through the oil-pumping crossroads of Aneth, rejoining US-160 about six miles north of the Four Corners Monument.

Though three of its four main access roads have been recently paved (with the exception of the road from the north, via Pleasant View, Colorado), Hovenweep National Monument is still sufficiently remote not to be wired for telephone service—though it does have an answering machine, and a pair of cellular phones for emergencies and visitor information.

fall returns to Telluride

ROAD TRIP RESOURCES

RECOMMENDED READING

BACKGROUND

Desert Solitaire, by Edward Abbey (Mc-Graw-Hill, 1968). One of the all-time classics of nature writing, this keenly observed, very funny, and magnificently passionate book is a vivid account of life on the otherworldly Colorado Plateau. Thirty-odd years since its publication, it may no longer seem quite so earth-shattering, but the fact that Abbey's original perceptions have become common sense is a tribute to his impact on our perceptions of people's place in the wilder scheme of things. Among his many other books are *The Monkey Wrench Gang,* the novel that inspired the radical Earth First! environmentalist movement, and *The Journey Home: Some Words in Defense of the American West,* a collection of essays, anecdotes, and vituperative epistles relating more of this self-described "agrarian anarchist" writer's lifelong love of the open spaces of the intermountain West.

Land of Little Rain, by Mary Austin (University of New Mexico Press, 1974). First published in 1903, this slim volume of stories recounts the varying aspects of life in the Owens Valley of California—at a time before all their water was siphoned off to Los Angeles. Deceptively simple, but rich in detail, the tales mix Native American myths, ghost town mysteries, homespun pioneer truths, and above all else a vivid sense of the natural world to portray a place that in many ways is a distillation of the greater Southwest region.

Scenes in America Deserta, by Reyner Banham (Gibbs Smith, 1982). In this lighthearted but eye-opening collection of essays and ideas, the late British architectural historian muses on desert resorts, railroad stations, cliff dwellings and everything else he finds in the desert Southwest.

The Thousand-Mile Summer, by Colin Fletcher (Howell-North, 1964). If you ever want to be grateful you have a car, read this account of a six-month-long backpacking trip from Mexico to Oregon by way of Death Valley and the High Sierra. (Actually, the book may well have the opposite effect, and make you swap your driver's seat for a pair of hiking boots.) Another evocative book by the same Welsh-born author is *The Man Who Walked Through Time,* describing his sojourn through the Grand Canyon.

Inventing the Southwest, by Kathleen L. Howard and Diana F. Pardue (Northland Publishing, 1996). Produced by the Heard Museum, this lushly illustrated, full-color book looks at the role of railroad companies and the hotelier Fred Harvey in the development of tourism in the Southwest.

A Sense of Place, A Sense of Time, by J. B. Jackson (Yale University Press, 1994). Discussing everything from the design of Pueblo Indian villages to the proliferation of semi-permanent "mobile homes," these essays by the late great pioneer of American landscape studies offer a provocative look at the everyday places of the desert Southwest.

Cadillac Desert, by Marc Reisner (Viking Penguin, 1986). Subtitled "The American West and its Disappearing Water," this powerful history of the ongoing water wars of California and the Southwest exposes the greed and corruption behind the blooming of the desert landscape. Tracing the role of the region's lifeblood—water—from John Wesley Powell's exploration of the Colorado River and its canyons through the building of the Glen Canyon dam and the reservoir that bears his name, this book is a crystal-clear look at the forces behind the ceaseless growth of Los Angeles, Las Vegas, and the other artificially sustained cities of the Sunbelt.

Cruising Paradise, by Sam Shepard (Knopf, 1996). Ideal reading for long sleepless nights in a desert motel room, this collection of short stories by the Pulitzer Prize-winning playwright and actor captures the dusty, drawling, directionless desolation of life in the middle of the Great American nowhere.

Cabeza de Vaca's Aventures in the Unknown Interior of America, by Alvar N. Cabaza de Vaca (University of New Mexico Press, 1983, translated by Cyclone Covey). Perhaps the very first southwestern road novel, this true account follows Spanish explorer Cabeza de Vaca from a 1528 Florida shipwreck through eight years of wandering the Gulf Coast, the American Southwest, and what is now northern Mexico. Some Indian tribes enslaved Cabeza de Vaca; others revered him as a miracle working medicine man. A fascinating look at the very early southwest and its inhabitants, the book was made into a visually stunning and nearly wordless film in 1993 by director Nicolas Echeverria.

GUIDEBOOKS

California Coastal Access Guide (University of California Press, 1997). Packed with over 100 maps, 200 photographs, and 300 pages of detailed practical and background information, this marvelous book contains everything you might want to know about the hundreds of publicly-accessible natural areas along California's 1,100-mile coastline.

Old US-80 Travelers Guide, by Eric J. Finley (Narrow Road Communications, 1997). Following what was once called the "Broadway of America" between Phoenix and San Diego, this handy little guide helps you find the many remaining stretches of atmospheric two-lane highway that survive alongside the modern I-8 and I-10 freeways.

Flattened Fauna: A Field Guide to Common Animals of Roads, Streets, and Highways, by Roger M. Knutson (Ten Speed Press, 1987). Lighthearted look at that under-studied ecosystem, the highway. Besides being a helpful guide to identifying the sundry dead objects along the roadside, the book also details the natural life and habitats of the unfortunate road-killed creatures.

Native Roads, by Fran Kosik (Creative Solutions Publishing, 1995). A complete driver's guide to exploring the Navajo and Hopi lands, this detailed book covers the native cultures and crafts as well as geology and history of the Four Corners region.

Highway 99: That Ribbon of Highway, Parts I and II, by Jill Livingston (Living Gold Press, 1998). Taking their titles from the Woodie Guthrie song "This Land is Your Land," this pair of books traces the route of Highway 99 from the top to the bottom of California, pointing out all the old bridges, welcome arches, giant oranges, and neon signs that make traveling the old road so much fun. Complete with accurate maps and directions, and dozens of historical and contemporary photographs, these books are essential companions for any trip through the heart of the Golden State.

Roadside History of Arizona, by Marshall Trimble (Mountain Press, 1986). One of a great series of breezily written, anecdote-rich books covering road-by-road history of each of the Southwestern states, this book answers all the who? what? where? when? and why? questions that arise when traveling. And if that's not enough knowledge for you, the same publishers do a series of Roadside Geology guides.

PERIODICALS

Arizona Highways. This monthly magazine, produced by the Arizona Department of Highways is full of fine photography, lively writing, and, best of all, no advertisements. Subscription information: 602/258-1000 or 800/543-5432.

Nevada Magazine. This glossy, entertaining bimonthly magazine is produced by the state-run Nevada Commission on Tourism, but is more lively and offbeat than you might expect from a government-issue publication. Subscription information: 775/687-5416 or 800/ 495-3281.

Out West: The Newspaper That Roams. For nearly 10 years, writer Chuck Woodbury has been traveling the back roads of the western U.S., documenting in a 32-page quarterly tabloid the many wild and wonderful things he finds there. Chuck, wife Rodica, daughter Emily, and a team of contributors cover the people they meet and the places they eat, photograph funny signs and roadside dinosaurs, and generally bring the open road alive, straight to your mailbox. They also run a very good mail-order bookstore. Contact: Out West, 9792 Edmonds Way, Suite 265, Edmonds WA 98020 (800/274-9378).

Route 66 Magazine. An impressive full-color quarterly, entirely dedicated to the Mother Road and to the people and places, past and present, that have made it such an icon of restless America. Strong graphics, lively writing, and not *too* many ads make it a great resource for armchair or front-seat readers. For subscription information, contact: Route 66 Magazine, 326 W. Route 66, Williams AZ 86046 (520/635-4322).

Sunset Magazine. Covering California and the Southwest for over 100 years, Sunset knows its way around the region's nooks and crannies, and regularly fills its pages with the best travel tips you'll find anywhere outside this book. Subscription information: 650/321-3600 or 800/777-0117.

ORGANIZATIONS

American Automobile Association is an indispensable resource, and no traveler in his or her right mind should hit the road without a membership card. Besides the free roadside assistance, 24 hours a day across the country, they also offer free maps, useful guidebooks, and tons of related information. Look in the Yellow Pages for a local office, or contact the national headquarters.

    American Automobile Association
    1000 AAA Drive
    Heathrow, FL 32746
    800/922-8228

Lincoln Highway Association is a group of old-roads aficionados who work to preserve remnants of the nation's first coast-to-coast highway and to promote its memory. They also get together for annual meetings to retrace the route.

    Lincoln Highway Association
    PO Box 308
    Franklin Grove, IL 61031
    815/456-3030

National Route 66 Federation is the only nationwide, nonprofit organization committed to revitalizing Route 66, and to promoting awareness of its historic role as the Main Street of America. Members receive a high-quality quarterly magazine, and all dues go directly toward lobbying governments to preserve what's left of Route 66.

    National Route 66 Federation
    PO Box 423
    Tujunga, CA 91043-0423
    818/352-7232

Santa Fe Trail Association works to promote public awareness of and appreciation for this historic trail between Kansas City and Santa Fe, which connected the young United States with Mexico.

    Santa Fe Trail Center
    RR 3
    Larned, KS 67550
    316/285-2054

Anyone interested in the cultural landscape lining America's highways and by-ways will want to join the **Society for Commercial Archaeology**, an all-volunteer organization working to preserve and interpret roadside culture. Studies cover everything from diners to giant roadside dinosaurs, and the enterprise is geared toward appreciation and enjoyment of quirks and crannies of the highway environment. Dues are $25 a year, and members receive a magazine and a quarterly newsletter, which details preservation efforts as well as get-togethers for annual tours of different regions.

Society for Commercial Archaeology
PO Box 235
Geneseo, NY 14454-0235
202/882-5424
www.sca-roadside.org

INFORMATION BY STATE

Arizona
Road conditions: 602/651-2400 (topic 7623)
Tourism info: 602/230-7733 or 888/520-3434

California
Road conditions: 916/445-7623 or 800/427-7623
Tourism info: 916/322-2881 or 800/862-2543

Colorado
Road conditions: 303/639-1234
Tourism info: 303/832-6171 or 800/265-6723

Nevada
Road conditions: 775/793-1313 or 702/486-3116
Tourism info: 775/687-4322 or 800/638-2328

New Mexico
Road conditions: 505/827-9325 or 800/432-4269
Tourism info: 505/827-7447 or 800/733-6396

Texas
Road conditions: 800/452-9292
Tourism info: 512/462-9191 or 800/452-9292

Utah
Road conditions: 801/964-6000
Tourism info: 801/538-1030 or 800/200-1160

ROAD TRIP TIME LINE

c. 3800-3600 B.C. . . . . The wheel is invented.

30,000 B.C.-A.D. 1800 . . . Native American trails crisscross North America.

10,000-8,000 B.C. . . . . Clovis Man hunts and gathers in what's now New Mexico.

600 B.C. . . . . Babylonians use tar to pave streets.

A.D. 700 . . . . The Anasazi, enigmatic ancestors of today's Pueblo Indians, establish cities around the Four Corners regon.

A.D. 1150 . . . . Pueblo villages of Acoma and Moenkopi established.

1540-42 . . . . Arriving overland from Mexico, Coronado explores southwestern deserts in search of the fabled Seven Cities of Cíbola.

1542 . . . . Juan Cabrillo explores the coast of California.

1579 . . . . Sailing from the Hawaiian Islands, Sir Francis Drake explores the coast of northern California.

1609 . . . . Spanish colony at Santa Fe, New Mexico established.

1770 . . . . Spain establishes first Franciscan missions in California.

1805-06 . . . . Zebulon Pike explores southern Great Plains and Rockies.

1821 . . . . Santa Fe Trail first opened by businessman William Becknell.

1826 . . . . Jedediah Strong Smith becomes the first white man to cross from the Rockies to California overland. He repeats the feat the following year, then dies in an ambush on the Santa Fe Trail across Texas.

1848 . . . . At the end of Mexican-American War, the Treaty of Guadalupe Hidalgo transfers Mexican claims to California and the Southwest over to the US. California gold rush, and migration of Mormons from Nauvoo to Utah, brings first significant numbers of American settlers to the region

1853 . . . . Gadsden Purchase completes present-day outline of lower 48 United States.

1858-61	Butterfield Overland Mail links St. Louis and Los Angeles via El Paso.
1860-61	Pony Express links Missouri and California.
May 10, 1869	Transcontinental railroad completed.
1884	Santa Fe Railroad links Los Angeles, Santa Fe, and Kansas City.
1886	Coca-Cola invented. Geronimo surrenders to General Miles.
1893	Southern Pacific Railroad reaches Los Angeles.
1900	Electric cars outnumber gasoline-powered cars 2 to 1. Steering wheel replaces the tiller for first time, on a Packard "Ohio."
1901	Oil discovered at Spindletop field in eastern Texas. Speedometers introduced by Oldsmobile.
1903	To win a $50 bet, Dr. Horatio Jackson, along with his chauffeur and dog, becomes first person to drive across the country, taking 65 days.
1904	Only 40,000 out of a total of over two million miles of U.S. roads are fully paved. Bicyclist organizations lead charge for better public roads. Henry Ford sets world land speed record of 91 mph.
1905	Total number of cars on roads: 75,000.
1909	Nation's first mile of rural highway is paved. Alice Ramsey becomes first woman to drive across the country—the trip took 41 days.
1912	Nation's first lane markings are painted onto the streets of Redlands, California.
1915	Total number of cars on roads: 2.3 million. The Lincoln Highway, the country's first coast-to-coast route, is marked from New York to San Francisco.
1916	General Pershing leads U.S. Army into Mexico in pursuit of Pancho Villa. Federal Aid Road Act establishes first federal funding for road building.
1919	First A&W Root Beer stand opens in Lodi, California. Dwight Eisenhower leads a military convoy across the country, which takes two months and points out the need for well-paved transcontinental roads.
1920	Beginning of Prohibition. Total number of cars on roads: 6.5 million.

1922 . . . . Balloon tires and gas gauges introduced. Ford Motor Company produces nearly half of nation's four million new cars and trucks.

1925 . . . . System of numbering federal highways is introduced, to replace route names. The shield symbol is designed by Michigan engineer Frank Rogers. World's first motel opens, in San Luis Obispo, California.

1926 . . . . Route 66 established, winding between Chicago and Los Angeles.

1927 . . . . Ford ceases production of Model T, having sold 27 million of them. Lincoln Highway is paved all the way from New York to California.

1933 . . . . End of Prohibition.

1940 . . . . Total number of cars on roads: 20 million. Arroyo Seco Parkway, now the Pasadena Freeway, opens.

1944 . . . . National System of Interstate and Defense Highways authorized by Congress. Basic wartime gasoline ration is two gallons per week. National speed limit is 35 mph.

1946 . . . . Bobby Troup composes "Route 66," which becomes a hit record for Nat King Cole.

1947 . . . . Henry Ford dies.

1949 . . . . VW Beetle introduced in the United States. In San Bernardino CA, brothers Richard and Maurice McDonald perfect cheap fast food: 15-cent hamburgers, 10-cent french fries.

1953 . . . . McDonald's opens first restaurant featuring the Golden Arches in Phoenix, Arizona, followed soon after by one in Downey, California, that still stands.

1954 . . . . Dwight Eisenhower adds phrase "under God" to the Pledge of Allegiance.

1956 . . . . Interstate Highway system inaugurated, planning 42,500 miles of freeways with federal funds paying 90% of the estimated $27 billion. (The cost so far has been over $125 billion.)

1961 . . . . Ray Kroc buys McDonald's for $2.7 million.

1963 . . . . California becomes first state to require emission controls on cars.

1964 . . . . Pontiac's GTO, with its triple-carbed, 350 horsepower V-8 engine, ushers in the era of the "muscle car."

1974 . . . . "Arab oil crisis" causes federal government to set a national speed limit of 55 mph. Cadillac Ranch is constructed outside Amarillo.

1975 . . . . Bruce Springsteen releases *Born to Run*.

1984 . . . . Chrysler introduces the original minivan. Last stretch of old Route 66 still in use, at Williams, Arizona, is bypassed by the I-40 freeway.

1997 . . . . "On the Road" journalist Charles Kuralt dies on the 4th of July, aged 62. Racing across the Black Rock Desert north of Reno NV, a British team lead by Richard Noble sets new land speed record of 763 mph.

1999 . . . . Congress sets aside over $200 billion for road and transit improvements, including the first appropriation, $1 million a year over 10 years, to help preserve Route 66 and the unique cultural landscape along it.

2000 . . . . The new millenium sees plans for cars to be banned from Yosemite, the South Rim of Grand Canyon, and other national parks.

Currently, there are over 175 million licensed drivers in the U.S., driving 200 million registered vehicles an estimated 2.5 trillion (2,500,000,000,000!) annual miles along four million miles of paved roads and highways.

LIST OF MAPS

SPECIAL TOPICS

INDEX AND INFORMATION

ACCOMMODATIONS

Best Western	800/528-1234
Comfort Inns	800/228-5150
Courtyard by Marriott	800/321-2211
Days Inn	800/325-2525
Econo Lodge	800/553-2666
Embassy Suites Hotels	800/362-2779
Fairfield Inns	800/228-2800
Friendship Inns	800/453-4511
HI Hostels	202/783-6161
Hampton Inns	800/426-7866
Hilton Hotels	800/445-8667
Holiday Inns	800/465-4329
Howard Johnson	800/654-2000
Hyatt Hotels	800/233-1234
La Quinta Inns	800/531-5900
Marriott Hotels	800/228-9290
Motel 6	800/466-8356
Quality Inns	800/228-5151
Ramada Inns	800/228-2828
Red Lion Inns	800/547-8010
Red Roof Inns	800/843-7663
Rodeway Inns	800/228-2000
Super 8 Motels	800/800-8000
TraveLodge	800/578-7878

AIRLINES

Alaska Airlines: 800/426-0333
America West: 800/235-2929
American Airlines: 800/433-7300
Continental: 800/525-0280
Delta Airlines: 800/221-1212
Southwest Airlines: 800/435-9792
United Airlines: 800/241-6522

CAMPING INFORMATION

Arizona State Parks: 602/542-4174
Bureau of Land Management: 202/452-5125
California State Parks: 916/653-6995 or 800/444-7275
Colorado State Parks: 303/866-3437
National Forest Service: 202/205-1706
National Park Service: 202/208-4747 or 800/365-2267
Nevada State Parks: 775/687-4384
New Mexico State Parks: 505/827-6364
Utah State Parks: 801/538-7220 or 800/322-3770

GREAT DRIVES

NATIONAL PARKS

STATE PARKS

Jamie Jensen has been immersed in road trip culture from an early age, thanks to a childhood spent drinking drive-in milk shakes and riding roller coasters in Los Angeles—before they tore everything down—and family road trips up and down the California coast, to the Sierra Nevada national parks, and all over the Southwest. After a three-year stint bumming around the country, making hay in Kansas, sailing boats on the Chesapeake Bay, painting houses in Boston, and living in the storeroom of a Manhattan music studio, he returned to California and earned a degree in Architecture from U.C. Berkeley. Rather than get a real job, he then moved to England, where he began writing about America. He now lives in Northern California, at the west end of US-50.

ACKNOWLEDGMENTS

A PROVERBIAL CAST OF THOUSANDS—in ranger stations, visitor centers, libraries, B&Bs and cafes all over California and the Southwest—has helped shape this book, providing directions, suggestions, story ideas and endless cups of coffee, and I can't thank you all enough for your kindness and hospitality. And to all the readers who've written in with helpful tips, snapshots, comments, corrections, and compliments—keep those pictures and postcards a'coming!

For making this book happen in the first place, I am grateful for the support and enthusiasm of the entire team at Avalon Travel Publishing, especially my editor Emily Lunceford, for fine-tuning my caffeinated prose and never flinching in the face of yet more last minute changes, and my guidebook-writing, road-tripping colleagues Kap Stann, Julian Smith, Barry Parr, and Andy Collins. Sincere thanks are also due Len Jenshel, for letting me use his marvelous photographs to illustrate this book; Kevin "Rootin' Around" Roe (and Debbie, and Big, Little and Hank!) for never-ending encouragement as well as musical accompaniment; to Doug Pappas for sharing his love and knowledge of the old roads, his library of photos and postcards, and his complete set of WPA travel guides; to Ron Thompson for all things Route 66; and to Richard Weingroff at the Federal Highway Adminstration, a one-man archive of everything to do with these wonderful old roads. And to all (well, most) of the people who live, work and play in the places I've passed through and written about—thanks for being there.

So much has happened in the years since I started work on this book that I don't know where to begin to acknowledge the help and support I've been given. I do know I owe my friends and extended family more kindness and hospitality than I could ever hope to repay, so here's a heartfelt "thank you" for welcoming me when I've dropped in out of the blue, in need of care and feeding. I'd also like to offer my sincere gratitude to the wonderful doctors and nurses of the Special Care Nurseries at the UC Davis Medical Center, and to LeNay at Great Beginnings, for looking after my newest traveling companions, Tom and Alex Jensen. And once again with feeling, I want to express my love and devotion to my wife, Catherine Robson, for a baker's dozen years (and counting) of seeing the bright side and making everything turn out right.

The images that serve as chapter frontispieces throughout this book were all made by New York-based photographer Len Jenshel, whose pictures are worth many more than 1,000 words. Most of these also appear in Len's book *Travels in the American West* (Smithsonian Press), and all vividly capture the magical essence of those often weird places where roads meet the wilds.

Pacific Coast Highway
Bixby Bridge Overlook, Big Sur; ©1994 Len Jenshel

Central Valley and National Parks
View of Mt. Shasta; ©1994 Len Jenshel

High Sierra and Death Valley: US-395
Dantes Point—Death Valley National Monument; ©1990 Len Jenshel

Great Basin and Sonora Desert: US-93
Great Basin National Park; ©1987 Len Jenshel

The Loneliest Road: US-50
Highway 50 NV/UT border; ©1987 Len Jenshel

The Mother Road: Route 66
near Chaco Culture National Historic Park; ©1988 Len Jenshel

Southern Pacific: US-80
City of Rocks State Park; ©1987 Len Jenshel

Canyonlands Loop: The Grand Circle
The Mittens Overlook, Monument Valley Navajo Tribal Park;
©1985 Len Jenshel

Four Corners Loop: Native America
Holbrook, AZ; ©1992 Len Jenshel

Road Trip Resources
Wheel Inn Truck Stop, Cabezon CA; ©1988 Len Jenshel

I would also like to take this opportunity to thank Seattle's "Ranger of the Lost Art," Doug Leen, for rescuing the New Deal-era WPA posters of the national parks, for bringing them back to life as prints and postcards, and for letting us reproduce them herein.

PHOTO AND ILLUSTRATION CREDITS

Amador County Museum 129; Apache Motel 362; Arizona Department of Library, Archives and Public Records, History and Archives Division, Phoenix, #90-0015 404; Arizona Office of Tourism 222, 293, 294, 367, 371, 377, 403; Arizona Office of Tourism/Chris Coe 302, 331, 341, 370, 376, 405, 406; Arizona Office of Tourism/Ranier Hackenberg 337; Melissa Brown 313; Buffalo Bill Historical Center, Cody WY 258; BunBoy Restaurant 193; California Department of Parks and Recreation 46, 48, 59, 126, 232, 241, 242, 278, 287; California Department of Parks and Recreation/Bob Mortensen 70; California Division of Tourism/Robert Holmes 85, 51, 53, 58, 67, 77, 92, 111, 112, 132, 139, 150, 151, 153, 170, 172, 181, 184, 186, 192; Carson City CVB 163; Jill Caven 428; Colorado Historical Society 269, 271; Colorado Springs CVB 270 (2); DACRA/ARAMARK 439; DACRA/Robert Royem Photography 438; DACRA/Rod Barker 437; Drive-Thru Tree Park 43; Eric J. Finley 330; Pedro E. Guerrero 216; Flagstaff Visitors Bureau 299; Jamie Jensen 33, 35, 37, 38, 43, 60, 68, 79, 81, 84, 101, 105, 108, 111, 122, 130, 131, 137, 139, 142, 148, 148, 150, 152 (both), 183, 202, 220, 226, 236, 237 (both), 239, 243, 247, 246, 249, 261, 265, 268, 277, 282 (all), 283, 284, 286, 294, 306 (all), 310, 319 (all), 326, 328, 330, 330, 332, 333, 336, 338, 340, 343, 344, 349, 363, 386, 400; Lake Tahoe Visitors Authority 241; Las Vegas News Bureau 209, 211; Lazy SOB Records 305; Jill Livingston 121, 145; Monterey Bay Aquarium 64; Monterey Bay Aquarium/Randy Wilder 63; NASA Dryden Flight Research Center 191 (all); Nevada City Chamber of Commerce 124; Nevada Tourism Commision 160, 161, 205, 208, 213; Out West Newspaper 288; Pasadena CVB 280; Palm Desert News Bureau 150; Bob Race 160, 171; Redwood Empire Association 49; Santa Cruz Parks and Recreation Department 61; Santa Fe Chamber Music Festival 412, 413; Santa Fe CVB 419; Santa Fe CVB/Chris Corrie 422, 431; Julian Smith 310, 358, 364, 363, 373, 373, 381, 382, 383, 385, 388, 392, 393, 394, 395; Taos CVB/Don Laine 426, 429; Page Teahan 442-443; Texas Department of Commerce 315, 317, 318; Texas Department of Commerce/Elizabeth Grivas 341; Texas Department of Commerce/Richard Reynolds 347; Metro Tucson CVB/Eddie Goldbaum Rios 334; Metro Tucson CVB/Gill Kenny 227, 337; Western Folklife Center 200; Mildred Wheeler 290; Wyoming Division of Cultural Resources 120

U.S.~METRIC CONVERSION

1 inch =	2.54 centimeters (cm)
1 foot =	.3048 meters (m)
1 yard =	0.914 meters
1 mile =	1.6093 kilometers (km)
1 km =	.6214 miles
1 fathom =	1.8288 m
1 chain =	20.1168 m
1 furlong =	201.168 m
1 acre =	.4047 hectares
1 sq km =	100 hectares
1 sq mile =	2.59 square km
1 ounce =	28.35 grams
1 pound =	.4536 kilograms
1 short ton =	.90718 metric ton
1 short ton =	2000 pounds
1 long ton =	1.016 metric tons
1 long ton =	2240 pounds
1 metric ton =	1000 kilograms
1 quart =	.94635 liters
1 US gallon =	3.7854 liters
1 Imperial gallon =	4.5459 liters
1 nautical mile =	1.852 km

To compute celsius temperatures, subtract 32 from Fahrenheit and divide by 1.8. To go the other way, multiply celsius by 1.8 and add 32.

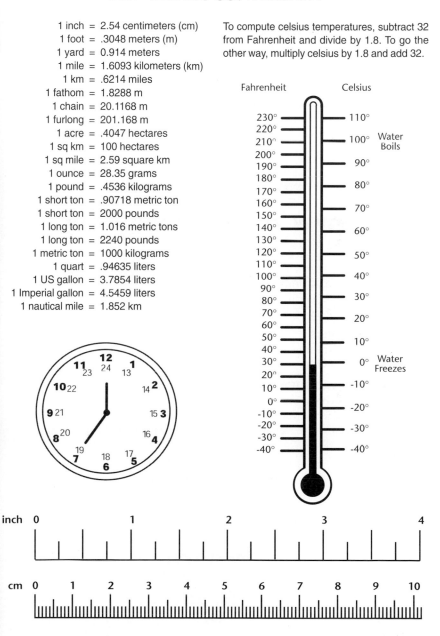

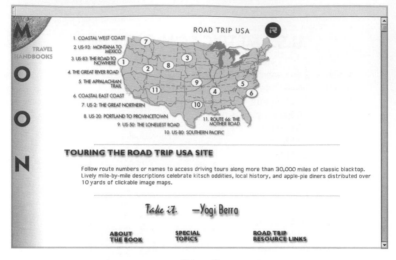

TOURING THE ROAD TRIP USA SITE

Follow route numbers or names to access driving tours along more than 30,000 miles of classic blacktop. Lively mile-by-mile descriptions celebrate kitsch oddities, local history, and apple-pie diners distributed over 10 yards of clickable image maps.

Take it. —Yogi Berra

ABOUT THE BOOK   SPECIAL TOPICS   ROAD TRIP RESOURCE LINKS

www.roadtripusa.com

Features on the Road Trip USA Web Site:

ROAD TRIP RESOURCE LINKS
A sampling of online resources—some quite practical, others just pulled from our list of favorites.

SPECIAL TOPICS
Colorful sidebars provide a wealth of trivia, anecdotes, and fascinating tidbits of local history.

CITY SURVIVAL GUIDE
The 11 cross-country routes covered in *Road Trip USA* pass near or through several major U.S. cities. Use these "survival guides" to find information on what to see, where to stay, what to eat, and where to find what's swinging.